Microsoft® 365 Excel®

ALL-IN-ONE

Microsoft® 365 Excel®

ALL-IN-ONE

by David H. Ringstrom, Michael Alexander,
Dick Kusleika, Paul McFedries, and
Ken Bluttman

Microsoft® 365 Excel® All-in-One For Dummies®

Published by: **John Wiley & Sons, Inc.**, 111 River Street, Hoboken, NJ 07030-5774, www.wiley.com

Copyright © 2025 by John Wiley & Sons, Inc. All rights reserved, including rights for text and data mining and training of artificial technologies or similar technologies.

Media and software compilation copyright © 2025 by John Wiley & Sons, Inc. All rights reserved, including rights for text and data mining and training of artificial technologies or similar technologies.

Published simultaneously in Canada

No part of this publication may be reproduced, stored in a retrieval system or transmitted in any form or by any means, electronic, mechanical, photocopying, recording, scanning or otherwise, except as permitted under Sections 107 or 108 of the 1976 United States Copyright Act, without the prior written permission of the Publisher or authorization through payment of the appropriate per-copy fee to the Copyright Clearance Center, Inc., 222 Rosewood Drive, Danvers, MA 01923, (978) 750-8400, fax (978) 750-4470, or on the web at www.copyright.com. Requests to the Publisher for permission should be addressed to the Permissions Department, John Wiley & Sons, Inc., 111 River Street, Hoboken, NJ 07030, (201) 748-6011, fax (201) 748-6008, or online at http://www.wiley.com/go/permissions.

The manufacturer's authorized representative according to the EU General Product Safety Regulation is Wiley-VCH GmbH, Boschstr. 12, 69469 Weinheim, Germany, e-mail: Product_Safety@wiley.com.

Trademarks: Wiley, For Dummies, the Dummies Man logo, Dummies.com, Making Everything Easier, and related trade dress are trademarks or registered trademarks of John Wiley & Sons, Inc. and may not be used without written permission. Microsoft 365 and Excel are trademarks or registered trademarks of Microsoft Corporation. All other trademarks are the property of their respective owners. John Wiley & Sons, Inc. is not associated with any product or vendor mentioned in this book. *Microsoft 365 Excel® All-in-One For Dummies®*, is an independent publication and is neither affiliated with, nor authorized, sponsored, or approved by, Microsoft Corporation.

LIMIT OF LIABILITY/DISCLAIMER OF WARRANTY: THE PUBLISHER AND THE AUTHOR MAKE NO REPRESENTATIONS OR WARRANTIES WITH RESPECT TO THE ACCURACY OR COMPLETENESS OF THE CONTENTS OF THIS WORK AND SPECIFICALLY DISCLAIM ALL WARRANTIES, INCLUDING WITHOUT LIMITATION WARRANTIES OF FITNESS FOR A PARTICULAR PURPOSE. NO WARRANTY MAY BE CREATED OR EXTENDED BY SALES OR PROMOTIONAL MATERIALS. THE ADVICE AND STRATEGIES CONTAINED HEREIN MAY NOT BE SUITABLE FOR EVERY SITUATION. THIS WORK IS SOLD WITH THE UNDERSTANDING THAT THE PUBLISHER IS NOT ENGAGED IN RENDERING LEGAL, ACCOUNTING, OR OTHER PROFESSIONAL SERVICES. IF PROFESSIONAL ASSISTANCE IS REQUIRED, THE SERVICES OF A COMPETENT PROFESSIONAL PERSON SHOULD BE SOUGHT. NEITHER THE PUBLISHER NOR THE AUTHOR SHALL BE LIABLE FOR DAMAGES ARISING HEREFROM. THE FACT THAT AN ORGANIZATION OR WEBSITE IS REFERRED TO IN THIS WORK AS A CITATION AND/OR A POTENTIAL SOURCE OF FURTHER INFORMATION DOES NOT MEAN THAT THE AUTHOR OR THE PUBLISHER ENDORSES THE INFORMATION THE ORGANIZATION OR WEBSITE MAY PROVIDE OR RECOMMENDATIONS IT MAY MAKE. FURTHER, READERS SHOULD BE AWARE THAT INTERNET WEBSITES LISTED IN THIS WORK MAY HAVE CHANGED OR DISAPPEARED BETWEEN WHEN THIS WORK WAS WRITTEN AND WHEN IT IS READ.

For general information on our other products and services, please contact our Customer Care Department within the U.S. at 877-762-2974, outside the U.S. at 317-572-3993, or fax 317-572-4002. For technical support, please visit https://hub.wiley.com/community/support/dummies.

Wiley publishes in a variety of print and electronic formats and by print-on-demand. Some material included with standard print versions of this book may not be included in e-books or in print-on-demand. If this book refers to media that is not included in the version you purchased, you may download this material at http://booksupport.wiley.com. For more information about Wiley products, visit www.wiley.com.

Library of Congress Control Number is available from the publisher.

ISBN 978-1-394-34463-5 (pbk); ISBN 978-1-394-34465-9 (ebk); ISBN 978-1-394-34464-2 (ebk)

SKY10122683_072425

Contents at a Glance

Introduction 1

Book 1: Getting Started with Excel 5
- CHAPTER 1: Getting Started with Spreadsheets 7
- CHAPTER 2: Carrying Out Basic Calculations 31
- CHAPTER 3: Formatting Cells and Worksheets 53
- CHAPTER 4: Organizing Data and Creating Tables 79
- CHAPTER 5: Navigating Worksheets and Workbooks 113

Book 2: Working with Formulas and Functions 129
- CHAPTER 1: Tapping Into Formula and Function Fundamentals ... 131
- CHAPTER 2: Saving Time with Function Tools 161
- CHAPTER 3: Building Array Formulas and Functions 177
- CHAPTER 4: Fixing Errors in Formulas 191

Book 3: Going Farther with Functions 207
- CHAPTER 1: Calculating Loans, Interest, and Depreciation 209
- CHAPTER 2: Performing Functional Math 241
- CHAPTER 3: Working with Date and Time Functions 271
- CHAPTER 4: Manipulating Text with Functions 291

Book 4: Analyzing Data 317
- CHAPTER 1: Using Basic Data Analysis Techniques 319
- CHAPTER 2: Working with Data Analysis Tools 343
- CHAPTER 3: Analyzing Table Data with Functions 365

Book 5: Summarizing, Visualizing, and Illustrating Data ... 377
- CHAPTER 1: Creating Charts 379
- CHAPTER 2: Creating and Using PivotTables 391
- CHAPTER 3: Performing PivotTable Calculations 413
- CHAPTER 4: Building PivotCharts 435

Book 6: Reporting and Querying Data 455

CHAPTER 1: Introducing Power Pivot 457
CHAPTER 2: Advanced Moves with PivotTables 469
CHAPTER 3: Working Directly with the Internal Data Model 499
CHAPTER 4: Adding Formulas to Power Pivot 513
CHAPTER 5: Meeting Power Query and Its Connection Types 531

Book 7: Creating Dashboards and Reports 559

CHAPTER 1: Getting in the Dashboard State of Mind 561
CHAPTER 2: Building a Super Model 575
CHAPTER 3: Dressing Up Your Data Tables 619
CHAPTER 4: Formatting Your Way to Visualizations 635
CHAPTER 5: Displaying Performance against a Target 663

Book 8: Automating Excel with Macros and VBA 679

CHAPTER 1: Macro Fundamentals 681
CHAPTER 2: Getting Cozy with the Visual Basic Editor 701
CHAPTER 3: The Anatomy of Macros 715
CHAPTER 4: Working with Workbooks 729

Index 753

Table of Contents

INTRODUCTION 1
    About This Book. 1
    Foolish Assumptions. 3
    Icons Used in This Book 3
    Beyond the Book. 3
    Where to Go from Here 4

BOOK 1: GETTING STARTED WITH EXCEL 5

CHAPTER 1: Getting Started with Spreadsheets 7
    Exploring Excel's User Interface 7
        Traversing the ribbon 9
        Customizing the Quick Access Toolbar 12
        Activating worksheets. 13
        Exploring the Status Bar. 13
    Entering and Editing Data 15
        Starting a task tracker. 15
        Applying basic formatting 17
        Leveraging worksheet functions 18
    Handling Workbook Operations 20
        Saving Excel workbooks 20
        Opening existing workbooks 21
        Creating new workbooks 22
        Using Excel templates. 22
    Managing Worksheet Tasks 23
        Renaming Excel worksheets 23
        Moving or copying worksheets 24
        Adding or deleting worksheets 25
        Hiding or unhiding worksheets. 26
        Grouping worksheets 27
    Collaborating with Others 27
        Sharing static copies of workbooks 27
        Coauthoring simultaneously 28
        Commenting collectively 29

CHAPTER 2: Carrying Out Basic Calculations 31
    Understanding Operators 31
        Analyzing arithmetic operators 32
        Comparing values with operators. 32

      Combining text...33
      Linking cells across sheets and workbooks....................33
  Exploring the Order of Operations..................................35
      Prioritizing with parentheses................................36
      Elevating with exponents....................................37
      Multiplying and dividing with precision......................38
      Adding and subtracting with ease............................39
  Contrasting Cell References..40
      Recognizing relative references..............................40
      Mastering mixed references.................................40
      Applying absolute references...............................40
  Replicating Formulas..41
      Copying with keyboard shortcuts............................41
      Automating with AutoFill....................................42
  Calculating Sums...44
      Computing amounts with AutoSum..........................44
      Totaling with SUM..44
      Adding or subtracting dates and times......................46
  Analyzing Data with Statistical Functions...........................47
      Calculating averages with AVERAGE.........................48
      Calculating a weighted average..............................48
      Calculating conditional averages............................49
      Finding the smallest and largest values......................51

CHAPTER 3: Formatting Cells and Worksheets.....................53
  Applying Basic Formatting Commands.............................54
  Exploring the Format Cells Dialog Box..............................55
      Formatting numbers..55
      Crafting custom number formats............................57
  Applying Cell Styles...59
      Modifying predefined styles.................................60
      Creating custom styles......................................60
      Applying and identifying cell styles..........................61
      Transferring cell styles between workbooks..................61
  Merging and Centering Cells......................................62
      Merging across columns....................................63
      Centering across a selection................................64
  Wrapping Text...64
  Tapping into Text Boxes..65
  Inserting Images...67
  Enhancing Accessibility...68
  Adjusting Row Heights and Column Widths........................69
  Hiding and Unhiding Rows and Columns..........................70
      Hiding rows and columns...................................71

        Unhiding rows and columns 71
        Grouping rows and columns 72
    Hiding and Unhiding Workbooks 74
    Modifying Page Setup 74
        Setting print ranges and page breaks 76
        Adding headers, footers, and print titles 77

CHAPTER 4: Organizing Data and Creating Tables 79
    Organizing Data 79
        Using the Sort feature 80
        Removing duplicates 86
        Finessing the Filter feature 88
        Calculating with SUBTOTAL 90
        Using the AGGREGATE function 92
        Summarizing lists with the Subtotal feature 94
        Jump-starting insights with Quick Analysis 96
    Creating Tables 97
        Comparing data ranges to Excel tables 98
        Creating Excel tables 99
        Automating formulas and features 104
        Unpacking table quirks 110
        Converting a table to a data range 112

CHAPTER 5: Navigating Worksheets and Workbooks 113
    Finding and Replacing Data within Cells 114
        Searching within worksheet cells 114
        Replacing text within worksheet cells 116
    Exploring with the Navigation Task Pane 116
    Jumping to Locations with Go To 118
    Targeting Specific Cells with Go To Special .118
    Navigating with the Name Box 120
    Activating Worksheets 120
    Reordering Worksheets 121
    Splitting Worksheet Windows 122
    Viewing Two or More Worksheets at Once 123
    Applying Custom Views 123
        Creating custom views 125
        Using the Custom Views Quick Access Toolbar shortcut 126
    Zooming In and Out 127

BOOK 2: WORKING WITH FORMULAS AND FUNCTIONS..................129

CHAPTER 1: Tapping Into Formula and Function Fundamentals..................131

Working with Excel Fundamentals..................132
    Understanding workbooks and worksheets..................132
    Introducing the Formulas tab..................135
    Working with rows, columns, cells, ranges, and tables..................137
    Formatting your data..................142
    Getting help..................143
Gaining the Upper Hand on Formulas..................143
    Entering your first formula..................144
    Understanding references..................146
    Copying formulas with the Fill Handle..................148
    Assembling formulas the right way..................149
Using Functions in Formulas..................152
    Looking at what goes into a function..................153
    Arguing with a function..................154
    Nesting functions..................158

CHAPTER 2: Saving Time with Function Tools..................161

Getting Familiar with the Insert Function Dialog Box..................162
Finding the Correct Function..................163
Entering Functions Using the Insert Function Dialog Box..................164
    Selecting a function that takes no arguments..................165
    Selecting a function that uses arguments..................166
    Entering cells, ranges, named areas, and tables as function arguments..................168
    Getting help in the Insert Function dialog box..................171
    Using the Function Arguments dialog box to edit functions..................172
Directly Entering Formulas and Functions..................172
    Entering formulas and functions in the Formula Bar..................173
    Entering formulas and functions directly in worksheet cells..................174

CHAPTER 3: Building Array Formulas and Functions..................177

Discovering Arrays..................178
Using Arrays in Formulas..................179
Changing the Shape of Arrays..................183
Working with Functions That Return Arrays..................186

CHAPTER 4: Fixing Errors in Formulas..................191

Catching Errors as You Enter Them..................191
    Getting parentheses to match..................192
    Avoiding circular references..................194

    Mending broken links...196
        Using the Error Checking feature for formulas................198
  Auditing Formulas...200
  Watching the Watch Window...203
  Evaluating and Checking Errors......................................204
  Making an Error Behave the Way You Want......................205

BOOK 3: GOING FARTHER WITH FUNCTIONS............207

CHAPTER 1: Calculating Loans, Interest, and Depreciation....209

  Understanding How Excel Handles Money.....................210
    Going with the cash flow......................................210
    Formatting for currency.......................................210
    Choosing separators..212
  Figuring Loan Calculations...213
    Calculating the payment amount............................214
    Calculating interest payments................................216
    Calculating payments toward principal......................217
    Calculating the number of payments.........................219
    Calculating the number of payments with PDURATION........221
    Calculating the interest rate.................................222
    Calculating the principal.....................................224
  Looking into the Future..226
  Depreciating the Finer Things in Life...............................228
    Calculating straight-line depreciation........................230
    Creating an accelerated depreciation schedule..............231
    Creating an even faster accelerated depreciation schedule.....233
    Calculating a midyear depreciation schedule................235
  Measuring Your Internals..237

CHAPTER 2: Performing Functional Math........................241

  Adding It All Together with the SUM Function...................242
  Rounding Out Your Knowledge.....................................246
    Just plain old rounding.......................................246
    Rounding in one direction....................................248
  Leaving All Decimals Behind with INT..............................253
  Leaving Some Decimals Behind with TRUNC......................254
  Looking for a Sign..255
  Ignoring Signs...256
  Using PI to Calculate Circumference and Diameter...............257
  Generating and Using Random Numbers.........................258
    The all-purpose RAND function..............................258
    Precise randomness with RANDBETWEEN....................260
  Creating a Sequence...261

Raising Numbers to New Heights..........................261
Multiplying Multiple Numbers............................263
Summing Things Up.....................................264
    Using SUBTOTAL....................................264
    Using SUMPRODUCT.................................266
    Using SUMIF and SUMIFS............................268

CHAPTER 3: Working with Date and Time Functions...........271

Understanding How Excel Handles Dates....................272
Formatting Dates.......................................273
Making a Date with DATE................................274
Breaking a Date with DAY, MONTH, and YEAR..............275
    Isolating the day...................................276
    Isolating the month................................278
    Isolating the year.................................278
Converting a Date from Text.............................278
Finding Out What TODAY Is..............................280
    Counting the days until your birthday................280
    Counting your age in days..........................281
Determining the Day of the Week........................281
Working with Workdays..................................283
    Determining workdays in a range of dates............283
    Workdays in the future.............................284
Understanding How Excel Handles Time...................285
Formatting Time..286
Deconstructing Time with HOUR, MINUTE, and SECOND......287
    Isolating the hour.................................288
    Isolating the minute...............................289
    Isolating the second...............................290
Finding the Time NOW...................................290

CHAPTER 4: Manipulating Text with Functions...............291

Breaking Apart Text.....................................291
    Bearing to the LEFT................................292
    Swinging to the RIGHT..............................293
    Staying in the MIDdle..............................293
    Splitting up.......................................295
    Finding the long of it with LEN....................295
Putting Text Together..................................296
    Putting text together with CONCATENATE..............296
    Putting text together with TEXTJOIN and a delimiter..298
Changing Text..299
    Making money......................................299
    Turning numbers into text..........................301

　　　　Repeating text 303
　　　　Swapping text. 304
　　　　Giving text a trim 308
　　　　Making a case. 309
　　Comparing, Finding, and Measuring Text 310
　　　　Going for perfection with EXACT. 310
　　　　Finding and searching. 312

BOOK 4: ANALYZING DATA 317

CHAPTER 1: Using Basic Data Analysis Techniques 319
　　What Is Data Analysis, Anyway?. 320
　　　　Cooking raw data. 320
　　　　Dealing with data. 320
　　　　Building data models 321
　　　　Performing what-if analysis 321
　　Analyzing Data with Conditional Formatting. 321
　　　　Highlighting cells that meet some criteria 322
　　　　Showing pesky duplicate values 323
　　　　Highlighting the top or bottom values in a range. 325
　　　　Analyzing cell values with data bars 326
　　　　Analyzing cell values with color scales .327
　　　　Analyzing cell values with icon sets. 328
　　　　Creating a custom conditional formatting rule. 329
　　　　Editing a conditional formatting rule 332
　　　　Removing conditional formatting rules 334
　　Summarizing Data with Subtotals. 335
　　Grouping Related Data. 337
　　Consolidating Data from Multiple Worksheets. 338
　　　　Consolidating by position. 339
　　　　Consolidating by category 340

CHAPTER 2: Working with Data Analysis Tools 343
　　Working with Data Tables 343
　　　　Creating a basic data table. 344
　　　　Creating a two-input data table. 346
　　　　Skipping data tables when calculating workbooks. 349
　　Analyzing Data with Goal Seek 349
　　Analyzing Data with Scenarios. 351
　　　　Creating a scenario 352
　　　　Applying a scenario 354
　　　　Editing a scenario 354
　　　　Deleting a scenario 355
　　Optimizing Data with Solver 355

Table of Contents **xiii**

Understanding Solver..356
Appreciating the advantages of Solver......................356
Knowing when to use Solver.................................356
Loading the Solver add-in..................................358
Optimizing a result with Solver............................359
Adding constraints to Solver...............................361
Saving a Solver solution as a scenario.....................364

CHAPTER 3: Analyzing Table Data with Functions...............365
Introducing the Database Functions.........................365
Retrieving a Value from a Table............................367
Summing a Column's Values..................................368
Counting a Column's Values.................................369
Averaging a Column's Values................................371
Determining a Column's Maximum and Minimum Values..........372
Multiplying a Column's Values..............................373
Deriving a Column's Standard Deviation.....................374
Calculating a Column's Variance............................375

BOOK 5: SUMMARIZING, VISUALIZING, AND ILLUSTRATING DATA...377

CHAPTER 1: Creating Charts...................................379
Introducing Excel Charts...................................379
Creating a Chart from Scratch..............................380
    Using Recommended Charts...............................380
    Building charts directly...............................382
Deconstructing and Customizing Charts......................383
    Customizing charts.....................................384
    Maintaining chart data.................................385
    Moving and resizing charts.............................387
    Transferring chart formatting and elements.............388
    Creating and applying chart templates..................389
    Managing templates.....................................390

CHAPTER 2: Creating and Using PivotTables....................391
Understanding PivotTables..................................391
Exploring PivotTable Features..............................394
Building a PivotTable from an Excel Range or Table.........395
Creating a PivotTable from External Data...................398
    Building a PivotTable from Microsoft Query.............398
    Building a PivotTable from a new data connection.......399
Refreshing PivotTable Data.................................401

  Refreshing PivotTable data manually. 401
  Refreshing PivotTable data automatically 401
 Adding Multiple Fields to a PivotTable Area 402
 Pivoting a Field to a Different Area. 403
 Grouping PivotTable Values. 404
  Grouping numeric values. 404
  Grouping date and time values. 405
  Grouping text values. 406
 Filtering PivotTable Values. 407
  Applying a report filter 407
  Filtering row or column items 408
  Filtering PivotTable values 409
  Filtering a PivotTable with a slicer. 410

CHAPTER 3: Performing PivotTable Calculations. 413
 Messing Around with PivotTable Summary Calculations 414
  Changing the PivotTable summary calculation. 414
  Trying out the difference summary calculation 416
  Applying a percentage summary calculation 418
  Adding a running total summary calculation 420
  Creating an index summary calculation. .422
 Working with PivotTable Subtotals. 425
  Turning off subtotals for a field. 425
  Displaying multiple subtotals for a field. 425
 Introducing Custom Calculations 427
  Formulas for custom calculations. 427
  Checking out the custom calculation types. 428
  Understanding custom calculation limitations 428
 Inserting a Custom Calculated Field 430
 Inserting a Custom Calculated Item 431
 Editing a Custom Calculation. 433
 Deleting a Custom Calculation 434

CHAPTER 4: Building PivotCharts 435
 Introducing the PivotChart. 436
  Understanding PivotChart pros and cons 436
  Taking a PivotChart tour. 437
  Understanding PivotChart limitations 438
 Creating a PivotChart 439
  Creating a PivotChart from a PivotTable 439
  Embedding a PivotChart on a PivotTable's worksheet. 439
  Creating a PivotChart from an Excel range or table. 441
 Working with PivotCharts. 443

      Moving a PivotChart to another sheet 443
      Filtering a PivotChart...444
      Changing the PivotChart type 446
      Adding data labels to your PivotChart 447
      Sorting the PivotChart...448
      Adding PivotChart titles 449
      Moving the PivotChart legend 451
      Displaying a data table with the PivotChart................452

BOOK 6: REPORTING AND QUERYING DATA 455

CHAPTER 1: Introducing Power Pivot 457
Understanding the Power Pivot Internal Data Model 458
Linking Excel Tables to Power Pivot 460
      Preparing Excel tables...461
      Adding Excel tables to the data model.....................462
      Creating relationships between Power Pivot tables...........464
      Managing existing relationships 466
      Using the Power Pivot data model in reporting 467

CHAPTER 2: Advanced Moves with PivotTables 469
Creating a PivotTable 470
      Changing and rearranging a PivotTable......................473
      Adding a report filter..474
      Keeping the PivotTable fresh.................................474
Customizing PivotTable Reports 476
      Changing the PivotTable layout..............................476
      Customizing field names 478
      Applying numeric formats to data fields 479
      Changing summary calculations..............................479
      Suppressing subtotals 481
      Showing and hiding data items...............................483
      Hiding or showing items without data 485
      Sorting the PivotTable...486
Understanding Slicers...488
Creating a Standard Slicer 490
Getting Fancy with Slicer Customizations 492
      Size and placement..492
      Data item columns 493
      Miscellaneous slicer settings 493
Controlling Multiple PivotTables with One Slicer 494
Creating a Timeline Slicer..495

CHAPTER 3: Working Directly with the Internal Data Model 499
    Directly Feeding the Internal Data Model 499
    Managing Relationships in the Internal Data Model 505
    Managing Queries and Connections 506
    Creating a New PivotTable Using the Internal Data Model.........506
    Filling the Internal Data Model with Multiple External Data Tables...508

CHAPTER 4: Adding Formulas to Power Pivot......................513
    Enhancing Power Pivot Data with Calculated Columns............513
        Creating your first calculated column 514
        Formatting calculated columns...........................516
        Referencing calculated columns in other calculations..........516
        Hiding calculated columns from end users..................517
    Utilizing DAX to Create Calculated Columns 518
        Identifying DAX functions that are safe for calculated columns...518
        Building DAX-driven calculated columns 520
        Sorting by month in Power Pivot–driven PivotTables 522
        Referencing fields from other tables 523
        Nesting functions......................................525
    Understanding Calculated Measures...........................526
        Creating a calculated measure 526
        Editing and deleting calculated measures..................529

CHAPTER 5: Meeting Power Query and Its Connection Types...531
    Power Query Basics 532
        Starting the query 532
        Understanding query steps..............................538
        Refreshing Power Query data 539
        Managing existing queries...............................540
    Understanding Column-Level Actions 542
    Understanding Table Actions 544
    Importing Data from Files 545
        Getting data from Excel workbooks 545
        Getting data from CSV and text files.......................546
        Getting data from PDF files 548
        Getting data from folders................................549
    Importing Data from Database Systems 550
        A connection for every database type 550
        Getting data from other data systems.....................551
        Walk-through: Getting data from a database 552

Managing Data Source Settings 553
Data Profiling with Power Query 555
    Data Profiling options 556
    Data Profiling quick actions 557

BOOK 7: CREATING DASHBOARDS AND REPORTS 559

CHAPTER 1: Getting in the Dashboard State of Mind 561

Defining Dashboards and Reports 561
    Defining reports 562
    Defining dashboards 562
Preparing for Greatness 564
    Establish the audience for, and purpose of, the dashboard 564
    Delineate the measures for the dashboard 565
    Catalog the required data sources 566
    Define the dimensions and filters for the dashboard 567
    Determine the need for drill-down features 568
    Establish the refresh schedule 568
A Quick Look at Dashboard Design Principles 568
    Rule number 1: Keep it simple 569
    Use layout and placement to draw focus 571
    Format numbers effectively 572
    Use titles and labels effectively 572

CHAPTER 2: Building a Super Model 575

Understanding Data Modeling Best Practices 576
    Separating data, analysis, and presentation 576
    Starting with appropriately structured data 579
    Avoiding turning your data model into a database 582
    Using tabs to document and organize your data model 584
    Testing your data model before building reporting
    components on top of it 585
Finding Excel Functions That Really Deliver 586
    The VLOOKUP function 586
    The HLOOKUP function 591
    The SUMPRODUCT function 592
    The CHOOSE function 595
Using Smart Tables That Expand with Data 598
    Converting a range to an Excel table 599
    Converting an Excel table back to a range 601
Introducing Dynamic Arrays 602
    Getting the basics of dynamic arrays 602
    Understanding spill ranges 604
    Referencing spill ranges 606

        Exploring Dynamic Array Functions 607
            The SORT function. 608
            The SORTBY function 608
            The UNIQUE function 610
            The FILTER function. 611
            The XLOOKUP function. 614

CHAPTER 3: Dressing Up Your Data Tables 619

        Table Design Principles. 620
            Use colors sparingly 620
            De-emphasize borders 621
            Use effective number formatting 624
            Subdue your labels and headers 625
        Getting Fancy with Custom Number Formatting 627
            Number formatting basics. 627
            Formatting numbers in thousands and millions 629
            Hiding and suppressing zeroes. 631
            Applying custom format colors 632
            Formatting dates and times. 633

CHAPTER 4: Formatting Your Way to Visualizations. 635

        Enhancing Reports with Conditional Formatting 635
            Applying basic conditional formatting .636
            Adding your own formatting rules manually. 642
            Showing only one icon 646
            Showing Data Bars and icons outside of cells. 648
            Representing trends with Icon Sets 650
        Using Symbols to Enhance Reporting 652
        Wielding the Magical Camera Tool 655
            Finding the Camera tool 656
            Using the Camera tool 656
            Enhancing a dashboard with the Camera tool 658
        Enhancing Excel Reports with Shapes 659
            Creating visually appealing containers with shapes. 659
            Layering shapes to save space 660
            Constructing your own infographic widgets with shapes 661

CHAPTER 5: Displaying Performance against a Target 663

        Showing Performance with Variances 663
        Showing Performance against Organizational Trends. 665
        Using a Thermometer-Style Chart 666

Using a Bullet Graph..667
    Creating a bullet graph..................................668
    Adding data to your bullet graph........................671
    Final thoughts on formatting bullet graphs................673
Showing Performance against a Target Range....................675

BOOK 8: AUTOMATING EXCEL WITH MACROS AND VBA 679

CHAPTER 1: Macro Fundamentals 681
Choosing to Use a Macro......................................682
Recording a Macro..682
    Examining the macro....................................684
    Editing the macro......................................685
    Testing the macro......................................686
    Comparing absolute and relative macro recording..........686
Understanding Macro Security..................................691
    Macro-enabled file extensions...........................691
    Trusted documents......................................692
    Trusted locations......................................692
Storing and Running Macros....................................693
    Storing macros in your Personal Macro Workbook...........694
    Assigning a macro to a button and other form controls....694
    Placing a macro on the Quick Access Toolbar.............696
Exploring Macro Examples......................................697
    Building navigation buttons.............................697
    Dynamically rearranging PivotTable data.................698
    Offering one-touch reporting options....................699

CHAPTER 2: Getting Cozy with the Visual Basic Editor 701
Working in the Visual Basic Editor.............................701
    VBE menu bar...702
    VBE toolbars...703
    Project Explorer.......................................703
    Code pane..703
    Immediate window.......................................703
Working with the Project Explorer..............................704
    Adding a new VBA module.................................704
    Removing a VBA module..................................706
Working with a Code Pane......................................706
    Minimizing and maximizing windows.......................706
    Getting VBA code into a module..........................707

    Customizing the VBE..709
        Editor tab 710
        Editor Format tab 712
        General tab..713
        Docking tab..714

CHAPTER 3: The Anatomy of Macros........................715
    A Brief Overview of the Excel Object Model 715
        Understanding objects 716
        Understanding collections 717
        Understanding properties 717
        Understanding methods 718
    A Brief Look at Variables 718
    Understanding Event Procedures..............................720
        Worksheet events 721
        Workbook events...723
    Error Handling in a Nutshell 724
        On Error GoTo SomeLabel..................................725
        On Error Resume Next 726
        On Error GoTo 0..726

CHAPTER 4: Working with Workbooks.......................729
    Installing Macros 730
        Event macros 730
        Personal Macro Workbook..................................730
        Standard macros 731
    Creating a New Workbook from Scratch 731
    Saving a Workbook When a Particular Cell Is Changed............733
    Saving a Workbook before Closing.............................735
    Protecting a Worksheet on Workbook Close.....................737
    Unprotecting a Worksheet...................................738
    Opening a Workbook to a Specific Tab 739
    Opening a Specific Workbook Chosen by the User 741
    Determining Whether a Workbook Is Already Open 742
    Determining Whether a Workbook Exists in a Directory...........745
    Closing All Workbooks at Once 746
    Printing All Workbooks in a Directory..........................747
    Preventing the Workbook from Closing until a
    Cell Is Populated 749
    Creating a Backup of the Current Workbook with Today's Date 750

INDEX..753

Introduction

Welcome to *Microsoft 365 Excel All-in-One For Dummies!* Whether you're just getting started with spreadsheets or you've been crunching numbers for many years, you've made the right choice with this book. Packed with tips, tricks, and real-world examples, it gives you the information you need to harness Excel's power and use the app's features to simplify your work, bring order to chaotic data, and unlock valuable insights.

About This Book

Microsoft 365 Excel All-in-One For Dummies contains the following eight minibooks:

- **Book 1: Getting Started with Excel** shows you how to get up and moving with Excel. You find out how to create Excel workbook files, populate the workbooks with worksheets, and enter and organize your data on the worksheets. You grasp how to carry out basic calculations, format cells and ranges, and create data tables.

- **Book 2: Working with Formulas and Functions** gives you a firm grounding in the essentials of formulas and functions, the tools you use to crunch your data. You find out how to use Excel's function tools to save time, how to build array formulas and functions to perform complex calculations across ranges in a single move, and how to fix the errors that tend to creep into formulas.

- **Book 3: Putting Functions to Work** digs deeper into functions, helping you tap the awesome power of the most widely used categories of functions. You learn to calculate loans, interest, and depreciation; perform mathematical operations ranging from the straightforward to the brain-bending; use date and time functions, such as calculating the number of workdays between two dates; and use functions to clean up, chop up, and otherwise manipulate text.

- **Book 4: Analyzing Data** launches you on the path to becoming an Excel data analyst. First, you grasp what data analysis consists of, meet tools such as conditional formatting and subtotals, and consolidate data across multiple worksheets either by position or by category. Next, you get the hang of data tables, the Goal Seek tool, the Scenarios feature, and the complex Solver add-in. After that, it's time to analyze data with Excel's database functions, which let you do everything from retrieving and summing values to calculating the standard deviation or variance of a column.

- » **Book 5: Summarizing, Visualizing, and Illustrating Data** shows you how to use Excel's tools for bringing drab and flat data to colorful, three-dimensional life. You start with charts and then get hands-on experience with the powerful PivotTable feature that enables you to slice, dice, and splice data. After you add the essentials of PivotTables to your toolkit, you find out how to create PivotCharts to present your PivotTable data visually.

- » **Book 6: Reporting and Querying Data** lays out how you can use Excel's reporting and querying tools to transform your raw data into meaningful insights that can guide your company's strategic decisions. First, you meet the Power Pivot feature and learn about the internal data model. Next, you learn advanced PivotTable moves, including how to customize reports, implement slicers, and create calculated columns and calculated measures. After that, you come to grips with using the Power Query tool to import data and transform it into the format you need.

- » **Book 7: Creating Dashboards and Reports** brings you up to speed on creating dashboards and reports to present your Excel data visually and interactively. After establishing the audience, the required data, and the schedule for refreshing that data, you build a super model and lay out the dashboard and report with the charts, tables, and key performance indicators (KPIs) that will deliver its message most effectively. Among the techniques you'll learn are how to use Excel's hidden Camera tool to build a compact but effective dashboard interface and how to create visuals that display performance against a target.

- » **Book 8: Automating Excel with Macros and VBA** gets you started recording macros and writing Visual Basic for Applications (VBA) code in Excel. Recording a macro is a quick and easy way to automate a straightforward action you need to perform over and over again. When you need to automate more complex tasks, you can write custom VBA code in the Visual Basic Editor programming environment that Microsoft includes with Excel.

Within this book, you may note that some web addresses break across two lines of text. If you're reading this book in print and want to visit one of these web pages, simply key in the web address exactly as it's noted in the text, pretending as though the line break doesn't exist. If you're reading this as an e-book, you've got it easy — just click the web address to be taken directly to the web page.

Foolish Assumptions

This book assumes that you're using Excel, most likely on the PC, because Excel for Windows is much more widely used than Excel for Mac. If you're using a Mac, you'll find that many things work the same way, though Excel for Mac is not quite as full-featured as Excel for Windows. In particular, look at Book 1, which includes coverage of essential moves in Excel for Mac.

Icons Used in This Book

This book uses the following icons to flag particularly important or helpful information.

The Tip icon highlights information that'll help you get your work done more quickly and accurately in Excel.

The Remember icon marks some basic concept that you'll want to keep tucked away somewhere in your brain.

The Warning icon points out places where you should be extra careful — for example, because you risk wiping out your valuable data.

Sometimes it's helpful to dig a little deeper into how Excel works. The Technical Stuff icon marks paragraphs that contain this kind of in-depth info. When you're focusing on getting things done, feel free to skip over these sections. But when you want to know the *why* behind the *how* of particular moves in Excel, come back and read them.

Beyond the Book

There's a huge amount of information in this book, but be sure to check out the free online Cheat Sheet, which puts key techniques and shortcuts at your fingertips. To find the Cheat Sheet, go to www.dummies.com and type **Microsoft 365 Excel All-in-One For Dummies Cheat Sheet** in the Search box.

We've also provided sample files to help you work through some of the examples in the chapters. To get the sample files, go to www.dummies.com/go/microsoft365excelaiofd.

Where to Go from Here

If you're just getting started with Excel, Book 1 is the place to begin. Turn the page and dig in. If you already work with Excel, you'll probably want to go straight to the topic on which you need help. Use the table of contents or the index to find what you need.

Getting Started with Excel

Contents at a Glance

CHAPTER 1: Getting Started with Spreadsheets 7
- Exploring Excel's User Interface 7
- Entering and Editing Data 15
- Handling Workbook Operations 20
- Managing Worksheet Tasks 23
- Collaborating with Others 27

CHAPTER 2: Carrying Out Basic Calculations 31
- Understanding Operators 31
- Exploring the Order of Operations 35
- Contrasting Cell References 40
- Replicating Formulas 41
- Calculating Sums 44
- Analyzing Data with Statistical Functions 47

CHAPTER 3: Formatting Cells and Worksheets 53
- Applying Basic Formatting Commands 54
- Exploring the Format Cells Dialog Box 55
- Applying Cell Styles 59
- Merging and Centering Cells 62
- Wrapping Text 64
- Tapping into Text Boxes 65
- Inserting Images 67
- Enhancing Accessibility 68
- Adjusting Row Heights and Column Widths 69
- Hiding and Unhiding Rows and Columns 70
- Hiding and Unhiding Workbooks 74
- Modifying Page Setup 74

CHAPTER 4: Organizing Data and Creating Tables 79
- Organizing Data 79
- Creating Tables 97

CHAPTER 5: Navigating Worksheets and Workbooks 113
- Finding and Replacing Data within Cells 114
- Exploring with the Navigation Task Pane 116
- Jumping to Locations with Go To 118
- Targeting Specific Cells with Go To Special 118
- Navigating with the Name Box 120
- Activating Worksheets 120
- Reordering Worksheets 121
- Splitting Worksheet Windows 122
- Viewing Two or More Worksheets at Once 123
- Applying Custom Views 123
- Zooming In and Out 127

> **IN THIS CHAPTER**
> » Getting oriented in Excel
> » Creating and saving workbooks
> » Working with spreadsheet templates
> » Entering and editing data
> » Sharing workbooks with others

Chapter 1
Getting Started with Spreadsheets

In this chapter, we show you how to get started with spreadsheets in Microsoft Excel. We cover the key features of the Excel interface, show you how to create and save Excel workbooks and enter and edit data in worksheets, and much more.

Exploring Excel's User Interface

Whenever you launch Excel, it eagerly greets you with a blank workbook featuring a single worksheet tab. You also see a tabbed command interface across the top that Microsoft calls the *ribbon* (see Figure 1-1). The ribbon includes a set of static tabs, along with other contextual tabs that pop up when Excel deems them necessary. Just above the ribbon sits a collection of icons known as the Quick Access Toolbar — your personal stash of frequently used commands, which we cover in the "Customizing the Quick Access Toolbar" section later in this chapter.

Below the ribbon, you see a row composed of three sections:

TIP

» **Name Box:** Most users rely on this area to see the address of the currently selected worksheet cell.

You can do a surprising number of things in the Name Box — more than two dozen! Chapter 5 of this minibook provides more details.

» **Insert Function button:** Excel's real power comes from its hundreds of worksheet functions, which let you crunch numbers from simple sums to complex calculations using inputs called *arguments*. Clicking this button opens a search-friendly dialog box, followed by another dialog box that walks you through building the formula step-by-step. The "Leveraging worksheet functions" section later in this chapter offers a straightforward way to get started.

» **Formula Bar:** This expandable section shows what's inside the selected worksheet cell. If a cell has a formula, you see the result in the cell, while the Formula Bar reveals the formula itself. You can edit cell contents directly in the Formula Bar or within the cell itself. To do so, double-click a cell or press F2 (Windows) or ⌘+U (macOS).

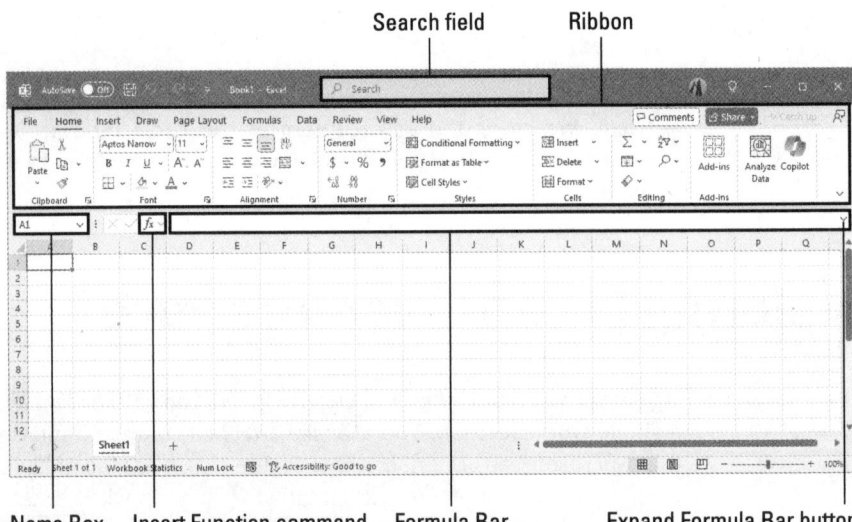

FIGURE 1-1: Microsoft Excel's user interface.

8   BOOK 1 **Getting Started with Excel**

TECHNICAL STUFF

Cells can contain up to 32,000 characters, including text, numbers, symbols, non-printable characters like carriage returns, and formulas.

TIP

The Expand Formula Bar button sits on the right-hand side of the Formula Bar. Clicking it — or pressing Ctrl+Shift+U (Windows) or ⌘+Shift+U (macOS) — expands the Formula Bar to show up to 11 rows, letting you see long formulas but reducing the number of visible worksheet rows. You can also resize the Formula Bar by dragging its bottom edge, balancing the need to see more cell contents and keeping more of the worksheet in view.

Below the Formula Bar lies the worksheet grid, made up of a fixed number of rows and columns. Rows are numbered from 1 to 1,048,576, while columns follow a lettered system: A through Z for the first 26, AA through AZ for the next 26, continuing on until the final column, XFD.

TECHNICAL STUFF

Every worksheet contains 1,048,576 rows and 16,384 columns — more than 17 billion cells in total — giving you plenty of room to get lost in data.

Traversing the ribbon

The ribbon in Excel is divided into two groups: the main tabs, which are always present, and the tool tabs, which appear when they're needed. The main tabs are as follows:

» **File:** Opens the Backstage View, where Excel handles all the behind-the-scenes business — opening, saving, printing, sharing workbooks, and tweaking settings.

» **Home:** This is where Excel keeps the most-used commands for formatting, editing, sorting, and filtering.

TIP

If all those icons are starting to blur together, think of ScreenTips as little cue cards. Hover over any ribbon or toolbar command, and Excel will remind you what it does. Windows users even get keyboard shortcuts — macOS users, not so much.

» **Insert:** Think of this as Excel's "Add Stuff" tab. Spice things up with shapes, images, and text boxes (see Chapter 3 of this minibook), or drop in PivotTables and slicers (see Book 5, Chapter 2) or PivotCharts (see Book 5, Chapter 4).

» **Page Layout:** Fine-tunes how your worksheet looks when printed — margins, scaling, and other settings that help you wrestle Excel into submission — *on paper, at least* (see Chapter 3 of this minibook).

CHAPTER 1 **Getting Started with Spreadsheets** 9

- **Formulas:** The command center for Excel's number-crunching wizardry. Dig into function libraries, troubleshoot formulas, and tweak calculation settings.

- **Data:** The Get & Transform Data section and Queries & Connections section let you pull in info from just about anywhere using Power Query (see Book 6, Chapter 5). The Data Types feature adds self-updating "smart" cells. The rest of the tab wrangles sorting, filtering (see Chapter 4 of this minibook), and what-if analysis, like scenario management (see Book 4, Chapter 2).

- **Review:** This tab helps you catch typos, flag accessibility issues (see Chapter 3 of this minibook), add comments (see the "Collaborating with Others" section of this chapter), and locking down spreadsheets to protect them.

- **View:** This tab lets you control what you see in Excel, including splitting worksheet windows (see Chapter 5 of this minibook), switching between custom views (Chapter 5 again), and adjusting zoom levels (Chapter 5 once more).

- **Help:** This tab connects you to support resources, troubleshooting information, and usage tips for Excel.

TECHNICAL STUFF

Depending on your rights and licensing, the Automate tab may appear, granting access to Office Scripts for automating repetitive tasks with JavaScript-based scripts. Any user can enable the Developer tab, packed with tools for creating and editing macros (see Book 8, Chapter 1).

SEARCHING EXCEL'S MENUS

If you're feeling adrift, get back on firm ground with Excel's multipurpose Search feature. Access it in one of the following ways:

- Click the Search field in Excel's title bar.
- Press Alt+Q (Windows) or ⌘+Ctrl+U (macOS).

Choose from suggestions based on recent or common actions, or start typing to generate a dynamic list of commands. To search within the worksheet, enter a term and select Find in Worksheet (Windows) or Find (macOS).

A second Search the Menus field appears when you right-click the worksheet frame or any cell. This search is limited to ribbon commands — use Find instead when hunting for data (covered in Chapter 5 of this minibook).

You can customize the ribbon by adding new command groups to existing tabs or creating entirely new tabs:

1. **Open the Customization dialog box:**

   - **Windows:** On the File tab of the ribbon, click Options, and then click Customize Ribbon to open the Excel Options dialog box. Alternatively, right-click the ribbon and select Customize the Ribbon.

   - **macOS:** Choose Excel⇨Preferences and click Ribbon & Toolbar (opens the Ribbon & Toolbar pane of the Excel Preferences dialog box).

2. **Show or hide tabs by toggling the check boxes in the Customize the Ribbon list.**

3. **Edit an existing tab:**

   a. Select a tab from the Customize the Ribbon list (defaults to Main Tabs). Select Tool Tabs or All Tabs to explore further.

   b. Click New Group (+ then New Group on macOS) to add a custom group.

   c. Rename it by clicking Rename (click . . . then Rename on macOS).

   d. Add commands by selecting them from the Choose Commands list and clicking Add >> (> on macOS). Use << Remove (< on macOS) to remove commands.

4. **To create a new tab, click New Tab (+ then New Tab on macOS), and then rename it and add groups and commands as needed.**

Here's a peek at some of the tool tabs that appear when a task calls for them:

» **Header & Footer:** This tab takes the stage when you decide what should grace the top or bottom of each page — because every sheet deserves a proper introduction and a grand finale (see Chapter 3 of this minibook).

» **Analyze:** This tab steps into the spotlight for PivotTables and PivotCharts (see Book 5, Chapters 2 through 4), giving you tools to connect, explore, and wrangle your data.

» **Design:** This tab makes a stylish appearance when you select a cell in an Excel table (see Chapter 4 of this minibook) or a PivotTable, or you click a chart or PivotChart.

» **Format:** This feature-specific tab appears for charts, PivotCharts, shapes, and images.

» **Query:** This tab enables you to edit, load, reuse, combine, and share data connections through Power Query (see Book 6, Chapter 5).

TECHNICAL STUFF

Enterprise and government users can — and frankly should — enable the Inquire add-in. This powerhouse of a tool helps you document workbooks, compare workbook versions, and fine-tune performance, making it a must-have for anyone wrangling complex spreadsheets.

Customizing the Quick Access Toolbar

The Quick Access Toolbar is a great way to give commands quickly, but to get the most out of it, you have to take the time to set it up. You can position the Quick Access Toolbar either above or below the ribbon. By default, it includes buttons for AutoSave, Save, Undo, and Redo. To make the Quick Access Toolbar your own:

» **Add a single command:** In Windows only, right-click the command on the ribbon and then click Add to Quick Access Toolbar.

» **Make extensive changes:**

- **Windows:** On the File tab of the ribbon, click Options to open the Excel Options dialog box, and then click Quick Access Toolbar.
- **macOS:** Choose Excel➪Preferences and click Ribbon & Toolbar to open the Ribbon & Toolbar pane of the Excel Preferences dialog box; then click the Quick Access Toolbar tab.

From there, you can shuffle icons, relocate the toolbar, and decide whether command labels should appear as ScreenTips.

» **Reset the Quick Access Toolbar** (if your customizations spiral into chaos):

- **Windows:** In the Excel Options dialog box, click Quick Access Toolbar. Then click the Reset button and click Reset Only Quick Access Toolbar.
- **macOS:** Click . . . on the Quick Access Toolbar tab of the Ribbon & Toolbar dialog box, and then click Reset Only Quick Access Toolbar.

One of our favorite areas to explore is the Commands Not in the Ribbon list within the Choose Commands From list. This hidden trove contains hundreds of commands left off the ribbon — either due to space constraints or feature deprecation. Here are a few gems we often add to the Quick Access Toolbar:

» **AutoFilter:** A one-click wonder that filters a normal range of cells based on whatever's in the selected cell. But don't get any wild ideas — this trick doesn't work within Excel tables (see Chapter 4 of this minibook).

» **Custom Views:** This feature lets you swap between saved worksheet and workbook layouts. We cover Custom Views in Chapter 5 of this minibook.

» **Full Screen:** Clears away the ribbon, Formula Bar, and Status Bar so you can focus on your data. Press Esc to bring everything back.

Activating worksheets

Each document you create in Excel is called a *workbook*, which consists of one or more *worksheets* — each represented by a tab at the bottom of the worksheet grid. Think of worksheets as pages in a ledger, neatly organized within your workbook.

Here are a few ways that you can activate a worksheet tab:

- **Click the tab.** Simple and straightforward.
- **Use the sheet navigation arrows.** Found just above the Status Bar, these arrows let you nudge the visible tabs left or right — provided you have more tabs than can fit comfortably on screen.
- **Use the Activate dialog box.** Right-click the sheet navigation arrows to summon the Activate dialog box. Pick a worksheet from the list and click OK — or double-click a sheet name to skip the extra step.

REMEMBER

The Activate dialog box lists only visible worksheets — so if a sheet is hidden, it won't show up there. To track down hidden worksheets, use the Navigation task pane (covered in Chapter 5 of this minibook). For more on making sheets disappear (or reappear), check out the upcoming "Hiding or unhiding worksheets" section.

Exploring the Status Bar

The Status Bar keeps you in the loop with various feedback mechanisms and quick-access tools. Here's a rundown of the default options (as shown in Figure 1-2):

- **Cell Mode Indicator:** Your cell's current mood, expressed in one word:
  - **Ready:** Just sitting there, minding its own business
  - **Enter:** Actively receiving data or a formula
  - **Point:** Waiting for you to pick cells for a formula
  - **Edit:** Mid-editing, hoping you don't regret your choices
- **AutoFilter Status:** Tells you how many records match your filter criteria — so you're not left wondering why half your data mysteriously vanished. Filtering gets the full treatment in Chapter 4 of this minibook.
- **Calculate Status:** Signals that some values may be outdated because Automatic Calculation is turned off or when Excel enters Manual Calculation mode due to a large dataset. Clicking it or pressing F9 (Windows only) recalculates outdated formulas in the open workbook.

TECHNICAL STUFF

Press Ctrl+Alt+F9 (Windows) or ⌘+Shift+= (macOS) to force a full recalculation of all formulas across all open workbooks. Windows users can also press Ctrl+Shift+Alt+F9 to rebuild the *dependency tree* (an internal structure that tracks relationships between formulas and the cells they reference) and then recalculate everything. Mac users can achieve a similar result by toggling Manual Calculation mode (choose Excel⇨Preferences and click Calculation) and then switching back to Automatic to force a full recalculation.

REMEMBER

Unlike most Status Bar features, the AutoFilter and Calculate settings can't be toggled on or off — they appear only when relevant.

» **Accessibility Assistant:** Indicates if an accessibility issue has been detected — click the icon to open the Accessibility Checker (see Chapter 3 of this minibook), where you can review and fix potential concerns so your workbook is inclusive and easy to navigate for all users.

» **AutoCalculate Functions:** Instantly crunches numbers when you select multiple cells, serving up average, count, numerical count, minimum, maximum, and sum.

TIP

Click any calculation in the Status Bar to copy the value to the Clipboard, letting you paste it elsewhere like the Excel wizard you are.

» **View Modes:** Located out on the right-hand side, these buttons let you switch between Normal (standard spreadsheet view), Page Layout (Excel's best guess at how your data will break across pages), and Page Break Preview (a true print preview, complete with headers and footers, so you can see exactly what will make it on the printed page).

» **Zoom Slider:** Located on the far right, this lets you zoom in until your data takes over the screen or zoom out until it vanishes into microscopic oblivion. The percentage zoom level appears next to it — click the number to open the Zoom dialog box for precise control.

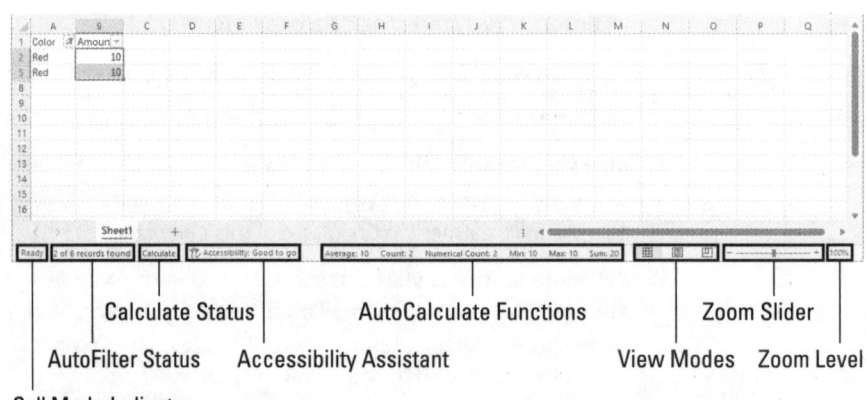

FIGURE 1-2: The Status Bar.

14 BOOK 1 **Getting Started with Excel**

You can customize the Status Bar by turning features on or off. Just right-click anywhere on it and toggle the options you want. You may want to enable the following options:

» **Sheet Number:** Displays where the current worksheet stands in the lineup — along with the total number of sheets in the workbook — for example, Sheet 3 of 27.

» **Workbook Statistics:** Click to open a dialog box that provides a quick summary of key details of the workbook, including the number of sheets, cells with data, tables, charts, and more.

» **Caps Lock, Num Lock, Scroll Lock Indicators:** These indicators let you know when you've engaged one of these settings.

   Scroll Lock is Excel for Windows's little gremlin, waiting for the perfect moment to ruin your day. When Scroll Lock is active, the arrow keys stop moving the selection and instead sends the whole worksheet gliding around like a greased-up air hockey puck. To disable it, press ScrLk again — if your keyboard even has one. If not, search for "On-Screen Keyboard" in Windows, and click ScrLk to wrestle back control.

» **Macro Recording:** When macro recording is enabled, a button appears that allows you to start or stop the Macro Recorder. Turn to Book 8, Chapter 1, to learn about macros and Visual Basic for Applications (VBA).

Entering and Editing Data

Next, try building a simple task tracker. This example introduces basic data entry, formatting, and formulas while providing a preview of features explored in more detail later in this book.

Starting a task tracker

Here's how to get started with building a task-tracking spreadsheet:

1. **Add the following column titles (referred to as *headers* in Excel) to a blank Excel worksheet.**

   - **Cell A1:** Task
   - **Cell B1:** Due Date
   - **Cell C1:** Priority

CHAPTER 1 **Getting Started with Spreadsheets** 15

- **Cell D1:** Status
- **Cell E1:** Time Spent (Hours)

> **TIP** Column headers organize data, make the spreadsheet easier to read, and improve ease of use with certain Excel features, such as sorting lists (see Chapter 4 of this minibook) and report writing with PivotTables (see Book 5, Chapter 2).

2. **Enter the following example tasks into the cells below:**
   - **A2:** Gym
   - **A3:** Tan
   - **A4:** Laundry
   - **A5:** Party

3. **In column B, add due dates for each task:**

   a. **In cell B2, type** 1/1 (the one day of the year that some folks actually go the gym)**, and then press Enter.**

   In unformatted cells, Excel converts entries in m/d or mm/dd format to d-mmm, with the hidden year defaulting to the current year. To display the full date in m/d/yyyy format, on the Home tab on the ribbon click the Number Format drop-down at the top of the Number group, and then click Short Date.

   b. **In cell B3, type** 04/01/2026**, and then press Enter.**

   Excel pranks you by dropping the leading zeroes — see Chapter 2 of this minibook for how to display them if needed.

   c. **Overwrite the values in cells B2:B3 with yesterday's date and today's date, respectively, using the m/d format.**

   Excel adds the current year automatically since both cells have date formats applied.

   d. **Drag the Fill Handle from cell B2, shown in Figure 1-3, to cell B5 to fill the series of dates.**

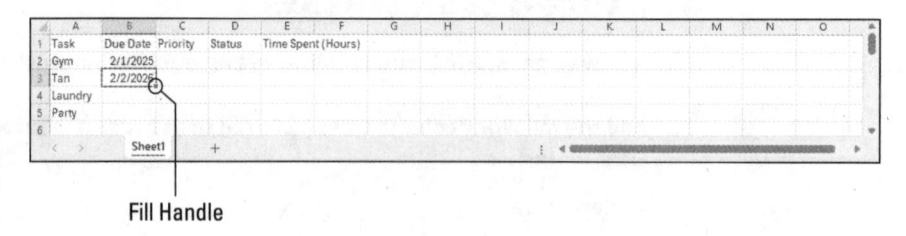

FIGURE 1-3: Use the Fill Handle.

Fill Handle

4. **Use column C to track priority:**
   - **C2:** High
   - **C3:** Medium
   - **C4:** Low
   - **C5:** High

   > **TIP:** As you may have noticed in cell D5, Excel can AutoFill entries based on similar entries within the current column of the current region — simply press Enter when the desired entry appears after typing matching characters.

5. **Use column D to track status:**
   - **D2:** Completed
   - **D3:** In Progress
   - **D4:** Pending
   - **D5:** Never Ending

6. **Use column E to track hours:**
   - **E2:** 2
   - **E3:** 1.5
   - **E4:** 3
   - **E5:** 4

Applying basic formatting

A common next step is to dress up data:

1. **Select the header cells (a necessary step before applying formatting):**
   - **Mouse action:** Click cell A1, hold down the left mouse button, and drag across to cell E1.
   - **Keyboard action:** Use the up-arrow key to return to cell A1, hold down Shift, and press the Right Arrow key to select across to cell E1.

   > **TIP:** To select the entire contiguous block of cells that surround the active cell, press Ctrl+A (Windows) or ⌘+A (macOS) to select the current region. If you press the shortcut again, Excel selects the entire worksheet.

2. **Apply basic formatting (see Chapter 2 of this minibook for more advanced formatting options):**

   - **Bold:** On the Home tab of the ribbon, click Bold. Alternatively, press Ctrl+B (Windows) or ⌘+B (macOS).

   - **Underline:** On the Home tab of the ribbon, click Underline. Alternatively, press Ctrl+U (Windows) or ⌘+U (macOS).

     Some commands, such as Underline, include a drop-down button that provides additional functionality, such as the Double Underline command.

   - **Center:** On the Home tab of the ribbon, click Center to align the text in the center of each cell. There's no built-in shortcut for center justification, but see the "Customizing the Quick Access Toolbar" section earlier in this chapter to create your own.

   Many formatting commands function as toggles, such as Bold or Underline. Other commands work in groups, so you need to choose an alternative option. For example, if text in a cell is right-aligned, you can't toggle right alignment off; instead, you can apply another alignment, such as left alignment.

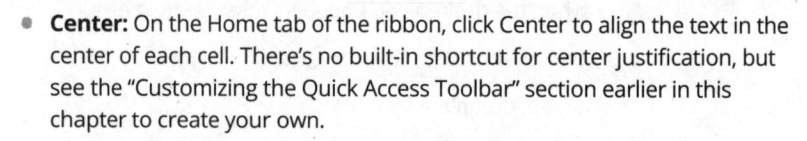

3. **Select cell E1, and then, on the Home tab of the ribbon, click Wrap Text.**

   Excel automatically adjusts the row height to ensure that all data within the cell is visible.

   Line breaks for wrapped text are based on the column width. To insert a manual line break, press Alt+Enter (Windows) or Option+Return (macOS).

4. **To format the hours with two decimal places, select cells E2:E5. Then, on the Home tab of the ribbon, click Comma Style (the button bearing a giant comma).**

   If necessary, adjust the decimal places by clicking Increase Decimal or Decrease Decimal on the Home tab of the ribbon.

5. **To adjust the width of column D, click the letter D at the top of the worksheet to select the entire column, and then go to the Home tab of the ribbon, click Format, and select AutoFit Column Width.**

   Alternatively, move the pointer over the column's right edge, so it changes to a double-headed arrow, and then double-click.

Leveraging worksheet functions

Worksheet functions are prepackaged formulas that crunch numbers, manipulate data, and make your life easier. They work by using specific values called *arguments,* which you feed into the function like ingredients in a recipe. Whether you're doing simple math or wrangling a monster-sized dataset, these functions have your back. You'll find them hanging out in the Function Library group of the Formulas tab of the ribbon.

For instance, the SUM function is an ideal way to add a total to cell E6. You can do this in two ways. The first is using the AutoSum command:

1. **Select the cell where the total should appear (for example, E6).**
2. **On the Home tab of the ribbon, click AutoSum.**

The second way is to use a manual formula:

1. **Type =SUM(in cell E6 to start the formula.**
2. **Select cells E2:E5 using one of these methods:**
   - Drag the mouse across E2:E5.
   - Use the up-arrow key to navigate to cell E5, hold Shift, and then navigate to cell E2.
   - Manually type **E2:E5** or **E5:E2**.
3. **Type) to close the formula, and then press Enter.**

Using either approach, the completed formula =SUM(E2:E5) appears. The SUM function has 255 arguments, but most users use only the first one:

» **number1:** The first range or amount to include in the total (for example, E2:E5).

» **number2...255:** Optional additional ranges or amounts.

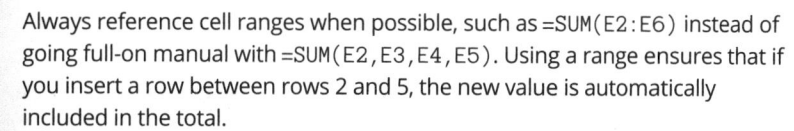

REMEMBER Always reference cell ranges when possible, such as =SUM(E2:E6) instead of going full-on manual with =SUM(E2,E3,E4,E5). Using a range ensures that if you insert a row between rows 2 and 5, the new value is automatically included in the total.

TIP The Table feature (see Chapter 4 of this minibook) includes a Total Row option, which creates total rows without manual formulas — and better yet, it automatically updates when additional amounts are added to the list.

CHAPTER 1 **Getting Started with Spreadsheets**

Here's how to create a slightly more complex formula:

1. **Type** Completion % **in cell G1.**
2. **Add this formula to cell G2:** =COUNTIF(D2:D5,"Completed")/COUNTA(A2:A5).

   The COUNTIF function (see Book 4, Chapter 3) counts the number of instances of the word *Completed* in cells D2:D5, while the COUNTA function counts the number of non-blank cells in A2:A5. As covered in Chapter 2 of this minibook, the / operator performs division.

   Similarly named worksheet functions can return wildly different results, so don't let Excel lull you into a false sense of security. Take COUNT, for example — it only tallies up numeric values, meaning =COUNT(A2:A5) would return 0 if the range contains nothing but text. So, if you were expecting a number and got ghosted instead, now you know why.

3. **Select cell G2 and then click Percent Style on the Home tab of the ribbon to format the result as a percent.**

Handling Workbook Operations

As noted earlier in this chapter, launching Excel conjures up a blank workbook featuring a single worksheet tab. You can dive straight into data entry or open an existing workbook instead. If you open an existing workbook, Excel discreetly sweeps that initial blank workbook away. Because you've likely put some effort into building a worksheet, let's make sure it's saved for later use.

Saving Excel workbooks

Here's how to save a workbook:

- **File menu:** On Windows, click the File tab on the ribbon, and then click either Save or Save As. On macOS, choose File➪Save or File➪Save As. If you've already saved the workbook, Save updates the existing version, whereas Save As allows you to save a copy under a new name.

If you save your workbook to OneDrive or SharePoint, you can toggle AutoSave on via the Quick Access Toolbar. After you enable AutoSave, Excel automatically saves your work every few seconds to a minute, ensuring you don't lose progress — even if Excel (or life) throws a curveball.

- **» Quick Access Toolbar:** Click Save or tap the Alt key in Windows and then type the shortcut that appears in a ScreenTip.
- **» Keyboard shortcut:** Press Ctrl+S (Windows) or ⌘+S (macOS). If you've already saved the workbook at least once, this shortcut updates the saved version. Otherwise, it opens the Save As dialog box, allowing you to specify the name and location for the workbook.

Opening existing workbooks

You can open an existing workbook in a couple of ways:

- **» Menu commands:** On Windows, on the File tab of the ribbon, click Open and then click Browse to summon the Open dialog box, where you can navigate through your digital filing cabinet, select a workbook, and then click Open. Alternatively, on Windows, on the File tab of the ribbon, click Home to browse recent workbooks. On macOS, choose File⇨Open to display the Open dialog box, or choose File⇨Recent⇨More to display the Recent tab of the Microsoft Excel dialog box.
- **» Keyboard shortcut:** Press Ctrl+O (Windows) or ⌘+O (macOS) to go straight to the Open dialog box. On macOS, press ⌘+Shift+O to display the Recent tab of the Microsoft Excel dialog box.

If you have multiple workbooks open, Excel typically shows only one at a time, but you're not stuck with that — you can view more than one simultaneously. Here's how to switch between workbooks or arrange them onscreen:

- **» Keyboard shortcut:** Press Ctrl+Tab (Windows) or ⌘+~ (macOS).
- **» View⇨Switch Windows⇨[Window Name]:** Lists all open workbooks, except the hidden ones, like the Personal Macro Workbook (covered in Book 8, Chapter 1).
- **» View⇨Arrange All:** Opens the Arrange All dialog box, where you can choose how to display your workbooks:
  - **Tiled:** Workbooks arranged in non-overlapping boxes
  - **Horizontal:** Workbooks stacked in rows, one above the other
  - **Vertical:** Workbooks placed in columns, side by side
  - **Cascade:** Workbooks stacked with overlapping windows, like a deck of cards

CHAPTER 1 Getting Started with Spreadsheets

Creating new workbooks

Need a new workbook? Here are a couple of ways to start fresh:

- » **Menu commands:** On Windows, you can create a new workbook by going to the File tab of the ribbon, clicking either Home or New, and then clicking Blank Workbook. On macOS, choose File➪New from the menu bar.
- » **Keyboard shortcut:** Press Ctrl+N (Windows) or ⌘+N (macOS).

Any of these approaches creates a new, blank workbook with a single worksheet tab — a clean slate, ready for whatever data you throw at it.

Using Excel templates

Excel workbook templates are ready-made designs that spare you from starting from scratch. They also double as cheat sheets for good spreadsheet design, with formatting and formulas baked in to keep things running smoothly. Here's how to grab one:

- » **File menu:**
    1. **On Windows, click the File tab of the ribbon, and then click New. On macOS, choose File➪New (Windows) or File➪New from Template.**

       The Template screen or Microsoft Excel dialog box opens.

    2. **Scroll through the suggested templates — macOS users have to scroll down more than one screen — or perform a keyword search using the Search for Online Templates field (Windows) or Search field (macOS).**

    3. **Click any template that seems to be a good match, and then click Create to generate a new workbook based on the template.**

- » **Worksheet tab context menu:** Windows users can right-click any worksheet tab, select Insert, choose a template from the General or Spreadsheet Solutions tabs (shown in Figure 1-4), and click OK to add it to the workbook.

- » **Microsoft website:** Head over to https://create.microsoft.com to explore a vast library of templates for Excel and other Microsoft 365 applications.

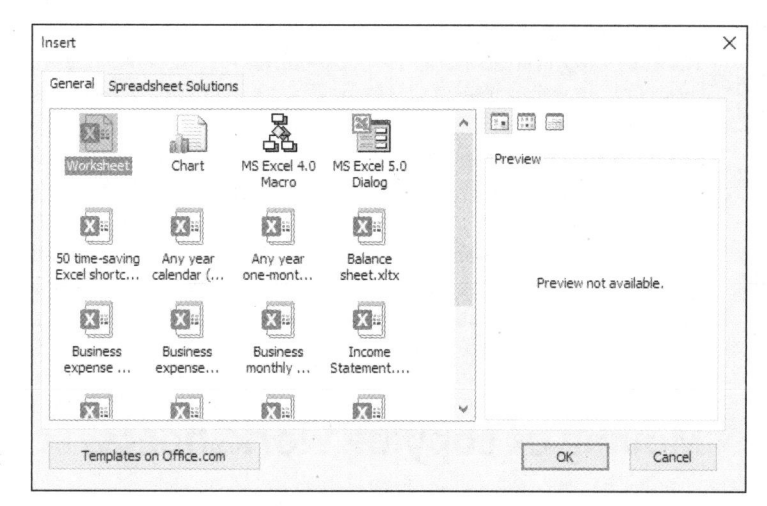

FIGURE 1-4: The Insert dialog box.

Managing Worksheet Tasks

A workbook must always have at least one visible worksheet — Excel won't let you delete the last sheet. You can rename, insert, remove, move, or copy worksheets.

TIP

You can perform most of these actions on multiple sheets at once. Check out the upcoming "Grouping worksheets" section to corral them.

Renaming Excel worksheets

Each tab name can be up to 31 characters long, but how many tabs you can see at once depends on their length and your screen resolution. Cram in long names, and you'll be scrolling like a hamster on a wheel. Keep them short, and you can fit more in view. You have three ways to rename an Excel worksheet:

- On the Home tab of the ribbon, click Format, and then click Rename Sheet.
- Right-click a worksheet tab and then choose Rename.
- Double-click a worksheet tab.

Any of these approaches enables you to edit a worksheet tab, which must have at least a single character. Press Enter or click any worksheet cell to apply your change or press Escape if you change your mind.

CHAPTER 1 **Getting Started with Spreadsheets** 23

TECHNICAL STUFF

The following characters are strictly banned from worksheet names: asterisk (*), colon (:), question mark (?), slashes (\ /), and square brackets ([ ]). But beyond that, Excel is surprisingly open-minded — even emojis are fair game. Try typing an invalid character, though, and Excel won't bother with a warning; it'll just silently toss your keystroke like it never happened.

REMEMBER

Excel won't let you name a worksheet "History" — not because it has a grudge against the past, but because Track Changes has already claimed it. And while we're at it, each worksheet tab must have a unique name within a workbook — no duplicates allowed no matter how much you want two sheets called "Stuff."

Moving or copying worksheets

You can shuffle worksheets within a workbook just by dragging their tabs to a new spot. One of our favorite disaster recovery methods in Excel is duplicating a worksheet — an instant fallback in case things go sideways. Our go-to move for this is holding down the Ctrl (Windows) or ⌘ (macOS) key while dragging a worksheet (or the first worksheet within a group of worksheets) into a new position, creating a copy without the hassle of menu diving. But if you prefer menus:

1. **Right-click the tab of the worksheet you want to move or copy, and then choose Move or Copy. Alternatively, select the worksheet, click the Home tab of the ribbon, click Format, and then click Move or Copy Sheet.**

   The Move or Copy dialog box appears, as shown in Figure 1-5.

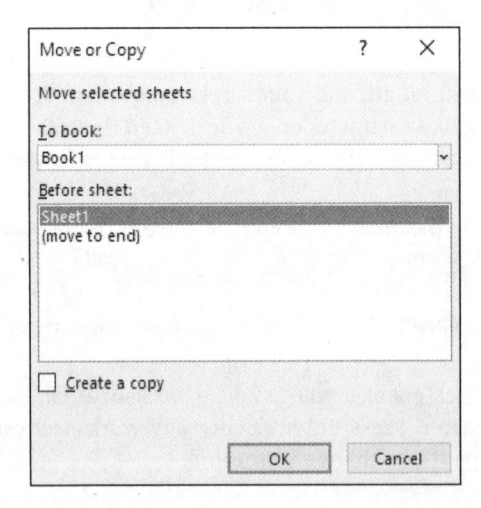

FIGURE 1-5: The Move or Copy dialog box.

BOOK 1 Getting Started with Excel

2. **To move the worksheet to another open workbook, select that workbook from the To Book list; to move the worksheet to a new workbook, choose (new book).**

   REMEMBER: You can move or copy worksheets only into a new workbook or an existing workbook that is currently open in Excel.

3. **To specify the worksheet's position, choose a location from the Before Sheet list.**

   If no selection is made, the worksheet is moved or copied to appear before the first sheet in the workbook.

4. **To make a copy of the worksheet or worksheets, select the Create a Copy check box.**

   Excel moves worksheets to the specified or default location if you don't select Create a Copy.

   REMEMBER: Moving or copying a worksheet can't be undone, but other prior actions remain reversible.

   WARNING: Take care when moving or copying worksheets between workbooks to prevent data loss. If you choose a destination in the To Book field without selecting Create a Copy, the worksheet is moved, not copied, and removed from the original workbook. The destination workbook becomes active, making it easy to overlook the change. Moving the last worksheet from a workbook causes Excel to close the workbook without a Save prompt.

5. **Click OK to apply the change.**

Adding or deleting worksheets

The number of worksheets that you can add to an Excel workbook depends on your computer's memory — in theory, you can keep adding them until your machine freezes. But just because you *can* doesn't mean you *should*. Stuffing a workbook with too many sheets can turn navigation into a nightmare and tank your efficiency. There are four ways to mindfully insert worksheets:

» On the Home tab of the ribbon, click the Insert drop-down and then click Insert Sheet.

» Right-click any worksheet tab, choose Insert, and then click OK.

» Click the New Sheet button that appears just above Excel's Status Bar, and to the right of the furthest onscreen worksheet tab.

» Press Shift+F11 (Windows) or Fn+Shift+F11 (macOS and some Windows keyboards).

CHAPTER 1 **Getting Started with Spreadsheets** 25

You can delete a worksheet in two ways:

- On the Home tab of the ribbon, click the Delete drop-down, and then click Delete sheet.
- Right-click a worksheet tab, and then choose Delete.

Blank worksheets that haven't been edited vanish instantly upon deletion, no questions asked. However, if a worksheet contains any edits, Excel warns you that it's about to be permanently deleted and asks if you're sure you want to proceed.

Deleting a worksheet is irreversible — you can't undo it or any actions taken before its deletion. After it's gone, it's truly gone.

Hiding or unhiding worksheets

If your workbook contains two or more worksheets, you can hide all but one. Formulas and features that reference hidden worksheets keep working as usual — hiding a sheet doesn't impact its functionality.

To hide a worksheet, right-click its tab (or the tab of the first worksheet in a group) and then click Hide. Alternatively, with the worksheet active, click the Home tab of the ribbon, click Format, click Hide & Unhide, and then click Hide Sheet. The worksheet vanishes from view, and you can no longer navigate to it — but don't worry, it's just hiding, not gone for good.

Use the following steps to unhide a hidden worksheet:

1. **Right-click a worksheet tab and select Unhide. Alternatively, click the Home tab of the ribbon, click Format, click Hide & Unhide, and then click Unhide Sheet.**

   The Unhide dialog box opens.

   The Unhide command or Unhide Sheet command is grayed out if no hidden worksheets are lurking in the workbook.

2. **Select a worksheet from the list and then click OK.**

   To unhide two or more worksheets, hold down Ctrl (Windows) or ⌘ (macOS) and then select the sheet names. To display all hidden worksheets, hold down the Shift key while you click the last worksheet.

In Chapter 5 of this minibook, we explain how you can hide and unhide worksheets via the Navigation task pane.

Grouping worksheets

The Group Sheets technique lets you boss around multiple worksheets at once, applying changes across all selected sheets in one go. It's a huge time-saver when you need to make identical updates to several worksheets, whether it's entering the same data, applying formatting, or crunching sets of numbers. You can also use this technique to hide multiple worksheets at once — because sometimes data is better left in the shadows. Here's how:

- » **All worksheets:** Right-click any tab and choose Select All Sheets.
- » **Selected worksheets:**
  - **Adjacent worksheets:** Select the first worksheet you want to group, and then hold down the Shift key and click the last sheet in the group.
  - **Nonadjacent worksheets:** Hold down the Ctrl (Windows) or ⌘ (macOS) key while clicking individual worksheet tabs.

When worksheets are grouped, the word *Group* appears in Excel's title bar, signaling that any changes you make apply to all selected sheets.

After completing your task, right-click any worksheet and choose Ungroup Sheets, or simply click a worksheet tab that isn't part of the group.

WARNING Editing grouped worksheets comes with a considerable risk of accidental data loss. Any action performed on one sheet is applied to all sheets in the group, which means you could unknowingly overwrite data in worksheets you're not even looking at. Always double-check that you're working on the intended sheets before making edits while the worksheets are grouped.

Collaborating with Others

Your spreadsheets don't have to be solitary — Excel makes sharing and collaborating easy. You can email versions back and forth or embrace coauthoring — inviting anyone anywhere to work on your spreadsheet in real time, without the endless email attachments.

Sharing static copies of workbooks

To send a noncollaborative copy of a workbook, choose File⇨Share and then choose between the Workbook or PDF options. Workbooks can still be edited in Excel, and changes won't affect your copy. You can't directly edit PDF files in Excel, though.

Coauthoring simultaneously

Simultaneous coauthoring allows multiple users to work on the same workbook at the same time, making collaboration easy. However, not every workbook is a good candidate. Workbooks saved locally (as opposed to on OneDrive or SharePoint) can't be coauthored. In addition, workbooks containing any of the following features cannot be coauthored:

- Macros (see Book 8, Chapter 1)
- Worksheet or workbook protection
- Legacy data connections (OLAP, Query Tables, Linked Tables)
- Data Model/Power Pivot (see Book 6, Chapter 1)

In addition, AutoSave must be enabled to use coauthoring. Here's how to get started in Excel for Windows:

1. **Open the workbook you want to share.**
2. **Click the Share button in the upper-right corner of the Excel window, and then click Share.**

   The Share command appears in the upper-right corner of the Excel window.

Depending on the workbook's status, either a single dialog box appears or two dialog boxes appear in sequence. Choose the option you prefer:

- **Share:** This dialog prompts you to save the workbook to a Microsoft cloud platform, like OneDrive or SharePoint. After you select a platform and name the workbook, the Send Link dialog box appears.
- **Send Link:** This dialog box contains three sections:
  - **Send Link:** Enter email addresses, draft a message, and control access. Use the Can Edit icon to toggle sharing permissions or click Sharing Settings to limit sharing to specific people, set an expiration date, or add a password.
  - **Copy Link:** Click Copy to generate a link to the workbook. Use the Anyone with the Link Can Edit option to manage permissions.
  - **Send a Copy:** Choose Excel workbook to share a noncollaborative copy or send the workbook as a PDF.

If you're on a Mac, choose File ➪ Share or click the Share button in the upper-right corner of the Excel window. If necessary, you're prompted to save your workbook to the cloud. After you've done so, choose File ➪ Share or File ➪ Share Again, and then choose a sharing option.

REMEMBER: You can spy on changes made by others in real time. Excel highlights the cells being edited and shows the name of the editor. If you want to take control later on Windows, click the File tab of the ribbon, click Info, click Manage Workbook, and click Manage Access. You can then update permissions or stop sharing.

Commenting collectively

Comments let you leave your brilliant thoughts in a spreadsheet and even invite others to chime in. Here's how to add one:

1. **Use one of the following methods:**
   - Right-click a cell and select New Comment.
   - On the Review tab of the ribbon, click New Comment.
   - Click New in the Comments task pane. (If needed, click the Review tab of the ribbon, and then click Show Comments.)

   A comment box appears on the worksheet grid, or in the Comments task pane.

2. **Type your message and then click Post Comment or press Ctrl+Enter.**

   To bring someone into the discussion, use an @mention by typing @ followed by their name. If they don't have access, Excel prompts you to share the workbook with them.

   Your workbook must be saved to OneDrive or SharePoint for @mentions to work.

REMEMBER: When a comment is added, a purple indicator appears in the upper-right corner of the cell. Hover over or click the cell to display the comment. Any user can add a reply to an existing comment. Replies are threaded, and each comment or reply is tagged with the author's name, helping collaborators track who said what and when.

To view all comments in a workbook, choose Review ⇨ Show Comments or click the Comments button in the upper-right corner of Excel. The Comments task pane appears, listing all comments and replies. Click a comment to activate the corresponding cell.

Use any of the following methods to edit a comment:

- » Hover over the cell that contains a comment, and then click Edit Comment.
- » Select a comment from the Comments task pane, and then click Edit Comment.
- » Right-click the underlying cell, and then choose Edit Comment from the context menu.

To mark a comment as resolved, click More Thread Options within the comment or Comments task pane, and then choose Resolve Thread. The in-cell comment indicator turns gray, and the comment is marked as Resolved in the Comment task pane. This keeps the discussion history intact while distinguishing it from active conversations. Click Reopen (which looks like the Undo command) to reactivate a comment.

To delete a comment:

- Hover over the cell that contains a comment, click More Thread Options, and then choose Delete Comment.
- Select a comment from the Comments task pane, choose More Thread Options, and then click Delete Comment.
- Right-click the underlying cell, and then choose Delete Comment.
- Click Delete Thread on a resolved comment in the Comments task pane

TIP: You can filter comments by @mentions, active threads, or resolved threads using the Filter button at the top of the Comments task pane.

NOTES VERSUS COMMENTS

In the good old days of Excel, what are now known as Notes used to be Comments. But here's the catch: Notes are one-way messages, like a sticky note that can't argue back, whereas Comments let you actually have a conversation. You can tell them apart by their indicators: Active Comments have a purple flag in the upper-right corner of the cell, whereas Notes sport a red triangle in the upper-left corner. Resolved Comments have a gray flag.

To manage your Comments and Notes, head to the Review tab of the ribbon. To upgrade your Notes to Comments, click the Review tab of the ribbon, click Notes, and then click Convert to Comments. To print all Comments and Notes, click the Page Layout tab of the ribbon, click Print Titles, select from the Comments and Notes field of the Sheet tab of the Page Setup dialog box, and then click Print.

IN THIS CHAPTER

» Performing mathematical operations

» Contrasting cell reference types

» Filling cells with formulas

» Summing and averaging

» Finding lowest and highest values

Chapter 2
Carrying Out Basic Calculations

This chapter covers operators, the symbols that guide Excel in crunching numbers; cell references, which save time and reduce frustration when used correctly; filling cells with formulas — both the hard and easy ways; and powerful statistical worksheet functions, preparing you for analytical adventures in later chapters.

Understanding Operators

Every formula begins with the equal sign (=), putting Excel on notice that a calculation is about to happen. If it's missing, Excel doesn't treat the entry as a formula; instead, Excel sees the entry as just a series of characters.

TIP To disable a formula without deleting it, type a single quote (') before the equal sign to convert the formula into text. This technique also helps preserve leading zeros in a number, ensuring that Excel treats the entry as text instead of dropping the zeros.

Analyzing arithmetic operators

Excel mixes in these operators to make arithmetic happen:

- **+ (plus sign):** Addition (for example, =1+1 or =A1+B1).
- **- (hyphen):** Subtraction (for example, =5-4 or =A1-B1) and negation (for example, =-8 or =-C1).
- *** (asterisk):** Multiplication (for example, =10*10 or =A1*B1).
- **/ (forward slash):** Division (for example, =13/14 or =A1/B1).

  REMEMBER: Excel displays the #DIV/0! error value when a formula attempts to divide by zero.

- **% (percent):** Percent (for example, 17% as a cell input or =18% within a formula).

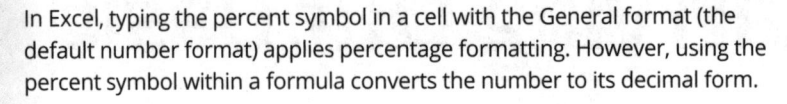

  REMEMBER: In Excel, typing the percent symbol in a cell with the General format (the default number format) applies percentage formatting. However, using the percent symbol within a formula converts the number to its decimal form.

Comparing values with operators

Whether within a logic function like IF or SUMIF, or directly in formulas, comparison operators return either TRUE or FALSE, based on whether the comparison holds. Here's the rundown on comparison operators:

- **= (equal sign):** Equal to (for example, =A1=B1)
- **> (greater-than sign):** Greater than (for example, =A1>B1)
- **< (less-than sign):** Less than (for example, =A1<B1)
- **>= (greater-than-or-equal-to sign):** Greater than or equal to (for example, =A1>=B1)
- **<= (less-than-or-equal-to sign:** Less than or equal to (for example, =A1<=B1)
- **<> (not-equal-to sign):** Not equal to (for example, =A1<>B1)

These examples use cell references, but you can apply these operators just as easily to compare the results of worksheet functions.

Combining text

Excel provides a single operator for joining text values:

& **(ampersand):** Combines text together (for example, =A1&B1)

For example, if cell A1 contains your first name and cell B1 contains your last name, the formula =A1&" "&B1 returns the two names joined together and separated by a space.

Linking cells across sheets and workbooks

Now, our discussion turns to the operators that connect cells, worksheets, and files. These little connectors are the backbone of linking data across your workbook and beyond, making complex calculations and references a breeze.

Exploring range operators

In Excel, ranges are cell references that span two or more cells. Of the four range operators, you most likely encounter the first two almost daily. The third one arises if you work with formulas that reference Excel tables, which we cover in Chapter 4 of this minibook. The fourth one is so rarified that you can't even see it and may never need to use it:

- **: (colon):** Indicates a range of cells or worksheets. Some examples include
  - **Referencing a range of cells:** =A1:A10 returns the information that currently appears in cells A1:A10 into a range of ten cells based upon where the formula is entered.
  - **Summing a range of cells:** =SUM(A1:A10) totals the values contained in cells A1 through A10 of the current worksheet.
- **, (comma):** Enables you to combine two or more noncontiguous ranges in a single formula, treating each range as a distinct argument for functions like SUM, AVERAGE and so on (for example, =SUM(A1:A10,C1:C10) and =AVERAGE(B2:M2,B12:M12)).
- **@ (at sign):** Serves two purposes — to force an implicit intersection in formulas by returning a single value from a range or array and to retrieve data from the current row in an Excel table (see Chapter 4 of this minibook).
- **(space):** Creates a range comprised of an intersection of common cells between two ranges. For example, =A3:C3 B1:B5 would return the value of cell B3, which is the only cell that overlaps between the two ranges.

In short, range operators enable you to build formulas that reference straightforward cell ranges, merge noncontiguous areas, or pinpoint intersecting cells.

Navigating sheet operators

For navigating worksheets, there's only one essential sheet operator to focus on, with a second one that may come in handy:

- **! (exclamation point):** Indicates a worksheet reference — for instance, the formula =Sheet1!A1 refers to cell A1 on the Sheet1 worksheet, while the formula =SUM(Sheet1!B2:M12) totals the values of cells B2 through M12 on Sheet1.

- **: (colon):** Indicates a worksheet drill-through reference, where a formula refers to the same cell or cells across multiple worksheets. Accordingly, the formula =SUM(Sheet1:Sheet5!B2) totals the values of cell B2 on Sheet1 through Sheet5. You can also reference a range of cells across worksheets, such as =SUM(Sheet1:Sheet5!B2:B12).

As you can see, the ! operator is used to separate worksheet names from cell references.

REMEMBER If a worksheet name contains spaces, it must be enclosed in single quotes — for example, ='Worksheet Name'!A1 or =SUM('Worksheet Name'!B2:M12). Excel automatically adds these single quotes if you navigate to another worksheet with your mouse, but remember to include them if you're typing a cell reference manually for a worksheet with spaces in its name.

Interpreting workbook operators

A *workbook link* is a reference in a formula that connects to data in another workbook. Workbook links create a dynamic connection between files, so formulas in Workbook B that reference cells in Workbook A automatically update to reflect changes in Workbook A.

This brings us to the one set of workbook operators that we want to share the lowdown on: [ ] (square brackets). Workbook names appear within square brackets before a worksheet name, such as ='[SourceWorkbook.xlsx]Sheet1'!A1. Notice how both the workbook name and the worksheet name appear within single quotes. This formula returns the value of cell A1 on a worksheet named Sheet1 from a workbook named SourceWorkbook.xlsx. Alternatively, a formula that sums cells B2:M12 from Sheet1 of SourceWorkbook.xlsx takes the form =SUM('[SourceWorkbook.xlsx]Sheet1'!B2:M12).

TECHNICAL STUFF

Workbook links undergo a bit of shape-shifting depending on whether the referenced workbook is currently open in Excel. The preceding examples show how workbook links look when the referenced workbook is open. However, if the workbook is closed, the file path appears in the link as something like this:

```
='C:\Users\David\Documents\[FruitSales.xlsx]Fruit Sales'!$A$1
```

This includes the full path to the file, enabling Excel to locate and pull in data from a closed workbook.

REMEMBER

Some operators serve multiple roles in Excel formulas. For instance, the equal sign (=) starts formulas but also acts as a comparison operator. Similarly, square brackets ([ ]) offset workbook names, enclose column names in structured references (see Chapter 4 of this minibook), and have yet another use touched on in the "Contrasting Cell References" section later in this chapter.

In short, workbook links enable automatic data transfer between workbooks.

Exploring the Order of Operations

Excel computes each formula from left to right but deviates as needed to follow the sacred sequence of PEMDAS (Parentheses, Exponents, Multiplication and Division, Addition and Subtraction). This sequence, also known as the *order of operations*, dictates exactly how calculations are performed in mathematical expressions and formulas. Here's how it works at a high level:

1. **Parentheses:** Excel calculates anything inside parentheses — including worksheet functions — first, ensuring key parts of a formula are prioritized.
2. **Exponents:** Any powers or roots are computed next.
3. **Multiplication and division:** These operations follow, processed from left to right.
4. **Addition and Subtraction:** Finally, Excel handles addition and subtraction, also from left to right.

By following this sequence, Excel ensures that formulas are evaluated systematically, helping you avoid unexpected or, worse, incorrect results.

To apply the concept: Imagine you've got $10,000 burning a hole in cell B1, ready to grow at 7 percent for one year. Follow these steps to create a formula that intentionally computes incorrectly, illustrating just how crucial Excel's order of operations can be:

1. **Enter the word** Principal **in cell A1 of a blank worksheet.**
2. **Enter** $10,000 **in cell B1.**
3. **Enter the word** Rate **in cell A2.**
4. **Enter** 7% **in cell B2.**

   TIP: Here's how to input percentages like a boss: Type a number with the % sign when entering a percentage — skip the hassle of decimal values like 0.07 and manual formatting. Excel handles both the input and formatting in one smooth move!

   TIP: Include the dollar sign ($) and comma (,) as you enter that value to get another two-for-one deal — both entering the number and formatting it in one swift move. Excel handles the heavy lifting, and your $10,000 looks as polished as your investment plan.

5. **Enter the words** Initial Formula **in cell A3.**
6. **Enter this formula into cell B3:** =1+B2*B1.

   Because Excel computes formulas from left to right, you may think it would add 1 and the value in cell B2 (7%) first, and then multiply that result by the value in cell B1 ($10,000), returning $10,700. But because of the order of operations, the formula returns $701 instead. Here's why: Excel first multiplies the value in cell B2 (7%) by cell B1 ($10,000), yielding $700, and then adds 1 to that result. This highlights the need for parentheses to ensure calculations flow as intended.

Prioritizing with parentheses

Portions of a formula wrapped in parentheses are calculated first. Worksheet functions, such as SUM, AVERAGE, or PMT, are also top priority, because they include parentheses. To create a beefed-up, and accurate, version of the formula that we just created:

1. **Enter the words** Revised Formula **in cell A4.**
2. **Enter this formula in cell B4:** =(1+B2)*B1.

   This time, the formula returns $10,700. The parentheses force Excel to add 1 plus the value in cell B2 (7%) first, resulting in 1.07. This intermediate result is then multiplied by the value in cell B1 ($10,000), producing the correct answer.

Parentheses ensure that Excel processes calculations in the intended order, giving you the expected outcome.

Elevating with exponents

Exponentiation is a mathematical operation that raises a number, known as the *base*, to the power of another number, known as the *exponent*. In short, the exponent tells you how many times to multiply the base by itself. For instance, the formula =2^3 is equivalent to =2*2*2, with both returning 8. As a reminder, exponents in Excel are represented by the ^ (caret) symbol.

Join us on a quick side quest to illustrate this concept before diving back into our investment calculations:

1. **Enter the word** Base **in cell D1.**
2. **Enter** 2 **into cell E1.**
3. **Enter the word** Exponent **in cell D2.**
4. **Enter** 3 **into cell E2.**
5. **Enter the word** Static **in cell D3.**
6. **Enter the formula** =2^3 **in cell E3.**

    The formula returns 8.

7. **Enter the word** Dynamic **in cell D4.**
8. **Enter the formula** =E1^E2 **in cell E4.**

    The formula also returns 8.

You can now calculate the power of any number by entering new values in cells E1 and E2. Now try this:

1. **Enter the words** Annual Compounding **in cell A5.**
2. **Enter this formula in cell B5:** =(1+B2)^30*B1.

    The formula, which assumes annual compounding, should return $76,122.55. It adds 1 to the value in cell B1 (representing the growth rate of 7%), raises this sum to the 30th power, and then multiplies that result by the initial investment in cell B2. This demonstrates the impact of compounding over 30 years at a consistent 7% growth rate.

The order of operations cuts both ways — a misplaced exponent can lead to a comically oversized result:

1. **Type** Exponential Error **in cell A6.**
2. **Enter this formula in cell B6:** =(1+B2)*B1^30.

   Excel first adds 1 to the growth rate in cell B2, 7%, giving an interim value of 1.07. Next it raises the value in cell B1 to the 30th power — before multiplying by 1.07. This yields a colossal number that could be presented in a couple of different ways:

   - **Currency format:** If cell B1 is formatted with a currency symbol, the resulting number will start with $1,070, followed by 118 zeros!
   - **Scientific notation:** If cell B1 has the General number format assigned, the result will be 1.07E+120.

   To avoid such exponential slipups, ensure that the exponent applies only to the 1+B2 portion, not the B1 portion.

Multiplying and dividing with precision

At this point, if you're thinking, "Wait a minute, most investments compound monthly instead of annually," you're spot on. It's time to add division.

Confession time: We committed what we consider a cardinal sin in Excel by embedding the exponent as a static value in this formula: =(1+B1)^30*B2. Hardcoding the 30 can make it tricky for users to understand the logic and edit as needed. Using a cell reference for the 30 exponent, rather than embedding it directly in the formula, makes future adjustments easier and provides transparency into what the formula is based on. Try this:

1. **Enter the words** Timeframe (years) **in cell A7.**
2. **Enter the number** 30 **in cell B7.**
3. **Enter the words** Monthly Compounding **in cell A8.**
4. **Enter this formula into cell B8:** =B1*(1+B2/12)^(B7*12).

   The formula, which allows for monthly compounding, should return $81,164.97. This setup takes advantage of compounding each month, slightly increasing the growth over 30 years at a 7% annual rate.

   Time to break it down:

   a. **Parentheses:** Excel evaluates the expression within the parentheses, (1+B2/12), first.

b. **Division:** Following the order of operations within the parentheses, Excel divides the annual growth rate in cell B2, 7%, by 12 to compute a monthly growth rate.

c. **Addition:** Excel adds the monthly growth rate to 1.

d. **Exponent:** Excel moves to the exponent, which is also enclosed in parentheses.

e. **Multiplication:** The expression (B7*12) multiplies the number of years (in cell B7) by 12, converting it into months. This monthly count represents the power to which we want to raise the monthly growth rate.

f. **Applying the exponent:** Now that the exponent has been computed, Excel raises (1+B2/12) to the power of (B7*12), giving the compounded growth factor over the entire investment period.

g. **Multiplying the principal:** Finally, Excel multiplies the result of the exponentiation by the principal amount in cell B1 (for example, $10,000). This yields the final investment value after compounding monthly for the specified period.

Adding and subtracting with ease

You've seen how Excel handles addition in the order of operations. Now let's subtract our initial investment from the future value we calculated:

1. **Enter the words** Return on Investment **in cell A9.**

2. **Enter this formula into cell B9:** =B1*(1+B2/12)^(B7*12)-B1, **or if that feels like too much math,** =B7-B2.

   Either way, the formula should return $71,164.97. This result comes from the future value of our investment, $81,164.97, minus the initial $10,000 — a tidy sum for our future selves!

REMEMBER
If you decide to be clever and copy the formula from cell B7 into cell B8 and then add –B2, you may get stopped in your tracks with a #NUM! error. The next section dives into why this happens and shows how creating absolute or mixed cell references can help you sidestep issues like this in the future.

TIP
If retyping the formula isn't on your agenda, click cell B7, select the entire formula in the Formula Bar, right-click, and select Copy. This allows you to paste the formula into cell B8 without triggering auto-adjustments in the cell references — which is what causes that #NUM! error. Then simply add –B2 at the end of the formula to complete the step.

Contrasting Cell References

Cell references are typically composed of a column letter and a row number, unless you're a true Excel aficionado who appreciates the R1C1 reference style!

TECHNICAL STUFF

The R1C1 style in Excel is a cell reference format where rows and columns are indicated by numbers (for example, R1C1 refers to row 1, column 1). This format is especially useful for creating dynamic formulas because it allows for relative references by indicating the number of rows or columns from the current cell, such as R[1]C[2] for one row down and two columns to the right.

Recognizing relative references

Relative references, like =A1 or =Sheet1!A1, adjust row and column references automatically when you copy a formula to a new location. This feature is helpful, saving you from manually updating countless cells. However, as the previous section illustrates, this convenience can sometimes backfire. For instance, copying a formula from cell B7 to B8 and encountering the #NUM! error value highlights how relative references can produce unintended results.

Mastering mixed references

Excel's mixed references let you lock either the row or the column. For example, copying =$A1 across a row keeps a fixed reference to column A; while copying it down a column allows the row number to adjust based on the formula's location. Likewise, =A$1 fixes the reference to row 1 when copied down a column, but the column reference adjusts when the formula is copied across a row.

Applying absolute references

Absolute references lock onto specific cells. Just double down on those dollar signs to create an absolute reference. For instance, =$A$1 always refers to cell A1, no matter where you copy the formula to within a worksheet. Even better, you don't have to painstakingly insert dollar signs in cell references by hand — there's a keyboard shortcut for that:

1. **Type =A1+A2 in cell B1, and then press Enter.**
2. **Double-click cell B1 or press F2 (Windows) or ⌘+U (macOS) to edit the formula.**

3. **Select A1 or the entire formula, and then press F4 (Windows) or ⌘+T (macOS):**

   - **First press:** =$A$1+A2 (absolute reference for A1) or =$A$1 : $A$2 (absolute reference for A1 and A2)
   - **Second press:** =A$1+A2 or =A$1+A$2 (row absolute)
   - **Third press:** =$A1+A2 or =$A1+$A2 (column absolute)
   - **Fourth press:** =A1+A2 (relative reference)

4. **Press Enter or continue editing.**

REMEMBER

Absolute references without a worksheet name behave relatively when copied to other worksheets. For instance, copying =$A$1 from Sheet1 to Sheet2 keeps it as =A1, referencing A1 on Sheet2, not Sheet1. To ensure accuracy, include the worksheet name in formulas you plan to copy across sheets (for example, =Sheet1!$A$1).

Replicating Formulas

Unlike in grade school, copying your homework — er, formulas — is both expected and encouraged in Excel! As we cover in the previous section, the $ operator ensures that formulas remain intact, even when Excel's helpfulness may otherwise get in the way. There are several efficient ways to transfer formulas from one place to another.

Copying with keyboard shortcuts

Formulas can be transferred between cells with ease:

- **Copy and Paste:** The Copy and Paste commands are on the Home tab of the ribbon. Select one or more cells and click Copy; then navigate to the new location and click Paste. To automate this repetitious task, press Ctrl+C (Windows) or ⌘+C (macOS) to copy, and then press Ctrl+V (Windows) or ⌘+V (macOS) to paste.

  TIP

  To paste like a pro, press Enter — just note that this shortcut clears the Clipboard after pasting.

- **Fill Formula from Above:** Press Ctrl+' (apostrophe) to copy the formula or cell contents — without the formatting — from the cell directly above into the current cell. This action pastes what's in the cell above into the current cell, making it a quick way to replicate formulas or values.

CHAPTER 2 **Carrying Out Basic Calculations** 41

- » **Fill Right:** Select any range of cells that span two or more columns and then press Ctrl+R (Windows) or ⌘+R (macOS) to copy the contents of the first column into the adjacent columns to the right.

- » **Fill Down:** Select a range of cells spanning two or more rows; then press Ctrl+D (Windows) or ⌘+D (macOS) to copy the contents of the first row into the rows below.

Automating with AutoFill

The AutoFill feature in Excel is an often overlooked time-saver with multiple uses across different contexts. This chapter focuses on formulas, so start by setting the scene:

1. **Select the cell containing the formula you want to copy.**

   Hypothetically, call it cell A1, and say that the formula is =ROW( ).

   TIP The ROW function returns the row number of the cell where the formula resides. You can also insert a cell reference, such as =ROW(A5), to return the row number of a specific cell.

2. **On the Home tab of the ribbon, click or press Ctrl+C (Windows) or ⌘+C (macOS).**

   The cell contents are copied to the Clipboard.

3. **Select the cells where you want to paste the formula.**

   To continue the example, select cells A2:A10.

4. **On the Home tab of the ribbon, click Paste. Alternatively, press Ctrl+V (Windows) or ⌘+V (macOS).**

Four steps. That's not too bad. But there's a quicker way:

1. **Navigate to cell A1 and double-click the Fill Handle, the black square in the lower-right corner of the cell.**

   The state of cells A2:A10 determine the outcome:

   - **If A2:A10 are blank:** Double-clicking the Fill Handle in A1 has no effect, because AutoFill references the current region, defined as the contiguous block of nonblank cells.

   - **If A2:A10 are nonblank:** Double-clicking the Fill Handle in A1 copies the contents of cell A1 down through cell A10.

2. **Enter a formula in cell B1, such as =COLUMN(), and then double-click the Fill Handle in B1.**

   The contents of cell B1 are copied down to cell B10.

Double-clicking the Fill Handle is a huge time-saver. Many users know how to drag the Fill Handle down (say, from B1 to B10), which is fine for a few cells but quickly becomes tedious when copying a formula down dozens, hundreds, or even thousands of rows.

Copying formulas is just one way to use AutoFill. Other uses arise when Excel detects a pattern in two or more selected cells:

» **Number series:** Select adjacent cells containing the numbers 1 and 2, and then double-click the Fill Handle to create a series. You can also drag the Fill Handle with the right mouse button to reveal the context menu shown in Figure 2-1.

» **Date series:** Select two dates and double-click the Fill Handle to create a date series. Figure 2-1 shows several date-related options that appear when you right-drag the Fill Handle over a date range.

» **Text patterns:** Pick a card, any card . . . we mean, select a month name or day of the week and drag down. Excel uses the Custom List feature (covered in Chapter 4 of this minibook) to populate a series of months or days. Numeric patterns also work — like Day 1, Week 1, or Quarter 1, with or without spaces — to create a series (for example, Day 1, Day 2, Week 1, Week 2, Quarter 1, Quarter 2, and so on).

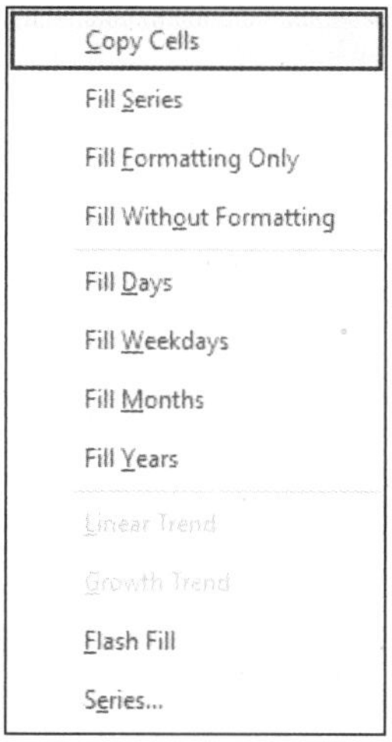

FIGURE 2-1: Context menu options for the Fill Handle.

CHAPTER 2 **Carrying Out Basic Calculations** 43

Calculating Sums

SUM is the function many users rely on most often in Excel. You can apply the SUM function manually or let Excel do the work with the AutoSum command.

Feel free to try these techniques with your own data, but here's a quick way to set up some sample data you can use in this section:

1. **Type 1 in cell A1 of a blank worksheet.**
2. **Type 3 in cell A2.**
3. **Select cells A1:A2 and drag the Fill Handle down through cell A10.**

   A series of odd numbers from 1 to 19 appears in the cells, adding up to a nice round total of 100.

Computing amounts with AutoSum

You can find the AutoSum command in the Editing group on the Home tab of the ribbon and the Function Library group on the Formulas tab of the ribbon. Here's how to try it out:

1. **Select a range of cells that contain numeric values, such as A1:A10.**
2. **Click the AutoSum button on the Home tab of the ribbon or press Alt+= (equal sign) (Windows) or ⌘+Shift+T (macOS).**

   The SUM function appears in the nearest blank cell to the selection. In this example, =SUM(A1:A10) appears in cell A11.

You can also sum rows and columns simultaneously:

1. **Select cells A1:A10, and then drag the Fill Handle to cell E10.**
2. **Select cells A1:F11, and then use AutoSum.**

   Excel adds totals to cells A11:F11, as well as cells F1:F10.

Totaling with SUM

The SUM function has the following arguments:

>> **number1:** The first number, cell reference, or range that you want to use

>> **number2...255:** Optional additional numbers, cell references, or ranges to include in the summation

Improving the integrity of totals

Users unfamiliar with Excel often use the SUM function in less than ideal ways. The preferred method is to reference a range of cells, like A1:A10, using a formula like =SUM(A1:A10). A less efficient approach is to reference each cell individually, like =SUM(A1,A2,A3,A4,A5,A6,A7,A8,A9,A10).

REMEMBER Using cell ranges ensures that any rows inserted between the first and last cell in the range are included in the total automatically. In contrast, listing each cell individually with commas requires manually updating the formula whenever a new row is added to include that row's amount. Even worse, deleting a referenced row replaces the cell reference with #REF!, which must be manually removed.

Although using cell ranges is best practice, there's still some risk: Rows inserted immediately above or below the range may be unintentionally excluded from the total.

You can, however, create a resizable range:

1. **Click the first row in the range that you're summing, click the Home tab of the ribbon, click Insert, and click Insert Sheet Rows.**

   If you're using the sample data from earlier in this section, row 1 is now blank and your amounts span cells A2:A11.

   TIP For a keyboard-based approach, press Shift+spacebar to select the row, and then press Ctrl++ (Windows) or ⌘+Shift++ (macOS) to insert a new row.

2. **Click the Home tab of the ribbon, click Format, and then click Row Height.**

   The Row Height dialog box opens.

3. **Enter 7.5 in the Row Height field and then click OK.**

   Row 1 is now half the height of a traditional row, helping discourage users from entering data there.

4. **Click the row just below your range, insert a new row, and change the row height as before.**

   If you're using the sample data, the SUM function that originated in cell A11 will now be in cell A13.

5. **Click the cell just below the lower buffer row, such as A13, and then click AutoSum or press Alt+= (Windows) or ⌘+Shift+T (macOS).**

   Excel creates a preview, highlighting the range it detects as relevant for summing, marked with a dashed outline to review or adjust before confirming.

6. **Drag the upper selector handle within the AutoSum outline up one cell to include the upper buffer row, and then press Enter.**

   The SUM function now has better integrity, encouraging users to insert new rows within the formula range rather than just outside it.

   REMEMBER: Solving one problem in Excel can sometimes create another. A green error indicator may appear in the cell containing the expanded range due to the rule about formulas referring to empty cells.

Adding numbers stored as text

One surefire way to pull your hair out is unexpectedly encountering numeric values stored as text. The SUM function treats these cells as blank, while formulas with arithmetic operators treat them as numeric values.

Here's a quick example that illustrates the nuance of numbers stored as text:

1. **Enter '1 into cell A1 of a blank worksheet and '2 into cell A2.**

   The apostrophe before each number instructs Excel to store the values as text.

2. **Click cell A3 and either use AutoSum, or type** =SUM(A1:A2).

   The formula returns 0.

3. **Enter this formula into cell A4:** =A1+A2.

   The formula returns 3.

   REMEMBER: This works in reverse for cells with nonnumeric characters. The SUM function still treats such cells as blank, while arithmetic operators referencing them cause formulas to return #VALUE!.

Adding or subtracting dates and times

In Excel, time "began" on December 31, 1899, which it treats as day zero, with January 1, 1900, as day 1. Each day adds 1 to the serial value, creating a system that tracks dates seamlessly. So, when you enter a date like 1/1/2026 into a cell, Excel displays it as entered, but behind the scenes, it gives a sly chuckle, thinking, "Pah! Silly humans, that's actually 46023."

This explains why you may occasionally see a series of seemingly random numbers instead of dates — Excel has simply removed the date formatting. To get your dates back in line, select the cells and choose Short Date from the Number Format drop-down on the Home tab of the ribbon. This drop-down typically shows General unless a different format has been applied to the active cell or selection.

To calculate dates in the future or past, simply add or subtract a whole number. You can also utilize a date-related worksheet function. For in-depth information on calculating dates and times, turn to Book 3, Chapter 3.

Analyzing Data with Statistical Functions

Excel isn't just for tallying expenses or managing inventory — it's packing some serious statistical muscle under the hood. In this section, we dig into the stats functions that help you slice, dice, and overanalyze data to your heart's content.

As always, you can crunch your own numbers, but if you don't have any lying around, here's how to generate a quick dataset:

1. **Type** Sunday **in cell A1 of a blank worksheet.**

2. **Click cell A1, and then drag the Fill Handle down through cell A21.**

   Every day of the week should now appear three times in column A.

3. **Enter your three favorite fruits into cells B1:B3.**

   If you're feeling uninspired, just go with Apple, Banana, and Cherry.

4. **Select cells B1:B3 and then double-click the Fill Handle.**

   The series of three fruits repeats all the way down to cell B21.

5. **Enter this formula into cell C1:** =RANDBETWEEN(1000,5000).

   A random number between 1,000 and 5,000 appears.

   RANDBETWEEN is a volatile function, meaning it recalculates automatically whenever a change occurs anywhere in the workbook. As a result, the contents of cell C1 keep changing as you work through this example.

6. **Select cell C1 and then double-click the Fill Handle.**

   The contents of cell C1 will be copied down to cell C21, creating a random set of numbers you can reference throughout the rest of this chapter.

   If you prefer to have a static set of numbers to work with, copy cells C1:C21 to the Clipboard and then press Ctrl+Shift+V in Windows. Alternatively, click the Home tab of the ribbon, click the Paste Special drop-down button, and then click Values.

Calculating averages with AVERAGE

The AVERAGE function calculates the arithmetic mean by adding up a group of numbers and dividing by the count of those numbers. The AVERAGE function includes the following arguments:

- **number1:** The first number, cell reference, or range that you want to reference
- **number2...255:** Optional additional numbers, cell references, or ranges to include in the average calculation

Though it may seem a bit ironic, here's how to use the AutoSum command to implement the AVERAGE function:

1. **Enter the word** AVERAGE **into cell E1.**
2. **Select cell F1, click the AutoSum drop-down on the Home tab of the ribbon, and then click Average.**

   A default formula, such as =AVERAGE(C1:E1), appears in Excels Formula Bar.
3. **Adjust the range by selecting cells C1:C21 and then pressing Enter.**

   The formula =AVERAGE(C1:C21) appears in cell F1, providing the arithmetic mean of the numbers in cells C1:C21.

Calculating a weighted average

Be prepared — this next formula has some heft to it. A weighted average is like a regular average but with a twist: Some values carry more weight, or importance, than others. Instead of just adding up all the numbers and dividing by how many there are, a weighted average considers how significant each value is.

Picture this: You're in a statistics class (of all things), and the grading breakdown looks like this:

- **Final exam:** Your score of 95 is 40 percent of your grade.
- **Homework:** Your score of 90 is 30 percent of your grade.
- **Group project:** Your score of 85 is 20 percent of your grade.
- **Class participation:** Your score of 80 is 10 percent of your grade.

In this setup, your final exam grade counts much more toward your overall grade than your class participation. To calculate the weighted average, you multiply each score by its weight, add the results together, and then divide by the sum of the weights, like so:

$$\text{Weighted Average} = \frac{(95 \times 0.4) + (90 \times 0.3) + (85 \times 0.2) + (80 \times 0.1)}{0.4 + 0.3 + 0.2 + 0.1}$$

The result of this calculation is 90, whereas a simple average of 95, 90, 85, and 80 would be 87.5. As you can see, the weighted average reflects the importance of each component.

Now that you've seen this on paper, try it out:

1. **Enter the categories — meaning** Final exam, Homework, Group project, **and** Class participation **— into cells H1:H4.**

2. **Enter the scores — meaning** 95, 90, 85, 80 **— into cells I1:I4.**

3. **Enter the weights — meaning** 0.4, 0.3, 0.2, 0.1 **— into cells J1:J4.**

4. **Select cells I1:I4 and then use the AutoSum command to add the average of the scores to cell I5.**

   The AVERAGE function returns 87.5.

5. **Enter the following formula into cell J5:** =SUMPRODUCT(I1:I4,J1:J4)/SUM(J1:J4).

   The weighted average formula returns 90, and breaks down as follows:

   - SUMPRODUCT(I1:I4,J1:J4): The SUMPRODUCT multiplies corresponding values in up to 255 ranges of cells and then adds up the results. In this case, the scores in cells I1:I4 are multiplied by the weights in cells J1:J4, and then SUMPRODUCT returns the sum of the multiplied amounts, providing the numerator for the division calculation that yields a weighted average.

   - SUM(J1:J4): The SUM function adds up the weights in cells J1:J4, providing the denominator for the weighted average calculation.

   This formula calculates the weighted average by dividing the weighted sum by the total weight, giving a balanced result that reflects each score's importance.

Calculating conditional averages

The AVERAGEIF function lets you calculate an average for values that meet a single condition. If you're ready to take it up a notch, the AVERAGEIFS function allows you to apply up to 127 conditions.

The AVERAGEIF function includes the following arguments:

- range: Two or more cells to average.
- criteria: Specifies which cells are averaged. This can be text, like "apples"; numbers, like 42; or comparison operators, like ">42" (in which case, the double quotes are required).
- average_range: An optional range of cells to average — Excel uses the range unless you specify otherwise.

Here's a quick rundown:

1. **Enter the word AVERAGEIF into cell E2.**
2. **Enter your favorite day of the week into cell E3.**

   Be sure to spell the day of the week in full, with no extra spaces at the end. Functions that rely on matches in Excel are, to say the least, exacting.

3. **Enter this formula in cell F3:** =AVERAGEIF(A1:A35,E3,C1:C35).

   The formula returns the average amount for your favorite day of the week.

Easy enough, eh? Kick it up a notch by adding a second criterion with AVERAGEIFS, which has the following arguments:

- average_range **(required):** The range of two or more cells to average
- criteria_range1 **(required):** The first range where Excel looks for the corresponding criteria
- criteria1 **(required):** The condition to match in criteria_range1
- criteria_range2...127 **(optional):** Additional ranges where Excel searches for additional criteria
- criteria2...127 **(optional):** Additional conditions to apply

To put it into action:

1. **Enter the word AVERAGEIFS into cell E5.**
2. **Enter the fruit of your choice in cell E6.**

   Any item that you typed in cells B1:B3 will do.

3. **Enter this formula in cell F5:** =AVERAGEIFS(C1:C35,A1:A35, E3,B1:B35,E5).

   The formula returns the average amount for the fruit of your choice on your favorite day of the week.

Finding the smallest and largest values

The MIN function uses the same arguments as SUM and AVERAGE. As you'd expect, MIN stands for *minimum,* pulling the smallest value from a range of numbers. You can use MINIF to retrieve the smallest value based on a single criterion and MINIFS for two or more criteria, just like AVERAGEIF and AVERAGEIFS. Or go to the other extreme with MAX, MAXIF, and MAXIFS.

You can get more nuanced and retrieve the second-smallest or third-largest values. For this, you can use the SMALL or LARGE functions. Both functions share the same arguments:

- » array: The range of two or more cells from which you want to return the *k*th value
- » k: The position (for example, second smallest, third largest) you'd like to retrieve from the array

IN THIS CHAPTER

» **Formatting cells**

» **Incorporating text boxes and images**

» **Managing rows and columns**

» **Hiding and unhiding worksheets and workbooks**

» **Improving worksheet accessibility**

» **Adjusting page layout settings**

Chapter **3**

Formatting Cells and Worksheets

This chapter focuses on giving your spreadsheets the glow-up they deserve. It begins with sprucing up cells to improve readability and dazzle the eye, offering tips on using text boxes to manage wordier rambles and jazzing things up with images and shapes. Formatting often acts as a double-edged sword — solving one problem while introducing others — but the Accessibility Checker helps manage some of these challenges. Later sections tackle the art of hiding (and unhiding) rows, columns, and even entire workbooks. The chapter winds up with page layout tweaks that result in polished printouts screaming, "I know what I'm doing!"

Applying Basic Formatting Commands

The Font section of the Home tab of the ribbon contains a collection of the most frequently used formatting commands in Excel:

- » **Font drop-down:** Displays a list of fonts.

- » **Font Size drop-down:** Displays a list of font sizes, with the option to type a custom size.

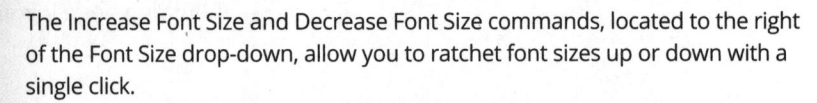

   TIP: The Increase Font Size and Decrease Font Size commands, located to the right of the Font Size drop-down, allow you to ratchet font sizes up or down with a single click.

- » **Bold:** When your text needs to make a statement, select a range of cells and on the Home tab of the ribbon, click Bold — or just press Ctrl+B (Windows) or ⌘+B (macOS).

- » **Italics:** Add a touch of flair by applying italics by clicking the Italics button on the Home tab of the ribbon or pressing Ctrl+I (Windows) or ⌘+I (macOS).

- » **Underline:** Emphasize your data by drawing a line beneath it by clicking the Underline button on the Home tab of the ribbon or pressing Ctrl+U (Windows) or ⌘+U (macOS). For double underline, click the Underline drop-down on the Home tab and then click Double Underline.

- » **Borders:** Set some boundaries around your data by clicking the Borders drop-down on the Home tab of the ribbon and then selecting a border option. If you need more customization, choose More Borders to open the Format Cells dialog box and select the Borders tab. The Borders command is "sticky," meaning it remembers the last border you applied within the active workbook.

- » **Fill Color:** Add a splash of color to your cells by clicking the Fill Color button on the Home tab of the ribbon. Like Borders, Fill Color is a sticky command.

- » **Font Color:** Draw attention by changing the font color of your data by clicking the Font Color button on the Home tab of the ribbon.

TIP: A dialog box launcher, labeled Font Settings, appears in the lower-right corner of the Font group of the ribbon. It opens the Format Cells dialog box to the Font tab. Other dialog box launchers of the ribbon provide similar access to additional settings.

If formatting doesn't look right, remember that commands like Bold, Italic, and Underline are toggles. Choosing the command, or pressing the keyboard shortcut, a second time removes the formatting. Another way to remove formatting is to click the Home tab of the ribbon, click Clear, and then click Clear Formatting, which removes all borders, fonts, colors, and number formatting, but retains any data or formulas. To have granular control over formatting, see the next section.

Exploring the Format Cells Dialog Box

The Format Cells dialog box gives you full control over the details of formatting. The easiest way to open this dialog box is to press Ctrl+1 (Windows) or ⌘+1 (macOS). If you want the hard way, click the Home tab of the ribbon, click Format, and then click Format Cells.

Formatting numbers

The Format Cells dialog box contains six tabs, but most of them are self-explanatory and only worth exploring if the ribbon's formatting commands don't meet your needs. The exception is the Number tab (see Figure 3-1), which can help you display numbers the way you want.

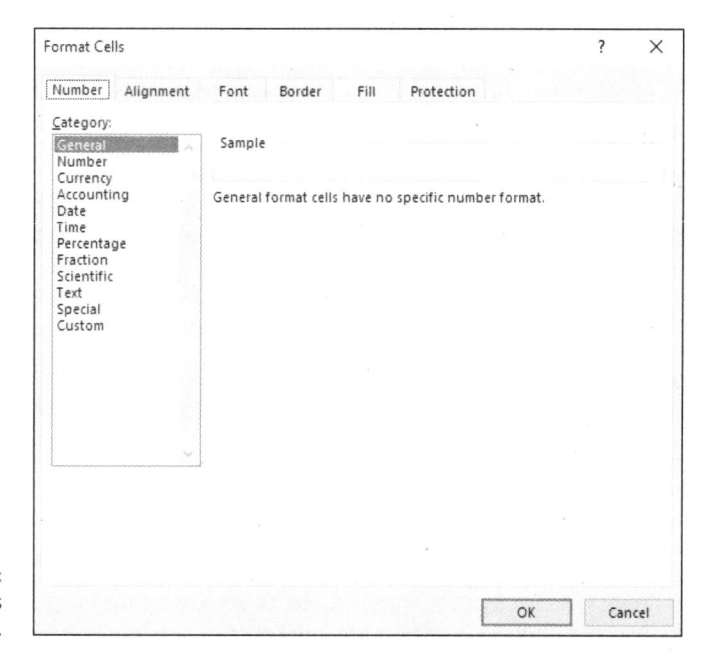

FIGURE 3-1: The Format Cells dialog box.

>> **General:** Numbers appear exactly as they're entered or computed.

>> **Number:** Use this format to display digits with no currency symbols. You can choose anywhere from 0 to 30 decimal places, enable the 1,000 separator if you'd like to keep those larger numbers readable, and choose an approach for formatting negative numbers.

REMEMBER: If others will be using your workbook, avoid using red formatting to indicate negative numbers — doing so can create accessibility challenges for users with color vision deficiencies.

» **Currency:** The Currency format lets you specify decimal places, currency symbols, and negative number styles, with the currency symbol positioned right next to the number.

» **Accounting:** Unlike Currency, the Accounting format displays the currency symbol aligned to the left edge of the cell and indents the numbers so that the digits align, even if negative values are shown in parentheses.

» **Date:** Use this section to display your numbers as actual dates, choosing from a variety of formats. Whether you need a short format like "3/15/26" or something more formal like "March 15, 2026" to document the Ides of March, beware — the Date section has you covered.

» **Time:** All formats include hours and minutes; you can optionally add seconds, AM/PM, or even go full drill sergeant with military time.

» **Percentage:** This format lets you display interest rates, completion rates, investment returns — so many ways to make your numbers pop.

REMEMBER: Excel makes a distinction between percents and percentages. The Percent Style command, prominently placed on the Home tab of the ribbon, quickly adds a percent symbol but hides all decimal places. If needed, you can then use the Increase Decimal command next to it to reveal decimal places. Alternatively, to format numbers as a percentage with two decimal places via the ribbon, click the Home tab, click the Number Format drop-down, and then click Percentage.

» **Fraction:** The Type list offers nine different fractional formats — ideal if you're calculating your share of a time-share or divvying up a pizza in complex fractions.

» **Scientific:** Scientific notation is a way to express very large or very small numbers using powers of 10, simplifying calculations and making the numbers easier to read and work with — if you're a scientist, that is.

» **Text:** The Text format calls cell contents as it sees it, meaning dates are shown as serial numbers, numbers are unformatted, and formulas are displayed instead of their results.

» **Special:** These deluxe number formats enable you to transform unformatted numeric values into zip codes, phone numbers, and Social Security numbers.

TECHNICAL STUFF: Number formats visually change what you see in a worksheet cell but don't alter the actual cell content. For example, if you save an Excel worksheet as a comma-separated values (CSV) file with a list that includes zip codes or Social Security numbers, Excel drops leading zeros. Even if the cell appears with the zero in Excel, the CSV file doesn't retain it.

» **Custom:** You can create a number format your way in this section. Custom number formats consist of four segments separated by semicolons: positive numbers, negative numbers, zero values, and text. You don't have to spell out all four formats, though; the previous segment applies to any missing segments.

REMEMBER

Custom number formats are applied only to cells that contain data. Empty cells remain unaffected by the format settings.

Crafting custom number formats

Geekiness alert! If you're not a number formatting enthusiast — like, *really* into formatting numbers — you may want to skip this section, because we're about to dive into some serious details here.

Here's a list of some (but not all) of the characters that you can use when rolling your own custom number formats:

» `0` **(zero):** Displays insignificant zeros — also known as *leading zeros* — when a number has fewer digits. For instance, `000` displays three digits, turning 7 into 007.

» `#` **(hash sign):** Displays only significant digits. For example, `#,##0` displays 5 as 5, but 5000 as 5,000.

» `,` **(comma):** As shown earlier, the comma can be used with the hash sign to add a thousands separator or to scale numbers. For example, the number format `#,` drops the thousands digits, displaying 10,000 as 10 or 10,000,000 as 10,000.

» `_` **(underscore):** Adds space equal to the width of the next character, commonly for alignment purposes. For instance, `_ )` aligns numbers with parentheses for negative values, mimicking the neat precision of the Accounting number format.

» `"Text"` **(quotation marks):** Enclose text in double quotes and use zeros or hash signs to format numbers (such as `0" Years"`), which displays 30 Years if you type **30** in a cell. Any formulas referencing cells formatted this way still treat the cell contents as numeric values, not text.

» **d:** Represents the day of the week or month within date formats:

- **d:** Returns the day of the month (for example, 5).
- **dd:** Includes a leading zero when applicable (for example, 05).

- **ddd:** Displays the first three letters of the day of the week (for example, Wed).

- **dddd:** Spells out the day of the week in full (for example, Wednesday).

» **m:** Represents the month of the year within date formats, or minutes within time formats:

- **m:** Returns the number of the month (for example, 1).

- **mm:** Includes a leading zero when applicable (for example, 01).

- **mmm:** Displays the first three letters of the month (for example, Jan).

- **mmmm:** Spells out the month in full (for example, January).

» **hh:mm:** Returns hours and minutes (for example, 05:27 for 5 hours and 27 minutes).

» **hh:mm:ss:** Returns hours, minutes, and seconds (for example, 05:27:38 for 5 hours, 27 minutes, and 38 seconds).

» **m:ss:** Returns minutes and seconds (for example, 27:38 for 27 minutes and 38 seconds).

» **y:** Represents the year portion within date formats:

- **y or yy:** Returns a two-digit year (for example, 26).

- **yyyy:** Returns a four-digit year (for example, 2026).

TIP

You can mix and match date format characters. For instance, `dddd, mmmm d, yyyy` returns Saturday, July 4, 2026, if a cell contains 7/4/2026. `"Balance Sheet as of "mmmm d, yyyy` causes Balance Sheet as of December 31, 2026, to appear within a cell that contains 12/31/2026.

» **[Color]:** Applies color to a number format, say `[Blue]0` to format numbers in blue. To take things further, use `[Green]0;[Black]-0;[Blue]0;[Yellow]@` to format positive numbers in green, negative numbers in black, zero values in blue, and text in yellow. Common colors include `[Red]`, `[Blue]`, `[Green]`, `[Yellow]`, `[Cyan]`, `[Magenta]`, and `[White]`.

» **Conditions** (`[>value]` **or** `[<value]`)**:** Sets conditions for displaying specific formats based on values — how fancy is this? For example, `[>=1000]0.0,"K";0` displays values 1,000 or greater in thousands (so 1.5K appears when a cell contains 1,500).

REMEMBER

Excel allows only up to two conditions within a custom number format. This means you can set formats for specific values or ranges, but you're limited to two conditional options within the format.

58 BOOK 1 **Getting Started with Excel**

Custom number formats are saved at the workbook level. This means that any custom formats you create in, say, Workbook A won't be available in Workbook B unless you copy and paste cells that use the format between workbooks. In the Format Cells dialog box, any custom number formats appear at the bottom of the Type list within the Number tab. As a reference, your custom formats start about five positions below the [h]:mm:ss format.

TIP

The next section explains how you can embed cell formatting, including custom number formats, into styles that can then be merged into other workbooks. This allows you to reuse consistent formatting across different workbooks seamlessly.

Applying Cell Styles

The Cell Styles feature (see Figure 3-2) is a straightforward way to apply consistent formatting across a workbook. Excel offers 47 built-in styles that are confined to the workbook where they're created, though there is a method for transferring styles between workbooks.

FIGURE 3-2: The Cell Styles gallery.

CHAPTER 3 **Formatting Cells and Worksheets** 59

Modifying predefined styles

Excel doesn't let you rename its built-in styles, but you can modify or delete them. If you plan to change the Normal style, know that changes to this style affect every unformatted cell across the entire workbook. Cells with any existing formatting remain unaffected by updates to the Normal style, though you can manually apply the Normal style to these cells if needed.

Here's how to format all worksheets within an Excel workbook by customizing the Normal style:

1. **To modify the Normal style, click the Home tab of the ribbon, click Cell Styles, and right-click Normal, and click Modify on the context menu; alternatively, if the Normal style is visible in the Styles group on the Home tab of the ribbon, right-click Normal, and then select Modify on the context menu.**

   The Style dialog box opens.

   Styles are combinations of settings from every tab in the Format Cells dialog box.

2. **Make the changes you want to make.**

   Your options include the following:

   - **Disabling unwanted style elements:** Deselect any check box within the Style Includes list to exclude that type of formatting from the style. This allows you to apply only certain attributes without overwriting other formatting you may have already set.
   - **Customizing a style:** Click Format to open the Format Cells dialog box, make any desired changes on the appropriate tab, and then click OK.

3. **Click OK to close the Styles dialog box.**

   The customizations you made now apply to every unformatted cell within the workbook.

   You can modify, but not rename, any of the predefined styles.

Creating custom styles

If you'd like a style that's entirely your own, Excel allows you to create custom cell styles:

1. **Use either of the following techniques to start a custom style:**
   - **On the Home tab of the ribbon, click the Cell Styles drop-down, right-click an existing style, and then click Duplicate to duplicate it.** This approach copies the formatting of the selected style, allowing you to apply a custom name.
   - **On the Home tab of the ribbon, click the Cell Styles drop-down, and then click New Cell Style.** This approach uses the formatting of the active cell as a starting point, which you can override as needed.

2. **Use the Style Name field to assign a name to the style.**

   You can enter up to 255 characters, though only the first 11 display within the Styles gallery. Hover over the style name to view the full name.

3. **Adjust style elements as needed, or click the Format button to open the Format Cells dialog box and further customize your style.**

4. **Click OK to close the Style dialog box.**

REMEMBER Custom cell styles are initially only available in the workbook where they were created. The upcoming "Transferring cell styles between workbooks" section shows how to move styles to other workbooks.

Applying and identifying cell styles

To apply a cell style, select one or more cells and then choose the desired style from the gallery. As you navigate through your workbook, the style applied to the active cell is highlighted in the Styles gallery, allowing you to identify it instantly.

TIP You can delete all styles except for Normal from the Cell Styles gallery, though manually removing the remaining 46 may be tedious. Additionally, these deletions apply only to the active workbook.

Transferring cell styles between workbooks

You can transfer custom cell styles to another workbook by copying and pasting one or more cells that use a custom cell style. Although this is quick, it doesn't work for built-in styles. However, customizations to built-in styles can be transferred this way:

1. **Open the workbook containing the cell styles you want to transfer.**

   Styles can be transferred only between open workbooks.

CHAPTER 3 **Formatting Cells and Worksheets** 61

2. **Open the workbook into which you want to transfer cell styles.**
3. **Click the Home tab of the Ribbon, click the Cell Styles drop-down, and then click Merge Styles.**

   The Merge Styles dialog box opens.

4. **Choose the workbook you want to merge styles from, and click OK.**

   If any built-in styles have been customized, or if any custom styles share the same name between the two workbooks, a prompt asks, `Merge Styles That Have the Same Names?`

5. **Choose one of the following responses:**

   - **Yes:** Overwrites all cell styles, both built-in and customized, in the current workbook.
   - **No:** Leaves existing styles intact and only adds new styles not present in the current workbook.
   - **Cancel:** Cancels the transfer of styles between workbooks.

   The cell styles can now be used in the new workbook. Any differences within the imported styles automatically apply to existing cells with a style applied, including unformatted cells, which default to the Normal style.

Merging and Centering Cells

Sometimes folks get wildly excited about corporate mergers, but in Excel, merging cells can open a can of worms. Merged cells present a paradox for Excel users: They're both immensely helpful and incredibly frustrating. Essentially, merging combines two or more worksheet cells into a single mega-cell.

Here's how to use the Merge & Center command:

1. **Type** The Greatest Financial Report of All Time **into cell A1 of a blank worksheet.**

   If you're feeling more reserved, simply type **Report Title** instead.

2. **Select cells A1:E1.**

   The cells that you select will become a merged cell.

3. **On the Home tab of the ribbon, click Merge & Center.**

   Cells A1:E1 are now merged, and the report title is centered across cells A1:E1.

WARNING: Be cautious when using Merge & Center on selections spanning multiple rows or columns. Excel displays a warning because merging cells in this manner retains only the contents of the upper-left cell, discarding data in all other rows and columns within the selection.

4. **To unmerge cells, select any cell within the merged range, click the Home tab of the ribbon, and then click Merge & Center again.**

   Just like bold, italic, and underline, the merge format in Excel toggles on and off with a single click.

Merging across columns

Excel users often take one germ of information about a feature and then dash off to the races. Case in point: When centering content across multiple rows, it's tempting — but unnecessary — to merge columns one row at a time. Here's a better approach:

1. **Type** Authored by a Most Excellent Spreadsheet User **into cell A2.**

   If you'd rather keep it low-key, simply type **Report Subtitle** instead.

2. **Select cells A1:E2.**

   These selected cells form two merged sections.

3. **On the Home tab of the ribbon, click the Merge & Center drop-down, and then click Merge Across.**

   Cells A1:E1 and A2:E2 are now merged.

4. **On the Home tab of the ribbon, click Center.**

   Merging and centering data across multiple rows requires this two-step process.

The Merge & Center drop-down list includes two other options: Merge combines cells without centering, and Unmerge Cells separates merged ranges back into individual cells. Simply clicking Merge & Center also unmerges cells if they're already merged. Additionally, you can merge or unmerge cells using the Merge check box on the Alignment tab in the Format Cells dialog box. However, when merging cells across two or more rows, you need to use the Merge Across command.

TIP: Check out the upcoming "Wrapping Text" section if you want to wrap text within a merged cell — but don't miss the "Tapping into Text Boxes" section after that for a more refined text management solution.

Centering across a selection

Center Across Selection is a formatting option in Excel that centers text across a selected range of cells without merging them. Unlike merged cells, which combine multiple cells into one, Center Across Selection keeps each cell in the range separate. This feature allows you to visually center content across the selection without the structural issues that come with merging, such as difficulty in sorting, AutoFilling, or selecting individual cells within the range. Even better, you can apply Center Across Selection across multiple rows simultaneously without losing any data.

So, pop that tab, baby, and take a swig of Center Across Selection:

1. **Select the range of cells where you want the text centered.**

    We'll select cells A1:E2 and then click Merge & Center to undo the havoc that we wreaked in the previous section.

2. **Press Ctrl+1 (Windows) or ⌘+1 (macOS).**

    On Windows, you can also click Alignment Settings, the small arrow in the lower-right corner of the Alignment group on the Home tab of the ribbon.

    The Format Cells dialog box opens.

3. **If the Alignment tab isn't already active, click it.**

4. **From the Horizontal list, choose Center Across Selection.**

5. **Click OK.**

This approach provides a visually centered effect while keeping each cell independent, making it a cleaner alternative to merging for certain layouts.

Wrapping Text

The Wrap Text command enables you to display long text within a single cell by wrapping it onto multiple lines, making it easier to read without spilling into adjacent cells. Users often utilize this feature in conjunction with merged cells to display a sentence, paragraph, or more of text within a spreadsheet (although the next section of this chapter spills the beans on a far more efficient and elegant approach).

Wrapping text is easy as pie:

1. **Select the range for which you want to apply the Wrap Text format.**
2. **On the Home tab of the ribbon, click the Wrap Text button to the Alignment group.**

   Excel wraps text within a cell and automatically adjusts the row height to ensure that all the text is displayed at once. This feature allows for easier readability of longer entries without needing to manually adjust row dimensions.

REMEMBER Always wrap text for column headings to keep your data organized and readable, while keeping headings in a single row to avoid unwanted side effects with certain Excel features.

Tapping into Text Boxes

The Text Box feature in Excel allows you to add a floating object — which resembles a scaled-down Word document — that can be positioned anywhere on your worksheet, independent of cell boundaries. This is especially useful for adding commentary, labels, or instructions. Text boxes eliminate the hassle of fitting text into merged cells; you can even choose whether a text box appears only onscreen or is included on printouts. Unlike text in worksheet cells, text boxes can be freely moved and resized.

To sum up, text boxes create a "blank space" that makes adding and manipulating text much easier than trying to work within a worksheet cell. So, slap on your favorite friendship bracelet, and brace yourself for the wonders of text boxes:

1. **On the Insert tab of the ribbon, click Text Box.**

   If Text Box doesn't appear directly on the ribbon, click the Text drop-down, and then click Text Box.

2. **Do one of the following:**

   - Click your worksheet to create a transparent text box that automatically expands as you type within it.
   - Click and drag on your worksheet to create a text box of your desired size with a solid white background.
   - Hold down the Alt key (Windows) or the Option key (macOS) while clicking and dragging to create a text box that aligns exactly over one or more cells.

3. **Type directly in the text box and adjust font, color, alignment, and other formatting as needed.**

   Select any text within the text box to display a formatting toolbar, select formatting from the Home tab of the ribbon, or press Ctrl+1 (Windows) or ⌘+1 (macOS) to open the Format Cells dialog box.

   REMEMBER Unlike merged cells, which require you to enable the Wrap Text format, text boxes automatically wrap text.

   TIP To format paragraphs within a text box, right-click inside the text box or on the selected text, then choose Paragraph. Similarly, to create a bulleted list, right-click inside the text box or on the selected text and choose an option from the Bullets submenu.

4. **To exit the text box, click any worksheet cell or another object.**

   To reactivate, click the text box. Use the selection handles to resize the text box or drag its edge to move it to a new location on your worksheet.

You can customize text boxes with borders, fill colors, and effects:

1. **Click a text box to select it.**

   The Shape Format tab appears on the ribbon.

2. **To change the background color, click the Shape Format tab of the ribbon, click Shape Fill, and then select an option.**

3. **To add or remove a border, click the Shape Format tab of the ribbon, click Shape Outline, and then select an option.**

4. **To really trick out your text box, click the Shape Format tab of the ribbon, click Shape Effects, and then select an option.**

   Options include shadow, reflection, 3-D formatting, and more.

5. **To precisely adjust the size of the text box, use the Height and Width fields on the Shape Format tab of the ribbon.**

Text boxes resize automatically by default when you insert or delete cells beneath them or when you sort or filter data. Additionally, text boxes appear on printouts if they're in the visible area. To control these characteristics, follow these steps:

1. **Click the Shape Format tab of the ribbon, click Rotate, and then click More Rotation Options; alternatively, right-click the text box and choose Format Shape.**

   The Format Shape task pane opens.

2. **Click Size & Properties to open the Size & Properties page of the task pane.**

3. **To keep the text box anchored in a specific location, expand the Properties section and select Don't Move or Size with Cells.**

   No matter what happens beneath, that text box should stay put.

4. **To prevent the text box from appearing on printouts, deselect the Print Object check box in the Properties section.**

   This is helpful for creating instructions that the user can view onscreen but won't see on paper.

Inserting Images

Here's how to display an image in a worksheet:

1. **On Windows, click the Insert tab of the ribbon, click Pictures, and then click Place in Cell to insert an image in a worksheet cell or click Place Over Cells to add an image that floats over the worksheet. Then choose the source of the image as explained in Step 2.**

   On macOS, click the Insert tab of the ribbon; click Pictures; and then specify the source by clicking Photo Browser, Picture from File, Stock Images, or Online Pictures.

2. **Choose one of the following options:**

   - **This Device:** Opens the Insert Picture dialog box, from which you can select an image that is stored locally

   - **Stock Images:** Opens the Stock Images window, from which you can choose images, icons, cutout people, stickers, illustrations, and cartoon people

   - **Online Pictures:** Opens the Online Pictures window, from which you can choose images from across the internet

   REMEMBER: Online pictures may be subject to copyright limitations. A Creative Commons Only option appears when you enter a search term, which limits your search to images that are generally free to use, but be sure to review licensing terms, which may require attribution, a link to the license, noting modifications, or other limitations.

Images placed within a worksheet cell may be too small to be recognizable. To resize such images, increase the row height and/or column width, or merge two or more cells to create a larger space within which the image can appear. To resize an image that floats above the worksheet, click the image, and then use the selection handles.

Toggle picture placement between embedding it within a cell or floating above the worksheet by clicking the picture and selecting the Place in Cell icon in the upper-right corner of the image, or by clicking within the cell and choosing Place Over Cell. The icons are similar.

Enhancing Accessibility

Accessible spreadsheets improve readability, navigation, and interaction, making it easier for users with — or without — visual, auditory, motor, or cognitive impairments to work with the content effectively.

Improving accessibility benefits everyone, not just those with disabilities, by enhancing overall usability and clarity. To support this effort, the Accessibility Assistant helps you identify and resolve accessibility issues within your spreadsheets, making your data more usable for everyone, including people with disabilities. This tool scans the active workbook for common accessibility issues — such as missing alternative (alt) text, merged cells, and low color contrast — and provides step-by-step guidance for fixing them. The Accessibility Assistant isn't perfect, but it's often helpful.

Here's how to launch the Accessibility Assistant:

1. **On the Review tab of the ribbon, click Check Accessibility; alternatively, click Accessibility: Investigate when this readout appears on Excel's Status Bar.**

   The Accessibility Assistant task pane and Accessibility Ribbon tab appear.

2. **Click any task pane section that displays a numeric count of issues.**

   The task pane highlights the affected area of the workbook and provides suggestions for resolving the issues.

Key aspects of accessibility in spreadsheets include the following:

» **Clear and descriptive column headers:** Proper labeling helps screen readers identify content and structure, while also ensuring that features like PivotTables and other Excel tools function correctly.

» **Alt text:** Adding descriptive text to images, charts, and other non-text elements provides context for users relying on screen readers. To add alt text, select a worksheet object that supports alt text, such as a chart or image, click the Accessibility tab of the ribbon, click Alt Text, and then add one or two detailed sentences or mark the object as decorative.

The Alt Text task pane becomes accessible only when a worksheet object is selected.

- **Limiting the use of merged cells:** Merged cells can disrupt navigation for assistive technology users.
- **Ensuring sufficient color contrast:** Using distinct colors improves readability, especially for users with color vision deficiencies. To select accessible colors, toggle the High Contrast Only option on when choosing fill or font colors.

Adjusting Row Heights and Column Widths

Excel applies two different measurements for row heights and column widths, each with its own logic:

- **Rows:** Row heights are based upon a typographic standard called *points*, which are equivalent to $1/72$ of an inch. This means that the standard row height of 15 points in Excel is equal to just over one-fifth of an inch.

  In Excel, increasing the font size within cells automatically increases the row height to fit the larger text. However, column widths remain unchanged, meaning wider text may spill over into adjacent columns. If you decrease the font size, Excel automatically reduces the row height, but never below the default height of 15. This ensures that the rows are always tall enough for standard readability.

- **Columns:** Column widths in Excel roughly correspond to the number of characters that can fit within a cell, based on the default font and size. A standard column width of 8.43 typically displays 8 to 9 characters in a cell. To accommodate additional characters, you'll need to widen the column.

Microsoft periodically updates Excel's default font to enhance readability and align with modern design standards. In 2022, it introduced Aptos Narrow as the default font, allowing slightly more text to appear in a cell without adjusting the column width.

To set your preferred default font and size on Windows, click the File tab of the ribbon, and then click Options to open the Excel Options dialog box. In the When Creating New Workbooks area, adjust the Use This as the Default Font and Font Size fields, and click OK. These settings apply to new workbooks you create from this point onward. On macOS, choose File ⇨ Preferences, and click General; select the font in the Default Font drop-down and the font size in the Font Size box; and then click the red Close button to close the Preferences window.

To adjust the default column width for the active worksheet, click the Home tab of the ribbon, click Format, click Default Width, enter a number, and then click OK.

You can let Excel decide how tall your rows and how wide your columns should be, or you can set them manually. Adjusting row heights and column widths is an either/or proposition — you can't change both at the same time — but the techniques are similar:

- » **Manual Adjustments:** Excel provides a couple of ways to automatically adjust row heights and column widths:
  - **Ribbon command:** On the Home tab of the ribbon, click Format and then click either Row Height or Column Width. Enter the desired height or width in the dialog box that opens, and click OK. Alternatively, you can right-click a row or column heading and select Row Height or Column Width to adjust manually.
  - **Mouse:** Select one or more rows or columns, and then click and hold the bottom edge of a selected row or the right edge of a selected column. Drag to adjust the height or width as needed.
- » **Automatic adjustments:** Excel provides two ways to automatically adjust row heights and column widths:
  - **Ribbon command:** Select one or more rows and/or columns, click the Home tab of the ribbon, click Format, and then click either Autofit Row Height or Autofit Column Width.
  - **Mouse:** Select one or more rows or columns, and then double-click the bottom border of any selected row or the right border of any selected column. Unlike the Ribbon command, double-clicking ensures that the tallest entry in each row or the widest entry in each column is fully displayed.

Hiding and Unhiding Rows and Columns

For rows and/or columns you're not ready to delete, the Hide Rows and Hide Columns commands let you keep data out of sight but readily accessible when needed.

Hiding rows and columns

Here's how to hide rows or columns by selecting cells:

1. **Select one or more cells within a worksheet.**
2. **On the Home tab of the ribbon, click Format, click Hide & Unhide, and then click either Hide Rows or Hide Columns.**

   The rows or columns containing the selected cells are hidden.

If Step 2 has too many clicks for your liking, try these shortcuts:

- Select one or more rows or columns in the worksheet, right-click the selection, and then choose Hide.
- Select cells, rows, or columns, and then press Ctrl+9 (Windows) or ⌘+9 (macOS) to hide rows; press Ctrl+0 (Windows) or ⌘+0 (macOS) to hide columns.

Unhiding rows and columns

Here's how to unhide rows or columns:

1. **Select surrounding rows or columns.**

   Highlight the rows or columns on both sides of the hidden ones.
2. **On the Home tab of the ribbon, click Format, click Hide & Unhide, and then click either Unhide Rows or Unhide Columns.**

   The hidden rows or columns reappear.

Nonetheless, if time is of the essence:

- Select an area that encompasses the hidden rows or columns, right-click the worksheet frame, and then choose Unhide.
- Select the hidden range and then press Ctrl+Shift+9 (Windows) or ⌘+Shift+9 (macOS) to unhide rows; for columns use Ctrl+Shift+0 (Windows) or ⌘+Shift+0 (macOS).

Hang with us on this next part — it could save you some frustration! Hidden rows and columns have a height or width of 0, which is key when it seems like the Unhide Rows or Unhide Columns commands are pranking you by not revealing

CHAPTER 3 Formatting Cells and Worksheets

the hidden areas. It's not that the commands are malfunctioning; instead, the column widths or row heights may be slightly above zero, creating the illusion of being hidden. When that happens, select an area around the hidden rows or columns and use the steps from the previous section to adjust their row height or column width.

To unhide only certain rows or columns within a group of hidden rows or columns while keeping others hidden, follow these steps:

1. **On the Home tab of the ribbon, click Find & Select and then click Go To; alternatively, press Ctrl+G (Windows) or ⌘+G (macOS).**

   The Go To dialog box opens.

2. **Type the address of a cell in a hidden row or column (for example, D1 to unhide column D) and click OK or press Enter.**

   You can also specify a range, like **D1:E1** to unhide columns D and E, or **3:5** to unhide rows 3 through 5.

   > **TIP:** If the Go To dialog box feels unwieldy, type a cell address or range directly into the Name Box and press Enter.

3. **On the Home tab of the ribbon, click Format, click Hide & Unhide, and then click either Unhide Rows or Unhide Columns; alternatively, use the unhide keyboard shortcuts from earlier in this section.**

   This lets you reveal specific rows or columns without exposing the entire hidden group.

Grouping rows and columns

Hiding and unhiding columns can be tedious and may inadvertently obscure data when users miss hidden columns within a range. Excel's Group feature addresses both issues, allowing you to hide or unhide columns and rows with a single click or keystroke. Expand (+) and Collapse (–) buttons appear next to or above the worksheet frame when rows or columns are grouped, making it easy to control data visibility.

Here's how to group individual rows or columns within a worksheet:

1. **Select cell(s), row(s) or column(s) within a worksheet.**
2. **On the Data tab of the ribbon, click Group; alternatively, press Shift+Alt+Right (Windows) or Option+Shift+Right (macOS).**

   The selection is grouped, with outline controls appearing in the upper-left corner, along with a collapse button for the group.

REMEMBER You can also select one or more cells instead of entire rows or columns before giving the Group command. In this case, Excel displays a Group dialog box, prompting you to specify Rows or Columns for the grouping.

WARNING Excel allows up to eight levels of grouping for both rows and columns. If you try to create a ninth level, you won't see an error prompt; instead, your clicks seem to disappear into the abyss.

If you're feeling lucky, you can give Excel a shot at outlining your worksheet:

1. **Select any cell within the area of the worksheet that you want to group columns and rows.**

   REMEMBER Most Excel commands, such as Group, operate on the current region, the contiguous block of rows and columns surrounding the active cell, unless you specifically select a range of two or more cells.

2. **On the Data tab of the ribbon, click the Group drop-down, and then click Auto Outline.**

   The rows and or columns within the current region or selection are grouped.

Certain aspects of Excel are just flat-out Kafkaesque, and the Group feature is Exhibit A. One tricky aspect of the Group and Auto Outline commands is that their actions can't be undone with the Undo command. To reverse grouping, you need to manually ungroup the rows or columns:

1. **Select one or more columns or rows within a group.**
2. **On the Data tab of the ribbon, click Ungroup.**

   The selected columns or rows are ungrouped, allowing you to remove specific rows or columns from a group without clearing the entire grouping.

To remove all groups from an area of the worksheet:

1. **Select any cell within the area of where you want to ungroup rows and columns.**
2. **On the Data tab of the ribbon, click the Ungroup drop-down, and then click Clear Outline.**

   All grouped rows or columns are removed from the selected area.

WARNING Here's where things get truly surreal. Not only can you not undo the Ungroup or Clear Outline commands, but they also wipe out the entire undo stack, erasing your ability to reverse any previous actions. And you thought we were being hyperbolic when we tossed around the term *Kafkaesque*.

CHAPTER 3 **Formatting Cells and Worksheets** 73

Hiding and Unhiding Workbooks

As we explain in Chapter 1 of this minibook, you can hide a worksheet by right-clicking its tab and then clicking Hide. Similarly, Excel lets you hide a workbook:

1. **Activate the workbook that you want to hide.**
2. **On the View tab of the ribbon, click Hide.**

REMEMBER: It's easy to lose track of hidden workbooks because they're out of sight. Rest assured, though — Excel prompts you to save any changes within hidden workbooks when you close the application. However, if you save a workbook while it's hidden, it reopens hidden, which can be confusing, especially if a colleague opens it unaware that it's hidden. You may even trigger a minor panic — we've managed to do it to ourselves!

Unhiding a workbook is just as easy. If the Unhide command on the View tab is disabled, you can stop here — no hidden workbooks are open on your computer. Otherwise, carry on:

1. **On the View tab of the ribbon, click Unhide.**

   The Unhide dialog box opens.

2. **Select from the Unhide Workbook list and click OK.**

   Excel unhides the workbook.

Modifying Page Setup

Page setup in Excel generally refers to adjusting the layout and appearance of a worksheet in preparation for printing. Most, but not all, page setup settings can be applied to multiple worksheets at once:

1. **Right-click any worksheet tab, and choose Select All Sheets.**

   All visible worksheets are selected.

   WARNING: The Select All Sheets command is one of those double-edged features in Excel that can save you a ton of time — but also cause a ton of grief if you don't respect it. This command enables Group mode, as indicated by the word *Group* in Excel's title bar. Any change you make to one worksheet applies to all worksheets in the group — a huge time-saver for setting print options, but pure havoc if you forget that Group mode is still on when making changes meant for just one specific worksheet. Ask us how we know.

2. **Modify the page layout settings as described later in this section.**

   Certain settings, such as defining the print area and specifying rows or columns to repeat at the top or left, must be set individually for each worksheet.

The Page Layout tab on the ribbon includes several commands related to managing page setup:

» **Margins:** Options include Last Custom Setting, Normal, Wide, and Narrow, along with Custom Margins, which displays the Margins tab of the Page Setup dialog box.

   TIP: Some inkjet printers offer edge-to-edge (borderless) printing, while most laser printers print within ¼ inch of the page edge. High-end models can go as close as ⅛ inch.

» **Orientation:** This drop-down list lets you toggle printouts between Portrait and Landscape.

» **Size:** To pick a paper size, click the Page Layout tab of the ribbon, and then click Size. And don't be fooled by the More Sizes command at the bottom — every size that's fit to print is already right there in the drop-down.

» **Print Area:** Set or clear the section of the worksheet you want to print. See "Setting print ranges and page breaks" for the scoop.

» **Breaks:** This drop-down list lets you set or remove page breaks.

» **Print Titles:** Opens the Page Setup dialog box, which offers far more options than the ribbon-based commands. This command lets you adjust way more than just titles.

» **Width:** Specifies the number of printed pages across that you'd like the print area to span.

» **Height:** Specifies the number of printed pages down that you'd like the print area to span.

» **Scale:** This field is disabled when either the Width or Height fields are set to anything other than Automatic but otherwise can be used to control the percentage that Excel zooms in (or out) when printing.

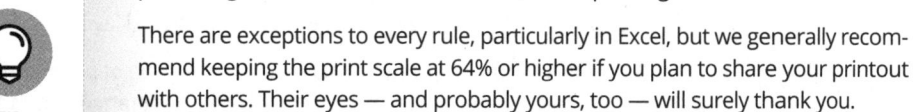

   TIP: There are exceptions to every rule, particularly in Excel, but we generally recommend keeping the print scale at 64% or higher if you plan to share your printout with others. Their eyes — and probably yours, too — will surely thank you.

» **Print Gridlines:** Select this check box to include gridlines on your printouts.

» **Print Headings:** Select this check box to include row numbers and column letters along the left and top edges of your printout.

Setting print ranges and page breaks

Print ranges in Excel let you specify areas of a worksheet to be printed, helping you focus on relevant sections and exclude unnecessary data. By default, Excel's print area extends from cell A1 to the last nonblank cell, but you can limit the printable area in two main ways:

» **Set Print Area:** Here's how to use the Page Layout tab of the ribbon to manage your print area:

   1. **Select the range of cells you want to print.**

      Don't be afraid to play favorites here — it's all about saving the trees.

   2. **On the Page Layout tab of the ribbon, click Print Area and then click Set Print Area.**

      Any cells outside this selected range are excluded from printouts.

» **Page Break Preview:** Drag and drop to adjust the print area visually:

   1. **On the View tab of the ribbon, click Page Break Preview.**

   2. **The print area is outlined by a bold blue border, which you can adjust by dragging with your mouse.**

      Page numbers in light gray help you see how pages are divided.

   3. **On the View tab of the ribbon, click Normal to return to Normal view.**

      Normal View is the default worksheet view, optimized for data entry and editing.

TIP: A third way to view or adjust the cell coordinates in the Print Area field is on the Sheet tab of the Page Setup dialog box, which appears when you click Print Titles on the Page Layout tab of the ribbon.

Savvy shoppers know to "try before you buy" — a philosophy you can apply to printouts by double-checking settings in two ways:

» **Page Layout:** On the View tab of the ribbon, click the Page Layout button. Page Layout View gives you a detailed, bird's-eye view of how your data will look on paper or in PDF, showing cells alongside the actual layout.

» **Print Preview:** Choose File ⇨ Print to access a mother lode of print settings. Most settings can be modified, except for the pesky print range and those dang rows and columns that you want to include on every page.

Adding headers, footers, and print titles

In Excel, page headers and footers consist of three sections — left, center, and right — at the top and bottom of each printed page, providing consistent labels across pages, such as document titles, page numbers, dates, or custom text. Headers appear above the top margin, while footers appear below the bottom margin.

To add headers and/or footers, follow these steps:

1. **On the Insert tab of the ribbon, click Header & Footer.**

   Excel enters Page Layout mode, displaying the Header & Footer tab of the ribbon. The header section appears, containing three sections: left, center, and right.

   If Excel warns you that Page Layout View is not compatible with Freeze Frames, click OK to unfreeze the worksheet panes.

2. **Click in the section where you'd like to place a header.**

3. **Add the header using commands from the Header & Footer tab:**

   - **Header:** A list of predefined headers. Options with commas span multiple sections.
   - **Footer:** Mirrors header options but inserts content into footer sections.
   - **Page Number:** Inserts the &[Page] placeholder for page numbers; you can add text around it (for example, Page &[Page]).
   - **Page Numbers:** Inserts the &[Pages] placeholder, which shows the total number of pages of the printout and can be combined with the Page Number placeholder (for example, Page &[Page] of &[Pages]).
   - **Current Date:** Inserts the &[Date] placeholder, which displays the date that the printout was created.
   - **Current Time:** Inserts the &[Time] placeholder, which displays the time that the printout was created.

     TIP Consider adding both date and time for clarity — insert the date, type a space-dash-space, and then add the time.

   - **File Path:** Inserts the &[Path]&[File] placeholders, which together display the file path and filename of the workbook on the printout.

CHAPTER 3 **Formatting Cells and Worksheets**

- **File Name:** Inserts the &[File] placeholder, which displays the workbook name on the printout.

- **Sheet Name:** Inserts the &[Tab] placeholder, which displays the worksheet name on the printout.

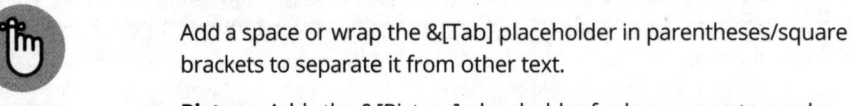

    > **REMEMBER:** Add a space or wrap the &[Tab] placeholder in parentheses/square brackets to separate it from other text.

- **Picture:** Adds the &[Picture] placeholder for logos or watermarks.

4. **When you finish working in the header, click in the worksheet.**

IN THIS CHAPTER

» Sorting data and eliminating duplicates

» Filtering data efficiently

» Tallying, outlining, and subtotaling

» Jump-starting analysis

» Creating Excel tables

» Optimizing formulas and features

» Reverting tables to standard ranges

Chapter **4**

Organizing Data and Creating Tables

In this chapter, we show you how to organize your data and how to create tables with it. In the first half of the chapter, you learn how to sort and filter data; how to eliminate duplicates; and how to use handy tools such as Subtotal, Remove Duplicates, and Quick Analysis. In the second half, you discover how to turn your data into Excel tables. Tables have one pesky quirk you need to be aware of, but apart from that, they generally automate repetitive tasks, improve spreadsheet integrity, and streamline navigation.

Organizing Data

> **TIP** To get started organizing data, open the sample workbook named `1.4.1 Organizing Data.xlsx` available for download at www.dummies.com/go/microsoft365excelaiofd.

Using the Sort feature

Sort is one of Excel's most-used features, as indicated by its presence on the Home tab of the ribbon. Within a spreadsheet, a basic sort refers to organizing data in a specific order based on specific criteria. By default, Excel applies the following hierarchy when sorting in ascending order:

- **Numbers:** Smallest to largest
- **Numbers Stored as Text:** Smallest to largest
- **Dates:** Oldest to newest
- **Special Characters:** Spaces, non-alphanumeric characters, and punctuation marks in Excel's determined order
- **Text:** A to Z, case insensitive
- **Logical values:** FALSE to TRUE
- **Error Values:** #N/A, #REF!, and so on
- **Blank cells:** Always sorted to the bottom of the list

For descending sorts, the order is reversed, except for blank cells, which remain at the bottom.

Getting started with basic sorting

Here's how to get some firsthand experience with sorting mixed data:

1. **Select any cell within cells A1:A20, click the Data tab on the ribbon, and click Sort A to Z. Alternatively, click the Home tab on the ribbon, click Sort & Filter, and then click Sort A to Z.**

   Column A is now sorted smallest to largest, causing the data in column B to appear in an even more random order.

2. **Select any cell within cells B1:B20, click the Data tab on the ribbon, and click Sort A to Z; alternatively, on the Home tab of the ribbon, click Sort & Filter, and then click Sort A to Z.**

   Column B is now sorted according to the default hierarchy described earlier, while column A is randomized.

3. **Select any cell within cells B1:B20, click the Data tab of the ribbon, and then click Sort Z to A; alternatively, on the Home tab of the ribbon, click Sort & Filter, and then click Sort Z to A.**

   The hierarchy is now reversed.

Feel free to expand on this structure to gain hands-on experience with Excel's sorting nuances.

Resolving sorting mishaps

If a sort goes awry, click Undo on the Quick Access Toolbar or press Ctrl+Z (Windows) or ⌘+Z (macOS). Then try these techniques:

- **Overcoming blank rows or columns:** Excel sorts data within the current region (contiguous cells around the selected one). For data with blank rows or columns, select the entire range before sorting.

- **Converting numbers or dates stored as text:** Select the data, click the Data tab on the ribbon, click Text to Columns, and then click Finish. Though intended for splitting text into columns, this wizard also transforms data formats.

- **Unmerging Cells:** Merged cells block sorting. To unmerge, select the range and click Merge & Center on the Home tab of the ribbon.

- **Leading or trailing spaces:** Extra spaces disrupt sorting, but you can remove them with the TRIM function (see Book 3, Chapter 4).

Creating custom sorts

Excel allows sorting on up to 64 columns or criteria. Sixty-four! That's the same number of squares on a chessboard — but hopefully your sorting game won't end in a stalemate. Here's how to expand the reference data in the `1.4.1 Organizing Data.xlsx` workbook in anticipation of a more complex sort:

1. **Type** Non-text **in cell C1.**

2. **Type** =NONTEXT(A2:A20) **in cell C2.**

   TRUE indicates non-text values in column A, while FALSE identifies text.

3. **Type** Month **in cell D1.**

4. **Type** January **in cell D2 and double-click the Fill Handle to extend the series of months down to cell D20.**

5. **Select cell C2, click the Data tab on the ribbon, and then click Sort A to Z; alternatively, on the Home tab of the ribbon click Sort & Filter, and then click Sort A to Z.**

   An error prompt states You can't change part of an array. The formula =ISNONTEXT(A2:A20) creates a dynamic array, making the data unsortable.

6. **Convert the list to static values:**

    a. **Press Ctrl+A (Windows) or ⌘+A (macOS) to select the entire list.**

    b. **Click Copy on the Home tab of the ribbon or press Ctrl+C (Windows) or ⌘+C (macOS).**

    c. **On the Home tab of the ribbon, click the Paste drop-down, and then click Values. Alternatively, press Ctrl+Shift+V (Windows).**

    The random numbers in column B are now static values, which is fine for this demonstration.

7. **Select cells A2:D8, and then click Fill Color on the Home tab of the ribbon to apply a color.**

8. **Select cells A14:D20, and then click the Fill Color drop-down on the Home tab of the ribbon and select another color.**

You're now ready to explore sorting in greater depth:

1. **Select any cell within A1:D20.**

2. **On the Data tab of the ribbon, click Sort; alternatively, on the Home tab of the ribbon, click Sort & Filter, and then click Custom Sort.**

    The Sort dialog box opens, as shown in Figure 4-1.

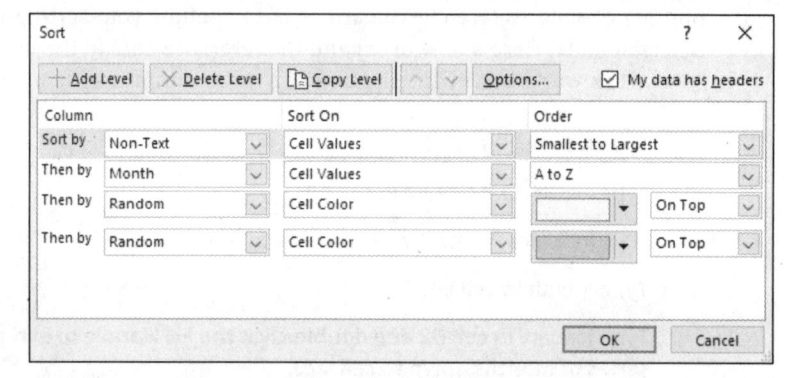

FIGURE 4-1: The Sort dialog box.

3. **If necessary, select the My Data Has Headers check box.**

    Excel often detects headers, but it may miss those spanning multiple rows.

82 BOOK 1 **Getting Started with Excel**

4. **From the Sort By drop-down, choose Non-Text.**

   The Sort On field defaults to Cell Values with other options, including Cell Color, Font Color, or Conditional Formatting Icon (referred to in Excel as Cell Icon). The Order field defaults to Smallest to Largest, but you can also choose Largest to Smallest, or Custom List.

   TECHNICAL STUFF: TRUE and FALSE are Boolean values equivalent to 1 and 0, respectively.

5. **Click Add Level, and then choose Month from the Then By drop-down menu.**

   The Sort On field defaults to Cell Values, and the Order field defaults to A to Z because the Month field is text-based.

6. **Click Add Level, and then choose Random from the second Then By drop-down list.**

7. **Choose Cell Color from the third Sort On drop-down list, and then choose a color from the No Cell Color drop-down list.**

8. **Click Copy Level, and then choose the other color from the No Cell Color drop-down list.**

   Copy Level provides a quick start for adding similar criteria to a sort.

9. **Click OK.**

   If your data has the months sorted alphabetically, that's expected — for now. No need to worry — we can sort it out!

   REMEMBER: Excel often frustrates users by following instructions literally, as seen with alphabetically sorted months.

10. **Click any cell within the list, click the Data tab on the ribbon, and then click Sort; alternatively, on the Home tab of the ribbon, click Sort & Filter, and then click Custom Sort.**

    The Sort dialog box opens.

11. **From the second Order drop-down list, choose Custom List.**

    The Custom Lists dialog box opens.

12. **Select the list that begins with January, February, March, and then click OK.**

    The Custom Lists dialog box closes, and the Order field displays a list of month names.

CHAPTER 4 **Organizing Data and Creating Tables** 83

13. **Click OK.**

    Your months are now sorted in calendar order as intended. Column C still groups non-text values first, followed by column D sorting by month. Cells D14:D19 show examples of the color order being applied.

Leveraging custom lists

If you've dragged the Fill Handle after typing a month or day, you've unknowingly used Excel's custom lists. Here's how to find the feature on Windows:

1. **On the File tab of the ribbon, click Options and then click Advanced.**

   The Advanced section of the Excel Options dialog box opens.

2. **Scroll all the way to the bottom.**

   You're in the right place when you see Lotus Compatibility settings — no yoga poses here, that's Lotus 1-2-3, Excel's predecessor.

3. **Click Edit Custom Lists.**

   The Custom Lists dialog box opens, as shown in Figure 4-2.

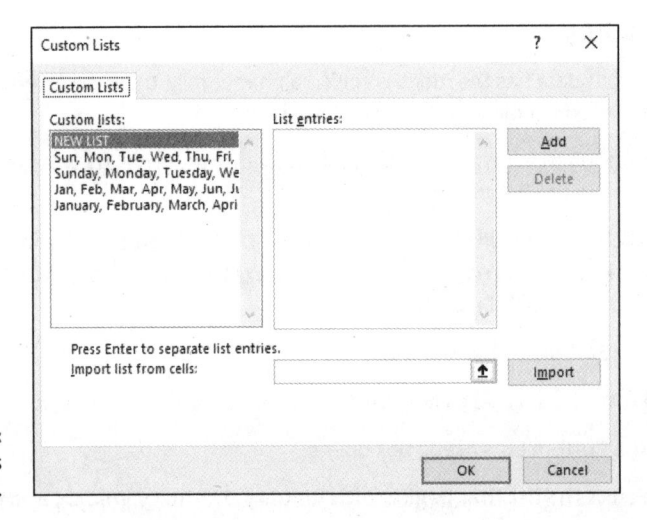

FIGURE 4-2: The Custom Lists dialog box.

Days and months are listed in read-only form, so you can't add an 8th day of the week or a 13th month.

4. **To create a new custom list, type up to 255 items into the List Entries field (pressing Enter after each one), or select a cell range and click Import.**

5. **Click OK twice.**

   The first OK saves your custom list, and the second exits the Excel Options dialog box.

TIP: On macOS, you access the Custom Lists feature by choosing Excel⇨Preferences to display the Preferences window; then click Custom Lists to display the Custom Lists pane.

You can use custom lists like days or months: Type an item into a cell and drag with the Fill Handle or use them to control the sort order of ranges and PivotTables.

Applying sort options

As noted earlier, text-based sorts are case-insensitive, so you may find that sometimes a lowercase instance will lead, while in others an uppercase instance will prevail. To confirm this behavior:

1. **Select any cell within B1:B20.**
2. **On the Data tab of the ribbon, click Sort A to Z; alternatively, on the Home tab of the ribbon, click Sort & Filter, and then click Sort A to Z.**

   The order of uppercase and lowercase letters (A, a, B, b, C, c) is random.

REMEMBER: The Sort A to Z and Sort Z to A commands reset and override any options previously set in the Custom Sort dialog box.

Here's how to force lowercase letters to appear before uppercase:

1. **Select any cell within your data.**
2. **On the Data tab of the ribbon, click Sort; alternatively, on the Home tab of the ribbon, click Sort & Filter and then click Custom Sort.**

   The Sort dialog box opens.
3. **Click Options.**

   The Sort Options dialog box opens, as shown in Figure 4-3.
4. **Enable the Case Sensitive option, and then click OK twice.**

   The order of lowercase and uppercase letters is now structured.

TIP: The Sort Options dialog box lets you sort data from left to right (by column instead of by row). When enabled, the Sort By drop-down list in the Sort dialog box prompts you to select a row number rather than a column heading.

CHAPTER 4 **Organizing Data and Creating Tables** 85

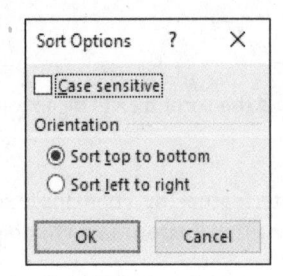

FIGURE 4-3: The Sort Options dialog box.

Removing duplicates

Excel's Remove Duplicates feature swiftly removes those pesky repetitions, leaving your dataset spotless and guilt-free. Work on a copy of your data if preserving the original list is important.

Removing duplicates from a single column

Here's how to remove duplicates from a single column:

1. **Select cells D1:D20.**

2. **Press Ctrl+C (Windows) or ⌘+C (macOS) or click Copy on the Home tab of the ribbon to copy the selected cells to the Clipboard.**

3. **Navigate to cell F1, click the Paste drop-down on the Home tab of the ribbon, and then click Value; alternatively, press Ctrl+Shift+V (Windows).**

   A copy of the data from A1:A20 should now appear in F1:F20.

   Always position your cursor within the list to remove duplicates. When pasting data into Excel, all cells are selected automatically; otherwise, selecting a single cell in the list suffices.

4. **On the Data tab of the ribbon, click Remove Duplicates.**

   The Remove Duplicates dialog box, shown in Figure 4-4, opens.

5. **If applicable, select the My Data Has Headers check box, and then click OK.**

   Excel displays one of two prompts:

   - **Summary of Action:** Shows the number of duplicates removed and the count of unique items that remain, with a note about empty cells and blanks.

   - **No Duplicate Values Found:** Indicates that the list consists entirely of unique items, such as when you're removing duplicates from a copy of cells A1:A20.

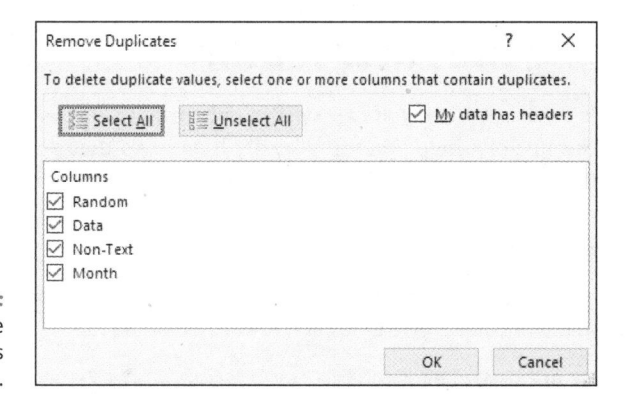

FIGURE 4-4:
The Remove Duplicates dialog box.

As noted, Remove Duplicates can shrink your original list unexpectedly. To backtrack, press Ctrl+Z (Windows) or ⌘+Z (macOS), or click the Undo command on the Quick Access Toolbar.

Eliminating duplicates across multiple columns

Duplicate data sneaks into lists as quickly as weeds sprout in a garden. You won't need a hoe, but removing duplicates across multiple columns demands care to avoid leaving behind any unwanted items. Here's how potential issues can arise:

1. **Copy cells A1:D20 and paste to cell H1 as values.**

2. **On the Data tab of the ribbon, click Remove Duplicates.**

   The Remove Duplicates dialog box opens.

3. **If applicable, select the My Data Has Headers check box, and then click OK.**

   Excel reports that no duplicate values were found because it treats each row as a separate record.

4. **On the Data tab of the ribbon, click Remove Duplicates again.**

5. **Click Unselect All, select Non-Text and Month, and then click OK.**

   This removes 5 duplicate rows, leaving 14. Columns J and K now contain each combination of TRUE or FALSE and a month name, while Columns H and I show the values from the first instance of each combination.

CHAPTER 4 **Organizing Data and Creating Tables**   87

Finessing the Filter feature

With Excel's Filter feature, you can swiftly cut through the noise to focus on the signal. In-cell buttons help you temporarily hide rows that don't meet your criteria. Here's a quick tour of the drop-down list that appears when you click one:

- **Sorting commands:** Sort A to Z, Sort Z to A, Sort by Color.

- **Sheet view commands:** Create individualized views for collaborative work on shared worksheets (see Chapter 5 of this minibook).

- **Filtering options:** Clear Filter, Filter by Color, and context-specific submenus like Text, Date, or Value filters. When Cell Icons (see Book 7, Chapter 4) are applied in a column, the Filter by Cell Icon option appears below Filter by Color.

- **Search field and check boxes:** Type full or partial criteria in the search field and refine your displayed data with check boxes.

Here's how to finesse and finagle the Filter feature:

1. **Click any cell within cells A1:D20.**

    For lists with blank rows or columns, select the entire range instead.

2. **To turn on the Filter feature, click the Data tab of the ribbon, and then click Filter; alternatively, on the Home tab of the ribbon, click Sort & Filter, and then click Filter.**

    If you prefer using the keyboard, press Ctrl+Shift+L (Windows) or ⌘+Shift+L (macOS).

    A filter button appears at the top of each column in the list.

3. **Click the filter button in cell D1, or select cell D1 and press Alt+↓ (Windows) or Option+↓ (macOS).**

4. **To narrow your view:**

    a. Clear the (Select All) check box.

    b. Select the January, February, and March check boxes.

    c. Click OK (Windows) or Close (macOS).

    Excel hides rows that don't match your selections, leaving only the rows with January, February, and March visible.

5. **Use the filter button in D1 (see Step 3) and type** A **in the Search field to filter the list for months containing the letter** *a*; **Then enter** p **to narrow the list to April.**

6. **Select the Add Current Selection to Filter check box, and then click OK.**

   Your visible rows now include January through April. You could've selected just the April check box, but the Add Current Selection to Filter check box allows for building complex filtering selections.

7. **Use the filter button in cell D1, select Filter by Color, and choose an option.**

   Filter by Color allows only one selection per column, unlike other filter settings.

This should give you a solid running start with filtering. From here, the possibilities are endless and your data stays in focus.

> **REMEMBER:** Hidden rows within filtered ranges remain protected during edits, letting you safely delete, format, or overwrite visible rows.

Clearing filters

Excel's Clear Filters command removes all filtering from your data, restoring visibility to all rows while keeping the filter buttons intact — no mutiny required. Compare this to turning off the Filter feature entirely:

1. **Select any cell within a filtered list.**

2. **To clear filters, on the Data tab of the ribbon, click Clear; alternatively, on the Home tab of the ribbon, click Sort & Filter, and then click Clear.**

   All rows become visible, but filter buttons remain.

   > **WARNING:** Don't confuse this with the Clear drop-down on the Home tab of the ribbon, which offers options to reset everything (Clear All), remove styles (Clear Formatting), erase data (Clear Contents), remove commentary (Clear Notes and Comments), or get rid of links (Clear Hyperlinks).

3. **Alternatively, to disable filters, click the Data tab of the ribbon, and then click Filter; alternatively, on the Home tab of the ribbon, click Sort & Filter, and then click Filter.**

   If you prefer using the keyboard, press Ctrl+Shift+L (Windows) or ⌘+Shift+L (macOS).

   All filter buttons are removed and your data is restored to its unfiltered state.

CHAPTER 4 **Organizing Data and Creating Tables** 89

Reapplying filters

When your data changes, use the Reapply command to refresh your filters:

1. **Filter the list in cells A1:D20 for January, February, and March.**

2. **Select the first three months in column D, type** December, **and then press Ctrl+Enter (Windows) or ⌘+Return (macOS).**

   All three cells are overwritten simultaneously.

3. **On the Data tab of the ribbon, click Reapply; alternatively, on the Home tab of the ribbon, click Sort & Filter, and then click Reapply.**

   The rows containing the edited data (for example, December) are now hidden because they no longer match the active filter criteria.

REMEMBER The Reapply command works with all filter types, including colors and cell icons. It's perfect for managing exception lists — adjust colors as items are cleared, and then use Reapply to reveal what's left to tackle.

Calculating with SUBTOTAL

Whether you're filtering data or doing math on visible cells only, SUBTOTAL is your go-to for precise, tailored calculations. Unlike most worksheet functions that act on all referenced cells, SUBTOTAL gives you the power to choose whether to include or exclude hidden rows. But wait, there's more! It can perform 11 different types of calculations. There are 255 arguments, but you'll typically only use the first two:

» `function_num`: A code specifying the calculation type. One- or two-digit codes include hidden rows; three-digit codes exclude them. Here are your options:

- **AVERAGE:** Calculates the average of the referenced cells (1 or 101).
- **COUNT:** Counts the number of numeric cells (2 or 102).
- **COUNTA:** Counts all nonblank cells (3 or 103).
- **MAX:** Finds the highest value (4 or 104).
- **MIN:** Finds the lowest value (5 or 105).
- **PRODUCT:** Multiplies all values together (6 or 106).
- **STDEV.S:** Calculates the standard deviation for a sample (7 or 107).
- **STDEV.P:** Calculates the standard deviation for an entire population (8 or 108).

- **SUM:** Adds up all values (9 or 109).
- **VAR.S:** Computes variance for a sample (10 or 110).
- **VAR.P:** Computes variance for an entire population (11 or 111).

Don't worry — typing the opening parenthesis brings up the `function_num` options, so no need to memorize the list.

» `ref1...ref254`: Up to 254 named ranges or ranges of cells.

Pairing SUBTOTAL with filters

Here's how to see how to use SUBTOTAL with a filtered list:

1. **Clear any existing filters (refer to the "Clearing filters" section, earlier in this chapter) or enable filter buttons if needed by selecting their check boxes.**

2. **Enter formulas:**

   a. Enter **=SUM(A2:A20)** in cell A22.

   b. Enter **=SUBTOTAL(9,A2:A20)** in cell A23.

   Both formulas return the same amount.

3. **Use the filter button in C1 to display only rows that contain** TRUE.

   The SUM function in cell A22 remains unchanged, while the SUBTOTAL function in cell A23 calculates the total for visible rows in the range A2:A20.

Now bear with us a second. You may be thinking, "Wait, isn't 9 supposed to *exclude* hidden rows?" Rest assured — we explain everything shortly!

Differentiating SUBTOTAL

Unlike most worksheet functions, the SUBTOTAL function adapts to your data's context, taking several factors into account:

» **Filtered datasets:** With filtered data, SUBTOTAL calculates values only in visible rows, regardless of using one-digit, two-digit, or three-digit function codes. For example:
  - `=SUBTOTAL(9, A2:20)` and `=SUBTOTAL(109, A2:A20)` produce the same result when applied to filtered lists.

CHAPTER 4 **Organizing Data and Creating Tables** 91

» **Manually hidden rows:** For manually hidden rows (those hidden without filters), use the appropriate function code to include or exclude them. For example, if rows 2 through 5 are manually hidden:

- =SUBTOTAL(9, A2:A20) includes *all rows*, hidden and visible, meaning cells A2:A5 are included in the result.

- =SUBTOTAL(109, A2:A20) tallies *only visible rows*, excluding those manually hidden, so amounts in cells A2:A5 are not included in the result.

» **Nonfiltered data:** The SUBTOTAL function in nonfiltered datasets automatically ignores nested SUBTOTAL and AGGREGATE functions, preventing double-counting data — a common pitfall in complex workbooks. For visual clarity, Figure 4-5 demonstrates how the SUBTOTAL function in cell F12 excludes the SUBTOTAL functions in cells F5 and F10.

FIGURE 4-5: The SUM function versus the SUBTOTAL function.

The SUBTOTAL function guards against formula errors. In Figure 4-6, if B5 excludes B2, both cells B5 and B12 return incorrect results. However, if F5 excludes F2, only F5 is wrong, but F12 remains accurate — minimizing the impact of errors.

Using the AGGREGATE function

If you're impressed by SUBTOTAL, you ain't seen nothin' yet. The AGGREGATE function includes all 11 operations from SUBTOTAL and adds 8 more, bringing the total to 19. Here's a breakdown of AGGREGATE's additional capabilities:

» **MEDIAN:** Returns the middle value in a range or the average of the two middle values for an even number of rows (12).

» **MODE.SNGL:** Finds the most frequently occurring value in a range (13).

» **LARGE:** Allows you to specify the *k*th largest value in a range (for example, the second largest) (14).

- **SMALL:** Returns the *k*th smallest value, acting as a counterpoint to LARGE (15).
- **PERCENTILE.INC:** Calculates the *k*th percentile of a range, including the minimum and maximum values (16).
- **QUARTILE.INC:** Returns the quartile of a dataset, using inclusive percentiles (17).
- **PERCENTILE.EXC:** Focuses on percentiles between the minimum and maximum, excluding both extremes (18).
- **QUARTILE.EXC:** Excludes the minimum and maximum values to calculate quartiles (19).

The arguments for the AGGREGATE function depend upon the form that you want to use. Here are the arguments if you use the Reference form, which references up to 253 ranges of cells:

- `function_num`: Specifies the operation (1–19).

  As with SUBTOTAL, an onscreen drop-down list the calculation types when you type the opening parenthesis.

- `options`: A single-digit number that determines which values to ignore:
  - **0 or omitted:** Ignore nested SUBTOTAL and AGGREGATE functions, which means include both hidden and visible rows.
  - **1:** Ignore hidden rows, nested SUBTOTAL and AGGREGATE functions.
  - **2:** Ignore error values, nested SUBTOTAL and AGGREGATE functions, which also means include both hidden and visible rows.
  - **3:** Ignore hidden rows, error values, nested SUBTOTAL and AGGREGATE functions, basically the whole enchilada.
  - **4:** Ignore nothing, which means nested SUBTOTAL and AGGREGATE functions are included in the result.
  - **5:** Ignore hidden rows, which means only include visible rows.
  - **6:** Ignore error values, which means that those pesky #N/A signs won't cause a cascade effect.
  - **7:** Ignore hidden rows and error values, meaning visible rows are considered, but error values like #DIV/0! are not.

  A second drop-down list appears after completing the `function_num` argument, allowing you to select which values to exclude, if any, for the calculation.

  - `ref1...ref253`: Up to 253 named ranges or ranges of cells.

Here are the arguments if you use the Array form, which lets you reference a single range or array, but includes an optional argument used with certain functions:

- `function_num`: Specifies the function to use (1-19).
- `options`: Determines exclusions (0-7).
- `array`: The range or array of data to evaluate.
- `k`: Required for functions like LARGE, SMALL, and percentiles, specifying the rank or position, sometimes referred to as `ref2`.

By way of example, the formula `=AGGREGATE(9,3,A2:A20)` sums the values in A2:A20, excluding hidden rows, error values, and nested SUBTOTAL or AGGREGATE functions. AGGREGATE gives you control: Sidestep error values, choose to include hidden rows, or calculate percentiles on the fly.

Summarizing lists with the Subtotal feature

How often have you manually added subtotals to a list and then calculated the grand total yourself? What if you never had to do that again? Meet the Subtotal feature — an efficient solution for handling totals (though it comes with some rough edges in formatting and removing subtotals). With Subtotal, you can

>> Create an interactive outline for your data.

>> Insert up to eight levels of subtotals within a list.

>> Add page breaks after each subtotal for easier organization.

>> Choose any operation covered in the "Calculating with SUBTOTAL" section.

Try out the Subtotal feature like this:

1. **Prepare your data for subtotaling:**

    - Turn off any existing filter buttons in A1:A20 (see the "Clearing filters" section, earlier in this chapter) to ensure the data is outlined.
    - Sort column D by month, either alphabetically or logically (see "Creating custom sorts," earlier in this chapter).

2. **On the Data tab of the ribbon, click Subtotal.**

    The Subtotal dialog box opens.

94 BOOK 1 **Getting Started with Excel**

3. **Configure subtotal settings:**

    a. **Select Month from the At Each Change In field.**

    Use this drop-down list to choose the field you want to subtotal.

    b. **Select Sum from the Use Function field.**

    This defaults to Sum if the last column contains numbers; otherwise, it defaults to Count.

    c. **Check Random and uncheck Month within the Add Subtotal To list.**

    The last column is selected by default.

4. **Adjust options:**

    a. **Leave Replace Current Subtotals on unless adding multiple levels of subtotals.**

    b. **Turn on Page Break Between Groups to insert a page break after each grouping (for example, Month).**

    c. **Turn off Summary Below Data to place subtotals at the top of each group.**

    By default, subtotals and the grand total appear below each group and the list.

5. **Click OK.**

If no filter buttons are present, outline controls now appear on the left-hand side of the screen. Use the + or − buttons to expand or collapse sections, or use the subtotal level buttons at the top to manage all sections. On the Data tab of the ribbon, click Ungroup Outline and then click Clear Outline to remove the outline.

Formatting subtotals

Formatting subtotal rows can take a twist. Unlike the Filter feature, which protects hidden rows, formatting outlined rows affects both hidden and visible rows. But you don't need to format each subtotal row individually. Instead:

> **» Option 1:** Filter the list on rows ending with Total, select and format the subtotal rows, and then clear the filter. Don't worry if subtotal amounts temporarily show as zeros — this happens when detail rows are hidden. The subtotals will reappear when the filter is removed.

CHAPTER 4 **Organizing Data and Creating Tables** 95

- **Option 2:** Collapse the list to show only subtotals, select the amounts, and use the Go To Special command to isolate visible cells:

  1. **On the Home tab of the ribbon, click Find & Select, click Go To Special, click Visible Cells Only, and then click OK.**

     Alternatively, press Alt+; (Windows) or ⌘+Shift+Z (macOS).

  2. **Apply your formatting as desired, and then click any other cell to finish.**

Removing subtotals

You can remove your subtotals with just a couple of clicks:

1. **Select any cell within the subtotaled list.**
2. **On the Data tab of the ribbon, click Subtotal.**

   The Subtotal dialog box opens.
3. **Click Remove All to clear the subtotals from the list.**

WARNING: Brace yourself — we're entering Dr. Jekyll and Mr. Hyde territory. Subtotal starts off as helpful and cheerful, offering to handle your totals, but its darker side emerges when you remove them. This action is irreversible and disables undo for prior actions, so plan carefully.

Jump-starting insights with Quick Analysis

The Quick Analysis feature provides a smooth entry point into several powerful analytical tools across Excel:

- **Conditional formatting:** See Book 4, Chapter 1.
- **Charts:** See Book 5, Chapter 1.
- **Totals:** Quick Analysis lets you add sums, averages, counts, running totals, or percentages to your list.
- **Tables:** For all things tables, see the second half of this chapter.
- **Sparklines:** You can create tiny charts that fit in worksheet cells.

Here's a speedy survey of the Quick Analysis feature:

1. **Select two or more cells and then click the Quick Analysis button or press Ctrl+Q (Windows).**

   On macOS, don't use ⌘+Q unless you want to quit Excel.

   The Quick Analysis Tool appears.

2. **Hover over any option to see a preview of the formatting or command, or be bold and make a selection.**

   To dismiss the Quick Analysis tool, click any worksheet cell or press Escape.

> **TIP** If the Quick Analysis button distracts you, you can turn it off. On Windows, click the File tab on the ribbon, click Options, deselect the Show Quick Analysis Options on Selection check box in the General section of the Excel Options dialog box, and click OK. On macOS, choose Excel⇨Preferences, click Edit to display the Edit Preferences pane, deselect the Show Quick Analysis Options on Selection check box, and then click the Close button.

Creating Tables

You likely have a list of data to transform into an Excel table, but if not, here's how to create a list to use throughout this chapter:

1. **Add headers:**

   a. **In cell A1, type** Month.

   b. **In cell B1, type** Quantity.

2. **Create a list of months:**

   a. **In cell A2, type** January.

   b. **Drag the Fill Handle in cell A2 down to cell A13 to AutoFill the remaining months.**

3. **Generate a series of amounts:**

   a. **In cell B2, type** 100.

   b. **In cell B3, type** 200.

c. **Select cells B2:B3, and then double-click the Fill Handle in cell B3 to automatically fill the series, completing it from 100 to 1200.**

Excel requires only two cells to identify and replicate a pattern.

Comparing data ranges to Excel tables

Nonblank areas of Excel worksheets are often referred to as *normal ranges* of cells or data ranges. In this era of "smart" everything, data in normal ranges could be considered "dumb," while data within Excel tables earns the "smart" label. Here's why:

- » Formulas or features referencing normal ranges need manual updates when data is added.
- » Standard cell references require navigation between sheets and result in unintelligible references that complicate auditing or revising.
- » Column headings in normal ranges scroll off-screen unless you use the Freeze Panes feature to lock rows in place.
- » In normal ranges, updating formulas requires manually copying changes up or down, risking skipped rows and errors.
- » Navigating to a normal range of cells often requires switching tabs and scrolling within the sheet to find the desired data.

With just a few mouse clicks — or even faster keyboard shortcuts — you can tackle repetitive tasks and improve data integrity. Excel tables also bring much-needed structure to spreadsheets. Before converting data into a table, ensure it meets these requirements:

- » A single row of unique and static column headings (headers in Excel) — formulas are not permitted here.
- » Contiguous data with no blank rows, columns, totals or subtotals.

Data rows within the table can include text, numbers, or formulas.

Excel tables can include only a header row, data rows, and (optionally) a total row. For subtotals, use the PivotTable feature (see Book 5, Chapter 2) or the Subtotal feature with a normal range of cells (see the "Calculating with SUBTOTAL" section, earlier in this chapter).

Creating Excel tables

Here's the process for creating an Excel table:

1. **Click any cell within a normal range of data, such as cell A1.**

2. **On the Insert tab of the ribbon, click Table; alternatively, press Ctrl+T (Windows) or ⌘+T (macOS).**

   The Create Table dialog box opens, as shown in Figure 4-6.

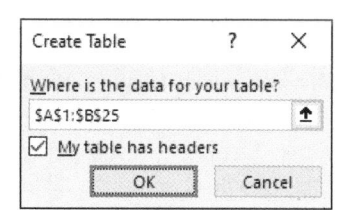

   FIGURE 4-6: The Create Table dialog box.

3. **If the first row of your data consists of column headings, ensure the My Table Has Headers check box is selected.**

   If My Table Has Headers is left unchecked, Excel adds generic headers like Column1, Column2, and so on. For multiple header rows, Excel treats only the first row as column headings; others are part of the data.

   REMEMBER

4. **Click OK to transform the data range into an Excel table.**

When the conversion is complete, several things happen:

- The contextual Table Design tab appears on the ribbon when your cursor is within the table. If Excel doesn't make the tab active when you need it, click the tab.

- A default table style with row banding is automatically applied — see the "Setting default table styles" section, later in this chapter, to customize it.

- Filter buttons (see the "Finessing the Filter feature" section, earlier in this chapter) appear in the header row.

- Column headers and filter buttons replace column letters in the worksheet frame when the header row scrolls off-screen and the active cell is within the table.

Resizing tables

In most cases, Excel tables automatically expand to include new data added immediately to the right or below:

1. **Click cell A13, and then drag the Fill Handle down to cell A25.**
2. **Select cells B12:B13, and then double-click the Fill Handle in cell B13 to automatically fill the series, extending it from 1200 to 2400.**

> **REMEMBER:** Tables don't expand automatically if you bring ranges closer together by deleting rows or columns between them.

If you need to resize a table manually, use one of these methods:

- » **Resizing Handle:** Click any cell within the table to reveal a small blue triangle in the bottom-right corner. Drag this handle to adjust the table's size as needed.
- » **Resize Table command:** On the Table Design tab of the ribbon, click Resize Table to open the Resize Table dialog box. Enter a new range in the field and click OK. You can't change the starting range of the table, but you can adjust the ending cell reference.

> **REMEMBER:** There's no need to turn the total row for a table off before resizing — Excel automatically repositions it to follow the new ending cell reference. For more about total rows, see the "Adding total rows" section later in this chapter.

Naming tables

What's in a name? Quite a lot — especially for tables. The first field in the Table Design tab, Table Name, contains a generic name, such as Table1. Although functional, these generic names quickly blend together, much like Sheet1 and Sheet2. Renaming tables keeps things clear. Table names must follow these rules:

- » They can include letters, numbers, underscores, and backslashes.
- » The first character must be a letter, underscore, or backslash.
- » They can't conflict with existing names in the workbook. For example, a table name can't match an existing named range. Also, a table name can't be a valid cell reference; for example:
  - TAX2026 is not a valid table name (it resembles a cell reference).
  - TAX_2026 is valid and follows the rules.

>> They can be a single letter, underscore, or backslash, but they can't be C or R, because these are shortcuts for selecting the column or row of the active cell in the Name Box.

Here's how to rename a table:

1. **Select any cell within an Excel table (for example, cell A1).**

   The first row of an Excel table is called the Header Row.

2. **Use the Table Name field to assign a name.**

   For example, enter the word **Sales** to name the table.

TIP: You can also rename tables by clicking the Formulas tab on the ribbon and then clicking Name Manager. In the Name Manager dialog box, select the name of a table and then click Edit to open the Edit Name dialog box.

Navigating to and from tables

Excel offers two quick ways to jump directly to your tables without scrolling endlessly through your data:

1. **Click any cell that isn't within a table (for example, cell J10).**

2. **Use one of these methods to navigate to a table:**

   - **Name Box:** Click the Name Box drop-down list (above the worksheet grid) and select a table name from the list, such as Sales.

   - **Go To command:** On the Home tab of the ribbon, click Find & Select, and then click Go To. Alternatively, press F5 or Ctrl+G (Windows) or ⌘+G (macOS). Then select a table name from the Go To list and click OK.

   If the worksheet containing the table is visible, Excel activates and selects the table's range of cells.

   TIP: Windows users can double-click a table name to save a step.

   REMEMBER: The Name Box displays names assigned to worksheet cells first (in alphabetical order), followed by table names in a second alphabetical sequence. This quirk arises only in workbooks that use both types of names.

3. **To return to your previous location, click the Home tab of the ribbon, click Find & Select, and then click Go To; alternatively, press F5 or Ctrl+G (Windows) or ⌘+G (macOS).**

   The Go To dialog box opens.

4. **Click OK.**

   The Reference field in the Go To dialog box contains the address of the cell location where you started, such as J10, letting you teleport back to your original position in the workbook with ease. This technique is particularly powerful and helpful in large workbooks.

Controlling table formatting

One aspect of Excel tables that often sends Excel users scrambling for Undo is banded row formatting. Although it's intended to highlight table areas and help track rows, it may just not be your aesthetic. Fortunately, you have options.

ADJUSTING TABLE FORMATTING MANUALLY

Follow these steps to remove or adjust the style of a single table:

1. **Select any cell within the table (for example, cell A1).**

   The Table Design tab appears on the ribbon.

2. **Change or remove the style:**

   a. **On the Table Design tab of the ribbon, click the Table Styles drop-down.**

   b. **Choose a new style or select None (upper-left) or Clear (bottom) to remove the formatting entirely.**

You can also adjust a table's style by toggling these options on the Table Design tab of the ribbon:

- **Header Row:** Enabled by default; displays column titles for the table.
- **Total Row:** Initially sums or counts the last column of the table (see the "Adding total rows" section, later in this chapter, for more information).
- **Banded Rows:** Enabled by default; shades every other row.
- **First Column:** Bolds the contents of the first column.
- **Last Column:** Bolds the contents of the last column.
- **Banded Columns:** Shades every other column.
- **Filter Buttons:** Enabled by default; toggles Filter Buttons (see the "Finessing the Filter feature" section, earlier in this chapter) on or off.

ESTABLISHING CUSTOM TABLE STYLES

You can't alter the built-in table styles, but you can use any existing style as a starting point:

1. **On the Table Styles tab of the ribbon, click the Table Styles drop-down.**
2. **Right-click any existing style and choose Duplicate.**

   The Modify Table Style dialog box opens, as shown in Figure 4-7.

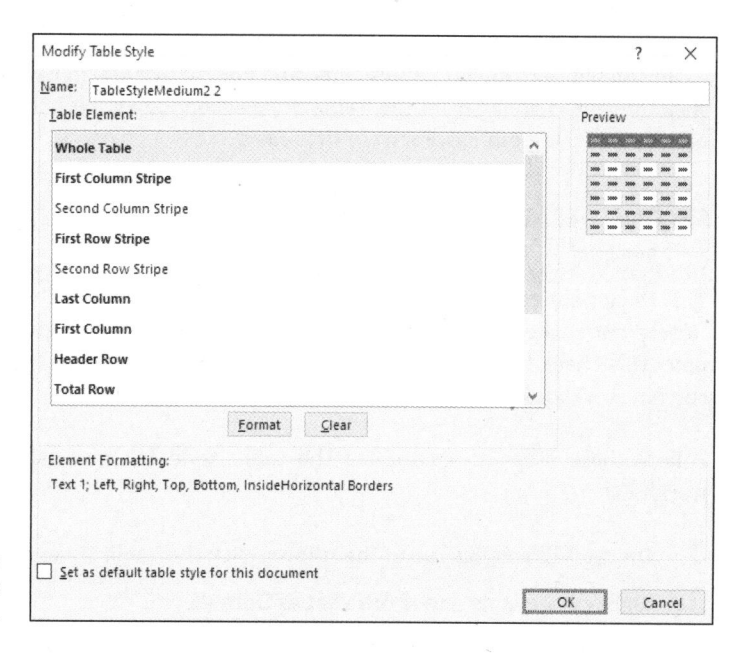

FIGURE 4-7: The Modify Table Style dialog box.

3. **Use the Name field to rename your new style.**
4. **Select a table element from the list and click Format.**

   An abbreviated version of the Format Cells dialog box opens.

   TIP: The Column Stripe and Row Stripe options enable you to choose a stripe size between 1 and 9.

5. **Customize the font, borders, and fill color for the selected table element, and then click OK.**
6. **Repeat steps 4 and 5 to customize additional table elements.**

7. **Click OK to close the Modify Table Style dialog box.**

   Going forward, the custom style appears at the top of the Table Styles drop-down list.

8. **Choose the new custom style from the Table Styles drop-down if you want to apply it to the active table.**

REMEMBER: Custom styles apply only to the active workbook. When transferring a table with a custom style to a new workbook — by moving or copying — Excel creates a new style in the destination, though formatting, such as fill colors, may differ.

TIP: As any fashionista knows, styles come and go. Thankfully, in Excel, you can right-click unwanted styles from the Table Styles drop-down list and choose Delete. If only decluttering our closets were that easy!

SETTING DEFAULT TABLE STYLES

You may be wondering why we didn't mention the Set as Default Table Style for This Document check box in the previous section. Sometimes, we like to test how closely our readers are paying attention — just one of our quirks. On a serious note, this check box allows you to define the default style for future tables in the current workbook.

Follow these steps to customize the table style for new tables in the active workbook:

1. **On the Table Styles tab of the ribbon, click the Table Styles drop-down.**
2. **Right-click a style and choose Set as Default.**

   If you prefer a no-frills approach, the first style listed in the Light section, labeled None in its ScreenTip, applies no formatting.

From now on, any tables you create in the active workbook reflect your own sense of style. However, custom table style defaults apply only to the active workbook, so you must repeat these steps in each workbook.

Automating formulas and features

The ease-of-use features discussed in the "Creating Excel tables" section earlier in this chapter — such as headings and filter buttons that integrate seamlessly into the worksheet frame and the intuitive navigation techniques — already make tables well worth the small price of admission. But these benefits are just the tip of the iceberg.

Adding total rows

Many of your Excel tables can be elevated by adding a total row. But hold on — before you reach for the equal sign or AutoSum command, manual formulas aren't necessary. Here's how to add and customize a total row within an Excel table:

1. **Select any cell within a table (for example, cell A1).**

   The Table Design tab appears on the ribbon.

2. **On the Table Design tab, select the Total Row check box.**

   A new row appears below the table, with the word *Total* in the first column and one of these amounts in the last column:

   - **Numeric total:** If it contains numbers, Excel automatically calculates the sum.
   - **Row count:** If it contains text or dates, Excel displays the count of non-blank cells.

3. **Adjust the total row as needed:**

   - **Remove column total:** Click the unwanted tally in the total row, select the AutoCalculate drop-down list, and choose None.
   - **Add column total:** Select a cell in the total row, click the AutoCalculate drop-down list, and choose a mathematical operation (for example, Average, Max, Min).

   The AutoCalculate drop-down relies on the SUBTOTAL function (see the "Calculating with SUBTOTAL" section, earlier in this chapter), which excludes hidden rows. Selecting More Functions opens the Insert Function dialog box, where most functions (unlike SUBTOTAL) include hidden rows in calculations.

Some Excel features seem to suffer from amnesia — turn them off and back on, and it's like starting from scratch. Not the total row, though — it remembers your choices. To add more data, turn the total row off on the Table Design tab of the ribbon, append your data, and turn it back on. If only life were this simple. . . .

Crafting calculated columns

What comes to mind when you hear "steely-eyed, cold, and calculated"? Maybe Gordon Gekko from *Wall Street*? Columns of formulas within a table don't need to be steely-eyed (though they may come across as a bit cold). But calculated? Absolutely — and that's precisely what makes them so powerful. Here's how to add a calculated column to a table:

1. **In cell C1, type** Price.

   The table expands by one column. Alternatively, you can insert a new column and then type the header name.

2. **Type a formula into the first data row of the new column (for example, type** =ROW() **in cell C2).**

   Notice how the formula is copied automatically through the last data row — this is a calculated column. In a normal range, you must copy the formula manually.

   TECHNICAL STUFF

   The ROW function returns the row number of a current row when the reference argument is omitted; otherwise, it returns the row number of the cell being referenced.

3. **Make a change to the formula in any other row of the table, so that a different amount is returned (for example, change cell C10 to** =ROW()*10**).**

   The change to the formula in cell C10 is applied to the rows above and below cell C10.

Leveraging structured references

In the movie *Groundhog Day*, a weatherman finds himself trapped in a time loop, reliving the same day over and over again until he learns to break free through personal growth. Similarly, many Excel users find themselves stuck in a loop of repetitive actions when using standard cell references, unaware of the efficiency that structured references can bring.

Structured reference formulas within Excel tables save time and enhance usability. Unlike standard cell references, they use table and column names. For instance, within the same table, formulas reference only column names, while references from outside the table include both table and column names. Here are some key benefits of using structured references:

- » **Automatic column references:** Column names inherently reference all data rows in a column, improving data integrity.
- » **Dynamic range adjustments:** Formula references reflect changes when rows are added or removed.
- » **Enhanced readability:** Table and column names clearly describe the data directly, making formulas easier to read and maintain.

Structured references include one or more of the following components:

» **Table name:** Identifies the table, such as Sales.

» **Column name:** The name of a specific column within the table, such as [Quantity].

» **Implicit intersection operator (@):** References the current row's value in a column, such as [@Price] or sometimes [@[Price]].

» **Item specifiers:** Define specific sections of a table:
- [#All]: Includes headers row, data, and totals.
- [#Headers]: Refers to the header row.
- [#Data]: Refers to the data rows (default for column references).
- [#Totals]: Refers to the total row.

Structured references combine adaptability and ease of use, making them ideal for maintaining and auditing formulas. Here's a quick example:

1. **In cell D1, type** Total.
2. **In cell D2, type an equal sign (=).**
3. **Select cell B1, and type an asterisk (*).**
4. **Select cell C1, and press Enter (Windows) or Return (macOS).**

    The formula =[@Quantity]*[@Price] is equivalent to =B2*C2 but easier to interpret. The implicit intersection operator (@) tells Excel to use the value for the current row in each column.

Here's how to dig deeper with dynamic arrays and structured references:

1. **Carry out the following steps in cell F1:**

    a. **Type** =UNIQUE(.

    The UNIQUE function lists distinct values.

    b. **Type** Sales **and then [to display the Formula AutoComplete list, as shown in Figure 4-8.**

    c. **Type [to display the Formula AutoComplete list, as shown in Figure 4-8.**

    The list shows options related to writing structured reference formulas, including column names in the Sales table, but it doesn't appear if the table name is incorrect.

FIGURE 4-8:
The structured reference version of the Formula AutoComplete list.

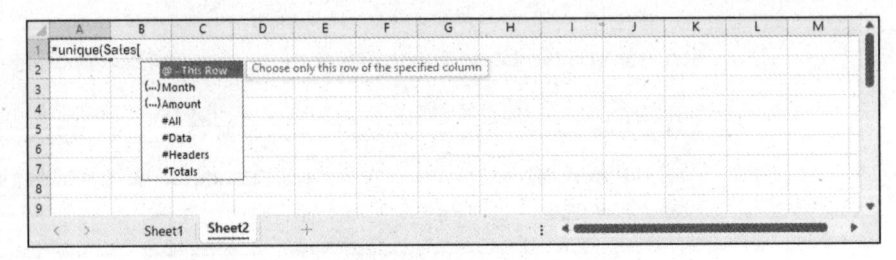

    d. **Use the arrow keys to select Month, and then press Tab.**

    e. **Type] to close the column name reference and press Enter.**

    Excel automatically adds the closing parenthesis for UNIQUE.

2. **Carry out the following steps in cell G1:**

    a. **Type** =SUMIF(.

    The SUMIF function adds values based on matching criteria in a list.

    b. **Type the table name** Sales.

    c. **Type [to display the Formula AutoComplete list.**

    d. **Use the arrow keys to select Month, and then press Tab.**

    e. **Type] to close the column name reference.**

    f. **Type a comma, and then type** F1#.

    The Spilled Range Operator (#), covered in Book 7, Chapter 2, enables you to reference the results of a dynamic array function, such as UNIQUE.

    g. **Type a comma (,), and then type the table name** Sales **again.**

    h. **Type [to display the Formula AutoComplete List.**

    i. **Use the arrow keys to select Amount, and then press Tab.**

    j. **Type] to close the column reference, and then press Enter.**

Notice that there's no need to leave cell F1 while writing this formula. Formula AutoComplete simplifies selecting table columns, while the Spilled Range Operator eliminates copying the formula down to F12.

Disabling structured references

To avoid structured references within Excel tables, type cell addresses directly within formulas or disable the feature entirely by following these steps:

1. **On the File tab of the ribbon, click Options, and then click Formulas.**

   The Formulas section of the Excel Options dialog box opens.

2. **Clear the check box for Use Table Names in Formulas.**

3. **Click OK.**

   This setting disables structured references, allowing you to use standard cell references exclusively.

Crafting self-expanding formulas

Structured references are the cat's meow for writing new formulas efficiently, but they offer little help for existing formulas with standard cell references. Fortunately, converting a normal range of data into an Excel table often improves the integrity of these older formulas.

WARNING

Before you start popping corks, note that this technique works only when formulas reference all rows — excluding column headers — before the range is converted into a table.

This demonstration highlights the integrity of formulas referencing normal ranges to those referencing Excel tables:

1. **Create two additional sets of reference data:**

   a. **Select cells B1:B4, and then click the Copy button on the Home tab of the ribbon or press Ctrl+C (Windows) or ⌘+C (macOS).**

   b. **Select cell I1, and then click the Paste button on the Home tab or press Ctrl+V (Windows) or ⌘+V (macOS).**

   A copy of cells B1:B4 appears in cells I1:I4, including the banded row formatting.

   c. **Click the Paste Options button and select Values. Alternatively, on the Home tab, click Clear and then click Clear Formats.**

   TIP

   Using Paste Special Values provides an alternative to steps b and c.

   d. **Copy and paste cells I1:I4 to cell K1.**

2. **Add labels and formulas that reference both ranges:**

   a. **Type** Normal Range **in cell M1 and** Excel Table **in cell M2.**

   b. **Type the formula** =SUM(I2:44) **in cell N1 and** =SUM(K2:K4) **in cell N2.**

   Both formulas return 600.

3. **Convert cells K1:K4 into an Excel table.**

   Refer to the "Creating Excel tables" section earlier in this chapter for a refresher if needed.

4. **Add new data by typing** 400 **in cells I5 and K5.**

   The formula in N2, referencing an Excel table, dynamically updates to 400. In contrast, the formula in P1, which references a normal range, remains stuck at 300, because it requires manual editing to include the additional data.

Unpacking table quirks

Here's a quick rundown of some common Excel commands that behave differently — or become unavailable — when working within a table:

» **Keyboard shortcuts:** Certain keyboard shortcuts behave differently within normal ranges of cells versus within tables:

- **Ctrl++ (Windows) or ⌘+Shift++ (macOS):** In a normal range of cells, this keyboard shortcut opens the Insert dialog box. Within a data row of a table, it inserts a new row, even if only a single cell is selected. It doesn't function in the header row of a table but inserts a new column when used in the total row.

- **Ctrl+– (Windows) or ⌘+– (macOS):** This keyboard combination deletes rows or columns, following the same behavior and nuances as the previous shortcut.

- **Ctrl+A (Windows) or ⌘+A (macOS):** In a normal range of cells, this keyboard combination selects the *current region* (the contiguous block of cells surrounding the active cell). Within a table, the combination works differently. If the active cell is in a header row or total row, this combination selects the entire table, including any header row and total row. If the active cell is in a data row, this combination selects all the data rows but not any header row and total row; press the combination again to add the header row and total row to the selection.

- **Ctrl+Space:** In a normal range of cells, selects the entire worksheet column. Within a table, selects all data rows in the current column; press the shortcut again to include the header and total rows.

- **Shift+Space:** In a normal range of cells, selects the entire worksheet row. Within a table, selects only the table row(s) for the current selection.

- **Disabled commands:** The following ribbon commands may be unavailable based upon context:

  - **Insert button on the Home tab:** You can't insert rows or columns within the header row of a table. However, this command works in any data or total row, where the Insert button displays two additional options: Insert Table Rows Above and Insert Table Columns to the Left.

  - **Delete button on the Home tab:** You can't delete the header row or any columns while the active cell is in the header row of a table. This command is available within data or total rows, where the Delete menu includes these additional choices: Delete Table Rows and Delete Table Columns.

  - **Merge & Center button on the Home tab:** The Merge & Center command is disabled within an Excel table, preventing you from merging cells in the table.

  - **Table button on the Insert tab:** The Table command is disabled when the active cell is within a table, because inserting one table within another is not allowed.

  - **Subtotal button on the Data tab:** The Subtotal feature (see the "Calculating with SUBTOTAL" section, earlier in this chapter) can't be used in tables. Use the Total Row functionality instead, which dynamically adjusts to filtered data for similar results.

  - **Custom Views button on the View tab:** The Custom Views feature is entirely disabled in workbooks containing Excel tables. Existing custom views remain intact but enter a "deep freeze," becoming accessible again when all tables are converted back to regular ranges of cells.

- **Mouse clicks:** In a normal range of cells or data row of a table, double-clicking the bottom edge of a cell moves the active cell selection to the last non-blank cell in that column. In contrast, selecting a single header cell and then double-clicking its bottom edge selects the entire column of the table.

TIP

As noted in the "Resizing tables" section, earlier in this chapter, tables should automatically expand to include new data. However, you can turn off this feature — either deliberately or by accident — by clicking the Stop Automatically Expanding Tables command on the AutoCorrect Options button's menu for a table. If this happens, you can reenable it easily. On Windows, click the File tab on the ribbon, click Options, click Proofing, and then click AutoCorrect Options. In the AutoCorrect Options dialog box, select the New Rows and Columns in Table check box on the AutoFormat As You Type tab, and then click OK to close each dialog box. On macOS, choose Excel ⇨ Preferences, click Tables & Filters to display the Tables & Filters pane, select the Automatically Expand Tables check box, and then click the Close button.

Converting a table to a data range

Excel tables offer numerous benefits, but there may be occasions where you need to revert them to normal ranges of cells. Here's how:

1. **Select a cell within the table.**

   The Table Design tab appears on the ribbon.

2. **Remove the formatting by clicking the Table Design tab on the ribbon, clicking the Table Styles drop-down, and then choosing None at the top or Clear at the bottom.**

   Both options remove table-specific formatting.

3. **Click the Table Design tab, click Convert to Range, and then click Yes to confirm.**

   If you have a change of heart, click Undo or press Ctrl+Z (Windows) or ⌘+Z (macOS) to restore the Table feature.

WARNING

Always remove styling from a table before converting it to a normal range. This prevents confusion and ensures that you or other users don't mistakenly assume that table automation features are still active.

> **IN THIS CHAPTER**
>
> » Finding and replacing data within cells
>
> » Exploring with the Navigation task pane
>
> » Navigating with Go To, Go To Special, and the Name Box
>
> » Activating and reordering worksheets
>
> » Splitting worksheet windows
>
> » Working with views and zoom

Chapter **5**

Navigating Worksheets and Workbooks

This chapter dives into ironing out the wrinkles in navigating worksheets and workbooks. Folding a fitted sheet remains beyond our expertise (and perhaps anyone's), but we provide guidance for leaping confidently from one spot in a spreadsheet to another. Taming unruly worksheets and workbooks becomes manageable with the Custom Views feature, which applies a buffet of settings in one fell swoop.

Finding and Replacing Data within Cells

The Find and Replace commands in Excel reside on separate tabs within the Find and Replace dialog box, shown in Figure 5-1. This handy tool lets you search for data across worksheets and replace all or part of a cell's contents. Use one of the following methods to open the corresponding tab:

» **Find tab:** On the Home tab of the ribbon, click Find & Select and then click Find. Alternatively, press Ctrl+F (Windows) or ⌘+F (macOS).

» **Replace tab:** On the Home tab of the ribbon, click Find & Select and then click Replace. Alternatively, press Ctrl+H (Windows) or ⌘+H (macOS).

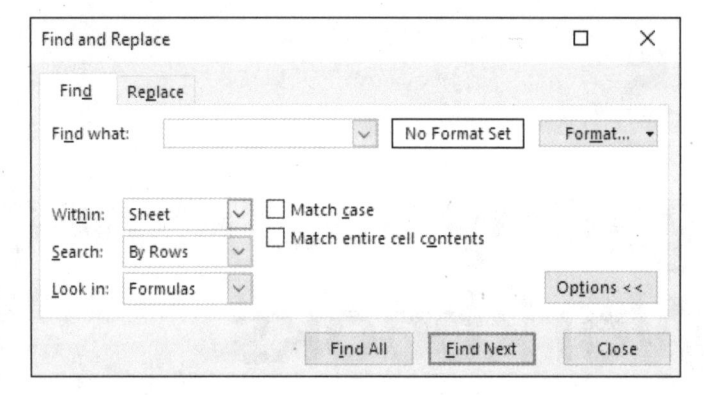

FIGURE 5-1: The Find and Replace dialog box.

Searching within worksheet cells

Here's how to ask the Find tab for exactly what you want:

» **Find What:** This field lets you specify the text or numbers you want to search for. It even includes a drop-down list of recent search criteria for quick access. Leave it blank if you're searching solely by formatting, or combine search criteria with formatting for a more targeted approach.

If the Find What field is the only option visible, click Options to reveal additional search choices.

» **Format:** Use the Format button to access three options:

- **Format:** This command opens the Format Cells dialog box, where you can define one or more formatting criteria for your search.

- **Choose Format from Cell:** Select a worksheet cell to use as a template for finding other cells with the same formatting.
- **Clear Find Format:** This command starts off disabled. It activates after you set one of the first two options, allowing you to clear any formatting criteria and start fresh.

» **Within:** Choose Sheet to search the current worksheet; choose Workbook to search the entire workbook.

» **Search:** Select By Rows or By Columns to steer the search direction within the worksheet.

» **Look In:** Refine your search by selecting one of the following options:

- **Formulas:** You can search formulas for specific cell references, function names, or other inputs.
- **Values:** You can search for either the raw contents of a cell or the calculated results.
- **Comments:** You can search comments (marked by a purple indicator in the upper-right corner of a cell) for @mentions or specific content.
- **Notes:** You can search notes (marked with a red triangle in the upper-right corner of a cell) for specific words or numbers — no strings attached.

» **Match Case:** This setting makes Excel pays close attention to whether text is uppercase or lowercase, ensuring that your search hits only the exact match.

» **Match Entire Cell Contents:** Includes only cells that match the exact contents of the Find What field. When this option is on, partial matches are not allowed, so searching for *pay* won't find *payroll*.

> **REMEMBER**
> The Match Case option and Match Entire Cell Contents options are sticky, which means they stay enabled until you turn them off. If you run into the `We couldn't find what you were looking for` message, double-check that these settings aren't stealthily sabotaging your search.

When you lock in your search criteria, Excel gives you two options:

» **Find Next:** Takes you directly to the first cell that matches your criteria.

» **Find All:** Displays a list of all matching cells, complete with clickable links for easy navigation. The list serves up details like the workbook, worksheet, cell name (if assigned), cell address, cell value, and formula (if applicable).

CHAPTER 5 **Navigating Worksheets and Workbooks** 115

Replacing text within worksheet cells

The Replace tab keeps most of the options from the Find tab, with a few key twists:

- » **Replace With:** Enables you to specify what to replace matches in the Find What field with.
- » **Replace Format button:** It's not explicitly labeled, but this second instance of the Format button lets you specify alternate formatting to apply to cells matching the search criteria.
- » **Look In:** This field allows you to choose only Formulas, which implicitly includes values.

REMEMBER You can't replace text in comments or notes — you can replace text only within worksheet cells.

If you prefer to play it safe, use the Find Next button to navigate to the first cell with a match, and then click Replace to make changes one at a time. But if you're feeling bold and a little rebellious, let a sinister laugh escape your lips as you devilishly hit Replace All, unleashing your changes across the entire worksheet or workbook in one dramatic swoop.

REMEMBER There's a middle ground: To limit where replacements happen, select two or more cells before opening the Find and Replace dialog box. If instant regret strikes because you replaced more than you intended, no worries — just click Undo on the Quick Access Toolbar or press Ctrl+Z (Windows) or ⌘+Z (macOS).

Exploring with the Navigation Task Pane

In a way, Find and Replace feels like hand-to-hand combat — intimate, cell-by-cell interactions. On the other hand, the Navigation task pane provides a space-age satellite view of your workbook and worksheets. Originally introduced by Microsoft as an accessibility feature to help users with assistive technologies navigate more effectively, this tool turns out to make all of us more efficient navigators in the Excel universe. The Navigation task pane appears only in Excel for Windows.

As shown in Figure 5-2, the Navigation task pane provides a complete list of all worksheets, including both hidden and visible ones. To display this task pane, click the View tab on the ribbon and choose Navigation. Powered by AI, this feature does require an internet connection — without it, you're left out in the cold, navigating within your workbook the old-school way.

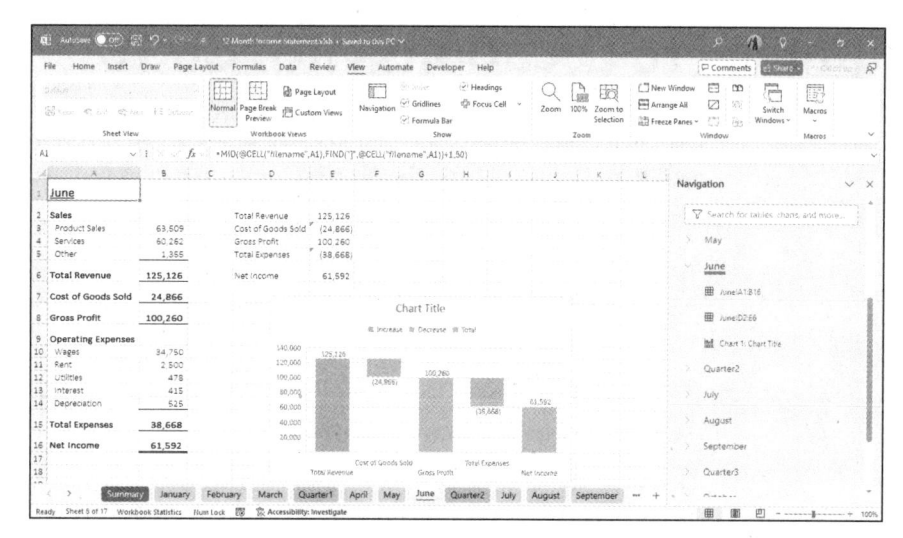

FIGURE 5-2:
The Navigation task pane.

The Navigation task pane provides the following information for every sheet in a workbook:

>> **Locations of non-blank cells:** This gives you a bird's-eye view of every cell or block of cells that isn't empty. Click any range address to jump straight there.

>> **Names of worksheet objects:** This lists noncell elements on the worksheet, making them easy to navigate to with a simple click. This includes images, PivotTables, charts, slicers, text boxes — anything that functions as an object rather than standard cell content. And yes, although PivotTables technically reside within worksheet cells, Excel still treats them as distinct objects.

To activate a worksheet, left-click its name, or right-click the name to bring up a context menu with the following commands:

>> **Rename:** Pick a fresh name for the worksheet in question.

>> **Delete:** Brings up a confirmation prompt asking if you're sure about removing the worksheet from the workbook — no take-backs after this!

>> **Hide (or Show):** Tuck a visible worksheet out of sight, or bring a hidden one back into the limelight.

CHAPTER 5 **Navigating Worksheets and Workbooks** 117

Jumping to Locations with Go To

Well, you can't collect $200, but you can jump to cell JAI1 if you like. There's no need to roll any dice here; the Go To command enables you to navigate to specific locations within a workbook:

1. **On the Home tab of the ribbon, click Find & Select and then click Go To; alternatively, press F5 or Ctrl+G (Windows) or ⌘+G (macOS).**

   The Go To dialog box opens.

2. **Enter the cell address, range name, or table name within the Reference field, or select it from the Go To list.**

3. **Click OK.**

REMEMBER: The Go To dialog box lets you navigate to specific cell locations but doesn't extend its reach to objects like charts, images, or PivotTables.

Targeting Specific Cells with Go To Special

When you need to target a specific cell type, use the Go To Special commands. Here's how:

1. **On the Home tab of the ribbon, click Find & Select and then click Go To Special.**

   The Go To Special dialog box, shown in Figure 5-3, opens.

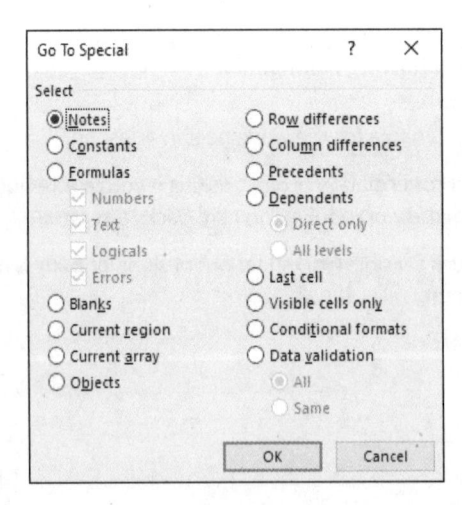

FIGURE 5-3: The Go To Special dialog box.

118   BOOK 1 Getting Started with Excel

2. **Choose any of the following options:**

   - **Notes:** Selects cells containing notes.

     REMEMBER: You can't select cell comments — anchored with purple indicators — using Go To Special.

   - **Constants:** Selects cells with non-formula data, such as text, numbers, or dates.

   - **Formulas:** Selects cells containing formulas — anything that kicks off with an equal sign (=).

     TIP: You can refine the constants or formulas options by specific types, such as numbers, text, logical values (TRUE/FALSE), or errors.

   - **Blanks:** Selects all blank cells within the selected range.

   - **Current Region:** Selects the block of contiguous data surrounding the active cell. This option shines when you're wrangling tables or data ranges.

     TIP: Press Ctrl+A (Windows) or ⌘+A (macOS) to instantly select the current region on the fly.

   - **Current Array:** Selects the output of an array formula, whether from modern dynamic array ranges or old-school Ctrl+Shift+Enter legacy array formulas.

   - **Objects:** Selects all graphical objects — shapes, charts, images, or text boxes — that gracefully float above the worksheet.

   - **Row Differences:** Selects cells in rows that differ from the first cell in the selection.

   - **Column Differences:** Selects cells in columns that differ from the first cell in the selection. Use this to quickly search vertically down columns for inconsistencies.

   - **Precedents:** Selects cells referenced by the active cell's formula. Perfect for tracing the origins of a calculation — like following breadcrumbs back to the source.

   - **Dependents:** Selects cells that rely on the active cell for their formulas. Useful for pinpointing where a cell's value influences other calculations.

     TIP: You can refine the Precedents and Dependents options by specifying Direct or Indirect relationships between cells.

   - **Last Cell:** Selects the last cell in the worksheet that contains data or formatting.

CHAPTER 5 **Navigating Worksheets and Workbooks** 119

- **Visible Cells Only:** Selects just the visible cells within a range, ignoring hidden rows or columns. This helps prevent accidental edits or deletions of hidden data.
- **Conditional Formats:** Selects cells with conditional formatting applied, making it easy to spot where rules are driving the formatting in your worksheet. (Book 4, Chapter 1 covers conditional formatting in detail.)
- **Data Validation:** Selects cells with data validation rules applied, making it handy for auditing drop-down lists or other data entry restrictions.

3. **Click OK.**

   Excel selects the corresponding cells or objects based on your choice, or you get a `No cells were found` message if nothing matches your search criteria.

Navigating with the Name Box

The Name Box is the field located to the left of the Formula Bar. Most Excel users assume its sole purpose is to display the address of the active cell, but it also enables you to perform other actions. Here are three highlights:

» **Navigating to a specific cell:** Type any cell address and press Enter to jump directly to a specific cell in the worksheet. You can type a cell range, such as **A1:B10**, to select a block of cells.

REMEMBER

Any misspelled cell references typed into the Name Box may unintentionally become names in your workbook. To clean them up, click the Formulas tab on the ribbon, click Name Manager, and then remove them.

» **Navigating to objects:** Type the name of an object that floats above the worksheet, such as Text Box 1 or Chart 1, to navigate to it.

» **Navigating to ranges or tables:** Click the Name Box drop-down list to display a list of named ranges and tables. Select any name to go straight to its location.

Activating Worksheets

Two sheet navigation arrows appear at the lower-left corner of the Excel window. They offer a few options:

» **Shifting worksheet tabs:** If your workbook contains more worksheet tabs than can be displayed onscreen, click the left or right arrows to move the tabs in the corresponding direction.

» **Displaying the Activate dialog box:** Right-click either navigation arrow to open the Activate dialog box, from which you can choose any visible worksheet, and then click OK.

» **Activating the first or last worksheet:** Hold Ctrl (Windows) or Option (macOS) and click the left navigation arrow to jump to the first worksheet in the workbook, or click the right navigation arrow to jump to the last worksheet.

TIP If you prefer the keyboard over the mouse, press Ctrl+Page Up (Windows) or Fn+⌘+up arrow (macOS) to activate the worksheet to the left, or Ctrl+Page Down (Windows) or Fn+⌘+down arrow (macOS) to move to the right. On some Windows keyboards, the Fn key may be required (for example, Fn+Ctrl+Page Up).

Reordering Worksheets

The easiest way to reposition a worksheet is to use your left mouse button to drag and drop the worksheet tab into a new position. You can also drag worksheets between Excel workbooks — hold down the Ctrl key (Windows) or the Option key (macOS) while you do so if you want to move a copy of a worksheet. To move or copy multiple worksheets, follow these steps:

1. **Activate the first worksheet that you want to move or copy.**

   To include additional worksheets:

   - Hold Shift and click the last worksheet tab in the group for contiguous selections.

   - Hold Ctrl (Windows) or ⌘ (macOS) and click individual tabs for noncontiguous selections.

2. **On the Home tab of the ribbon, click Format and then click Move or Copy Sheet; alternatively, right-click one of the selected sheet tabs and choose Move or Copy.**

   The Move or Copy dialog box opens.

3. **Select the destination workbook from the To Book list if needed:**

   - Choose a specific workbook currently open in Excel.

   - Select (new book) to move the sheets into a new, blank workbook.

4. **From the Before Sheet list, select where to place the worksheet(s) within the tab sequence.**

   The default is the beginning unless specified otherwise.

5. **Select the Create a Copy check box if you want to duplicate the worksheet(s) rather than move them.**

   WARNING

   Tread carefully here; if you inadvertently skip over the Create a Copy check box, you could end up moving worksheets from one workbook to another, instead of copying. Given that the receiving workbook is automatically activated, it's very easy to overlook the fact that the worksheets are no longer present in the original workbook. If this happens, you can't undo the move; instead, use the Move or Copy dialog box to copy the worksheet back from the recipient workbook to the donor workbook.

6. **Click OK.**

Splitting Worksheet Windows

Splitting a window in Excel lets you view two or four areas of your worksheet at once. Here's how to split a worksheet window:

1. **Position your cursor where you want the split to occur:**

   - **Two panes (left and right):** Select any cell in the first visible column except cell A1.
   - **Two panes (upper and lower):** Select any cell in the first visible row except cell A1.
   - **Four panes:** Select cell A1 or any cell not in the first column or first row.

2. **On the View tab of the ribbon, click Split.**

   Depending upon your choices, one or two split bars appear.

   To reposition the split, move the pointer over a split bar or the cross of the two split bars so that it turns into a double-headed or four-headed arrow. Then drag the split bar or the cross to where you want it.

You can now scroll the panes independently, reducing navigation time and increasing efficiency. To remove the split, double-click a split bar or the cross, or click the View tab on the ribbon and click Split again.

TIP: To fix the split or splits in place, click the View tab of the ribbon, click Freeze Panes, and then click Freeze Panes.

Viewing Two or More Worksheets at Once

When you need to work in two or more places at once in the same workbook, use the New Window command to open a new window:

1. **Open or activate a workbook that contains at least two worksheets.**

   Or go rogue and stick with a workbook that only has one worksheet — this technique can serve as an alternative to the Split feature covered earlier.

2. **On the View tab on the ribbon, click New Window.**

   The new window may open on top of the original, which may mislead you into thinking that nothing has happened.

3. **Arrange the windows:**

   - **Separate Monitors:** Grab the window by its title bar and drag it to the desired monitor.
   - **Same Monitor:** On the View tab of the ribbon, click Arrange All to open the Arrange Windows dialog box; select Tiled, Horizontal, Vertical, or Cascade; select the Windows of Active Workbook check box if you want to arrange only those windows; and then click OK.

REMEMBER: Creating additional windows doesn't mean you've opened the workbook multiple times. It simply allows you to view and work on different parts of the same workbook simultaneously.

Applying Custom Views

Custom Views is one of Excel's often-overlooked gems, an automation feature that lets you carry out any combination of tasks across an entire workbook. Custom Views stores a snapshot of settings — kind of like a preset filter, and so much more, for your workbook — that you can apply with a single click. These settings can include any combination of the following:

>> **Hiding or unhiding worksheets:** The hidden or visible status of all worksheets at the time a view is created is saved. When you select the view, Excel

applies these settings, allowing you to hide or unhide multiple worksheets in one fell swoop.

Worksheets that are added after the creation of a custom view are not affected when the view is applied.

» **Hiding or unhiding rows and columns:** Each custom view saves and reapplies the hidden or visible status of every row and column in the workbook.

» **Adjusting the Zoom level:** Each custom view saves the Zoom level of a worksheet, letting you toggle how much data is displayed onscreen.

» **Applying page layout settings:** Each custom view saves the page layout settings for every worksheet. For instance, you can toggle between printing a worksheet in portrait for one scenario and landscape for another. This flexibility lets you cater to your boss's preference for wide margins (to allow for commentary) while you keep margins near zero for your own printouts.

» **Applying filters:** Custom views capture the status of the filter buttons (meaning on or off), as well as any filters applied to any columns within the worksheet. Filtering is a fantastic way to zero in on important data, but as covered in Chapter 4 of this minibook, it can become a tad tedious when done manually.

» **Activating a cell:** Custom views save the location of the active cell when the view is created and return you to that cell when the view is applied.

» **Sizing and positioning the active window:** Custom views store and apply the position of the active window within a workbook. Be mindful of the active window's state when creating a view to avoid surprises.

» **Selecting cells:** Custom views remember a remarkable amount of information about your workbook, including the currently selected range of cells. This can be both a blessing and a curse. If you clicked the Select All button to unhide rows and columns before creating a view and left the cells selected, every cell will be selected each time you apply the view. On the flip side, if you frequently copy a specific block of cells, custom views are an excellent way to have Excel tee up your data, ready for a quick copy and paste.

You can't use the Custom Views feature if your workbook contains an Excel table, as covered in Chapter 4 of this minibook. Another limitation is that custom views can't override worksheet or workbook protection, so you can't use custom views to hide or unhide rows or columns on protected worksheets. If you try, Excel warns you: `Some view settings could not be applied`.

SHEET VIEW

Sheet View lets you see the worksheet exactly how you want, while your coworkers see it their way. The Sheet View feature, available for workbooks saved to OneDrive or SharePoint, allows two or more users to apply individualized sorting and filtering settings to a worksheet. Unlike custom views, which apply to the entire workbook, Sheet View focuses on a single worksheet.

Even better, Sheet View works with the Table feature. To use it, click the View tab on the ribbon, click Sheet View, and then click New. After sorting or filtering the data, click the View tab on the ribbon and click Keep to assign a name to the view. You can create as many views as you want, but remember that anyone else with access to the workbook can see and apply your views, too.

Creating custom views

Here's how to create some custom views to hide and unhide worksheets:

1. **Open a workbook that has two or more worksheets within it.**
2. **Check for hidden worksheets by clicking the Home tab on the ribbon, clicking Format, clicking Hide & Unhide, and confirming that the Unhide Sheet command is disabled.**

   Alternatively, right-click any worksheet tab and confirm that the Unhide command is disabled.
3. **If the Unhide Sheet command or the Unhide command is enabled, choose that command to open the Unhide dialog box, select all the hidden worksheets, and then click OK.**
4. **Select the cell you'd like activated when the custom view is applied.**
5. **Click the View tab on the ribbon, and then click Custom Views.**

   The Custom Views dialog box opens.

   REMEMBER: If the Custom Views command is disabled, it means your workbook contains an Excel table. You can either forgo using custom views or convert the tables back to ranges (see Chapter 4 of this minibook).
6. **Click Add.**

   The Add View dialog box opens.

7. **Assign a name, such as All Worksheets, to the view; turn off Print Settings and/or Hidden Rows, Columns, and Filter Settings if you want to exclude them.**

   Any other aspects that Custom Views captures — such as cell selection, window position, hidden or visible sheets, and so on — are automatically captured and applied, with no option to disable them.

8. **Click OK to create the view.**

9. **Hide at least one worksheet within the workbook by right-clicking the worksheet's tab and then clicking Hide.**

   Feel free to adjust other settings captured by Custom Views.

10. **On the View tab of the ribbon, click Custom Views.**

11. **On the View tab of the ribbon, click Custom Views again, click Add, and create a second view (for example, VIP Worksheets Only).**

12. **On the View tab of the ribbon, click Custom Views once more.**

13. **Select the first view that you created and then click Show.**

    Applying a Custom View restores settings as they were at the time the view was saved, but it doesn't restrict how you use your workbook. You can freely switch between the views as needed while continuing to work.

Using the Custom Views Quick Access Toolbar shortcut

In Excel for Windows, you can give yourself easy access to custom views by adding a Custom Views drop-down list to your Quick Access Toolbar:

1. **Click the drop-down at the right end of the Quick Access Toolbar, and then click More Commands.**

   The Quick Access Toolbar tab of the Excel Options dialog box appears.

2. **From the Customize Quick Access Toolbar drop-down list, select the current workbook.**

   By default, changes to the toolbar apply to all workbooks. Selecting a specific workbook lets you create a toolbar that appears only when that workbook is open — and it travels with the file, so your colleagues who use Excel for Windows can benefit from your handiwork.

3. **From the Choose Commands From list, select Commands Not in the ribbon.**

4. **Scroll down and select Custom Views.**

   TIP: To jump directly to the Custom Views command, click the list and type **D**. This highlights the first command starting with *D* and ensures that Custom Views appears onscreen.

5. **Click Add or double-click Custom Views.**

   Custom Views appears on the list on the right.

6. **Click OK.**

Going forward, you can select a custom view directly from your Quick Access Toolbar instead of having to display the Views tab of the ribbon and click Custom Views. A bonus: The drop-down always shows the most recently applied view — something the Custom Views dialog box doesn't provide.

Zooming In and Out

To control worksheet zoom, use these three commands in the Zoom section of the View tab of the ribbon:

- **Zoom:** Opens the Zoom dialog box, where you can choose preset zoom options or use a custom field to adjust the zoom to as high as 400% or as low as 10%.

  REMEMBER: No, you don't necessarily need to get your eyes checked — Excel's Page Break Preview command automatically adjusts the zoom level of a worksheet to 60%. Conversely, Page Layout changes the zoom level to 100%, overriding any custom zoom level you may have applied. Rest assured, switching back to Normal view restores the zoom to your specified level, or 100% if you haven't set one.

  TECHNICAL STUFF: Excel begins displaying range names directly on the worksheet at 39% zoom or lower. At this zoom level, instead of showing cell content, Excel replaces it with the defined range names, making it easier to identify and navigate named ranges in your worksheet.

- **100%:** This resets the zoom level to the default, 100%.

» **Zoom to Selection:** When you're dealing with off-screen columns or rows, select the cells you want always visible, click the View tab of the ribbon, and then click Zoom to Selection. Excel adjusts the zoom level (up or down) so your selected range fits perfectly onscreen.

> **TIP** A Zoom Slider control appears on the right-hand side of Excel's Status Bar, showing the current worksheet zoom level. Click the number to open the Zoom dialog box, or use the slider to refine your zoom level. If you tend to click this slider by accident, right-click the Status Bar, and then click Zoom Slider on the context menu to remove its check mark.

Working with Formulas and Functions

Contents at a Glance

CHAPTER 1: Tapping Into Formula and Function Fundamentals 131
  Working with Excel Fundamentals 132
  Gaining the Upper Hand on Formulas 143
  Using Functions in Formulas 152

CHAPTER 2: Saving Time with Function Tools 161
  Getting Familiar with the Insert Function Dialog Box 162
  Finding the Correct Function 163
  Entering Functions Using the Insert Function Dialog Box 164
  Directly Entering Formulas and Functions 172

CHAPTER 3: Building Array Formulas and Functions 177
  Discovering Arrays 178
  Using Arrays in Formulas 179
  Changing the Shape of Arrays 183
  Working with Functions That Return Arrays 186

CHAPTER 4: Fixing Errors in Formulas 191
  Catching Errors as You Enter Them 191
  Auditing Formulas 200
  Watching the Watch Window 203
  Evaluating and Checking Errors 204
  Making an Error Behave the Way You Want 205

IN THIS CHAPTER

» Getting the skinny on the Excel basics

» Writing formulas

» Working with functions in formulas

Chapter 1
Tapping Into Formula and Function Fundamentals

Excel is to computer programs what a Ferrari is to cars: sleek on the outside and a lot of power under the hood. Excel is also like a truck. It can handle all your data — lots of it. In fact, in Excel, a single worksheet has 17,179,869,184 places to hold data. Yes, that's what we said — more than 17 *billion* data placeholders. And that's on just *one* worksheet!

TIP The number of available rows and columns may be fewer depending on how much memory your computer has.

Excel is used in all types of businesses. And you know how that's possible? By being able to store and work with any kind of data. It doesn't matter whether you're in finance or sales, whether you organize wilderness trips or run an online store, or whether you're keeping track of wedding RSVPs or the scores of your favorite sports teams — Excel can handle it all! Its number-crunching ability is just awesome. And it's so easy to use!

But just putting a bunch of information on worksheets doesn't crunch the numbers or give you sums, results, or analyses. In this minibook, we show you how to build formulas and how to use the dozens of built-in functions that Excel provides. That's where the real power of Excel is — making sense of your data.

Don't worry about making mistakes. We did when we were ramping up. Besides, Excel is very forgiving. It usually tells you when you've made a mistake, and sometimes it even helps you correct it. How many programs do that? But first, the basics. This chapter is the springboard you need to use the rest of this minibook, as well as the following minibook. We wish books like this had been around when we were introduced to computers. We had to stumble through a lot of this.

Working with Excel Fundamentals

Before you can write any formulas or crunch any numbers, you have to know where the data goes and how to find it again. We wouldn't want your data to get lost! Knowing how worksheets store your data and present it is critical to your analysis efforts.

Understanding workbooks and worksheets

In Excel, a *workbook* is the same as a file. Excel opens and closes workbooks, just as a word processor program opens and closes documents. When you start up Excel, you're presented with a selection of templates to choose from, the first one being the standard blank workbook. You're also given a selection of recent files to select from. After you open a new or already created workbook, click the File tab at the upper left of the screen to view basic functions such as opening, saving, printing, and closing your Excel files (not to mention a number of other nifty functions to boot!). Figure 1-1 shows the contents presented on the Info tab.

TIP The default Excel file extension is `.xlsx`. However, you may see files with the older `.xls` extension; these older files work fine in the latest version of Excel. You may also see Excel files with the `.xlsm` extension; those are fine to use, too.

Start Excel and click the Blank Workbook icon to create a new blank workbook. When you have more than one workbook open, you pick the one you want to work on by clicking it on the Windows taskbar.

A worksheet is where your data actually goes. A workbook contains at least one worksheet. Figure 1-2 shows an open workbook that has two sheets, aptly named Sheet1 and Sheet2. To the right of these worksheet tabs is the New Sheet button (it looks like a plus sign), used to add worksheets to the workbook.

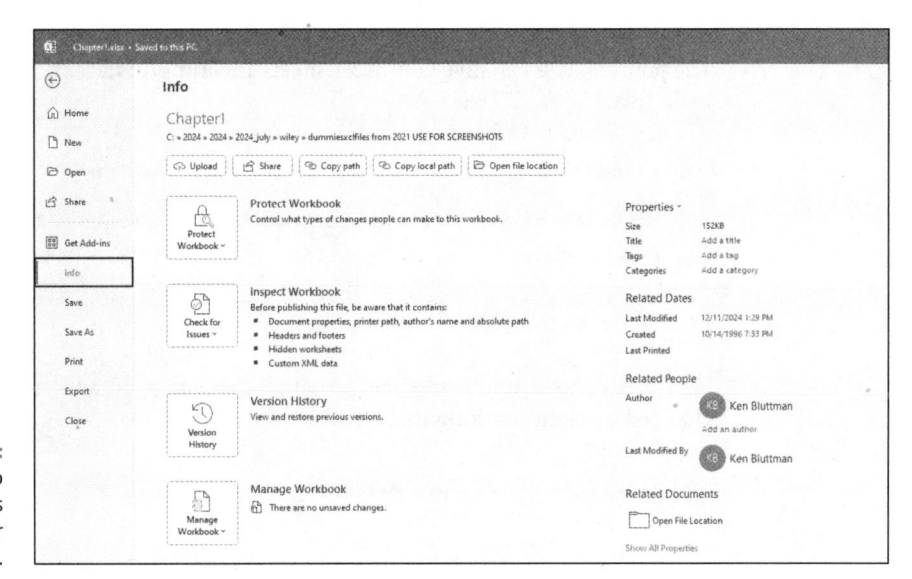

FIGURE 1-1:
The Info tab shows details about your Excel file.

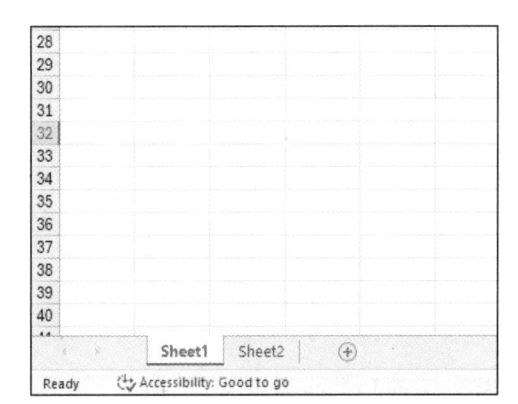

FIGURE 1-2:
Looking at a workbook and worksheets.

At any given moment, one worksheet is always on top. In Figure 1-2, Sheet1 is on top. Another way of saying this is that Sheet1 is the *active worksheet.* There is always one and only one active worksheet. To make another worksheet active, just click its tab.

TIP

Worksheet, spreadsheet, and just plain old *sheet* are used interchangeably to mean the worksheet.

What's really cool is that you can change the names of worksheets. Names like Sheet1 and Sheet2 just aren't very exciting. How about Baseball Card Collection or Last Year's Taxes? Well, actually, Last Year's Taxes isn't too exciting, either.

CHAPTER 1 **Tapping Into Formula and Function Fundamentals** 133

The point is, you can give your worksheets meaningful names. You have two ways to do this:

» Double-click the worksheet tab and then type a new name.

» Right-click the worksheet tab, select Rename from the menu, and then type a new name.

Press Enter to complete the name change.

Figure 1-3 shows one worksheet name already changed and another about to be changed by right-clicking its tab.

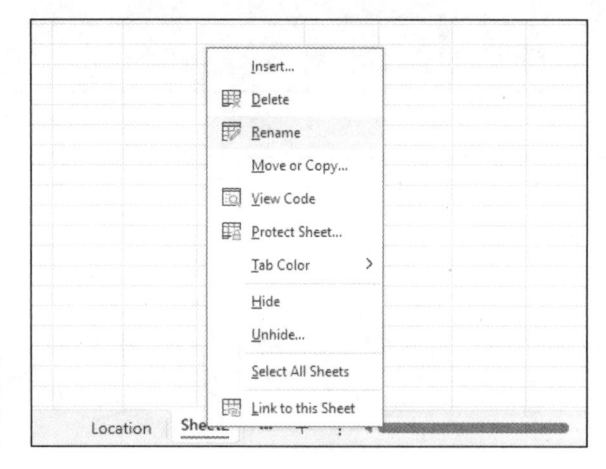

FIGURE 1-3: Changing the name of a worksheet.

TIP A worksheet name can't exceed 31 characters.

You also can change the color of worksheet tabs. Right-click the tab and select Tab Color from the menu. Color-coding tabs is a great way to organize your work.

To insert a new worksheet into a workbook, click the New Sheet button, which is located after the last worksheet tab. To delete a worksheet, just right-click the worksheet's tab and select Delete from the menu.

WARNING Don't delete a worksheet unless you really mean to. You can't get it back after it's gone.

You can insert many new worksheets. The limit of how many is based on your computer's memory, but you should have no problem inserting 200 or more. Of course, we hope you have a good reason for having so many, which brings us to the next point.

Worksheets enable you to organize your data. Use them wisely, and you'll find it easy to manage your data. For example, say that you're the boss (we thought you'd like that!), and over the course of a year you track information about 30 employees. You may have 30 worksheets — one for each employee. Or you may have 12 worksheets — one for each month. Or you may just keep all the information on one worksheet. How you use Excel is up to you, but Excel is ready to handle whatever you throw at it.

> **TIP** You can set how many worksheets a new workbook has as the default. To do this, select the File tab at the upper left of the screen and click Options. The Excel Options dialog box opens. Select the General tab. In the When Creating New Workbooks section, use the Include This Many Sheets spinner control to select a number.

Introducing the Formulas tab

The ribbon sits at the top of Excel. Items on the ribbon appear as menu headers along the top of the Excel screen, but they actually work more like tabs. Click them, and no menus appear. Instead, the ribbon presents the items that are related to the clicked ribbon tab.

Figure 1-4 shows the Formulas tab of the ribbon. In the figure, the Formulas tab is set to show formula-based methods. At the left side of the tab, functions are categorized. One of the categories is opened to show how you can access a particular function.

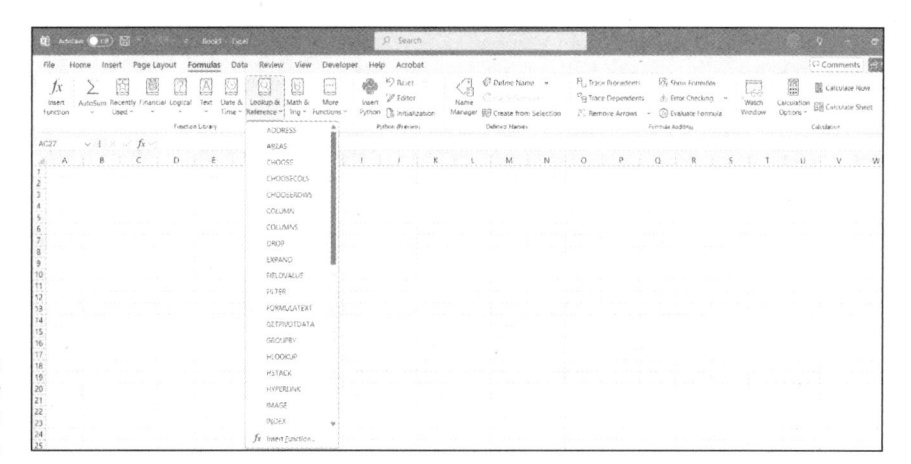

FIGURE 1-4: Getting to know the Formulas tab of the ribbon.

CHAPTER 1 **Tapping Into Formula and Function Fundamentals**

The following groups are along the bottom of the Formulas tab:

- » **Function Library:** This group includes the Function Wizard, the AutoSum feature, and the categorized functions.

- » **Defined Names:** These features manage *named areas,* which are cells or ranges on worksheets to which you assign meaningful names for easy reference.

- » **Formula Auditing:** These features are for checking and correcting formulas. Also in this group is the Watch Window, which lets you keep an eye on the values in designated cells, but within one window. In Figure 1-5, you can see that a few cells have been assigned to the Watch Window. If any values change, you can see this in the Watch Window. Note how the watched cells are on sheets that are not the current active sheet. Neat! By the way, you can move the Watch Window around the screen by clicking the title area of the window and dragging it with the mouse.

- » **Calculation:** This group is where you manage calculation settings, such as whether calculation is automatic or manual.

Book	Sheet	Name	Cell	Value
Book2.xlsx	Location		C3	
Book2.xlsx	Inventory		B5	87
Book2.xlsx	Inventory		C5	105

FIGURE 1-5: Eyeing the Watch Window.

TIP

Another great feature that goes hand in hand with the ribbon is the Quick Access Toolbar. The Quick Access Toolbar sits just above the left side of the ribbon. On it are icons that perform actions with a single click. The icons are ones you select by using the Quick Access Toolbar tab in the Excel Options dialog box. You can put the toolbar above or below the ribbon by clicking the Customize Quick Access Toolbar drop-down arrow on the Quick Access Toolbar and choosing either Show Above the ribbon or Show Below the ribbon. This drop-down list also contains other options for the Quick Access Toolbar.

Working with rows, columns, cells, ranges, and tables

A *worksheet* contains cells. Lots of them. Billions of them. This may seem unmanageable, but it's actually pretty straightforward. Figure 1-6 shows a worksheet that contains data. Each *cell* can contain data or a formula. In Figure 1-6, the cells contain data. Some or even all cells could contain formulas, but that's not the case here.

	A	B	C	D
1	CLIENT	NAME OF PET	TYPE OF PET	DATE OF LAST VISIT
2				
3	Caryl Whaley	Paws	Cat	4/10/2021
4	Dave Konneker	Sugar	Cat	4/10/2021
5	Portia Coyle	Queenie	Dog	4/7/2021
6	Steven Trailer	Winger	Bird	4/7/2021
7	Gwendolin Gauder	Honey	Cat	4/5/2021
8	Avis Javinsky	Tweetie	Bird	4/4/2021
9	Talli Evert	Hunter	Cat	3/27/2021
10	Alma Pruett	Proud King	Horse	3/20/2021
11	Del Moore	Nelson	Monkey	3/19/2021
12	Mayta Pellman	Tiger	Cat	3/18/2021
13	Aurora McCracken	Pretty Girl	Bird	3/17/2021
14	Hugh Blastick	Missy	Cat	3/17/2021
15	Seiji Davis	Basil	Cat	3/14/2021
16	Greg Batin	Baby	Cat	3/8/2021
17	Ilene Lochead	Coiler	Snake	3/8/2021
18	Bernie Vambreck	Boxer	Dog	3/5/2021
19	Faris Alameda	Wally	Dog	3/5/2021
20	Trisha Hill	Climber	Cat	3/5/2021
21	Edna Wells	Royal	Dog	3/4/2021
22	William Albissonno	Parsnip	Cat	3/2/2021
23	Muriel Rosenkantz	Little Lil	Bird	2/28/2021

FIGURE 1-6: Looking at what goes into a worksheet.

Columns have letter headers — A, B, C, and so on. You can see these listed horizontally just above the area where the cells are. After you get past the 26th column, a double-letter system is used — AA, AB, and so on. After all the two-letter combinations are used up, a triple-letter scheme is used. Rows are listed vertically down the left side of the screen and use a numbering system.

Cells are located at the intersection of rows and columns. Cell A1 is the cell at the intersection of column A and row 1. A1 is the cell's *address.* There is always an *active cell* — that is, a cell in which any entry would go into if you started typing. The active cell has a border around it. Also, the contents of the active cell appear in the *Formula Box.*

CHAPTER 1 **Tapping Into Formula and Function Fundamentals** 137

GETTING TO KNOW THE FORMULA BAR

Taken together, the Formula Box and the Name Box make up the Formula Bar. You use the Formula Bar quite a bit as you work with formulas and functions. The Formula Box is used to enter and edit formulas. The Formula Box is the long entry box that starts in the middle of the bar. When you enter a formula into this box, you can click the little check-mark button to finish the entry. The check-mark button is enabled only when you're entering a formula. Pressing Enter also completes your entry; clicking the X cancels the entry.

An alternative is to enter a formula directly into a cell. The Formula Box displays the formula as it's being entered into the cell. When you want to see just the contents of a cell that has a formula, make that cell active and look at its contents in the Formula Box. Cells that have formulas don't normally display the formula; instead, they display the result of the formula. When you want to see the actual formula, the Formula Box is the place to do it. The Name Box, on the left side of the Formula Bar, is used to select named areas in the workbook.

REMEMBER When we speak of, or reference, a *cell*, we're referring to its address. The address is the intersection of a column and row. To talk about cell D20 means to talk about the cell that you find at the intersection of column D and row 20.

In Figure 1-6, the active cell is C7. You have a couple ways to see this. For starters, cell C7 has a border around it. Also, notice that the column head C and row number 7 are shaded. Just above the column headers are the Name Box and the Formula Box. The Name Box is all the way to the left and shows the active cell's address of C7. To the right of the Name Box, the Formula Box shows the contents of cell C7.

TIP If the Formula Bar is not visible, choose View➪Show➪Formula Bar or select the Formula Bar check box in the Show group on the View tab of the ribbon.

A *range* is usually a group of adjacent cells, although noncontiguous cells can be included in the same range (but that's mostly for rocket scientists and those obsessed with treating data like jigsaw puzzle pieces). For your purposes, assume a range is a group of continuous cells. Make a range right now! Here's how:

1. **Position the mouse pointer over the first cell where you want to define a range.**
2. **Press and hold the left mouse button.**
3. **Move the pointer to the last cell of your desired area.**
4. **Release the mouse button.**

Figure 1-7 shows what happened when we did this. We selected a *range* of cells. The address of this range is A3:D21.

	A	B	C	D
1	CLIENT	NAME OF PET	TYPE OF PET	DATE OF LAST VISIT
2				
3	Caryl Whaley	Paws	Cat	4/10/2021
4	Dave Konneker	Sugar	Cat	4/10/2021
5	Portia Coyle	Queenie	Dog	4/7/2021
6	Steven Trailer	Winger	Bird	4/7/2021
7	Gwendolin Gauder	Honey	Cat	4/5/2021
8	Avis Javinsky	Tweetie	Bird	4/4/2021
9	Talli Evert	Hunter	Cat	3/27/2021
10	Alma Pruett	Proud King	Horse	3/20/2021
11	Del Moore	Nelson	Monkey	3/19/2021
12	Mayta Pellman	Tiger	Cat	3/18/2021
13	Aurora McCracken	Pretty Girl	Bird	3/17/2021
14	Hugh Blastick	Missy	Cat	3/17/2021
15	Seiji Davis	Basil	Cat	3/14/2021
16	Greg Batin	Baby	Cat	3/8/2021
17	Ilene Lochead	Coiler	Snake	3/8/2021
18	Bernie Vambreck	Boxer	Dog	3/5/2021
19	Faris Alameda	Wally	Dog	3/5/2021
20	Trisha Hill	Climber	Cat	3/5/2021
21	Edna Wells	Royal	Dog	3/4/2021
22	William Albissonno	Parsnip	Cat	3/2/2021
23	Muriel Rosenkantz	Little Lil	Bird	2/28/2021
24	Iola Cramer	Ira	Bird	2/26/2021
25	Russell Triplett	Crawford	Dog	2/25/2021
26	Ramesh Carvalho	Purry	Cat	2/20/2021
27	Kin Sigman	Runner	Dog	2/13/2022

FIGURE 1-7: Selecting a range of cells.

REMEMBER

A range address looks like two cell addresses put together, with a colon (:) in the middle — and that's what it is! A range address starts with the address of the cell in the upper left of the range, then has a colon, and ends with the address of the cell in the lower right.

One more detail about ranges: You can name them. This feature is great because it enables you to think about a range in terms of what it's used for, instead of what its address is. Also, if you don't take the extra step of assigning a name, the range will be gone as soon as you click anywhere on the worksheet. When a range is given a name, you can repeatedly use the range by using its name.

Say you have a list of clients on a worksheet. What's easier — thinking of exactly which cells the list occupies, or thinking that there's your list of clients?

Throughout this minibook and the next minibook, we use areas made of cell addresses and ranges, which have been given names. It's time to get your feet wet creating a named area. Follow these steps:

1. **Position the mouse pointer over a cell, click and hold the left mouse button, and drag the pointer around.**

2. **Release the mouse button when you're done.**

   You've selected an area of the worksheet.

3. **Click Define Name in the Defined Names group on the Formulas tab of the ribbon.**

   The New Name dialog box opens. Figure 1-8 shows you how it looks so far.

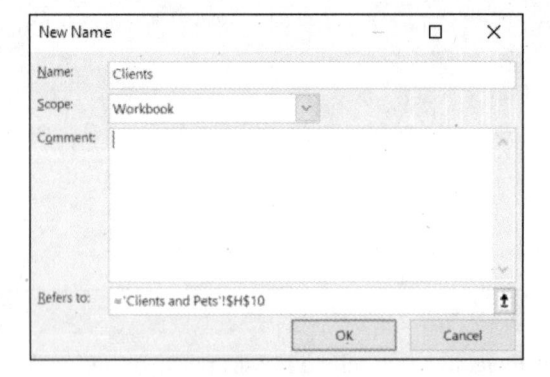

FIGURE 1-8: Adding a name to the workbook.

4. **Name the area or keep the suggested name. You can change the suggested name as well.**

   Excel guesses that you want to name the area with the value it finds in the top cell of the range. That may or may not be what you want. Change the name if you need to. In Figure 1-8, we changed the name to Clients.

   TIP: An alternative method of naming an area is to select it, type the name in the Name Box (on the left side of the Formula Bar), and press Enter.

5. **Click OK.**

That's it. Hey, you're already on your way to being an Excel pro! Now that you have a named area, you can easily select your data at any time. Just go to the Name Box and select it from the list. Figure 1-9 shows how to select the Clients area.

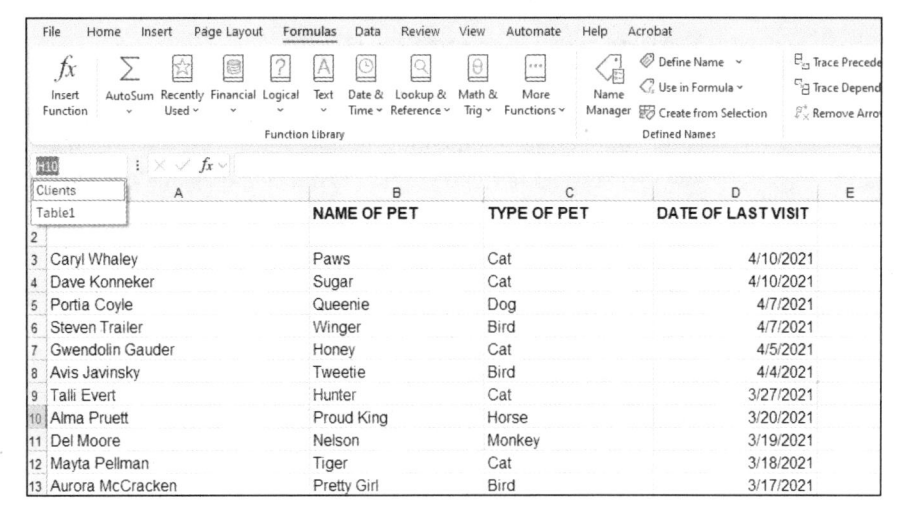

FIGURE 1-9:
Using the Name Box to find the named area.

	A	B	C	D
1		NAME OF PET	TYPE OF PET	DATE OF LAST VISIT
3	Caryl Whaley	Paws	Cat	4/10/2021
4	Dave Konneker	Sugar	Cat	4/10/2021
5	Portia Coyle	Queenie	Dog	4/7/2021
6	Steven Trailer	Winger	Bird	4/7/2021
7	Gwendolin Gauder	Honey	Cat	4/5/2021
8	Avis Javinsky	Tweetie	Bird	4/4/2021
9	Talli Evert	Hunter	Cat	3/27/2021
10	Alma Pruett	Proud King	Horse	3/20/2021
11	Del Moore	Nelson	Monkey	3/19/2021
12	Mayta Pellman	Tiger	Cat	3/18/2021
13	Aurora McCracken	Pretty Girl	Bird	3/17/2021

Tables work in much the same way as named areas. Tables have a few features that are unavailable to simple named areas. With tables, you can indicate that the top row contains header labels. Further, tables default to have filtering ability. Figure 1-10 shows a table on a worksheet, with headings and filtering ability.

Item	East	West	North	South
Gadgets	4	5	7	5
Gizmos	3	5	8	5
Things	2	6	7	5

FIGURE 1-10:
Trying a table.

With filtering, you can limit which rows show, based on which values you select to display.

> **TIP**
> The Tables group on the Insert tab of the ribbon contains the Table button for inserting a table.

CHAPTER 1 Tapping Into Formula and Function Fundamentals 141

Formatting your data

Of course, you want to make your data look all spiffy and shiny. Bosses like that. Is the number 98.6 someone's temperature? Is it a score on a test? Is it 98 dollars and 60 cents? Is it a percentage? Any of these formats is correct:

- 98.6
- $98.60
- 98.6%

Excel lets you format your data just the way you need to. Formatting options are in the Number group on the Home tab of the ribbon.

Figure 1-11 shows how formatting helps in the readability and understanding of a worksheet. Cell B1 has a monetary amount and is formatted with the Accounting style. Cell B2 is formatted as a percentage (the actual value in cell B2 is .05). Cell B7 is formatted as currency. The currency format displays a negative value in parentheses (this is just one of the formatting options for currency). Book 3, Chapter 1 explains more about formatting currency data.

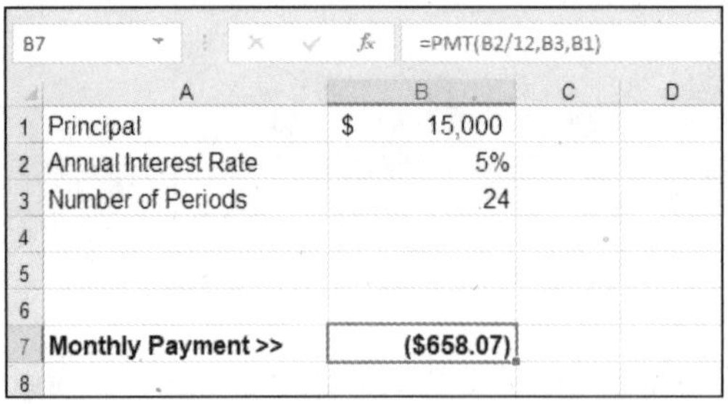

FIGURE 1-11: Formatting data.

In addition to setting formatting on the Home tab of the ribbon, you can use the Format Cells dialog box (see Figure 1-12). This is the place to go for all your formatting needs beyond what's available on the Home tab of the ribbon. You can even use the dialog box to create custom formats. You can get to the Format Cells dialog box two ways:

- On the Home tab of the ribbon, click the drop-down list in the Number group and then select More Number Formats.
- Right-click any cell and select Format Cells from the pop-up menu.

We discuss this dialog box and formatting more extensively in Book 1, Chapter 3.

FIGURE 1-12:
Using the Format Cells dialog box for advanced formatting options.

Getting help

Excel is complex — you can't deny that. And lucky for all of us, help is just a key press away. Yes, literally one key press — just press the F1 key.

This starts the Help system. From there, you can search on a keyword or browse through the Help table of contents. Later, when you're working with Excel functions, you can get help on specific functions directly by clicking the Help on This Function link in the Insert Function dialog box. (Chapter 2 of this minibook covers the Insert Function dialog box in detail.)

Gaining the Upper Hand on Formulas

Okay, time to get to the nitty-gritty of what Excel is all about. Sure, you can just enter data and leave it as is. You can even generate some pretty charts from it. But getting answers from your data, or creating a summary of your data, or applying what-if tests — all of these tasks require formulas.

To be specific, in Excel a *formula* calculates something or returns some result based on data in one or more worksheets. These worksheets can be in more than one workbook. A formula is placed in a cell and must start with an equal sign (=) to tell Excel that it's a formula and not data. Sounds simple, and it is.

Let's look at some very basic formulas. Table 1-1 shows a few formulas and explains what they do.

TABLE 1-1 **Basic Formulas**

Formula	What It Does
=2+2	Returns the number 4.
=A1+A2	Returns the sum of the values in cells A1 and A2, whatever those values may be. If either A1 or A2 has text in it, an error is returned.
=D5	The cell that contains this formula displays the value that is in cell D5. If you try to enter this formula into cell D5 itself, you create a circular reference, which is a no-no. (See Chapter 4 of this minibook for more on circular references.)
=SUM(A2:A5)	Returns the sum of the values in cells A2, A3, A4, and A5. This formula uses the SUM function to sum up all the values in the range.

> **TIP** We use the word *return* to refer to the result of the formula or function calculation. So saying "The formula returns 7" is the same as saying "The formula calculated the answer to be 7."

Entering your first formula

Ready to enter your first formula? Make sure Excel is running and a worksheet is in front of you, and then follow these steps:

1. **Click an empty cell.**
2. **Type** =10+10.
3. **Press Enter.**

That was easy, wasn't it? You should see the *result* of the formula — the number 20.

Try another formula. This time you'll create one that adds the value of two cells:

1. **Click any cell.**
2. **Type any number.**
3. **Click another cell.**
4. **Type another number.**

5. **Click a third cell.**

   This cell will contain the formula.

6. **Type =.**

7. **Click the first cell.**

   This is an important point in the creation of the formula. The formula is being written by both your keyboard entry and your mouse clicks. The formula should look about half complete, with an equal sign immediately followed by the address of the cell you just clicked. Figure 1-13 shows what this looks like. In the example, the value 15 has been entered into cell B3 and the value 35 into cell B6. The formula was started in cell E3. Cell E3 so far has =B3 in it.

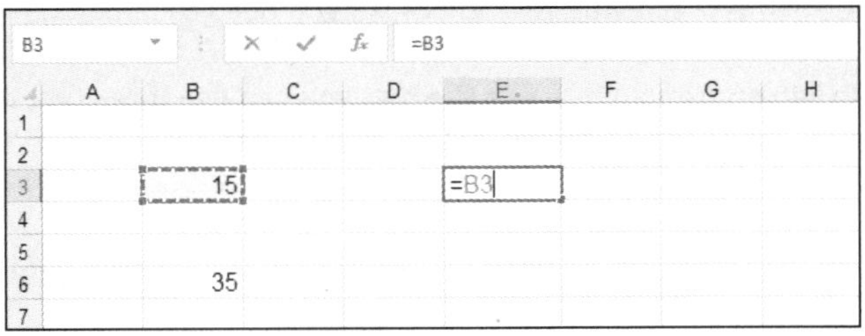

FIGURE 1-13: Entering a formula that references cells.

8. **Type +.**

9. **Click the cell that has the second entered value.**

   In this example, this is cell B6. The formula in cell E3 now looks like this: =B3+B6. You can see this in Figure 1-14.

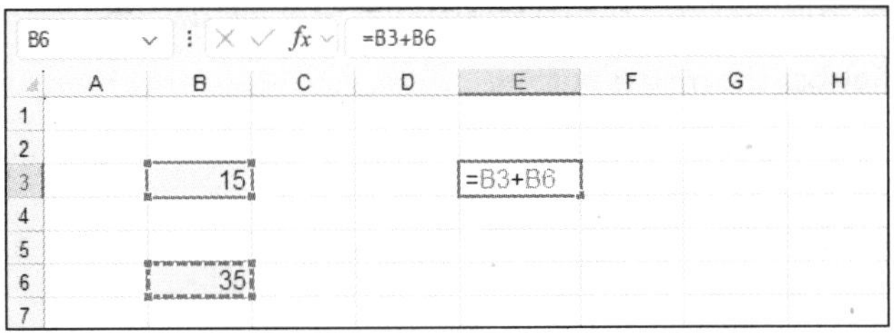

FIGURE 1-14: Completing the formula.

10. **Press Enter.**

    This ends the entry of the function. All done! Congratulations!

Figure 1-15 shows how the example ended up. Cell E3 displays the result of the calculation. Also notice that the Formula Box displays the contents of cell E3, which really is the formula.

CHAPTER 1 Tapping Into Formula and Function Fundamentals   145

FIGURE 1-15:
A finished formula.

Understanding references

References abound in Excel formulas. You can reference cells. You can reference ranges. You can reference cells and ranges on other worksheets. You can reference cells and ranges in other workbooks. Formulas and functions are at their most useful when you're using references, so you need to understand them.

And if that isn't enough to stir the pot, you can use three types of cell references: relative, absolute, and mixed. Okay, one step at a time here. Try a formula that uses a range.

Formulas that use ranges often have a function in the formula, so use the SUM function here:

1. **Enter some numbers in many cells going down one column.**

2. **Click another cell where you want the result to appear.**

3. **Type =SUM(.**

   This starts the function.

4. **Click the first cell that has an entered value, hold down the left mouse button, and drag the mouse pointer over all the cells that have values.**

5. **Release the mouse button.**

   The range address appears where the formula and function are being entered.

6. **Type).**

7. **Press Enter.**

   Give yourself a pat on the back!

TIP Wherever you drag the mouse to enter the range address into a function, you can also just type the address of the range, if you know what it is.

146 BOOK 2 **Working with Formulas and Functions**

Excel is *dynamic* when it comes to cell addresses. If you have a cell with a formula that references a different cell's address, and you copy the formula from the first cell to another cell, the address of the reference inside the formula changes. Excel updates the reference inside the formula to match the number of rows and/or columns that separate the original cell (where the formula is being copied from) from the new cell (where the formula is being copied to). This may be confusing, so try an example so you can see this for yourself:

1. **In cell B2, type** 100.
2. **In cell C2, type** =B2*2.
3. **Press Enter.**

   Cell C2 now returns the value 200.

4. **If C2 is not the active cell, click it once so it becomes the active cell.**
5. **Press Ctrl+C, or click the Copy button in the Clipboard group on the Home tab of the ribbon.**
6. **Click cell C3.**
7. **Press Ctrl+V, or click the Paste button in the Clipboard group on the Home tab of the ribbon.**
8. **If you see a strange moving line around cell C2, press the Esc key.**

   Cell C3 should be the active cell, but if it isn't, just click it once. Look at the Formula Box. The contents of cell C3 are =B3*2, and not the =B2*2 that you copied.

TIP Did you see a moving line around a cell? That line is called a *marquee,* and it's a reminder that you're in the middle of a cut or copy operation; the marquee goes around the cut or copied data.

What happened? Excel, in its wisdom, assumed that if a formula in cell C2 references the cell B2 — one cell to the left — the same formula put into cell C3 is supposed to reference cell B3 — also one cell to the left.

When you're copying formulas in Excel, *relative addressing* is usually what you want, as with the relative address to cell B2 in this example. That's why it's the default behavior. Sometimes you don't want relative addressing, and you want *absolute addressing,* which is making a cell reference fixed to an absolute cell address so it doesn't change when the formula is copied.

CHAPTER 1 **Tapping Into Formula and Function Fundamentals** 147

In an absolute cell reference, a dollar sign ($) precedes both the column letter and the row number. You can also have a mixed reference in which the column is absolute and the row is relative, or vice versa. To create a mixed reference, you place the dollar sign in front of just the column letter or row number that you don't want Excel to change. Table 1-2 has some examples.

TABLE 1-2 Referencing Cells

Reference Type	Formula	What Happens After Copying the Formula
Relative	=A1	Either, or both, the column letter A and the row number 1 can change.
Absolute	=$A$1	The column letter A and the row number 1 can't change.
Mixed	=$A1	The column letter A does not change. The row number 1 can change.
Mixed	=A$1	The column letter A can change. The row number 1 can't change.

Copying formulas with the Fill Handle

As long as we're on the subject of copying formulas around, take a look at the Fill Handle. You're gonna love this one! The *Fill Handle* is a quick way to copy the contents of a cell to other cells with just a single click and drag.

The active cell always has a little square box in the lower-right side of its border. That's the Fill Handle. When you move the mouse pointer over the Fill Handle, the mouse pointer changes to a cross. If you click and hold the left mouse button, you can drag up, down, or across over other cells. When you release the mouse button, Excel copies the contents of the active cell automatically to the cells you dragged over.

A picture is worth a thousand words, so take a look at Figure 1-16, which shows a worksheet that adds some numbers. Cell E4 has this formula: =B4+C4+D4. This formula needs to be placed in cells E5 through E15. Look closely at cell E4. The Fill Handle is in the lower-right corner. We're about to use the Fill Handle to drag the formula to the other cells. Clicking and holding down the left mouse button and then dragging to cell E15 does the trick.

Figure 1-17 shows what the worksheet looks like after the Fill Handle is used to get the formula into all the cells. This is a real time-saver. Also, you can see that the formula in each cell of column E correctly references the cells to its left. This is the intention of using relative referencing. For example, the formula in cell E15 ended up with this formula: =B15+C15+D15.

FIGURE 1-16: Getting ready to drag the formula down.

FIGURE 1-17: Populating cells with a formula by using the Fill Handle.

Assembling formulas the right way

There's a saying in the computer business: Garbage in, garbage out. And that applies to how formulas are put together. If a formula is constructed the wrong way, it returns an incorrect result or an error.

Two types of errors can occur in formulas. In one type, Excel can calculate the formula, but the result is wrong. In the other type, Excel can't calculate the formula.

A formula can work and still produce an incorrect result. Excel doesn't report an error because there is no error for it to find. Often, this is the result of not using parentheses properly in the formula. Take a look at the examples in Table 1-3.

CHAPTER 1 Tapping Into Formula and Function Fundamentals 149

TABLE 1-3 ## Order of Operations

Formula	Result
=7+5*20+25/5	112
=(7+5)*20+25/5	245
=7+5*(20+25)/5	52
=(7+5*20+25)/5	26.4

All of these formulas are valid, but the placement of parentheses makes a difference in the outcome. You have to take into account the order of mathematical operators when writing formulas. Here's the order of precedence:

1. Parentheses
2. Exponents
3. Multiplication and division
4. Addition and subtraction

This is a key point to remember about formulas. It's easy to just accept a returned answer. After all, Excel is smart, right? Wrong! Like all computer programs, Excel can do only what it's told to do. If you tell it to calculate an incorrect but structurally valid formula, it will do so. So mind your p's and q's — er, your parentheses and mathematical operators — when building formulas.

The second type of error occurs when a mistake in the formula or in the data the formula uses prevents Excel from calculating the result. Excel makes your life easier by telling you when such an error occurs. To be precise, it does one of the following:

» It displays a message when you try to enter a formula that isn't constructed correctly.

» It returns an error message in the cell when there is something wrong with the result of the calculation.

Figure 1-18 shows what happened when we tried to finish entering a formula that had the wrong number of parentheses.

Excel finds an uneven number of open and closed parentheses. Therefore, the formula can't work (it doesn't make sense mathematically), and Excel tells you so. Watch for these messages; they often offer solutions.

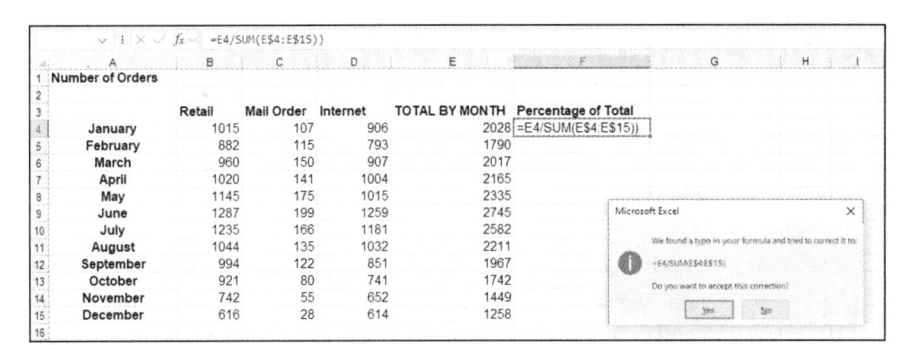

FIGURE 1-18:
Getting a message from Excel.

On the other side of the fence are errors in returned values. If you got this far, the formula's syntax passed muster, but something went awry nonetheless. Possible errors include the following:

- Trying to perform a mathematical operation on text
- Trying to divide a number by 0 (a mathematical no-no)
- Trying to reference a nonexistent cell, range, worksheet, or workbook
- Entering the wrong type of information into an argument function

This is by no means an exhaustive list of possible error conditions, but you get the idea. So, what does Excel do about it? There are a handful of errors that Excel displays in cells with the problem formulas (see Table 1-4).

Chapter 4 of this minibook discusses catching and handling formula errors in detail.

TABLE 1-4   Error Types

Error Type	When It Happens
#DIV/0!	You're trying to divide by 0.
#N/A!	A formula or a function inside a formula can't find the referenced data.
#NAME?	Text in a formula isn't recognized.
#NULL!	You used a space instead of a comma in formulas that reference multiple ranges. A comma is necessary to separate range references.
#NUM!	A formula has numeric data that is invalid for the operation type.
#REF!	A reference is invalid.
#VALUE!	You used the wrong type of operand or function argument.

CHAPTER 1 **Tapping Into Formula and Function Fundamentals**   151

Using Functions in Formulas

Functions are like little utility programs that do a single thing. For example, the SUM function sums numbers, the COUNT function counts, and the AVERAGE function calculates an average.

There are functions to handle many needs: working with numbers, working with text, working with dates and times, working with finance, and so on. Functions can be combined and nested (one goes inside another). Each function returns a value, and this value can be combined with the results of another function or formula. The possibilities are nearly endless.

But functions don't exist on their own. They're always a part of a formula. Now, that can mean that the formula is made up completely of the function or that the formula combines the function with other functions, data, operators, or references. But functions must follow the formula golden rule: *Start with the equal sign.* Look at the examples in Table 1-5.

TABLE 1-5 Using Functions in Formulas

Function/Formula	Result
=SUM(A1:A5)	Returns the sum of the values in the range A1:A5. This is an example of a function serving as the whole formula.
=SUM(A1:A5)/B5	Returns the sum of the values in the range A1:A5 divided by the value in cell B5. This is an example of mixing a function's result with other data.
=SUM(A1:A5)+AVERAGE(B1:B5)	Returns the sum of the range A1:A5 added with the average of the range B1:B5. This is an example of a formula that combines the result of two functions.

Ready to write your first formula with a function in it? Use the following steps to write a function that creates an average:

1. **Enter some numbers in a column's cells.**
2. **Click an empty cell where you want to see the result.**
3. **Type =AVERAGE(.**

    This starts the function.

    Note: Excel presents a list of functions that have the same spelling as the function name you type. The more letters you type, the shorter the list becomes. The advantage is, for example, typing the letters *AV*, pressing the down arrow to select the AVERAGE function, and then pressing the Tab key.

4. **Click the first cell with an entered value and, while holding the left mouse button, drag the mouse pointer over the other cells that have values and then release the mouse button.**

   An alternative is to enter the range of those cells.

5. **Type).**

6. **Press Enter.**

If all went well, your worksheet should look like ours, in Figure 1-19. Cell B11 has the calculated result, but look up at the Formula Box, and you can see the actual function as it was entered.

FIGURE 1-19: Entering the AVERAGE function.

Formulas and functions are dependent on the cells and ranges to which they refer. If you change the data in one of the cells, the result returned by the function updates. You can try this now. In the example you just did with making an average, click one of the cells with the values and enter a different number. The returned average changes.

REMEMBER

A formula can consist of nothing but a single function — preceded by an equal sign, of course.

Looking at what goes into a function

Most functions take inputs — called *arguments* or *parameters* — that specify the data the function is to use. Some functions take no arguments, some take one, and others take many; it all depends on the function. The argument list is always enclosed in parentheses following the function name. If there's more than one argument, the arguments are separated by commas. Look at a few examples in Table 1-6.

CHAPTER 1 **Tapping Into Formula and Function Fundamentals**   153

TABLE 1-6 Arguments in Functions

Function	Comment
=NOW()	Takes no arguments.
=AVERAGE(A6,A11,B7)	Can take up to 255 arguments. Here, three cell references are included as arguments. The arguments are separated by commas.
=AVERAGE(A6:A10,A13:A19,A23:A29)	In this example, the arguments are range references instead of cell references. The arguments are separated by commas.
=IPMT(B5,B6,B7,B8)	Requires four arguments. Commas separate the arguments.

Some functions have required arguments and optional arguments. You must provide the required ones. The optional ones are, well, optional. But you may want to include them if their presence helps the function return the value you need.

The IPMT function is a good example. Four arguments are required, and two more are optional. You can read more about the IPMT function in Book 3, Chapter 1. You can read more about function arguments in Chapter 2 of this minibook.

Arguing with a function

Memorizing the arguments that every function takes would be a daunting task. If you could pull that off, you could be on television! But back to reality. You don't have to memorize arguments because Excel helps you select what function to use and then tells you which arguments are needed.

Figure 1-20 shows the Insert Function dialog box. You access this great helper by clicking the Insert Function button on the Formulas tab of the ribbon. The dialog box is where you select a function to use.

The dialog box contains a listing of all available functions — and there are a lot of them! So, to make matters easier, the dialog box gives you a way to search for a function by a keyword, or you can filter the list of functions by category.

TIP If you know which category a function belongs in, you can click the function category button on the Formulas tab and select the function from the menu.

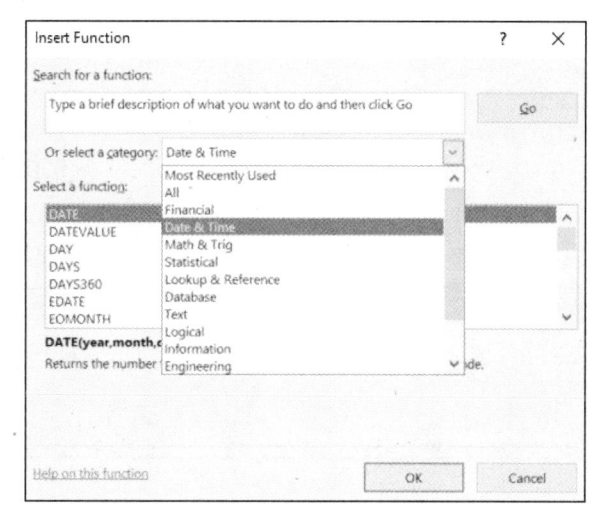

FIGURE 1-20:
The Insert Function dialog box.

Here's an example of how to use the Insert Function dialog box to multiply a few numbers:

1. **Enter three numbers in three different cells.**
2. **Click an empty cell where you want the result to appear.**
3. **Click the Insert Function button on the Formulas tab of the ribbon.**

   As an alternative, you can just click the little *fx* button on the Formula Bar. The Insert Function dialog box opens.

4. **From the category drop-down list, select either All or Math & Trig.**
5. **In the list of functions, find and select the PRODUCT function.**
6. **Click OK.**

   The Insert Function dialog box closes and the Function Arguments dialog box (shown in Figure 1-21) opens. Here, you can enter as many arguments as needed. Initially, the dialog box may not look like it can accommodate enough arguments. You need to enter three in this example, but it looks like there's only room for two. This is like musical chairs!

   More argument entry boxes appear as you need them. First, though, how do you enter the argument?

CHAPTER 1 **Tapping Into Formula and Function Fundamentals** 155

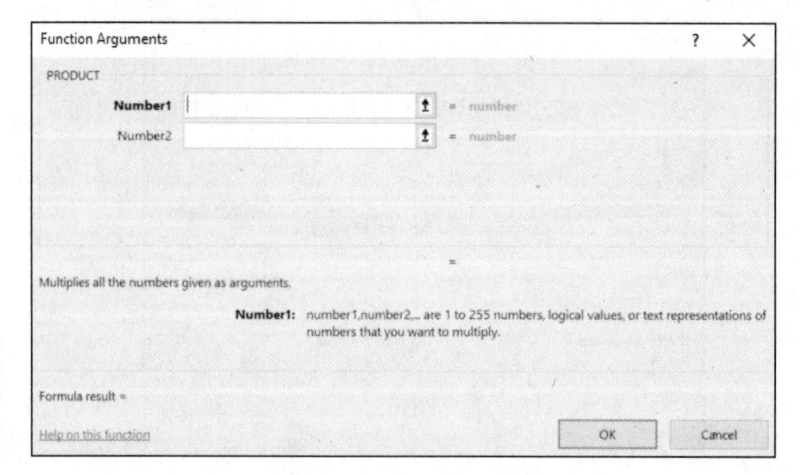

FIGURE 1-21:
Getting ready to enter some arguments to the function.

7. **Enter the argument in one of two ways:**

   - Type the numbers or cell references in the boxes.
   - Use those funny-looking squares to the right of the entry boxes.

   In Figure 1-21, two entry boxes are ready to go. To the left of them are the names Number1 and Number2. To the right of the boxes are the little squares. These squares are actually called *RefEdit controls.* They make argument entry a snap. All you do is click one, click the cell with the value, and then press Enter.

8. **Click the RefEdit control to the right of the Number1 entry box.**

   The Function Arguments dialog box shrinks to just the size of the entry box.

9. **Click the cell with the first number.**

   Figure 1-22 shows what the screen looks like at this point.

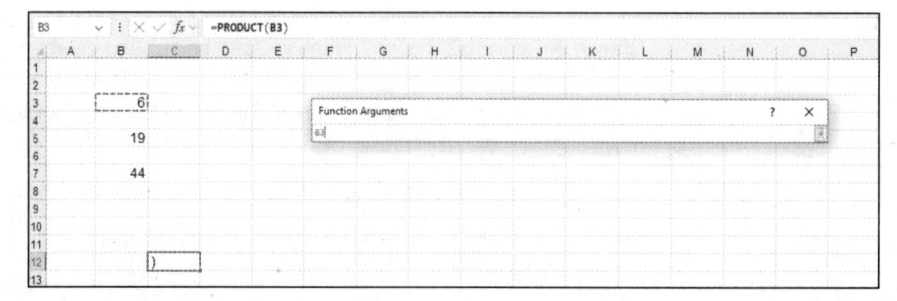

FIGURE 1-22:
Using RefEdit to enter arguments.

10. **Press Enter.**

    The Function Arguments dialog box expands to its previous size, now with the argument entered in the box. The argument is not the value in the cell, but the address of the cell that contains the value — exactly what you want.

156   BOOK 2 **Working with Formulas and Functions**

11. **Repeat Steps 7–9 to enter the other two cell references.**

    Figure 1-23 shows what the screen should look like now.

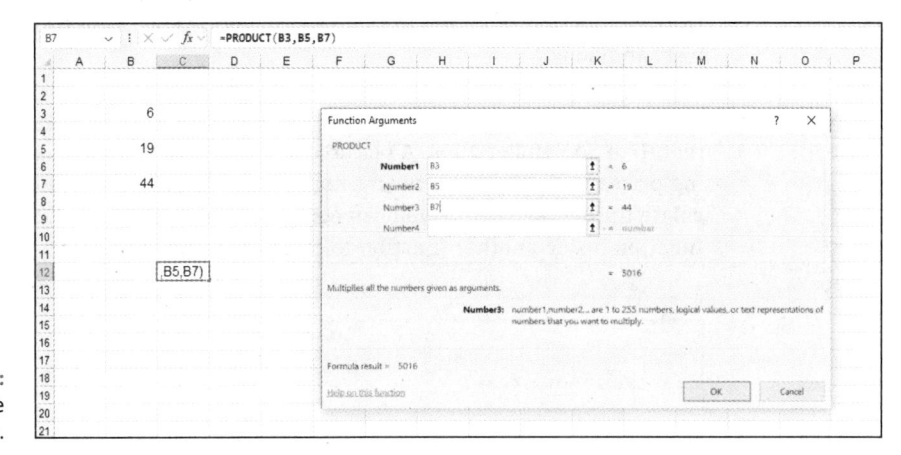

    FIGURE 1-23: Completing the function entry.

    > **TIP** The number of entry boxes and associated RefEdit controls grow to match the number of needed entry boxes.

12. **Click OK or press Enter to complete the function.**

    Figure 1-24 shows the result of all this hoopla. The PRODUCT function returns the result of the individual numbers being multiplied together.

    FIGURE 1-24: Math was never this easy!

    > **TIP** You don't have to use the Insert Function dialog box to enter functions into cells. It's just there for convenience. As you become familiar with certain functions that you use repeatedly, you may find it faster to just type the function directly in the cell.

CHAPTER 1 Tapping Into Formula and Function Fundamentals   157

Nesting functions

A *nested function* is tucked inside another function as one of its arguments. Nested functions let you return results you would have a hard time getting otherwise. (Nested functions are used in examples in various places in this minibook and the next minibook.)

Figure 1-25 shows the daily closing price for the Standard & Poor's 500 for the month of September 2004. A possible analysis is to see how many times the closing price was higher than the average for the month. Therefore, you need to calculate the average before you can compare any single price. Embed the AVERAGE function inside another function to calculate the average first.

FIGURE 1-25: Nesting functions.

When a function is nested inside another, the inner function is calculated first. Then that result is used as an argument for the outer function.

The COUNTIF function counts the number of cells in a range that meet a condition. The condition in this case is that any single value in the range is greater than (>) the average of the range. The formula in cell D7 is =COUNTIF(B5:B25,">"&AVERAGE(B5:B25)). The AVERAGE function is evaluated first; then the COUNTIF function is evaluated, using the returned value from the nested function as an argument.

Nested functions are best entered directly. The Insert Function dialog box doesn't make it easy to enter a nested function. In the following example, you use the AVERAGE function to find the average of the largest values from two sets of numbers. The nested function in this example is MAX. You enter the MAX function twice within the AVERAGE function. Follow these steps:

1. **Enter a few different numbers in one column.**
2. **Enter a few different numbers in a different column.**
3. **Click an empty cell where you want the result to appear.**
4. **Type** =AVERAGE(.

   This starts the function entry.
5. **Type** MAX(.
6. **Click the first cell in the second set of numbers, press the left mouse button, drag over all the cells of the first set, and release the mouse button.**

   The address of this range enters into the MAX function.
7. **Type**).

   This ends the first MAX function.
8. **Enter a comma (,).**
9. **Type** MAX(.
10. **Click the first cell in the second set of numbers, press the left mouse button, drag over all the cells of the second set, and release the mouse button.**

    The address of this range enters into the MAX function.
11. **Type**).

    This ends the second MAX function.
12. **Type**).

    This ends the AVERAGE function.
13. **Press Enter.**

Figure 1-26 shows the result of your nested function. Cell C14 has this formula: =AVERAGE(MAX(B4:B10),MAX(D4:D10)).

FIGURE 1-26: Getting a result from nested functions.

> When you use nested functions, the outer function is preceded with an equal sign (=) if it's the beginning of the formula. Any nested functions are *not* preceded with an equal sign.

> You can nest functions up to 64 levels.

> **IN THIS CHAPTER**
>
> » Displaying the Insert Function dialog box
>
> » Finding the function you need
>
> » Using the Function Arguments dialog box
>
> » Entering formulas and functions

Chapter 2
Saving Time with Function Tools

Excel has so many functions that it's both a blessing and a curse. You can do many things with Excel functions — if you can remember them all! Even if you remember many function names, memorizing all the arguments the functions can use is a challenge.

REMEMBER *Arguments* are pieces of information that functions use to calculate and return a value.

Never fear: Microsoft hasn't left you in the dark when it comes to figuring out which arguments to use. Excel has a great utility to help you insert functions, and their arguments, into your worksheet. This makes it a snap to find and use the functions you need. You can save both time and headaches — and make fewer errors to boot — so read on!

Getting Familiar with the Insert Function Dialog Box

The Insert Function dialog box (shown in Figure 2-1) is designed to simplify the task of using functions in your worksheet. The dialog box not only helps you locate the proper function for the task at hand but also provides information about the arguments that the function takes. If you use the Insert Function dialog box, you don't have to type functions directly in worksheet cells. Instead, the dialog box guides you through a (mostly) point-and-click procedure — a good thing, because if you're anything like us, you need all the help you can get.

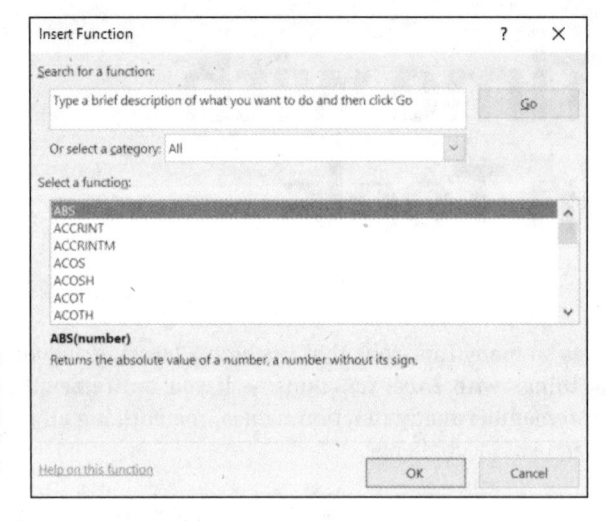

FIGURE 2-1: Use the Insert Function dialog box to easily enter functions in a worksheet.

In the Insert Function dialog box, you can browse functions by category or scroll the complete alphabetical list. A search feature — in which you type a word or phrase in the Search for a Function box, click the Go button, and see what comes up — is helpful. When you select a function in the Select a Function box, a brief description of what the function does appears under the list. You can also click the Help on This Function link at the bottom of the dialog box to view more detailed information about the function.

You can get to the Insert Function dialog box in three ways:

- Click the Insert Function button on the Formulas tab of the ribbon.
- On the Formula Bar, click the smaller Insert Function button (which looks like *fx*).

>> Click the small arrow on the AutoSum button on the Home tab or the Formulas tab of the ribbon, and select More Functions (see Figure 2-2). AutoSum has a list of commonly used functions that you can insert with a click.

FIGURE 2-2: The AutoSum button offers quick access to basic functions and the Insert Function dialog box.

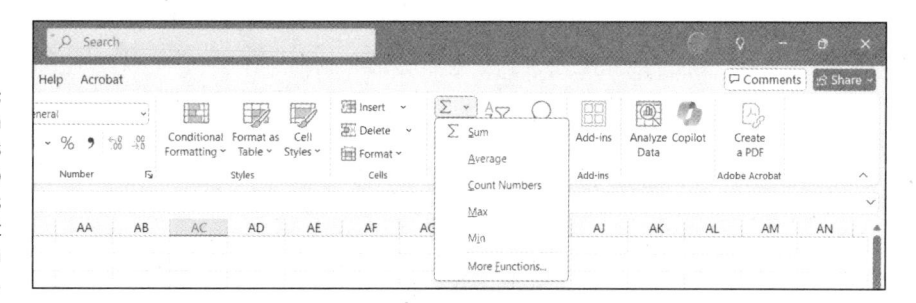

Finding the Correct Function

The first step in using a function is finding the one you need! Even when you do know the one you need, you may not remember all the arguments it takes. You can find a function in the Insert Function dialog box in two ways:

>> **Search:** Type one or more keywords or a phrase in the Search for a Function box, and then click the Go button.

- If a match is made, the Or Select a Category drop-down list displays Recommended, and the Select a Function box displays a list of the functions that match your search.

- If no match is made, the Or Select a Category drop-down list displays Most Recently Used functions, and the most recently used functions appear in the Select a Function dialog box. The Search for a Function box displays a message to rephrase the text entered for the search.

>> **Browse:** Click the Or Select a Category down arrow, and from the drop-down list, select All or an actual function category. When you select an actual category, the Select a Function box updates to show just the functions in that category. You can look through the list to find the function you want. Alternatively, if you know the category, you can select it on the Formulas tab of the ribbon.

Table 2-1 lists the categories in the Or Select a Category drop-down list. Finding the function you need is different from knowing which function you need. Excel is great at giving you the functions, but you do need to know what to ask for.

CHAPTER 2 **Saving Time with Function Tools** 163

TABLE 2-1 Function Categories in the Insert Function Dialog Box

Category	Type of Functions
Most Recently Used	The last several functions you used.
All	The entire function list, sorted alphabetically.
Financial	Functions for managing loans, analyzing investments, and so on.
Date & Time	Functions for calculating days of the week, elapsed time, and so on.
Math & Trig	A considerable number of mathematical functions.
Statistical	Functions for using descriptive and inferential statistics.
Lookup & Reference	Functions for obtaining facts about and data on worksheets.
Database	Functions for selecting data in structured rows and columns.
Text	Functions for manipulating and searching text values.
Logical	Boolean functions (AND, OR, and so on).
Information	Functions for getting facts about worksheet cells and the data therein.
Web	A few functions that are useful when sharing data with web services.
Engineering	Engineering and some conversion functions. These functions are also provided in the Analysis ToolPak.
Cube	Functions used with online analytical processing (OLAP) cubes.
Compatibility	Some functions were updated in more recent versions of Excel. The functions in this category are the older versions that remain compatible with Excel 2007 and earlier versions.
User Defined	Any available custom functions created in Visual Basic for Applications (VBA) code or from add-ins. This category appears only when there are user-defined functions.

Entering Functions Using the Insert Function Dialog Box

The previous section shows you how to search for or select a function. Now it's time to use the Insert Function dialog box to actually insert a function. The dialog box makes it easy to enter functions that take no arguments and functions that *do* take arguments. Either way, the dialog box guides you through the process of entering the function.

Sometimes, function arguments are not values but references to cells, ranges, named areas, or tables. The Insert Function dialog box enables you to add such references to your functions easily.

Selecting a function that takes no arguments

Some functions return a value, period. No arguments are needed for these functions. This means you don't have to have some arguments ready to go. What could be easier? Here's how to enter a function that does not take any arguments. The TODAY function is used in the following example:

1. **Position the cursor in the cell where you want the results to appear.**
2. **Click the Insert Function button on the Formulas tab of the ribbon to open the Insert Function dialog box.**
3. **From the Or Select a Category drop-down list, select All.**
4. **Scroll through the Select a Function list until you see the TODAY function, and click it.**

   The Insert Function dialog box (see Figure 2-3) opens.

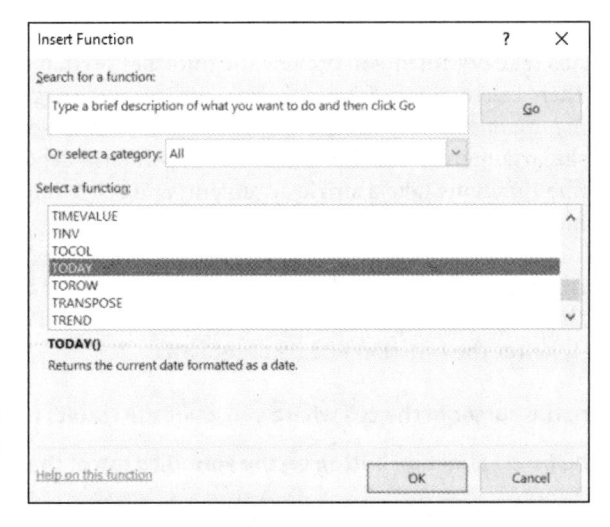

FIGURE 2-3: The Insert Function dialog box.

5. **Click OK.**

   The Insert Function dialog box closes, and the Function Arguments dialog box (see Figure 2-4) opens. The dialog box tells you that this function doesn't take any arguments.

6. **Click OK.**

   The Function Arguments dialog box closes, and the function entry is complete. The function's result appears in the cell as a date, such as 11/13/2025.

FIGURE 2-4:
The Function Arguments dialog box shows that the TODAY function takes no arguments.

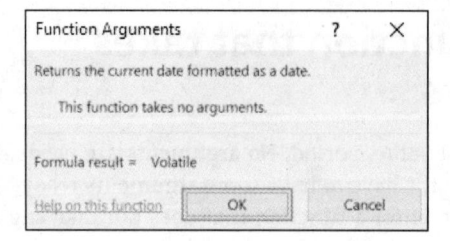

You may have noticed that the Function Arguments dialog box says that the Formula result will equal Volatile. This is nothing to be alarmed about — it just means the answer can be different each time you use the function. For example, TODAY will return a different date tomorrow than today.

Most functions do take arguments. The few that do *not* take arguments can return a result without needing any information. For example, the TODAY function just returns the current date. It doesn't need any information to figure this out.

Selecting a function that uses arguments

Most functions take arguments to provide the information that the functions need to perform their calculations. Some functions use a single argument; others use many. (*Taking arguments* and *using arguments* are interchangeable terms.) Most functions take arguments, but the number of arguments depends on the actual function. Some functions take a single argument, and other functions can take up to 255 arguments.

The following example shows how to use the Insert Function dialog box to enter a function that *does* use arguments. The example uses the PRODUCT function. Here's how to enter the function and its arguments:

1. **Position the cursor in the cell where you want the results to appear.**

2. **Click the Insert Function button on the Formulas tab of the ribbon.**

   The Insert Function dialog box opens.

3. **From the Or Select a Category drop-down list, select Math & Trig.**

4. **Scroll through the Select a Function list until you see the PRODUCT function and then click it.**

5. **Click OK.**

   The Insert Function dialog box closes, and the Function Arguments dialog box (see Figure 2-5) opens. This dialog box tells you that this function can take up to 255 arguments, yet there appears to be room for only 2. As you enter arguments, the dialog box provides a scroll bar to manage multiple arguments.

166   BOOK 2 Working with Formulas and Functions

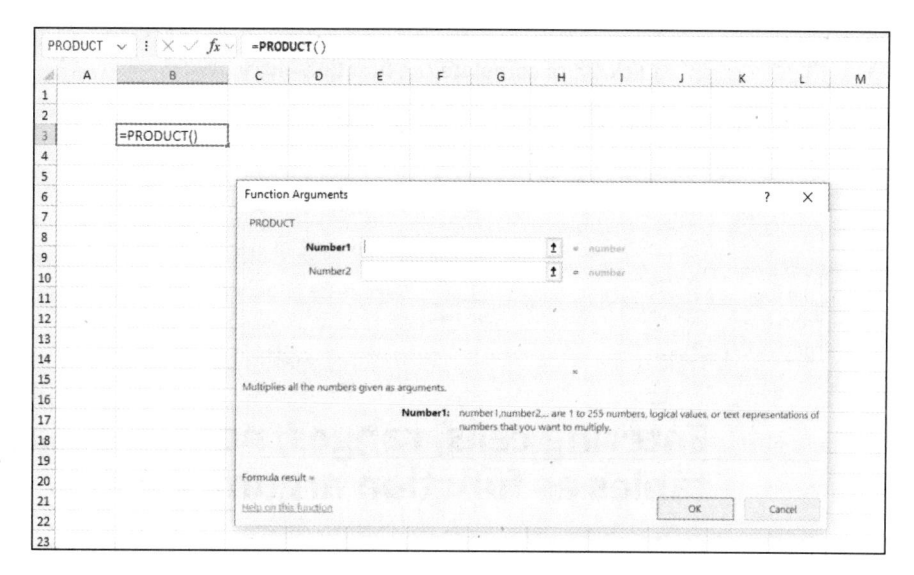

FIGURE 2-5:
Ready to input function arguments.

6. **In the Function Arguments dialog box, enter a number in the Number1 box.**

7. **Enter another number in the Number2 box.**

   You're entering actual arguments. As you enter numbers in the dialog box, a scroll bar appears, letting you add more arguments. Enter as many arguments as you like, up to 255. Figure 2-6 shows that we entered eight arguments. Also look at the lower left of the dialog box. As you enter functions, the formula result is instantly calculated. Wouldn't it be nice to be that smart?

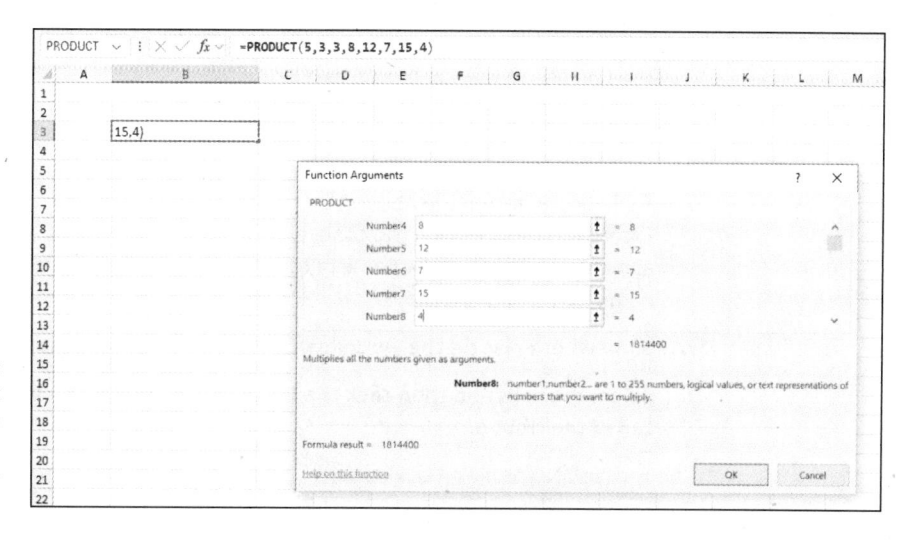

FIGURE 2-6:
Getting instant results in the Function Arguments dialog box.

CHAPTER 2 Saving Time with Function Tools   167

8. **Click OK to complete the function entry.**

   Figure 2-7 shows the worksheet's result.

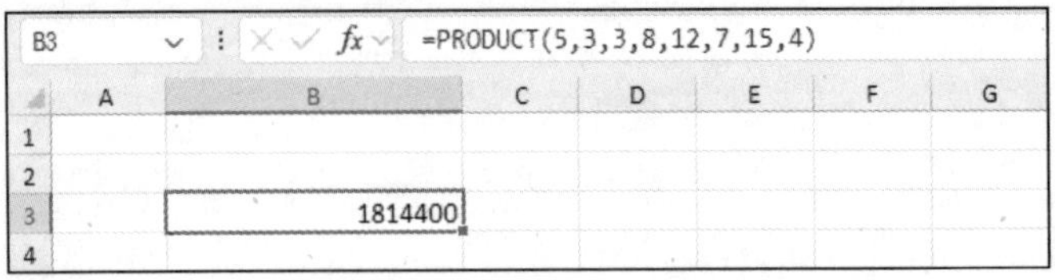

FIGURE 2-7: Getting the final answer from the function.

Entering cells, ranges, named areas, and tables as function arguments

Excel is so cool. Not only can you provide single cell references as arguments, but also, in many cases, you can enter an entire range reference, or the name of an area or table, as a single argument! What's more, you can enter these arguments by using either the keyboard or the mouse.

This example demonstrates using both single cell and range references as well as a named area and table as arguments. For this example, we use the SUM function. Here's how to use the Insert Function dialog box to enter the function and its arguments:

1. **Enter some numbers in a worksheet in contiguous cells.**

2. **Select the cells and then click the Table button on the Insert tab of the ribbon.**

   The Create Table dialog box opens.

3. **Click OK to complete making the table.**

   The ribbon should display table styles and other options. (If it doesn't, click the Table Design tab on the ribbon.) On the left end of the ribbon is the name that Excel gave the table. You can change the name of the table, as well as the appearance. Jot down the name of the table. You need to reenter the table name further in these steps.

4. **Somewhere else on the worksheet, enter numbers in contiguous cells.**

5. **Select the cells and then click the Define Name button on the Formulas tab of the ribbon.**

   The New Name dialog box opens.

6. **Enter a name for the area.**

   We used the name MyArea. Figure 2-8 shows how the worksheet is shaping up.

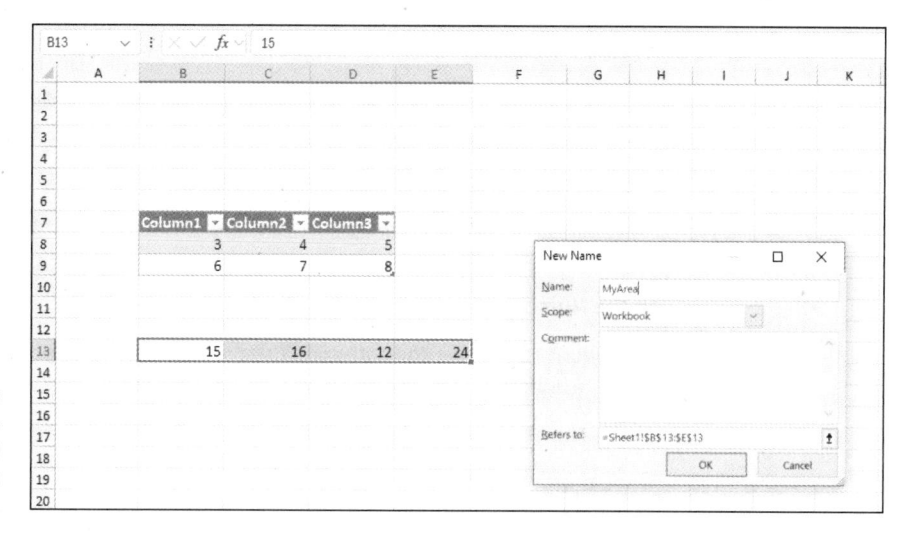

   FIGURE 2-8: Adding a table and a named area to a worksheet.

7. **Enter some more numbers in contiguous cells, either across a row or down a column.**

8. **Enter a single number in cell A1.**

9. **Click an empty cell where you want the result to appear.**

10. **Click the Insert Function button on the Formulas tab of the ribbon.**

    The Insert Function dialog box opens.

11. **Select the SUM function.**

    SUM is in the All category, in the Math & Trig category, and possibly in the Recently Used category.

12. **Click OK.**

    The Function Arguments dialog box opens.

    REMEMBER

    To the right of each number box is a small up-arrow button — a special Excel control sometimes called *RefEdit*. Clicking a RefEdit button allows you to leave the dialog box, select a cell or range on the worksheet, and then go back to the dialog box. Whatever cell or range you click or drag over on the worksheet is brought into the entry box as a reference.

CHAPTER 2 **Saving Time with Function Tools** 169

You can type cell and range references, named areas, and table names directly in the number boxes as well. You can also click directly on cells or ranges on the worksheet. The RefEdit controls are there to use if you want to work with the mouse instead.

13. **Click the RefEdit button to the right of the Number1 box.**

    The dialog box shrinks so that the only control visible is the field where you enter data.

14. **Click cell A1, where you entered a number, and press Enter.**

    The Function Arguments dialog box reopens, with the A1 reference now entered in the Number1 box.

15. **In the Number2 box, type the name of your named area.**

    If you don't remember the name you used, click the RefEdit button to the right of the Number2 box to select the area on the worksheet.

16. **In the Number3 box, enter your table name and press Enter.**

    If you don't remember the name you used, click the RefEdit button to the right of the Number3 box to select the table.

17. **In the Number4 box, enter a range from the worksheet where some values are located and press Enter.**

    It doesn't matter if this range is part of a named area or table. Click the RefEdit button to the right of the Number4 box if you want to just drag the mouse over a range of numbers. Your screen should look similar to Figure 2-9.

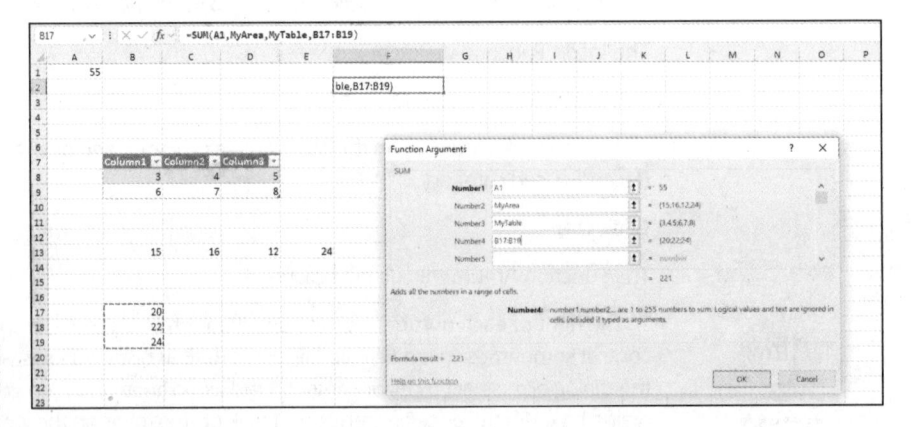

FIGURE 2-9: Entering arguments.

18. **Click OK.**

    The final sum from the various parts of the worksheet displays in the cell where you entered the function. Figure 2-10 shows how the example worksheet turned out.

FIGURE 2-10: Calculating a sum based on cell and range references.

Congratulations! You successfully inserted a function that took a cell reference, a range reference, a named area, and a table name. You're harnessing the power of Excel. Look at the result — the sum of many numbers located in various parts of the worksheet. Just imagine how much summing you can do. You can have up to 255 inputs, and if necessary, each one can be a *range* of cells.

TIP

You can use the Insert Function dialog box at any time while entering a formula. This is helpful when the formula uses some values and references in addition to a function. Just open the Insert Function dialog box when the formula entry is at the point where the function goes.

Getting help in the Insert Function dialog box

The number of functions and their exhaustive capabilities give you the power to do great things in Excel. However, from time to time, you may need guidance on how to get functions to work. Luckily for you, help is just a click away.

Both the Insert Function dialog box and the Function Arguments dialog box have a link to the Help system. At any time, you can click the Help on This Function link in the lower-left corner of the dialog box and get help on the function you're using. The Help system has many examples. Often, reviewing how a function works leads you to other, similar functions that may be better suited to your situation.

Using the Function Arguments dialog box to edit functions

Excel makes entering functions with the Insert Function dialog box easy. But what do you do when you need to change a function that has already been entered in a cell? What about adding arguments or taking some away? There is an easy way to do this! Follow these steps:

1. **Click the cell with the existing function.**

2. **Click the Insert Function button.**

   The Function Arguments dialog box opens. This dialog box is already set to work with your function. In fact, the arguments that have already been entered in the function are displayed in the dialog box as well!

3. **Add, edit, or delete arguments, as follows:**

   - To add an argument (if the function allows), use the RefEdit control to pick up the extra values from the worksheet. Alternatively, if you click the bottom argument reference, a new box opens below it, and you can enter a value or range in that box.
   - To edit an argument, simply click it and change it.
   - To delete an argument, click it and press the Backspace key.

4. **Click OK when you're finished.**

   The function is updated with your changes.

Directly Entering Formulas and Functions

As you get sharp with functions, you'll likely bypass the Insert Function dialog box altogether and enter functions directly. One place you can do this is in the Formula Bar. Another way is to just type in a cell.

Entering formulas and functions in the Formula Bar

When you place your entry in the Formula Bar, the entry is really going into the active cell. However, because the active cell can be anywhere, you may prefer entering formulas and functions directly in the Formula Bar. That way, you know that the entry will land where you need it.

Before you enter a formula in the Formula Box (on the right end of the Formula Bar), the Name Box on the left lets you know where the entry will end up. The cell receiving the entry may not be in the visible area of the worksheet. It could be a million rows down and thousands of columns to the right! After you start entering the formula, the Name Box becomes a drop-down list of functions; this list is useful for nesting functions. As you enter a function in the Formula Box, you can click a function in the Name Box's drop-down list (see Figure 2-11), and Excel inserts the function into the entry you started in the Formula Box. Adding a function via the Name Box is a great way to assemble nested functions.

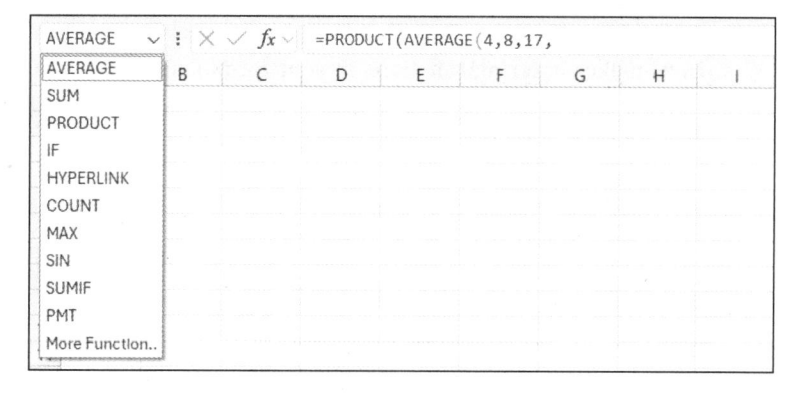

FIGURE 2-11: Entering a formula in the Formula Box has its conveniences.

When your entry is finished, press Enter or click the little check-mark Enter button to the left of the Formula Box.

In between the Name Box and the Formula Box are three small buttons. From left to right, they do the following:

>> Cancel the entry.
>> Complete the entry.
>> Display the Insert Function dialog box.

REMEMBER: The Cancel button and Enter Function button are enabled only when you enter a formula, a function, or just plain old values in the Formula Box or directly in a cell.

Entering formulas and functions directly in worksheet cells

Perhaps the easiest entry method is typing the formula directly in a cell. Just type formulas that contain no functions and press Enter to complete the entry. Try this simple example:

1. **Click a cell where the formula is to be entered.**

2. **Enter this simple math-based formula:**

   =6+(9/5)*100

3. **Press Enter.**

   The answer is 186. (See Chapter 1 of this minibook for more information about the order of mathematical operators.)

Excel makes entering functions in your formulas as easy as a click. As you type the first letter of a function in a cell, a list of functions starting with that letter appears in the Formula Box (see Figure 2-12).

FIGURE 2-12: Entering functions has never been this easy.

The desired function in this example is MIN, which returns the minimum value from a group of values. As soon as you type *M* (after entering the equal sign if this is the start of a formula entry), the list in Figure 2-12 appears, showing all the functions beginning with *M*. Now either keep typing the full function name or scroll to MIN and press the Tab key. Figure 2-13 shows just what happens when you do the latter: Excel completes MIN completed and provides the required syntax structure. In Figure 2-13, the MIN function is used to find the minimum value in the range A7:A15 (which is multiplied by the sum of the values in A1 plus A2). Entering the closing parenthesis and then pressing Enter completes the function. The formula in D5 is =(A1+A2)*MIN(A7:A15). In this example, the answer is 1,222.

FIGURE 2-13: Completing the direct-in-the-cell formula entry.

Excel's capability to show a list of functions based on spelling is called *Formula AutoComplete*.

You can turn Formula AutoComplete on or off in the Excel Options dialog box by following these steps:

1. **Select the File tab at the left end of the ribbon.**
2. **Click Options.**

   The Excel Options dialog box opens.

3. **In the Excel Options dialog box, select the Formulas tab.**
4. **In the Working with Formulas section, select or deselect the Formula AutoComplete check box.**
5. **Click OK.**

IN THIS CHAPTER

» **Understanding arrays**

» **Creating formulas that use arrays**

» **Using functions that return arrays of data**

Chapter 3

Building Array Formulas and Functions

Excel is really quite sophisticated; its many built-in functions make your work easier. On top of that, Excel allows you to tell functions to work on entire sets of values, called *arrays*, which makes for even more clever analysis.

An *array* is a set of two or more values (for example, the contents of two or more worksheet cells, or even the contents of two or more worksheet ranges). Certain functions use arrays for arguments.

You may be thinking, "Hey, how is this different from just entering a bunch of arguments?" You're right in the comparison. For example, the SUM function can take up to 255 arguments. Isn't this the same as giving the function an array with 255 values? Well, yes and no. It's the same idea, but using the array approach can streamline your work, as you soon see.

There is even another side to array functions. Some of the functions *return* an array. Yes, that's right. Most of the time a function returns a single value into a single cell. In this chapter, we show you how a function returns a group of values into multiple cells.

Discovering Arrays

An array is like a box. It can hold a number of items. In Excel, an array holds a collection of values or cell references. These arrays are used exclusively in formulas and functions. That is, the association of some values as one cohesive group exists just for the purpose of calculating results. An array differs from the named areas (named ranges of cells) that you can create in Excel. Named areas become part of the worksheet and can be referenced at any time.

Named areas are set using the New Name dialog box, shown in Figure 3-1. By contrast, there is no such dialog box or method to create arrays that can be referenced from functions or formulas. Arrays, instead, are embedded in formulas.

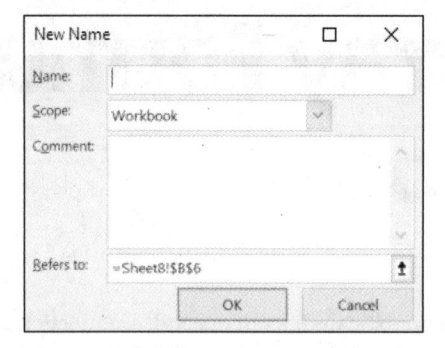

FIGURE 3-1: Creating a named area with the New Name dialog box.

Named areas are easily referenced in formulas. For example, if a workbook contains a named area Sales, the values of all the cells in Sales can be summed up like this:

```
=SUM(Sales)
```

Assume that Sales contains three cells with these values: 10, 15, and 20. These values can be entered directly in the SUM function like this:

```
=SUM(10,15,20)
```

This is almost an array, but not quite. Excel recognizes a group of values to be an array when they're enclosed in braces: { and }. Therefore, to enter the array of values into the function, you make an entry that looks like this:

```
=SUM({10,15,20})
```

Essentially, the braces tell Excel to treat the group of values as an array. So far, you may be wondering about the usefulness of an array, but in the next section, we show you how using arrays with standard functions such as SUM can provide sophisticated results.

REMEMBER To enter values as an array within a function, enclose them in braces. Braces have a curly look and are not to be confused with brackets: [and]. On a typical keyboard, braces and brackets are on the same keys. Holding the Shift key while pressing the brace/bracket key provides the brace.

However, getting the braces into the formula takes a particular keystroke, as you see in the next section. You don't type braces directly.

Using Arrays in Formulas

You can use arrays when entering formulas and functions. Typically, the arguments to a function are entered in a different manner, which we demonstrate in this section. Using arrays can save entry steps and deliver an answer in a single formula, which is useful in situations that normally require a set of intermediate calculations from which the final result is calculated.

Here's an example of an array coming in handy: The SUM function is normally used to add a few numbers together. Summing up a few numbers doesn't require an array formula per se, but what about summing up the results of other calculations? This next example shows how using an array simplifies getting to the final result.

Figure 3-2 shows a small portfolio of stocks. Column A has the stock symbols, column B has the number of shares per stock, and column C has a recent price for each stock.

	A	B	C
2	Stock	# of Shares	Price
4	IBM	100	$120.82
5	MSFT	200	$25.71
6	YHOO	200	$17.21
7	INTC	300	$19.88
8	BA	150	$25.37

FIGURE 3-2: A stock portfolio.

The task is to find out the *total* value of the portfolio. The typical way to do this is to

1. **Multiply the number of shares of each stock by its price.**
2. **Sum up the results from Step 1.**

Figure 3-3 shows a common way to do this. Column D contains formulas to calculate the value of each stock in the portfolio. This is done by multiplying the number of shares of each stock by its price. For example, cell D4 contains the formula =B4*C4. Cell D10 sums up the interim results with the formula =SUM(D4:D8).

FIGURE 3-3: Calculating the value of a stock portfolio the old-fashioned way.

Stock	# of Shares	Price		
IBM	100	$120.82	$12,082.00	
MSFT	200	$25.71	$5,142.00	
YHOO	200	$17.21	$3,442.00	
INTC	300	$19.88	$5,964.00	
BA	150	$25.37	$3,805.50	
			$30,435.50	Total Value

The method shown in Figure 3-3 requires creating additional calculations — those in column D. These calculations are necessary if you need to know the value of each stock, but not if all you need to know is the value of the portfolio as a whole.

Fortunately, alternatives to this standard approach exist. One is to embed the separate multiplicative steps directly in the SUM function, like this:

```
=SUM(B4*C4,B5*C5,B6*C6,B7*C7,B8*C8)
```

That works, but it's bloated, to say the least. What if you had 20 stocks in the portfolio? Forget it!

Another alternative is the SUMPRODUCT function. This function sums the products, just as the other methods shown here do. The limitation, however, is that SUMPRODUCT can be used only for summing. It can't, for example, give you an average.

In many situations such as this one, your best bet is to use an array function. Figure 3-4 shows the correct result from using the SUM function entered as an array function. Notice that the formula in the Formula Box begins and ends with a brace.

FIGURE 3-4:
Calculating the value of a stock portfolio using an array function.

The syntax is important. Two ranges are entered in the function: One contains the cells that hold the number of shares, and the other contains the cells that have the stock prices. These are multiplied in the function by entering the multiplication operator, which is an asterisk (*):

{=SUM(B4:B8*C4:C8)}

We've pressed Ctrl+Shift+Enter to turn the whole thing into an array function. You use that special keystroke combination when you finish the formula, not before. Note the lack of subtotals (per stock) in cells D4:D8. Compare Figure 3-4 to Figure 3-3, and you can see the difference.

REMEMBER

Use Ctrl+Shift+Enter to turn a formula into an array formula. You must use the key combination after entering the formula instead of pressing Enter. The key combination takes the place of pressing Enter.

Here's how you use an array with the SUM function:

1. **Enter two columns of values.**

   The two lists must be the same size.

2. **Position the cursor in the cell where you want the result to appear.**

3. **Type =SUM(to start the function.**

   Note that you do *not* enter a brace in this step.

4. **Click the first cell in the first list, hold the left mouse button down, drag the pointer over the first list, and then release the mouse button.**

5. **Type the multiplication operator (*).**

6. **Click the first cell of the second list, hold down the left mouse button, and drag the pointer over the second list.**

7. **Release the mouse button.**
8. **Type).**
9. **Press Ctrl+Shift+Enter to enter the function.**

   Don't just press Enter by itself when using an array with the SUM function.

REMEMBER

Array functions are useful for saving steps in mathematical operations. So, you can apply these examples to a number of functions, such as AVERAGE, MAX, MIN, and so on.

As another example, suppose you run a fleet of taxis, and you need to calculate the average cost of gasoline per mile driven. This number is easy to calculate for a single vehicle. You just divide the total spent on gasoline by the total miles driven for a given period of time. The calculation looks like this:

cost of gasoline per mile = total spent on gasoline ÷ total miles driven

How can you easily calculate this amount for a fleet of vehicles? Figure 3-5 shows how this is done. The vehicles are listed in column A, the total miles driven for the month are listed in column B, and the total amounts spent on gasoline are listed in column C.

	A	B	C
			C21 fx {=AVERAGE(C6:C17/B6:B17)}
1	The Happy Taxi Company		
2	Mileage and Gasoline for October - December 2019		
3			
4			
5	TAXI	MILES DRIVEN	AMOUNT SPENT ON GAS
6	Taxi 1	4020	$702.32
7	Taxi 2	3355	$602.15
8	Taxi 3	3800	$624.84
9	Taxi 4	2487	$428.36
10	Taxi 5	3661	$620.75
11	Taxi 6	4050	$715.92
12	Taxi 7	3742	$622.30
13	Taxi 8	3410	$585.65
14	Taxi 9	2880	$472.12
15	Taxi 10	3100	$526.45
16	Taxi 11	2844	$487.98
17	Taxi 12	3854	$671.15
18			
19			
20			
21	Average Gasoline Expense per Mile Driven:		$0.17
22			

FIGURE 3-5: Making an easy calculation using an array formula.

One single formula in cell C21 answers the question. When you use the AVERAGE function in an array formula, the result is returned without the need for any intermediate calculations. The formula looks like this:

{=AVERAGE(C6:C17/B6:B17)}

Changing the Shape of Arrays

Did you know you can add to an array or take away from one? Yep! Let's say you have an array spread over a given number of rows and columns. You can add additional rows and/or columns to the array using the EXPAND function.

Figure 3-6 shows an area of data that extends from row 5 to row 9, and from column B to column E. The data in row 5 through row 11 and column G through column K are the result of using EXPAND.

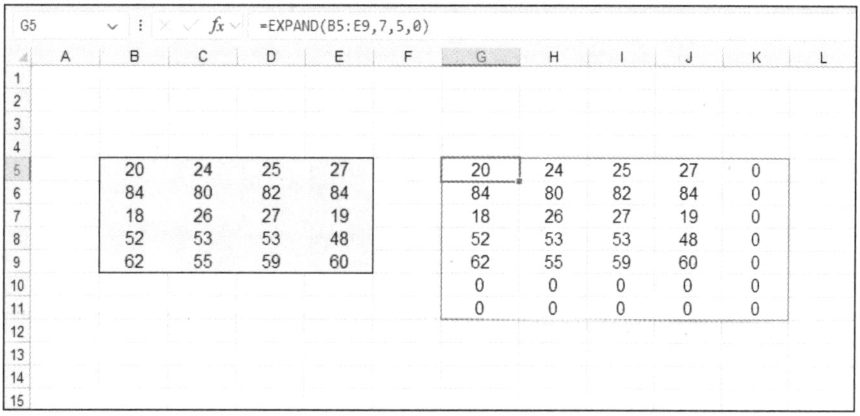

FIGURE 3-6: Expanding an array or range.

The EXPAND function increases the size of an array. The function takes four arguments: the array (specified as a range), the number of rows to add, the number of columns to add, and what value to put in the added cells.

The formula used in Figure 3-6 is

=EXPAND(B5:E9,7,5,0)

In the example shown in Figure 3-6, the second and third function arguments indicate the new size of the array, not how many rows or columns to add. In this case, the starting row count is 5 and the starting column count is 4. By using the numbers 7 and 5 as the arguments, two rows and one column were added. The cells are given the value of 0 because that's what the fourth function argument set.

The DROP function does the opposite of the EXPAND function. DROP takes away a specified number of rows and/or columns from an array. There are three arguments: the array (specified as a range), the number of rows to remove, and the number of columns to remove. The number of rows and number of columns must be 0 or a negative number. A positive number for either the rows or columns produces an error.

Figure 3-7 shows an area of data that extends from row 5 to row 12, and from column B to column E. The data in row 5 through row 7 and column G through column J are the result of using the DROP function. The formula used in cell G5 is

=DROP(B5:E12,-5,0)

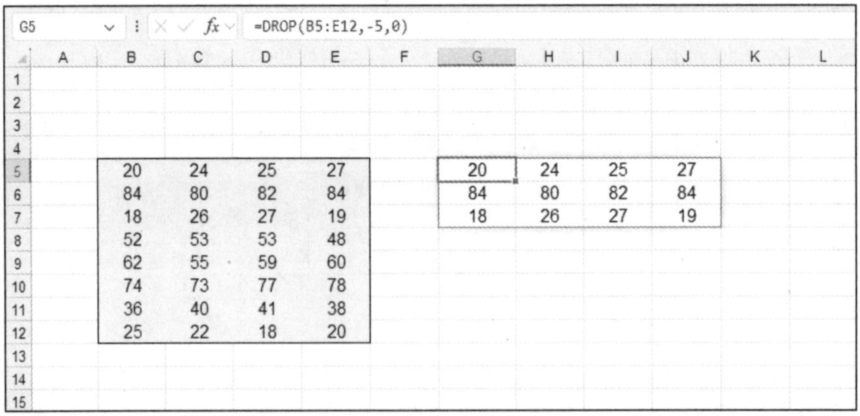

FIGURE 3-7: Shrink an array with DROP.

> **TIP** Both EXPAND and DROP place the newly sized array in another place on the sheet. The original array is left intact.

Sometimes not all the data is important, and instead just one part of an array needs scrutiny. Well, guess what? Excel provides the TAKE function for this very purpose.

Figure 3-8 shows a large array of data that is 12 rows by 6 columns. In this scenario the needed data is just an inner part of the array composed of 4 rows and 4 columns.

184   BOOK 2 Working with Formulas and Functions

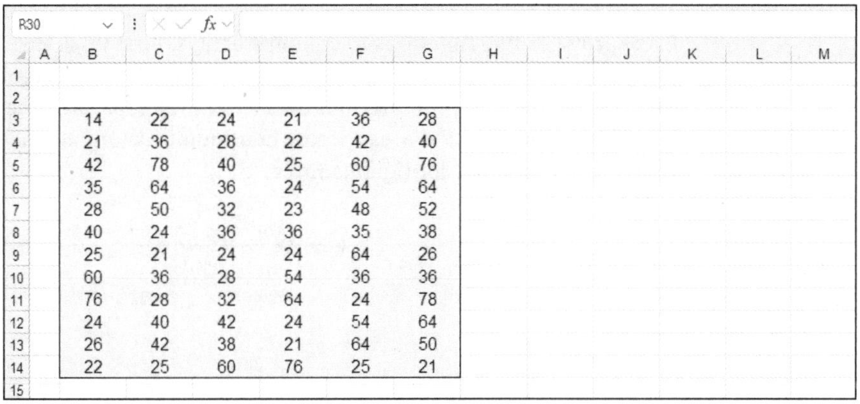

FIGURE 3-8:
Only a small section of this array is relevant.

Using the TAKE function, the needed data area is placed into another part of the sheet. Kinda cool! Figure 3-9 shows how the data appears now as a separate array.

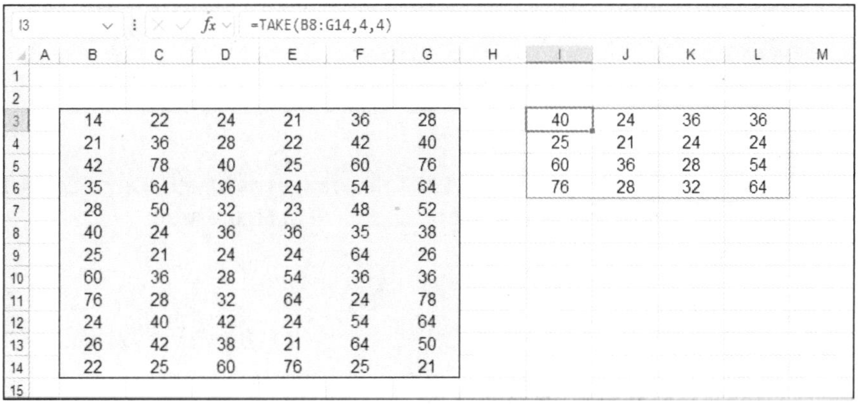

FIGURE 3-9:
The TAKE function has created an array of just the needed information.

TAKE has just three arguments: the range, the number of rows to take, and the number of columns to take.

The TAKE function used in Figure 3-9 is

```
=TAKE(B8:G14,4,4)
```

TIP You can use negative numbers as function arguments in TAKE. This results in data being taken from the right or bottom of the array.

CHAPTER 3 **Building Array Formulas and Functions** 185

Excel provides two functions to combine arrays. First up is HSTACK, which simply combines arrays horizontally into one array area. VSTACK combines arrays vertically. In Figure 3-10, the original data is in four separate areas. HSTACK is used in cell J4 to combine the areas across contiguous columns, and VSTACK is used to combine the areas in contiguous rows.

FIGURE 3-10: Using HSTACK and VSTACK.

Both HSTACK and VSTACK take ranges as function arguments. Here's the formula using HSTACK in cell J4, as shown in Figure 3-10:

```
=HSTACK(B4:B5,D4:D5,F4:F5,H4:H5)
```

Working with Functions That Return Arrays

A few functions actually return arrays of data. Instead of providing a single result, as most functions do, these functions return several values. The number of actual returned values is directly related to the function's arguments. The returned values go into a range of cells.

REMEMBER

Excel array functions accept arrays as arguments and possibly return arrays of data.

186 BOOK 2 Working with Formulas and Functions

A good example of this is the TRANSPOSE function. This interesting function is used to reorient data. Data situated a given way in columns and rows is transposed (changed to be presented in rows and columns instead). Figure 3-11 shows how this works.

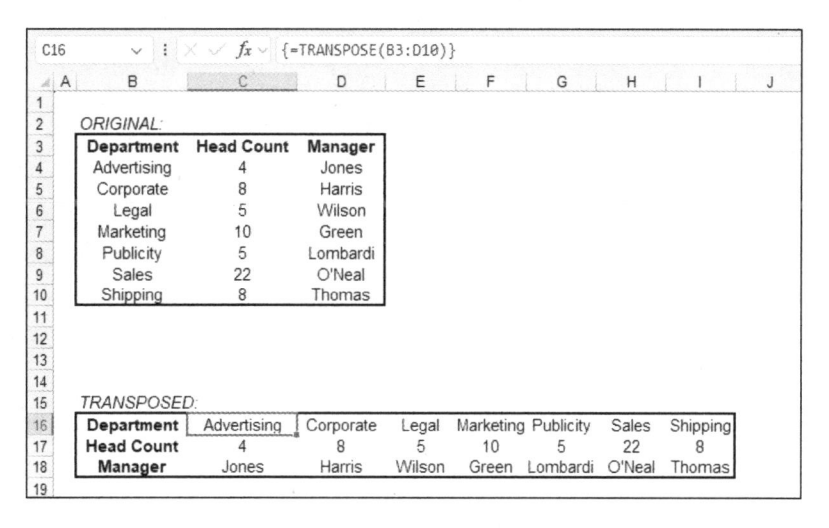

FIGURE 3-11: Transposing data.

Cells B3 through D10 contain information about departments in a company. Departments are listed going down column B. Note that the area of B3 through D10 specifically occupies three columns and eight rows. The header row is included in the area.

Cells B16 through I18 contain the transposed data. It's the same data, but now it occupies eight columns and three rows. In total number of cells, it's the same size as the original area. Just as important is that the area is made up of the same dimensions, just reversed. That is, a 3-by-8 area became an 8-by-3 area. The number of cells remains 24. However, the transposed area has not been altered to be 6 by 4, 2 by 12, or any other two dimensions that cover 24 cells.

Every single cell in the B16:I18 range contains the same formula: {=TRANSPOSE(B3:D10)}. However, we entered the function only once.

In detail, here's how you can use the TRANSPOSE function:

1. **Enter some data that occupies at least two adjacent cells.**

    Creating an area of data that spans multiple rows and columns is best for seeing how useful the function is.

CHAPTER 3 Building Array Formulas and Functions

2. **Elsewhere on the worksheet, select an area that covers the same number of cells but has the length of the sides of the original area reversed.**

   For example:

   - If the original area is 2 columns and 6 rows, select an area that is 6 columns and 2 rows.

   - If the original area is 1 column and 2 rows, select an area that is 2 columns and 1 row.

   - If the original area is 200 columns and 201 rows, select an area that is 201 columns and 200 rows.

   - If the original area is 5 columns and 5 rows, select an area that is 5 columns and 5 rows. (A square area is transposed into a square area.)

   Figure 3-12 shows an area of data and a selected area ready to receive the transposed data. The original data area occupies 11 columns and 3 rows. The selected area is 3 columns by 11 rows.

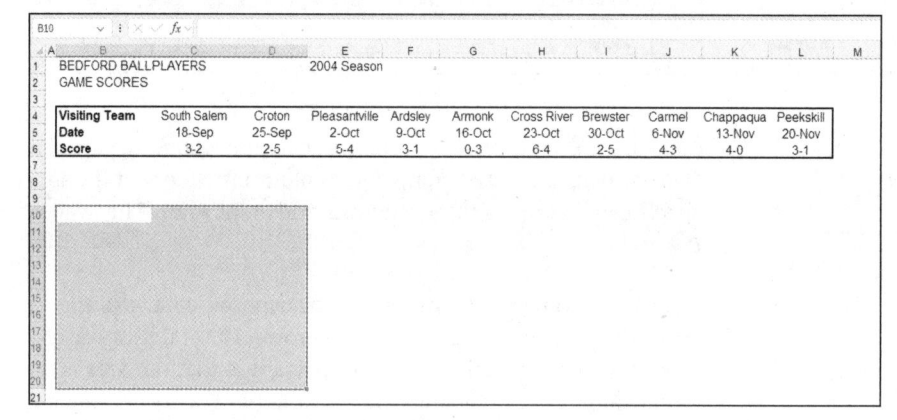

   FIGURE 3-12: Preparing an area to receive transposed data.

3. **Type =TRANSPOSE(to start the function.**

   Because the receiving area is already selected, the entry goes into the first cell of the area.

4. **Click the first cell in the original data, drag the pointer over the entire original data area while keeping the mouse button down, and release the mouse button when the area is selected.**

   The function now shows the range of the original area. Figure 3-13 shows how the entry should appear at this step.

BOOK 2 Working with Formulas and Functions

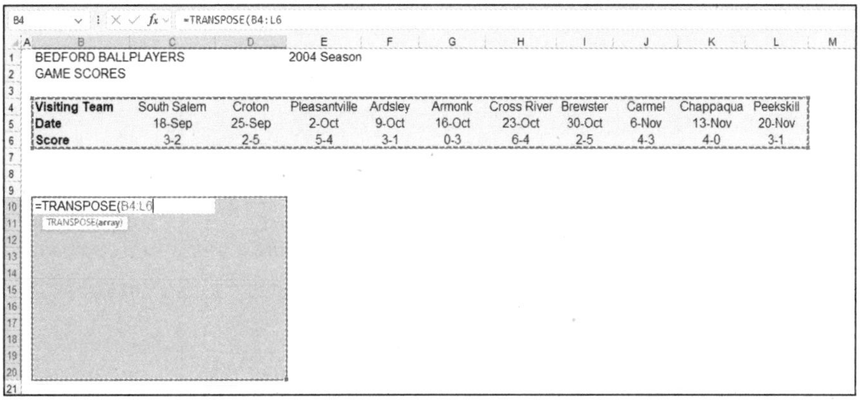

FIGURE 3-13: Completing the function.

5. Type).
6. **Press Ctrl+Shift+Enter to end the function.**

Note that the transposed data doesn't necessarily take on the formatting of the original area. You may need to format the area. Figure 3-14 shows the result of using TRANSPOSE and then formatting the transposed data.

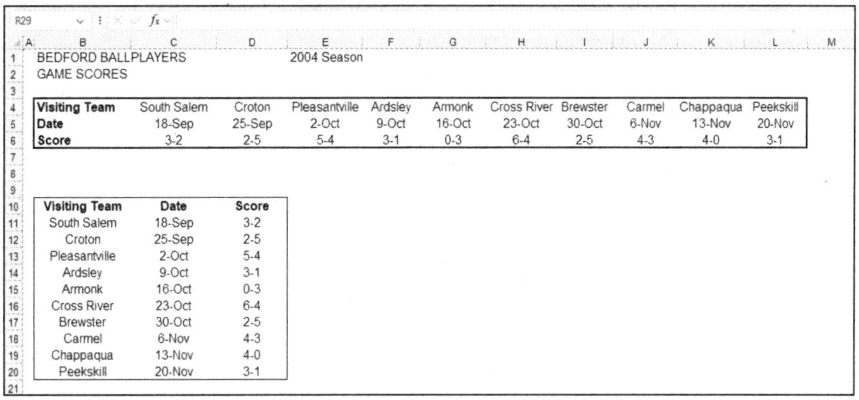

FIGURE 3-14: Transposed data after formatting.

Wait! Isn't this a waste of time? Excel can easily transpose data when you use the Paste Special dialog box. Simply copying a range of data and using this dialog box to paste the data gives the same result as the TRANSPOSE function. Or does it?

Figure 3-15 shows the Paste Special dialog box with the Transpose check box selected. Selecting this check box transposes the data. You don't even have to select the correct number of rows and columns where the transposed data will land. It just appears transposed, with the active cell as the upper-left corner of the area.

CHAPTER 3 **Building Array Formulas and Functions** 189

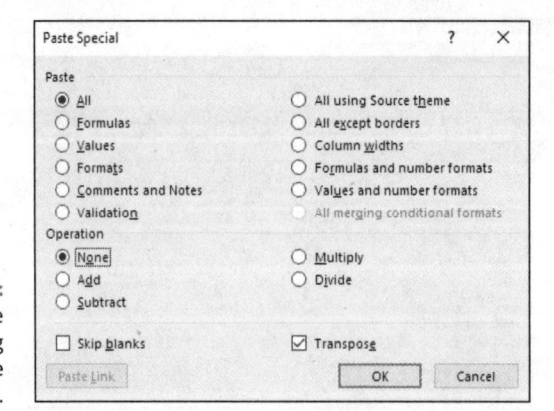

FIGURE 3-15:
Using the Paste Special dialog box to transpose data.

However, when data is transposed with the Paste Special dialog box, the actual data is *copied* to the new area. By contrast, the TRANSPOSE function pastes a formula that references the original data — and that's the key point. When data is changed in the original area, the change is reflected in the new, transposed area if the TRANSPOSE function was used.

REMEMBER

You can transpose data in two ways. The area filled with the TRANSPOSE function references the original data and will update as original data is changed. Using the Paste Special dialog box to transpose data creates values that don't update when the original data changes.

190 BOOK 2 **Working with Formulas and Functions**

> **IN THIS CHAPTER**
>
> » Preventing errors with Excel
>
> » Following the flow of cell and range references to and from formulas
>
> » Keeping an eye on changes with the Watch Window
>
> » Stepping through a calculation to find the error
>
> » Displaying user-friendly error messages

Chapter **4**

Fixing Errors in Formulas

Excel would be nothing if it didn't enable you to create formulas. Creating formulas is, after all, the real purpose of a worksheet: to allow you to build a solution that pertains to your specific needs. Without formulas, Excel would be no more than a place to store information. Boring!

Excel allows formulas to have up to 8,192 characters. This means you can create some monster formulas! Formulas can reference cells that have formulas that reference other cells that have formulas that reference . . . well, you get the idea!

Ah, but this comes at a price: How can you track down errors in long formulas? How can you avoid them in the first place? In this chapter, we explain how Excel steers you away from entering problematic formulas and discuss how to correct completed formulas that aren't working the way you intended.

Catching Errors as You Enter Them

Excel is keeping an eye on you when you enter formulas. But don't be worried! This is a good thing. You aren't being graded. Excel is helping you, not testing you.

All formulas start with an equal sign. When you complete an entry by pressing Enter or Tab (or clicking another cell), Excel scans the entry. If the entry did, indeed, start with an equal sign, Excel immediately looks for three major problems, which we cover in the following sections.

Getting parentheses to match

In a mathematical formula, each open parenthesis must have a matching closed parenthesis. Excel checks your formulas to make sure they comply. Figure 4-1 shows a simple business calculation that requires parentheses to make sense. The result is based on multiplying units by price per unit, adding an additional purchase amount to that, applying a discount, and finally applying tax.

In math terms, here is how the formula works:

$$(\text{units sold} \times \text{price per unit} + \text{additional purchases}) \times \text{discount} \times (1 + \text{tax rate})$$

The placement of the parentheses is critical to making the formula work. Excel won't sense a problem if any particular parenthesis is in the wrong place as long as there are matching numbers of open and closed parentheses. For example, using the cells and values from Figure 4-1, Table 4-1 shows some possibilities of valid formulas that return incorrect answers.

FIGURE 4-1: Using parentheses in a formula.

WARNING Correct parentheses placement and a firm understanding of mathematical-operator precedence are critical to calculating correct answers. Brush up on these basic math concepts if you aren't sure how to construct your formulas.

TABLE 4-1　Valid Formulas That Return Incorrect Answers

Formula	Result
=B3*(B4+B6)*B8*(1+B9)	5626.84
=B3*B4+(B6*B8)*(1+B9)	549.13
=(B3*B4+B6*B8)*(1+B9)	589.96
=(B3*B4+B6)*(B8*1+B9)	299.15

TIP There is a great mnemonic for orders of operation: *Please excuse my dear Aunt Sally*. It's meant to help you remember parentheses, exponents, multiplication, division, addition, and subtraction (PEMDAS).

What if, during entry, you leave out a parenthesis? When you try to complete the entry, Excel pops up a warning and a suggestion. In this example, we intentionally left out the first closed parenthesis. Here is the *incorrect* formula: =(B3*B4+B6*B8*(1+B9).

Figure 4-2 shows how Excel catches the error and offers a solution.

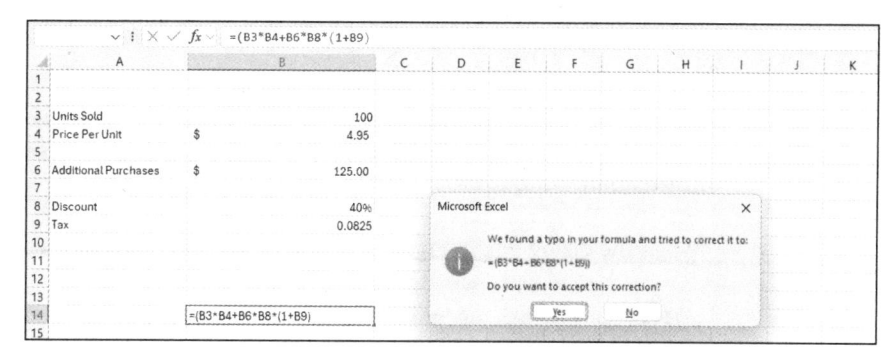

FIGURE 4-2: Fixing mismatched parentheses.

Don't be hasty! The correction proposed by Excel corrects the mismatched parentheses but does not create the correct formula. Look closely at the following example of a proposed correction by Excel: =(B3*B4+B6*B8*(1+B9)).

What you really need is this: =(B3*B4+B6)*B8*(1+B9).

Excel simply added the missing parenthesis to the end of the formula. A good idea, but not good enough. If the proposed correction were accepted, a result of 549.13 would be returned in this example. The correct answer is 268.46. In this case, you should reject the proposal and fix the formula yourself.

CHAPTER 4 **Fixing Errors in Formulas** 193

WARNING: Never assume that Excel's proposed formula corrections are right for you. Carefully review the proposed correction, and accept or reject it accordingly.

Avoiding circular references

A *circular reference* occurs when a cell refers to itself, whether directly or indirectly. For example, if you enter =100+A2 in cell A2, a direct circular reference has been created. An *indirect circular reference* is when the formula in a given cell refers to one or more other cells that in return refer to the original cell. For example, a formula in A1 refers to A2, A2 refers to A3, and A3 refers back to A1.

Figure 4-3 shows a worksheet that has a direct circular reference. Cell D10 is meant to sum the values above it but mistakenly includes itself in the sum: =SUM(D4:D10). Excel reports the problem in the message box shown in Figure 4-3.

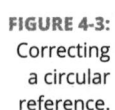

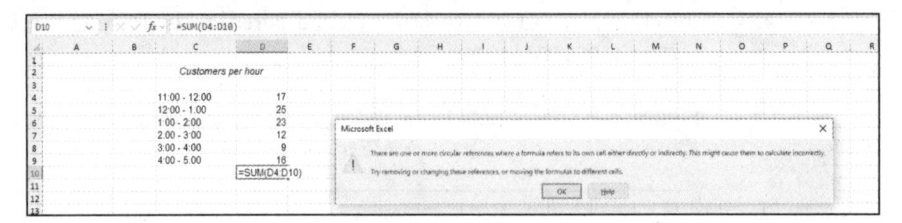

FIGURE 4-3: Correcting a circular reference.

TIP: If Automatic Calculation is turned off, the circular reference goes unnoticed until you do a manual recalculation (by pressing F9) or change the setting to Automatic Calculation.

When the dialog box in Figure 4-3 opens, you have two choices:

» Clicking OK lets the formula entry complete, but the result won't be correct. In fact, you may just end up with a zero.

» Clicking Help takes you to Excel Help's Circular Reference topic.

Figure 4-4 shows the Formulas tab of the Excel Options dialog box. This is where you set calculation — automatic or manual. Note that the Enable Iterative Calculation check box is here as well. When this option is checked, circular references are allowed. How they calculate values in this case is dependent on the Maximum Iterations and Maximum Change settings.

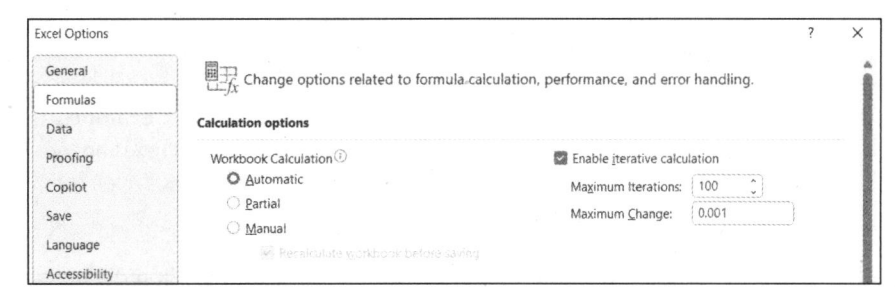

FIGURE 4-4: Setting calculation and iteration options.

Checking and applying iterations on the Calculation tab of the Excel Options dialog box enables you to use circular references in your formulas. These references are useful for certain advanced calculations that are beyond the scope of this mini-book (see Excel Help for more information).

Excel has an approach to hunting down circular references. The Formulas tab of the ribbon has a group named Formula Auditing. In this group is an Error Checking drop-down list that shows any circular references (see Figure 4-5).

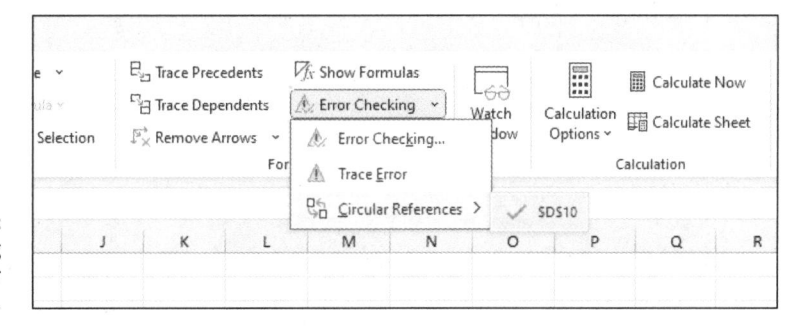

FIGURE 4-5: Hunting down circular references.

The drop-down list lists circular references, and clicking one takes you to the listed cell with the circular reference. This enables you to get to circular references easily instead of having to review all your formulas. Hey, that's a time-saver!

You may notice that the circular reference error message appears only the first time you enter a circular reference formula. Excel's behavior after that is to place a zero in the cell with the problematic formula. However, Excel still notifies you of the issue — it's in the Status Bar and in the Error Checking drop-down list, as shown in Figure 4-5.

CHAPTER 4 **Fixing Errors in Formulas** 195

Mending broken links

Formulas can reference external workbooks. For example, a formula could be written like this: `='C:\Inventory\[Inventory.xlsx]Engine Parts'!$D$8`. The formula uses the value in the external workbook `Inventory.xlsx`. But what if Excel can't find the workbook?

When a formula references an unfound workbook, a dialog box opens to let you navigate to an appropriate workbook elsewhere. Figure 4-6 shows that the dialog box has opened after the `Inventory.xlsx` file is referenced. This file couldn't be found, and Excel is prompting you to find it.

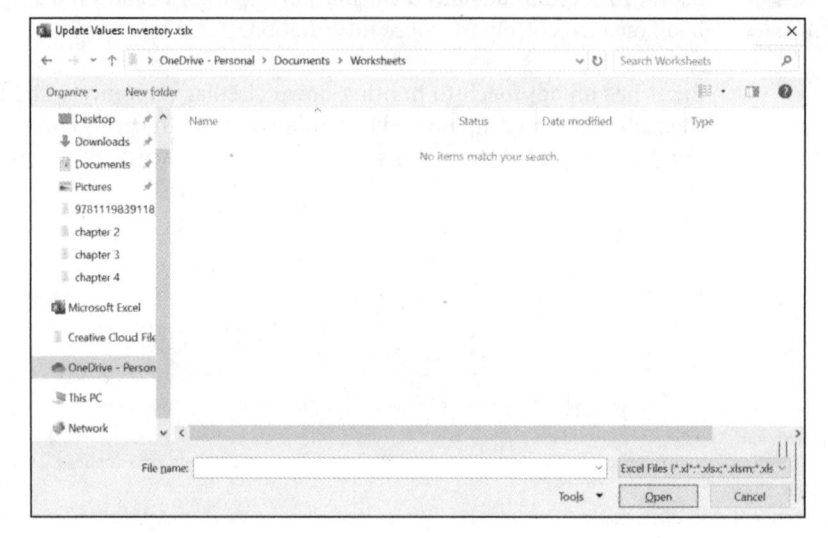

FIGURE 4-6: Browsing for an unfound external workbook.

The Workbook Links pane gives you other options for handling broken links. Click the Data tab of the ribbon, and click Workbook Links in the Queries & Connections group. The Workbook Links pane opens on the right, as shown in Figure 4-7.

The options in the Workbook Links pane work like this:

» **Refresh All:** When external workbooks are where they should be, clicking Refresh All gets the values from the external workbooks, and the cells with those formulas are recalculated. When there are broken links, a message appears alerting you that the external file can't be found.

» **Break All:** Clicking Break All breaks all existing external links, including ones that are working. Use with caution.

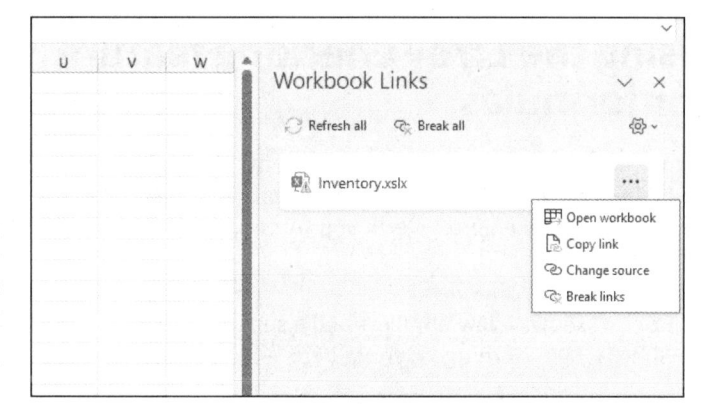

FIGURE 4-7:
Using the Workbook Links pane to correct external reference problems.

The following options work with a single external reference. There are one or more workbooks listed in the pane. Each workbook has an ellipsis button (three dots). Clicking the ellipsis button shows the following options (refer to Figure 4-7):

- **Open Workbook:** In the case of broken links, this option does nothing because the external workbook can't be found. An error message confirms this.

- **Copy Link:** This option simply copies the link to the unfound external workbook. This helps to review the link and make changes as needed.

- **Change Source:** This option displays the Change Source dialog box, which lets you select an external workbook to use. Selecting a workbook in this dialog box actually alters the formula that references the external workbook. This is the best option if you want to permanently fix a broken link.

- **Break Links:** This option converts formulas that contain external links to the calculated values. In other words, the cells that contain formulas with external links are replaced with values; the formulas are removed. Make sure this is what you want to do. You can't undo this action, and it can be a serious mistake if you do it unintentionally. Excel displays a warning dialog box, as shown in Figure 4-8, if you choose this option.

FIGURE 4-8:
Confirming that you mean to break links.

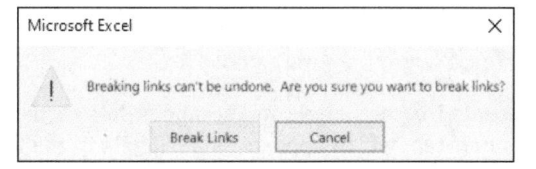

CHAPTER 4 Fixing Errors in Formulas   197

Using the Error Checking feature for formulas

Some errors are immediately apparent, such as mismatched parentheses (explained earlier). Other types of entries aren't blatant errors, but they *resemble* errors. In this case, Excel alerts you to the possible problem and lets you choose how to handle it.

Figure 4-9 shows a few numbers and a sum at the bottom. The formula in cell B10 is =SUM(B4:B9). Nothing is wrong here — no possible error yet.

	A	B
1	Employee	Sales
2		
3		
4	Cindy	2200
5	Juan	2300
6	Tara	2450
7	Bill	2400
8	Gary	2300
9	Sally	2500
10	TOTAL SALES	14150
11		

FIGURE 4-9: Calculating a sum with no possible error.

Note that in Figure 4-9, the headings row is not adjacent to the rows of information. Rows 2 and 3 are between the headings and the data. This is not unusual — it just leads to a clean-looking report.

However, watch what happens if you accidentally enter a value in the area between the headings and the data. The formula in cell B10 calculates values starting in row 4. When a value is entered in cell B3, Excel alerts you that there may be an error. You can see this in Figure 4-10. A small triangle is now visible in the upper-left corner of cell B10 — the cell with the formula.

Clicking cell B10 and moving the pointer over the triangle causes a small symbol with an exclamation point to appear. Clicking the symbol displays a list of choices, as shown in Figure 4-11.

TECHNICAL STUFF

An error is represented by a triangle in the upper-left corner of a cell. This is different from a smart tag, which appears as a triangle in the lower-right corner of a cell. Smart tags lead to helpful options based on the contents of the cell. See Excel Help for more information on smart tags.

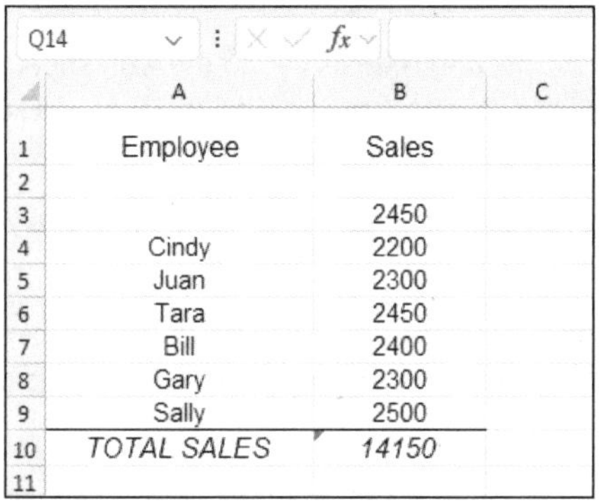

FIGURE 4-10:
Excel detects a possible error.

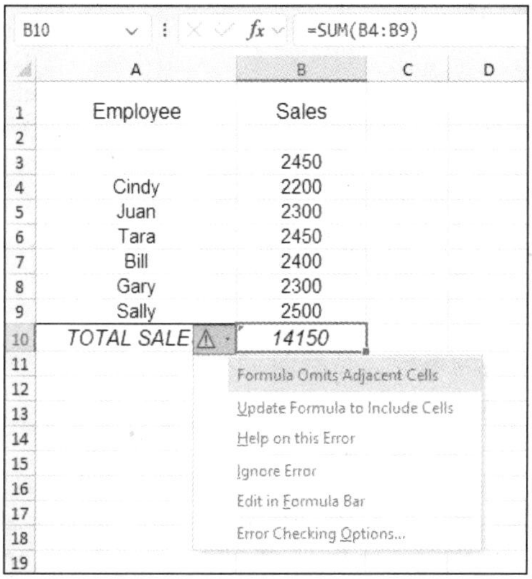

FIGURE 4-11:
Deciding what to do with the possible error.

The first item in the list is just a statement of the problem. In this example, the statement is Formula Omits Adjacent Cells. Sure enough, it does just that! But is it an error? Did you mean to enter the extra value in cell B3? Perhaps it has some other meaning or use.

The other items in the list give you options:

» **Update Formula to Include Cells:** Automatically changes the formula to include the extra cell in this example. So, the formula in cell B10 changes from =SUM(B4:B9) to =SUM(B3:B9). Of course, the calculated sum changes as well.

» **Help on This Error:** Steers you to Excel's Help system.

CHAPTER 4 Fixing Errors in Formulas   199

» **Ignore Error:** Closes the list and returns you to the worksheet. The triangle is removed from the cell in question. You've told Excel that you know what you're doing, and you want Excel to butt out. Good job!

» **Edit in Formula Bar:** Places the cursor in the Formula Bar so you can easily edit the formula.

» **Error Checking Options:** Displays the Formulas tab of the Excel Options dialog box. On this tab, you set options for how Excel handles errors.

Auditing Formulas

With Excel, you can create some fairly complex solutions. A cell can contain a formula that uses values from multitudes of other cells and ranges. Working through long, complex formulas to track down problems can be quite tedious. The good news is that Excel has a way to help!

Formulas may contain precedents and may serve as dependents to other formulas:

» *Precedents* are cells or ranges that affect the active cell's value.

» *Dependents* are cells or ranges affected by the active cell.

It's all relative! A cell often serves as both a precedent and a dependent. Figure 4-12 shows a simple worksheet with some values and some calculations. Cell B9 contains the formula =SUM(B3:B8). Cell F9 contains the formula =SUM(F3:F8). Cell B18 contains the formula =B9-F9.

» Cells B3:B8 are precedents of B9, but at the same time, cell B9 is dependent on all the cells in B3:B8.

» Cells F3:F8 are precedents of F9, but at the same time, cell F9 is dependent on all the cells in F3:F8.

» Cells B9 and F9 are precedents of B18, but at the same time, cell B18 is dependent on cells B9 and F9.

To help you follow and fix formulas, Excel provides formula auditing tools. The Formula Auditing group on the Formulas tab of the ribbon has three buttons that let you use formula auditing. Figure 4-13 shows the worksheet from Figure 4-12 with visible precedent and dependent lines. The methods for displaying these lines are shown on the ribbon.

FIGURE 4-12: Understanding precedents and dependents.

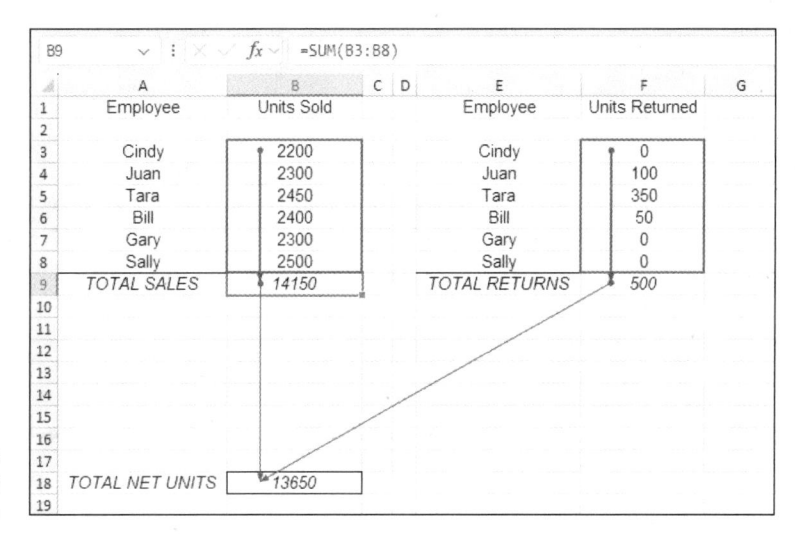

FIGURE 4-13: Tracing formulas.

Precedent and dependent lines are always inserted from or to the active cell. From the active cell:

>> To see what other cells are referenced in the active cell's formula, click the Trace Precedents button.

>> To see which other cells contain a reference to the active cell, click the Trace Dependents button.

CHAPTER 4 Fixing Errors in Formulas   201

The Remove Arrows drop-down list has three choices:

- Remove Arrows
- Remove Precedent Arrows
- Remove Dependent Arrows

In Figure 4-13, cells B9 and F9 have arrows that originate in the cells above. This shows the flow of precedents into the given cells. The arrow head rests in the cell that has the formula that contains the references of the precedents.

On the other hand, cells B9 and F9 themselves then have lines coming from them and ending as arrow heads in cell B18. Therefore, B9 and F9 serve as precedents to cell B18. Put another way, cell B18 is dependent on cells B9 and F9.

TIP

Double-clicking a tracer arrow activates the cell on one end of the line. Double-clicking again activates the cell on the other end.

Tracing precedents and dependents can lead to some interesting conclusions about a worksheet. Complex formulas can be difficult to follow, but by displaying tracer arrows, you can better see what's going on. Figure 4-14 shows a piece of a worksheet used in a financial solution. The active cell, H2, has a complex formula in it, as you can see by looking at the Formula Bar. The tracer arrows show that numerous precedents are feeding the formula in the active cell.

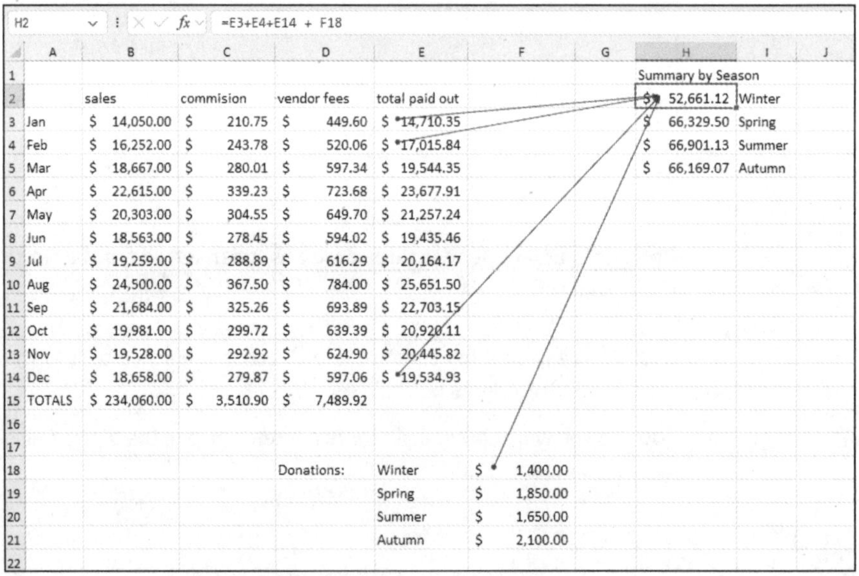

H2 fx =E3+E4+E14 + F18

	A	B	C	D	E	F	G	H	I	J
1								Summary by Season		
2		sales	commision	vendor fees	total paid out			$ 52,661.12	Winter	
3	Jan	$ 14,050.00	$ 210.75	$ 449.60	$ 14,710.35			$ 66,329.50	Spring	
4	Feb	$ 16,252.00	$ 243.78	$ 520.06	$ 17,015.84			$ 66,901.13	Summer	
5	Mar	$ 18,667.00	$ 280.01	$ 597.34	$ 19,544.35			$ 66,169.07	Autumn	
6	Apr	$ 22,615.00	$ 339.23	$ 723.68	$ 23,677.91					
7	May	$ 20,303.00	$ 304.55	$ 649.70	$ 21,257.24					
8	Jun	$ 18,563.00	$ 278.45	$ 594.02	$ 19,435.46					
9	Jul	$ 19,259.00	$ 288.89	$ 616.29	$ 20,164.17					
10	Aug	$ 24,500.00	$ 367.50	$ 784.00	$ 25,651.50					
11	Sep	$ 21,684.00	$ 325.26	$ 693.89	$ 22,703.15					
12	Oct	$ 19,981.00	$ 299.72	$ 639.39	$ 20,920.11					
13	Nov	$ 19,528.00	$ 292.92	$ 624.90	$ 20,445.82					
14	Dec	$ 18,658.00	$ 279.87	$ 597.06	$ 19,534.93					
15	TOTALS	$ 234,060.00	$ 3,510.90	$ 7,489.92						
16										
17										
18				Donations:	Winter	$ 1,400.00				
19					Spring	$ 1,850.00				
20					Summer	$ 1,650.00				
21					Autumn	$ 2,100.00				
22										

FIGURE 4-14: Examining the components of a complex formula.

When a cell references a cell on a different worksheet, an icon that looks like a worksheet appears at the end of the precedent line. This serves as a visual clue that the formula is composed of values from more than the current worksheet.

The tracer arrows make it easy to see the values that are feeding the formula and, therefore, make it easier to look for the source of a problem. For example, cell H2 may be returning a negative number as an answer. The formula adds certain values. Positive numbers added with a negative number may return a negative number as the result of the calculation. Therefore, just looking for a negative number among the values at the end of the tracer arrows may help identify the problem, perhaps within just a few seconds!

Watching the Watch Window

The Watch Window lets you watch the calculated results of a formula but without the limitation of having the cell be in the viewing area of Excel. This feature is helpful when you're working on correcting formulas that use precedents that are scattered about the worksheet or workbook.

First, to set up a watch, follow these steps:

1. **Click the Watch Window button on the Formulas tab of the ribbon.**
2. **In the Watch Window, click the Add Watch button.**

   The Add Watch dialog box opens.

3. **Use the RefEdit control (the square button to the right of the entry box) to specify the cell(s), or type in the cell address or range.**
4. **Click the Add button in the Add Watch dialog box to set up the watch.**

Figure 4-15 shows the Watch Window with a watch already in place. Cell C6 of the Costs worksheet is being watched. The formula uses precedents from both the Orders worksheet and the Shipping worksheet. The Watch Window sits on top of the workbook and stays visible regardless of which worksheet is active. This means, for example, that you could try different values on the Orders worksheet and see the result in the calculation in Costs!C6, but without having to bounce around the worksheets to see how new values alter the calculated result.

FIGURE 4-15: Using the Watch Window to keep an eye on a formula's result.

Book	Sheet	Name	Cell	Value	Formula
Chapter4...	Costs		C6	115	=IF(MAX(Orders!B2:B29)>200,MAX(Orders!B2:B29)*Shipping!C22,Shipping!C24)

To delete a watch, perform these steps:

1. **Select a watch from the list of watches in the Watch Window.**
2. **Click the Delete Watch button.**

Evaluating and Checking Errors

The Evaluate Formula dialog box walks you through the sequential steps used in calculating a result from a formula. These steps are useful for tracking down errors in formulas that are long or have precedents. For example, the formula =IF(MAX(Orders!B2:B29)>200,MAX(Orders!B2:B29)*Shipping!C22,Shipping!C24) refers to different worksheets. Using the Evaluate Formula dialog box makes it easy to see how Excel works out this formula. The step-by-step approach lets you see what is done at each step.

Figure 4-16 shows the Evaluate Formula dialog box at the start of evaluating the formula. To display the Evaluate Formula dialog box, simply click the Evaluate Formula button in the Formula Auditing group of the Formulas tab of the ribbon. With each successive click of the Evaluate button, the Evaluation box displays the interim results. The Step In and Step Out buttons are enabled during the steps that work on the precedents.

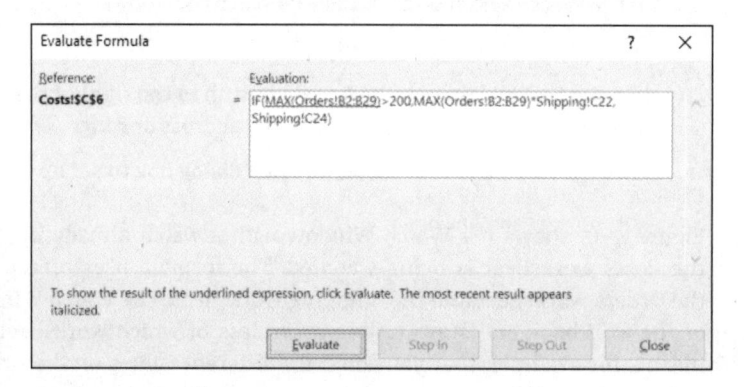

FIGURE 4-16: Evaluating a formula.

The Evaluate Formula dialog box is great for really seeing how each little step feeds into the final calculated result. Using this dialog box lets you pinpoint exactly where a complex formula has gone sour.

A similar error-hunting tool is the Error Checking dialog box, shown in Figure 4-17. (Excel really wants to help you!)

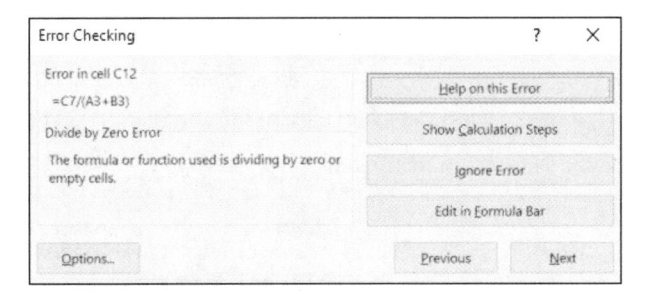

FIGURE 4-17:
Checking the cause of an error.

> **TIP** You can get to the Error Checking dialog box by choosing Error Checking from the Error Checking drop-down list on the Formulas tab of the ribbon.

The dialog box has a handful of buttons that let you analyze the error and make decisions about it:

- **Help on This Error** starts the Excel Help system.
- **Show Calculation Steps** opens the Evaluate Formula dialog box.
- **Ignore Error** ensures that Excel no longer cares about the error. The cell may still display an error symbol, but Excel doesn't give a hoot, and you probably won't either, because you clicked the button.
- **Edit in Formula Bar** places the cursor in the Formula Bar, making it easy for you to edit the formula.
- **Options** opens the Excel Options dialog box.
- **Previous and Next** cycle through the multiple errors on the worksheet, assuming that it contains more than one error.

> **TIP** The Error Checking drop-down list hosts the Trace Error command. Only precedents are pointed out by the tracer lines. This makes it easy to see the cells that feed into a cell that has an error.

Making an Error Behave the Way You Want

Excel has a neat function: IFERROR. Don't confuse it with ISERROR, which is similar but not as slick. Figure 4-18 shows how IFERROR one-ups ISERROR. In the figure, F7 has the dreaded Divide by Zero error.

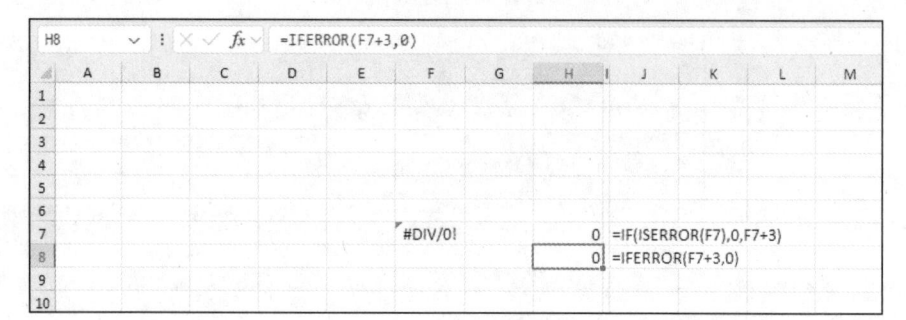

FIGURE 4-18: Two ways to prevent an error from being seen.

Cell H7 has the tried-and-true way to make the error *not* look like an error. Using the ISERROR function nested inside an IF function takes care of the error's appearance, as shown in cell H7 (which refers to cell F7). Cell H8 achieves the same result with the IFERROR function. Cells J7 and J8, respectively, show the formulas that are in cells H7 and H8.

- In cell H7 is =IF(ISERROR(F7),0,F7+3).
- In cell H8 is =IFERROR(F7+3,0).

The main distinction is that IFERROR, as a single function, does what used to take two functions. With IFERROR, the first argument is being tested. If the test makes sense, Excel goes with it. Otherwise, Excel uses the second argument.

TIP IFERROR can return a message. For example, consider this: =IFERROR(F7+3,"Somebody Goofed!").

3
Going Farther with Functions

Contents at a Glance

CHAPTER 1: Calculating Loans, Interest, and Depreciation 209
    Understanding How Excel Handles Money 210
    Figuring Loan Calculations 213
    Looking into the Future 226
    Depreciating the Finer Things in Life 228
    Measuring Your Internals 237

CHAPTER 2: Performing Functional Math 241
    Adding It All Together with the SUM Function 242
    Rounding Out Your Knowledge 246
    Leaving All Decimals Behind with INT 253
    Leaving Some Decimals Behind with TRUNC 254
    Looking for a Sign 255
    Ignoring Signs 256
    Using PI to Calculate Circumference and Diameter 257
    Generating and Using Random Numbers 258
    Creating a Sequence 261
    Raising Numbers to New Heights 261
    Multiplying Multiple Numbers 263
    Summing Things Up 264

CHAPTER 3: Working with Date and Time Functions 271
    Understanding How Excel Handles Dates 272
    Formatting Dates 273
    Making a Date with DATE 274
    Breaking a Date with DAY, MONTH, and YEAR 275
    Converting a Date from Text 278
    Finding Out What TODAY Is 280
    Determining the Day of the Week 281
    Working with Workdays 283
    Understanding How Excel Handles Time 285
    Formatting Time 286
    Deconstructing Time with HOUR, MINUTE, and SECOND 287
    Finding the Time NOW 290

CHAPTER 4: Manipulating Text with Functions 291
    Breaking Apart Text 291
    Putting Text Together 296
    Changing Text 299
    Comparing, Finding, and Measuring Text 310

IN THIS CHAPTER

» Formatting monetary values

» Working with loan calculations

» Determining what an investment is worth

» Using different depreciation methods

» Evaluating business opportunities

Chapter 1
Calculating Loans, Interest, and Depreciation

Taking out a car loan, a mortgage, or another type of loan involves planning how you want to manage the loan payments. In the simplest terms, all you may need to know is the amount of your monthly payment. But knowing the components of a loan and being able to compare one loan with another can help you manage your financial resources in your own best interest.

In this chapter, we show you how to use the financial functions in Excel to crunch the numbers for your loans. You supply these functions the relevant numbers: the principal amount, the interest rate, the *period* (how often you make a payment), and the length of the loan. Then the functions return an answer, such as your payment amount.

What if you have some extra money? You can put it in the bank, you can pay off a debt, or you can purchase something. Excel helps you figure out the best course of action by using the IRR function. The IRR function lets you boil down each option to a single value that you can then use to compare opportunities and select the best one.

For the business set, Excel has a number of functions to help create depreciation schedules. Look no further than the SLN, SYD, DB, and DDB functions for help in this area. Brush up on these, and you can talk shop with your accountant!

Understanding How Excel Handles Money

Excel is a lot more than a simple adding machine. It has great tools for working with money values and a number of ways of presenting the amounts. For example, Excel makes it easy for you to make sure that your financial amounts are displayed with two decimal places. You can even work with different currencies from around the world.

Going with the cash flow

Excel works with money on a cash-flow basis. In other words, money amounts are treated either as a cash flow *in* (money you receive) or a *cash flow out* (money you pay out). Yes, there always seem to be too many of the latter and not enough of the former — but hey, you can't blame Excel for that!

Excel represents cash flows *in* as positive numbers and cash flows *out* as negative numbers. For example, when you calculate the payments on a loan, the situation is as follows:

» The amount of the loan is entered as a positive value, because this is money you'll receive from the bank or whoever is giving you the loan.

» The monthly payment that Excel calculates is a negative value, because this is money that you'll be paying out.

Formatting for currency

One of Excel's shining strengths is accepting, manipulating, and reporting on monetary data. As such, Excel provides robust formatting for numeric data, including the ability to control the placement of commas and decimals, and even how to format negative values.

People are used to seeing money amounts formatted with a currency symbol and a certain number of decimal places. In the United States and Canada, that's the dollar sign and two decimal places. Let's face it — $199.95 looks like money, but

199.950 does not. Excel makes formatting cells to display money amounts as easy as clicking a button. To format amounts as dollars, follow these steps:

1. **Select the cell(s) you want to format.**
2. **Click the Dollar ($) button in the Number group on the Home tab of the ribbon.**

This technique assigns Excel's default Accounting format to the selected cells. Here's the default currency format in the United States:

- A dollar sign, aligned to the left of the cell
- Two decimal places
- Negative numbers enclosed in parentheses

The default format depends on your locale, which is a setting of the operating system. If you're in Italy, for example, the locale should be set so that the default currency format is the euro (€).

But suppose you don't want the default currency formatting. Perhaps you're in the United States working on a spreadsheet for the London office. You can specify the currency symbol, the number of decimal places, and how negative values are shown by following these steps:

1. **Select the cell(s) you want to format.**
2. **Right-click the cell(s) and choose Format Cells from the context menu.**
3. **In the Format Cells dialog box, select the Number tab, shown in Figure 1-1.**
4. **In the Category list, click Currency.**
5. **Use the Decimal Places spinner control to select the desired number of decimal places.**
6. **From the Symbol drop-down list, select the desired currency symbol.**
7. **In the Negative Numbers list, select the desired format for negative numbers.**
8. **Click OK.**

> **TIP** The Currency and Accounting formats are similar except for a couple of key points. Currency provides choices for displaying negative values; Accounting uses one fixed display with parentheses. Currency places the currency symbol next to the number; Accounting places the currency symbol at the left of the cell.

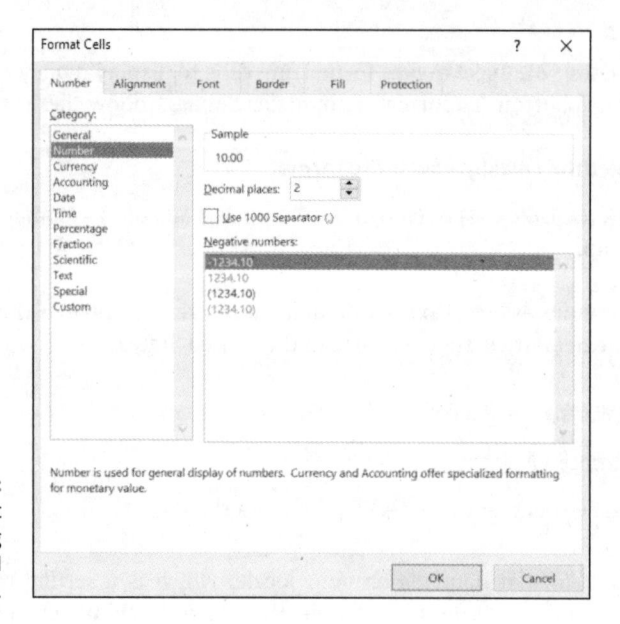

FIGURE 1-1:
Using the Format Cells dialog box to control numeric display.

Choosing separators

When numbers are formatted as currency, two separator symbols are typically used — one separates thousands and the other separates the decimal part of the value. In the United States, commas are used for thousands and the period is used for the decimal, as follows:

$12,345.67

Other countries have different ways of doing this. In many European countries, for example, the period is used to separate thousands, and the comma is used for the decimal. In addition, the currency symbol is often at the end of the number. An amount in euros, for example, may be formatted as follows:

12.345,67€

In almost all situations, the operating system's locale settings result in the automatic use of the proper separators. If you need to change the separators from the defaults, do so in the Regional and Language Options section of the Windows Control Panel. *Note:* These instructions are for computers running the Windows 10 operating system or later versions.

1. **In the Windows Search box on the taskbar, type** Control Panel **and then click Control Panel in the search results.**
2. **Click the Clock and Region link.**

212 BOOK 3 Going Farther with Functions

3. **Click the Region link.**

   The Region dialog box opens.

4. **Click the Additional Settings button.**

   The Customize Format dialog box opens.

5. **Select the Currency tab.**

6. **Choose the settings you want.**

7. **Click OK to close the Customize Format dialog box.**

8. **Click OK again to close the Region dialog box.**

TIP

You can change settings for numbers, currency, dates, and time in the Customize Format dialog box.

Figuring Loan Calculations

Loans are part of almost everyone's life. At the personal level, you may need to deal with car loans, education loans, and a mortgage. From a business perspective, companies from the smallest to the largest often use loans to fund new equipment, expansion, and so on. No matter what kind of loan you need, Excel has the tools that permit you to evaluate loans and calculate specific details.

Most loans have the following five factors:

- **Loan principal:** This is the amount you're borrowing. For example, if you're interested in a loan for $5,000, the loan principal is $5,000.

- **Interest rate:** This is the cost to borrow the principal. This is how lenders make money. The interest rate is a fee, so to speak, that a borrower pays to a lender. Usually, but not always, the interest rate is expressed as a percent per year.

- **Payment period:** Loans are usually paid back by paying a periodic amount. Most often, the period is monthly.

- **Duration of the loan:** This is the count of payment periods. For example, a loan may have 36 monthly payments.

- **Payment:** This is the amount you pay each payment period.

CHAPTER 1 Calculating Loans, Interest, and Depreciation 213

Each of these factors is related to all the others. If you borrow more, your monthly payments will be higher — that's no surprise. If you get a low interest rate, you may be able to pay off your loan in less time, which may be something to consider!

The functions used to calculate loan factors work with the same group of inputs, namely the five factors just listed. The functions typically accept three or four inputs as data and then calculate the desired value, kind of like the way algebra works.

Calculating the payment amount

The PMT function tells you the periodic payment amount for your loan. If you know the principal, interest rate, and number of payments for a loan, you can use the PMT function to calculate the payment amount. But first, a word about interest rates.

Most loan interest rates are expressed as an annual rate. However, Excel needs the interest rate per payment *period* to calculate properly. For example, if you're calculating for a loan with monthly payments, you need the monthly interest rate. You can easily get this number by dividing the annual interest rate by 12, the number of months in a year.

To calculate a loan payment, follow these steps:

1. **Enter the loan principal, annual interest rate, and number of payment periods in separate cells of the worksheet.**

    You can add labels to adjacent cells to identify the values, if desired.

2. **Position the cursor in the cell where you want the results to display.**

3. **Type =PMT(to begin the function entry.**

    A small pop-up menu shows the arguments used in the function.

4. **Click the cell where you entered the interest rate, or just type the cell address.**

5. **Type /12 to divide the annual interest rate to get the monthly interest rate.**

6. **Type a comma (,).**

7. **Click the cell where you entered the number of payments, or type the cell address.**

8. **Type a comma (,).**

9. **Click the cell where you entered the principal amount, or type the cell address.**

10. **Type) and press Enter.**

WARNING

Watch those percentages! Remember that a percent is really one one-hundredth, so 5 percent is the numerical value 0.05. You can format values to display as percentages in Excel, but you have to enter the proper value.

Figure 1-2 shows how we set up a worksheet with values and returned the periodic payment amount for a loan. The amount is expressed as a negative number because payments are cash flow out. For example, you may be considering taking out a loan from the bank for some house additions. Using real numbers, the loan may be structured like this:

» A loan amount of $15,000 (the principal)

» An annual interest rate of 5 percent

» A monthly payment period

» A payment period of 24 payments

FIGURE 1-2: The PMT function calculates the loan payment amount.

This summarizes four of the key parameters. The PMT function figures out the fifth: the periodic payment, which is the amount you have to shell out each month.

Although the PMT function returns the constant periodic payback amount for a loan, note that each payment actually consists of two portions. One portion goes toward reducing the principal, and the other portion is the interest payment. As if this weren't already confusing enough!

TECHNICAL STUFF

You may notice some new terms when using this function: Pv, Fv, and Nper. In financial terminology, *present value* (Pv) refers to the value of a transaction at the present moment. When you're dealing with a loan, for example, the present value is the amount you receive from the loan — in other words, the principal. The term

CHAPTER 1 **Calculating Loans, Interest, and Depreciation**   215 *future value* (Fv) refers to the value of a transaction at some point in the future, such as the amount you'll accumulate by saving $50 a month for five years. *Nper* stands for the number of payment periods in the loan.

Calculating interest payments

The IPMT function tells you the interest payment for a given period. In each payment period during a typical loan, the payment consists of a portion set to reduce the principal of the loan, with the other portion of the payment being the interest on the principal. The amount of interest varies payment by payment. In a typical loan, the portion of the payment that is interest is highest in the first period; that portion is reduced in each successive period.

The IPMT function takes four inputs: the principal, the interest rate, the number of payments for the loan, and the number of the payment you're interested in. For example, a loan may have 24 payments, and you're interested in how much interest is included in the 12th payment. For some types of loans, the interest is tax deductible, so this information may literally be worth something!

Here are the steps to use the IPMT function:

1. **Enter the following information in separate cells on the worksheet:**
   - Loan principal
   - Annual interest rate
   - Number of payment periods
   - Number of the actual period for which you want to calculate the interest

   You can use cells anywhere you want on the worksheet, but putting the data in a column is usually clearest. Add labels to adjacent cells to identify the values, if you want.

2. **Position the cursor in the cell where you want the results to appear.**

3. **Type** =IPMT(**to begin the function entry.**

4. **Click the cell where you entered the interest rate, or just type the cell address.**

5. **Type** /12.

   This divides the annual interest rate to get the monthly interest rate.

6. **Type a comma (,).**

7. Click the cell where you entered the number of the payment to analyze, or just type the cell address.

8. Type a comma (,).

9. Click the cell where you entered the number of payments, or just type the cell address.

10. Type a comma (,).

11. Click the cell where you entered the principal amount, or just type the cell address.

12. Type) and press Enter.

The IPMT function returns the interest portion of the amount of the specified payment. This amount is smaller than the full periodic payment amount. How much smaller depends on which sequential payment is being examined. The remainder of the payment — the part that is not interest — goes to reduce the principal.

You can use two optional arguments with IPMT:

>> **Future value:** This is the amount you want the loan to be worth at the end of its life. The default is 0, meaning the loan is fully paid off.

>> **Type:** This tells the function whether payments are applied at the end of the period or the beginning of the period. A value of 0 indicates the end of the period; a value of 1 indicates the beginning of the period. The default is 0.

These optional arguments, when used, become the fifth and sixth arguments, respectively.

Calculating payments toward principal

The PPMT function tells you the payment on principal for a given period. In each payment period during a typical loan, the payment consists of a portion that goes toward reducing the principal of the loan and another portion that is interest. With the PPMT function, you can find out the amount that reduces the principal.

The ratio of the interest portion to the payment on principal portion varies payment by payment. In a typical loan, the portion of the payment that is interest is highest in the first period, and it's reduced in each successive period. Turning that around, the last payment is almost all toward paying down the principal.

The PPMT function takes four inputs: the principal, the interest rate, the number of payments for the loan, and the number of the payment in question. For example, a loan may have 36 payments, and you're interested in how much principal is included in just the last payment. Here are the steps to use this function:

1. **Enter the loan principal, the annual interest rate, the number of payment periods, and the number of the actual period for which the interest is to be calculated in separate cells within the worksheet.**

   You can add labels to adjacent cells to identify the values, if you want.

2. **Position the cursor in the cell where you want the results to appear.**

3. **Type** =PPMT(**to begin the function entry.**

4. **Click the cell where you entered the interest rate, or just type the cell address.**

5. **Type** /12 **to divide the annual interest rate to get the monthly interest rate.**

6. **Type a comma (,).**

7. **Click the cell where you entered the number of the payment to analyze, or just type the cell address.**

8. **Type a comma (,).**

9. **Click the cell where you entered the number of payments, or just type the cell address.**

10. **Type a comma (,).**

11. **Click the cell where you entered the principal amount, or just type the cell address.**

12. **Type**) **and press Enter.**

The PPMT function returns the amount of the payment that reduces the principal. This amount is smaller than the full periodic payment amount. How much smaller depends on which sequential payment is being examined. The remainder of the payment is the interest charge.

TIP The PMT function tells how much each payment is. The IPMT function tells you the interest portion. The PPMT tells you the principal portion. For any given payment period, the amounts returned by IPMT and PPMT should equal the amount returned by PMT.

You can use two optional arguments with PPMT:

> **Future value:** This is the amount you want the loan to be worth at the end of its life. The default is 0.

> **Type:** This tells the function whether payments are applied at the end of the period or the beginning of the period. A value of 0 indicates the end of the period; a value of 1 indicates the beginning of the period. The default is 0.

These optional arguments, when used, become the fifth and sixth arguments, respectively.

Calculating the number of payments

The NPER function tells you how many payments are necessary to pay off a loan. This information is useful when you know how much you can afford to pay per month and you need to know how long it will take to pay off the loan. The inputs for this function are the principal, the interest rate, and the periodic payment amount.

Here's how to use the NPER function:

1. **Enter the following in separate cells on your worksheet:**
   - Loan principal
   - Annual interest rate
   - Periodic payment amount (the amount you can afford to pay)

   Enter the periodic payment amount as a negative number because payments are cash flow out. You can add labels to adjacent cells to identify the values, if you want.

2. **Position the cursor in the cell where you want the results to display.**

3. **Type** =NPER(**to begin the function entry.**

4. **Click the cell where you entered the interest rate, or just type the cell address.**

5. **Type** /12 **to divide the annual interest rate to get the monthly interest rate.**

6. **Type a comma (,).**

CHAPTER 1 Calculating Loans, Interest, and Depreciation   219

7. **Click the cell where you entered the periodic payment amount, or just type the cell address.**

8. **Type a comma (,).**

9. **Click the cell where you entered the principal amount, or just type the cell address.**

10. **Type) and press Enter.**

Figure 1-3 shows how we set up a worksheet with values and used the NPER function to find out how many payments are necessary to pay off a loan. In this example, we assume you can afford to pay $200 per month for a loan. The amount you need is $4,000, and you're able to get a 6 percent interest rate.

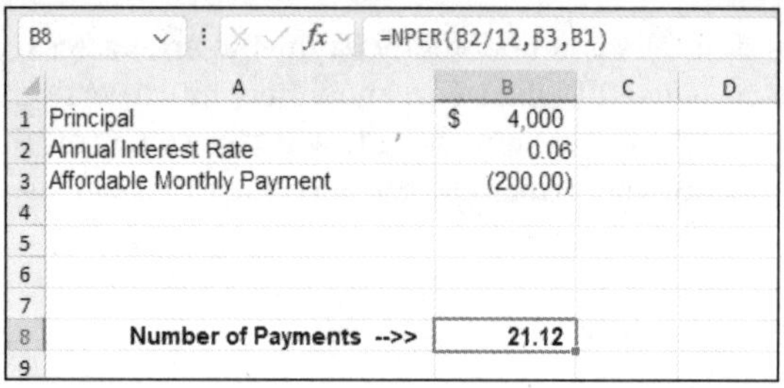

FIGURE 1-3: The NPER function calculates the number of payments for a loan.

With this set of assumptions, the NPER function returns a value of 21.12 months to pay off the loan. We don't think anyone will mind if you round that off to 21 months. Knowing you'll pay off the loan in less than two years may very well allow you to plan ahead for some other activity at that time. Did someone say "Vegas"?

You can use two optional arguments with NPER:

- » **Future value:** This is the amount you want the loan to be worth at the end of its life. The default is 0.

- » **Type:** This tells the function whether payments are applied at the end of the period or the beginning of the period. A value of 0 indicates the end of the period; a value of 1 indicates the beginning of the period. The default is 0.

These optional arguments, when used, become the fifth and sixth arguments, respectively.

Calculating the number of payments with PDURATION

This function is a twist on determining the number of payments. Instead of using a periodic payment amount in the calculation, PDURATION uses the *present value of the loan* (the borrowed amount) and the *future value of the loan* (what you will have paid in total when the loan is paid off). This calculation is useful if and when you know just three pieces of information:

>> The loan principal

>> The annual interest rate

>> The amount paid back (the combined principal and interest)

The result PDURATION gives you is the number of periods based on the previously listed factors.

Here's how to use the PDURATION function:

1. **Enter the following in separate cells of your worksheet:**
   - Loan principal
   - Annual interest rate
   - Expected total amount you will have paid back at the end of the loan

2. **Position the cursor in the cell where you want the results to display.**

3. **Type** =PDURATION(**to begin the function entry.**

4. **Click the cell where you entered the interest rate, or just type the cell address.**

5. **Type** /12 **to divide the annual interest rate to get the monthly interest rate.**

6. **Type a comma (,).**

7. **Click the cell where you entered the principal, or just type the cell address.**

8. **Type a comma (,).**

9. **Click the cell where you entered the payback amount, or just type the cell address.**

10. **Type) and press Enter.**

CHAPTER 1 Calculating Loans, Interest, and Depreciation   221

Figure 1-4 shows how we set up a worksheet with values and used the PDURATION function to find out how many payments are necessary to pay off a loan. In this example, we assume that the amount paid off is $4,400 (which includes principal and interest). The amount borrowed is $4,000, and the annual interest rate is 6 percent.

FIGURE 1-4: The PDURATION function calculates the number of payments for a loan.

The number of payments is 22.92, so we'll call that 23 payments — just under two years.

Calculating the interest rate

The RATE function tells you what the interest rate is on a loan. This function is great for comparing loan offers. Although a loan offer always includes an interest rate, you may want to use Excel to double-check to ensure that some other fees aren't included in the payments. Then you can compare different loan scenarios to see which one offers the true lowest interest rate. You don't want to pay more than necessary!

TIP Some lenders charge fees as well as an annual interest rate. When these fees are figured in, the *effective interest rate* will be higher than the stated interest rate. You can use the RATE function to determine the effective interest rate for a loan. If it's the same as the stated interest rate, you know no fees are being added.

The inputs for this function are the principal, the number of payments, and the fixed amount of the periodic payment. Here's how to use the RATE function:

1. **Enter the following in separate cells of the worksheet:**

    - Loan principal
    - Number of payment periods
    - Amount you will pay each month

    Enter the monthly payment amount as a negative number because it's cash flow out. You can add labels to adjacent cells to identify the values, if you want.

2. Position the cursor in the cell where you want the results to appear.
3. Type =RATE(to begin the function entry.
4. Click the cell where you entered the number of periods, or just type the cell address.
5. Type a comma (,).
6. Click the cell where you entered the monthly payment amount, or just type the cell address.
7. Type a comma (,).
8. Click the cell where you entered the principal amount, or just type the cell address.
9. Type) and press Enter.

The RATE function returns the interest rate *per period*. This number can be misleading. The periodic interest amount may be small enough that it's displayed as 0 percent if the formatting in the cell isn't set to display enough decimal points.

To find out the annual rate, simply take the number returned by RATE and multiply it by 12. To do this, follow these steps:

1. Position the cursor in the cell where you want the annual interest rate to appear.
2. Type =.
3. Click the cell where the RATE function returned the periodic interest rate.
4. Type *.
5. Type 12.
6. Press Enter.

As an example, assume a loan principal of $15,000 with a monthly payment of $650. The loan is to be paid off in 24 months. Figure 1-5 shows a worksheet with these figures. The periodic interest rate is calculated with the RATE function, and the annual rate is calculated by multiplying the periodic interest rate by 12.

CHAPTER 1 Calculating Loans, Interest, and Depreciation   223

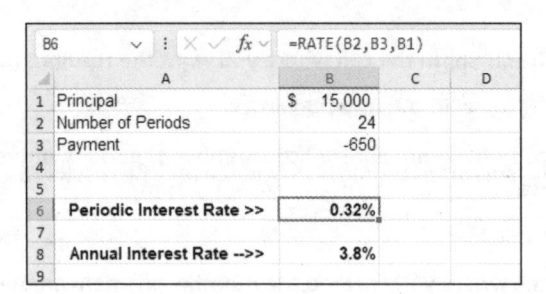

FIGURE 1-5: The RATE function calculates the periodic interest rate.

	A	B	C	D
1	Principal	$ 15,000		
2	Number of Periods	24		
3	Payment	-650		
4				
5				
6	Periodic Interest Rate >>	0.32%		
7				
8	Annual Interest Rate -->>	3.8%		
9				

Cell B6: `=RATE(B2,B3,B1)`

You can use three optional arguments with RATE:

» **Future value:** This is the amount you want the loan to be worth at the end of its life. The default is 0.

» **Type:** This tells the function whether payments are applied at the end of the period or the beginning of the period. A value of 0 indicates the end of the period. A value of 1 indicates the beginning of the period. The default is 0.

» **Guess:** This estimates what the interest rate should be. The function may need this value to determine a result. (See Excel's Help system for more information.) The default value is 0.1 (for 10 percent).

These optional arguments, when used, become the fourth, fifth, and sixth arguments, respectively.

Calculating the principal

The PV function tells you what the principal amount of a loan is when you know the other loan factors, such as the interest rate and the number of payment periods. You can use PV to determine how much you can borrow when you already know how much you can pay each month and how long you can make payments.

The inputs for this function are the interest rate, the number of payment periods, and the monthly payment amount. The interest rate used in the function is the periodic rate, not the annual rate.

Here's how to use the PV function:

1. **Enter the following in separate cells of your worksheet:**
    - Annual interest rate
    - Number of payment periods
    - Periodic payment amount

Enter the periodic payment amount as a negative number because payments are cash flow out. You can add labels to adjacent cells to identify the values, if desired.

2. **Position the cursor in the cell where you want the results to appear.**

3. **Type =PV(to begin the function entry.**

4. **Click the cell where you entered the interest rate, or just type the cell address.**

5. **Type /12 to divide the annual interest rate to get the monthly interest rate.**

6. **Type a comma (,).**

7. **Click the cell where you entered the number of payments, or just type the cell address.**

8. **Type a comma (,).**

9. **Click the cell where you entered the periodic payment amount, or just type the cell address.**

10. **Type) and press Enter.**

As an example, assume a monthly payment amount of $600. The annual interest rate is 5 percent. There are 24 monthly payments. Figure 1-6 shows a worksheet with these figures.

FIGURE 1-6: The PV function calculates the principal amount of a loan.

	A	B
1	Annual Interest Rate	0.05
2	Number of Payments	24
3	Payment	(600.00)
4		
5		
6	Principal Loan Amount --->>	$ 13,676

Formula bar: =PV(B1/12,B2,B3)

With these assumptions, the loan principal is $13,676. Altering any of the parameters causes PV to return a different amount of principal. For example, raising the interest rate to 7.5 percent tells you that you can borrow only $13,333. Although you may often think of how much you're borrowing, having interest in the interest is just as important!

You can use two optional arguments with PV:

- » **Future value:** This is the amount you want the loan to be worth at the end of its life. The default is 0.

- » **Type:** This value tells the function whether payments are applied at the end of the period or the beginning of the period. A value of 0 indicates the end of the period; a value of 1 indicates the beginning of the period. The default is 0.

These optional arguments, when used, become the fourth and fifth arguments, respectively.

Looking into the Future

The FV function tells you what an investment will be worth in the future. The function takes an initial amount of money and also takes into account additional periodic fixed payments. You also specify a rate of return — the interest rate — and the returned value tells you what the investment will be worth after a specified period of time.

For example, you start a savings account with a certain amount — say, $1,000. Every month you add $50 to the account. The bank pays an annual interest rate of 5 percent. At the end of two years, what is the value of the account?

This is the type of question the FV function answers. The function takes five arguments:

- » **Interest rate:** This argument is the annual interest rate. When entered in the function, it needs to be divided by the number of payments per year — presumably 12, if the payments are monthly.

- » **Number of payments:** This argument is the total number of payments in the investment. These payments are the ones beyond the initial investment; don't include the initial investment in this figure. If payments occur monthly and the investment is for three years, there are 36 payments.

- » **Payment amount:** This argument is the fixed amount contributed to the investment each payment period.

- » **Initial investment (also called present value, or PV):** This argument is the amount the investment starts with. A possible value is 0, which means no initial amount is used to start the investment. This is an optional argument. If left out, 0 is assumed.

- **How payments are applied:** The periodic payments may be applied at either the beginning of each period or the end of each period. This argument affects the result to a small but noticeable degree. Either a 0 or a 1 can be entered. A 0 tells the function that payments occur at the end of the period; a 1 tells the function that payments occur at the start of the period. This is an optional argument. If it's left out, 0 is assumed.

REMEMBER: When using the FV function, be sure to enter the initial investment amount and the periodic payment amount as negative numbers. Although you're investing these monies, you're essentially paying out (even if it's into your own account). Therefore, these are cash flows out.

Here's how to use the FV function:

1. **Type the following data in separate cells of the worksheet:**
   - Annual interest rate
   - Number of payment periods
   - Periodic payment amount
   - Initial investment amount

   You can add labels to adjacent cells to identify the values, if desired.

2. **Position the cursor in the cell where you want the results to appear.**

3. **Type =FV(to begin the function entry.**

4. **Click the cell where you typed the annual interest rate, or type the cell address.**

5. **Type /12 to divide the annual interest rate to get the monthly interest rate.**

6. **Type a comma (,).**

7. **Click the cell where you typed the total number of payments, or type the cell address.**

8. **Type a comma (,).**

9. **Click the cell where you typed the periodic payment amount, or type the cell address.**

10. **Type a comma (,).**

11. **Click the cell where you typed the initial investment amount, or type the cell address.**

12. **(Optional) Type a comma (,) and then type either 0 or 1 to identify whether payments are made at the beginning of the period (0) or at the end of the period (1).**

13. **Type) and press Enter.**

Figure 1-7 shows how much an investment is worth after two years. The investment is begun with $1,000, and $50 is added each month. The interest rate is 5 percent. The value of the investment at the end is $2,364.24. The actual layout was $2,200 ($1,000 + [$50 × 24]). The account has earned $164.24.

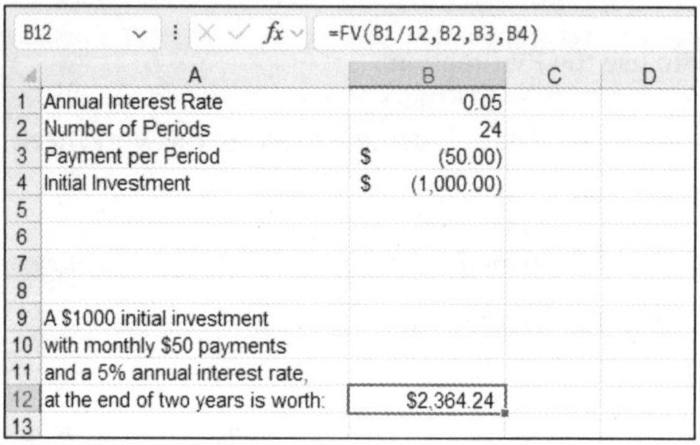

FIGURE 1-7: Earning extra money in an investment.

Depreciating the Finer Things in Life

Depreciation is the technique of allocating the cost of an asset over the useful period that the asset is used. Depreciation is applied to *capital assets*, which are tangible goods that provide usefulness for a year or more.

Vehicles, buildings, and equipment are the types of assets that depreciation can be applied to. A tuna sandwich is not a capital asset because its usefulness is going to last for just the few minutes it takes someone to eat it — although the person eating it may expect to capitalize on it!

Take the example of a business purchasing a delivery truck. The truck costs $35,000. It's expected to be used for 12 years; this is known as the *life* of the asset. At the end of 12 years, the vehicle's estimated worth will be $8,000. These figures follow certain terminology used in the depreciation formulas:

» **Cost:** This is the initial cost of the item ($35,000). This could include not just the price of the item, but also costs associated with getting and installing the item, such as delivery costs.

- **Salvage:** This is the value of the item at the end of the useful life of the item ($8,000).

- **Life:** This is the number of periods that the depreciation is applied to. This is usually expressed in years (in this case, 12 years).

Depreciation is calculated in different ways. Some techniques assume that an asset provides the majority of its usefulness during the early periods of its life. Depreciation in this case is applied on a sliding scale from the first period to the last. The bulk of the depreciation gets applied in the first few periods. This is known as an *accelerated depreciation schedule*. Sometimes, the depreciation amount runs out sooner than the asset's life. Alternatively, depreciation can be applied evenly over all the periods. In this case, each period of the asset's life has an equal amount of depreciation to apply. The different depreciation methods are summarized in Table 1-1.

TABLE 1-1   Depreciation Methods

Method	Comments	Excel Functions That Use the Method
Straight Line	Evenly applies the depreciable cost (Cost − Salvage) among the periods. Uses the formula (Cost − Salvage) ÷ Number of Periods.	SLN
Sum of Years' Digits	First sums up the periods, literally. For example, if there are five periods, the method first calculates the sum of the years' digits as 1 + 2 + 3 + 4 + 5 = 15. This method creates an accelerated depreciation schedule. See Excel Help for more information.	SYD
Double Declining Balance	Creates an accelerated depreciation schedule by doubling the straight-line depreciation rate but then applies it to the running declining balance of the asset cost, instead of to the fixed depreciable cost.	DDB, DB

TIP   The *depreciable cost* is the original cost minus the salvage value.

Figure 1-8 shows a worksheet with three different methods. The methods use the example of a delivery truck that costs $35,000, is used for 12 years, and has an ending value of $8,000. An important calculation in all these methods is the *depreciable cost*, which is the original cost minus the salvage value. In this example, the depreciable cost is $27,000, calculated as $35,000 − $8,000.

In the three depreciation methods shown in Figure 1-8 — Straight Line, Sum of Years' Digits, and Double Declining Balance — all end with the accumulated depreciation at the end of life equal to the depreciable cost, or the cost minus the salvage.

CHAPTER 1 **Calculating Loans, Interest, and Depreciation**   229

FIGURE 1-8: Depreciating an asset.

	A	B	C	D	E	F	G	H	I
1						Depreciation Methods			
2	Cost of Asset	$ 35,000							
3	Salvage Value	$ 8,000							
4	Life (in years)	12							
5									
6				Straight Line		Sum of Years' Digits		Double Declining Balance	
7									
8		Year							
9		1		$2,250.00		$4,153.85		$5,833.33	
10		2		$2,250.00		$3,807.69		$4,861.11	
11		3		$2,250.00		$3,461.54		$4,050.93	
12		4		$2,250.00		$3,115.38		$3,375.77	
13		5		$2,250.00		$2,769.23		$2,813.14	
14		6		$2,250.00		$2,423.08		$2,344.29	
15		7		$2,250.00		$2,076.92		$1,953.57	
16		8		$2,250.00		$1,730.77		$1,627.98	
17		9		$2,250.00		$1,384.62		$139.88	
18		10		$2,250.00		$1,038.46		$0.00	
19		11		$2,250.00		$692.31		$0.00	
20		12		$2,250.00		$346.15		$0.00	
21									
22		Total Depreciation		$27,000.00		$27,000.00		$27,000.00	

D9: =SLN($B$2,$B$3,$B$4)

However, each method arrives at the total in a different way. The Straight Line method simply applies an even amount among the periods. The Sum of Years' Digits and Double Declining Balance methods accelerate the depreciation. In fact the Double Declining Balance method does it to such a degree that all the depreciation is accounted for before the asset's life is over.

Calculating straight-line depreciation

The SLN function calculates the depreciation amount for each period of the life of the asset. The arguments are simple: just the cost, salvage, and the number of periods. In Figure 1-8, each cell in the range D9:D20 has the same formula: =SLN($B$2,$B$3,$B$4). Because straight-line depreciation provides an equal amount of depreciation to each period, it makes sense that each cell uses the formula verbatim. The answer is the same regardless of the period. (This approach differs from the accelerated depreciation methods that follow.)

REMEMBER

Using dollar signs ($) in front of column and row indicators fixes the cell address so it won't change when you copy the function to another cell.

Here's how to use the SLN function:

1. **Type three values in a worksheet:**

   - Cost of an asset
   - Salvage value (always less than the original cost)
   - Number of periods in the life of the asset (usually years)

2. **Type =SLN(to begin the function entry.**
3. **Click the cell that has the original cost, or type its address.**
4. **Type a comma (,).**
5. **Click the cell that has the salvage amount, or type its address.**
6. **Type a comma (,).**
7. **Click the cell that has the number of periods, or type its address.**
8. **Type) and press Enter.**

The returned value is the amount of depreciation per period. Each period has the same depreciation amount. The same formula, referencing the same cells (using $ for absolute referencing), is in each cell in the D9:D20 range.

Creating an accelerated depreciation schedule

The SYD function creates an accelerated depreciation schedule (that is, more depreciation is applied in the early periods of the asset's life). The method uses an interesting technique of first summing up the years' digits. So, for a depreciation schedule that covers five years, a value of 15 is first calculated as 1 + 2 + 3 + 4 + 5 = 15. If the schedule is for ten years, the first step of the method is to calculate the sum of the digits 1 through 10, like this: 1 + 2 + 3 + 4 + 5 + 6 + 7 + 8 + 9 + 10 = 55.

Then the years'-digit sum is used as the denominator in calculations with the actual digits themselves to determine a percentage per period. The digits in the calculations are the reverse of the actual periods. In other words, in a five-year depreciation schedule, the depreciation for the first period is calculated as (5 ÷ 15) × Depreciable Cost. The second-period depreciation is calculated as (4 ÷ 15) × Depreciable Cost. The following table makes it clear, with an assumed five-year depreciation on a depreciable cost of $6,000 and a salvage value of $0:

Period	Calculation	Result
1	(5 ÷ 15) × 6,000	$2,000
2	(4 ÷ 15) × 6,000	$1,600
3	(3 ÷ 15) × 6,000	$1,200
4	(2 ÷ 15) × 6,000	$800
5	(1 ÷ 15) × 6,000	$400

Guess what? You don't even need to know how this works! Excel does all the figuring for you. The SYD function takes four arguments: the cost, the salvage, the life (the number of periods), and the period to be calculated.

SYD returns the depreciation for a single period. Earlier in this chapter, we show you that the SLN function also returns the depreciation per period, but because all periods are the same, the SLN function doesn't need to have an actual period entered as an argument.

The SYD function returns a different depreciation amount for each period, so the period must be entered as an argument. In Figure 1-8, each formula in the range F9:F20 uses the SYD function but has a different period as the fourth argument. For example, cell F9 has the formula =SYD($B$2,$B$3,$B$4,B9), and cell F10 has the formula =SYD($B$2,$B$3,$B$4,B10). The last argument provides a different value.

Here's how to use the SYD function to calculate the depreciation for one period:

1. **Type three values in a worksheet:**
   - Cost of an asset
   - Salvage value (always less than the original cost)
   - Number of periods in the life of the asset (usually years)
2. **Type** =SYD(**to begin the function entry.**
3. **Click the cell that has the original cost, or type its address.**
4. **Type a comma (,).**
5. **Click the cell that has the salvage amount, or type its address.**
6. **Type a comma (,).**
7. **Click the cell that has the number of periods, or type its address.**
8. **Type a comma (,).**
9. **Type a number for the period for which to calculate the depreciation.**
10. **Type) and press Enter.**

The *returned value* is the amount of depreciation for the entered period. To calculate the depreciation for the entire set of periods, type a formula with the SYD function in the same number of cells as there are periods. In this case, each cell has a different period entered for the fourth argument. To make this type of entry easy to do, type the first three arguments as absolute cell addresses. In other words, use the dollar sign ($) in front of the row and column indicators. Leave the fourth argument in the relative address format.

In cell F9 in Figure 1-8, the formula is =SYD($B$2,$B$3,$B$4,B9). Note that the first three arguments are fixed to the cells B2, B3, and B4. With this formula entered in cell F9, simply dragging the formula (using the Fill Handle in the lower-right corner of the cell) down to F20 fills the range of cells that need the calculation. The fourth argument changes in each row. For example, cell F20 has this formula: =SYD($B$2,$B$3,$B$4,B20).

Creating an even faster accelerated depreciation schedule

The Double Declining Balance method provides an accelerated depreciation schedule but calculates the amounts differently from the Sum of Years' Digits method.

Although rooted in the doubling of the Straight Line method (which is not an accelerated method), the calculation for each successive period is based on the remaining value of the asset after each period instead of on the depreciable cost. Because the remaining value is reduced each period, the schedule for each period is different.

The DDB function takes five arguments. The first four are required:

- Cost
- Salvage
- Life (the number of periods)
- Period for which the depreciation is to be calculated

The fifth argument is the factor. A factor of 2 tells the function to use the Double Declining Balance method. Other values can be used, such as 1.5. The factor is the rate at which the balance declines. A smaller value (than the default of 2) results in a longer time for the balance to decline. When the fifth argument is omitted, the value of 2 is the default.

The DDB function returns a different depreciation amount for each period, so the period must be typed as an argument. In Figure 1-8, each formula in the range H9:H20 uses the DDB function but has a different period as the fourth argument. For example, cell H9 has the formula =DDB($B$2,$B$3,$B$4,B9) and cell H10 has the formula =DDB($B$2,$B$3,$B$4,B10). The last argument provides a different value.

As shown in Figure 1-8, earlier in this chapter, the Double Declining Balance method provides an even more accelerated depreciation schedule than the Sum of Years' Digits method does. In fact, the depreciation is fully accounted for before the asset has reached the end of its life.

Here's how to use the DDB function to calculate the depreciation for one period:

1. **Type three values in a worksheet:**
   - Cost of an asset
   - Salvage value (always less than the original cost)
   - Number of periods in the life of the asset (usually years)
2. **Type =DDB(to begin the function entry.**
3. **Click the cell that has the original cost, or type its address.**
4. **Type a comma (,).**
5. **Click the cell that has the salvage amount, or type its address.**
6. **Type a comma (,).**
7. **Click the cell that has the number of periods.**
8. **Type a comma (,).**
9. **Type a number for the period for which to calculate the depreciation.**
10. **If a variation on the Double Declining Balance method is desired, type a comma (,) and a value other than 2.**
11. **Type) and press Enter.**

The returned value is the amount of depreciation for the entered period. To calculate the depreciation for the entire set of periods, you need to type a formula with the DDB function in the same number of cells as there are periods. In this case, each cell would have a different period entered for the fourth argument. One of the best approaches is to use absolute addressing for the first three function arguments. Then, when you fill the rest of the cells by dragging or copying, the references to original cost, salvage amount, and number of periods stay constant. You can see an example of absolute addressing in the Formula Bar in Figure 1-8.

> **TIP** There is no hard-and-fast rule for selecting the best depreciation method. However, it makes sense to use one that matches the depreciating value of the asset. For example, cars lose a good deal of their value in the first few years, so applying an accelerated depreciation schedule makes sense.

Calculating a midyear depreciation schedule

Most assets are not purchased, delivered, and put into service on January 1. Excel provides a depreciation function, DB, that accounts for the periods being offset from the calendar year. The DB function takes five arguments. The first four are the typical ones: the cost, the salvage, the life (the number of periods), and the period for which the depreciation is to be calculated. The fifth argument is the number of months in the first year. The fifth argument is optional; when it's left out, the function uses 12 as a default.

For the fifth argument, a value of 3 means the depreciation starts in October (October through December is three months), so the amount of depreciation charged in the first calendar year is small. A value of 11 means that the depreciation starts in February (February through December is 11 months).

Figure 1-9 shows a depreciation schedule created with the DB function. Note that the life of the asset is 12 years (in cell B4) but that the formula is applied to 13 different periods. Including an extra year is necessary because the first year is partial. The remaining months must spill into an extra calendar year. The depreciation periods and the calendar years are offset.

FIGURE 1-9: Offsetting depreciation periods from the calendar.

	A	B	D
1			
2	Cost of Asset	$35,000	
3	Salvage Value	$8,000	
4	Life (in years)	12	
5			
6			Fixed Depreciation
7			
8		Year	
9		1	$1,691.67
10		2	$3,863.77
11		3	$3,415.57
12		4	$3,019.36
13		5	$2,669.12
14		6	$2,359.50
15		7	$2,085.80
16		8	$1,843.85
17		9	$1,629.96
18		10	$1,440.88
19		11	$1,273.74
20		12	$1,125.99
21		13	$580.63
22			
23			
24		Total Depreciation	$26,999.83

D9 =DB($B$2,$B$3,$B$4,B9,5)

CHAPTER 1 Calculating Loans, Interest, and Depreciation

The example in Figure 1-9 is for an asset put into service in August. Cell D9 has the formula =DB($B$2,$B$3,$B$4,B9,5). The fifth argument is 5, which indicates that the first-year depreciation covers five months: August, September, October, November, and December.

Here's how to use the DB function to calculate the depreciation for one period:

1. **Type three values in a worksheet:**
   - Cost of an asset
   - Salvage value (always less than the original cost)
   - Number of periods in the life of the asset (usually years)
2. **Type =DB(to begin the function entry.**
3. **Click the cell that has the original cost, or type its address.**
4. **Type a comma (,).**
5. **Click the cell that has the salvage amount, or type its address.**
6. **Type a comma (,).**
7. **Click the cell that has the number of periods.**
8. **Type a comma (,).**
9. **Type a number for the period for which to calculate the depreciation.**
10. **Type a comma (,).**
11. **Type the number of months within the first year that the depreciation is applied to.**
12. **Type) and press Enter.**

The returned value is the amount of depreciation for the entered period. To calculate the depreciation for the entire set of periods, you need to type a formula with the DB function in the same number of cells as there are periods. However, you should make space for an additional period (refer to Figure 1-9).

TIP Type the constant arguments of the function with absolute addressing (the dollar signs used in front of row numbers or column letters). This makes the function easy to apply across multiple cells by copying the formula. The references to the pertinent function arguments stay constant.

Measuring Your Internals

Which is better to do: Pay off your credit card or invest in Uncle Ralph's new business venture? You're about to finance a car. Should you put down a large down payment? Or should you put down a small amount and invest the rest? How can you make decisions about alternative financial opportunities like these?

The IRR function helps answer these types of questions. The IRR function analyzes the cash flows in and out of an investment and calculates an interest rate that is the effective result of the cash flows. In other words, all the various cash flows are accounted for, and one interest rate is returned. Then you can compare this figure with other financial opportunities.

Perhaps Uncle Ralph's business venture will provide a 10 percent return on your investment. On the other hand, the credit card company charges you 12 percent on your balance. In this case, paying off the credit card is wiser. Why? Because earning 10 percent is pointless when you're just losing 12 percent elsewhere. Uncle Ralph will understand, won't he?

The IRR function takes two arguments:

>> **An array of cash flows:** Following the cash-flows standard, money coming in is entered as a positive value, and money going out is entered as a negative value. Assuming that the particular cash flows in and out are entered on a worksheet, the first argument to the function is the range of cells. This argument is required.

>> **A guess at what the result should be:** We know this sounds crazy, but Excel may need your help here (though most times, it won't). The IRR function starts by guessing the result and calculating how closely the guess matches the data. Then it adjusts the guess up or down and repeats the process (a technique called *iteration*) until it arrives at the correct answer. If Excel doesn't figure it out in 20 tries, the #NUM! error is returned. In this case, you could type a guess in the function to help it along. For example, 0.05 indicates a guess of 5 percent, 0.15 indicates a guess of 15 percent, and so on. You can type a negative number, too. For example, typing –0.05 tells the function that you expect a 5 percent loss. If you don't type a guess, Excel assumes 0.1 (10 percent).

Figure 1-10 shows a business venture that has been evaluated with IRR. The project is to create and market T-shirts. Assorted costs, such as paying artists, are cash flows out, typed as negative numbers. The one positive value in cell B7 is the expected revenue.

FIGURE 1-10: Calculating the return on a business venture.

	A	B	C D	E	F	G
1						
2						
3		$ (2,500.00)	Creative (Payment for Artists)			
4		$ (3,500.00)	T-shirt Production			
5		$ (2,000.00)	Marketing			
6		$ (400.00)	Administrative Costs			
7		$11,960.00	Expected Revenue			
8						
9		12%	INTERNAL RATE OF RETURN			
10						

Cell B9: `=IRR(B3:B7)`

The IRR function has been used to calculate an expected rate of return. The formula in cell B9 is =IRR(B3:B7). The entered range includes all the cash flows, in and out.

This project has an internal rate of return of 12 percent. By the way, the investment amount in this case is the sum of all the cash flows out: $8,400. Earning back $11,960 makes this a good investment. The revenue is significantly higher than the outlay.

REMEMBER Even though a business opportunity seems worthy after IRR has been applied, you must consider other factors. For example, you may have to *borrow* the money to invest in the business venture. The real number to look at is the internal rate of return of the business venture less the cost of borrowing the money to invest.

However, the project can now be compared with other investments. Another project may calculate to a higher internal rate of return. Then the second project would make sense to pursue. Of course, don't forget the fun factor. Making T-shirts may be worth giving up a few extra points!

TIP When you're comparing opportunities with the IRR function, a higher returned value is a better result than a lower internal rate of return.

Figure 1-11 compares the business venture in Figure 1-10 to another investment opportunity. The second business venture is a start-up videography business for weddings and other events. There is a significant outlay for equipment and marketing. An internal rate of return is calculated for the first year, and then for the first and second year together. Cell H10 has the formula =IRR(H3:H5), and cell H11 has the formula =IRR(H3:H6). It's clear that even within the first year, the second business venture surpasses the first.

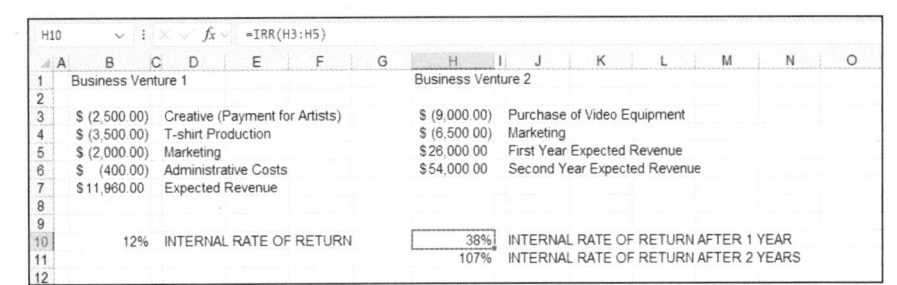

FIGURE 1-11: Comparing business opportunities.

	A	B	C D	E	F	G	H	I J	K	L	M	N	O
1		Business Venture 1					Business Venture 2						
3		$ (2,500.00)	Creative (Payment for Artists)				$ (9,000.00)	Purchase of Video Equipment					
4		$ (3,500.00)	T-shirt Production				$ (6,500.00)	Marketing					
5		$ (2,000.00)	Marketing				$26,000.00	First Year Expected Revenue					
6		$ (400.00)	Administrative Costs				$54,000.00	Second Year Expected Revenue					
7		$11,960.00	Expected Revenue										
10			12%	INTERNAL RATE OF RETURN				38%	INTERNAL RATE OF RETURN AFTER 1 YEAR				
11								107%	INTERNAL RATE OF RETURN AFTER 2 YEARS				

This is how to use the IRR function:

1. **Type a series of cash-flow values:**

   - Money paid out, such as the initial investment, as a negative value
   - Money coming in, such as revenue, as a positive value

2. **Type =IRR(to begin the function entry.**

3. **Drag the cursor over the range of cells containing the cash flows, or type the range address.**

4. **(Optional) Type a guess to help the function.**

   To do this, type a comma (,) and then type a decimal value to be used as a percentage (such as 0.2 for 20 percent). You can type a positive or negative value.

5. **Type) and press Enter.**

Considering that internal rate of return is based on cash flows, in and out, it's prudent to include paying yourself, as well as accounting for investments back in the business. Salary is cash flow out; investment is cash flow in.

> **IN THIS CHAPTER**
>
> » Summing, rounding, and truncating values
>
> » Using or removing a number's sign
>
> » Calculating the circumference, diameter, and area of a circle
>
> » Returning random numbers
>
> » Performing sophisticated multiplication
>
> » Using SUBTOTAL, SUMIF, and SUMIFS

Chapter 2
Performing Functional Math

Excel is excellent for working with advanced math and complex calculations. You can do so many complex things with Excel that it's easy to forget that Excel is great at basic math, too.

Need the sum of a batch of numbers? No problem. Need to round a number? Read on! In this chapter, we show you not just how to sum and round numbers, but also how to use these methods in ways that give you just the answers you need. Then we move on to some of the more advanced math functions. You won't use these functions every day, but they're just the right thing when you need them.

Adding It All Together with the SUM Function

Just adding numbers together is something Excel is great at. Oh, you can use your calculator to add numbers as well, but think about it: On a calculator you enter a number, press the + button, enter another number, press the + button, and so on. Eventually you press the = button, and you get your answer. But if you make an entry mistake in the middle, you have to start all over!

The SUM function in Excel adds numbers together in a more efficient way. First, you list all your numbers on the worksheet. You can see them all and verify that they're correct. Then you use the SUM function to add them all together. Here's how:

1. **Type some numbers in a worksheet.**

   These numbers can be both integer and *real* (decimal) values. You can add labels to adjacent cells to identify the values, if you want.

2. **Position the cursor in the cell where you want the results to appear.**

3. **Type =SUM(to begin the function entry.**

4. **Click a cell where you typed a number.**

5. **Type a comma (,).**

6. **Click a cell where you typed another number.**

7. **Repeat steps 5 and 6 until you've entered all the numbers into the function.**

8. **Type) and press Enter.**

Figure 2-1 shows an example of how these steps help sum up amounts that aren't situated next to one another on a worksheet. Cell F6 contains the sum of values in cells C2, E2, G2, and I2.

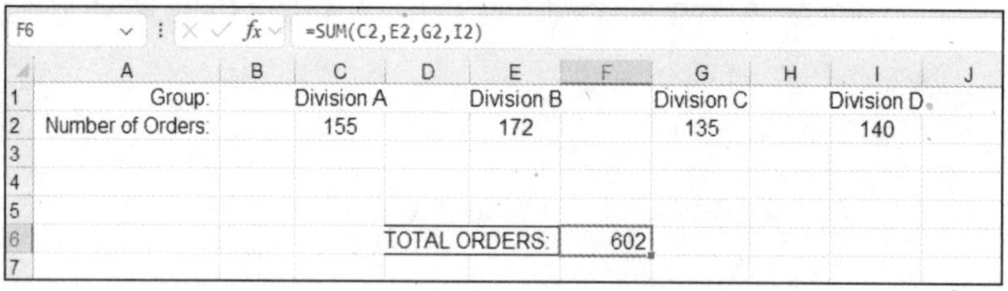

FIGURE 2-1: Using the SUM function to add noncontiguous numbers.

Using SUM is even easier when the numbers you're adding are next to one another in a column or row. The SUM function lets you type a range of cells in place of single cells in the arguments of the function. So, adding a list of contiguous numbers is as easy as giving SUM a single argument. Here's how to type a range as a single argument:

1. **Type some numbers in a worksheet.**

   Be sure the numbers are contiguous in a row or column. You can add labels to adjacent cells to identify the values, if desired, but this doesn't affect the SUM function.

2. **Position the cursor in the cell where you want the results to appear.**

3. **Type =SUM(to begin the function entry.**

4. **Type the range address that contains the numbers.**

   Alternatively, you can click the first cell with a number, hold down the left mouse button, and drag the mouse over the range of cells.

5. **Type) and press Enter.**

Using a range address or a named range in the function is a real time-saver — and it's easier on the fingers, too. Figure 2-2 shows how a single range is used with the SUM function. Look at the Formula Bar, and you'll see that the entire function's syntax is =SUM(B6:B12). A single range takes the place of multiple individual cell addresses.

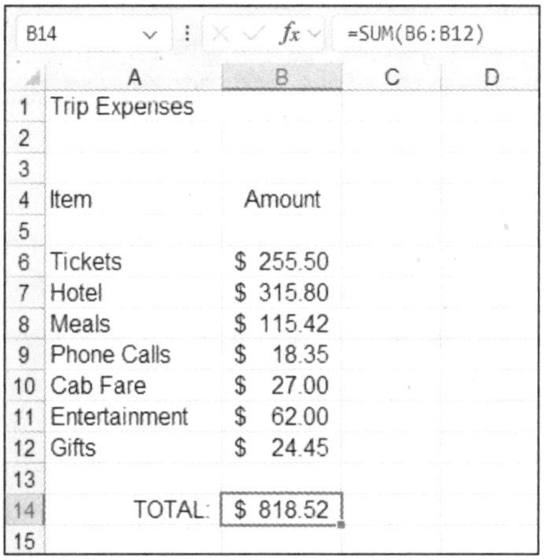

FIGURE 2-2: Calculating a sum from a range of cells.

CHAPTER 2 **Performing Functional Math** 243

You can sum multiple ranges in a single formula, which is great when multiple distinct contiguous cell ranges all must feed a grand total. Figure 2-3 shows just such a situation.

FIGURE 2-3: Calculating a sum of multiple ranges.

To use SUM to add the values in multiple ranges, follow these steps:

1. **Type some lists of numbers in a worksheet.**

   You can add labels to adjacent cells to identify the values, if desired.

2. **Position the cursor in the cell where you want the results to appear.**

3. **Type =SUM(to begin the function entry.**

4. **Click the first cell in a range, hold down the left mouse button, drag the mouse over all the cells in the range, and then release the mouse button.**

5. **Type a comma (,).**

6. **Click the first cell in another range, hold down the left mouse button, drag the mouse over all the cells in this range, and then release the mouse button.**

7. **Repeat steps 5 and 6 until you've entered all the ranges into the function.**

8. **Type) and press Enter.**

The completed function entry should look similar to the entry shown in the Formula Bar in Figure 2-3. Ranges are separated by commas, and a grand sum is in the cell where the function was typed.

TIP

When entering ranges into a formula, you can either type them or use the mouse to drag over the range.

Excel has a special button, the AutoSum button, that makes it easier to use the SUM function. The AutoSum button is on both the Home tab and the Formulas tab of the ribbon. The AutoSum feature works best with numbers that are in a vertical or horizontal list. In a nutshell, AutoSum creates a range reference for the SUM function to use. AutoSum makes its best guess about what the range should be. Often, it gets it right — but sometimes, you have to help it along.

Using AutoSum is as easy as clicking and then pressing Enter. Figure 2-4 shows that the AutoSum button on the ribbon has been clicked, and Excel, in its infinite wisdom, guessed correctly that the operation is to sum cells B6:B13. At this point, the operation is incomplete. Pressing Enter finishes the formula.

FIGURE 2-4: Using AutoSum to guess a range for the SUM function.

TIP You can click the check mark to the left of the formula, in the Formula Bar, to complete the operation.

Follow these steps to use AutoSum:

1. **Type some lists of numbers in a worksheet.**

    You can add labels to adjacent cells to identify the values, if desired.

2. **Position the cursor in the cell where you want the results to appear.**

3. **Click the AutoSum button.**

    AutoSum enters a suggested range in the SUM function.

4. **Change the suggested range, if necessary, by typing it with the keyboard or using the mouse to drag over a range of cells.**

5. **Press Enter or click the check mark on the Formula Bar to complete the function.**

CHAPTER 2 **Performing Functional Math** 245

TIP It's easy to use AutoSum to tally multiple ranges, such as those shown in Figure 2-3. Before ending the function with the Enter key or the check mark in the Formula Bar, instead type a comma and then drag the mouse over another range. Do this for as many ranges as you need to sum. Finally, finish the function by pressing Enter or clicking the check mark in the Formula Bar.

By the way, the AutoSum button can do more than addition. If you click the down arrow on the button, you can quickly enter any of four other functions: AVERAGE, COUNT, MAX, or MIN.

Rounding Out Your Knowledge

Excel calculates answers to many decimal places. Unless you're doing rocket science, you probably don't need such precise answers. Excel has a great set of functions for rounding numbers so they're usable for the rest of us.

Just plain old rounding

Easy to use, the ROUND function is the old tried-and-true method for rounding off a number. It takes two arguments. One argument is the number to round (typically, this is a cell reference), and the other argument indicates how many decimal places to round to.

The ROUND function rounds up or down, depending on the number being rounded. When the value is less than the halfway point of the next significant digit, the number is rounded down. When the value is at or greater than the halfway point, the number is rounded up, as follows:

- 10.4 rounds down to 10.
- 10.6 rounds up to 11.
- 10.5 also rounds up to 11.

Table 2-1 shows some examples of the ROUND function.

TABLE 2-1 Using the ROUND Function

Example of Function	Result	Comment
=ROUND(12.3456,1)	12.3	The second argument is 1. The result is rounded to a single decimal place.
=ROUND(12.3456,2)	12.35	The second argument is 2. The result is rounded to two decimal places. Note that the full decimal of .3456 becomes .35 because the .0456 portion of the decimal value rounds to the closest second-place decimal, which is .05.
=ROUND(12.3456,3)	12.346	The second argument is 3. The result is rounded to three decimal places. Note that the full decimal or .3456 becomes .346 because the .0056 portion of the decimal value rounds to the closest third-place decimal, which is .006.
=ROUND(12.3456,4)	12.3456	The second argument is 4. There are four decimal places. No rounding takes place.
=ROUND(12.3456,0)	12	When the second argument is 0, the number is rounded to the nearest integer. Because 12.3456 is closer to 12 than to 13, the number rounds to 12.
=ROUND(12.3456,-1)	10	When negative values are used in the second argument, the rounding occurs on the left side of the decimal (the integer portion). A second argument value of -1 tells the function to round to the closest value of 10. In this example, that value is 10 because 12 is closer to 10 than to 20.

To use the ROUND function, follow these steps:

1. **In a cell of your choice, type a number that has a decimal portion.**
2. **Position the cursor in the cell where you want the results to appear.**
3. **Type =ROUND(to begin the function entry.**
4. **Click the cell where you typed the number.**
5. **Type a comma (,).**
6. **Type a number to indicate how many decimal places to round to.**
7. **Type) and press Enter.**

REMEMBER

Rounding functions make the most sense when the first argument is a cell reference, not an actual number. Think about it: If you know what a number should appear as, you would just type the number. You wouldn't need a function to round it.

Rounding in one direction

Excel has a handful of functions that always round numbers up or always round numbers down. That is, when Excel is rounding a number, the functions that round down always give a result that is lower than the number itself. Functions that round up, of course, always give a higher number. These functions are useful when letting the good ol' ROUND function determine which way to round just won't work.

A few of these rounding functions not only round in the desired direction but also allow you to specify some additional ways of rounding. The EVEN and ODD functions, for example, round to the closest even or odd number, respectively. The CEILING and FLOOR functions let you round to a multiple. We cover EVEN, ODD, CEILING, and FLOOR later in this section.

Directional rounding, pure and simple

ROUNDUP and ROUNDDOWN are similar to the ROUND function. The first argument to the function is the cell reference of the number to be rounded. The second argument indicates the number of decimal places to round to. But unlike with plain old ROUND, the rounding direction is not based on the halfway point of the next significant digit but on which function you use.

For example, =ROUND(4.22,1) returns 4.2, but =ROUNDUP(4.22,1) returns 4.3. =ROUNDDOWN(4.22,1), however, returns 4.2 because 4.2 is less than 4.22. Table 2-2 shows some examples of ROUNDUP and ROUNDDOWN.

TABLE 2-2 Using the ROUNDUP and ROUNDDOWN Functions

Example of Function	Result	Comment
=ROUNDUP(150.255,0)	151	The second argument is 0. The result is rounded up to the next higher integer, regardless of the fact that the decimal portion would normally indicate that the rounding would go to the next lower integer.
=ROUNDUP(150.255,1)	150.3	The second argument is 1. The result is rounded to a single decimal place. Note that the full decimal of .255 rounds up to .3. This would also happen with the standard ROUND function.
=ROUNDUP(150.255,2)	150.26	The second argument is 2. The result is rounded to two decimal places. Note that the full decimal of .255 becomes .26. This would also happen with the standard ROUND function.
=ROUNDUP(150.255,3)	150.255	The second argument is 3, and there are three decimal places. No rounding takes place.

Example of Function	Result	Comment
=ROUNDDOWN(155.798,0)	155	The second argument is 0. The result is rounded down to the integer portion of the number, regardless of the fact that the decimal portion would normally indicate that the rounding would go to the next higher integer.
=ROUNDDOWN(155.798,1)	155.7	The second argument is 1. The result is rounded to a single decimal place. Note that the full decimal of .798 rounds down to .7. The standard ROUND function would round the decimal up to .8.
=ROUNDDOWN(155.798,2)	155.79	The second argument is 2. The result is rounded to two decimal places. Note that the full decimal of .798 becomes .79. The standard ROUND function would round the decimal up to .8.
=ROUNDDOWN(155.798,3)	155.798	The second argument is 3, and there are three decimal places. No rounding takes place.

To use the ROUNDUP and ROUNDDOWN functions, follow these steps:

1. **In a cell of your choice, type a number with a decimal portion.**
2. **Position the cursor in the cell where you want the results to appear.**
3. **Type** =ROUNDUP(**or** =ROUNDDOWN(**to begin the function entry.**
4. **Click the cell where you typed the number.**
5. **Type a comma (,).**
6. **Type a number to indicate how many decimal places to round to.**
7. **Type) and press Enter.**

Rounding to the multiple of choice

The FLOOR and CEILING functions take directional rounding to a new level. With these functions, the second argument is a multiple to which to round to. What does that mean?

Well, imagine this: You're a human resources manager, and you need to prepare a summary report of employee salaries. You don't need the figures to be reported down to the last penny — just rounded to the closest $250 multiple. Either FLOOR or CEILING can do this. For this example, you can use FLOOR to round down to the closest multiple of $250 that is less than the salary, or you can use CEILING to round up to the next $250 multiple greater than the salary. Figure 2-5 shows how FLOOR and CEILING return rounded values.

	A	B	C	D	E
1			Salary Rounded to Nearest 250	Salary Rounded to Nearest 250	
2			Using FLOOR	Using CEILING	
3					
4					
5	Employee ID	Salary			
6	W234	$ 54,677	$ 54,500	$ 54,750	
7	N552	$ 36,125	$ 36,000	$ 36,250	
8	P310	$ 28,900	$ 28,750	$ 29,000	
9	B533	$ 31,950	$ 31,750	$ 32,000	
10	R390	$ 48,305	$ 48,250	$ 48,500	
11	R418	$ 78,500	$ 78,500	$ 78,500	
12	W602	$ 60,252	$ 60,250	$ 60,500	
13	C177	$ 58,900	$ 58,750	$ 59,000	
14	T542	$ 36,550	$ 36,500	$ 36,750	
15	T833	$ 38,740	$ 38,500	$ 38,750	
16	M405	$ 52,580	$ 52,500	$ 52,750	
17					

FIGURE 2-5: Using FLOOR and CEILING to round to a desired multiple.

FLOOR and CEILING exceed the rounding ability of ROUND, ROUNDUP, and ROUNDDOWN. These three functions can use the positioning of digit placeholders in how they work. For example, =ROUND(B4,-3) tells the ROUND function to round on the thousandth position. On the other hand, FLOOR and CEILING can round to whatever specific multiple you set.

The FLOOR function rounds toward 0, returning the closest multiple of the second argument that is lower than the number itself.

The CEILING function works in the opposite direction. CEILING rounds its first argument, the number to be rounded, to the next multiple of the second number that is in the direction away from 0.

A few examples will make this clear. Table 2-3 shows how you can use FLOOR and CEILING.

You can use FLOOR and CEILING to round negative numbers, too. FLOOR rounds toward 0, and CEILING rounds away from 0. FLOOR decreases a positive number as it rounds it toward 0 and also decreases a negative number toward 0, although in absolute terms, FLOOR actually *increases* the value of a negative number. Weird, huh?

CEILING does the opposite. It increases a positive number away from 0 and also increases a negative number away from 0, which in absolute terms means the number is getting smaller.

WARNING

For both the FLOOR and CEILING functions, the first and second arguments must match signs. Trying to apply a positive number with a negative multiple, or vice versa, results in an error.

TABLE 2-3 **Using FLOOR and CEILING for Sophisticated Rounding**

Example of Function	Result	Comment
=FLOOR(30.17,0.05)	30.15	The second argument says to round to the next 0.05 multiple, in the direction of 0.
=FLOOR(30.17,0.1)	30.1	The second argument says to round to the next 0.1 multiple, in the direction of 0.
=FLOOR(-30.17,-0.1)	-30.1	The second argument says to round to the next 0.1 multiple, in the direction of 0.
=CEILING(30.17,0.05)	30.2	The second argument says to round to the next 0.05 multiple, away from 0.
=CEILING(30.17,0.1)	30.2	The second argument says to round to the next 0.1 multiple, away from 0.
=CEILING(-30.17,-0.1)	-30.2	The second argument says to round to the next 0.1 multiple, away from 0.

Follow these steps to use the FLOOR and CEILING functions:

1. **Type a number in any cell.**
2. **Position the cursor in the cell where you want the results to appear.**
3. **Type** =FLOOR(or =CEILING(**to begin the function entry.**
4. **Click the cell where you type the number.**
5. **Type a comma (,).**
6. **Type a number that is the next multiple you want to round the number to.**

   For example, to get the floor value, at the ones place, make sure 1 is the second argument. The first argument should, of course, be a number larger than 1 and should be a decimal value, like this: =FLOOR(19.77,1). This returns 19 as the floor, but hey — don't hit the ceiling about it!

7. **Type) and press Enter.**

Rounding to the next even or odd number

The EVEN and ODD functions round numbers away from 0. The EVEN function rounds a number to the next higher even integer. ODD rounds a number to the next higher odd integer. Table 2-4 has examples of how these functions work.

TABLE 2-4　Rounding to Even or Odd Integers

Example of Function	Result	Comment
=EVEN(3)	4	Rounds to the next even integer, moving away from 0.
=EVEN(4)	4	Because 4 is an even number, no rounding takes place. The number 4 itself is returned.
=EVEN(4.01)	6	Rounds to the next even integer, moving away from 0.
=EVEN(-3.5)	-4	Rounds to the next even integer, moving away from 0.
=ODD(3)	3	Because 3 is an odd number, no rounding takes place. The number 3 itself is returned.
=ODD(4)	5	Rounds to the next odd integer, moving away from 0.
=ODD(5.01)	7	Rounds to the next odd integer, moving away from 0.
=ODD(-3.5)	-5	Rounds to the next odd integer, moving away from 0.

The EVEN function is helpful in calculations that depend on multiples of two. Say you're in charge of planning a school trip. You need to figure out how many bus seats are needed for each class. A seat can fit two children. When a class has an odd number of children, you still have to count that last seat as taken, even though only one child will sit there.

Say the class has 17 children. This formula tells you how many seats are needed: =EVEN(17)/2. The EVEN function returns the number 18 (the next higher integer), and that result is divided by 2 because 2 children fit on each seat. The answer is 9 seats are needed for a class of 17 children.

To use the EVEN and ODD functions, follow these steps:

1. **Position the cursor in the cell where you want the results to appear.**
2. **Type** =EVEN(**or** =ODD(**to begin the function entry.**
3. **Click a cell where you typed a number, or type a number.**
4. **Type) and press Enter.**

Leaving All Decimals Behind with INT

The INT function rounds a number down to the next lower integer. The effect is as if the decimal portion is just dropped, and often, INT is used to facilitate just that: dropping the decimal.

INT comes in handy when all you need to know is the integer part of a number or the integer part of a calculation's result. For example, you may be estimating what it will cost to build a piece of furniture. You have the prices for each type of raw material, and you just want a ballpark total.

Figure 2-6 shows a worksheet in which a project has been set up. Column A contains item descriptions, and column B has the price for each item. Columns C and D contain the parameters for the project. That is, column C contains the count of each item needed, and column D has the amount to be spent for each item — that is, the price per item multiplied by the number of items needed.

FIGURE 2-6: Using INT to drop unnecessary decimals.

	A	B	C	D
1	Item	Price per Unit	Units Needed	Cost
3	Lumber	$ 6.99	12	$ 83.88
4	Hinges	$ 4.49	24	$ 107.76
5	Knobs	$ 4.99	4	$ 19.96
8			Project Cost	$ 211.00

D8 =INT(SUM(D3:D5))

The sums to be spent are then summed into a project total. If you added the item sums as they are — 83.88, 107.76, and 19.96 — you would get a total of $211.60. Instead, the INT function is used to round the total to a ballpark figure of $211.

In cell D8, INT is applied to the total sum, like this:

```
=INT(SUM(D3:D5))
```

The INT function effectively drops the decimal portion, .60, and returns the integer part, 211. The project estimate is $211.

INT takes only the number as an argument. INT can work on positive or negative values, but it works a little differently with negative numbers. When working with negative numbers, INT actually rounds down. When INT is working with positive numbers, the effect appears the same as just dropping the decimal. With negative numbers, the function drops the decimal portion and subtracts 1.

CHAPTER 2 Performing Functional Math   253

With negative numbers, the function produces an integer that is farther away from 0. Therefore, a number such as –25.25 becomes –26. Here are some examples:

- INT(25.25) returns 25.
- INT(25.75) returns 25.
- INT(-25.25) returns -26.
- INT(-25.75) returns -26.

To use the INT function, follow these steps:

1. **In a cell of your choice, type a number that has a decimal portion.**
2. **Position the cursor in the cell where you want the results to appear.**
3. **Type =INT(to begin the function entry.**
4. **Click the cell where you typed the number.**
5. **Type) and press Enter.**

TIP INT can also be used to return just the decimal part of a number. Subtracting the integer portion of a number from its full value leaves just the decimal as the answer. For example, =10.95-INT(10.95) is 0.95.

Leaving Some Decimals Behind with TRUNC

The TRUNC function drops a part of a number. The function takes two arguments. The first argument is the number to be changed. The second argument indicates how much of the number is to be dropped. A value of 2 for the second argument says to leave two decimal places remaining. A value of 1 for the second argument says to leave one decimal place remaining.

TRUNC doesn't round as it truncates numbers. Here are some examples:

- =TRUNC(212.65,2) returns 212.65.
- =TRUNC(212.65,1) returns 212.6.
- =TRUNC(212.65,0) returns 212.

You can even use TRUNC to drop a portion of the number from the integer side. To do this, you type negative values for the second argument, like this:

» =TRUNC(212.65,-1) returns 210.

» =TRUNC(212.65,-2) returns 200.

> **TIP** Assuming TRUNC has no decimal argument, then the INT and TRUNC functions work exactly the same way for positive numbers. The only difference is when negative numbers are being changed. Then INT's rounding produces a different result than TRUNC's truncation.

Looking for a Sign

Excel's SIGN function tells you whether a number is positive or negative. The SIGN function doesn't alter the number in any way, but it's used to find out information about the number.

SIGN does actually return a number, but it isn't a variation of the number being tested in the function. SIGN returns only three numbers:

» 1 if the number being tested is positive

» -1 if the number being tested is negative

» 0 if the number being tested is 0

Consider these examples:

» =SIGN(5) returns 1.

» =SIGN(-5) returns -1.

» =SIGN(0) returns 0.

To use the SIGN function, follow these steps:

1. **Position the cursor in the cell where you want the results to appear.**
2. **Type =SIGN(to begin the function entry.**
3. **Click a cell where you typed a number, or type a number.**
4. **Type) and press Enter.**

CHAPTER 2 Performing Functional Math

Ignoring Signs

The ABS function returns the absolute value of a number. The absolute value is always a positive. The absolute value of a positive number is the number itself. The absolute value of a negative number is the number but with the sign changed to positive. For example, =ABS(100) returns 100, as does =ABS(-100).

The ABS function is handy in a number of situations. For example, sometimes imported data comes in as negative values, which need to be converted to their positive equivalents. Or, when you're working with cash flows, you can use the ABS function to present cash flows as positive numbers.

A common use of the ABS function is to calculate the difference between two numbers when you don't know which number has the greater value to begin with. Say you need to calculate the difference between scores for two contestants. Score 1 is in cell A5, and score 2 is in cell B5. The result goes in cell C5. The formula in cell C5 would be =A5-B5.

Plugging in some numbers, assume that score 1 is 90 and score 2 is 75. The difference is 15. Okay, that's a good answer. What happens when score 1 is 75 and score 2 is 90? The answer is -15. This answer is mathematically correct but not presented in a useful way. The difference is still 15, not -15. When you use the ABS function, the result is always returned as positive. Therefore, for this example, the best formula coding is this: =ABS(A5-A6).

Now, whether score 1 is greater than score 2 or score 2 is greater than score 1, the correct difference is returned.

To use the ABS function, follow these steps:

1. **Position the cursor in the cell where you want the results to appear.**
2. **Type =ABS(to begin the function entry.**
3. **Click a cell where you typed a number, or type a number.**
4. **Type) and press Enter.**

Using PI to Calculate Circumference and Diameter

Pi is the ratio of a circle's circumference to its diameter. A circle's *circumference* is its outer edge, and it's equal to the complete distance around the circle. A circle's *diameter* is the length of a straight line running from one side of the circle, through the middle, and reaching the other side.

Dividing a circle's circumference by its diameter returns a value of approximately 3.14159, known as *pi*. Pi is represented with the Greek letter π.

Mathematicians have proved that pi is an *irrational number* — in other words, that it has an infinite number of decimal places. They've calculated the value of pi to many thousands of decimal places, but you don't need that level of precision in most calculations. Many people use the value 3.14159 for pi, but the PI function in Excel does a bit better than that. Excel returns a value of pi accurate to 15 digits — that is 14 decimal places in addition to the integer 3, namely 3.14159265358979. This function has no input arguments. The function uses this syntax:

```
=PI()
```

If you know the circumference of a circle, you can calculate its diameter with this formula:

diameter = circumference ÷ π

If you know the diameter of a circle, you can calculate its circumference with this formula:

circumference = diameter × π

If you know the diameter of a circle, you can calculate the area of the circle. A component of this calculation is the *radius*, which is one-half of the diameter. The formula is

area = (diameter × 0.5)^2 × π

Generating and Using Random Numbers

Random numbers are, by definition, unpredictable. That is, given a series of random numbers, you can't predict the next number from what has come before. Random numbers are quite useful for trying formulas and calculations. Suppose you're creating a worksheet to perform various kinds of data analysis. You may not have any real data yet, but you can generate random numbers to test the formulas and charts in the worksheet.

For example, an actuary may want to test some calculations based on a distribution of people's ages. Random numbers between 18 and 65 can be used for this task. You don't have to manually type fixed values between 18 and 65, because Excel can generate them automatically via the RAND function.

The all-purpose RAND function

The RAND function is simple; it takes no arguments and returns a decimal value between 0 and 1. That is, RAND never actually returns 0 or 1; the value is always in between these two numbers. The function is entered like this:

```
=RAND()
```

The RAND function returns values such as 0.136852731, 0.856104058, or 0.009277161. "Yikes!" you may be thinking. "How do these numbers help if you need values between 18 and 65?" Actually, it's easy with a little extra math.

There is a standard calculation for generating random numbers within a determined range:

```
=RAND()*(high number-low number)+low number
```

Using 18 and 65 as a desired range of numbers, the formula looks like this: =RAND()*(65-18)+18. This formula returns values such as 51.71777896 and 27.20727871.

Almost usable! But what about the long decimal portions of these numbers? Some people lie about their ages, but we've never heard someone say they're 27.2 years old!

All that is needed now for this 18-to-65 age example is to include the INT or ROUND function. INT simply discards the decimal portion of a number. ROUND allows control of how to handle the decimal portion.

The syntax for using the INT function with the RAND function follows:

```
=INT((high number-low number+1)*RAND()+low number)
```

Here's the syntax for using the ROUND function with the RAND function:

```
=ROUND(RAND()*(high number-low number)+low number,0)
```

Try it yourself! Here's how to use RAND and INT together:

1. **Position the pointer in the cell where you want the results displayed.**
2. **Type** =INT((**to begin the formula.**
3. **Click the cell that has the highest number to be used, or type such a value.**
4. **Type a hyphen (-).**
5. **Click the cell that has the lowest number to be used, or type such a value.**
6. **Type** +1)*RAND()+**.**
7. **Again, click the cell that has the lowest number to be used, or type the value.**
8. **Type) and press Enter.**

A random number, somewhere in the range between the low and high number, is returned.

Table 2-5 shows how returned random numbers can be altered with the INT and ROUND functions.

TABLE 2-5 **Using INT and ROUND to Process Random Values**

Value	Value Returned with INT	Value Returned with ROUND
51.71777896	51	52
27.20727871	27	27
24.61657068	24	25
55.27298686	55	55
49.93632709	49	50
43.60069745	43	44

Table 2-5 points out how the INT and ROUND functions return different numbers. For example, 51.71777896 is more accurately rounded to 52. Bear in mind that the second argument in the ROUND function (0 in this case) has an effect on how the rounding works. A 0 tells the ROUND function to round the number to the nearest integer, up or down to whichever integer is closest to the number.

A last but not insignificant note about using the RAND function: It's subject to the recalculation feature built into worksheets. In other words, each time the worksheet calculates, the RAND function is rerun and returns a new random number. The calculation setting in your worksheet is probably set to automatic. You can check this by looking at the Calculation Options section on the Formulas tab of the Excel Options dialog box. On a setting of Automatic, the worksheet recalculates with every action. The random generated numbers keep changing, which can become quite annoying if this isn't what you intended to have happen. However, you probably *did* want the number to change — otherwise, why use something "random" in the first place?

Luckily, you can generate a random number but have it remain fixed regardless of the calculation setting. The method is to type the RAND function, along with any other parts of a larger formula, directly in the Formula Bar. After you type your formula, press the F9 key and then press Enter. This tells Excel to calculate the formula and type the returned random number as a fixed number instead of a formula. If you press Enter or finish the entry in some way without pressing the F9 key, you have to type it again.

Precise randomness with RANDBETWEEN

Using the RAND function returns a value between 0 and 1, and when you use it with other functions, such as ROUND, you can get a random number within a range that you specify. If you just need a quick way to get an integer (no decimal portion!) within a given range, use RANDBETWEEN.

The RANDBETWEEN function takes two arguments: the low and high numbers of the desired range. It works only with integers. You can put real numbers in the range, but the result will still be an integer.

To use RANDBETWEEN, follow these steps:

1. **Position the pointer in the cell where you want the results displayed.**
2. **Type** =RANDBETWEEN(**to begin the formula.**
3. **Click the cell that has the low number of the desired range, or type such a value.**

4. **Type a comma (,).**
5. **Click the cell that has the highest number of the desired range, or type such a value.**
6. **Type) and press Enter.**

For example, =RANDBETWEEN(10,20) returns a random integer between 10 and 20.

Creating a Sequence

The SEQUENCE function is a nifty helper that creates a repeating sequence over a given number of rows and columns. There are four arguments. The first argument is the number of rows, and the second argument is the number of columns to be filled in with the sequence. The third and fourth arguments indicate the starting number and increment of the sequence.

In the following example, an area covering six rows and four columns will show a sequence starting with 10 and incrementing by 2:

```
=SEQUENCE(6,4,10,2)
```

The area covers 24 cells (6 x 4). The first cell will show 10, and the last cell will show 56.

The third and fourth arguments of the SEQUENCE function are optional. If either is left out, the default becomes 1. For example this use of SEQUENCE fills a 5 x 5 area that starts with 7 and then increments each cell by 1:

```
=SEQUENCE(5,5,7,1)
```

Raising Numbers to New Heights

There is an old tale about a king who loved chess so much, he decided to reward the inventor of chess by granting any request he had. The inventor asked for a grain of wheat for the first square of the chessboard on Monday, two grains for the second square on Tuesday, four grains for the third square on Wednesday, eight grains for the fourth square on Thursday, and so on, each day doubling the amount until the 64th square was filled with wheat. The king thought this was a silly request. The inventor could've asked for riches!

What happened was that the kingdom quickly ran out of wheat. By the 15th day, the number equaled 16,384. By the 20th day, the number was 524,288. On the 64th day, the number would've been an astonishing 9,223,372,036,854,780,000, but the kingdom had run out of wheat at least a couple of weeks earlier!

This "powerful" math is literally known as raising a number to a power. The *power*, in this case, means how many times a number is to be multiplied by itself. The notation is typically a superscript (2^3 for example). Another common way of noting the use of a power is with the caret symbol: 2^3. The verbiage for this is *two to the third power* or *two to the power of three*.

In the chess example, 2 is raised to a higher power each day. Table 2-6 shows the first ten days.

TABLE 2-6 The Power of Raising Numbers to a Power

Day	Power That 2 Is Raised To	Power Notation	Basic Math Notation	Result
1	0	2^0	1	1
2	1	2^1	2	2
3	2	2^2	2 × 2	4
4	3	2^3	2 × 2 × 2	8
5	4	2^4	2 × 2 × 2 × 2	16
6	5	2^5	2 × 2 × 2 × 2 × 2	32
7	6	2^6	2 × 2 × 2 × 2 × 2 × 2	64
8	7	2^7	2 × 2 × 2 × 2 × 2 × 2 × 2	128
9	8	2^8	2 × 2 × 2 × 2 × 2 × 2 × 2 × 2	256
10	9	2^9	2 × 2 × 2 × 2 × 2 × 2 × 2 × 2 × 2	512

The concept is easy enough. Each time the power is incremented by 1, the result doubles. Note that the first entry raises 2 to the 0 power. Isn't that strange? Well, not really. Any number raised to the 0 power equals 1. Also note that any number raised to the power of 1 equals the number itself.

Excel provides the POWER function, with the following syntax:

```
=POWER(number,power)
```

Both the number and power arguments can be integers or real numbers, and negative numbers are allowed.

> **TIP**
> In a worksheet, you can use either the POWER function or the caret. For example, in a cell you can type =**POWER(4,3)** or =**4^3**. The result is the same either way. You insert the caret by holding Shift and pressing the number 6 key on the keyboard.

Multiplying Multiple Numbers

The PRODUCT function is useful for multiplying up to 255 numbers at a time. The syntax follows:

```
=PRODUCT(number1,number2,...)
```

Cell references can be included in the argument list, as well as actual numbers, and of course, they can be mixed. Therefore, all these variations work:

```
=PRODUCT(A2,B15,C20)
=PRODUCT(5,8,22)
=PRODUCT(A10,5,B9)
```

In fact, you can use ranges of numbers as the arguments. In this case, the notation looks like this:

```
=PRODUCT(B85:B88,C85:C88,D86:D88)
```

Here's how to use the PRODUCT function:

1. **Type some values in a worksheet.**

    You can include many values, going down columns or across in rows.

2. **Position the pointer in the cell where you want the results displayed.**
3. **Type** =PRODUCT(**to begin the function.**
4. **Click a cell that has a number.**

    Alternatively, you can hold down the left mouse button and drag the pointer over a range of cells with numbers.

5. **Type a comma (,).**
6. **Repeat steps 4 and 5 up to 254 times.**
7. **Type) and press Enter.**

CHAPTER 2 Performing Functional Math   263

The result you see is calculated by multiplying all the numbers you selected. Your fingers would probably hurt if you had done this on a calculator.

Figure 2-7 shows this on a worksheet. Cell C10 shows the result of multiplying 12 numbers, although only three arguments, as ranges, have been used in the function.

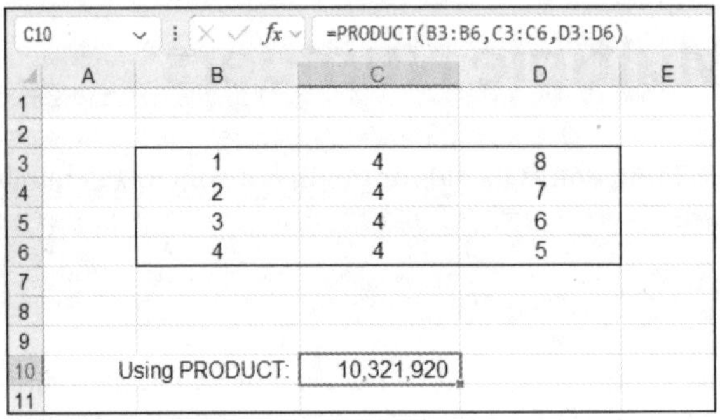

FIGURE 2-7: Putting the PRODUCT function to work.

Summing Things Up

Aha! Just when you think you know how to sum numbers (really, haven't you been doing this since your early school years?), we present a fancy-footwork summing that makes you think twice before going for that quick total.

The functions here are very cool — very "in" with the math crowd. To be a true Excel guru, try the SUBTOTAL, SUMPRODUCT, SUMIF, and SUMIFS functions shown here, and then strut your stuff around the office!

Using SUBTOTAL

The SUBTOTAL function is very flexible. It doesn't perform just one calculation; it can do any of 11 calculations depending on what you need. What's more, SUBTOTAL can perform these calculations on up to 255 ranges of numbers. This gives you the ability to get exactly the type of summary you need without creating a complex set of formulas. The syntax of the function follows:

```
=SUBTOTAL(function number,range1,range2,...)
```

The first argument determines which calculation is performed. It can be any of the values shown in Table 2-7. The remaining arguments identify the ranges containing the numbers to be used in the calculation.

264 BOOK 3 Going Farther with Functions

TABLE 2-7 **Argument Values for the SUBTOTAL Function**

Function Number for First Argument	Function	Description
1	AVERAGE	Returns the average value of a group of numbers
2	COUNT	Returns the count of cells that contain numbers and also numbers within the list of arguments
3	COUNTA	Returns the count of cells that are not empty within the list of arguments
4	MAX	Returns the maximum value in a group of numbers
5	MIN	Returns the minimum value in a group of numbers
6	PRODUCT	Returns the product of a group of numbers
7	STDEV.S	Returns the standard deviation from a sample of values
8	STDEV.P	Returns the standard deviation from an entire population, including text and logical values
9	SUM	Returns the sum of a group of numbers
10	VAR.S	Returns variance based on a sample
11	VAR.P	Returns variance based on an entire population

Figure 2-8 shows examples of using the SUBTOTAL function. Raw data values are listed in column A. The results of using the function in a few variations are listed in column C. Column E displays the actual function entries that returned the respective results in column C.

TIP Using named ranges with the SUBTOTAL function is useful. For example, =SUBTOTAL(1,October_Sales,November_Sales,December_Sales) makes for an easy way to calculate the average sale of the fourth quarter.

A second set of numbers can be used for the function number (the first argument in the SUBTOTAL function). These numbers start with 101 and are the same functions as shown in Table 2-7. For example, 101 is AVERAGE, 102 is COUNT, and so on. The 1 through 11 function numbers consider all values in a range. The 101 through 111 function numbers tell the function to ignore values that are in hidden rows or columns.

	A	B	C	D	E	F	G	H	I
1	4								
2	8								
3	12		14		=SUBTOTAL(1,A1:A6)				
4	16		26		=SUBTOTAL(1,A1:A12)				
5	20								
6	24		10		=SUBTOTAL(2,A1:A10)				
7	28								
8	32		40		=SUBTOTAL(4,A1:A10)				
9	36								
10	40								
11	44		12.111		=SUBTOTAL(7,A1:A10)				
12	48								
13	52								
14	56		220		=SUBTOTAL(9,A1:A10)				
15	60		640		=SUBTOTAL(9,A1:A10,A15:A20)				
16	64								
17	68								
18	72								
19	76								
20	80								
21									

FIGURE 2-8: Working with the SUBTOTAL function.

Using SUMPRODUCT

The SUMPRODUCT function provides a sophisticated way to add various products across ranges of values. It doesn't just add the products of separate ranges; it produces products of the values positioned in the same place in each range and then sums up those products. The syntax of the function follows:

=SUMPRODUCT(Range1,Range2,...)

The arguments to SUMPRODUCT must be ranges, although a range can be a single cell or value. What is required is that all the ranges be the same size, both rows and columns. Up to 255 ranges are allowed, and at least 2 are required.

SUMPRODUCT works by first multiplying elements, by position, across the ranges and then adding all the results. To see how this works, take a look at the three ranges of values in Figure 2-9. We put letters in the ranges instead of numbers to make this easier to explain.

	A	B	C	D	E	F	G	H	I	J
1										
2		A	D		H	K		N	Q	
3		B	E		I	L		O	R	
4		C	F		J	M		P	S	
5										

FIGURE 2-9: Following the steps used by SUMPRODUCT.

Suppose that you typed the following formula in the worksheet:

```
=SUMPRODUCT(B2:C4,E2:F4,H2:I4)
```

The result would be calculated by the following steps:

1. Multiplying A times H times N and saving the result.
2. Multiplying D times K times Q and saving the result.
3. Multiplying B times I times O and saving the result.
4. Multiplying E times L times R and saving the result.
5. Multiplying C times J times P and saving the result.
6. Multiplying F times M times S and saving the result.
7. Adding all six results to get the final answer.

> **WARNING**: Be careful when you're using the SUMPRODUCT function. It's easy to mistakenly assume that the function adds products of individual ranges. It doesn't. SUMPRODUCT returns the sums of products across positional elements.

As confusing as SUMPRODUCT seems, it actually has a sophisticated use. Imagine that you have a list of units sold by product and another list of the products' prices. You need to know total sales (that is, the sum of the amounts), in which an amount is units sold times unit price.

In the old days of spreadsheets, you would use an additional column to first multiply each unit sold figure by its price. Then you would sum those intermediate values. Now, with SUMPRODUCT, the drudgery is over. The single use of SUMPRODUCT gets the final answer in one step. Figure 2-10 shows how one cell contains the needed grand total. No intermediate steps are necessary.

Item	Units Sold	Price per Unit
Desks	15	$60
Tables	10	$85
Chairs	22	$25
Sofas	6	$450
Bookcases	24	$30
		$ 5,720

D11: =SUMPRODUCT(C3:C7,D3:D7)

FIGURE 2-10: Being productive with SUMPRODUCT.

CHAPTER 2 **Performing Functional Math** 267

Using SUMIF and SUMIFS

SUMIF is one of the real gemstones of Excel functions. It calculates the sum of a range of values, including only those values that meet a specified criterion.

Suppose that you use a worksheet to keep track of all your food-store purchases. For each shopping trip, you put the date in column A, the amount in column B, and the name of the store in column C. You can use the SUMIF function to tell Excel to add all the values in column B only where column C contains Great Grocery. That's it. SUMIF gives you the answer. Neat!

Figure 2-11 shows this example. The date of purchase, place of purchase, and amount spent are listed in three columns. SUMIF calculates the sum of purchases at Great Grocery. Here's how the function is written for the example:

```
=SUMIF(C3:C15,"Great Grocery",B3:B15)
```

FIGURE 2-11: Using SUMIF for targeted tallying.

Here are a couple of important points about the SUMIF function:

REMEMBER

» The second argument can accommodate several variations of expressions, such as including greater than (>) or less than (<) signs or other operators. For example, if a column has regions such as North, South, East, and West, the criteria could be <>North, which would return the sum of rows that are *not* for the North region.

» Unpredictable results occur if the ranges in the first and third arguments don't match in size.

Try it yourself! Here's how to use the SUMIF function:

1. **Type two ranges of data in a worksheet.**

   At least one should contain numerical data. Make sure both ranges are the same size.

2. **Position the pointer in the cell where you want the results displayed.**

3. **Type =SUMIF(to begin the function.**

4. **Hold down the left mouse button and drag the pointer over one of the ranges.**

   This is the range that can be other than numerical data.

5. **Type a comma (,).**

6. **Click one of the cells in the first range.**

   This is the criterion.

7. **Type a comma (,).**

8. **Hold down the left mouse button and drag the pointer over the second range.**

   This is the range that must contain numerical data.

9. **Type) and press Enter.**

The result you see is a sum of the numeric values where the items in the first range matched the selected criteria.

The example in Figure 2-11 sums values when the store is Great Grocery but does not use the date in the calculation. What if you need to know how much was spent at Great Grocery in April only? Excel provides a function for this, of course: SUMIFS.

SUMIFS lets you apply multiple "if" conditions to a sum. The format of SUMIFS is a bit different from that of SUMIF. SUMIFS uses this structure:

```
=SUMIFS(range to be summed,criteria range 1,criteria 1,criteria
   range 2,criteria 2)
```

The structure requires the range of numerical values to be typed first, followed by pairs of criteria ranges and the criteria itself. In Figure 2-12, the formula is

```
=SUMIFS(B3:B15,A3:A15,"<5/1/2020",C3:C15,"Great Grocery")
```

CHAPTER 2 Performing Functional Math   269

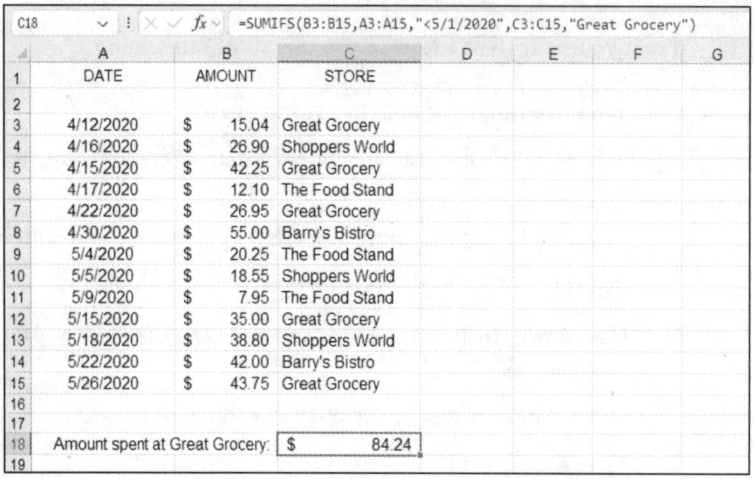

	A	B	C	D	E	F	G
1	DATE	AMOUNT	STORE				
2							
3	4/12/2020	$ 15.04	Great Grocery				
4	4/16/2020	$ 26.90	Shoppers World				
5	4/15/2020	$ 42.25	Great Grocery				
6	4/17/2020	$ 12.10	The Food Stand				
7	4/22/2020	$ 26.95	Great Grocery				
8	4/30/2020	$ 55.00	Barry's Bistro				
9	5/4/2020	$ 20.25	The Food Stand				
10	5/5/2020	$ 18.55	Shoppers World				
11	5/9/2020	$ 7.95	The Food Stand				
12	5/15/2020	$ 35.00	Great Grocery				
13	5/18/2020	$ 38.80	Shoppers World				
14	5/22/2020	$ 42.00	Barry's Bistro				
15	5/26/2020	$ 43.75	Great Grocery				
16							
17							
18	Amount spent at Great Grocery:	$ 84.24					
19							

Cell C18 formula: `=SUMIFS(B3:B15,A3:A15,"<5/1/2020",C3:C15,"Great Grocery")`

FIGURE 2-12: Using SUMIFS to get a multiple filtered sum.

The function uses B3:B15 as the source of values to sum. A3:A15 is the first criteria range, and <5/1/2020 is the criteria. This tells the function to look for any date that is earlier than May 1, 2020 (which filters the dates to just April). This is followed by a second criteria range and value: In C3:C15, look just for Great Grocery. The final sum of $84.24 adds just three numbers — 15.04, 42.25, and 26.95 — because these are the only values in April for Great Grocery.

> **IN THIS CHAPTER**
>
> » Handling and formatting dates
> » Working with days, months, and years
> » Getting the value of today
> » Determining the day of the week
> » Handling and formatting time values
> » Working with hours, minutes, and seconds
> » Getting the current time

Chapter 3
Working with Date and Time Functions

Often, when working with Excel, you need to manage dates and times. Perhaps you have a list of dates when you visited a client and you need to count how many times you were there in September. On the other hand, maybe you're tracking a project over a few months and you want to know how many days are in between the milestones.

Excel has a number of useful date and time functions to make your work easier! This chapter explains how Excel handles dates and times, how to compare and subtract dates, how to work with parts of a date (such as the month or year), and even how to convert a date written as text into a real date value. We also show you how to work with times and perform calculations on time values.

Understanding How Excel Handles Dates

Imagine that on January 1, 1900, you started counting by ones, each day adding one more to the total. This is just how Excel thinks of dates. January 1, 1900, is one; January 2, 1900, is two; and so on. We'll always remember 25,404 as the day man first walked on the moon, and 36,892 as the start of the new millennium!

TECHNICAL STUFF

The millennium actually started on January 1, 2001. The year 2000 is the last year of the 20th century. Representing dates as a serial number — specifically, the number of days between January 1, 1900, and the date in question — may seem odd, but there are very good reasons for it. Excel can handle dates from January 1, 1900, to December 31, 9999. Using the serial numbering system, that's 1 through 2,958,465!

Because Excel represents dates in this way, it can work with dates in the same manner as numbers. For example, you can subtract one date from another to find out how many days are between them. Likewise, you can add 14 to today's date to get a date two weeks in the future. This trick is very useful, but people are used to seeing dates represented in traditional formats, not as numbers. Fortunately, Excel uses date serial numbers only behind the scenes, and what you see in your workbook are dates in the standard date formats such as Jan 20, 2021 and 1/20/21.

TIP

In Excel for Mac, the serial numbering system begins on January 1, 1904.

The way years are handled requires special mention. When a year is fully displayed in four digits, such as 2025, there is no ambiguity. However, when a date is written in a shorthand style, such as in 3/1/25, it isn't clear what the year is. It could be 2025 or it could be 1925. Suppose that 3/1/25 is a shorthand entry for someone's birthday. On March 1, 2028, they're either 3 years old or 103 years old. In those countries that write dates as mm/dd/yy, this would be March 1, 1925, or March 1, 2025.

Excel and the Windows operating system have a default way of interpreting shorthand years. Windows has a setting in the Customize Regional Options dialog box located in the Control Panel. This setting guides how Excel interprets years. If the setting is 1950 through 2049, 3/1/25 indicates the year 2025, but 3/1/45 indicates the year 1945, not 2045.

Here's how to open the Customize Regional Options dialog box and set the cutoff year:

1. **Use the Windows search feature to find and open Control Panel.**
2. **Select Clock and Region.**

3. **Select Region.**

   The Region dialog box opens.

4. **Select the Formats tab.**

5. **Click the Additional Settings button.**

   The Customize Format dialog box opens.

6. **Select the Date tab.**

7. **In the Calendar section, select a four-digit ending year (such as 2049) to indicate the latest year that will be used when interpreting a two-digit year.**

8. **Click Apply and then click OK to close each dialog box.**

> **TIP** To ensure full accuracy when working with dates, always type the full four digits for the year.

Formatting Dates

When you work with dates, you probably need to format cells in your worksheet. It's great that Excel tells you that June 1, 2026, is serially represented as 46174, but you probably don't want that in a report. To format dates, you use the Format Cells dialog box, as shown in Figure 3-1.

To format the currently selected cells as dates, follow these steps:

1. **If it's not already displayed, select the Home tab at the top of the Excel screen.**

2. **Click the small arrow at the lower-right corner of the Number section.**

   The Format Cells dialog box appears, revealing the Number tab.

3. **From the Category list, select Date.**

4. **From the Type list, select an appropriate format.**

   Now you can turn the useful but pesky serial dates into a user-friendly format.

> **TIP** When you type a date in a cell using one of the standard date formats, Excel recognizes it as a date and automatically assigns a Date format to the cell. You may want to use the Number tab in the Format Cells dialog box to assign a different Date format.

CHAPTER 3 Working with Date and Time Functions 273

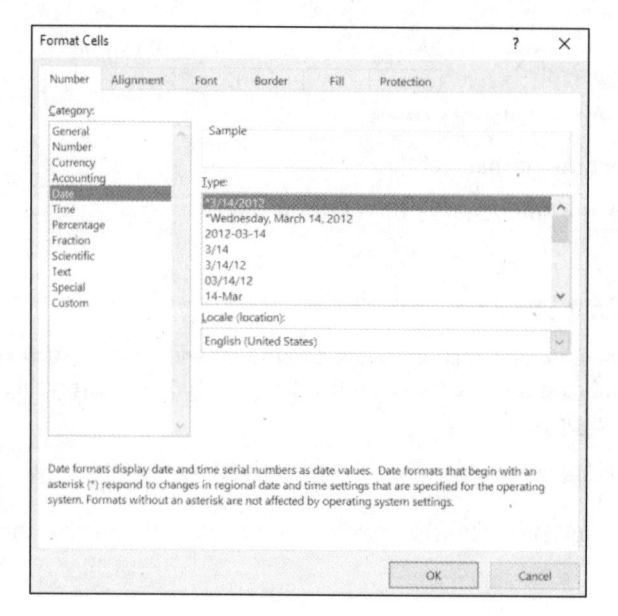

FIGURE 3-1: Using the Format Cells dialog box to control how dates are displayed.

Making a Date with DATE

You can use the DATE function to create a complete date from separate year, month, and day information. The DATE function can be useful because dates don't always appear as, well, dates, in a worksheet. You may have a column of values between 1 and 12 that represents the month and another column of values between 1 and 31 for the day of the month. A third column may hold years — in either two-digit shorthand or the full four digits.

The DATE function combines individual day, month, and year components into a single usable date. This makes using and referencing dates in your worksheet easy.

Follow these steps to use the DATE function:

1. **Click the cell where you want the results displayed.**
2. **Type** =DATE(**to begin the function entry.**
3. **Click the cell that has the year.**
4. **Type a comma (,).**
5. **Click the cell that has the number (1–12) that represents the month.**
6. **Type a comma (,).**

274 BOOK 3 *Going Farther with Functions*

7. Click the cell that has the number (1–31) that represents the day of the month.

8. Type) and press Enter.

Figure 3-2 displays a fourth column of dates that were created by using DATE and the values from the first three columns. The fourth column of dates has been formatted so the dates are displayed in a standard format, not as a raw date serial number.

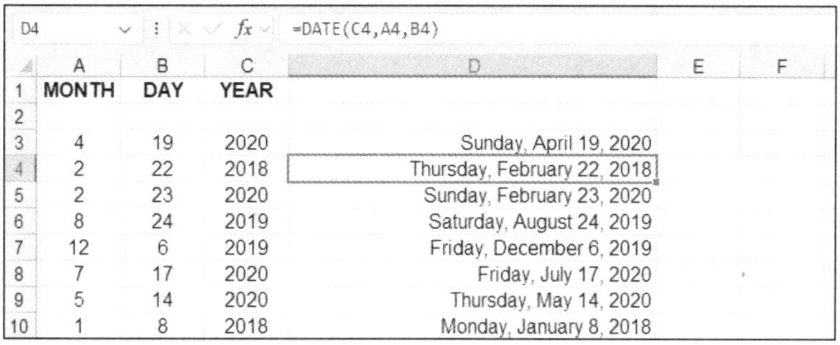

FIGURE 3-2:
Using the DATE function to assemble a date from separate month, day, and year values.

DATE provides some extra flexibility with the month number. Negative month numbers are subtracted from the specified year. For example, the function =DATE(2021,-5,15) returns the date July 15, 2020, because July 2020 is five months before the first month of 2021. Numbers greater than 12 work the same way. =DATE(2021,15,1) returns March 1, 2022, because March 2022 is 15 months after the first month of 2021.

Day numbers work the same way. Negative day numbers are subtracted from the first of the specified month, and numbers that are greater than the last day of the specified month wrap into later months. Thus, =DATE(2021,2,30) returns March 2, 2021, because February does not have 30 days. Likewise, =DATE(2021,2,40) returns March 12, 2021.

Breaking a Date with DAY, MONTH, and YEAR

That which can be put together can also be taken apart. In the preceding section, we show you how to use the DATE function to create a date from separate year, month, and day data. In this section, you find out how to do the reverse:

CHAPTER 3 Working with Date and Time Functions 275

Split a date into individual year, month, and day components by using the YEAR, MONTH, and DAY functions, respectively. In Figure 3-3, the dates in column A are split apart by day, month, and year, respectively, in columns B, C, and D.

	A	B	C	D
	Date	DAY	MONTH	YEAR
1	1/1/2021	1	1	2021
2	5/22/2019	22	5	2019
3	3/13/2020	13	3	2020
4	9/28/2020	28	9	2020
5	9/3/2019	3	9	2019
6	4/10/2020	10	4	2020
7	3/9/2019	9	3	2019
8	8/15/2019	15	8	2019
9	7/31/2019	31	7	2019

FIGURE 3-3: Splitting apart a date with the DAY, MONTH, and YEAR functions.

Isolating the day

Isolating the day part of a date is useful when just the day but not the month or year is relevant. Suppose that you own a store and want to figure out whether more customers come to shop in the first half or the second half of the month. You're interested in this trend over several months. So, the task may be to average the number of sales by the day of the month only.

The DAY function is useful for this because you can use it to return just the day for a lengthy list of dates. Then you can examine results by the day only.

Here's how to use the DAY function:

1. **Position the pointer in the cell where you want the results displayed.**
2. **Type =DAY(to begin the function entry.**
3. **Click the cell that has the date.**
4. **Type) and press Enter.**

    Excel returns a number between 1 and 31.

Figure 3-4 shows how the DAY function can be used to analyze customer activity. Column A contains a full year's sequential dates (most of which are not visible in the figure). In column B, the day part of each date has been isolated. Column C shows the customer traffic for each day.

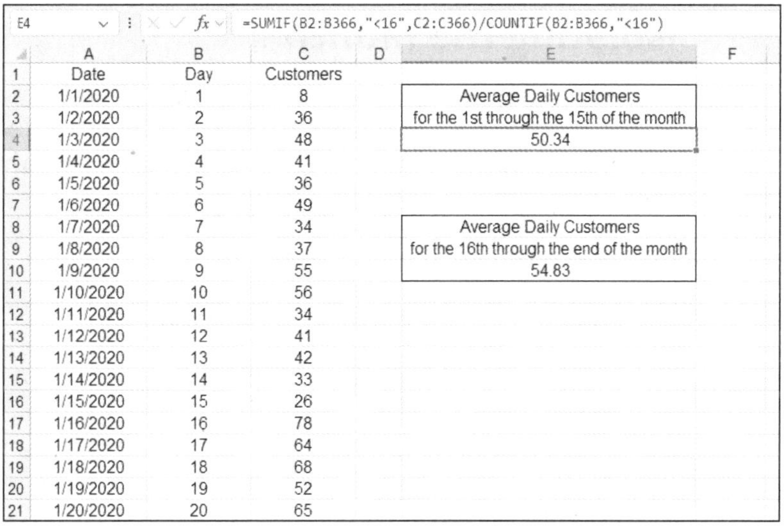

	A	B	C	D	E	F
1	Date	Day	Customers			
2	1/1/2020	1	8		Average Daily Customers	
3	1/2/2020	2	36		for the 1st through the 15th of the month	
4	1/3/2020	3	48		50.34	
5	1/4/2020	4	41			
6	1/5/2020	5	36			
7	1/6/2020	6	49			
8	1/7/2020	7	34		Average Daily Customers	
9	1/8/2020	8	37		for the 16th through the end of the month	
10	1/9/2020	9	55		54.83	
11	1/10/2020	10	56			
12	1/11/2020	11	34			
13	1/12/2020	12	41			
14	1/13/2020	13	42			
15	1/14/2020	14	33			
16	1/15/2020	15	26			
17	1/16/2020	16	78			
18	1/17/2020	17	64			
19	1/18/2020	18	68			
20	1/19/2020	19	52			
21	1/20/2020	20	65			

E4: =SUMIF(B2:B366,"<16",C2:C366)/COUNTIF(B2:B366,"<16")

FIGURE 3-4: Using the DAY function to analyze customer activity.

This is all the information you need to analyze whether there is a difference in the amount of customer traffic between the first half and second half of the month.

Cells E4 and E10 show the average daily customer traffic for the first half and second half of the month, respectively. The value for the first half of the month was obtained by adding all the customer values for day values in the range 1 to 15 and then dividing by the total number of days. The value for the second half of the month was done the same way, using day values in the range 16 to 31.

The day parts of the dates, in column B, were key to these calculations:

» In cell E4, the calculation is =SUMIF(B2:B366,"<16",C2:C366)/COUNTIF(B2:B366"<16").

» In cell E10, the calculation is =SUMIF(B2:B366,">15",C2:C366)/COUNTIF(B2:B366,">15").

The SUMIF function is discussed in Chapter 2 of this minibook. The COUNTIF function works in a similar way to SUMIF: It counts only the cells that match the criteria you specify.

The DAY function has been instrumental in showing that more customers visit the fictitious store in the second half of the month. This type of information is great for helping a store owner plan staff assignments, sales specials, and so on.

Isolating the month

Isolating the month part of a date is useful when just the month, but not the day or year, is relevant. For example, you may have a list of dates on which more than five of your employees call in sick and need to determine whether this event is more common in certain months than others.

Use the MONTH function this way:

1. **Click the cell where you want the results displayed.**
2. **Type** =MONTH(**to begin the function entry.**
3. **Click the cell that has the date.**
4. **Type) and press Enter.**

   Excel returns a number between 1 and 12.

Isolating the year

Isolating the year part of a date is useful when only the year, but not the day or month, is relevant. In practice, this is less used than the DAY or MONTH functions because date data is often — though not always — from the same year.

Follow these steps to use the YEAR function:

1. **Click the cell where you want the results displayed.**
2. **Type** =YEAR(**to begin the function entry.**
3. **Click the cell that has the date.**
4. **Type) and press Enter.**

   Excel returns the four-digit year.

Converting a Date from Text

You may have data in your worksheet that looks like a date but is not represented as an Excel date value. For example, if you type 01-24-26 in a cell, Excel would have no way of knowing whether this is January 24, 2026, or the code for your combination lock. If it looks like a date, you can use the DATEVALUE function to convert it to an Excel date value.

In practice, any standard date format typed into a cell is recognized by Excel as a date and converted accordingly. However, there may be cases such as when text dates are imported from an external data source or data is copied and pasted into Excel for which you need DATEVALUE.

TECHNICAL STUFF

Why not type dates as text data? Although they may look fine, you can't use them for any of Excel's powerful date calculations without first converting them to date values.

The DATEVALUE function recognizes almost all commonly used ways that dates are written. Here are some ways that you may type August 14, 2026:

» 8/14/26

» 14-Aug-2026

» 2026/08/14

DATEVALUE can convert these and several other date representations to a date serial number.

After you've converted the dates to a date serial number, you can use the dates in other date formulas or perform calculations with them as described in other parts of this chapter.

To use the DATEVALUE function, follow these steps:

1. **Click the cell where you want the date serial number located.**
2. **Type =DATEVALUE(to begin the function entry.**
3. **Click the cell that has the text format date.**
4. **Type) and press Enter.**

   The result is a date serial number unless the cell where the result is displayed has already been set to a date format.

Figure 3-5 shows how some nonstandard dates in column A have been converted to serial numbers with the DATEVALUE function in column B. Then column C displays these serial numbers formatted as dates.

Do you notice something funny in Figure 3-5? Normally, you aren't able to type a value such as the one in cell A4 — 02-28-21 — without losing the leading 0. The cells in column A had been changed to the Text format. This format tells Excel to leave your entry as is. The Text format is one of the choices in the Category list in the Format Cells dialog box (refer to Figure 3-1).

CHAPTER 3 **Working with Date and Time Functions** 279

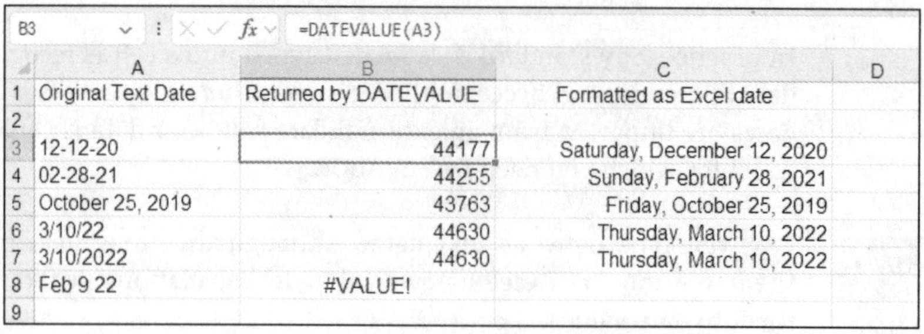

FIGURE 3-5: Converting dates to their serial equivalents with the DATEVALUE function.

Note also that the text date in cell A8, Feb 9 22, could not be converted by DATEVALUE, so the function returned the error message #VALUE#. Excel is great at recognizing dates, but it isn't perfect! In cases such as this, you have to format the date another way so DATEVALUE can recognize it.

Finding Out What TODAY Is

When working in Excel, you often need to use the current date. Each time you print a worksheet, for example, you may want the day's date to show. The TODAY function fills the bill perfectly. It simply returns the date from your computer's internal clock. To use the TODAY function, follow these steps:

1. **Click the pointer in the cell where you want the result.**
2. **Type** =TODAY().
3. **Press Enter.**

That's it! You now have the date from your computer. If your computer's clock isn't set correctly, don't blame Excel. As with all dates in Excel, what you really end up with is a serial number, but the Date formatting displays the date in a readable fashion.

As with all functions in Excel, you can embed functions in other functions. For example, if you need to know just the current date's month, you can combine the TODAY function with the MONTH function, like this:

```
=MONTH(TODAY())
```

Counting the days until your birthday

After a certain age, a lot of people wish their birthdays wouldn't come around so often, but if you still like birthdays, you can use Excel to keep track of how many days are left until the next one. Typed in a cell, this formula tells you how many days are left until your birthday (assuming that your next birthday is May 5, 2022):

```
=DATE(2022,5,5)-TODAY()
```

Use the DATE function to type the day, month, and year of your next birthday. This prevents Excel from interpreting a shorthand entry, such as 5/5/2022, as a mathematical operation on its own.

If the formula were =5/5/2022-TODAY(), Excel would calculate an incorrect answer because the formula effectively says, "Divide 5 by 5, divide that result by 2022, and then subtract the serial number of today's date." The answer would be incorrect.

REMEMBER Using the DATE function to represent dates in which a mathematical operation is performed is a good idea.

Counting your age in days

When your birthday finally rolls around, someone may ask how old you are. Maybe you'd rather not say. Here's a way to respond, but in a way that leaves some doubt: Answer by saying how old you are in days!

Excel can help you figure this out. All you have to do is count the number of days between your birth date and the current date. A simple formula tells you this:

```
=TODAY()-DATE(birth year,birth month,birth day)
```

Here's an example, assuming that your birthday is March 18, 1976:

```
=TODAY()-DATE(1976,3,18)
```

Determining the Day of the Week

The Beatles recorded a song called "Eight Days a Week," but for the rest of us, seven days is the norm. The WEEKDAY function helps you figure out which day of the week a date falls on. Now you can figure out whether your next birthday falls on a Friday. Or you can make sure that a planned business meeting doesn't fall on a weekend.

Here's how to use the WEEKDAY function:

1. **Click the cell where you want the results displayed.**
2. **Type =WEEKDAY(to begin the function entry.**
3. **Click the cell that has the date for which you want to find the weekday.**
4. **Type) and press Enter.**

   WEEKDAY returns a number between 1 and 7. By default, 1 represents Sunday; 2, Monday; 3, Tuesday; 4, Wednesday; 5, Thursday; 6, Friday; and 7, Saturday.

TIP If you'd rather have the week start on Monday, you can include a second, optional, argument that tells WEEKDAY to return 1 for Monday, 2 for Tuesday, and so on:

```
=WEEKDAY(A1,2)
```

The WEEKDAY function lets you extract interesting information from date-related data. For example, maybe you're on a diet, and you're keeping a tally of how many calories you consume each day for a month. Then you start wondering "On which days do I eat the most?" Figure 3-6 shows a worksheet that calculates the average calories consumed on each day of the week over a month's time. A glance at the results shows that Saturdays and Sundays are not your high-calorie-consumption days; it's Wednesdays and Thursdays that you have to watch out for.

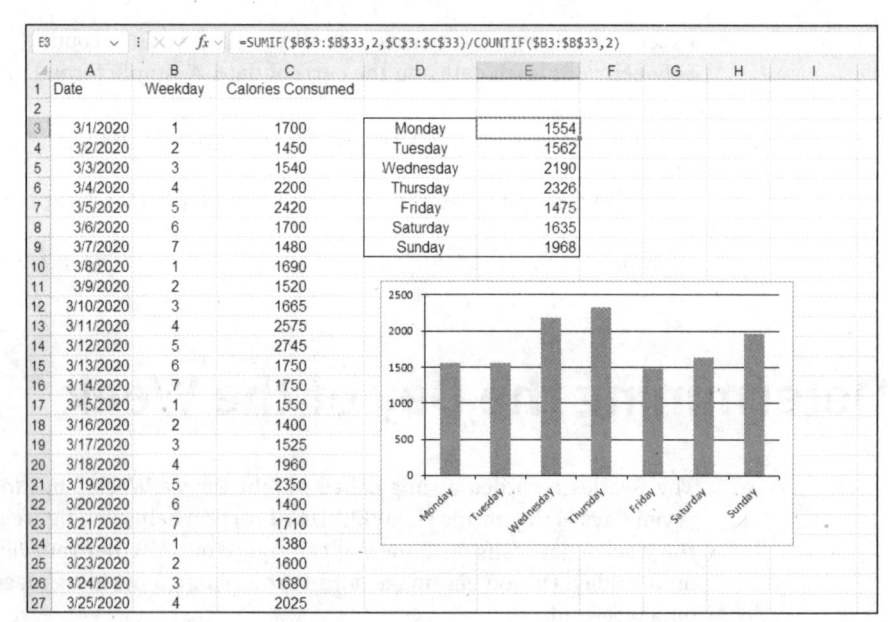

FIGURE 3-6: Using WEEKDAY tells you which day of the week a date falls on.

282 BOOK 3 **Going Farther with Functions**

Working with Workdays

Most weeks have five workdays — Monday through Friday — and two weekend days. (We know — some weeks seem to have 20 workdays, but that's just your imagination!) Excel has two functions that let you perform workday-related calculations.

Determining workdays in a range of dates

The NETWORKDAYS function tells you how many working days are in a range of dates. Do you ever sit at your desk and stare at the calendar, trying to count how many working days are left in the year? Excel can answer this vital question for you!

NETWORKDAYS counts the number of days, omitting Saturdays and Sundays, in a range of dates that you supply. You can add a list of dates that should not be counted, if you want. This optional list is where you can put holidays, vacation time, and so on.

Figure 3-7 shows an example using NETWORKDAYS. Cells C3 and C4 show the start and end dates, respectively. In this example, the start date is provided by the TODAY function. Therefore, the result always reflects a count that starts from the current date. The end date is the last day of the year. The function in cell C6 is =NETWORKDAYS(C3,C4,C10:C23).

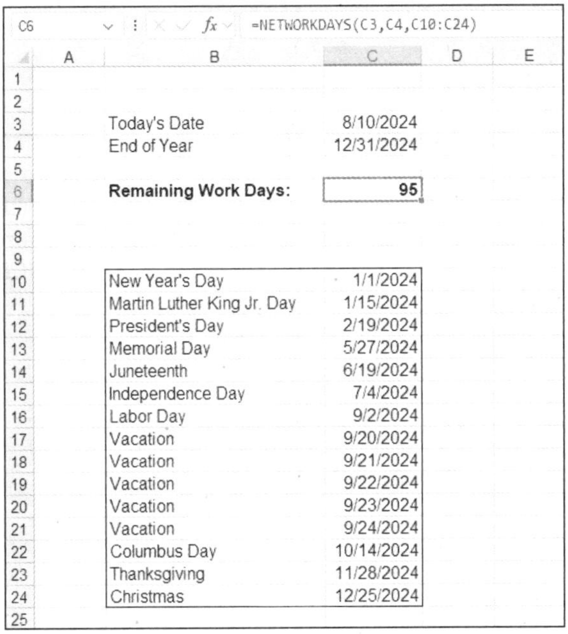

FIGURE 3-7: Counting workdays with NETWORKDAYS.

The function includes the cells that have the start and end dates. Then there is a range of cells: C10 through C23. These cells have dates that should not be counted in the total of workdays: holidays and vacations. You can put anything in these cells, but they have to be Excel dates. If a date specified in this list falls on a workday, NETWORKDAYS doesn't count it. If it falls on a weekend, it wouldn't be counted anyway, so it's ignored.

To use NETWORKDAYS, follow these steps:

1. **Click the cell where you want the results displayed.**
2. **Type** =NETWORKDAYS(**to begin the function entry.**
3. **Click the cell that has the start date for the range of dates to be counted.**
4. **Type a comma (,).**
5. **Click the cell that has the end date for the range of dates to be counted.**

    If you want to add a list of dates to exclude, continue to steps 6 and 7; otherwise, go to Step 8.

6. **Type a comma (,).**
7. **Click and drag the pointer over the cells that have the dates to exclude.**
8. **Type) and press Enter.**

    The result is a count of days, between the start and end dates, that do not fall on Saturday or Sunday and are not in an optional list of exclusion dates.

Workdays in the future

Sometimes, you're given a deadline ("Have that back to me in 20 working days"), or you give it to someone else. Fine, but what's the date 20 working days from now? The WORKDAY function comes to the rescue. You specify a start date, the number of working days, and an optional list of holidays that are not to be counted as working days. (This list works just the same as for the NETWORKDAYS function, discussed in the previous section.)

To use WORKDAYS, follow these steps:

1. **Click the cell where you want the results displayed.**
2. **Type** =WORKDAY(**to begin the function entry.**

3. **Click the cell that has the start date for the calculation.**
4. **Type a comma (,).**
5. **Click the cell that has the number of workdays or type the number directly in the formula.**

   If you want to add a list of dates to exclude in the count, continue to steps 6 and 7; otherwise, go to Step 8.

6. **Type a comma (,).**
7. **Click and drag the pointer over the cells that have the dates to be excluded.**
8. **Type) and press Enter.**

   The result is a date that is the specified number of workdays from the start date, not counting dates in the optional list of exclusion dates.

Understanding How Excel Handles Time

At the beginning of this chapter, we explain how Excel uses a serial number system to work with dates. Well, guess what? The same system is used to work with time. The key difference is that although dates are represented by the integer portion of a serial number, time is represented by the decimal portion.

What does this mean? Consider this: 43466. That is the serial number representation for January 1, 2019. Notice, though, that there is no indication of the time of day. The assumed time is 12 a.m. (midnight), the start of the day. You can, however, represent specific times if needed.

Excel uses the decimal side of the serial number to represent time as a fraction of the 24-hour day. Thus, 12 p.m. (noon) is 0.5, and 6 p.m. is 0.75. Table 3-1 shows some more examples and reveals how dates and time information are combined in a single serial number.

Time is represented in a decimal value — up to five digits to the right of the decimal point. A value of 0 is the equivalent of 12 a.m. A value of 0.5 is the equivalent of 12 p.m. — the midpoint of the day. The value of 0.99931 is the same as the 23rd hour and the *start* of the 59th minute. A value of 0.99999 is the same as the 23rd hour, the 59th minute, and the 59th second — in other words, 1 second before the start of the next day.

TABLE 3-1 **How Excel Represents Time**

Date and Time	Serial Format
January 1, 2019 12:00 a.m.	43466
January 1, 2019 12:01 a.m.	43466.00069
January 1, 2019 10:00 a.m.	43466.41667
January 1, 2019 12:00 p.m.	43466.5
January 1, 2019 4:30 p.m.	43466.6875
January 1, 2019 10:00 p.m.	43466.91667
January 1, 2019 11:59 p.m.	43466.99931

Can you represent time without a date? You bet! Use a value less than 1 for this purpose. For example, the serial number 0.75 represents 6 p.m. with no date specified.

Representing time as a serial number provides the same advantages as it does for dates: the ability to add and subtract times. For example, given a date/time serial number, you can create the serial number for the date/time one and a half days later by adding 1.5 to it.

Formatting Time

When you work with time values, you probably need to format cells in your worksheet so the times display in a standard format that people will understand. The decimal numbers don't make sense to us human folk. To format time, you use the Number tab of the Format Cells dialog box.

To format time, follow these steps:

1. **If it isn't already displayed, select the Home tab of the ribbon.**
2. **Click the small arrow in the lower-right corner of the Number section.**

   The Format Cells dialog box appears, with the Number tab displayed.
3. **Select Time in the Category list.**
4. **Select an appropriate format in the Type list.**

TIP: You can display time in several ways. Excel can format time so that hours in a day range from 1 a.m. to 12 a.m. and then 1 p.m. to 12 p.m. Alternatively, the hour can be between 0 and 23, with values 13 through 23 representing 1 p.m. through 11 p.m. The latter system, known to some as *military time* or *24-hour time*, is commonly used in computer systems.

Note that Excel stores a date and time together in a single serial number. Therefore, some of the formatting options in the time and date categories display a complete date and time.

Deconstructing Time with HOUR, MINUTE, and SECOND

Any moment in time really is a combination of an hour, a minute, and a second. You can use Excel's HOUR, MINUTE, and SECOND functions to break apart a time into these three components. The worksheet in Figure 3-8 shows a date and time in several rows going down column A. The same dates and times are shown in column B, with a different format. Columns C, D, and E show the hour, minute, and second, respectively, from the values in column A.

	A	B	C	D	E
1	Date and Time	Date and Time	Hour	Minute	Second
2	In General Format	in Date and Time Format			
3					
4					
5	44028.89935	7/16/2020 9:35:04 PM	21	35	4
6	43981.55234	5/30/2020 1:15:22 PM	13	15	22
7	44088.2303	9/14/2020 5:31:38 AM	5	31	38
8	43837.3452	1/7/2020 8:17:05 AM	8	17	5
9	43838.33802	1/8/2020 8:06:45 AM	8	6	45
10	43935.6486	4/14/2020 3:33:59 PM	15	33	59
11	44149.36667	11/14/2020 8:48:00 AM	8	48	0
12	44060.839	8/17/2020 8:08:10 PM	20	8	10
13	44012.13837	6/30/2020 3:19:15 AM	3	19	15
14	43917.04307	3/27/2020 1:02:01 AM	1	2	1

FIGURE 3-8: Splitting time with the HOUR, MINUTE, and SECOND functions.

TIP: Note that if the date/time serial number contains a date part, HOUR, MINUTE, and SECOND ignore it — all they care about is the time part.

Isolating the hour

Extracting the hour from a time is useful in workbooks that tally hourly events. A common use of this occurs in call centers. If you've ever responded to an infomercial or a pledge drive, you may realize that a group of workers wait for incoming phone calls such as the one you made. A common metric in this type of business is the number of calls per hour.

Figure 3-9 shows a worksheet that summarizes calls per hour. Calls have been tracked for October 2012. The incoming call dates and times are listed in column A. In column B, the hour of each call has been isolated with the HOUR function. Columns D and E show a summary of calls per hour over the course of the month.

FIGURE 3-9: Using the HOUR function to summarize results.

	A	B	C	D	E
1	Date and Time of Call	Hour of Call			
2					
3	10/1/2012 10:01 AM	10		Hour	Number of Calls
4	10/1/2012 10:05 AM	10		10:00 AM	52
5	10/1/2012 10:10 AM	10		11:00 AM	77
6	10/1/2012 10:14 AM	10		12:00 PM	49
7	10/1/2012 10:19 AM	10		1:00 PM	41
8	10/1/2012 10:24 AM	10		2:00 PM	42
9	10/1/2012 10:28 AM	10		3:00 PM	42
10	10/1/2012 10:33 AM	10		4:00 PM	42
11	10/1/2012 10:37 AM	10		5:00 PM	40
12	10/1/2012 10:42 AM	10		6:00 PM	42
13	10/1/2012 10:47 AM	10		7:00 PM	41
14	10/1/2012 10:51 AM	10		8:00 PM	65
15	10/1/2012 10:56 AM	10		9:00 PM	64
16	10/1/2012 11:00 AM	11		10:00 PM	45
17	10/1/2012 11:05 AM	11		11:00 PM	42
18	10/1/2012 11:10 AM	11			
19	10/1/2012 11:11 AM	11			

Formula in E4: `=COUNTIF($B$3:$B$1100,"=10")`

In Figure 3-9, the values in column E are calculated by the COUNTIF function. There is a COUNTIF for each hour from 10 a.m. through 11 p.m. Each COUNTIF looks at the range of numbers in column B (the hours) and counts the values that match the criteria. Each COUNTIF uses a different hour value for its criteria. Following is an example:

```
=COUNTIF($B$3:$B$1100,"=16")
```

To use the HOUR function, follow these steps:

1. **Select the cell where you want the result displayed.**
2. **Type =HOUR(to begin the function entry.**
3. **Click the cell that has the full time (or date/time) entry.**

4. **Type) and press Enter.**

   Excel returns a number between 0 and 23.

Isolating the minute

Isolating the minute part of a time is necessary in workbooks that track activity down to the minute. A timed test is a perfect example. Remember when the teacher would yell, "Pencils down"?

Excel can easily calculate how long something takes by subtracting one time from another. In the case of a test, the MINUTE function helps with the calculation because how long something took in minutes is being figured out. Figure 3-10 shows a list of times it took for students to take a test. All students started the test at 10 a.m. Then, when each student finished, the time was noted. The test *should* have taken a student no more than 15 minutes.

	A	B	C	D
1	Student ID	Start Time	End Time	Finished on Time
3	S2223	10:00 AM	10:18 AM	No
4	G7854	10:00 AM	10:12 AM	Yes
5	A4973	10:00 AM	10:14 AM	Yes
6	M4211	10:00 AM	10:20 AM	No
7	H7840	10:00 AM	10:22 AM	No
8	G4381	10:00 AM	10:10 AM	Yes
9	J4009	10:00 AM	10:11 AM	Yes
10	T5545	10:00 AM	10:15 AM	Yes
11	W9329	10:00 AM	10:13 AM	Yes
12	M8050	10:00 AM	10:16 AM	No
13	S2377	10:00 AM	10:23 AM	No
14	R1967	10:00 AM	10:14 AM	Yes

D3 fx =IF(MINUTE(C3)-MINUTE(B3)<=15,"Yes","No")

FIGURE 3-10: Calculating minutes elapsed with the MINUTE function.

For each data row, column D contains a formula that subtracts the minute in the end time (in column C) from the start time (in column B). This math operation is embedded in an IF statement. If the result is 15 or less, Yes appears in column D; otherwise, No appears.

```
=IF(MINUTE(C3)-MINUTE(B3)<=15,"Yes","No")
```

Like the HOUR function, the MINUTE function takes a single time or date/time reference as its argument.

Isolating the second

Isolating the second from a date value is useful in situations in which highly accurate time calculations are needed. In practice, this isn't a common requirement in Excel worksheets.

Follow these steps to use the SECOND function:

1. **Position the pointer in the cell where you want the results displayed.**
2. **Type** =SECOND(**to begin the function entry.**
3. **Click the cell that has the time value or enter a time value.**
4. **Type) and press Enter.**

Finding the Time NOW

Sometimes when you're working in Excel, you need to access the current time. For example, you may be working on a client project and need to know how much time you've spent on it. Use the NOW function when you first open the workbook, and use it again when you're finished. Subtracting one value from the other provides the elapsed time.

To use the NOW function, follow these steps:

1. **Select the cell where you want the result.**
2. **Type** =NOW().
3. **Press Enter.**

TIP You must take one additional step to make the preceding NOW time calculation work. When you get the current time at the start, copy the value and then use Paste Special to paste it back as a value. This strategy prevents the time from constantly updating. You can also do this by selecting the cell, clicking the Formula Bar, and then pressing F9.

NOW provides not just the current time, but also the current date. This is similar to the TODAY function. TODAY returns the current date — without the current time. NOW returns the full current date and time.

IN THIS CHAPTER

» **Assembling, altering, and formatting text**

» **Figuring out the length of text**

» **Comparing text**

» **Searching for text**

Chapter 4
Manipulating Text with Functions

A rose is still a rose by any other name. Or maybe not, when you use Excel's sophisticated text-manipulation functions to change it into something else. Case in point: You can use the REPLACE function to change a rose into a tulip or a daisy, literally!

Did you ever have to work on a list in which people's full names are in one column, but you need to use only their last names? You could extract the last names to another column manually, but that strategy gets pretty tedious for more than a few names. What if the list contains hundreds of names? This is just one example of text manipulations that you can do easily and quickly with Excel's text functions.

Breaking Apart Text

Excel has three functions that are used to extract part of a text value (often referred to as a *string*). The LEFT, RIGHT, and MID functions let you get to the parts of a text value that their name implies, extracting part of a text value from the left, the right, or the middle. Mastering these functions gives you the power to literally break text apart.

How about this? You have a list of codes of inventory items. The first three characters are the vendor ID, and the other characters are the part ID. You need just the vendor IDs. How do you do this? Or how do you get the part numbers not including the vendor IDs? Excel functions to the rescue!

Bearing to the LEFT

The LEFT function lets you grab a specified number of characters from the left side of a larger string. All you do is tell the function what or where the string is and how many characters you need to extract.

Figure 4-1 demonstrates how the LEFT function isolates the vendor ID in a hypothetical product code list (column A). The vendor ID is the first three characters in each product code. You want to extract the first three characters of each product code and put them in column B. You put the LEFT function in column B with the first argument, specifying where the larger string is (column A) and the second argument specifying how many characters to extract (three). See Figure 4-1 for an illustration of this worksheet with the LEFT formula visible in the Formula Bar. (What's column C in this worksheet? We get to that in the next section.)

FIGURE 4-1:
Getting the three left characters from a larger string.

What if you ask LEFT to return more characters than the entire original string contains? No problem. In this case, LEFT simply returns the entire original string. The same is true for the RIGHT function, explained in the next section.

The LEFT function is really handy and so easy to use. Try it yourself:

1. **Position the cursor in the cell where you want the extracted string displayed.**

2. **Type =LEFT(to start the function.**

3. **Click the cell containing the original string or type its address.**

4. **Type a comma (,).**

5. **Type a number.**

    This number tells the function how many characters to extract from the left of the larger string. If you type a number that is equal to or larger than the number of characters in the string, the whole string is returned.

6. **Type) and press Enter.**

Swinging to the RIGHT

Excel does not favor sides. Because there is a LEFT function, there also is a RIGHT function. RIGHT extracts a specified number of characters from the right of a larger string. It works pretty much the same way as the LEFT function.

Column C in Figure 4-1 uses the RIGHT function to extract the rightmost four characters from the product codes. Cell C4, for example, has this formula: =RIGHT(A4,4).

Here's how to use the RIGHT function:

1. **Position the cursor in the cell where you want the extracted string displayed.**

2. **Type =RIGHT(to start the function.**

3. **Click the cell containing the original string or type its address.**

4. **Type a comma (,).**

5. **Type a number.**

    This number tells the function how many characters to extract from the right of the larger string. If you type a number that is equal to or larger than the number of characters in the string, the whole string is returned.

6. **Type) and press Enter.**

> **REMEMBER:** Use LEFT and RIGHT to extract characters from the start or end of a text string. Use MID to extract characters from the middle.

Staying in the MIDdle

MID is a powerful text-extraction function. It lets you pull out a portion of a larger string — from anywhere within the larger string. The LEFT and RIGHT functions allow you to extract from the start or end of a string, but not the middle. MID gives you essentially complete flexibility.

CHAPTER 4 **Manipulating Text with Functions**   293

MID takes three arguments: the larger string (or a reference to one), the character position to start at, and how many characters to extract. Here's how to use MID:

1. **Position the cursor in the cell where you want the extracted string displayed.**
2. **Type =MID(to start the function.**
3. **Click the cell that has the full text entry or type its address.**
4. **Type a comma (,).**
5. **Type a number to tell the function which character to start the extraction from.**

    This number can be anything from 1 to the full count of characters of the string. Typically, the starting character position used with MID is greater than 1. Why? If you need to start at the first position, you may as well use the simpler LEFT function. If you type a number for the starting character position that is greater than the length of the string, nothing is returned.

6. **Type a comma (,).**
7. **Type a number to tell the function how many characters to extract.**

    If you type a number that is greater than the remaining length of the string, the full remainder of the string is returned. For example, if you tell MID to extract characters 2 through 8 of a six-character string, MID returns characters 2 through 6.

8. **Type) and press Enter.**

Table 4-1 shows some examples of how MID works.

TABLE 4-1   How MID Works

Example	Result
=MID("APPLE",4,2)	LE
=MID("APPLE",4,1)	L
=MID("APPLE",2,3)	PPL
=MID("APPLE",5,1)	E

Figure 4-2 shows how the MID function helps isolate the fourth and fifth characters in the hypothetical inventory shown in Figure 4-1. These characters could represent a storage-bin number for the inventory item. The MID function makes it easy to extract this piece of information from the larger product code.

D4 | fx =MID(A4,4,2)

	A	B	C	D	E
1	**INVENTORY CONTROL**				
2					
3	**Product Code**	**Vendor**	**Internal Tracking Number**	**Bin Number**	
4	WES7164	WES	7164	71	
5	NER6578	NER	6578	65	
6	NER8400	NER	8400	84	
7	APP5333	APP	5333	53	
8	POW9655	POW	9655	96	
9	WES2141	WES	2141	21	
10	APP7496	APP	7496	74	
11	POW1500	POW	1500	15	
12	POW1600	POW	1600	16	

FIGURE 4-2: Using MID to pull characters from any position in a string.

Splitting up

The TEXTSPLIT function is useful when you have a bunch of text-based information all stuffed into one cell. Ugh, is that ugly! Well, as long as the individual parts of the text are separated with a consistent delimiter such as a comma, then game on!

TEXTSPLIT has two required arguments: the cell that contains the data, and the delimiter character. Figure 4-3 shows how TEXTSPLIT is used to break apart a string of names contained in one cell.

The formula in cell D6 is

```
=TEXTSPLIT(B6,",")
```

D6 | fx =TEXTSPLIT(B6,",")

	A	B	C	D	E	F	G	H	I	J
1										
2										
3										
4										
5		**Employees in one cell**		**Employees in separate cells**						
6		Mark,Sarah,Bill, Heather, Steve,Tammy		Mark	Sarah	Bill	Heather	Steve	Tammy	
7										
8										

FIGURE 4-3: Using TEXTSPLIT to break apart a string of text.

Finding the long of it with LEN

The LEN function returns a string's length. It takes a single argument: the string being evaluated. LEN is often used with other functions, such as LEFT or RIGHT.

Manipulating text sometimes requires a little math. For example, you may need to calculate how many characters to isolate with the RIGHT function. A common configuration of functions to do this is RIGHT, SEARCH, and LEN, like this:

```
=RIGHT(A1,LEN(A1)-SEARCH(" ",A1))
```

This formula calculates the number of characters to return as the full count of characters less the position where the space is. Used with the RIGHT function, this formula returns the characters to the right of the space.

REMEMBER The LEN function is often used with other functions, notably LEFT, RIGHT, and MID. In this manner, LEN helps determine the value of an argument to the other function.

Here's how to use LEN:

1. **Position the cursor in the cell where you want the results to appear.**
2. **Type** =LEN(**to begin the function.**
3. **Perform one of these steps:**
   - Click a cell that contains text.
   - Type the cell's address.
   - Type a string enclosed in double quotation marks.
4. **Type) and press Enter.**

Putting Text Together

Excel has two functions that take separate snippets of text and put them together into one string. Think of it as a family reunion! These two functions are quite similar, but TEXTJOIN requires a delimiter and CONCATENATE does not.

Putting text together with CONCATENATE

The CONCATENATE function pulls multiple strings together into one larger string. A good use of this is when you have a column of first names and a column of last names and you need to put the two together to use as full names.

CONCATENATE takes up to 255 arguments. Each argument is a string or a cell reference, and the arguments are separated by commas. The function doesn't insert anything, such as a space, between the strings. If you need to separate the substrings, as you would with the first name and last name example, you must explicitly insert the separator. Figure 4-4 makes this clear. You can see that the second argument to the CONCATENATE function is a space.

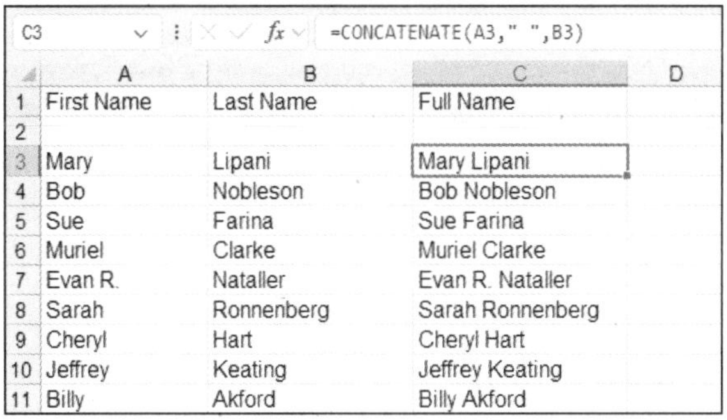

FIGURE 4-4: Putting strings together with CONCATENATE.

In Figure 4-4, the full names displayed in column C are concatenated from the first and last names in columns A and B, respectively. In the function's arguments, type a space between the references to cells in columns A and B. You type a space by enclosing a space between double quotation marks, like this: " ".

To use CONCATENATE, follow these steps:

1. **Position the cursor in an empty column, in the same row as the first text entry, and type** =CONCATENATE(**to start the function.**

2. **Click the cell that has the *first* name or type its address.**

3. **Type a comma (,).**

4. **Type a space inside double quotation marks.**

   It should look like this: " ".

5. **Type a comma (,).**

6. **Click the cell that has the *last* name or type its address.**

7. **Type) and press Enter.**

8. **Use the Fill Handle to drag the function into the rows below, as many rows as there are text entries in the first column.**

CHAPTER 4 Manipulating Text with Functions   297

Putting text together with TEXTJOIN and a delimiter

The TEXTJOIN function puts different pieces of text together and includes a required delimiter argument to boot. In fact, the first argument in the function is the delimiter. Table 4-2 lists the arguments of TEXTJOIN.

TABLE 4-2 TEXTJOIN arguments

Argument	Comment
Delimiter (required)	Can be any character or symbol, including a space.
Ignore Empty Cells (required)	True or False. The default is True.
Text 1 (required)	This can be a range or an actual string of text.
Text 2 and on (optional)	More pieces of text to join together. These can be cell or range addresses or actual strings of text.

Figure 4-5 shows how TEXTJOIN combines separate city names into one string. The delimiter is a dash. Just to make it interesting, Miami has been added as actual text instead of a cell reference. The formula in cell H6 is

```
=TEXTJOIN("-",TRUE,B6:F6,"Miami")
```

FIGURE 4-5: Putting strings together with TEXTJOIN.

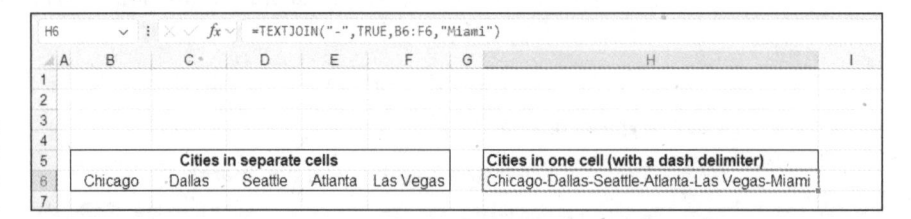

There is another way to concatenate strings. You can use the ampersand (&) character instead and skip using either CONCATENATE or TEXTJOIN. For example, this formula works fine for combining text from two different cells: =A3 & " " & B3.

Changing Text

There must be a whole lot of issues about text. We say that because a whole lot of functions let you work with text. There are functions that format text, replace text with other text, and clean text. (Yes, text needs a good scrubbing at times.) There are functions just for making lowercase letters into uppercase, and uppercase letters into lowercase.

Making money

Formatting numbers as currency is a common need in Excel. The Format Cells dialog box or the Currency Style button in the Number Formatting options on the Home tab of the ribbon are the usual places to go to format cells as currency. Excel also has the DOLLAR function. On the surface, DOLLAR seems to do the same thing as the similar currency formatting options, but it has some key differences:

- **DOLLAR converts a number to text.** Therefore, you can't perform math on a DOLLAR value. For example, a series of DOLLAR amounts can't be summed into a total.

- **DOLLAR displays a value from another cell.** As its first argument, DOLLAR takes a cell address or a number typed directly in the function. DOLLAR is handy when you want to preserve the original cell's formatting. In other words, you may need to present a value as currency in one location but also let the number display in its original format in another location. DOLLAR lets you take the original number and present it as currency in another cell — the one you place the DOLLAR function in.

- **DOLLAR includes a rounding feature.** DOLLAR has a bit more muscle than the currency style. DOLLAR takes a second argument that specifies how many decimal places to display. When negative values are typed for the second argument, this serves to apply rounding to the digits on the left side of the decimal point.

Figure 4-6 shows how the DOLLAR function can display various numeric values just the way you want. At the bottom of the worksheet is an area of detailed revenues. At the top is a summary that uses DOLLAR.

TIP Unless a cell has been formatted otherwise, you can tell the type of entry by alignment. Text aligns to the left; numbers align to the right.

FIGURE 4-6: Using DOLLAR to round numbers and format them as currency.

	A	B	C	D	E	F	G	H
1								
2		Total Revenue, First Quarter						
3								
4			East	West				
5		January	$3,087	$5,118				
6		February	$3,280	$5,752				
7		March	$4,241	$5,847				
8-12								
13		Revenue by Division and Item, for the first quarter						
14		Division	Month	Toys	Video Games	Bicycles	Total	
15		East	January	1173.15	622.55	1290.99	3086.69	
16		East	February	1055.92	689.05	1535.01	3279.98	
17		East	March	1614.25	946.82	1680.24	4241.31	
18			TOTAL	3843.32	2258.42	4506.24	10607.98	
19								
20		West	January	2150.78	866.68	2100.94	5118.4	
21		West	February	2454.12	1022.52	2275.75	5752.39	
22		West	March	2327.85	1028.95	2489.75	5846.55	
23			TOTAL	6932.75	2918.15	6866.44	16717.34	

Cell C5 formula: =DOLLAR(G15,0)

Specifically, the cells in the range C5:D7 use the DOLLAR function to present values from the detail area and also round them to no decimals. For example, cell C5 contains =DOLLAR(G15,0). Table 4-3 shows some examples of how the rounding feature works.

TABLE 4-3 The Rounding Feature

Example	Result
=DOLLAR(1234.56,2)	$1,234.56
=DOLLAR(1234.56,1)	$1,234.6
=DOLLAR(1234.56,0)	$1,235
=DOLLAR(1234.56,-1)	$1,230
=DOLLAR(1234.56,-2)	$1,200
=DOLLAR(1234.56,-3)	$1,000

Using DOLLAR is easy. Follow these steps:

1. **Position the cursor in the cell where you want the results to appear.**
2. **Type =DOLLAR(to begin the function entry.**

3. **Click a cell that contains a number or type a number.**
4. **Type a comma (,).**
5. **Type a number to indicate the number of decimal places to display.**

    If the number is 0, no decimal places are displayed. Numbers less than 0 force rounding to occur to the left of the decimal point.

6. **Type) and press Enter.**

TECHNICAL STUFF

The DOLLAR function is named DOLLAR in countries that use dollars, such as the United States and Canada. In versions of Excel designed for countries that use a different currency, the name of the function should match the name of the currency.

Turning numbers into text

The TEXT function is a bit like the DOLLAR function in that it converts a number value to text data, but it gives you more formatting options for your results. TEXT can format numbers as currency, like DOLLAR, but it's not limited to this.

The first TEXT argument is a number or reference to a cell that contains a number. The second argument is a formatting pattern that tells the function how to format the number. You can see some formatting patterns in the Custom category on the Number tab of the Format Cells dialog box (shown in Figure 4-7).

FIGURE 4-7: Formatting options in the Format Cells dialog box.

CHAPTER 4 **Manipulating Text with Functions** 301

Excel lets you create custom formatting patterns so you can present your data just the way you need to. For example, you can specify whether numbers use a thousands separator, whether decimal values are always displayed to the third decimal place, and so on.

These patterns are created with the use of a few key symbols. A pound sign (#) is a placeholder for a number — that is, a single digit. Interspersing pound signs with fixed literal characters (such as a dollar sign, a percent sign, a comma, or a period) establishes a pattern. For example, this pattern — $#,###.# — says to display a dollar sign in front of the number, to use a comma for a thousands separator, and to display one digit to the right of the decimal point. Some formatting options used with the TEXT function are shown in Table 4-4. Look up custom number formatting in Excel Help for more information on custom format patterns, or go to www.microsoft.com and search for guidelines for custom number formats.

TABLE 4-4 **Formatting Options for the TEXT Function**

Format	Displays
=TEXT(1234.56,"#.##")	1234.56
=TEXT(1234.56,"#.#")	1234.6
=TEXT(1234.56,"#")	1235
=TEXT(1234.56,"$#")	$1235
=TEXT(1234.56,"$#,#")	$1,235
=TEXT(1234.56,"$#,#.##")	$1,234.56
=TEXT(0.4,"#%")	40%
=TEXT("3/15/2005","mm/dd/yy")	03/15/05
=TEXT("3/15/2005","mm/dd/yyyy")	03/15/2005
=TEXT("3/15/2005","mmm-dd")	Mar-15

Figure 4-8 shows how the TEXT function is used to format values that are incorporated into sentences. Column C contains the formulas that use TEXT. For example, C4 has this formula: ="We spent " & TEXT(B4,"$#,#.#0") & " on " & A4. Cell C8 has this formula: ="We opened the office on " & TEXT(B8,"mmm d,yyyy").

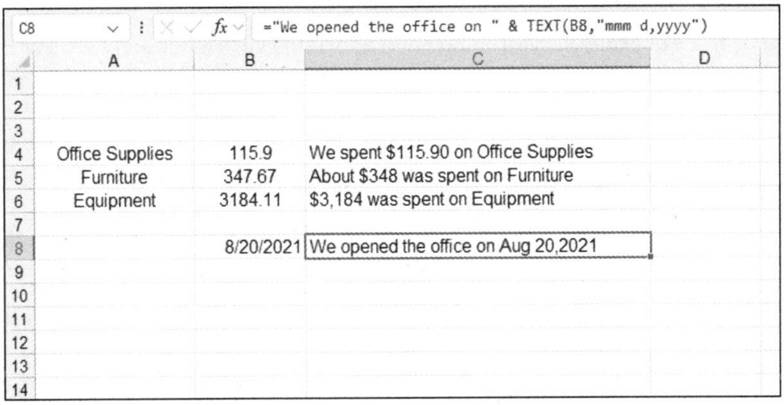

	A	B	C	D
1				
2				
3				
4	Office Supplies	115.9	We spent $115.90 on Office Supplies	
5	Furniture	347.67	About $348 was spent on Furniture	
6	Equipment	3184.11	$3,184 was spent on Equipment	
7				
8		8/20/2021	We opened the office on Aug 20,2021	

C8: `="We opened the office on " & TEXT(B8,"mmm d,yyyy")`

FIGURE 4-8: Using TEXT to report in a well-formatted manner.

Here's how to use TEXT:

1. **Position the cursor in the cell where you want the results to appear.**
2. **Type =TEXT(to begin the function entry.**
3. **Click a cell that contains a number or a date or type its address.**
4. **Type a comma (,).**
5. **Type a double quotation mark (") and then type a formatting pattern.**

   See the Format Cells dialog box (the Custom category of the Number tab) for guidance.

6. **Type a double quotation mark (") after the pattern is typed.**
7. **Type) and press Enter.**

The VALUE function does the opposite of TEXT; it converts strings to numbers. Excel does this by default anyway, so we don't cover the VALUE function here. You can look it up in Excel's Help system if you're curious about it.

Repeating text

REPT is a nifty function that does nothing other than repeat a string of text. REPT has two arguments:

» The string or a reference to a cell that contains text
» The number of times to repeat the text

CHAPTER 4 **Manipulating Text with Functions** 303

For example, you could enter a formula such as =REPT("*",120) to enter a string of 120 asterisks. Try it out:

1. **Position the cursor in the cell where you want the results to appear.**
2. **Type** =REPT(**to begin the function entry.**
3. **Click a cell that contains text or type text enclosed in double quotation marks.**

    Typically, you would type a character (such as a period or an asterisk), but any text will work.

4. **Type a comma (,).**
5. **Type a number to tell the function how many times to repeat the text.**
6. **Type) and press Enter.**

Swapping text

Two functions — REPLACE and SUBSTITUTE — replace a portion of a string with other text. The functions are nearly identical in concept but are used in different situations.

> **TIP** Both REPLACE and SUBSTITUTE replace text within other text. Use REPLACE when you know the position of the text you want to replace. Use SUBSTITUTE when you don't know the position of the text you want to replace.

REPLACE

REPLACE takes four arguments:

>> The target string as a cell reference

>> The character position in the target string at which to start replacing

>> The number of characters to replace

>> The string to replace with (doesn't have to be the same length as the text being replaced)

For example, if cell A1 contains the string Our Chicago office has closed., the formula =REPLACE(A1,5,7,"Dallas") returns the string Our Dallas office has closed.

Figure 4-9 shows how to use REPLACE with the Inventory Control data first shown in the "Breaking Apart Text" section. A new task is at hand. For compatibility with a new computer system, you have to modify the product codes in the inventory data with two dashes between the vendor ID and the internal tracking number. The original codes are in column A. Use a combination of REPLACE and LEFT functions to get the job done: =REPLACE(A4, 1, 3, LEFT(A4,3) & "--").

	A	B	C	D
1	INVENTORY CONTROL			
2				
3	Product Code	Vendor	Internal Tracking Number	New Product Code
4	WES7164	WES	7164	WES--7164
5	NER6578	NER	6578	NER--6578
6	NER8400	NER	8400	NER--8400
7	APP5333	APP	5333	APP--5333
8	POW9655	POW	9655	POW--9655
9	WES2141	WES	2141	WES--2141
10	APP7496	APP	7496	APP--7496
11	POW1500	POW	1500	POW--1500
12	POW1600	POW	1600	POW--1600

FIGURE 4-9: Using REPLACE to change text.

These arguments replace the original three characters in each product code with the same three characters followed by two dashes. Figure 4-9 shows how REPLACE alters the product codes. In the figure, the first three product code characters are replaced with themselves and the dashes. The LEFT function and the dashes serve as the fourth argument of REPLACE.

Keep in mind a couple of points about REPLACE:

REMEMBER

>> **You need to know where the text being replaced is in the larger text.** Specifically, you have to tell the function at what position the text starts and how many positions it occupies.

>> **The text being replaced and the new text taking its place don't have to be the same length.**

Here's how to use the REPLACE function:

1. **Position the cursor in the cell where you want the result to appear.**
2. **Type** =REPLACE(**to begin the function entry.**
3. **Click a cell that contains the full string of which a portion is to be replaced.**
4. **Type a comma (,).**

5. **Type a number to tell the function the starting position of the text to be replaced.**

6. **Type a comma (,).**

7. **Type a number to tell the function how many characters are to be replaced.**

8. **Type a comma (,).**

9. **Click a cell that contains text or type text enclosed in double quotation marks.**

   This is the replacement text.

10. **Type) and press Enter.**

> **TIP** You can also use REPLACE to delete text from a string. Simply specify an empty string ("") as the replacement text.

SUBSTITUTE

Use the SUBSTITUTE function when you don't know the position in the target string of the text to be replaced. Instead of telling the function the starting position and number of characters (as you do with REPLACE), you just tell it what string to look for and replace.

SUBSTITUTE takes three required arguments and a fourth optional argument:

» A reference to the cell that contains the target text string

» The string within the target string that is to be replaced

» The replacement text

» An optional number to tell the function which occurrence of the string to replace

The fourth argument tells SUBSTITUTE which occurrence of the text to be changed (the second argument) and actually replaced with the new text (the third argument). The text to be replaced may appear more than once in the target string. If you omit the fourth argument, all occurrences are replaced. This is the case in the first example in Table 4-5; all spaces are replaced with commas. In the last example in Table 4-5, only the second occurrence of the word two is changed to the word three.

TABLE 4-5   **Applying the SUBSTITUTE Function**

Example	Returned String	Comment
=SUBSTITUTE("apple banana cherry fig", " ",",")	apple,banana, cherry,fig	All spaces are replaced with commas.
=SUBSTITUTE("apple banana cherry fig", " ",",",1)	apple,banana cherry fig	The first space is replaced with a comma. The other spaces remain as they are.
=SUBSTITUTE("apple banana cherry fig", " ",",",3)	apple banana cherry,fig	The third space is replaced with a comma. The other spaces remain as they are.
=SUBSTITUTE("There are two cats and two birds.","two","three")	There are three cats and three birds.	Both occurrences of two are replaced with three.
=SUBSTITUTE("There are two cats and two birds.","two","three",2)	There are two cats and three birds.	Only the second occurrence of two is replaced with three.

Try it yourself! Follow these steps:

1. **Position the cursor in the cell where you want the result to appear.**
2. **Type** =SUBSTITUTE(**to begin the function entry.**
3. **Click a cell that contains text or type its address.**

    This is the full string of which a portion is to be replaced.

4. **Type a comma (,).**
5. **Click a cell that contains text or type text enclosed in double quotation marks.**

    This is the portion of text that is to be replaced.

6. **Type a comma (,).**
7. **Click a cell that contains text or type text enclosed in double quotation marks.**

    This is the replacement text. If you want to specify which occurrence of text to change, continue to steps 8 and 9; otherwise, go to Step 10.

8. **Type a comma (,).**
9. **Type a number that tells the function which occurrence to apply the substitution to.**
10. **Type) and press Enter.**

TIP You can use SUBSTITUTE to remove spaces from text. In the second argument (what to replace), type a space enclosed in double quotation marks. In the third argument, type two double quotation marks *with nothing between them*; this is known as an *empty string*.

Giving text a trim

Spaces have a way of sneaking in and ruining your work. The worst thing is that you often can't even see them! When the space you need to remove is at the beginning or end of a string, use the TRIM function to remove them. The function simply clips any leading or trailing spaces from a string. It also removes extra spaces from within a string; a sequence of two or more spaces is replaced by a single space.

Figure 4-10 shows how this works. In column A is a list of names. Looking closely, you can see that some unwanted spaces precede the names in cells A5 and A10. Column B shows the correction using TRIM. The formula in cell B5 is =TRIM(A5).

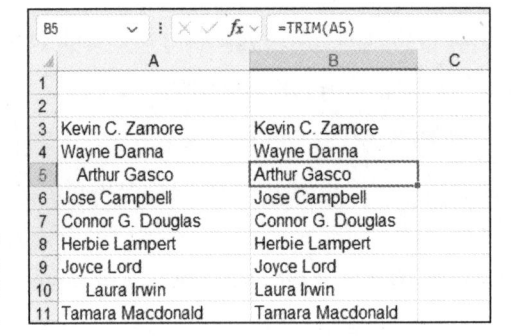

FIGURE 4-10: Removing spaces with the TRIM function.

TRIM takes just one argument: the text to be cleaned of leading and trailing spaces. Here's how it works:

1. **Position the cursor in the cell where you want the result to appear.**
2. **Type =TRIM(to begin the function entry.**
3. **Click a cell that contains the text that has leading or trailing spaces, or type the cell address.**
4. **Type) and press Enter.**

WARNING

Be on the lookout: Although you generally use TRIM to remove leading and trailing spaces, it removes extra spaces in the middle of a string. If two or more spaces are next to each other, TRIM removes the extra spaces and leaves one space in place. This is usually a good thing — most times, you don't want extra spaces in the middle of your text. But what if you do? Table 4-6 shows a couple of alternatives to remove a leading space, if it's there, without affecting the middle of the string.

TABLE 4-6 **Removing Spaces**

Formula to Remove Leading Space	Comment
`=IF(LEFT(E10,1)=" ",SUBSTITUTE(E10," ","",1), E10)`	If a space is found in the first position, substitute an empty string; otherwise, just return the original string.
`=IF(LEFT(E10,1)=" ",RIGHT(E10,LEN(E10)-1), E10)`	If a space is found in the first position, return the right side of the string, less the first position. (See "Finding the long of it with LEN," earlier in this chapter.)

Making a case

In school, you were taught to use an uppercase letter at the start of a sentence as well as for proper nouns. But that was a while ago, and now the brain cells are a bit fuzzy. Lucky thing Excel has a way to help fix case.

Three functions alter the case of text: UPPER, LOWER, and PROPER. All three functions take a single argument — the text that will have its case altered. Table 4-7 shows a few examples.

TABLE 4-7 **Changing Text Case**

Formula	Result
`=LOWER("The Cow Jumped Over The Moon")`	the cow jumped over the moon
`=UPPER("the cow jumped over the moon")`	THE COW JUMPED OVER THE MOON
`=PROPER("the cow jumped over the moon")`	The Cow Jumped Over The Moon

Try this:

1. **Type a sentence in a cell.**

    Any old sentence will do, but don't make any letters uppercase. For example, type **excel is great** or **computers give me a headache**.

CHAPTER 4 **Manipulating Text with Functions** 309

2. **Position the cursor in an empty cell.**
3. **Type =UPPER(to start the function.**
4. **Click the cell that has the sentence or type its address.**
5. **Type) and press Enter.**
6. **In another empty cell, type =PROPER(to start the function.**
7. **Click the cell that has the sentence or type its address.**
8. **Type) and press Enter.**

   You should now have two cells that show the sentence with a case change. One cell has the sentence in uppercase; the other cell has the sentence, in proper case.

TIP

Perhaps you noticed another possibility that needs to be addressed. What about when just the first word needs to start with an uppercase letter and the rest of the string is all lowercase? Some people refer to this as *sentence case*. You can create sentence case by using the UPPER, LEFT, RIGHT, and LEN functions. (LEN is explained earlier in this chapter.) With the assumption that the text is in cell B10, here's how the formula looks:

```
=UPPER(LEFT(B10,1)) & RIGHT(B10,LEN(B10)-1)
```

In a nutshell, the UPPER function is applied to the first letter, which is isolated with the help of the LEFT function. This result is concatenated with the remainder of the string. You know how much is left by using the LEN function to get the length of the string and using the RIGHT function to get all the characters from the right, less one.

Comparing, Finding, and Measuring Text

Excel has many functions that manipulate text, but sometimes you just need to find out about the text before you do anything else! A handful of functions determine whether text matches other text, let you find text inside other text, and tell you how long a string is. These functions are *passive* — that is, they don't alter text.

Going for perfection with EXACT

The EXACT function lets you compare two strings of text to see whether they're the same. The function takes two arguments — the two strings of text — and returns a true or false value. EXACT is case-sensitive, so two strings that contain the same letters but with differing case produce a result of false. For example, `Apple` and `APPLE` are not identical.

EXACT is great for finding changes in data. Figure 4-11 shows two lists of employees, one for each year, in columns A and B. Are they identical? You could spend a number of minutes staring at the two lists. (That would give you a headache!) Or you can use EXACT. The cells in column C contain the EXACT function, used to check column A against column B. The returned values are true for the most part. This means there is no change.

FIGURE 4-11: Comparing strings with the EXACT function.

	A	B	C
2	Employees 2020	Employees 2021	Exact?
4	Steve Moulin	Steve Moulin	TRUE
5	Victor Cushman	Victor Cushman	TRUE
6	Anthony H. Elmore	Anthony H. Elmore	TRUE
7	Nancy Aguilera	Nancy Aguilera	TRUE
8	Raymond Majolin	Ray Majolin	FALSE
9	Kristie Graber	Kristie Graber	TRUE
10	Sal Rizzo	Sal Rizzo	TRUE
11	Ed Woodworth	Ed Woodworth	TRUE
12	Pat Carter	Pat Wilson	FALSE
13	Kimberly K. Layman	Kimberly K. Layman	TRUE
14	Ernest DeGraw	Ernest DeGraw	TRUE
15	Lynn Alandale	Lynn Alandale	TRUE
16	Corrina Harran	Corrina Harran	TRUE
17	Mark Branson	Mark Bransonn	FALSE
18	Nina Garonznik	Nina Garonznik	TRUE
19	Steve Hallerman	Steve Hallerman	TRUE
20	Mary Astor	Mary Astor	TRUE

A few names are different in the second year. Marriage, divorce, misspellings — the mismatched data could be because of any of these. EXACT returns false for these names, which means they aren't identical in the two lists and should be checked manually.

Here's how you use EXACT:

1. **Position the cursor in the cell where you want the results to appear.**
2. **Type =EXACT(to begin the function entry.**
3. **Click a cell that contains text or type its address.**
4. **Type a comma (,).**

CHAPTER 4 **Manipulating Text with Functions** 311

5. **Click another cell that has text or type its address.**
6. **Type) and press Enter.**

REMEMBER: If you get a true result with EXACT, the strings are identical. A false result means they're different.

TIP: What if you want to compare strings without regard to case? In other words, APPLE and apple would be considered the same. Excel doesn't have a function for this, but the result is easily obtained with EXACT and UPPER. The idea is to convert both strings to uppercase and compare the results:

```
=EXACT(UPPER("APPLE"), UPPER("apple"))
```

You could use LOWER here instead, if you want.

Finding and searching

Two functions, FIND and SEARCH, work in a quite similar fashion. A couple of differences are key to figuring out which to use. Both FIND and SEARCH find one string inside a larger string and tell you the position at which it was found (or produce #VALUE if it is not found). The differences are shown in Table 4-8.

TABLE 4-8 Comparing FIND and SEARCH

FIND	SEARCH
Case-sensitive. It will not, for example, find At inside heat.	Not case-sensitive.
You cannot use the wildcards * and ?.	You can use the wildcards * and ?.

FIND

FIND takes three arguments:

- The string to find
- The larger string to search in
- The position in the larger string to start looking at (optional)

If the third argument is left out, the function starts looking at the beginning of the larger string. Table 4-9 shows some examples.

TABLE 4-9 **Finding One String inside Another String**

Value in Cell A1	Function	Result
Happy birthday to you	=FIND("Birthday",A1)	#VALUE!
Happy birthday to you	=FIND("birthday",A1)	7
Happy birthday to you	=FIND("y",A1)	5
Happy birthday to you	=FIND("y",A1,10)	14

In the first example using FIND, an error is returned. The #VALUE! error is returned if the text can't be found. Birthday is not the same as birthday, at least to the case-sensitive FIND function.

SEARCH

The SEARCH function takes the same arguments as FIND. The two common wildcards you can use are the asterisk (*) and the question mark (?). An asterisk tells the function to accept any number of characters (including zero characters). A question mark tells the function to accept any single character. It is not uncommon to see more than one question mark together as a wildcard pattern. Table 4-10 shows several examples.

TABLE 4-10 **Using the SEARCH Function**

Value in Cell A1	Function	Result	Comment
Happy birthday to you	=SEARCH("Birthday",A1)	7	*birthday* starts in position 7.
Happy birthday to you	=SEARCH("y??",A1)	5	The first place where a *y* is followed by any two characters is at position 5. This is the last letter in *Happy*, a space, and the first letter in *birthday*.
Happy birthday to you	=SEARCH("yo?",A1)	19	The first place where *yo* is followed by any single character is the word *you*.
Happy birthday to you	=SEARCH("b*d",A1)	7	The search pattern is the letter *b*, followed by any number of characters, followed by the letter *d*. This starts in position 7.
Happy birthday to you	=SEARCH("*b",A1)	1	The asterisk says search for any number of characters before the letter *b*. The start of characters before the letter *b* is at position 1. Using an asterisk at the start is not useful. It will either return a *1* or an error if the fixed character(s) (the letter *b* in this example) is not in the larger text.

(continued)

TABLE 4-10 *(continued)*

Value in Cell A1	Function	Result	Comment
Happy birthday to you	=SEARCH("t*",A1)	10	The asterisk says search for any number of characters after the letter *t*. Because the search starts with a fixed character, its position is the result. The asterisk serves no purpose here.
Happy birthday to you	=SEARCH("t",A1,12)	16	Finds the position of the first letter *t*, starting after position 12. The result is the position of the first letter in the word *to*. The letter *t* in birthday is ignored because it's before position 13.

Back in Figure 4-4, we show you how to concatenate first and last names. What if you have full names to separate into first names and last names? SEARCH to the rescue! (Does that make this a search-and-rescue mission?)

Isolating the first name from a full name is straightforward. You just use LEFT to get characters up to the first space. The position of the first space is returned from the SEARCH function. Here's how this looks:

```
=LEFT(A3,SEARCH(" ",A3)-1)
```

Getting the last names is just as simple — *not!* When the full name has only first and last names (no middle name or initials), you need SEARCH, RIGHT, and LEN, like this:

```
=RIGHT(A3,LEN(A3)-SEARCH(" ",A3))
```

However, this doesn't work for middle names or initials. What about Franklin D. Roosevelt? If you rely on the last name being after the first space, the last name becomes D. Roosevelt. An honest mistake, but you can do better. What you need is a way to test for the second space and then return everything to the right of that space. There are likely a number of ways to do this; here's ours:

```
=IF(ISERROR(SEARCH(" ",RIGHT(A3,LEN(A3)-SEARCH(" ",A3)))),RIGHT(A3,LEN(A3)-SEARCH(" ",A3)),RIGHT(A3,LEN(A3)-SEARCH(" ",A3,SEARCH(" ",A3)+1)))
```

Admittedly, it's a doozy. But it gets the job done. Here's an overview of what this formula does:

- » It's an IF function, so it tests for either true or false.
- » The test is if an error is returned from SEARCH for trying to find a space to the right of the first space:

```
ISERROR(SEARCH(" ",RIGHT(A3,LEN(A3)-SEARCH(" ",A3))))
```

- » If the test is true, there is no other space. This means there is no middle initial, so just return the portion of the name after the first space:

```
RIGHT(A3,LEN(A3)-SEARCH(" ",A3))
```

- » If the test is false, there is a second space, and the task is to return the portion of the string after the second space. SEARCH tells both the position of the first space and the second space. This is done by nesting one SEARCH inside the other. The inner SEARCH provides the third argument — where to start looking from. A 1 is added so the outer SEARCH starts looking for a space one position after the first space:

```
RIGHT(A3,LEN(A3)-SEARCH(" ",A3,SEARCH(" ",A3)+1))
```

Your eyes have probably glazed over, but that's it!

The monster formula isolates last names from full names that include a middle initial. A task for you to try, if you have any working brain cells left, is to write a formula that isolates the middle initial, if there is one. Here's how to use FIND or SEARCH:

1. **Position the cursor in the cell where you want the results to appear.**
2. **Type** =FIND(**or** =SEARCH(**to begin the function entry.**
3. **Type a string of text that you want in a larger string, enclosed with double quotation marks, or click a cell that contains the text.**
4. **Type a comma (,).**
5. **Click a cell that contains the larger text or type its address.**

    If you want the function to begin searching at the start of the larger string, go to Step 7. If you want to have the function begin the search in the larger string at a position other than 1, go to Step 6.

6. **Type a comma (,) and the position number.**
7. **Type) and press Enter.**

4 Analyzing Data

Contents at a Glance

CHAPTER 1: Using Basic Data Analysis Techniques 319
  What Is Data Analysis, Anyway? 320
  Analyzing Data with Conditional Formatting 321
  Summarizing Data with Subtotals 335
  Grouping Related Data 337
  Consolidating Data from Multiple Worksheets 338

CHAPTER 2: Working with Data Analysis Tools 343
  Working with Data Tables 343
  Analyzing Data with Goal Seek 349
  Analyzing Data with Scenarios 351
  Optimizing Data with Solver 355

CHAPTER 3: Analyzing Table Data with Functions 365
  Introducing the Database Functions 365
  Retrieving a Value from a Table 367
  Summing a Column's Values 368
  Counting a Column's Values 369
  Averaging a Column's Values 371
  Determining a Column's Maximum and Minimum Values 372
  Multiplying a Column's Values 373
  Deriving a Column's Standard Deviation 374
  Calculating a Column's Variance 375

IN THIS CHAPTER

- » Learning about data analysis
- » Analyzing data by applying conditional formatting
- » Adding subtotals to summarize data
- » Grouping related data
- » Combining data from multiple worksheets

Chapter 1
Using Basic Data Analysis Techniques

You are awash in data. Information multiplies around you so fast that you wonder how to make sense of it all. You think, "I know what to do. I'll paste the data into Excel. That way, at least the data will be nicely arranged in the worksheet cells, and I can add a little formatting to make things somewhat palatable." That's a fine start, but you're often called upon to do more with your data than make it merely presentable. Your boss, your customer, or perhaps just your curiosity requires you to divine some inner meaning from the jumble of numbers and text that litter your workbooks. In other words, you need to *analyze* your data to see what nuggets of understanding you can unearth.

This chapter gets you started down that data analysis path by exploring a few straightforward but useful analytic techniques. After discovering what data analysis entails, you investigate a number of Excel data analysis techniques, including conditional formatting, data bars, color scales, and icon sets. From there, you dive into some useful methods for summarizing your data, including subtotals, grouping, and consolidation. Before you know it, that untamed wilderness of a worksheet will be nicely groomed and landscaped.

What Is Data Analysis, Anyway?

Data analysis is the application of tools and techniques to organize, study, reach conclusions, and sometimes make predictions about a specific collection of information. For example, a sales manager might use data analysis to study the sales history of a product, determine the overall trend, and produce a forecast of future sales. A scientist might use data analysis to study experimental findings and determine the statistical significance of the results. A family might use data analysis to find the maximum mortgage it can afford or how much it must put aside each month to finance retirement or the kids' education.

Cooking raw data

The point of data analysis is to understand information on some deeper, more meaningful level. By definition, *raw data* is a mere collection of facts that, by themselves, tell you little or nothing of any importance. To gain some understanding of the data, you must manipulate the data in some meaningful way. The purpose of manipulating data can be something as simple as finding the sum or average of a column of numbers or as complex as employing a full-scale regression analysis to determine the underlying trend of a range of values. Both are examples of data analysis, and Excel offers a number of tools — from the straightforward to the sophisticated — to meet even the most demanding needs.

Dealing with data

The *data* part of *data analysis* is a collection of numbers, dates, and text that represents the raw information you have to work with. In Excel, this data resides inside a worksheet, which makes the data available for you to apply Excel's satisfyingly large array of data analysis tools.

Most data analysis projects involve large amounts of data, and the fastest and most accurate way to get that data onto a worksheet is to import it from a non-Excel data source. In the simplest scenario, you can copy the data from a text file, a Word table, or an Access datasheet and then paste it into a worksheet. However, most business and scientific data is stored in large databases, so Excel offers tools to import the data you need into your worksheet.

After you have your data in the worksheet, you can use the data as is to apply many data analysis techniques. However, if you convert the range into a *table*, Excel treats the data as a simple database and enables you to apply a number of database-specific analysis techniques to the table.

Building data models

In many cases, you perform data analysis on worksheet values by organizing those values into a *data model*, a collection of cells designed as a worksheet version of some real-world concept or scenario. The model includes not only the raw data but also one or more cells that represent some analysis of the data. For example, a mortgage amortization model would have the mortgage data — interest rate, principal, and term — and cells that calculate the payment, principal, and interest over the term. For such calculations, you use formulas and Excel's built-in worksheet functions.

Performing what-if analysis

One of the most common data analysis techniques is *what-if analysis,* for which you set up worksheet models to analyze hypothetical situations. The *what-if* part means that these situations usually come in the form of a question: "What happens to the monthly payment if the interest rate goes up by 2 percent?" or "What will the sales be if you increase the advertising budget by 10 percent?" Excel offers four what-if analysis tools: data tables, Goal Seek, Solver, and scenarios, all of which we cover in the next chapter.

Analyzing Data with Conditional Formatting

Many Excel worksheets contain hundreds of data values. You could try to make sense of such largish sets of data by creating complex formulas and wielding Excel's powerful data analysis tools. However, just as you wouldn't use a steamroller to crush a tin can, sometimes these sophisticated techniques are too much tool for the job. For example, what if all you want are answers to simple questions such as the following:

- » Which cell values are less than zero?
- » What are the top ten values?
- » Which cell values are above average, and which are below average?

These simple questions aren't easy to answer just by glancing at the worksheet, and the more numbers you're dealing with, the harder it gets. To help you eyeball your worksheets and answer these and similar questions, Excel lets you apply conditional formatting to the cells. Excel applies this special format only to cells that satisfy some condition, which Excel calls a *rule.* For example, you could apply formatting to display all negative values in a red font, or you could apply a filter to show only the top ten values.

Highlighting cells that meet some criteria

A *conditional format* is formatting that Excel applies only to cells that meet the criteria you specify. For example, you can tell Excel to apply the formatting only if a cell's value is greater or less than some specified amount, between two specified values, or equal to some value. You can also look for cells that contain specified text, dates that occur during a specified time frame, and more.

When you set up your conditional format, you can specify the font, border, and background pattern. This formatting helps to ensure that the cells that meet your criteria stand out from the other cells in the range. Here are the steps to follow:

1. **Select the range you want to work with.**

    Select just the data values you want to format. Don't select any surrounding data.

2. **On the Home tab of the ribbon, click Conditional Formatting, click Highlight Cells Rules, and then select the rule you want to use for the condition.**

    You have seven rules to play around with:

    - *Greater Than:* Applies the conditional format to cells that have a value larger than a value that you specify.

    - *Less Than:* Applies the conditional format to cells that have a value smaller than a value that you specify.

    - *Between:* Applies the conditional format to cells that have a value that is greater than or equal to a minimum value that you specify and less than or equal to a maximum value that you specify.

    - *Equal To:* Applies the conditional format to cells that have a value that is the same as a value that you specify.

    - *Text That Contains:* Applies the conditional format to cells that include the text that you specify.

    - *A Date Occurring*: Applies the conditional format to cells that have a date value that meets the condition that you specify (such as Yesterday, Last Week, or Next Month).

    - *Duplicate Values:* I cover duplicate values in the next section.

A dialog box appears, the name of which depends on the rule you click. For example, Figure 1-1 shows the dialog box for the Greater Than rule.

	A	B	C	D	E	F	G	H	I	J	K
2	Country Name	2007	2008	2009	2010	2011	2012	2013	2014	2015	2016
3	Afghanistan	13.7	3.6	21.0	8.4	6.1	14.4	3.9	2.7	1.3	2.4
4	Albania	5.9	3.8	3.4	3.7	2.6	1.4	1.0	1.8	2.2	3.4
5	Algeria	3.4	2.4	1.6	3.6	2.9	3.4	2.8	3.8	3.8	3.3
6	American Samoa	2.0	-2.6	-4.2	0.4	0.3	-4.4	-2.8	0.9	1.2	-2.6
7	Andorra	0.0	-8.6	-3.7	-5.4	-4.6	-1.6	0.4	2.3	0.8	1.2
8	Angola	22.6	13.8	2.4	3.4	3.9	5.2	6.8	4.8	3.0	-0.7
9	Antigua and Barbuda	9.3	0.0							4.1	5.3
10	Arab World	4.6	5.8							3.4	3.2
11	Argentina	9.0	4.1							2.6	-2.2
12	Armenia	13.7	6.9							3.2	0.2
13	Australia	3.7	3.7							2.4	2.8
14	Austria	3.6	1.5							1.1	1.5
15	Azerbaijan	25.0	10.8	9.4	4.9	0.1	2.2	5.8	2.0	1.1	-3.1
16	Bahamas, The	1.4	-2.3	-4.2	1.5	0.6	3.1	-0.6	-1.2	-3.1	0.2
17	Bangladesh	7.1	6.0	5.0	5.6	6.5	6.5	6.0	6.1	6.6	7.1
18	Barbados	1.8	0.4	-4.0	0.3	0.5	0.3	0.0	0.0	0.9	2.0
19	Belarus	8.6	10.2	0.2	7.8	5.5	1.7	1.0	1.7	-3.8	-2.6

FIGURE 1-1: The Greater Than dialog box and some highlighted values.

3. **Type the value to use for the condition.**

   You can also click the up-arrow button that appears to the right of the text box and select a worksheet cell that contains the value. Also, depending on the operator, you may need to specify two values.

4. **Use the right drop-down list to select the formatting to apply to cells that match your condition.**

   If you're feeling creative, you can make up your own format by selecting the Custom Format command.

5. **Click OK.**

   Excel applies the formatting to cells that meet the condition you specified.

TIP

Excel enables you to specify multiple conditional formats for the same range. For example, you can set up one condition for cells that are greater than some value and a separate condition for cells that are less than some other value. You can apply unique formats to each condition. Keep the range selected and follow steps 2 through 6 to configure the new condition.

Showing pesky duplicate values

You use conditional formatting mostly to highlight numbers greater than or less than some value, or dates occurring within some range. However, you can use conditional formatting also to look for duplicate values in a range. Why would you want to do that? The main reason is that many range or table columns require unique values. For example, a column of student IDs or part numbers shouldn't have duplicates.

Unfortunately, scanning such numbers and picking out the repeat values is hard. Not to worry! With conditional formatting, you can specify a font, border, and background pattern that ensures that any duplicate cells in a range or table stand out from the other cells. Here's what you do:

1. **Select the range that you want to check for duplicates.**

2. **On the Home tab of the ribbon, click Conditional Formatting, click Highlight Cells Rules, and select Duplicate Values.**

   The Duplicate Values dialog box appears. The left drop-down list has Duplicate selected by default, as shown in Figure 1-2. However, if you want to highlight all the unique values instead of the duplicates, select Unique from this list.

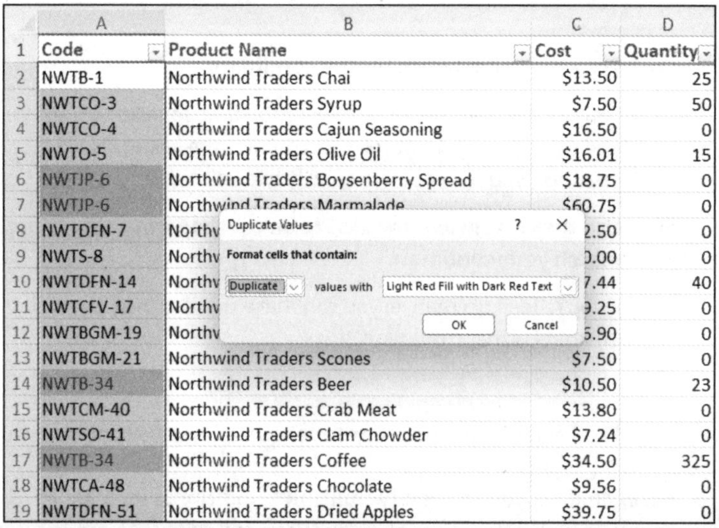

FIGURE 1-2: Use the Duplicate Values rule to highlight worksheet duplicates.

3. **In the right drop-down list, select the formatting to apply to the cells with duplicate values.**

   You can create your own format by choosing the Custom Format command. In the Format Cells dialog box, use the Font, Border, and Fill tabs to specify the formatting you want to apply, and then click OK.

4. **Click OK.**

   Excel applies the formatting to any cells that have duplicate values in the range.

324   BOOK 4 Analyzing Data

Highlighting the top or bottom values in a range

When analyzing worksheet data, looking for items that stand out from the norm is often useful. For example, you may want to know which sales reps sold the most last year or which departments had the lowest gross margins. To quickly and easily view the extreme values in a range, you can apply a conditional format to the top or bottom values of that range.

You can apply such a format by setting up a *top/bottom rule*, in which Excel applies a conditional format to those items that are at the top or bottom of a range of values. For the top or bottom values, you can specify a number (such as the top five or ten) or a percentage (such as the bottom 20 percent). Here's how it works:

1. **Select the range you want to work with.**
2. **On the Home tab of the ribbon, click Conditional Formatting, click Top/Bottom Rules, and then select the type of rule you want to create.**

   You have six rules to mess with:

   - *Top 10 Items:* Applies the conditional format to cells that rank in the top *X*, where *X* is a number that you specify (the default is 10).
   - *Top 10 %:* Applies the conditional format to cells that rank in the top *X*%, where *X* is a number that you specify (the default is 10).
   - *Bottom 10 Items:* Applies the conditional format to cells that rank in the bottom *X*, where *X* is a number that you specify (the default is 10).
   - *Bottom 10 %:* Applies the conditional format to cells that rank in the bottom *X*%, where *X* is a number that you specify (the default is 10).
   - *Above Average:* Applies the conditional format to cells that rank above the average value of the range.
   - *Below Average:* Applies the conditional format to cells that rank below the average value of the range.

   A dialog box appears, the name of which depends on the rule you selected. For example, Figure 1-3 shows the dialog box for the Top Ten Items rule.

3. **Type the value to use for the condition.**

   You can also click the spin buttons that appear to the right of the text box. Note that you don't need to enter a value for the Above Average and Below Average rules.

FIGURE 1-3:
The Top 10 Items dialog box with the top five values highlighted.

4. **In the right drop-down list, select the formatting to apply to cells that match your condition.**

   When you set up your top/bottom rule, select a format that ensures that the cells that meet your criteria will stand out from the other cells in the range. If none of the predefined formats suits your needs, you can always choose Custom Format and then use the Format Cells dialog box to create a suitable formatting combination. Use the Font, Border, and Fill tabs to specify the formatting you want to apply, and then click OK.

5. **Click OK.**

   Excel applies the formatting to cells that meet the condition you specified.

Analyzing cell values with data bars

In some data analysis scenarios, you may be interested more in the relative values within a range than the absolute values. For example, if you have a table of products that includes a column showing unit sales, you may want to compare the relative sales of all products.

Comparing relative values is often easiest if you visualize the values. One of the easiest ways to visualize data in Excel is to use *data bars*, a data visualization feature that applies colored horizontal bars to each cell in a range of values; these bars appear *behind* (that is, in the background of) the values in the range. The length of the data bar in each cell depends on the value in that cell: The larger the value, the longer the data bar.

326   BOOK 4 Analyzing Data

Follow these steps to apply data bars to a range:

1. **Select the range you want to work with.**
2. **On the Home tab of the ribbon, click Conditional Formatting, click Data Bars, and then select the fill type of data bars you want to create.**

   You can apply two type of data bars:

   - *Gradient Fill:* The data bars begin with a solid color and then gradually fade to a lighter color.
   - *Solid Fill:* The data bars are a solid color.

   Excel applies the data bars to each cell in the range. Figure 1-4 shows an example in the Units column.

	A	B	C
1	Product Name	Units	$ Total
2	Northwind Traders Almonds	20	$ 200
3	Northwind Traders Beer	487	$ 6,818
4	Northwind Traders Boysenberry Spread	100	$ 2,500
5	Northwind Traders Cajun Seasoning	40	$ 880
6	Northwind Traders Chai	40	$ 720
7	Northwind Traders Chocolate	200	$ 2,550
8	Northwind Traders Chocolate Biscuits Mix	85	$ 782
9	Northwind Traders Clam Chowder	290	$ 2,799
10	Northwind Traders Coffee	650	$ 29,900
11	Northwind Traders Crab Meat	120	$ 2,208
12	Northwind Traders Curry Sauce	65	$ 2,600
13	Northwind Traders Dried Apples	40	$ 2,120
14	Northwind Traders Dried Pears	40	$ 1,200
15	Northwind Traders Dried Plums	75	$ 263
16	Northwind Traders Fruit Cocktail	40	$ 1,560
17	Northwind Traders Gnocchi	10	$ 380
18	Northwind Traders Green Tea	275	$ 822
19	Northwind Traders Long Grain Rice	40	$ 280
20	Northwind Traders Marmalade	40	$ 3,240
21	Northwind Traders Mozzarella	90	$ 3,132
22	Northwind Traders Olive Oil	25	$ 534

FIGURE 1-4: The higher the value, the longer the data bar.

TIP If your range includes right-aligned values, gradient-fill data bars are a better choice than solid-fill data bars. Why? Because even the longest gradient-fill bars fade to white toward the right edge of the cell, so your range values will mostly appear on a white background, making them easier to read.

Analyzing cell values with color scales

Getting some idea about the overall distribution of values in a range is often useful. For example, you may want to know whether a range has many low values and just a few high values. Color scales can help you analyze your data in this way. A *color scale* compares the relative values in a range by applying shading to each cell, where the color reflects each cell's value.

Color scales can also tell you whether your data includes *outliers* (values that are much higher or lower than the others). Similarly, color scales can help you make value judgments about your data. For example, high sales and low numbers of product defects are good, whereas low margins and high employee turnover rates are bad.

To apply a color scale to a range of values, do the following:

1. **Select the range you want to format.**
2. **On the Home tab of the ribbon, click Conditional Formatting, click Color Scales, and then select the color scale that has the color scheme you want to apply.**

   Color scales come in two varieties: three-color scales and two-color scales.

   TIP If your goal is to look for outliers, go with a three-color scale because it helps the outliers stand out more. A three-color scale is also useful if you want to make value judgments about your data, because you can assign your own values to the colors (such as positive, neutral, and negative). Use a two-color scale when you want to look for patterns in the data, because a two-color scale offers less contrast.

   Excel applies the color scale to each cell in your selected range.

Analyzing cell values with icon sets

Symbols that have common or well-known associations are often useful for analyzing large amounts of data. For example, a check mark usually means that something is good or finished or acceptable, whereas an X means that something is bad or unfinished or unacceptable. Similarly, a green circle is positive, whereas a red circle is negative (think traffic lights). Excel puts these and other symbolic associations to good use with the *icon sets* feature. You can use icon sets to visualize the relative values of cells in a range.

REMEMBER With icon sets, Excel adds a particular icon to each cell in the range, and that icon tells you something about the cell's value relative to the rest of the range. For example, the highest values might be assigned an upward-pointing arrow; the lowest values, a downward-pointing arrow; and the values in between, a horizontal arrow.

Here's how you apply an icon set to a range:

1. **Select the range you want to format with an icon set.**
2. **On the Home tab of the ribbon, click Conditional Formatting, click Icon Sets, and then select the type of icon set you want to apply.**

   Icon sets come in four categories:

   - *Directional:* Indicates trends and data movement
   - *Shapes:* Points out the high (green) and low (red) values in the range
   - *Indicators:* Adds value judgments
   - *Ratings:* Shows where each cell resides in the overall range of data values

   Excel applies the icons to each cell in the range, as shown in Figure 1-5.

FIGURE 1-5: Excel applies an icon based on each cell's value.

	A	B
1	Student ID	Grade
2	64947	✓ 82
3	69630	66
4	18324	✗ 52
5	89826	✓ 94
6	63600	✗ 40
7	25089	62
8	89923	✓ 88
9	13000	75
10	16895	66
11	24918	62
12	45107	71
13	64090	✗ 53
14	94395	74
15	58749	65

Creating a custom conditional formatting rule

The conditional formatting rules in Excel — highlight cells rules, top/bottom rules, data bars, color scales, and icon sets — offer an easy way to analyze data through visualization. However, you can also tailor your formatting-based data analysis by creating a custom conditional formatting rule that suits how you want to analyze and present the data.

REMEMBER Custom conditional formatting rules are ideal for situations in which normal value judgments — that is, that higher values are good and lower values are bad — don't apply. In a database of product defects, for example, lower values are better than higher ones. Similarly, data bars are based on the relative numeric values in a range, but you may prefer to base them on the relative percentages or on percentile rankings.

To get the type of data analysis you prefer, follow these steps to create a custom conditional formatting rule and apply it to your range:

1. **Select the range you want to analyze with a custom conditional formatting rule.**

2. **On the Home tab of the ribbon, click Conditional Formatting, and click New Rule.**

   The New Formatting Rule dialog box opens.

3. **In the Select a Rule Type box, select the type of rule you want to create.**

4. **Use the controls in the Edit the Rule Description box to edit the rule's style and formatting.**

   The controls you see depend on the rule type you selected in Step 3. For example, if you select Icon Sets, you see the controls shown in Figure 1-6.

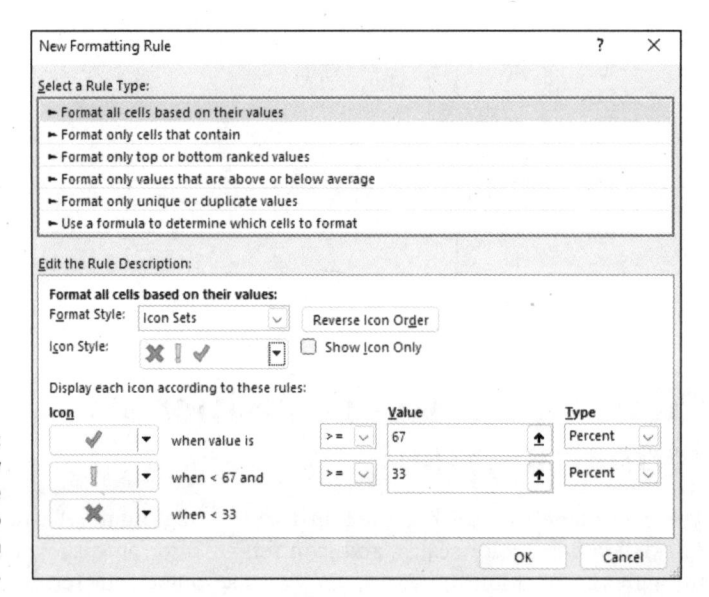

FIGURE 1-6: Use the New Formatting Rule dialog box to create a custom rule.

> **TIP** With Icon Sets, select Reverse Icon Order (as shown in the figure) if you want to reverse the normal icon assignments.

5. **Click OK.**

   Excel applies the conditional formatting to each cell in the range.

HIGHLIGHT CELLS BASED ON A FORMULA

You can apply conditional formatting based on the results of a formula. That is, you set up a logical formula as the conditional formatting criteria. For each cell in which that formula returns TRUE, Excel applies the formatting you specify; for all the other cells, Excel doesn't apply the formatting.

In most cases, you use a comparison formula, or you use an IF function, often combined with another logical function such as AND or OR. In each case, your formula's comparison value must reference only the first value in the range. For example, if the range you're working with is a set of dates in A2:A100, the comparison formula =WEEKDAY(A2)=6 would apply conditional formatting to every cell in the range that occurs on a Friday.

The following steps show you how to apply conditional formatting based on the results of a formula:

1. **Select the range you want to work with.**
2. **On the Home tab of the ribbon, click Conditional Formatting, and click New Rule.**

   The New Formatting Rule dialog box opens.
3. **Select Use a Formula to Determine Which Cells to Format.**
4. **In the Format Values Where This Formula Is True text box, type the logical formula.**

   The figure shows an example of using a formula to apply conditional formatting.

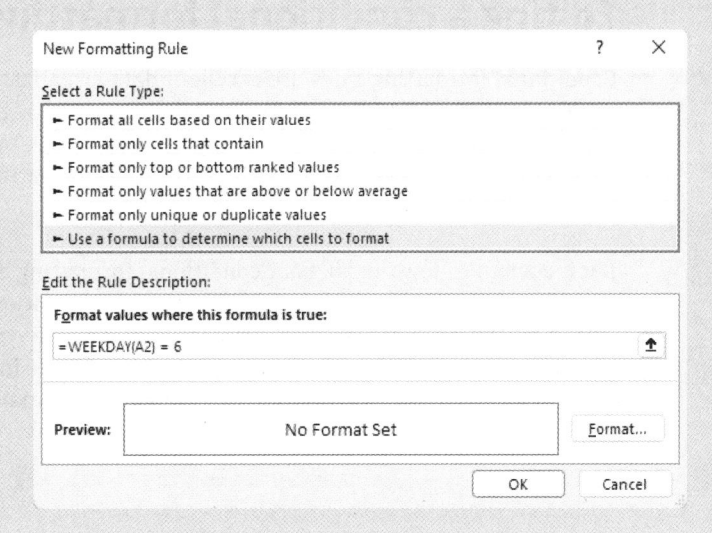

(continued)

CHAPTER 1 Using Basic Data Analysis Techniques   331

(continued)

5. **Choose Format.**

    The Format Cells dialog box opens.

6. **Define the rule's style and formatting, and then click OK.**

7. **Click OK to close the New Formatting Rule dialog box.**

    Excel applies the conditional formatting to each cell in the range in which the logical formula returns TRUE.

When you're messing around with formula-based rules, one useful technique is to apply a conditional format based on a formula that compares all the cells in a range to one value in that range. The simplest case is a formula that applies conditional formatting to those range cells that are equal to a cell value in the range. Here's the logical formula to use for such a comparison:

    =range=cell

Here, *range* is an absolute reference to the range of cells you want to work with, and *cell* is a relative reference to the comparison cell. For example, to apply a conditional format to those cells in the range A1:A50 that are equal to the value in cell A1, you would use the following logical formula:

    =$A$1:$A$50=A1

Editing a conditional formatting rule

Conditional formatting rules are excellent data visualization tools that can make analyzing your data easier and faster. Whether you're highlighting cells based on criteria, showing cells in the top or bottom of a range, or using features such as data bars, color scales, and icon sets, conditional formatting enables you to interpret your data quickly.

But it doesn't follow that all your conditional formatting experiments will be successful ones. For example, you may find that the conditional formatting you used isn't working out because it doesn't let you visualize your data the way you'd hoped. Similarly, a change in data may require a change in the condition you used. Whatever the reason, you can edit your conditional formatting rules to ensure that you get the best visualization for your data. Here's how:

1. **Select a cell in the range that includes the conditional formatting rule you want to edit.**

   You can select a single cell, multiple cells, or the entire range.

2. **On the Home of the ribbon, click Conditional Formatting, and click Manage Rules.**

   The Conditional Formatting Rules Manager dialog box, shown in Figure 1-7, opens.

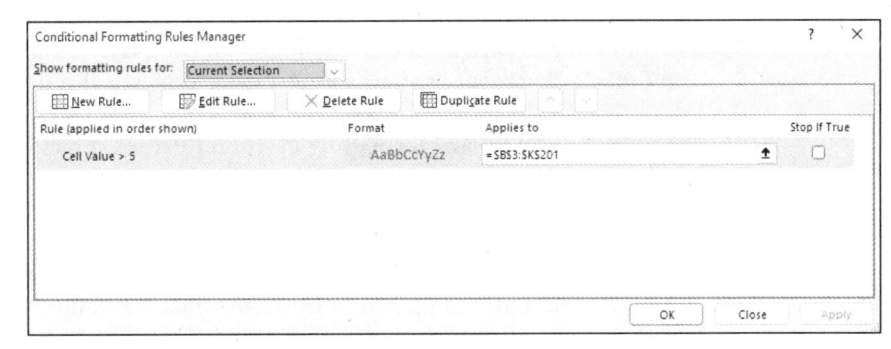

   FIGURE 1-7: Use the Conditional Formatting Rules Manager dialog box to edit your rules.

3. **Select the rule you want to modify.**

   If you don't see the rule, click the Show Formatting Rules For drop-down list and then select This Worksheet. The list that appears displays every conditional formatting rule that you've applied in the current worksheet.

4. **Choose Edit Rule.**

   The Edit Formatting Rule dialog box appears.

5. **Make your changes to the rule.**

6. **Click OK.**

   Excel returns you to the Conditional Formatting Rules Manager dialog box.

7. **Click OK.**

   Excel updates the conditional formatting.

WARNING

If you have multiple conditional formatting rules applied to a range, the visualization is affected by the order in which Excel applies the rules. Specifically, if a cell already has a conditional format applied, Excel doesn't overwrite that format with a new one. For example, suppose that you have two conditional formatting rules applied to a list of student grades: one for grades over 90 and one for grades over 80. If you apply the over-80 conditional format first, Excel will never apply the

CHAPTER 1 **Using Basic Data Analysis Techniques** 333

over-90 format because those values are already covered by the over-80 format. The solution is to change the order of the rules. In the Conditional Formatting Rules Manager dialog box, select the rule that you want to modify and then click the Move Up and Move Down button to set the order you want. If you want Excel to stop processing the rest of the rules after it has applied a particular rule, select that rule's Stop If True check box.

Removing conditional formatting rules

Conditional formatting rules are useful critters, but they don't work in all scenarios. For example, if your data is essentially random, conditional formatting rules won't magically produce patterns in that data. You may also find that conditional formatting isn't helpful for certain collections of data or certain types of data. Or you may find conditional formatting useful for getting a handle on your dataset but then prefer to remove the formatting.

Similarly, although the data visualization aspect of conditional formatting rules is part of the appeal of this Excel feature, as with all things visual, you can overdo it. That is, you may end up with a worksheet that has multiple conditional formatting rules and, therefore, some unattractive and confusing combinations of highlighted cells, data bars, color scales, and icon sets.

If, for whatever reason, you find that a range's conditional formatting isn't helpful or is no longer required, you can remove the conditional formatting from that range by following these steps:

1. **Select a cell in the range that includes the conditional formatting rule you want to trash.**

    You can select a single cell, multiple cells, or the entire range.

2. **On the Home tab of the ribbon, click Conditional Formatting, and click Manage Rules.**

    The Conditional Formatting Rules Manager dialog box opens.

3. **Select the rule you want to remove.**

    If you don't see the rule, use the Show Formatting Rules For list to select This Worksheet, which tells Excel to display every conditional formatting rule that you've applied in the current worksheet.

4. **Choose Delete Rule.**

    Excel removes the rule from the range.

5. **Click OK.**

TIP

If you have multiple rules defined and want to remove them all, click the Home tab of the ribbon, click Conditional Formatting, select Clear Rules, and then select either Clear Rules from Selected Cells or Clear Rules from Entire Sheet.

Summarizing Data with Subtotals

Although you can use formulas and worksheet functions to summarize your data in various ways — including sums, averages, counts, maximums, and minimums — if you're in a hurry, or if you just need a quick summary of your data, you can get Excel to do the work for you. The secret here is a feature called *automatic subtotals*, which are formulas that Excel adds to a worksheet automatically.

REMEMBER

Excel sets up automatic subtotals based on data groupings in a selected field. For example, if you ask for subtotals based on the Customer field, Excel runs down the Customer column and creates a new subtotal each time the name changes. To get useful summaries, you should sort the range on the field containing the data groupings you're interested in.

Follow these steps to summarize your data with subtotals:

1. **Select a cell within the range you want to subtotal.**
2. **Click the Data tab of the ribbon, and click Subtotal.**

   If you don't see the Subtotal command, click the Outline button, and then click Subtotal on the drop-down list. The Subtotal dialog box appears.

3. **In the At Each Change In list, select the column you want to use to group the subtotals.**
4. **In the Use Function list, select Sum.**
5. **In the Add Subtotal To list, select the check box for the column you want to summarize.**

   In Figure 1-8, for example, each change in the Customer field displays the sum of that customer's Total cells.

6. **Click OK.**

   Excel calculates the subtotals and adds them into the range. Note, too, that Excel also adds outline symbols to the range. We talk about outlining in a bit more detail in the next section.

Figure 1-9 shows some subtotals applied to a range.

CHAPTER 1 **Using Basic Data Analysis Techniques** 335

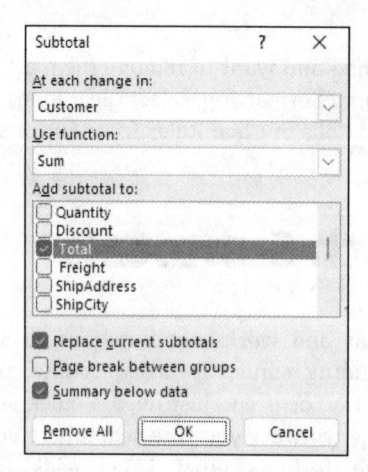

FIGURE 1-8:
Use the Subtotal dialog box to apply subtotals to a range.

FIGURE 1-9:
Some subtotals applied to the Total column for each customer.

	A	B	C	E	F	G	H	I
1	Customer	Country	Region	Unit Price	Quantity	Discount	Total	Freight
2	Cactus Comidas para llevar	Argentina		$ 46.00	7	0%	$ 322.00	$ 19.76
3	Cactus Comidas para llevar	Argentina		$ 7.75	20	0%	$ 155.00	$ 19.76
4	Cactus Comidas para llevar	Argentina		$ 15.00	10	0%	$ 150.00	$ 2.84
5	Cactus Comidas para llevar	Argentina		$ 45.60	8	0%	$ 364.80	$ 31.51
6	Cactus Comidas para llevar	Argentina		$ 14.00	20	0%	$ 280.00	$ 31.51
7	**Cactus Comidas para llevar Total**						$ 1,271.80	
8	Océano Atlántico Ltda.	Argentina		$ 6.00	5	0%	$ 30.00	$ 1.27
9	Océano Atlántico Ltda.	Argentina		$ 21.35	20	0%	$ 427.00	$ 49.56
10	Océano Atlántico Ltda.	Argentina		$ 30.00	6	0%	$ 180.00	$ 49.56
11	Océano Atlántico Ltda.	Argentina		$ 34.80	5	0%	$ 174.00	$ 49.56
12	Océano Atlántico Ltda.	Argentina		$ 21.00	30	0%	$ 630.00	$ 217.86
13	Océano Atlántico Ltda.	Argentina		$ 81.00	15	0%	$ 1,215.00	$ 217.86
14	Océano Atlántico Ltda.	Argentina		$ 18.00	10	0%	$ 180.00	$ 217.86
15	Océano Atlántico Ltda.	Argentina		$ 13.00	15	0%	$ 195.00	$ 217.86
16	**Océano Atlántico Ltda. Total**						$ 3,031.00	
17	Rancho grande	Argentina		$ 81.00	5	0%	$ 405.00	$ 90.85
18	Rancho grande	Argentina		$263.50	2	0%	$ 527.00	$ 90.85
19	Rancho grande	Argentina		$ 17.45	6	0%	$ 104.70	$ 63.77
20	Rancho grande	Argentina		$ 32.00	6	0%	$ 192.00	$ 63.77
21	Rancho grande	Argentina		$ 19.50	20	0%	$ 390.00	$ 63.77
22	**Rancho grande Total**						$ 1,618.70	

REMEMBER

Note that in the term *automatic subtotals,* the word *subtotals* is misleading because it implies that you can summarize your data only with totals. Not even close! Using "subtotals," you can also count the values (all the values or just the numeric values), calculate the average of the values, determine the maximum or minimum value, and calculate the product of the values. For statistical analysis, you can also calculate the standard deviation and variance, both of a sample and of a population. To change the summary calculation, follow Steps 1 to 3, open the Use Function drop-down list, and then select the function you want to use for the summary.

336   BOOK 4 **Analyzing Data**

Grouping Related Data

To help you analyze a worksheet, you may be able to control what parts of the worksheet are displayed by grouping the data based on the worksheet formulas and data. Grouping the data creates a worksheet outline, which works similarly to the outline feature in Microsoft Word. In a worksheet outline, you can *collapse* sections of the sheet to display only summary cells (such as quarterly or regional totals), or *expand* hidden sections to show the underlying detail. Note that when you add subtotals to a range, as we describe in the preceding section, Excel automatically groups the data and displays the outline tools.

REMEMBER

Not all worksheets can be grouped, so you need to make sure that your worksheet is a candidate for outlining:

» **The worksheet must contain formulas that reference cells or ranges directly adjacent to the formula cell.** Worksheets with SUM functions that subtotal cells above or to the left are particularly good candidates for outlining.

» **There must be a consistent pattern to the direction of the formula references.** For example, a worksheet with formulas that always reference cells above or to the left can be outlined. Excel won't outline a worksheet with, say, SUM functions where some of the range references are above the formula cell and some are below.

Here are the steps to follow group-related data:

1. **Display the worksheet you want to outline.**
2. **Click the Data tab of the ribbon, click the Group down arrow, and select Auto Outline.**

    If you don't see the Group command, click the Outline button, click the Group down arrow, and then click Auto Outline. (If you accidentally click Group instead of clicking the down arrow, the Group dialog box opens. Just click Cancel to dismiss that.) Excel outlines the worksheet data.

Excel uses *level bars* to indicate the grouped ranges and *level numbers* to indicate the various levels of the underlying data available in the outline (see Figure 1-10).

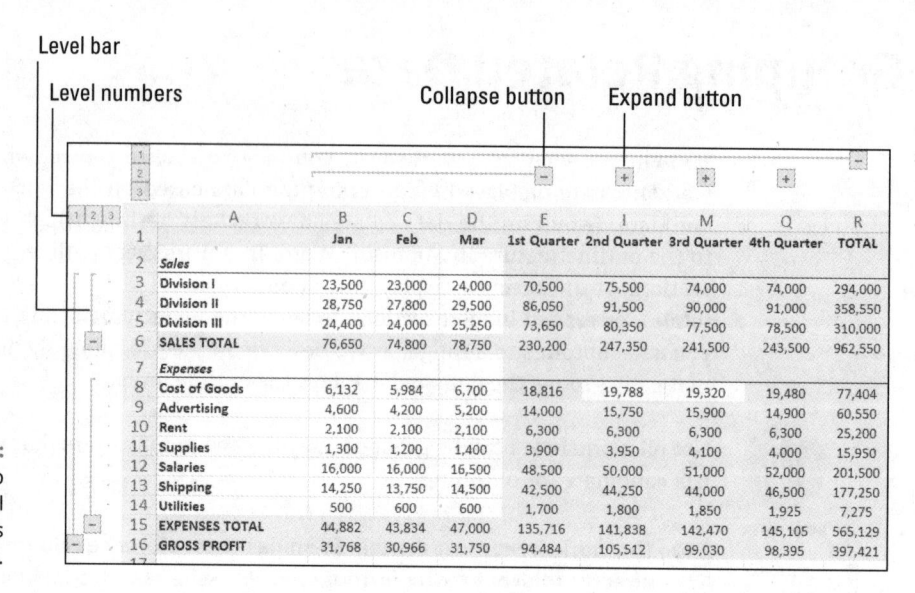

FIGURE 1-10:
When you group a range, Excel displays its outlining tools.

Here are some ways you can use the outline to control the range display:

» Click the – (collapse) button to hide the range indicated by the level bar.

» Click the + (expand) button for a collapsed range to view it again.

» Click a level number to collapse multiple ranges on the same outline level.

» Click a level number to display multiple collapsed ranges on the same outline level.

Consolidating Data from Multiple Worksheets

Companies often distribute similar worksheets to multiple departments to capture budget numbers, inventory values, survey data, and so on. Those worksheets must then be combined into a summary report showing company-wide totals. Combining multiple worksheets into a summary report is called *consolidating* the data.

Sounds like a lot of work, right? It sure is, if you do it manually, so forget that. Instead, Excel can consolidate your data automatically. You can use the consolidate feature to consolidate the data in either of two ways:

» **By position:** Excel consolidates the data from two or more worksheets, using the same range coordinates on each sheet. Use this method if the worksheets you're consolidating have an identical layout.

» **By category:** Excel consolidates the data from two or more worksheets by looking for identical row and column labels in each sheet. Reach for this method if the worksheets you're consolidating have different layouts but common labels.

In both cases, you specify one or more *source ranges* (the ranges that contain the data you want to consolidate) and a *destination range* (the range where the consolidated data will appear).

Consolidating by position

Here are the steps to trudge through if you want to consolidate multiple worksheets by position:

1. **Create a new worksheet that uses the same layout — including row and column labels — as the sheets you want to consolidate.**

   The identical layout in this new worksheet is your destination range.

2. **If necessary, open the workbooks that contain the worksheets you want to consolidate.**

   If the worksheets you want to consolidate are in the current workbook, you can skip this step.

3. **In the new worksheet from Step 1, select the upper-left corner of the destination range.**

4. **Click the Data tab of the ribbon, and click Consolidate.**

   The Consolidate dialog box opens.

5. **In the Function list, select the summary function you want to use.**

6. **In the Reference text box, select one of the ranges you want to consolidate.**

7. **Click Add.**

   Excel adds the range to the All References list, as shown in Figure 1-11.

8. **Repeat steps 6 and 7 to add all the consolidation ranges.**

9. **Click OK.**

   Excel consolidates the data from the source ranges and displays the summary in the destination range.

CHAPTER 1 **Using Basic Data Analysis Techniques** 339

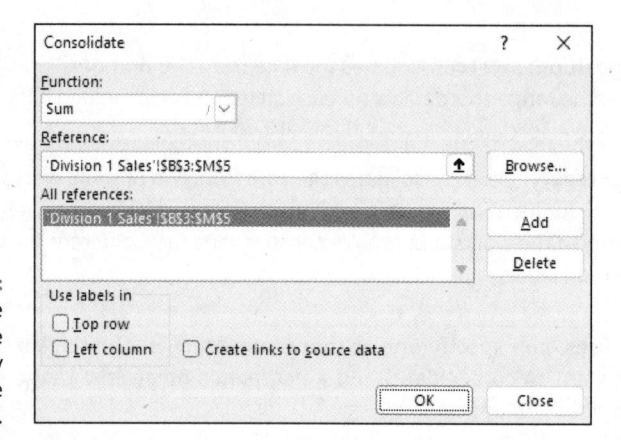

FIGURE 1-11: Consolidate multiple worksheets by adding a range from each one.

> **TIP**
>
> If the source data changes, you probably want to reflect those changes in the consolidation worksheet. Instead of running the entire consolidation over again, a much easier solution is to select the Create Links to Source Data check box in the Consolidate dialog box. You can then update the consolidation worksheet by clicking Refresh All on the Data tab of the ribbon.

Consolidating by category

Here are the steps to follow to consolidate multiple worksheets by category:

1. **Create a new worksheet for the consolidation.**

    You use this worksheet to specify your destination range.

2. **If necessary, open the workbooks that contain the worksheets you want to consolidate.**

    If the worksheets you want to consolidate are in the current workbook, you can skip this step.

3. **In the new worksheet from Step 1, select the upper-left corner of the destination range.**

4. **Click the Data tab of the ribbon, and click Consolidate.**

    The Consolidate dialog box appears.

5. **In the Function list, select the summary function you want to use.**

6. **In the Reference text box, select one of the ranges you want to consolidate.**

   When you're selecting the range, be sure to include the row and column labels in the range.

7. **Click Add.**

   Excel adds the range to the All References list.

8. **Repeat steps 6 and 7 to add all the consolidation ranges.**

9. **If you have labels in the top row of each range, select the Top Row check box.**

10. **If you have labels in the leftmost column of each range, select the Left Column check box.**

11. **Click OK.**

    Excel consolidates the data from the source ranges and displays the summary in the destination range.

IN THIS CHAPTER

» **Creating basic and two-input data tables**

» **Analyzing your data using the Goal Seek tool**

» **Creating and running scenarios**

» **Optimizing your data with the Solver tool**

Chapter 2
Working with Data Analysis Tools

When it comes to data analysis, you're best off getting Excel to perform most — or, ideally, all — of the work. After all, Excel is a complex, powerful, and expensive piece of software, so why shouldn't it take on the lion's share of the data analysis chores? Sure, you still have to get your data into the worksheet, but after you've done that, it's time for Excel to get busy.

In this chapter, you investigate some built-in Excel tools that will handle most of the data analysis dirty work. We show you how to build two different types of data tables, give you the details on using the very cool Goal Seek tool, delve into scenarios and how to use them for fun and profit, and take you on a tour of the powerful Solver add-in.

Working with Data Tables

If you want to study the effect that different input values have on a formula, one solution is to set up the worksheet model and then manually change the formula's input cells. For example, if you're calculating a loan payment, you can enter different interest rate values to see what effect changing the value has on the payment.

The problem with modifying the values of a formula input is that you see only a single result at one time. A better solution is to set up a *data table,* which is a range that consists of the formula you're using and multiple input values for that formula. Excel automatically creates a solution to the formula for each different input value.

REMEMBER

Data tables are an example of *what-if analysis,* which is perhaps the most basic method for analyzing worksheet data. With what-if analysis, you first calculate a formula D, based on the input from variables A, B, and C. You then say, "What happens to the result if I change the value of variable A?" "What happens if I change B or C?" and so on.

Creating a basic data table

The most basic type of data table is one that varies only one of the formula's input cells. Not even remotely surprisingly, this basic version is known far and wide as a *one-input data table.* To create a one-input data table, follow these steps:

1. **Type the input values.**

   - To enter the values in a column, start the column one cell down and one cell to the left of the cell containing the formula, as shown in Figure 2-1.

   - To enter the values in a row, start the row one cell up and one cell to the right of the cell containing the formula.

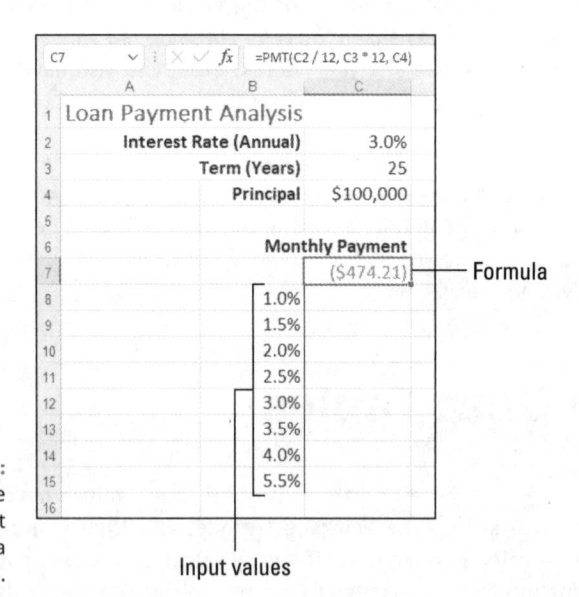

FIGURE 2-1:
This data table has the input values in a column.

344 BOOK 4 **Analyzing Data**

2. **Select the range that includes the input values and the formula.**

   In the example shown in Figure 2-1, you'd select the range B7:C15.

3. **Click the Data tab of the ribbon, click What-If Analysis, and select Data Table.**

   The Data Table dialog box opens.

4. **Enter the address of the *input cell* (the cell referenced by the formula that you want the data table to vary).**

   That is, for whatever cell you specify, the data table will substitute each of its input values into that cell and calculate the formula result. You have two choices:

   - If you entered the input values in a row, enter the input cell's address in the Row Input Cell text box.

   - If the input values are in a column, enter the input cell's address in the Column Input Cell text box. In the example shown in Figure 2-1, the data table's input values are annual interest rates, so the column input cell is C2, as shown in Figure 2-2.

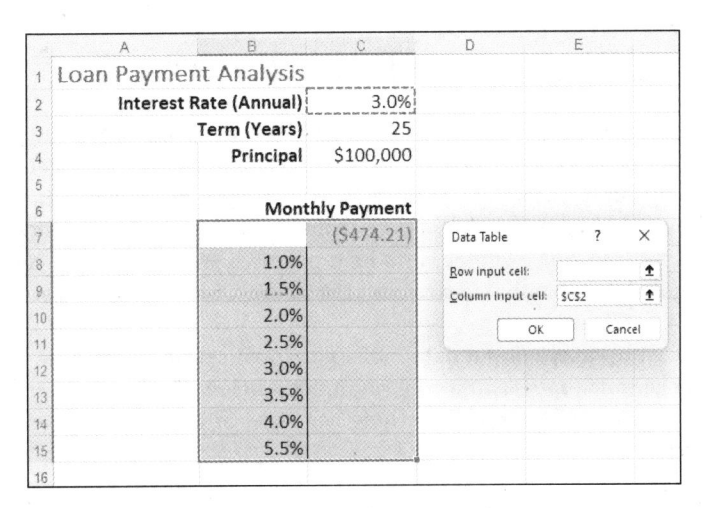

FIGURE 2-2: Enter the address of the input cell.

5. **Click OK.**

   Excel fills the input table with the results. Figure 2-3 shows the results of the example data table.

CHAPTER 2 Working with Data Analysis Tools   345

	A	B	C
1	Loan Payment Analysis		
2	Interest Rate (Annual)		3.0%
3	Term (Years)		25
4	Principal		$100,000
5			
6			Monthly Payment
7			($474.21)
8		1.0%	($376.87)
9		1.5%	($399.94)
10		2.0%	($423.85)
11		2.5%	($448.62)
12		3.0%	($474.21)
13		3.5%	($500.62)
14		4.0%	($527.84)
15		5.5%	($614.09)
16			

FIGURE 2-3: The data table results.

WARNING: When you see the data table results, you might find that all the calculated values are identical. What gives? The problem most likely is Excel's current calculation mode. Click the Formulas tab of the ribbon, click Calculation Options, and select Automatic; the data table results should recalculate to the correct values.

Creating a two-input data table

Instead of requiring you to vary a single formula input at a time — as in the one-input data table we discuss in the preceding section — Excel also lets you kick things up a notch by enabling you to set up a *two-input* data table. As you may have guessed, a two-input data table is one that varies two formula inputs at the same time. For example, in a loan payment worksheet, you could set up a two-input data table that varies both the interest rate and the term.

To set up a two-input data table, you must set up two ranges of input cells. One range must appear in a column directly below the formula, and the other range must appear in a row directly to the right of the formula. Here are the steps to follow:

1. **Type the input values:**

   - To enter the column values, start the column one cell down and one cell to the left of the cell containing the formula.

   - To enter the row values, start the row one cell up and one cell to the right of the cell containing the formula.

   Figure 2-4 shows an example.

346 BOOK 4 **Analyzing Data**

FIGURE 2-4:
For a two-input data table, enter one set of values in a column and the other in a row.

2. **Select the range that includes the input values and the formula.**

   In the example shown in Figure 2-4, you'd select the range B7:F15.

3. **Click the Data tab of the ribbon, click What-If Analysis, and select Data Table.**

   The Data Table dialog box opens.

4. **In the Row Input Cell text box, enter the cell address of the input cell that corresponds to the row values you entered.**

   In the example shown in Figure 2-4, the row values are term inputs, so the input cell is C3 (see Figure 2-5).

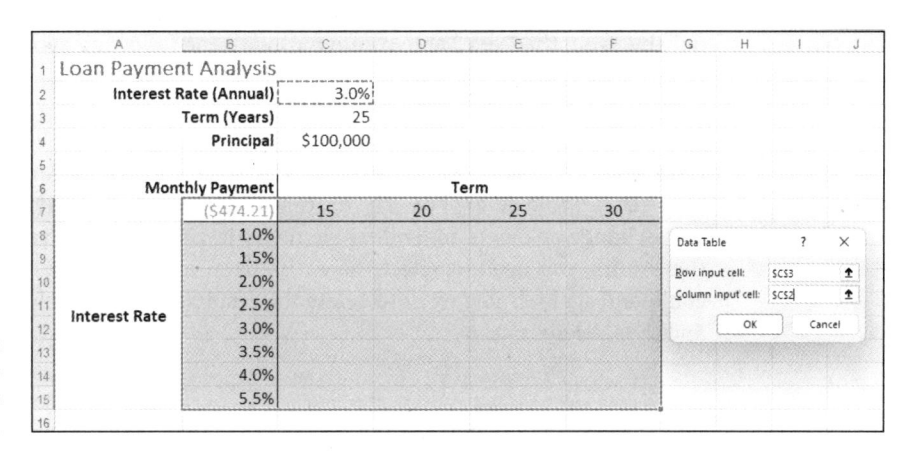

FIGURE 2-5:
Enter the addresses of the input cells.

CHAPTER 2 Working with Data Analysis Tools   347

5. **In the Column Input Cell text box, enter the cell address of the input cell you want to use for the column values.**

   In the example shown in Figure 2-4, the column values are interest rate inputs, so the input cell is C2 (refer to Figure 2-5).

6. **Click OK.**

   Excel displays the results. Figure 2-6 shows the results of the example two-input data table.

	A	B	C	D	E	F
1	Loan Payment Analysis					
2		Interest Rate (Annual)	3.0%			
3		Term (Years)	25			
4		Principal	$100,000			
5						
6		Monthly Payment			Term	
7		($474.21)	15	20	25	30
8		1.0%	($598.49)	($459.89)	($376.87)	($321.64)
9		1.5%	($620.74)	($482.55)	($399.94)	($345.12)
10		2.0%	($643.51)	($505.88)	($423.85)	($369.62)
11	Interest Rate	2.5%	($666.79)	($529.90)	($448.62)	($395.12)
12		3.0%	($690.58)	($554.60)	($474.21)	($421.60)
13		3.5%	($714.88)	($579.96)	($500.62)	($449.04)
14		4.0%	($739.69)	($605.98)	($527.84)	($477.42)
15		5.5%	($817.08)	($687.89)	($614.09)	($567.79)

C8 cell contains: {=TABLE(C3,C2)}

FIGURE 2-6: The two-input data table results.

TECHNICAL STUFF

When you run the Data Table command, Excel enters an array formula in the interior of the data table. The formula is a TABLE function (a special function available only by using the Data Table command) with the following syntax:

```
{=TABLE(row_input_ref, column_input_ref)}
```

Here, `row_input_ref` and `column_input_ref` are the cell references you entered in the Data Table dialog box. The braces ({ }) indicate an array, which means you can't change or delete individual elements in the results. If you want to change the results, you need to select the entire data table and then run the Data Table command again. If you want to delete the results, you must select the entire array and then delete it.

Skipping data tables when calculating workbooks

Because a data table is an array, Excel treats it as a unit, so a worksheet recalculation means that the entire data table is always recalculated. Such a recalculation isn't a big problem for a small data table that has just a few dozen formulas. However, it's not uncommon to have data tables with hundreds or even thousands of formulas, and these larger data tables can slow down worksheet recalculation.

If you're working with a large data table, you can reduce the time it takes for Excel to recalculate the workbook if you configure Excel to bypass data tables when it's running the recalculation. Here are the two methods you can use:

» Click the Formulas tab of the ribbon, click Calculation Options, and select Automatic Except for Data Tables.

» Choose File ⇨ Options to open the Excel Options dialog box, choose Formulas, select the Automatic Except for Data Tables option, and then click OK.

Now every time you calculate a workbook, Excel bypasses the data tables.

TIP When you want to recalculate a data table, you can repeat either of the preceding procedures and then choose the Automatic option. On the other hand, if you prefer to leave the Automatic Except for Data Tables option selected, you can still recalculate the data table by selecting any cell in the data table and either clicking Calculate Now on the Formulas tab of the ribbon or pressing F9.

Analyzing Data with Goal Seek

What if you already know the formula result you need and you want to produce that result by tweaking one of the formula's input values? For example, suppose that you know that you need to have $200,000 saved for your children's college education. In other words, you want to start an investment now that will be worth $200,000 at some point in the future.

This is called a *future value* calculation, and it requires three parameters:

» The term of the investment

» The interest rate you earn on the investment

» The amount of money you invest each year

CHAPTER 2 **Working with Data Analysis Tools** 349

Assume that you need that money 18 years from now and that you can make a 4 percent annual return on your investment. Here's the question that remains: How much should you invest each year to make your goal?

Sure, you could waste large chunks of your life guessing the answer. Fortunately, you don't have to, because you can put Excel's Goal Seek tool to work. Goal Seek works by trying dozens of possibilities — called *iterations* — that enable it to get closer and closer to a solution. When Goal Seek finds a solution (or finds a solution that's as close as it can get), it stops and shows you the result.

You must do three things to set up your worksheet for Goal Seek:

- » Set up one cell as the *changing cell,* which is the formula input cell value that Goal Seek will manipulate to reach the goal. In the college fund example, the formula cell that holds the annual deposit is the changing cell.
- » Set up the other input values for the formula and give them proper initial values. In the college fund example, you enter 4 percent for the interest rate and 18 years for the term.
- » Create a formula for Goal Seek to use to reach the goal. In the college fund example, you use the FV function, which calculates the future value of an investment given an interest rate, term, and regular deposit.

When your worksheet is ready for action, here are the steps to follow to get Goal Seek on the job:

1. **Click the Data tab of the ribbon, click What-If Analysis, and click Goal Seek.**

   The Goal Seek dialog box appears.

2. **In the Set Cell box, enter the address of the cell that contains the formula you want Goal Seek to work with.**

3. **In the To Value text box, enter the value that you want Goal Seek to find.**

4. **In the By Changing Cell box, enter the address of the cell that you want Goal Seek to modify.**

   Figure 2-7 shows an example model for the college fund calculation as well as the completed Goal Seek dialog box.

5. **Click OK.**

   Goal Seek adjusts the changing cell value until it reaches a solution. When it's done, the formula shows the value you entered in Step 3, as shown in Figure 2-8.

6. **Click OK to accept the solution.**

FIGURE 2-7:
Using Goal Seek to calculate the annual deposit required to end up with $200,000 in a college fund.

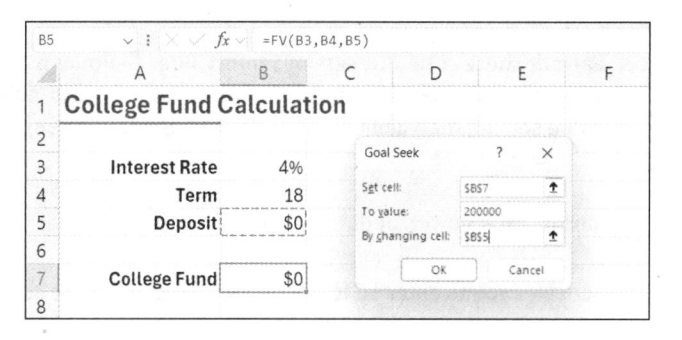

FIGURE 2-8:
Goal Seek took all of a second or two to find a solution.

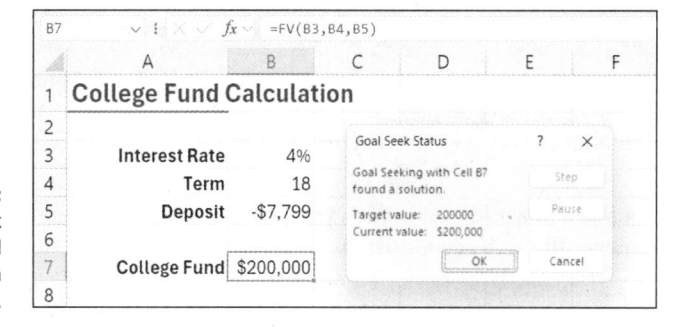

In some cases, Goal Seek might not find an exact solution to your model. Goal Seek stops after 100 iterations or if the current result is within 0.001 of the desired result.

You can get a more accurate solution by increasing the number of iterations that Goal Seek can use, by reducing the value that Goal Seek uses to mark a solution as close enough, or both. Choose File ⇨ Options and then choose Formulas. Increase the value of the Maximum Iterations spin button, decrease the value in the Maximum Change text box, or both, and then click OK.

Analyzing Data with Scenarios

Many formulas require a number of input values to produce a result. Previously in this chapter, in the "Working with Data Tables" section, we talk about using data tables to quickly see the results of varying one or two of those input values. Handy stuff, for sure, but when you're analyzing a formula's results, manipulating three or more input values at a time and performing this manipulation in some systematic way often help. For example, one set of values might represent a best-case approach, whereas another might represent a worst-case approach.

CHAPTER 2 **Working with Data Analysis Tools**   351

In Excel, each of these coherent sets of input values — known as *changing cells* — is called a *scenario*. By creating multiple scenarios, you can quickly apply these different value sets to analyze how the result of a formula changes under different conditions.

Excel scenarios are a powerful data analysis tool for a number of reasons:

- » Excel enables you to enter up to 32 changing cells in a single scenario, so you can create models that are as elaborate as you need.
- » No matter how many changing cells you have in a scenario, Excel enables you to show the scenario's result with just a few taps or clicks.
- » Because the number of scenarios you can define is limited only by the available memory on your computer, you can effectively use as many scenarios as you need to analyze your data model.

REMEMBER

When building a worksheet model, you can use a couple of techniques to make the model more suited to scenarios:

- » Group all your changing cells in one place and label them.
- » Make sure that each changing cell is a constant value. If you use a formula for a changing cell, another cell could change the formula result and throw off your scenarios.

Creating a scenario

If scenarios sound like your kind of data analysis tool, follow these steps to create a scenario for a worksheet model that you've set up:

1. **Click the Data tab of the ribbon, click What-If Analysis, and click Scenario Manager.**

   The Scenario Manager dialog box appears.

2. **Click Add.**

   The Add Scenario dialog box appears.

3. **In the Scenario Name box, type a name for the scenario.**

4. **In the Changing Cells box, enter the cells you want to change in the scenario.**

   You can type the address of each cell or range, separating each by a comma, or you can select the changing cells directly in the worksheet.

5. **In the Comment box, enter a description for the scenario.**

   Your scenarios appear in the Scenario Manager dialog box, and for each scenario, you see its changing cells and its description. The description is often very useful, particularly if you have several scenarios defined, so be sure to write a detailed description to help you differentiate your scenarios later on.

   Figure 2-9 shows a worksheet model for a mortgage analysis and a filled-in Add Scenario dialog box.

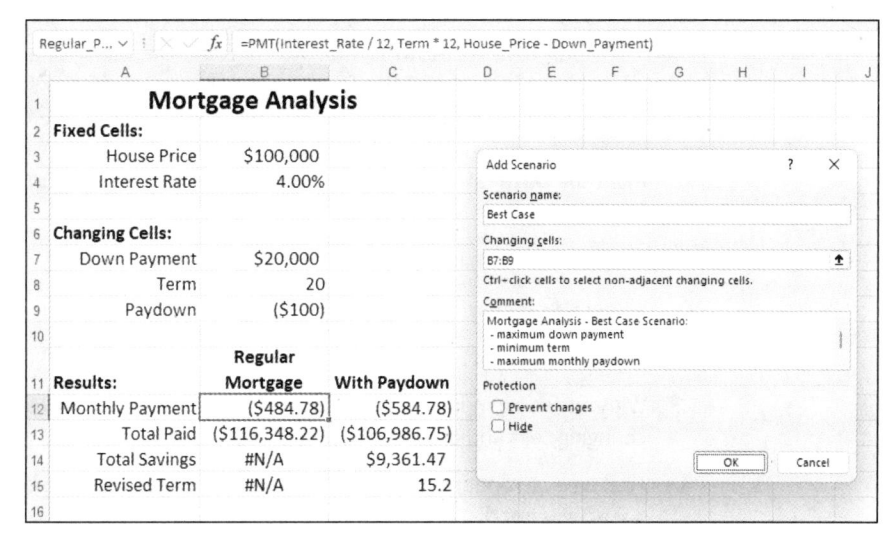

   FIGURE 2-9: Creating a scenario for a mortgage analysis.

6. **Click OK.**

   The Scenario Values dialog box appears.

7. **In the text boxes, enter a value for each changing cell.**

   Figure 2-10 shows some example values for a scenario.

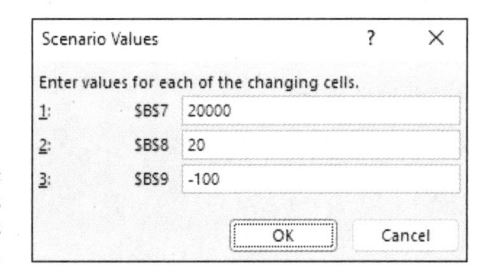

   FIGURE 2-10: Example values for a scenario's changing cells.

CHAPTER 2 Working with Data Analysis Tools

8. **To add more scenarios, click Add and then repeat steps 3 through 7.**
9. **Click OK.**

   The Scenario Values dialog box closes and the Scenario Manager dialog box returns, showing the scenarios you've added.

10. **Click Close.**

Applying a scenario

The real value of a scenario is that no matter how many changing cells you've defined or how complicated the formula is, you can apply any scenario with just a few straightforward steps. Don't believe us? Here, we'll prove it:

1. **Click the Data tab of the ribbon, click What-If Analysis, and click Scenario Manager.**

   The Scenario Manager dialog box appears.

2. **Select the scenario you want to display.**
3. **Click Show.**

   Without even a moment's hesitation, Excel enters the scenario values into the changing cells and displays the formula result.

4. **Feel free to repeat steps 2 and 3 to display other scenarios. (When it's this easy, why not?)**
5. **When you've completed your analysis, click Close.**

Editing a scenario

If you need to make changes to a scenario, you can edit the name, the changing cells, the description, and the scenario's input values. Here are the steps to follow:

1. **Click the Data tab of the ribbon, click What-If Analysis, and click Scenario Manager.**

   The Scenario Manager dialog box appears.

2. **Select the scenario you want to modify.**
3. **Click Edit.**

   The Edit Scenario dialog box appears.

4. **Modify the scenario name, changing cells, and comment, as needed.**

5. **Click OK.**

   The Scenario Values dialog box appears.

6. **Modify the scenario values, as needed.**

7. **Click OK.**

   Excel returns you to the Scenario Manager dialog box.

8. **Click Close.**

Deleting a scenario

If you have a scenario that has worn out its welcome, you should delete it to reduce clutter in the Scenario Manager dialog box. Here are the steps required:

1. **Click the Data tab of the ribbon, click What-If Analysis, and click Scenario Manager.**

   The Scenario Manager dialog box appears.

2. **Select the scenario you want to remove.**

   WARNING: Excel does not ask you to confirm the deletion, so double- or triple-check that you've selected the correct scenario.

3. **Click Delete.**

   Scenario Manager gets rids of the scenario.

4. **Click Close.**

Optimizing Data with Solver

Spreadsheet tools such as Goal Seek that change a single variable are useful, but unfortunately most problems in business aren't so simple. You'll usually face formulas with at least two and sometimes dozens of variables. Often, a problem will have more than one solution, and your challenge will be to find the *optimal* solution (that is, the one that maximizes profit, minimizes costs, or matches other criteria). For these bigger challenges, you need a more muscular tool. Excel has just the answer: Solver, a sophisticated optimization program that enables you to find the solutions to complex problems that would otherwise require high-level mathematical analysis.

CHAPTER 2 **Working with Data Analysis Tools** 355

Understanding Solver

Solver, like Goal Seek, uses an iterative method to perform its calculations. Using iteration means that Solver tries a solution, analyzes the results, tries another solution, and so on. However, this cyclic iteration isn't just guesswork on Solver's part. That would be silly. No, Solver examines how the results change with each new iteration and, through some sophisticated mathematical processes (which, thankfully, happen way in the background and can be ignored), can usually tell in what direction it should head for the solution.

Appreciating the advantages of Solver

Yes, Goal Seek and Solver are both iterative, but that doesn't make them equal. In fact, Solver brings a number of advantages to the table:

» **Solver enables you to specify multiple adjustable cells.** You can use up to 200 adjustable cells in all.

» **Solver enables you to set up constraints on the adjustable cells.** For example, you can tell Solver to find a solution that not only maximizes profit but also satisfies certain conditions, such as achieving a gross margin between 20 percent and 30 percent or keeping expenses less than $100,000. These conditions are said to be *constraints* on the solution.

» **Solver seeks not only a desired result (the "goal" in Goal Seek) but also the optimal one.** For example, looking for an optimal result might mean that you can find a solution that's the maximum or minimum possible.

» **For complex problems, Solver can generate multiple solutions.** You can then save these different solutions under different scenarios.

Knowing when to use Solver

Okay, we'll be straight with you: Solver is a powerful tool that most Excel users don't need. It would be overkill, for example, to use Solver to compute net profit given fixed revenue and cost figures. Some problems, however, require nothing less than the Solver approach. These problems cover many different fields and situations, but they all have the following characteristics in common:

» **They have a single *objective cell* (also called the *target cell*) that contains a formula you want to maximize, minimize, or set to a specific value.** This formula could be a calculation such as total transportation expenses or net profit.

» **The objective cell formula contains references to one or more** *variable cells* **(also called** *unknowns* **or** *changing cells***).** Solver adjusts these cells to find the optimal solution for the objective cell formula. These variable cells might include items such as units sold, shipping costs, or advertising expenses.

» **Optionally, there are one or more** *constraint cells* **that must satisfy certain criteria.** For example, you might require that advertising be less than 10 percent of total expenses, or that the discount to customers be an amount between 40 percent and 60 percent.

For example, Figure 2-11 shows a worksheet data model that's all set up for Solver. The model shows revenue (price times units sold) and costs for two products, the profit produced by each product, and the total profit. The question to be answered here is this: How many units of each product must be sold to get a total profit of $0? This is known in business as a *break-even analysis*.

	A	B	C
1			
2		Inflatable Dartboard	Dog Polisher
3	Price	$24.95	$19.95
4	Units	1	1
5	Revenue	$25	$20
6			
7	Unit Cost	$12.50	$9.50
8	Variable Costs	$12	$9
9	Fixed Costs	$100,000	$75,000
10	Total Costs	$100,012	$75,009
11			
12	Product Profit	-$99,987	-$74,989
13			
14	Total Profit	-$174,975	

FIGURE 2-11: The goal for this data model is to find the break-even point (where total profit is $0).

That sounds like a straightforward Goal Seek task, but this model has a tricky aspect: the variable costs. Normally, the variable costs of a product are its unit cost times the number of units sold. If it costs $10 to produce product A and you sell 10,000 units, the variable costs for that product are $100,000. However, in the real world, such costs are often mixed up among multiple products. For example, if you run a joint advertising campaign for two products, the costs are borne by both products. Therefore, this model assumes that the costs of one product are related to the units sold of the other.

CHAPTER 2 **Working with Data Analysis Tools** 357

Here, for example, is the formula used to calculate the costs of the Inflatable Dartboard (cell B8):

```
=B7*B4-C4
```

In other words, the variable costs for the Inflatable Dartboard are reduced by one dollar for every unit sold of the Dog Polisher. The latter's variable costs use a similar formula (in cell C8):

```
=C7*C4-B4
```

Having the variable costs related to multiple products puts this data model outside of what Goal Seek can do, but Solver is up to the challenge. Here are the special cells in the model that Solver will use:

- » The objective cell is C14; the total profit and the target solution for this formula is 0 (that is, the break-even point).
- » The changing cells are B4 and C4, which hold the number of units sold for each product.
- » For constraints, you may want to add that both the product profit cells (B12 and C12) should also be 0.

Loading the Solver add-in

An *add-in* is software that adds one or more features to Excel. Installing add-ins gives you additional Excel features that aren't available on the ribbon by default. Bundled add-in software is included with Excel but isn't automatically installed when you install Excel. Several add-ins come standard with Excel, including Solver.

You install bundled add-ins by using the Excel Options dialog box; you can find them in the Add-Ins section. After they're installed, add-ins are available right away. They usually appear on a tab related to their function. For example, Solver appears on the Data tab.

Here are the steps to follow to load the Solver add-in:

1. **Choose File ⇨ Options.**

    The Excel Options dialog box opens.

2. **Choose Add-ins.**

3. **In the Manage list, select Excel Add-ins and then select Go.**

   The Add-Ins dialog box opens.

4. **Select the Solver Add-in check box.**

5. **Click OK.**

   Excel adds a Solver button to the Data tab's Analysis group.

Optimizing a result with Solver

You set up your Solver model by using the Solver Parameters dialog box. In the Set Objective field, you specify the objective cell. You use the options in the To group to tell Solver what you want from the objective cell: the maximum possible value, the minimum possible value, or a specific value. Finally, you use the By Changing Variable Cells box to specify the cells that Solver can use to plug in values to optimize the result.

WARNING: When Solver finds a solution, you can choose either Keep Solver Solution or Restore Original Values. If you choose Keep Solver Solution, Excel permanently changes the worksheet. You can't undo the changes.

With your Solver-ready worksheet model prepared, here are the steps to follow to find an optimal result for your model using Solver:

1. **Click the Data tab of the ribbon and click Solver.**

   The Solver Parameters dialog box appears.

2. **In the Set Objective box, enter the address of your model's objective cell.**

   In the example in the "Knowing when to use Solver" section, earlier in this chapter (refer to Figure 2-11), the objective cell is B14. Note that if you click the cell to enter it, Solver automatically enters an absolute cell address (for example, $B$14 instead of B14). Solver works fine either way.

3. **In the To group, select an option:**

   - *Max:* Returns the maximum possible value.
   - *Min:* Returns the minimum possible value.
   - *Value Of:* Enter a number to set the objective cell to that number.

   For the example model, we selected Value Of and entered **0** in the text box.

CHAPTER 2 **Working with Data Analysis Tools**

4. **In the By Changing Variable Cells box, enter the addresses of the cells you want Solver to change while it looks for a solution.**

   In the example, the changing cells are B4 and C4. Figure 2-12 shows the completed Solver Parameters dialog box. (What about constraints? We talk about those in the next section.)

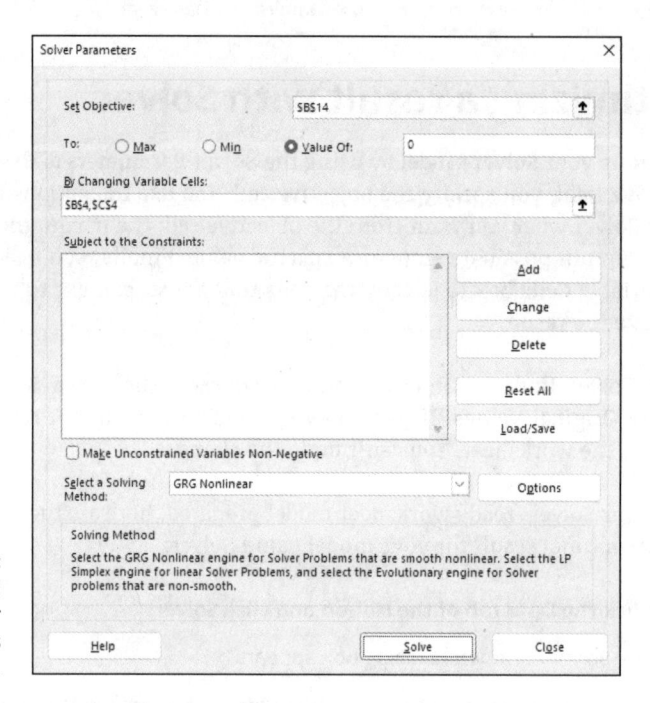

FIGURE 2-12: The completed Solver Parameters dialog box.

5. **In the Select a Solving Method drop-down list, make sure GRG Nonlinear is selected.**

   GRG Nonlinear is the default solving method and the best for general use. For advanced use of Solver, you can choose Simplex LP on a worksheet that has a linear model or Evolutionary on a worksheet that has a nonlinear and nonsmooth model. If the previous sentence sounds like gibberish to you, stick with GRG Nonlinear.

6. **Click Solve.**

   Solver gets down to business. As Solver works on the problem, the Show Trial Solution dialog boxes might show up one or more times.

7. **In any Show Trial Solution dialog box that appears, click Continue to move things along.**

   When the optimization is complete, Excel displays the Solver Results dialog box, shown in Figure 2-13.

8. **Select the Keep Solver Solution option.**

   If you don't want to accept the result, select the Restore Original Values option instead.

9. **Click OK.**

You can ask Solver to display one or more reports that give you extra information about the results. In the Solver Results dialog box, use the Reports list to select each report you want to view:

- **Answer:** Displays information about the model's objective cell, variable cells, and constraints. For the objective cell and variable cells, Solver shows the original and final values.

- **Sensitivity:** Attempts to show how sensitive a solution is to changes in the model's formulas. The layout of the Sensitivity report depends on the type of model you're using.

- **Limits:** Displays the objective cell and its value, as well as the variable cells and their addresses, names, and values.

Adding constraints to Solver

The real world puts restrictions and conditions on formulas. A factory might have a maximum capacity of 10,000 units a day, the number of employees in a company can't be a negative number, and your advertising costs might be restricted to 10 percent of total expenses.

Similarly, suppose that you're running a break-even analysis on two products, as we discuss in the preceding section. If you run the optimization without any restrictions, Solver might reach a total profit of 0 by setting one product at a slight loss and the other at a slight profit, where the loss and profit cancel each other out. In fact, if you take a close look at Figure 2-13, this is exactly what Solver did. To get a true break-even solution, you might prefer to see both product profit values as 0.

Such restrictions and conditions are examples of what Solver calls *constraints*. Adding constraints tells Solver to find a solution so that these conditions are not violated.

CHAPTER 2 **Working with Data Analysis Tools**

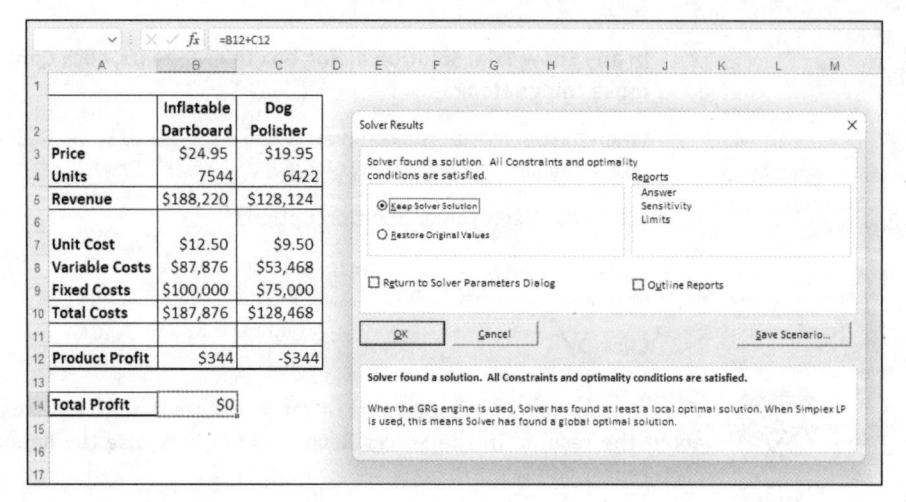

FIGURE 2-13:
The Solver Results dialog box and the solution to the break-even problem.

	A	B	C
1			
2		Inflatable Dartboard	Dog Polisher
3	Price	$24.95	$19.95
4	Units	7544	6422
5	Revenue	$188,220	$128,124
6			
7	Unit Cost	$12.50	$9.50
8	Variable Costs	$87,876	$53,468
9	Fixed Costs	$100,000	$75,000
10	Total Costs	$187,876	$128,468
11			
12	Product Profit	$344	-$344
13			
14	Total Profit	$0	

Solver Results: Solver found a solution. All Constraints and optimality conditions are satisfied.

Here's how to run Solver with constraints added to the optimization:

1. **Click the Data tab of the ribbon and click Solver.**

   The Solver Parameters dialog box opens.

2. **Use the Set Objective box, the To group, and the By Changing Variable Cells box to set up Solver as we describe in the preceding section, "Optimizing a result with Solver."**

3. **Click Add.**

   The Add Constraint dialog box opens.

4. **In the Cell Reference box, enter the address of the cell you want to constrain.**

   You can type the address or select the cell on the worksheet.

5. **In the drop-down list, select the operator you want to use.**

   Most of the time, you use a comparison operator, such as equal to (=) or greater than (>). Use the int (integer) operator when you need a constraint, such as total employees, to be an integer value instead of a real number (that is, a number with a decimal component; you can't have 10.5 employees!). Use the bin (binary) operator when you have a constraint that must be either TRUE or FALSE (or 1 or 0).

6. **If you chose a comparison operator in Step 5, in the Constraint box, enter the value by which you want to restrict the cell.**

   Figure 2-14 shows an example of a completed Add Constraint dialog box. In the example model, this constraint tells Solver to find a solution such that the product profit of the Inflatable Dartboard (cell B12) is equal to 0.

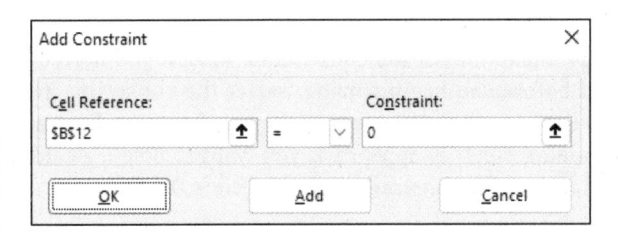

FIGURE 2-14:
The completed Add Constraint dialog box.

7. **To specify more constraints, click Add and repeat steps 4 through 6, as needed.**

   For the example, you add a constraint that asks for the Dog Polisher product profit (cell C12) to be 0.

8. **Click OK.**

   Excel returns to the Solver Parameters dialog box and displays your constraints in the Subject to the Constraints list box.

9. **Click Solve.**

10. **In any Show Trial Solution dialog box that appears, click Continue to move things along.**

    Figure 2-15 shows the example break-even solution with the constraints added. Note that not only is the Total Profit cell (B14) set to 0, but so are the two Product Profit cells (B12 and C12).

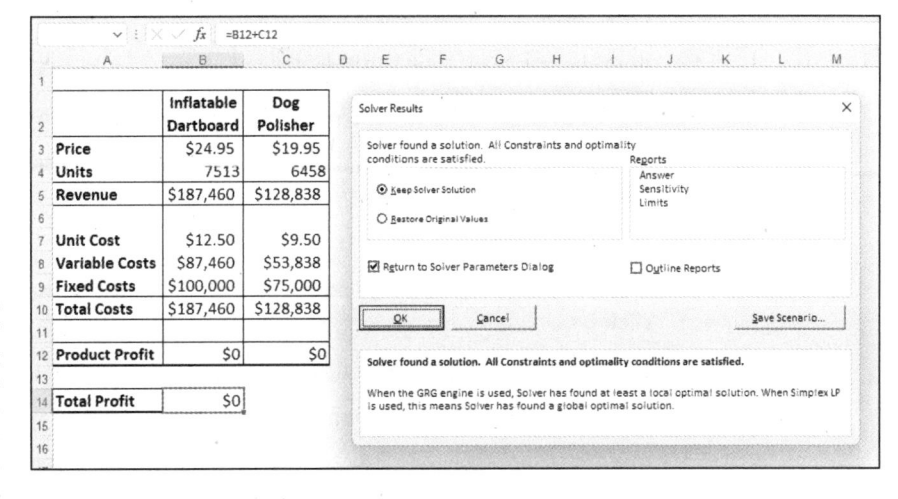

FIGURE 2-15:
The Solver Results dialog box and the final solution to the break-even problem.

11. **Select the Keep Solver Solution option.**

    If you don't want to accept the result, select the Restore Original Values option instead.

12. **Click OK.**

CHAPTER 2 Working with Data Analysis Tools   363

REMEMBER You can add a maximum of 100 constraints. Also, if you need to make a change to a constraint before you begin solving, select the constraint in the Subject to the Constraints list box, click Change, and then make your adjustments in the Change Constraint dialog box that appears. If you want to delete a constraint that you no longer need, select the constraint and then click Delete.

Saving a Solver solution as a scenario

REMEMBER Whenever you have a spreadsheet model that uses a coherent set of input values — known as *changing cells* — you have what Excel calls a *scenario*. With Solver, these changing cells are its variable cells, so a Solver solution amounts to a kind of scenario. However, Solver doesn't give you an easy way to save and rerun a particular solution. To work around this problem, you can save a solution as a scenario that you can then later recall using Excel's scenario manager feature.

Follow these steps to save a Solver solution as a scenario:

1. **Click the Data tab of the ribbon and click Solver.**

   The Solver Parameters dialog box opens.

2. **Use the Set Objective box, the To group, the By Changing Variable Cells box, and the Subject to the Constraints list to set up Solver as we describe in the "Optimizing a result with Solver" section, earlier in this chapter.**

3. **Click Solve.**

4. **Anytime the Show Trial Solution dialog box appears, click Continue.**

   When the optimization is complete, Excel displays the Solver Results dialog box.

5. **Click Save Scenario.**

   Excel displays the Save Scenario dialog box.

6. **In the Scenario Name dialog box, type a name for the scenario and then click OK.**

   Excel returns you to the Solver Results dialog box.

7. **Select the Keep Solver Solution option.**

   If you don't want to accept the result, select the Restore Original Values option instead.

8. **Click OK.**

IN THIS CHAPTER

» Summing, counting, and averaging column values

» Getting the maximum and minimum column values

» Multiplying column values

» Deriving the standard deviation and variance of column values

Chapter **3**

Analyzing Table Data with Functions

After you've imported your data and converted it to an Excel range, you may find yourself asking a most unmusical question: Now what? The "What do I do next?" conundrum is particularly relevant to tables that contain a vast sea of numbers. You're sure that those numbers must contain some important information for you to glean, but how do you get at it? You're sure that the data has something useful to say about your business, but how do you hear it?

The answer to all these questions is to put Excel to work analyzing the table. Excel handily provides a special set of functions — called *database functions* — especially for the statistical analysis of information stored in Excel tables. In this chapter, you find out about these database functions and see how to take advantage of them to get your table to spill its secrets.

Introducing the Database Functions

The database functions all use the same three arguments (see Table 3-1).

TABLE 3-1 Database Function Arguments

Argument	Description
database	The range of cells that make up the table you want to work with. You can use the table name or the table range address. If you go with the table name, be sure to reference the entire table by using the syntax `Table[#All]` (where `Table` is the name of your table).
field	A reference to the table column on which you want to perform the operation. You can use either the column header or the column number (where the leftmost column is 1, the next column is 2, and so on). If you use the column name, enclose it in quotation marks (for example, `"Unit Price"`).
criteria	The range of cells that hold the criteria you want to work with. You can use either a range name, if one is defined, or the range address.

To create a criteria range, you insert three or four blank rows above your table headers, copy your table headers, select the first cell of the first row of those blank rows, and then paste the copied headers there. For example, Figure 3-1 shows two ranges; the bigger range beginning in cell A7 is a table named Inventory, whereas the smaller range in A4:G5 is the criteria range.

	A	B	C	D	E	F	G
4	Product Name	Category	On Hold	On Hand	Unit Cost	List Price	Value
5							
6							
7	Product Name	Category	On Hold	On Hand	Unit Cost	List Price	Value
8	Chai	Beverages	25	25	$13.50	$18.00	$337.50
9	Syrup	Confections	0	50	$7.50	$10.00	$375.00
10	Cajun Seasoning	Confections	0	0	$16.50	$22.00	$0.00
11	Olive Oil	Condiments	0	15	$16.01	$21.35	$240.19
12	Boysenberry Spread	Condiments	0	0	$18.75	$25.00	$0.00
13	Dried Pears	Fruits	0	0	$22.50	$30.00	$0.00
14	Curry Sauce	Sauces/Soups	0	0	$30.00	$40.00	$0.00
15	Walnuts	Produce	0	40	$17.44	$23.25	$697.50
16	Fruit Cocktail	Produce	0	0	$29.25	$39.00	$0.00
17	Chocolate Biscuits Mix	Confections	0	0	$6.90	$9.20	$0.00
18	Marmalade	Condiments	0	0	$60.75	$81.00	$0.00
19	Scones	Grains/Cereals	0	0	$7.50	$10.00	$0.00
20	Beer	Beverages	23	23	$10.50	$14.00	$241.50
21	Crab Meat	Seafood	0	0	$13.80	$18.40	$0.00
22	Clam Chowder	Seafood	0	0	$7.24	$9.65	$0.00

FIGURE 3-1: A table and its criteria range.

Now you can enter your criteria, which consists of one or more comparison expressions that you enter into the cells below the copied header of each column you want to work with:

>> **Enter the comparison expressions on the same row.** This tells Excel to apply the database function to the *field* rows that match all the comparison expressions you enter.

366 BOOK 4 Analyzing Data

» **Enter the comparison expressions on separate rows.** This tells Excel to apply the database function to the `field` rows that match at least one of the comparison expressions you enter.

Retrieving a Value from a Table

As part of your data analysis, retrieving a single value from a table to use in a formula is often useful. For example, if you have a table that lists the inventory of all your products, you may want to check how much of a particular product is on hand now to decide whether to reorder that product. Similarly, you may want to calculate a product's gross margin given its list price and unit cost:

```
(List Price - Unit Cost) / List Price
```

Whenever you need a value from the table to use in a formula, use the DGET function. DGET retrieves a value from a table according to the criteria you specify. The function uses the following syntax:

```
DGET(database, field, criteria)
```

For example, consider the Inventory table shown in Figure 3-1. Suppose you want to know how many units are on hand of the product named Beer. To set up the criteria range, you enter **Beer** below the Product Name field, as shown in Figure 3-2. With that done, you can build your DGET function, which is in cell B1 in Figure 3-2:

```
DGET(Inventory[#All], "On Hand", A4:G5)
```

This DGET function is saying to Excel, in effect, "Take a look at the entire table named Inventory, locate the row that has Beer in the Product Name column, and then retrieve the value in the On Hand column. Thanks in advance." Sure enough, DGET returns the value 23 to cell B1 because that's the On Hand value of the Beer product.

TIP By the way, if no record in your list matches your selection criteria, DGET returns the #VALUE error message. For example, if you construct selection criteria that look for Northwind Traders Lager, DGET returns #VALUE because that product doesn't exist. Also, if multiple records in your list match your selection criteria, DGET returns the #NUM error message. For example, if you enter ***Chocolate*** in the Product Name field of the criteria range, that string matches all the products that have Chocolate in the name. Two such products exist, so DGET returns the #NUM error message.

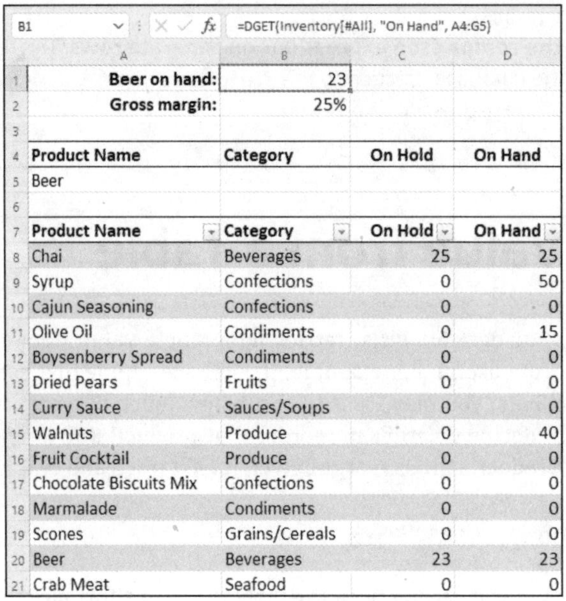

FIGURE 3-2: Use DGET to retrieve a value from a table based on your criteria.

Summing a Column's Values

In Book 1, Chapter 4, you find out how to create a table and add subtotals to it. That technique is fine if all you want to do is view the sum, but what if you want to use the sum in a formula or as part of a table summary? Yep, Excel's SUM function would work, but what if you want the sum of only those items that meet some criteria? For example, in an inventory table, what if you want to know the total value of just the items in the Beverages category?

Ah, for that you need the DSUM function, which adds values from a table based on the criteria you specify. The function uses the standard database function syntax:

```
DSUM(database, field, criteria)
```

For example, to get the total value of just the products in the Beverages category, you set up your criteria range with the string Beverages under the Category header (see Figure 3-3). With that value in place, you build your DSUM function (as shown in cell B1 in Figure 3-3):

```
DSUM(Inventory2[#All], "Value", A3:G4)
```

FIGURE 3-3:
Use DSUM to add a column's values based on your criteria.

	A	B	C	D	E	F	G
1	Total value of Beverages:	$12,041.50					
2							
3	Product Name	Category	On Hold	On Hand	Unit Cost	List Price	Value
4		Beverages					
5							
6	Product Name	Category	On Hold	On Hand	Unit Cost	List Price	Value
7	Chai	Beverages	25	25	$13.50	$18.00	$337.50
8	Syrup	Confections	0	50	$7.50	$10.00	$375.00
9	Cajun Seasoning	Confections	0	0	$16.50	$22.00	$0.00
10	Olive Oil	Condiments	0	15	$16.01	$21.35	$240.19
11	Boysenberry Spread	Condiments	0	0	$18.75	$25.00	$0.00
12	Dried Pears	Fruits	0	0	$22.50	$30.00	$0.00
13	Curry Sauce	Sauces/Soups	0	0	$30.00	$40.00	$0.00
14	Walnuts	Produce	0	40	$17.44	$23.25	$697.50
15	Fruit Cocktail	Produce	0	0	$29.25	$39.00	$0.00
16	Chocolate Biscuits Mix	Confections	0	0	$6.90	$9.20	$0.00
17	Marmalade	Condiments	0	0	$60.75	$81.00	$0.00
18	Scones	Grains/Cereals	0	0	$7.50	$10.00	$0.00
19	Beer	Beverages	23	23	$10.50	$14.00	$241.50
20	Crab Meat	Seafood	0	0	$13.80	$18.40	$0.00

You might be wondering why the table name changed from Inventory in the DGET example to Inventory2 in the DSUM example. That's because, when writing this chapter, I used a separate worksheet in the same workbook for each database function. Each table name in a workbook must be unique, so I added a number to the name on each worksheet after the first.

TIP

DSUM isn't the only way to total stuff based on criteria. Excel also offers the SUMIF and SUMIFS functions, which you can read about in Book 3, Chapter 2.

Counting a Column's Values

If you select some values in a table column, Excel's Status Bar will gladly display a Count item, which tells you how many cells you selected. Fine and dandy, but data analysis is usually a bit more sophisticated than that. For example, in an inventory table, suppose you want to know many products are low in stock (that is, have fewer than 10 in the On Hand column)?

That kind of calculation falls under the bailiwick of both the DCOUNT and DCOUNTA functions, which count records in a table that match criteria you specify:

```
DCOUNT(database, field, criteria)
DCOUNTA(database, field, criteria)
```

CHAPTER 3 **Analyzing Table Data with Functions** 369

What's the difference? DCOUNT counts the numeric values in `field`, whereas DCOUNTA counts all the nonblank items in `field`.

For example, to get the count of the products that have low stock, you set up your criteria range with the expression <10 under the On Hand header (see Figure 3-4) and then add the DCOUNT function (as shown in cell B1 in Figure 3-4):

```
DCOUNT(Inventory3[#All], "On Hand", A3:G4)
```

FIGURE 3-4: Use DCOUNT (or DCOUNTA) to tally a column's values based on your criteria.

TIP

If you just want to count records in a list, you can omit the `field` argument from the DCOUNT and DCOUNTA functions. When you don't specify a column name or number, the function counts the records in the table that match your criteria without regard to whether some field stores a value or is nonblank. For example, both of the following functions return the value 25:

```
DCOUNT(Inventory3[#All],, A3:G4)
DCOUNTA(Inventory3[#All],, A3:G4)
```

Note: To omit an argument, leave the space between the two commas empty.

TIP

Excel has a seemingly uncountable number of ways to count things. Besides DCOUNT, you can also use COUNT, COUNTA, COUNTIF, COUNTIFS, and COUNT-BLANK. Check out Excel's online help at https://support.microsoft.com/excel for more information about these functions.

370 BOOK 4 **Analyzing Data**

Averaging a Column's Values

The DAVERAGE function calculates an average for values in an Excel list. The unique and truly useful feature of DAVERAGE is that you can specify that you want only table records that meet specified criteria included in your average. DAVERAGE uses the following syntax:

```
DAVERAGE(database, field, criteria)
```

As an example of how the DAVERAGE function works, return to the Inventory table and ask a basic question: What's the average unit cost value for those products in the Beverages and Produce categories? To answer this query, you type **Beverages** under the Category header in the criteria range, and then type **Produce** below the Beverages cell, as shown in Figure 3-5. Remember that when you enter criteria using multiple rows, Excel selects those rows in the table that match at least one of the conditions. So, in the example, we're asking Excel to look for only those products that have either Beverages or Produce in the Category column. Here's the DAVERAGE function that returns the average Unit Cost for those products (see cell B1 in Figure 3-5):

```
DAVERAGE(Inventory4[#All], "Unit Cost", A3:G5)
```

FIGURE 3-5: Use DAVERAGE to average a column's values based on your criteria.

CHAPTER 3 Analyzing Table Data with Functions   371

Note that we expanded the *criteria* range to include both rows 4 and 5.

TIP
Excel offers various functions for calculating averages, including not only the AVERAGE function, but also the MEAN, MEDIAN, and MODE functions.

Determining a Column's Maximum and Minimum Values

In data analysis work, it's often useful to look for *outliers*, which are values that are either much greater or much less than the average. One way to check for such anomalous values is to find the largest and smallest values in a column. You can certainly calculate such maximums and minimums using every value in the column, but if you're interested only in the values that meet some criteria, use the DMAX and DMIN functions. These functions find the largest and smallest values, respectively, in a table column for those rows that match the criteria you specify. Both functions use the same standard-issue database function syntax:

```
DMAX(database, field, criteria)
DMIN(database, field, criteria)
```

As an example of how the DMAX and DMIN functions work, suppose you have an inventory table with a Value column that's the product of the number of units on hand and the unit cost. (For example, a product with 100 units on hand and a $5 unit cost has a total value of $500.) Here's a question for you: What are the maximum and minimum values for those items in the Produce category that are in stock?

To answer the preceding question, you type **Produce** under the Category header in the criteria range and then type **>0** below the On Hand header, as shown in Figure 3-6. Remember that when you enter multiple conditions on a single row, Excel matches only those rows in the table that match all the conditions. So, in the example, we're asking Excel to look for only those products that have Produce in the Category column and a value greater than 0 in the On Hand column.

Here are the DMAX and DMIN functions that return the maximum and minimum, respectively, for those products (see cells B1 and B2 in Figure 3-6):

```
DMAX(Inventory5[#All], "Value", A4:G5)
DMIN(Inventory5[#All], "Value", A4:G5)
```

372 BOOK 4 Analyzing Data

FIGURE 3-6:
Use DMAX and DMIN to return a column's largest and smallest values based on your criteria.

	A	B	C	D	E	F	G
1	Maximum value:	$697.50					
2	Minimum value:	$5.00					
3							
4	Product Name	Category	On Hold	On Hand	Unit Cost	List Price	Value
5		Produce		>0			
6							
7	Product Name	Category	On Hold	On Hand	Unit Cost	List Price	Value
8	Chai	Beverages	25	25	$13.50	$18.00	$337.50
9	Syrup	Confections	0	50	$7.50	$10.00	$375.00
10	Cajun Seasoning	Confections	0	0	$16.50	$22.00	$0.00
11	Olive Oil	Condiments	0	15	$16.01	$21.35	$240.19
12	Boysenberry Spread	Condiments	0	0	$18.75	$25.00	$0.00
13	Dried Pears	Produce	0	0	$22.50	$30.00	$0.00
14	Curry Sauce	Sauces/Soups	0	0	$30.00	$40.00	$0.00
15	Walnuts	Produce	0	40	$17.44	$23.25	$697.50
16	Fruit Cocktail	Produce	0	0	$29.25	$39.00	$0.00
17	Chocolate Biscuits Mix	Confections	0	0	$6.90	$9.20	$0.00
18	Marmalade	Condiments	0	0	$60.75	$81.00	$0.00
19	Scones	Grains/Cereals	0	0	$7.50	$10.00	$0.00
20	Beer	Beverages	23	23	$10.50	$14.00	$241.50
21	Crab Meat	Seafood	0	0	$13.80	$18.40	$0.00

> **TIP**
>
> Excel provides several other functions for finding the minimum or maximum value, including MAX, MAXA, MIN, and MINA.

Multiplying a Column's Values

Lots of table data contains the results of surveys or polls, meaning that the table values are percentages. One way you may want to interrogate such data is to ask, "Given two percentages, in what percentage are both true in the surveyed population?" For example, if your survey says that 50 percent of people like item A and 50 percent of people like item B, what percentage of people like both items A and B? You get the answer by multiplying the percentages, so in this case, 25 percent of the surveyed population like both A and B.

You can perform this kind of table multiplication using the DPRODUCT function, which uses the usual syntax:

```
DPRODUCT(database, field, criteria)
```

For example, Figure 3-7 shows the results of a survey that asked people whether they liked certain items. What percentage of people like any two of the items? To calculate this answer, you set up a criteria range for the Item field and then add the items in separate rows below the Item header. In Figure 3-7, for example,

CHAPTER 3 **Analyzing Table Data with Functions** 373

you can see that we entered Soggy cereal in the first row and Commuting in the second row. Here's the DPRODUCT function that calculates the answer (see cell B1 in Figure 3-7):

```
DPRODUCT(A6:B11, 2, A2:A4)
```

FIGURE 3-7: Use DPRODUCT to multiply a column's values based on your criteria.

	A	B
1	% who like the items below:	8.19%
2	Item	
3	Soggy cereal	
4	Commuting	
5		
6	Item	% of People Who Like:
7	Kumquats	6%
8	Leaf blowers	0.01%
9	Puppies	99%
10	Soggy cereal	39%
11	Commuting	21%
12	Statistics	2%
13		

Deriving a Column's Standard Deviation

One of the most important statistical measures is the *standard deviation*, which tells you how much the values in a collection vary with respect to the average. A low standard deviation means that the data values are grouped near the average, and a high standard deviation means that the values are spread out from the average.

For your table data analysis fun, the DSTDEV and DSTDEVP functions calculate the standard deviation: DSTDEV calculates the standard deviation when you're working with a sample of the population, whereas DSTDEVP calculates the standard deviation when you're working with the entire population. As with other database statistical functions, the unique and useful feature of DSTDEV and DSTDEVP is that you can specify that you want the calculation to include only those table records that meet your specified criteria.

REMEMBER

The DSTDEV and DSTDEVP functions use the same syntax:

```
=DSTDEV(database, field, criteria)
=DSTDEVP(database, field, criteria)
```

For example, in the Inventory table, suppose you want to know the standard deviation of the Value column for products in the Condiments category and where the Value column is greater than 0. To set up this calculation, you enter **Condiments** under the criteria range's Category header and the expression **>10** under the Value header (see Figure 3-8), and then you add the DSTDEV function (as shown in cell B1 in Figure 3-8):

```
DSTDEV(Inventory6[#All], "Value", A3:G4)
```

	A	B	C	D	E	F	G
1	Standard deviation	$213.77					
2							
3	Product Name	Category	On Hold	On Hand	Unit Cost	List Price	Value
4		Condiments					>0
5							
6	Product Name	Category	On Hold	On Hand	Unit Cost	List Price	Value
7	Chai	Beverages	25	25	$13.50	$18.00	$337.50
8	Syrup	Confections	0	50	$7.50	$10.00	$375.00
9	Cajun Seasoning	Confections	0	0	$16.50	$22.00	$0.00
10	Olive Oil	Condiments	0	15	$16.01	$21.35	$240.19
11	Boysenberry Spread	Condiments	0	0	$18.75	$25.00	$0.00
12	Dried Pears	Produce	0	0	$22.50	$30.00	$0.00
13	Curry Sauce	Sauces/Soups	0	0	$30.00	$40.00	$0.00
14	Walnuts	Produce	0	40	$17.44	$23.25	$697.50
15	Fruit Cocktail	Produce	0	0	$29.25	$39.00	$0.00
16	Chocolate Biscuits Mix	Confections	0	0	$6.90	$9.20	$0.00
17	Marmalade	Condiments	0	0	$60.75	$81.00	$0.00
18	Scones	Grains/Cereals	0	0	$7.50	$10.00	$0.00
19	Beer	Beverages	23	23	$10.50	$14.00	$241.50
20	Crab Meat	Seafood	0	0	$13.80	$18.40	$0.00

FIGURE 3-8: Use DSTDEV (or DSTDEVP) to derive the standard deviation of a column's values based on your criteria.

TIP If you want to calculate standard deviations without applying selection criteria, use one of Excel's non-database statistical functions, such as STDEV, STDEVA, STDEVP, or STDEVPA.

Calculating a Column's Variance

The *variance* of a set is a measure of how dispersed the data is. The variance is the square of the standard deviation, so it's rarely used because it doesn't make intuitive sense. (For example, what does it mean to say that a result is in "dollars squared" or "years squared"?)

DVAR calculates the variance when your data is a sample of a larger population, whereas DVARP calculates the variance when your data is the entire population. As with other database statistical functions, using DVAR and DVARP enables you to specify that you want only the table records that meet selection criteria included in your calculations.

REMEMBER As with standard deviation calculations, don't pick one of the two variance functions based on a whim, the weather outside, or how you're feeling. If you're calculating a variance using a sample or a subset of items from the entire dataset or population, you use the DVAR function. To calculate a variance when you're dealing with all the items in the population, use the DVARP function.

The DVAR and DVARP functions use the same syntax:

```
=DVAR(database, field, criteria)
=DVARP(database, field, criteria)
```

For example, in the Inventory table, suppose you want to know the variance of the Unit Cost column for products in the Confections category. To set up this calculation, you enter **Confections** under the criteria range's Category header and then add the DVAR function in cell B1:

```
DVAR(Inventory7[#All], "Unit Cost", A3:G4)
```

TIP If you want to calculate variances without applying selection criteria, use one of the Excel nondatabase statistical functions, such as VAR, VARA, VARP, or VARPA.

5 Summarizing, Visualizing, and Illustrating Data

Contents at a Glance

CHAPTER 1: Creating Charts 379
    Introducing Excel Charts 379
    Creating a Chart from Scratch 380
    Deconstructing and Customizing Charts 383

CHAPTER 2: Creating and Using PivotTables 391
    Understanding PivotTables 391
    Exploring PivotTable Features 394
    Building a PivotTable from an Excel Range or Table 395
    Creating a PivotTable from External Data 398
    Refreshing PivotTable Data 401
    Adding Multiple Fields to a PivotTable Area 402
    Pivoting a Field to a Different Area 403
    Grouping PivotTable Values 404
    Filtering PivotTable Values 407

CHAPTER 3: Performing PivotTable Calculations 413
    Messing Around with PivotTable Summary Calculations 414
    Working with PivotTable Subtotals 425
    Introducing Custom Calculations 427
    Inserting a Custom Calculated Field 430
    Inserting a Custom Calculated Item 431
    Editing a Custom Calculation 433
    Deleting a Custom Calculation 434

CHAPTER 4: Building PivotCharts 435
    Introducing the PivotChart 436
    Creating a PivotChart 439
    Working with PivotCharts 443

> **IN THIS CHAPTER**
>
> » **Learning the essentials of Excel charts**
>
> » **Creating charts**
>
> » **Modifying and personalizing charts**

Chapter **1**

Creating Charts

Excel offers a powerful array of tools for visualizing and summarizing data, including a wide variety of regular charts, in-cell graphics such as sparklines, PivotTables, and PivotCharts. In this chapter, you first explore the essentials of regular charts and how to create and format them. You then learn how to modify and personalize charts so they look and act the way you prefer.

To learn about PivotTables, turn to Chapter 2 of this minibook. And if you want to know about PivotCharts, turn to Chapter 4 of this minibook.

Introducing Excel Charts

Excel charts are visual representations of worksheet data, designed to spotlight trends, patterns, and comparisons. These versatile tools come in many flavors, from trusty bar and line charts to specialized options like scatter plots.

Seasoned users can craft their go-to favorites using commands on the Insert tab of the ribbon, while the Recommended Charts feature acts as a helpful sidekick, suggesting the best way to graphically showcase your data when inspiration runs dry. And don't worry about buyers' remorse — switching to a different chart type is quick and easy, especially when your boss takes one look and says, "Huh?"

This exploration of charts riffs off one of the most data-driven sports in America: baseball. Much like every pitch, swing, and hit is analyzed to uncover patterns and trends, Excel charts allow you to visualize and break down your data with the precision of a seasoned statistician.

Excel charts are referred to as *objects*, meaning they float above the worksheet. This design makes charts easy to move around, but keep in mind that they can obscure any data sitting beneath them.

Creating a Chart from Scratch

Before you can create a chart, you need some data. If you need a sample dataset before stepping into the batter's box, follow these steps to whip one up:

1. **Type Inning 1 into cell B1 of a blank worksheet.**
2. **Drag the Fill Handle for cell B1 across to cell D1.**

   The headers Inning 1, Inning 2, and Inning 3 appear in cells B1:D1.
3. **Type Fastball and Curveball into cells A2 and A3, respectively.**
4. **Type 3, 5, and 7 into cells B2, C2, and D2, respectively.**
5. **Type 6, 8, and 10 into cells B3, C3, and D3, respectively.**

   When entering data across rows, press Tab or Right Arrow instead of Enter to jump to the cell in the next column.

Using Recommended Charts

Recommended Charts was one of Excel's earliest forays into artificial intelligence (AI) over a decade ago. This feature helps you transform a dataset into a polished chart without breaking a sweat:

1. **Select any cell within your dataset (for example, cell A1).**

   By default, Excel charts use the contiguous block of cells surrounding the active cell as their data source. This means you can skip preselecting your data — unless there are blank rows or columns, which may lead to some awkward gaps in your chart.

2. **Click the Insert tab of the ribbon, and then click Recommended Charts.**

   In Excel for Windows, the Recommended Charts tab of the Insert Chart dialog box opens, as shown in Figure 1-1. In macOS, an abbreviated drop-down list offers a few suggestions.

3. **Take a quick detour to the All Charts tab (see Figure 1-2), your comprehensive playbook for exploring the 50-odd chart types Excel has to offer.**

4. **Select the Recommended Charts tab, and click any chart in the scrollable list on the left to display a larger preview of the chart along with an explanation of the story it tells and when to use it.**

   All charts in the Insert Chart dialog box are based on your data.

5. **Click OK to confirm your choice and close the Insert Chart dialog box.**

   A new chart now graces your worksheet.

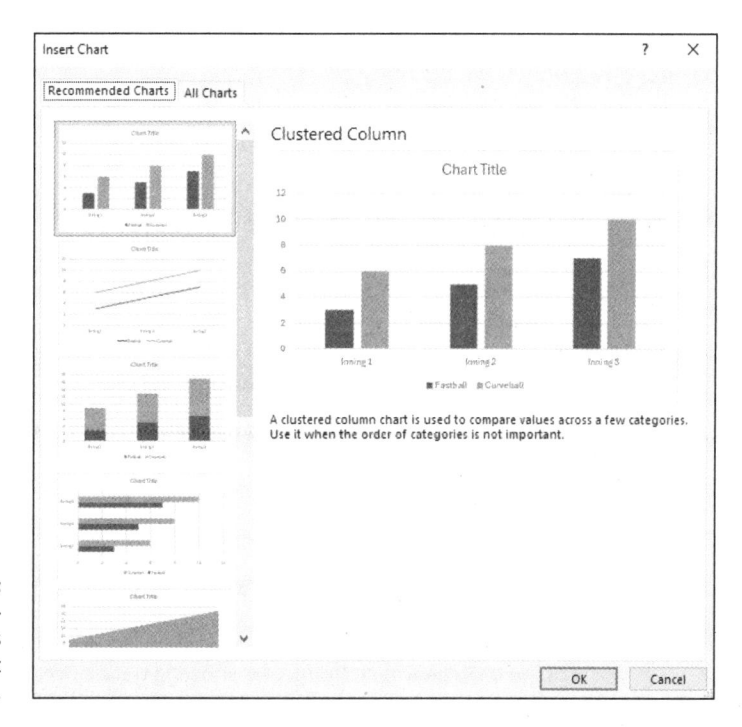

FIGURE 1-1: The Recommended Charts tab of the Insert Chart dialog box.

CHAPTER 1 Creating Charts   381

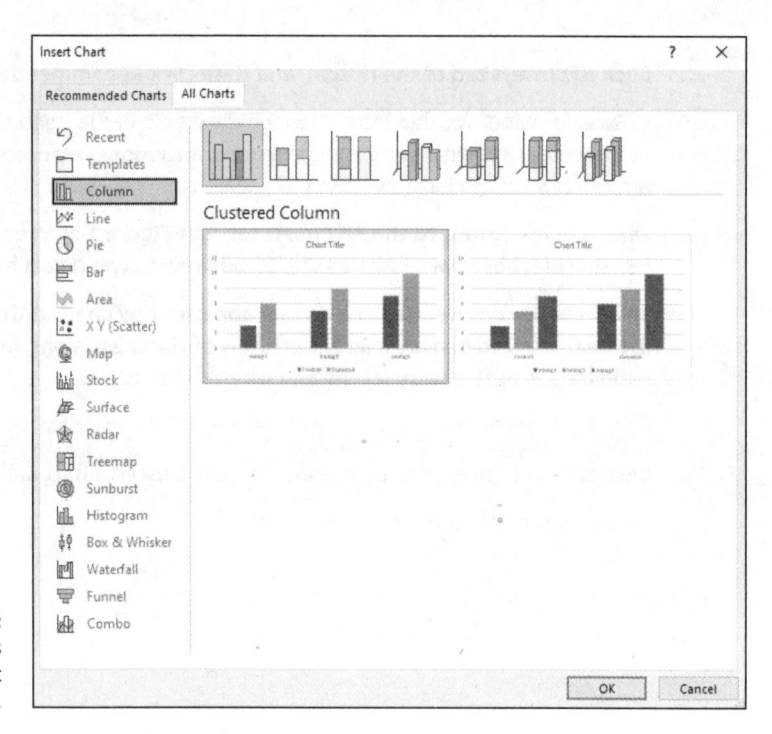

FIGURE 1-2:
The All Charts tab of the Insert Chart dialog box.

Building charts directly

Instead of using the Recommended Charts command, you can insert a chart directly from the Insert tab of the ribbon:

1. **Click any cell in your data range (for example, A1).**
2. **Select the Insert tab of the ribbon, and then choose a chart category drop-down:**

   - **Insert Column or Bar Chart:** Use these charts to visually compare values across a few categories.

     Press Alt-F1 (Windows) or Fn+Option+F1 (macOS) to create a column chart on the fly in the active worksheet.

   - **Insert Line or Area Chart:** Perfect for showing trends over time or categories, like tracking runs scored inning by inning.

   - **Insert Pie or Doughnut Chart:** These round charts give you virtual slices of your data.

   - **Insert Hierarchy Chart:** Featuring Treemap and Sunburst charts. These are great for visualizing hierarchies, such as how data is organized into categories and subcategories.

- **Insert Statistic Chart:** Baseball geeks, rejoice! Here reside the Histogram and Box and Whisker chart types, ideal for analyzing performance metrics.

- **Insert Scatter (X, Y) or Bubble Chart:** Show relationships between two sets of values, like comparing batting averages and on-base percentages.

- **Insert Waterfall, Funnel, Stock, Surface, or Radar Chart:** This category catches the specialized chart types that didn't make it onto any other teams.

- **Insert Combo Chart:** This is a chart that lets you display data using bar and line charts together.

- **Maps:** This drop-down features a single Filled Map option, perfect for comparing values across geographic regions. But beware of the More Map Charts option — it's a trap! Excel just loops you back to the same Filled Map chart.

The chart lands on your worksheet, ready for you to jazz up with labels, colors, or whatever flair your heart desires.

REMEMBER

Excel gives you a sneak peek at your chart, but if your screen resolution blocks part of the preview, don't sweat it. Just resize your window or grab a bigger monitor.

Deconstructing and Customizing Charts

Depending on the chart you pick, a standard set of default elements rolls out (see Figure 1-3):

>> **Chart area:** The outer borders of your chart's world — like the outfield fence, it defines the boundaries while leaving space for the action in the middle.

>> **Chart title:** The name of the chart, telling your audience what it contains.

>> **Horizontal (Category) Axis:** Also known as the *x*-axis, this is the baseline that groups your data.

>> **Legend:** The chart's dugout lineup card, translating colors and symbols so fans (and you) can follow the game.

>> **Plot area:** The infield of your chart — where the action happens.

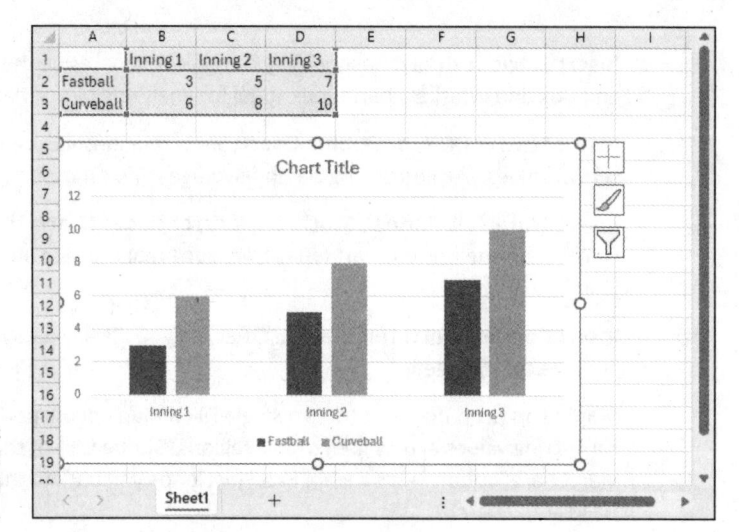

FIGURE 1-3:
A standard Clustered Columns chart.

Customizing charts

The Chart Design tab and Format tab appear in the ribbon whenever you click a chart, accompanied by the following three buttons — the Chart Elements button (top), the Chart Styles button (middle), and the Chart Filters button (bottom) — shown in Figure 1-3:

> » **Chart Elements:** Think of the Chart Elements menu as your chart's coach, ready to swap players in and out of the lineup to create a winning combination. Whether you're fine-tuning your chart for the big leagues or just tinkering in the minors, this menu has you covered.
>
> The first layer of the menu acts like a manager calling plays from the dugout — toggle features on or off with a simple click. Hover over a chart element to display options to fine-tune that feature. To reach the full set of options available, click the More Options command, which opens the Format task pane for the feature.
>
> Here's the lineup of chart elements you can adjust by clicking the Chart Elements button or by clicking the Chart Design tab on the ribbon and then clicking Add Chart Element:
>
> - **Axes:** The first and third base lines of your chart, keeping everything in play and defining the *x*-axis (horizontal, category labels) and *y*-axis (vertical, value numbers). Enabled by default.
> - **Axis Titles:** These titles provide extra context for your axes. Optional, but they can be a game changer for clarity.
> - **Chart Title:** Use the title to explain your chart's purpose.

- **Data Labels:** The play-by-play announcers of your chart, calling out exact numbers at each data point. Disabled by default, because sometimes less is more.
- **Data Table:** The raw numbers beneath the action of the chart. Ideal for when you want both the game highlights and the stat sheet.
- **Error Bars:** The ballpark range for your data points, showing the potential variation or uncertainty in the numbers.
- **Gridlines:** The chalk lines of your chart, giving structure to the field. Horizontal lines appear by default, but you can add vertical ones, too.
- **Legend:** Your chart's playbook, decoding colors and shapes into understandable categories.
- **Trend line:** The trend line reveals patterns or the overall direction in your data.
- **Up/Down Bars:** On a line chart or stock chart, these bars highlight the highs and lows between two series over time.

» **Chart Styles:** The Chart Styles button lets you adjust color palettes for a cohesive theme, with more advanced options available through the Format menu if you're ready to channel your inner graphic designer.

» **Chart Filters:** Filters enable you to highlight specific data series or points. Much like the Filter feature in worksheets (see Book 1, Chapter 4), just remember to click Apply to lock in your lineup.

REMEMBER

Hiding rows or columns in your worksheet can result in data points or series vanishing from the chart.

With this roster of tools, charts go from rookie status to championship contenders. With these options at your disposal, striking out isn't even on the table!

Maintaining chart data

Data marches on, just like the accumulation of baseball statistics, which means you may need to periodically add more data to your charts. Carry out these steps to build on the chart from the "Creating a Chart from Scratch" section, earlier in this chapter:

1. **Enter** Slider **into cell A4.**
2. **Enter** 5, 7, and 9 **into cells B4, C4, and D4, respectively.**
3. **Select cells A4:D4.**

4. **Click the Home tab of the ribbon and then click Copy. Alternatively, press Ctrl+C (Windows) or ⌘+C (macOS).**

5. **Click the chart and then press Ctrl+V (Windows) or ⌘+V (macOS).**

   A new data series appears on the chart.

6. **Select cells C1:D4 and then drag the Fill Handle from cell D4 to cell E4.**

   A fourth inning appears within the data range but doesn't appear on the chart.

7. **Click the chart and then drag the selector handle in cell D4 to cell E4.**

   The new data appears on the chart.

8. **Select cells C1:E4 and then drag the Fill Handle from cell E4 to cell F4.**

9. **Click the chart to activate the object, click the Chart Design tab of the ribbon, and then click Select Data.**

   The Select Data Source dialog box opens, as shown in Figure 1-4.

10. **Select cells A1:F4 in the worksheet to update the chart's data range.**

11. **Click OK to close the Select Data Source dialog box.**

    The Select Source Data dialog box also enables you to add or remove data series and control the display of horizontal (category) axis labels.

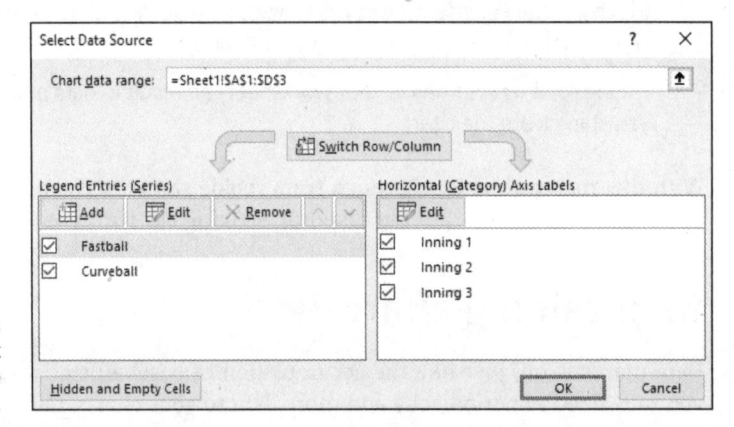

FIGURE 1-4: The Select Data Source dialog box.

If you need to create a chart that expands itself automatically when new data series are available, base the chart on a table and select the Include New Rows and Columns in Table check box on the AutoFormat As You Type tab of the AutoCorrect dialog box. See Book 1, Chapter 4 for information on tables.

Moving and resizing charts

Charts are a switch-hitter feature in Excel, typically floating above worksheet cells but ready to transition into a *chart sheet* (a blank canvas with a worksheet-style tab but no grid of cells) instead. Chart sheets make charts more accessible compared to those embedded within worksheets.

To move a chart within a worksheet, click anywhere in the chart area and drag the chart to its new location. Alternatively, use cut and paste: Right-click the chart and select Cut to cut the chart to the Clipboard, then right-click the cell where you want the upper-left corner of the chart to land and click Paste.

To move a chart to a chart sheet or another worksheet, follow these steps:

1. **Click the chart to activate it as an object.**
2. **Click the Chart Design tab of the ribbon, and then click Move Chart.**

   The Move Chart dialog box opens, as shown in Figure 1-5.

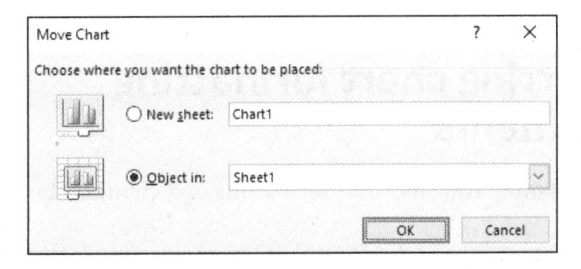

FIGURE 1-5: The Move Chart dialog box.

3. **Choose your desired location:**
   - **New Sheet:** Moves the chart to a chart sheet.
   - **Object In:** Moves the chart to any existing worksheet within the current workbook.
4. **Click OK to close the dialog box and complete the move.**

   You can't undo any prior actions, including moving a chart, after using the Move Chart dialog box.

WARNING

Charts can be resized as well, letting you create Little League–size graphs or go all out with full-size charts ready for the big leagues. To begin, click a chart to activate the object, and then use either of the following techniques:

>> **Use the resizing handles.** Drag any of the eight resizing handles to change the size of the chart.

CHAPTER 1 Creating Charts   387

TIP Hold down Alt (Windows) or Option (macOS) while resizing to snap the chart to the worksheet grid. To snap multiple charts on Windows, click the Page Layout tab of the ribbon, click Align, and then click Snap to Grid. On macOS, click the Shape Format tab of the ribbon, click Align, and then click Snap to Grid. Going forward, charts automatically align to the underlying worksheet grid as you resize.

REMEMBER Snap to Grid stays enabled as a permanent setting until you repeat the steps to turn it off.

» **Change the shape height and/or width.** Update the Shape Height and Shape Width fields in the Size group of the Format tab of the ribbon to specify the chart's dimensions in inches. For more detailed adjustments, right-click the chart; click Format Chart Area, click Size & Properties, and click Size; and then fine-tune the settings as needed.

TIP To adjust the dimensions of two or more charts simultaneously, hold down Ctrl (Windows) or ⌘ (macOS) while clicking each chart. Then use the Shape Height and Shape Width fields on the Shape Format tab of the ribbon to set uniform dimensions.

Transferring chart formatting and elements

Excel enables you to transfer most formatting and elements between charts:

1. **Click the chart area of the chart that has the desired formatting and elements.**

2. **Click the Home tab of the ribbon and click Copy; alternatively, right-click the chart area and click Copy.**

3. **Click the chart area of the chart that you want to update.**

4. **Click the Home tab of the ribbon, click the drop-down arrow below the Paste button, and then click Paste Special.**

   An abbreviated version of the Paste Special dialog box opens, as shown in Figure 1-6.

5. **Select the Formats radio button and then click OK.**

REMEMBER All formatting is applied from the first chart to the second chart, and the mix of chart elements on the second chart is adjusted to match those of the first chart. Excel adds to the second chart any extra elements the first chart has and removes from the second chart any elements the first chart doesn't have.

FIGURE 1-6:
The abbreviated version of the Paste Special dialog box.

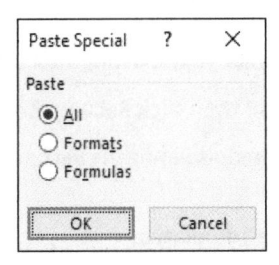

WARNING

If you choose the Paste command instead of Paste Special, or select the All radio button or the Formulas radio button, you may paste more than you bargained for — merging the data from both charts together. Fortunately, you can erase your error by choosing Undo or pressing Ctrl+Z (Windows) or ⌘+Z (macOS).

Creating and applying chart templates

In Excel for Windows (but not macOS), chart templates are the pinch hitters of the game, ready to step in at a moment's notice. These templates bundle a chart type, chart elements, and formatting into a single package that you can apply with just a few mouse clicks, helping you give your charts a consistent look and feel. Follow these steps:

1. **Click a chart, such as the sample chart expanded on in the "Maintaining chart data" section, earlier in this chapter.**

2. **On the Chart Design tab of the ribbon, click the drop-down button on the right side of the Chart Styles gallery, and then select a style from the gallery or customize the chart formatting to your liking.**

3. **Still on the Chart Design tab, click Add Chart Element, click Data Table, and then click the With Legend Keys item or the No Legend Keys item, as needed.**

   A data table appears on the chart.

   The Data Table option isn't available for certain chart types, such as Pie or Waterfall Charts.

   TIP

4. **Right-click the chart area — not a chart element, such as the plot area — and then choose Save As Template.**

   The Save Chart Template dialog box opens.

5. **Assign a name to the chart template file and then click Save.**

   Chart template files have a `.crtx` file extension and can't be opened directly in Excel. You can, however, update a template by saving over an existing copy.

   TECHNICAL STUFF

CHAPTER 1 Creating Charts   389

6. **Click any cell within the source data for your existing chart.**
7. **Click the Insert tab of the ribbon, and then click Recommended Charts.**

   The Change Chart Type dialog box opens, displaying the Recommended Charts tab.

8. **Select the All Charts tab, and choose Templates.**
9. **Choose a chart template and then click OK (or get a running start by double-clicking the template).**

   A new chart appears on the worksheet that includes all formatting and chart elements bundled into the template.

   > **TIP:** To apply a template to an existing chart, click the chart, click the Chart Design tab on the ribbon, and then click Change Chart Type. The Change Chart Type dialog box opens to the All Charts tab, from which you can make a selection from the Templates section.

Managing templates

You can mark a single chart template as the default template in Excel for Windows, and then start new charts by way of a keyboard shortcut:

1. **Click the Insert tab of the ribbon, and then click Recommended Charts.**
2. **Select the All Charts tab, and choose Templates.**
3. **Right-click your preferred template and click Set as Default Chart.**
4. **Click OK.**

   You can now insert that type of chart quickly: Select any cell within the range of data that you want to chart, and then press Alt+F1. A chart using the default template settings appears in your worksheet.

   > **TIP:** A Manage Templates button appears at the bottom of both the Insert Chart and Change Chart Type dialog boxes when you click Templates on the sidebar. This button opens a Windows Explorer window, allowing you to back up, copy, or remove templates as needed.

> **IN THIS CHAPTER**
>
> » Getting to know PivotTables
>
> » Using an Excel table to build a PivotTable
>
> » Using external data to build a PivotTable
>
> » Putting the "pivot" in PivotTable
>
> » Grouping and filtering PivotTables

Chapter 2
Creating and Using PivotTables

Excel tables and external databases can contain thousands of records. Let's face it: Figuring out how to glean useful insights from that much data will either keep you awake at night or cause nightmares if you do sleep. Want to get some quality shut-eye? No need for sleeping pills when Excel offers a powerful and versatile data analysis tool called a *PivotTable*, which enables you to take those thousands of records and summarize them in a concise tabular format. You can then manipulate the layout of — or *pivot* — the PivotTable to see different views of your data.

This chapter shows you everything you need to know to get started with what is arguably Excel's most useful data analysis tool. You learn how to create Pivot-Tables, refresh them, pivot them, group them, filter them, and much more.

Understanding PivotTables

In a general sense, PivotTables condense a large amount of information into a report that tells you something useful or interesting. For example, check out the table shown in Figure 2-1. This table contains more than 100 records, each of which is an order from a sales promotion. That's not a ton of data in the larger scheme of things, but trying to make sense of even this relatively small dataset just by eyeballing the table's contents is futile. For example, how many earbuds were sold via social media advertising? Who knows?

SUMMER SALES PROMOTION - ORDERS

Date	Product	Quantity	Net $	Promotion	Advertisement
6/1/2022	Smartphone case	11	$119.70	1 Free with 10	Social media
6/1/2022	HDMI cable	6	$77.82	Extra Discount	Blog network
6/1/2022	USB car charger	15	$100.95	Extra Discount	Search
6/1/2022	HDMI cable	11	$149.71	1 Free with 10	Blog network
6/2/2022	USB car charger	22	$155.40	1 Free with 10	Blog network
6/2/2022	USB car charger	3	$20.19	Extra Discount	Search
6/2/2022	Earbuds	5	$33.65	Extra Discount	Social media
6/2/2022	Smartphone case	22	$239.36	1 Free with 10	Search
6/2/2022	HDMI cable	10	$129.70	Extra Discount	Blog network
6/5/2022	USB car charger	22	$155.40	1 Free with 10	Blog network
6/5/2022	Smartphone case	8	$82.96	Extra Discount	Social media
6/5/2022	Smartphone case	22	$239.40	1 Free with 10	Social media
6/5/2022	Earbuds	55	$388.50	1 Free with 10	Blog network
6/5/2022	USB car charger	25	$168.25	Extra Discount	Search
6/5/2022	HDMI cable	22	$299.42	1 Free with 10	Blog network
6/5/2022	Smartphone case	11	$131.67	1 Free with 10	Search
6/6/2022	USB car charger	33	$256.41	1 Free with 10	Blog network
6/6/2022	Smartphone case	11	$119.70	1 Free with 10	Blog network
6/6/2022	HDMI cable	22	$329.34	1 Free with 10	Blog network
6/6/2022	Earbuds	20	$134.60	Extra Discount	Blog network
6/7/2022	Smartphone case	102	$1,057.74	Extra Discount	Search
6/7/2022	USB car charger	55	$427.35	1 Free with 10	Blog network
6/7/2022	Earbuds	25	$168.25	Extra Discount	Search

FIGURE 2-1: Some great data, but how do you make sense of it?

Ah, but now look at Figure 2-2, which shows a PivotTable built from the order data. This report tabulates the number of units sold for each product based on each type of promotion. From here, you can quickly see that 322 earbuds were sold via social media advertising. *That* is what PivotTables do.

Promotion (All)

Sum of Quantity	Column Labels			
Row Labels	**Blog network**	**Search**	**Social media**	**Grand Total**
Earbuds	555	562	322	1439
HDMI cable	719	587	402	1708
Smartphone case	546	460	338	1344
USB car charger	1596	1012	752	3360
Grand Total	**3416**	**2621**	**1814**	**7851**

FIGURE 2-2: The PivotTable creates order out of data chaos.

PivotTables help you analyze large amounts of data by performing three operations: grouping the data into categories, summarizing the data using calculations, and filtering the data to show just the records you want to work with:

» **Grouping:** A PivotTable is a powerful data analysis tool in part because it automatically groups large amounts of data into smaller, more manageable chunks. For example, suppose you have a data source with a Region field in which each item contains one of four values: East, West, North, and South. The original data may contain thousands of records, but if you build your PivotTable using the Region field, the resulting table has just four rows — one each for the four unique Region values in your data.

You can also create your own grouping after you build your PivotTable. For example, if your data has a Country field, you can build the PivotTable to group all records that have the same Country value. Then you could further group the unique Country values into continents: North America, South America, Europe, and so on.

» **Summarizing:** In conjunction with grouping data according to the unique values in one or more fields, Excel also displays summary calculations for each group. The default calculation is Sum, which means that for each group, Excel totals all the values in some specified field. For example, if your data has a Region field and a Sales field, a PivotTable can group the unique Region values and display the total of the Sales values for each one. Excel has other summary calculations, including Count, Average, Maximum, Minimum, and Standard Deviation.

Even more powerful, a PivotTable can display summaries for one grouping broken down by another. For example, suppose your sales data also has a Product field. You can set up a PivotTable to show the total sales for each product, broken down by region.

» **Filtering:** A PivotTable also enables you to view just a subset of the data. For example, by default, the PivotTable's groupings show all unique values in the field. However, you can manipulate each grouping to hide the unique values that you don't want to view. Each PivotTable also comes with a report filter that enables you to apply a filter to the entire PivotTable. For example, suppose your sales data also includes a Customer field. By placing this field in the PivotTable's report filter, you can filter the PivotTable report to show just the results for a single Customer.

CHAPTER 2 Creating and Using PivotTables   **393**

Exploring PivotTable Features

You can get up to speed with PivotTables quickly after you learn a few key concepts. You need to understand the features that make up a typical PivotTable, particularly the four areas — row, column, data, and filter — to which you add fields from your data. Figure 2-3 points out the following PivotTable features:

- **Row area:** Displays vertically the unique values from a field in your data.
- **Column area:** Displays horizontally the unique values from a field in your data.
- **Value area:** Displays the results of the calculation that Excel applied to a numeric field in your data.
- **Row field header:** Identifies the field contained in the row area. You also use the row field header to filter the field values that appear in the row area.
- **Column field header:** Identifies the field contained in the column area. You also use the column field header to filter the field values that appear in the column area.
- **Value field header:** Specifies both the calculation (such as Sum) and the field (such as Quantity) used in the value area.
- **Filter area:** Displays a drop-down list that contains the unique values from a field. When you select a value (or multiple values) from the list, Excel filters the PivotTable results to include only the records that match the selected value(s).

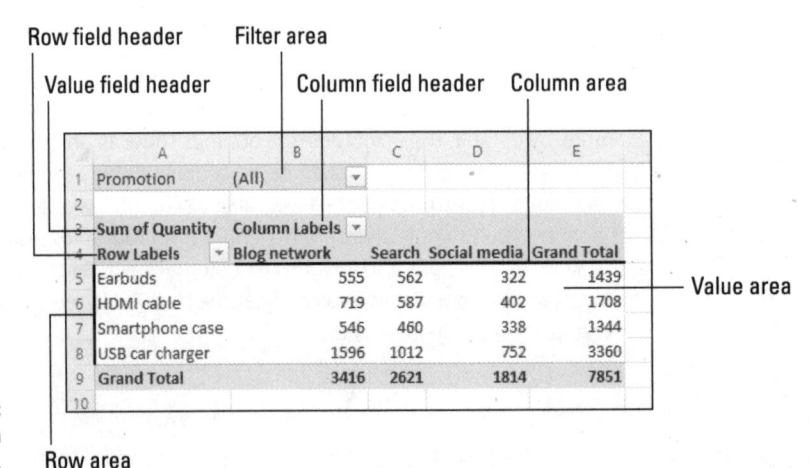

	A	B	C	D	E
1	Promotion	(All)			
2					
3	Sum of Quantity	Column Labels			
4	Row Labels	Blog network	Search	Social media	Grand Total
5	Earbuds		555	562	322	1439
6	HDMI cable		719	587	402	1708
7	Smartphone case		546	460	338	1344
8	USB car charger		1596	1012	752	3360
9	Grand Total		3416	2621	1814	7851

FIGURE 2-3: The features of a typical PivotTable.

394 BOOK 5 **Summarizing, Visualizing, and Illustrating Data**

Building a PivotTable from an Excel Range or Table

If the data you want to analyze exists as an Excel range or table, you can use the Summarize with PivotTable command to quickly build a PivotTable report based on your data. You just need to specify the location of your source data and then choose the location of the resulting PivotTable.

Here are the steps to follow:

1. **Select a cell in the range or table that you want to use as the source data.**

   If you're using a range, make sure each column of data has a heading.

2. **On the Table Design tab of the ribbon, click Summarize with PivotTable.**

   If your data resides in a regular Excel range instead of a table, you can still do the PivotTable thing. Select any cell in the range, click the Insert tab on the ribbon, and then click PivotTable.

   > **TIP**
   > While we have your attention, we should also point out the Insert tab's Recommended PivotTables command. This command displays a dialog box that shows several predefined PivotTable layouts. These may not mean anything to you now if you're new to PivotTables, but keep the Recommended PivotTables command in mind down the road; it may save you a bit of time.

   The PivotTable from Table or Range dialog box opens.

3. **Select the New Worksheet radio button.**

   Alternatively, if you want to add the PivotTable to an existing location, select the Existing Worksheet radio button and then use the Location range box to select the worksheet and cell where you want the PivotTable to appear.

4. **Click OK.**

   Excel creates a blank PivotTable and displays the PivotTable Fields task pane, as shown in Figure 2-4. This pane contains two main areas:

   - A list of the column headers from your table, each of which has a check box to its left. These are your PivotTable fields.

   - Four boxes representing the four areas of the PivotTable: Filters, Columns, Rows, and Values. To complete the PivotTable, your job is to add one or more fields to some (or even all) of these areas.

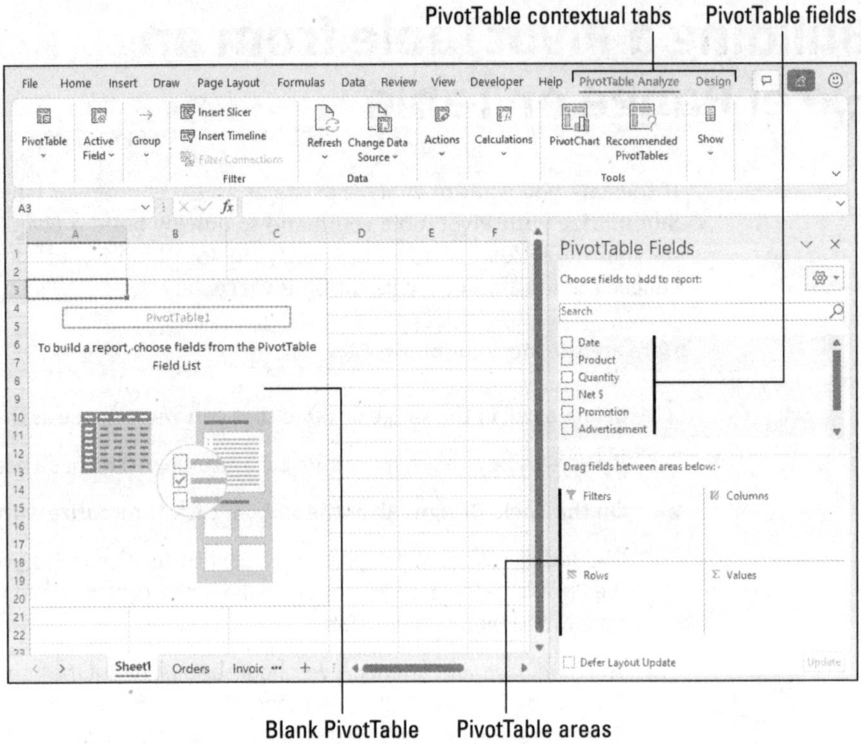

FIGURE 2-4: You start with a blank PivotTable and the PivotTable Fields task pane.

5. **Drag a field that contains text values and drop it in the Rows area.**

   For example, using the fields shown in Figure 2-4, you could drop the Product field into the Rows area.

   Excel adds a button for the field to the Rows area and displays the field's unique values to the PivotTable's row area.

6. **Drag a field that contains numeric values and drop it in the Values area.**

   For example, using the fields shown in Figure 2-4, you could drop the Quantity field into the Values area.

   Excel adds a button for the field to the Values area and sums the numeric values based on the row values.

7. **If desired, drag fields and drop them in the Columns area and the Filters area.**

   For example, using the fields shown in Figure 2-4, you could drop the Advertisement field into the Columns area and the Promotion field into the Filters area.

   Excel adds a button for the field to the Columns area and displays the field's unique values to the PivotTable's column area.

396 BOOK 5 **Summarizing, Visualizing, and Illustrating Data**

Each time you drop a field in an area, Excel adds a button for the field to that area and updates the PivotTable to include the new data.

TIP Excel offers a few shortcut techniques for building PivotTables:

» Select the check box for a text or date field to add it to the Rows area automatically.

» Select the check box for a numeric field to add it to the Values area automatically.

» Right-click a field and then select the area that you want to use.

Figure 2-5 shows a completed PivotTable, with fields in all four areas. Note, too, that when you select a cell in the PivotTable, Excel displays two contextual tabs on the ribbon — the PivotTable Analyze tab and the Design tab — that offer lots of goodies for manipulating and formatting your PivotTable.

	A	B	C	D	E
1	Promotion	(All)			
2					
3	Sum of Quantity	Column Labels			
4	Row Labels	Blog network	Search	Social media	Grand Total
5	Earbuds		555	562	322	1439
6	HDMI cable		719	587	402	1708
7	Smartphone case		546	460	338	1344
8	USB car charger		1596	1012	752	3360
9	Grand Total		3416	2621	1814	7851

PivotTable Fields
Choose fields to add to report:
☑ Product
☑ Quantity
☐ Net $
☑ Promotion
☑ Advertisement

Drag fields between areas below:

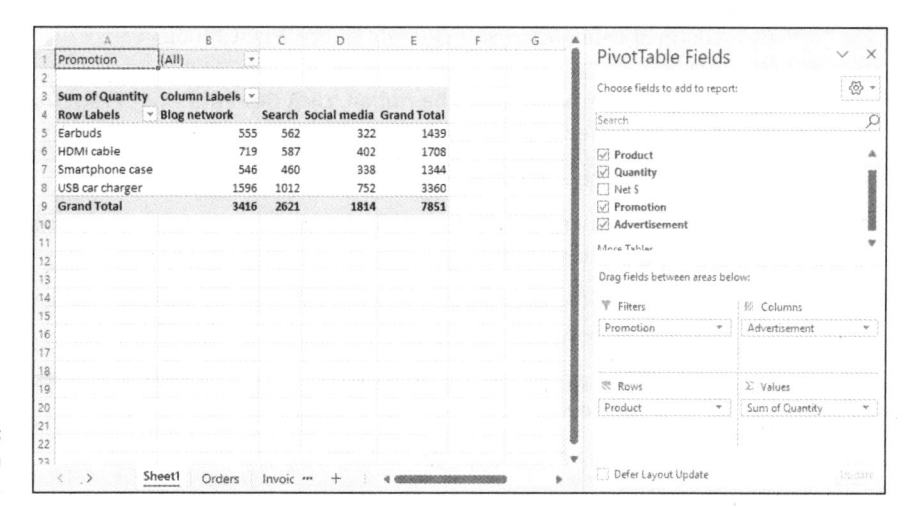

Filters: Promotion
Columns: Advertisement
Rows: Product
Values: Sum of Quantity

FIGURE 2-5: The features of a typical PivotTable.

To remove a field from a PivotTable area, you have three ways to proceed:

» Drag the field from the area and out of the PivotTable Fields task pane.

» Deselect the field's check box in the PivotTable Fields task pane.

» In the PivotTable Fields task pane area where the field resides, click the field button to drop down the field menu, and then click Remove Field. For example, to remove the Advertisement field shown in Figure 2-5, click the Advertisement field button in the Columns area and then click Remove Field.

Creating a PivotTable from External Data

The data you're analyzing may exist not in an Excel range or table but rather outside Excel, in a relational database management system (RDBMS) such as Microsoft Access or SQL Server. With these programs, you can set up a table, a query, or another object that defines the data you want to work with. Then, instead of building a PivotTable from data in an Excel worksheet, you create the PivotTable using the external data source. This feature enables you to build reports from extremely large datasets and from RDBMSs.

As we describe in the next two sections, you can specify the external data source for your new PivotTable by using Microsoft Query or by creating a new data connection.

Building a PivotTable from Microsoft Query

Here are the steps to follow to build a PivotTable based on an external data source defined using Microsoft Query's Query Wizard tool:

1. **On the Data tab of the ribbon, click Get Data, click From Other Sources, and then click From Microsoft Query.**

   The Choose Data Source dialog box opens.

2. **Use Query Wizard to define the external data you want to summarize in your PivotTable.**

   Follow the prompts in Query Wizard to specify the data source you want to use and the data you want to return from it.

3. **When you get to the Query Wizard – Finish dialog box, select the Return Data to Microsoft Excel radio button and click Finish.**

   The Import Data dialog box opens, as shown in Figure 2-6.

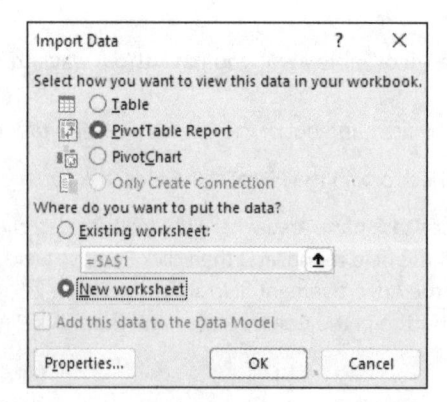

FIGURE 2-6: Import the external data to a PivotTable Report.

4. **Select the PivotTable Report radio button, select the New Worksheet radio button, and click OK.**

   Excel creates a blank PivotTable and displays the PivotTable Fields task pane.

5. **Drag a text field and drop it in the Rows area.**

   Excel adds the field's unique values to the PivotTable's row area.

6. **Drag a numeric field and drop it in the Values area.**

   Excel sums the numeric values based on the row values.

7. **If desired, drag fields and drop them in the Columns area and the Filters area.**

   Each time you drop a field in an area, Excel updates the PivotTable to include the new data.

REMEMBER When you create a PivotTable from external data, you don't need the external data to be imported to Excel. The external data resides only in the new PivotTable — you don't see the actual data in your workbook.

The most common drawback to using external data is that you often have no control over the data source. For example, if you try to refresh the PivotTable, as we describe in the next section, Excel may display an error message. If you suspect that the problem is a change to the database login data, click OK to display the Login dialog box and then find out the new login name and password from the database administrator. Alternatively, the problem may be that the database file has been moved or renamed. Click OK in the error message and then click Database in the Login dialog box. Next, in the Select Database dialog box, find and select the database file.

Building a PivotTable from a new data connection

You can also summarize external data in a PivotTable by creating a connection to the source data. Here's how it works:

1. **On the Insert tab of the ribbon, click PivotTable and then click From External Data Source.**

   Be sure to click the PivotTable button's drop-down arrow to display its menu.

   The PivotTable from an External Source dialog box opens.

2. **Click Choose Connection.**

   The Existing Connections dialog box opens.

CHAPTER 2 **Creating and Using PivotTables** 399

3. **Click Browse for More.**

   The Select Data Source dialog box opens.

4. **Click New Source.**

   The Data Connection Wizard opens.

5. **Click the type of data source you want to connect to and then click Next.**

   The wizard steps you follow from here depend on the data source type you selected. For example, to connect to an Access database, you follow these steps:

   a. Select ODBC DSN and then click Next to open the Connect to ODBC Data Source dialog box.

   b. Select MS Access Database and then click Next to open the Select Database dialog box.

   c. Select the Access database file you want to connect to and then click OK to open the Select Database and Table dialog box.

   d. Select the table you want to use and then click Next to open the Save Data Connection File and Finish dialog box.

6. **(Optional) Edit the file name, description, friendly name, and search keywords.**

7. **Click Finish.**

   Excel saves your new data connection and returns you to the PivotTable from an External Source dialog box.

   In the future, when you click the Insert tab of the ribbon, click PivotTable, click From External Data Source, and then click Choose Connection, your saved connections appear in the Existing Connections dialog box so you can reuse them without having to run through the Data Connection Wizard.

8. **Select the New Worksheet radio button and then click OK.**

   Excel creates a blank PivotTable and displays the PivotTable Fields task pane.

9. **Drag a text field and drop it in the Rows area.**

   Excel adds the field's unique values to the PivotTable's row area.

10. **Drag a numeric field and drop it in the Values area.**

    Excel sums the numeric values based on the row values.

11. **If desired, drag fields and drop them in the Columns area and the Filters area.**

    Each time you drop a field in an area, Excel updates the PivotTable to include the new data.

Refreshing PivotTable Data

Whether your PivotTable is based on financial results, survey responses, or a database of collectibles such as rare books or cubic zirconia jewelry, the underlying data is probably not static. That is, the data changes over time as new results come in, new surveys are undertaken, and new items are added to the collection. You can ensure that the data analysis represented by the PivotTable remains up-to-date by refreshing the PivotTable.

Excel offers two methods for refreshing a PivotTable: manual and automatic. A manual refresh is one that you perform, usually when you know that the source data has changed, or if you just want to be sure that the latest data is reflected in your PivotTable report. An automatic refresh is one that Excel handles for you.

Refreshing PivotTable data manually

To refresh your PivotTable data manually, you have two choices:

> **Update a single PivotTable.** Select any cell in the PivotTable, click the PivotTable Analyze tab of the ribbon and then click Refresh. You can also press Alt+F5.

> **Update every PivotTable in the workbook.** Select a cell in any PivotTable, click the PivotTable Analyze tab of the ribbon, click Refresh, and then click Refresh All. You can also update all PivotTables by pressing Ctrl+Alt+F5.

Excel dutifully updates the PivotTable data.

Refreshing PivotTable data automatically

Here are the steps to follow to convince Excel to refresh your PivotTable data automatically:

1. **Select any cell in the PivotTable.**
2. **On the PivotTable Analyze tab of the ribbon, click PivotTable and then click Options.**

   TIP You can also right-click any cell in the PivotTable and then choose PivotTable Options.

   The PivotTable Options dialog box opens.
3. **Click the Data tab.**

CHAPTER 2 Creating and Using PivotTables   401

4. **Select the Refresh Data When Opening the File check box, as shown in Figure 2-7, and then click OK.**

   From now on, Excel will automatically refresh the PivotTable data each time you open the workbook.

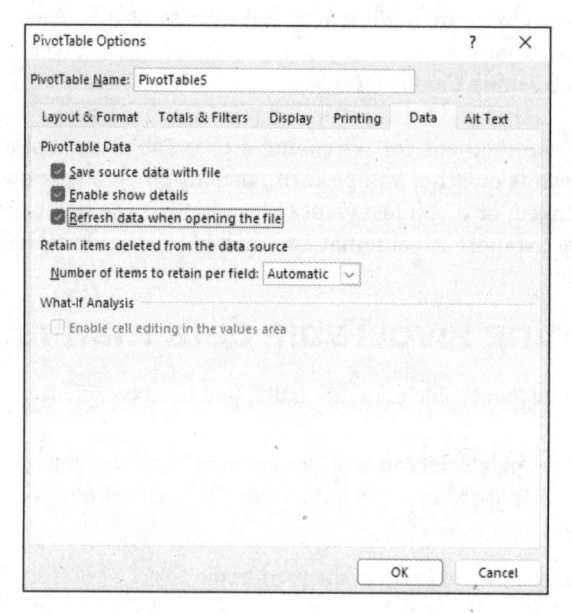

FIGURE 2-7: Select Refresh Data When Opening the File to tell Excel to refresh a PivotTable automatically whenever you open its workbook.

TIP If your PivotTable is based on external data, you can set up a schedule that automatically refreshes the PivotTable at a specified interval. Select any cell in the PivotTable, click the PivotTable Analyze tab of the ribbon, click Refresh, and then click Connection Properties. In the Connection Properties dialog box, on the Usage tab, select the Refresh Every check box, use the spin buttons to specify the refresh interval, in minutes, and then click OK.

WARNING Note, however, that when you set up an automatic refresh, it may be best not to have the source data updated too frequently. Depending on where the data resides and how much data you're working with, the refresh could take some time, which may slow down the rest of your work.

Adding Multiple Fields to a PivotTable Area

You can add two or more fields to any of the PivotTable areas. Having multiple fields is a powerful feature that enables you to perform further analysis of your data by viewing the data differently. For example, suppose you're analyzing the results of a sales campaign that ran different promotions in several types of advertisements (such as the partial table shown previously in Figure 2-1). A basic PivotTable may show you the sales for each product (the row field) according to the advertisement used (the column field). You may also be interested in seeing, for each product, the breakdown in sales for each promotion. You can do that by adding the Promotion field to the row area.

REMEMBER

Excel doesn't restrict you to just two fields in any area. Depending on your data analysis requirements, you're free to add three, four, or more fields to any Pivot-Table area.

Select a cell in the PivotTable and then use any of the following techniques to add another field to a PivotTable area:

>> **Add a field to the Rows area.** In the PivotTable Fields task pane, select the check box of the text or date field that you want to add.

>> **Add a field to the Value area.** In the PivotTable Fields task pane, select the check box of the numeric field that you want to add.

>> **Add a field to any area.** In the PivotTable Fields task pane, drag the field and drop it in the area where you want the field to appear.

TIP

After you add a second field to the row or column area, you can change the field positions to change the PivotTable view. In the PivotTable Fields task pane, drag the button of the field you want to move and then drop the field above or below an existing field button.

When you add a second field to the value area, Excel moves the labels, such as Sum of Quantity and Sum of Net $, into the column area for easier reference. This is also reflected in the addition of a Values button in the Columns area of the PivotTable Fields task pane. This enables you to pivot the values in the report, as I describe in the next section.

Pivoting a Field to a Different Area

A PivotTable is a powerful data analysis tool because it can take hundreds or even thousands of records and summarize them into a compact, comprehensible report. However, unlike most of the other data analysis features in Excel, a PivotTable is not a static collection of worksheet cells. Instead, you can move a PivotTable's fields from one area of the PivotTable to another. Moving fields to various areas enables you to view your data from different perspectives, which can greatly enhance the analysis of the data. Moving a field within a PivotTable is called *pivoting* the data.

The most common way to pivot the data is to move fields between the row and column areas. However, you can also pivot data by moving a row or column field to the filter area. Either way, you perform the pivot by dragging the field from its current box in the PivotTable Fields task pane and then dropping it in the area where you want it moved.

You can move any row, column, or filter field to the PivotTable's value area. Moving a field to this location may seem strange because row, column, and page fields are almost always text values, and the default value area calculation is Sum. How can you sum text values? You can't, of course. Instead, the default Excel PivotTable summary calculation for text values is Count. So, for example, if you drag the Promotion field and drop it in the value area, Excel creates a second value field named Count of Promotion.

Grouping PivotTable Values

To make a PivotTable with a large number of row or column items easier to work with, you can group the items. For example, you can group months into quarters, thus reducing the number of items from 12 to 4. Similarly, a report that lists dozens of countries can group those countries by continent, thus reducing the number of items to four or five, depending on where the countries are located. Finally, if you use a numeric field in the row or column area, you may have hundreds of items, one for each numeric value. You can improve the report by creating just a few numeric ranges.

Grouping numeric values

Grouping numeric values is useful when you use a numeric field in a row or column field. Excel enables you to specify numeric ranges into which the field items are grouped. For example, suppose you have a PivotTable of invoice data that shows the extended price (the row field) and the salesperson (the column field). It would be useful to group the extended prices into ranges and then count the number of invoices each salesperson processed in each range.

Follow these steps to group numeric values in a PivotTable field:

1. **Select any item in the numeric field you want to group.**
2. **On the PivotTable Analyze tab of the ribbon, click Group Field.**

    The Grouping dialog box opens, as shown in Figure 2-8.

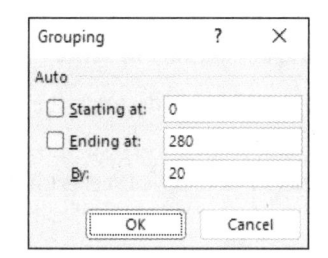

FIGURE 2-8: The Grouping dialog box.

3. **In the Starting At text box, enter the starting numeric value.**

   When you enter a new starting numeric value, Excel deselects the Starting At check box.

   Alternatively, select the Starting At check box to have Excel extract the minimum value of the numeric items and place that value in the text box.

4. **In the Ending At text box, enter the ending numeric value.**

   When you enter a new ending numeric value, Excel deselects the Ending At check box.

   Alternatively, select the Ending At check box to have Excel extract the maximum value of the numeric items and place that value in the text box.

5. **In the By text box, enter the size you want to use for each grouping.**

6. **Click OK.**

   Excel groups the numeric values.

Grouping date and time values

If your PivotTable includes a field with date or time data, you can use Excel's grouping feature to consolidate that data into more manageable or useful groups. Follow these steps:

1. **Select any item in the date or time field you want to group.**

2. **On the PivotTable Analyze tab of the ribbon, click Group Field.**

   The Grouping dialog box opens.

3. **In the Starting At text box, enter the starting date or time.**

   When you enter a new starting date or time, Excel deselects the Starting At check box.

   Alternatively, select the Starting At check box to have Excel extract the earliest date or time and place that value in the text box.

CHAPTER 2 **Creating and Using PivotTables**   405

4. **In the Ending At text box, enter the ending date or time.**

   When you enter a new ending date or time, Excel deselects the Ending At check box.

   Alternatively, select the Ending At check box to have Excel extract the latest date or time and place that value in the text box.

5. **In the By list, select the grouping you want, such as Months for dates or Hours for times.**

   If you select Days, you can also use the Number of Days spin buttons to set the days you want to use for the grouping interval.

   To use multiple groupings, select each type of grouping you want to use.

6. **Click OK.**

   Excel groups the date or time values.

Grouping text values

One common problem that arises when you work with PivotTables is that you often need to consolidate items, but you have no corresponding field in the data. For example, the data may have a Country field, but what if you need to consolidate the PivotTable results by continent? Your source data isn't likely to include a Continent field. Similarly, your source data may include employee names, but you may need to consolidate the employees according to the people they report to. What happens if your source data doesn't include, say, a Supervisor field?

The solution in both cases is to use the grouping feature to create custom groups. For the country data, you can create custom groups named North America, South America, Europe, and so on. For the employees, you can create a custom group for each supervisor.

Here are the steps to follow to create such a custom grouping for text values:

1. **Select the items that you want to include in the group.**

2. **On the PivotTable Analyze tab of the ribbon, click Group Selection.**

   Excel creates a new group named Group*n* (where *n* means that this is the *n*th group you've created; the first group is Group1, the second is Group2, and so on) and restructures the PivotTable.

3. **Select the cell that contains the group label, type a new name for the group, and then press Enter.**

   Excel renames the group.

4. **Repeat Steps 1 to 3 for the other items in the field until you've created all your groups.**

Filtering PivotTable Values

By default, each PivotTable report displays a summary of all the records in your source data, which is usually what you want to see. However, you may have situations in which you need to focus more closely on some aspect of the data. You can focus on a specific item (or on just a few items) from one of the source data fields by taking advantage of the PivotTable's report filter field.

Applying a report filter

Suppose you're dealing with a PivotTable that summarizes data from thousands of customer invoices over some period of time. A basic PivotTable may tell you the total amount sold for each product that you carry. That's interesting, but what if you want to see the total amount sold for each product in a specific country? If the Product field is in the PivotTable's row area, you can add the Country field to the column area. However, you may have dozens of countries, so adding the field to the column area isn't an efficient solution. Instead, you can add the Country field to the report filter and tell Excel to display the total sold for each product for the specific country that you're interested in.

Follow these steps to apply a PivotTable report filter:

1. **Select the filter field's drop-down arrow.**

    A list of the report filter field values appears.

2. **Select the report filter you want to view.**

    In Figure 2-9, we used the report filter list to select Canada.

    If you want to display data for two or more report filters, select the Select Multiple Items check box and then repeat Step 2 to select the other report filters.

    To return later to showing all the items in the report field, select (All) in the filter field's drop-down list.

3. **Click OK.**

    Excel filters the PivotTable to show only the data for the report filter you selected.

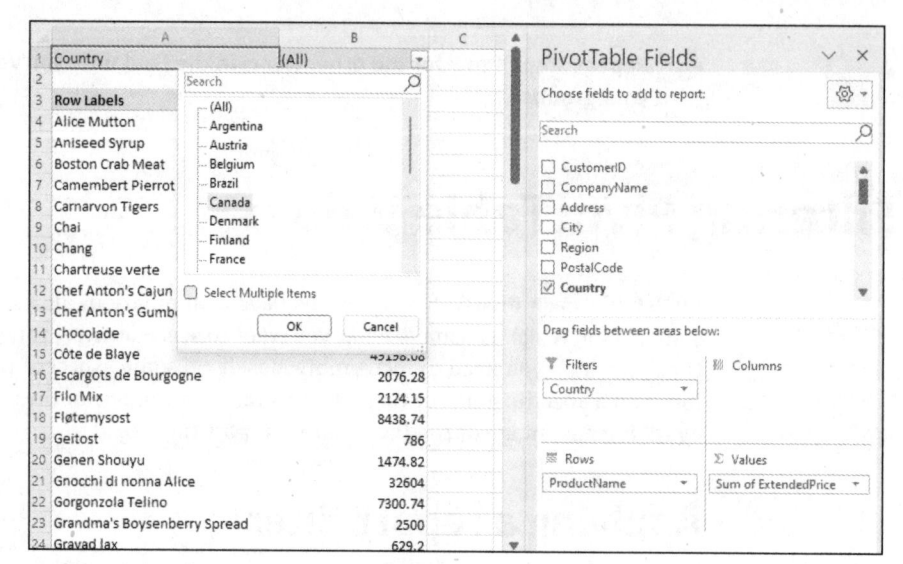

FIGURE 2-9:
From the filter field's drop-down list, select a report filter.

Filtering row or column items

By default, your PivotTable shows all the items in whatever row and column fields you added to the report layout. Seeing all the items is usually what you want because the point of a PivotTable is to summarize all the data in the original source. However, sometimes you may not want to see every item. For example, in a PivotTable report that includes items from the ProductName field in the row area, you may want to see only those products with names that begin with the letter G or that contain the word *tofu*.

When you modify a PivotTable report to display only a subset of the row or column items, you're applying to the report a *label filter*, which is different from a *report filter*, which filters the entire PivotTable, as described in the preceding section. Excel offers a number of label filters for text, including Equals, Does Not Equal, Begins With, Ends With, Contains, Greater Than, and Less Than.

If your PivotTable report includes a date field in the row or column area, you can apply a date filter to that field. Excel offers many different date filters, including Before, After, Between, Today, Yesterday, Last Week, Last Month, Last Quarter, This Year, and Year to Date.

Follow these steps to apply a label filter to row or column items:

1. **Click the drop-down arrow in the header of the field you want to filter.**

    The field's Sorting & Filtering menu appears.

2. **Select Label Filters and then select the filter type you want to apply, such as Begins With.**

   The Label Filter dialog box opens.

3. **Type the filter criteria and then click OK.**

   Some filters, such as Between, require you to type two criteria values.

   Excel filters the PivotTable report.

To remove a row or column label filter, click the drop-down arrow in the field's header and then select Clear Filter from *Field*, where *Field* is the name of the filtered field.

Filtering PivotTable values

Excel enables you to apply *value filters* that restrict the values you see in the value area. For example, you may want to see only those values that are larger than some amount or that fall between two specified amounts. Excel offers several value filters, including Equals, Does Not Equal, Greater Than, Greater Than or Equal To, Less Than, Less Than or Equal To, Between, and Not Between.

Similarly, you may be interested in only the highest or lowest values that appear in the PivotTable. For example, you may want to see just the top ten values. You can generate such a report by using Excel's Top 10 Filter, which filters the PivotTable to show just the top ten items based on the values in the value field.

For example, suppose you have a PivotTable report based on a database of invoices that shows the total sales for each product. The basic report shows all the products, but if you're interested in only the top performers for the year, you can activate the Top 10 Filter feature to see the ten products that sold the most. Despite its name, the Top 10 Filter can display more than just the top ten data values. You can specify any number between 1 and 2,147,483,647, and you can ask Excel to show the bottommost values instead of the topmost ones.

Follow these steps to apply a value filter to your PivotTable:

1. **Click the drop-down arrow in the header of any row or column field.**

   The field's Sorting & Filtering menu appears.

2. **Select Value Filters and then select the filter type you want to apply, such as Top 10.**

   The dialog box for that value filter opens — for example, the Top 10 Filter dialog box.

3. **Specify the filter criteria and then click OK.**

   Excel filters the PivotTable report.

To remove a value filter, click the drop-down arrow in the header of the filtered field, click Value Filters, and then click Clear Filter.

Filtering a PivotTable with a slicer

As mentioned previously in this chapter, you can filter a PivotTable by using the report filter, which applies to the entire PivotTable, or by using either a label filter or a value filter, which applies only to the filter field. Whether it applies to the entire PivotTable or just the filter field, the filter is usable only with the PivotTable in which it's defined. However, requiring the same filter in multiple PivotTable reports is not unusual. For example, if you're a sales manager responsible for sales in a particular set of countries, you may often need to filter a PivotTable to show data from just those countries. Similarly, if you work with a subset of your company's product line, you may often have to filter PivotTable reports to show the results from just those products.

Applying these kinds of filters to one or two PivotTables isn't difficult or time consuming, but if you have to apply the same filter over and over again, the process gets old in a hurry. To combat this repetition, Excel offers a PivotTable feature called the slicer. A *slicer* is similar to a report filter, except it's independent of any PivotTable. This means you can use a single slicer to filter multiple PivotTables. Nice! Slicers also enable you to see at a glance which filters you've applied and which fields are not available.

First, here are the steps to follow to create a slicer to filter a PivotTable:

1. **Select a cell in your PivotTable.**
2. **On the PivotTable Analyze tab of the ribbon, click Insert Slicer.**

   The Insert Slicers dialog box opens and displays a check box for every field in your PivotTable report.
3. **Select the check box beside each field for which you want to create a slicer, and then click OK.**

   Excel displays one slicer for each field you selected. Each slicer is a box that contains a list of the items from its associated field. By default, all items in the slicer are selected, so no filtering has yet been applied to the PivotTable. Your mission is to use the slicer to select just the field items you want to see in the PivotTable.

Also, the Slicer contextual tab appears when a slicer has the focus, and you can use the controls in this tab to customize each slicer.

4. **Select a field item that you want to include in your filter.**

   If you want to include multiple items in your filter, click the first item, hold down Ctrl, click the other items, and then release Ctrl. Alternatively, click the Multi-Select icon (labeled in Figure 2-10; you can also toggle Multi-Select by pressing Alt+S).

   Excel filters the PivotTable based on the field items you selected in each slicer. Figure 2-10 shows an example.

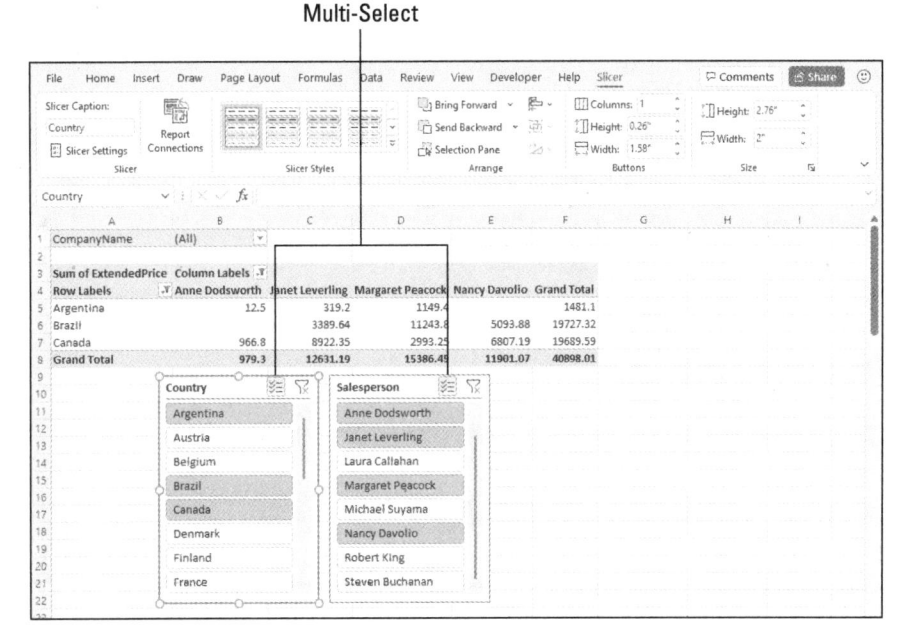

FIGURE 2-10: Excel filters the PivotTable to show just the selected items in each slicer.

If a field contains lots of items, you may have to scroll a long way in the slicer to locate the item you want. In this case, configuring the slicer to display its items in multiple columns is often easier. Select the title of the slicer to select it, click the Options tab, and then click the Column spin buttons to set the number of columns.

If you find that you no longer need to use a slicer, you should remove it to avoid cluttering the PivotTable window. Either select the slicer and press Delete, or right-click the slicer and then select Remove *Slicer*, where *Slicer* is the name of the slicer (which is usually the field name). If you want to temporarily hide the slicer, select any slicer, click the Slicer tab of the ribbon, click Selection Pane to display the Selection task pane, and then click the eye icon beside the slicer to hide it.

CHAPTER 2 **Creating and Using PivotTables** 411

IN THIS CHAPTER

» Trying some PivotTable summary calculations

» Working with PivotTable subtotals

» Using custom PivotTable calculations

» Creating a custom calculated PivotTable field and item

Chapter 3
Performing PivotTable Calculations

The near-ridiculous power and flexibility of a PivotTable is in contrast with the relative simplicity of what a PivotTable does, which is to take a mountain of data and turn it into a molehill of a report. With that report in place, the fun part begins when you pivot fields, group items, and filter the report (all of which we describe in painstaking detail in Chapter 2 of this minibook). Pivoting, grouping, and filtering represent the most visible aspects of a PivotTable's power, but lots of impressive things happen behind the PivotTable scene as well. These "hidden" features include the massive number of calculations that Excel performs to summarize all that data so succinctly. And you can harness that raw calculation horsepower for your own ends.

In this chapter, you open the PivotTable's hood to check out its calculation engine. You explore how the calculations work, swap out some parts to try different calculations, and even learn how to soup things up with your own custom calculations. Vroom vroom!

Messing Around with PivotTable Summary Calculations

The calculation that Excel uses to populate the PivotTable data area is called the *summary calculation*. Most of the time, the default Sum calculation will get the job done, but Excel offers lots of options for taking the summary calculation to a higher analytical level. The next few sections fill you in on those options.

Changing the PivotTable summary calculation

The default summary calculation depends on the type of field you add to the data area:

» If you add a numeric field to the data area, Excel uses Sum as the default summary calculation.

» If you use a text field in the data area, Excel uses Count as the default summary calculation.

Sum and Count aren't the only calculation choices, however. If your data analysis requires a different calculation, you can configure the data field to use any one of Excel's 11 built-in summary calculations. Here's the complete list:

» **Average:** Calculates the mean value in a numeric field

» **Count:** Displays the total number of cells in the source field

» **Count Numbers:** Displays the total number of numeric values in the source field

» **Max:** Displays the largest value in a numeric field

» **Min:** Displays the smallest value in a numeric field

» **Product:** Multiplies the values in a numeric field

» **StdDev:** Calculates the standard deviation of a population sample, which tells you how much the values in the source field vary with respect to the average

» **StdDevp:** Calculates the standard deviation when the values in the data field represent the entire population

» **Sum:** Adds the values in a numeric field

- **Var:** Calculates the variance of a population sample, which is the square of the standard deviation
- **Varp:** Calculates the variance when the values in the data field represent the entire population

Here are the steps to follow to try a different summary calculation:

1. **Select any cell in the data field.**
2. **On the PivotTable Analyze tab of the ribbon, click Field Settings.**

   The Value Field Settings dialog box opens with the Summarize Values By tab displayed, as shown in Figure 3-1.

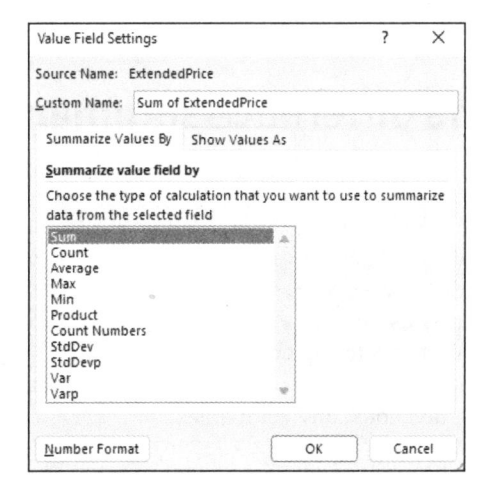

FIGURE 3-1: Use the Value Field Settings dialog box to choose a summary calculation.

3. **In the Summarize Value Field By list, select the summary calculation you want to use.**
4. **Click OK.**

   Excel recalculates the PivotTable results and renames the value field label to reflect the new summary calculation.

TIP Another way to change the PivotTable summary calculation is to right-click any cell in the value field, choose the Summarize Values By command, and then select the calculation you want to use from the submenu that appears. If you don't see the calculation, choose the More Options command to open the Value Field Settings dialog box.

When you build your PivotTable, you may find that the results don't pass the smell test. For example, the numbers may appear to be far too small. In that case, check the summary calculation that Excel has applied to the field to see whether it's using Count instead of Sum. If the data field includes one or more text cells or one or more blank cells, Excel defaults to the Count summary function instead of Sum. If your field is supposed to be numeric, check the data to see whether any text values or blank cells are showing up.

When you add a second field to the row or column area, Excel displays a subtotal for each item in the outer field. (The *outer field* is the field farthest from the value area: the leftmost field if you have two fields in the row area, or the topmost field if you have two fields in the column area. The other field is called the *inner field* because it's closest to the value area.) By default, the subtotals show the sum of the data results for each outer field item. However, the same 11 summary calculations — from Average to Varp — are also available for subtotals.

Trying out the difference summary calculation

The built-in summary calculations — Sum, Count, and so on — apply over an entire field. However, a major part of data analysis involves comparing one item with another. If you're analyzing sales to customers, for example, knowing how much you sold this year is useful, but even more useful is to compare this year's sales with last year's. Are the sales up or down? By how much? Are the sales up or down with all customers or only some? These fundamental questions help managers run departments, divisions, and companies.

Excel offers two difference calculations that can help with this kind of analysis:

- **Difference From:** Compares one numeric item with another and returns the difference between them
- **% Difference From:** Compares one numeric item with another and returns the percentage difference between them

Before you set up a difference calculation, you need to decide which field in your PivotTable to use as the comparison field, or *base field,* and which item in that field to use as the basis for all the comparisons, which is called the *base item.* For example, take a peek at Figure 3-2, which uses the Order Date field to show the sales in 2022 and the sales in 2021. In this example, Order Date is the base field and 2021 is the base item.

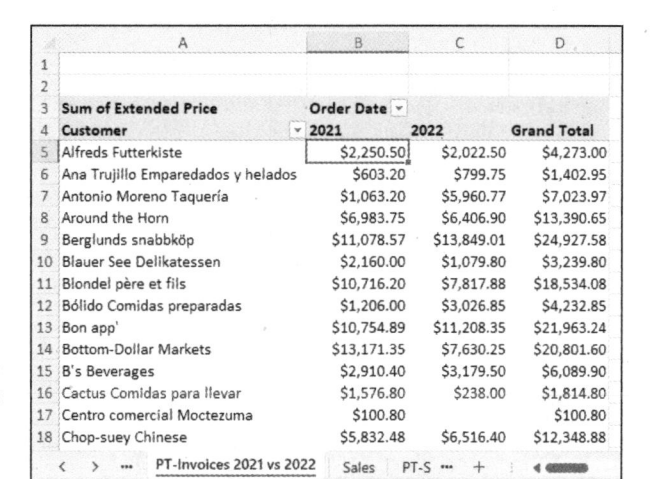

FIGURE 3-2:
A PivotTable that shows sales in two years: 2021 and 2022.

	A	B	C	D
3	Sum of Extended Price	Order Date		
4	Customer	2021	2022	Grand Total
5	Alfreds Futterkiste	$2,250.50	$2,022.50	$4,273.00
6	Ana Trujillo Emparedados y helados	$603.20	$799.75	$1,402.95
7	Antonio Moreno Taquería	$1,063.20	$5,960.77	$7,023.97
8	Around the Horn	$6,983.75	$6,406.90	$13,390.65
9	Berglunds snabbköp	$11,078.57	$13,849.01	$24,927.58
10	Blauer See Delikatessen	$2,160.00	$1,079.80	$3,239.80
11	Blondel père et fils	$10,716.20	$7,817.88	$18,534.08
12	Bólido Comidas preparadas	$1,206.00	$3,026.85	$4,232.85
13	Bon app'	$10,754.89	$11,208.35	$21,963.24
14	Bottom-Dollar Markets	$13,171.35	$7,630.25	$20,801.60
15	B's Beverages	$2,910.40	$3,179.50	$6,089.90
16	Cactus Comidas para llevar	$1,576.80	$238.00	$1,814.80
17	Centro comercial Moctezuma	$100.80		$100.80
18	Chop-suey Chinese	$5,832.48	$6,516.40	$12,348.88

Here are the steps to follow to apply a difference summary calculation to a PivotTable:

1. **Select any cell in the value field.**
2. **On the PivotTable Analyze tab of the ribbon, click Field Settings.**

   The Value Field Settings dialog box opens with the Summarize Values By tab displayed.

3. **Click the Show Values As tab.**
4. **In the Show Values As list, select Difference From.**

   If you want to see the difference in percentage terms, select % Difference From instead.

   TIP Another way to select the Difference Summary calculation is to right-click any cell in the value field, select Show Values As, and then select Difference From.

5. **In the Base Field list, select the field from which you want Excel to calculate the difference.**
6. **In the Base Item list, select a base item.**

   Figure 3-3 shows a completed Show Values As tab for the example PivotTable.

7. **Click OK.**

   Excel recalculates the PivotTable results to show the difference summary calculation. Figure 3-4 shows the PivotTable from Figure 3-2 with the Difference From calculation applied.

CHAPTER 3 **Performing PivotTable Calculations** 417

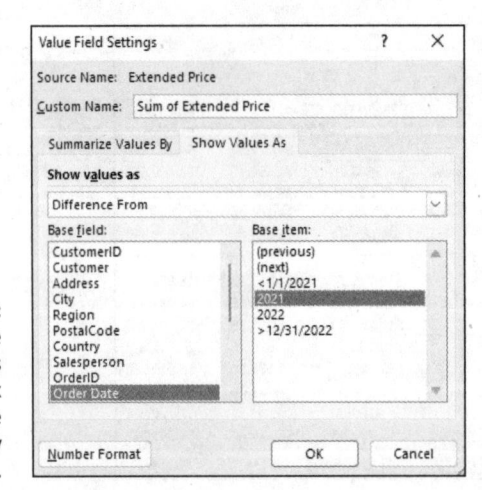

FIGURE 3-3:
Use the Value Field Settings dialog box to choose a summary calculation.

FIGURE 3-4:
The PivotTable from Figure 3-2 is now using the Difference From calculation.

Applying a percentage summary calculation

When analyzing data, comparing two or more items as a percentage is often helpful because percentage calculations enable you to make apples-to-apples comparisons between values. For example, if your PivotTable shows quarterly sales by region (see Figure 3-5), you may want to know how the results in the second, third, and fourth quarters compare, as a percentage, to the results from the first quarter.

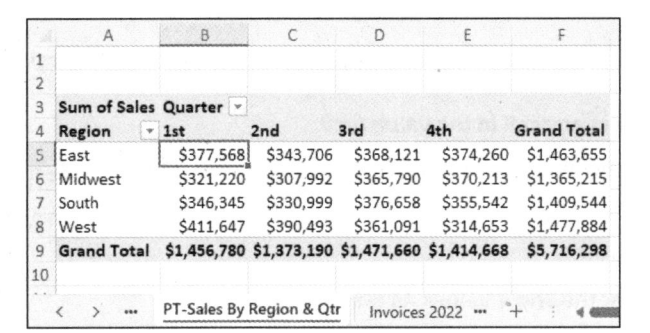

FIGURE 3-5:
A PivotTable that shows quarterly sales by region.

	A	B	C	D	E	F
1						
2						
3	Sum of Sales	Quarter				
4	Region	1st	2nd	3rd	4th	Grand Total
5	East	$377,568	$343,706	$368,121	$374,260	$1,463,655
6	Midwest	$321,220	$307,992	$365,790	$370,213	$1,365,215
7	South	$346,345	$330,999	$376,658	$355,542	$1,409,544
8	West	$411,647	$390,493	$361,091	$314,653	$1,477,884
9	Grand Total	$1,456,780	$1,373,190	$1,471,660	$1,414,668	$5,716,298

That kind of comparison sounds hard, but you can use Excel's percentage calculations to quickly view data items as a percentage of some other item or as a percentage of the total in the current row, column, or PivotTable. Excel offers seven percentage calculations that can help you perform this kind of analysis:

» **% Of:** Returns the percentage of each value with respect to a selected base item.

» **% of Row Total:** Returns the percentage that each value in a row represents of the total value of the row.

» **% of Column Total:** Returns the percentage that each value in a column represents of the total value of the column.

» **% of Grand Total:** Returns the percentage that each value represents of the PivotTable grand total.

» **% of Parent Row Total:** If you have multiple fields in the row area, this calculation returns the percentage that each value in an inner row represents with respect to the total of the parent item in the outer row.

» **% of Parent Column Total:** If you have multiple fields in the column area, this calculation returns the percentage that each value in an inner column represents with respect to the total of the parent item in the outer column.

» **% of Parent Total:** If you have multiple fields in the row or column area, this calculation returns the percentage of each value with respect to a selected base field in the outer row or column.

If you use the % Of calculation, you must also choose a base field and a base item upon which Excel will calculate the percentages. If you use the % of Parent Total calculation, you must also choose a base field.

CHAPTER 3 **Performing PivotTable Calculations** 419

Here are the steps to follow to apply a percentage summary calculation:

1. **Select any cell in the value field.**
2. **On the PivotTable Analyze tab of the ribbon, click Field Settings.**

   The Value Field Settings dialog box opens with the Summarize Values By tab displayed.
3. **Click the Show Values As tab.**
4. **In the Show Values As list, select the percentage calculation you want to use and then do the following:**

   - **If you selected % Of:** In the Base Field list, select the field from which you want Excel to calculate the percentages. In the Base Item list, select a base item. Click OK.

   - **If you selected % of Parent Total:** In the Base Field list, select the field from which you want Excel to calculate the percentages. Click OK.

   - **If you selected any other option in the list:** Click OK.

   Excel recalculates the PivotTable results to show the percentage summary calculation. Figure 3-6 shows the PivotTable from Figure 3-5 with the % Of calculation applied with Quarter as the base field and 1st as the base item.

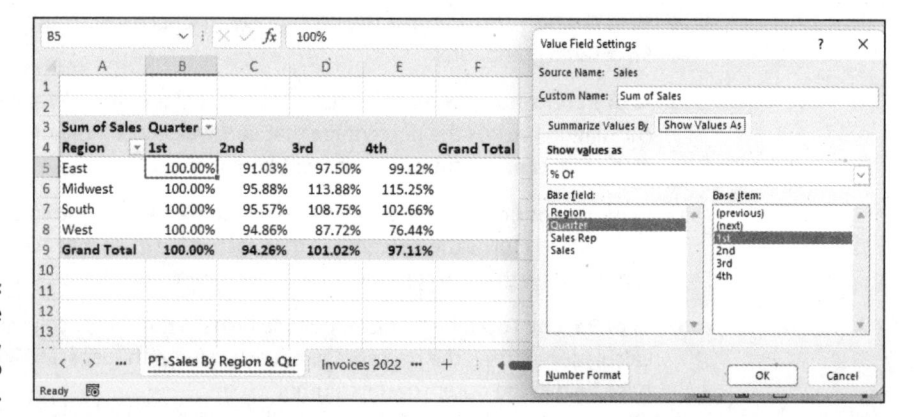

FIGURE 3-6: The PivotTable from Figure 3-5, now using the % Of calculation.

Adding a running total summary calculation

A *running total* is the cumulative sum of the values that appear in a set of data. Most running totals accumulate over a period of time. For example, suppose you have 12 months of sales figures. In a running total calculation, the first value is the first month of sales, the second value is the sum of the first and second months, the third value is the sum of the first three months, and so on.

You use a running total in data analysis when you need to see a snapshot of the overall data at various points. For example, suppose you have a sales budget for each month. As the fiscal year progresses, comparing the running total of the budget figures with the running total of the actual sales tells you how your department or company is doing with respect to the budget. If sales are consistently below budget, you may consider lowering prices, offering customers extra discounts, or increasing your product advertising.

Creating a running total seems like a job best left to a complex Excel formula. Sure, you could create such a formula, but we're happy to report that you don't have to bother with any of that. That's because Excel offers a built-in Running Total In summary calculation that you can apply to your PivotTable results. No muss and not even any fuss.

REMEMBER

The Running Total In summary applies not just to the Sum calculation but also to related calculations, such as Count and Average.

Before you configure your PivotTable to use a Running Total In summary calculation, you must choose the field on which to base the accumulation, called the *base field*. This field will most often be a date field, but you can also create running totals based on other fields, such as customer, division, or product.

Here are the steps to follow to apply a Running Total In summary calculation to a PivotTable:

1. **Select any cell in the value field.**

   Figure 3-7 shows a value field cell selected in a PivotTable of monthly order totals.

2. **On the PivotTable Analyze tab of the ribbon, click Field Settings.**

   The Value Field Settings dialog box opens, displaying the Summarize Values By tab.

3. **Click the Show Values As tab.**

4. **In the Show Values As list, select Running Total In.**

   If you want to see the running total in percentage terms, select % Running Total In instead.

   TIP

   Another way to select the Running Total In summary calculation is to right-click any cell in the value field, click Show Values As, and then click Running Total In.

	A	B
1	CategoryName	(All)
2		
3	OrderDate	Sum of ExtendedPrice
4	Jan	$53,981.61
5	Feb	$42,386.08
6	Mar	$41,921.21
7	Apr	$53,032.95
8	May	$50,506.46
9	Jun	$39,637.61
10	Jul	$44,811.34
11	Aug	$53,497.15
12	Sep	$55,629.24
13	Oct	$65,354.48
14	Nov	$44,928.54
15	Dec	$71,398.41
16	Grand Total	$617,085.08

FIGURE 3-7: A PivotTable showing monthly order totals.

5. **In the Base Field list, select the field from which you want Excel to accumulate the running totals.**

6. **Click OK.**

   Excel recalculates the PivotTable results to show the running totals. Figure 3-8 shows the PivotTable from Figure 3-7 with the Running Total In calculation applied using OrderDate as the base field.

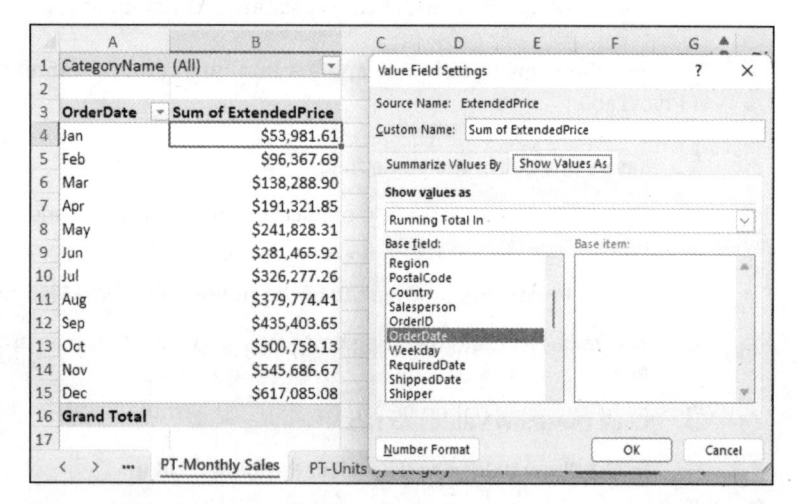

	A	B
1	CategoryName	(All)
2		
3	OrderDate	Sum of ExtendedPrice
4	Jan	$53,981.61
5	Feb	$96,367.69
6	Mar	$138,288.90
7	Apr	$191,321.85
8	May	$241,828.31
9	Jun	$281,465.92
10	Jul	$326,277.26
11	Aug	$379,774.41
12	Sep	$435,403.65
13	Oct	$500,758.13
14	Nov	$545,686.67
15	Dec	$617,085.08
16	Grand Total	

FIGURE 3-8: The PivotTable from Figure 3-7, with the Running Total In calculation applied.

Creating an index summary calculation

One of the most crucial aspects of data analysis is determining the relative importance of the results of your calculations. This determination is particularly vital in a PivotTable, whose results summarize a large amount of data but on the surface provide no clue as to the relative importance of the various value area results.

For example, suppose your PivotTable shows the units sold for various product categories broken down by region (see Figure 3-9). Suppose further that in Oregon, you sold 30 units of produce and 35 units of seafood. Does this mean that seafood sales are relatively more important in the Oregon market than produce sales? Not necessarily. To determine relative importance, you must take into account the larger picture, such as the total units sold of both produce and seafood across all states. Suppose the produce total is 145 units and the seafood total is 757 units. In that case, you can see that the 30 units of produce sold in Oregon represents a much higher portion of total produce sales than does Oregon's 35 units of seafood. A proper analysis would also take into account the total units sold in Oregon and the total units sold overall (the PivotTable's Grand Total).

FIGURE 3-9: A PivotTable showing units sold by category and region.

Sum of Quantity	Region			
CategoryName	Idaho	Oregon	Washington	Grand Total
Beverages	301	71	182	554
Condiments	240	32	99	371
Confections	359	79	72	510
Dairy Products	343	86	54	483
Grains/Cereals	247	42	25	314
Meat/Poultry	337	6	96	439
Produce	110	30	5	145
Seafood	637	35	85	757
Grand Total	2574	381	618	3573

Determining the relative importance of a PivotTable's results sounds headache-inducingly complex, but Excel offers the built-in Index calculation, which handles everything without the need for aspirin. The Index calculation determines the *weighted average* (the average taking into account the relative importance of each value) of each cell in the PivotTable results.

Put your math geek hat on because here's the formula Excel uses:

```
(Cell Value) * (Grand Total) / (Row Total) * (Column Total)
```

In the Index calculation results, the higher the value, the more important the cell in the overall PivotTable report.

CHAPTER 3 **Performing PivotTable Calculations** 423

Follow these steps to apply the Index summary calculation to a PivotTable:

1. **Select any cell in the value field.**
2. **On the PivotTable Analyze tab of the ribbon, click Field Settings.**

   The Value Field Settings dialog box opens with the Summarize Values By tab displayed.
3. **Click the Show Values As tab.**
4. **In the Show Values As list, select Index.**

   Alternatively, right-click any cell in the value field, click Show Values As, and then click Index.

   TIP
5. **Click OK.**

   Excel recalculates the PivotTable results to show the Index results.

TIP

Working with the Index calculation results is much easier if you format the data field to show just two decimal places. Select any cell in the value field, click the PivotTable Analyze tab of the ribbon, click Field Settings, click Number Format, select Number in the Category list, make sure that 2 appears in the Decimal places field, click OK, and then click OK again.

Figure 3-10 shows the PivotTable from Figure 3-9 with the Index calculation applied (and all the Index calculations reduced to two decimal places for easier reading). Note that under Oregon, the index value for the Produce category is 1.94, whereas the index value for Seafood is 0.43, which tells you that produce sales in Oregon are relatively more important than seafood sales.

	A	B	C	D	E
1	Country	USA			
2					
3	Sum of Quantity	Region			
4	CategoryName	Idaho	Oregon	Washington	Grand Total
5	Beverages	0.75	1.20	1.90	1
6	Condiments	0.90	0.81	1.54	1
7	Confections	0.98	1.45	0.82	1
8	Dairy Products	0.99	1.67	0.65	1
9	Grains/Cereals	1.09	1.25	0.46	1
10	Meat/Poultry	1.07	0.13	1.26	1
11	Produce	1.05	1.94	0.20	1
12	Seafood	1.17	0.43	0.65	1
13	Grand Total	1	1	1	1

FIGURE 3-10: The PivotTable from Figure 3-9, with the Index calculation applied.

Working with PivotTable Subtotals

When you add a second field to the row or column area, as we describe in Chapter 2 of this minibook, Excel displays subtotals for the items in the outer field. Having these outer field subtotals available is a useful component of data analysis because it shows you not only how the data breaks down according to the items in the second (inner) field but also the total of those items for each item in the first (outer) field. However, Excel lets you turn off subtotals that you don't want to see, and it lets you add multiple subtotals. The next two sections provide the details.

Turning off subtotals for a field

If you kick things up a notch and add a third field to the row or column area, Excel displays two sets of subtotals: one for the second (middle) field and one for the first (outer) field. And for every extra field you add to the row or column area, Excel mindlessly adds yet another set of subtotals.

Believe me, a PivotTable displaying two or more sets of subtotals in one area is no picnic to read. Do yourself a favor and reduce the complexity of the PivotTable layout by turning off the subtotals for one or more of the fields. Here's how:

1. **Select any cell in the field you want to work with.**
2. **On the PivotTable Analyze tab of the ribbon, click Field Settings.**

   The Field Settings dialog box opens with the Subtotals & Filters tab displayed.
3. **In the Subtotals group, select the None radio button.**

   Alternatively, right-click any cell in the field and then deselect the Subtotal "*Field*" command, where *Field* is the name of the field.
4. **Click OK.**

   Excel hides the field's subtotals.

Displaying multiple subtotals for a field

When you add a second field to the row or column area, as we discuss in Chapter 2 of this minibook, Excel displays a subtotal for each item in the outer field, and that subtotal uses the Sum calculation. If you prefer to see the Average for each item or the Count, you can change the field's summary calculation; see the section "Changing the PivotTable summary calculation," earlier in this chapter.

However, a common data analysis task is to view items from several different points of view. That is, you study the results by eyeballing not just a single summary calculation, but several: Sum, Average, Count, Max, Min, and so on.

That's awesome of you, but it's not all that easy to switch from one summary calculation to another. To avoid this problem, Excel enables you to view multiple subtotals for each field, with each subtotal using a different summary calculation. It's true. You can use as many of Excel's 11 built-in summary calculations as you need. That said, using StdDev and StDevp at the same time doesn't make sense, because the former is for sample data and the latter is for population data. The same is true for the Var and Varp calculations.

Okay, here are the steps to follow to add multiple subtotals to a field:

1. **Select any cell in the field you want to mess with.**
2. **On the PivotTable Analyze tab of the ribbon, click Field Settings.**

    The Field Settings dialog box opens with the Subtotals & Filters tab displayed.

3. **In the Subtotals group, select the Custom radio button.**
4. **In the list that appears below the Custom options, select each calculation that you want to appear as a subtotal.**

    Alternatively, right-click any cell in the field and then deselect the Subtotal "*Field*" command, where *Field* is the name of the field.

5. **Click OK.**

    Excel recalculates the PivotTable to show the subtotals you selected. Figure 3-11 shows an example PivotTable showing the Sum, Average, Max, and Min subtotals.

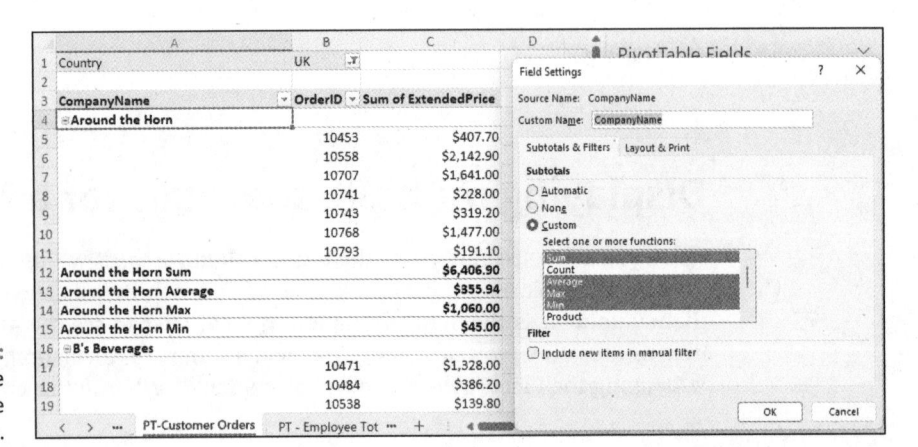

FIGURE 3-11:
A PivotTable with multiple subtotals.

Introducing Custom Calculations

A *custom calculation* is a formula that you define to produce PivotTable values that wouldn't otherwise appear in the report if you used only the source data and Excel's prefab summary calculations. Custom calculations let you extend your data analysis to include results that are tailored to your company, your department, or the daily whims of your boss.

For example, suppose your PivotTable shows employee sales by quarter and you want to award a 10 percent bonus to each employee with sales of more than $50,000 in any quarter. That's awfully generous of you! To help, you can create a custom calculation that checks for sales greater than $50,000 and then multiplies those by 0.1 to get the bonus number.

A custom calculation is an Excel formula applied to your source data to produce a summary result. In other words, in most cases the custom calculation is just like Excel's built-in PivotTable summary calculations, except that you define the specifics of the calculation. Because you're creating a formula, you can use most of Excel's formula power, which gives you tremendous flexibility to create custom calculations that suit your data analysis needs. And by placing these calculations in the PivotTable itself — as opposed to, for example, adding them to your source data — you can easily update the calculations as needed and refresh the report results.

Formulas for custom calculations

Custom calculations are formulas with certain restrictions imposed; see the section "Understanding custom calculation limitations," later in this chapter, for more details. A custom calculation formula always begins with an equal sign (=), followed by one or more operands and operators:

- **Operands:** The values that the formula uses as the raw material for the calculation. In a custom PivotTable calculation, the operands can be numbers, worksheet functions, or fields from your data source.
- **Operators:** The symbols that the formula uses to perform the calculation. In a custom PivotTable calculation, the available operators include addition (+), subtraction (–), multiplication (*), division (/), and comparison operators such as greater than (>) and less than or equal to (<=).

Checking out the custom calculation types

When building a custom calculation for a PivotTable, Excel offers two types:

- **Calculated field:** A new data field in which the values are the result of a custom calculation formula. You can display the calculated field along with another data field or on its own. A calculated field is really a custom summary calculation, so in almost all cases, the calculated field references one or more fields in the source data. See the section "Inserting a Custom Calculated Field," later in this chapter.

- **Calculated item:** A new item in a row or column field in which the values are the result of a custom calculation. In this case, the calculated item's formula references one or more items in the same field. See the section "Inserting a Custom Calculated Item," later in this chapter, for more on working with a custom calculated item.

Understanding custom calculation limitations

Custom calculations — whether they're calculated fields or calculated items — are powerful additions to your PivotTable analysis toolbox. However, although custom calculation formulas look like regular worksheet formulas, you can't assume that you can do everything with a custom PivotTable formula that you can do with a worksheet formula. In fact, Excel imposes a number of limitations on custom formulas.

The major limitation inherent in custom calculations is that, with the exception of constant values such as numbers, you can't reference anything outside the PivotTable's source data:

- You can't use a cell reference, range address, or range name as an operand in a custom calculation formula.

- You can't use any worksheet function that requires a cell reference, range, or defined name. However, you can still use many of Excel's worksheet functions by substituting either a PivotTable field or a PivotTable item in place of a cell reference or range name. For example, if you want a calculated item that returns the average of items named Jan, Feb, and Mar, you could use the following formula:

  ```
  =AVERAGE(Jan, Feb, Mar)
  ```

- » You can't use the PivotTable's subtotals, row totals, column totals, or grand total as an operand in a custom calculation formula.

You also need to understand how references to other PivotTable fields work in your calculations and what limitations you face when using field references:

- » **Field references:** When you reference a PivotTable field in your formula, Excel interprets this reference as the *sum* of that field's values. For example, the formula =Sales + 1 does not add 1 to each Sales value and return the sum of these results; that is, Excel doesn't interpret the formula as =Sum of (Sales + 1). Instead, the formula adds 1 to the sum of the Sales values, and Excel interprets the formula as =(Sum of Sales) + 1.

- » **Field reference problems:** The fact that Excel defaults to a Sum calculation when you reference another field in your custom calculation can lead to problems. The trouble is that summing certain types of data doesn't make sense. For example, suppose you have inventory source data with UnitsInStock and UnitPrice fields. You want to calculate the total value of the inventory, so you create a custom field based on the following formula:

```
=UnitsInStock * UnitPrice
```

Unfortunately, this formula doesn't work because Excel treats the UnitPrice operand as Sum of UnitPrice. Adding the prices together doesn't make sense, so your formula produces an incorrect result.

Finally, Excel imposes the following limitations on the use of calculated items:

- » A formula for a calculated item can't reference items from any field except the one in which the calculated item resides.
- » You can't insert a calculated item into a PivotTable that has at least one grouped field. You must ungroup all the PivotTable fields before you can insert a calculated item.
- » You can't group a field in a PivotTable that has at least one calculated item.
- » You can't insert a calculated item into a filter field. Also, you can't move a row or column field that has a calculated item into the filter area.
- » You can't insert a calculated item into a PivotTable in which a field has been used more than once.
- » You can't insert a calculated item into a PivotTable that uses the Average, StdDev, StdDevp, Var, or Varp summary calculations.

Inserting a Custom Calculated Field

A custom calculated field may look much like an Excel worksheet formula, but you don't enter the formula for a calculated field into a worksheet cell. Instead, Excel offers the Calculated Field feature, which provides a dialog box for you to name the field and construct the formula. Excel then stores the formula along with the rest of the PivotTable data.

Here are the steps to follow to insert a custom calculated field into a PivotTable:

1. **Select any cell in the PivotTable's value area.**
2. **On the PivotTable Analyze tab of the ribbon, click Fields, Items, & Sets and then click Calculated Field.**

   The Insert Calculated Field dialog box opens.
3. **In the Name text box, enter a name for the calculated field.**
4. **In the Formula text box, start the formula.**

   Begin with an equal sign (=) and then add any constants or worksheet functions you need to get started.
5. **When you get to the point in your formula at which you need to add a field, select a field in the Fields list and then click Insert Field.**

   You can also double-click the field to add it to the formula.
6. **Keep building your formula, repeating Step 5 to add fields as needed.**
7. **When the formula is complete, click Add.**

   Figure 3-12 shows an example formula for a custom calculated field. In this case, the formula uses an IF function to check whether the ExtendedPrice field is greater than 50,000. If it is, the formula returns the ExtendedPrice value multiplied by 0.1; otherwise, it returns 0.

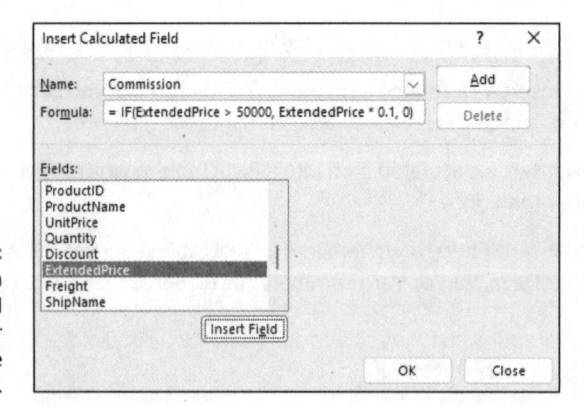

FIGURE 3-12: A custom calculated field, ready for insertion into the PivotTable.

8. **Click OK.**

   Excel adds the calculated field to the PivotTable's data area, as shown in Figure 3-13. Excel adds the calculated field to the PivotTable Fields task pane.

	A	B	C
1	Country	(All)	
2			
3	Row Labels	Sum of ExtendedPrice	Sum of Commission
4	Andrew Fuller	$70,444.14	$ 7,044.41
5	Anne Dodsworth	$26,310.39	$ -
6	Janet Leverling	$108,026.13	$ 10,802.61
7	Laura Callahan	$56,032.60	$ 5,603.26
8	Margaret Peacock	$128,809.78	$ 12,880.98
9	Michael Suyama	$43,126.37	$ -
10	Nancy Davolio	$93,148.04	$ 9,314.80
11	Robert King	$60,471.19	$ 6,047.12
12	Steven Buchanan	$30,716.44	$ -
13	Grand Total	$617,085.08	$ 61,708.51

FIGURE 3-13: The custom calculated field in action.

> **WARNING** When you add a calculated field to the PivotTable, Excel also applies the custom calculation to the Grand Total value (refer to Figure 3-13). Unfortunately, this total is often inaccurate, and you should be careful not to assume that it's correct. The problem is that it's not a sum of the values in the calculated field, as you may think. Instead, Excel applies the calculated field's formula to the sum of whatever field(s) you referenced in the formula. In the example shown in Figure 3-13, Excel applies the formula to the Sum of Extended Price field's Grand Total value, which is not the correct way to calculate the total commission. If you want to see the correct total for the calculated field, set up a formula outside the PivotTable that sums the values.

Inserting a Custom Calculated Item

If your data analysis requires PivotTable results that are not available using just the data source fields and Excel's built-in summary calculations, no problem: You can insert a calculated item that uses a custom formula to derive the results you need. Sweet!

A calculated item uses a formula similar to an Excel worksheet formula, but you don't enter the formula for a calculated item into a worksheet cell. Instead, Excel offers the Calculated Item command, which displays a dialog box in which you name the item and construct the formula. Excel then stores the formula along with the rest of the PivotTable data.

The Calculated Item feature creates just a single item in a field. However, feel free to add as many calculated items as you need. For example, suppose you want to compare the sales of nonvegan items (such as meat, poultry, dairy, and seafood) with vegan items (grains, cereals, produce, and beverages). One approach would be to create one calculated item that returns the average sales of the nonvegan items and a second calculated item that returns the average sales of the vegan items.

Here are the steps to follow to insert a custom calculated item into a PivotTable:

1. **Select any cell in the field to which you want to insert the item.**
2. **On the PivotTable Analyze tab of the ribbon, click Fields, Items, & Sets and then click Calculated Item.**

   The Insert Calculated Item dialog box opens.
3. **In the Name text box, enter a name for the calculated field.**
4. **In the Formula text box, start the formula.**

   Begin with an equal sign (=) and then add any constants or worksheet functions you need to get started.
5. **When you get to the point in your formula at which you need to add a field, select the field in the Fields list and then click Insert Field.**

   You can also double-click the field to add it to the formula.
6. **When you get to the point in your formula at which you need to add an item, select the item in the Items list and then click Insert Item.**

   You can also double-click the item to add it to the formula.
7. **Keep building your formula, repeating Steps 5 and 6 to add fields and items as needed.**
8. **When the formula is complete, click Add.**

   Figure 3-14 shows an example formula for a custom calculated item. In this case, we use the AVERAGE function to calculate the average of several nonvegan food categories.
9. **Click OK.**
10. **Click OK.**

    Excel adds the calculated item to the PivotTable field. Figure 3-15 shows two calculated items added to the PivotTable's row field. Note, as well, that when you select a custom calculated item, Excel shows the item's custom formula in the Formula Bar.

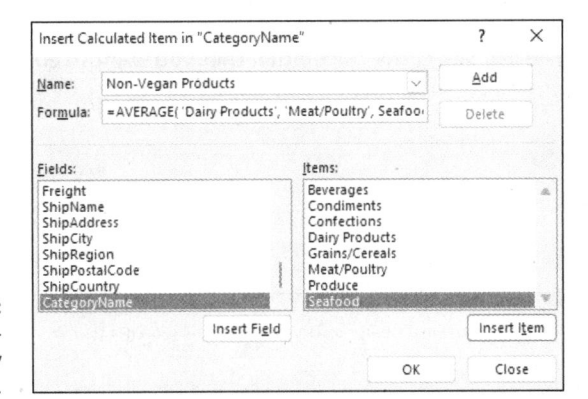

FIGURE 3-14:
A custom calculated item, ready for action.

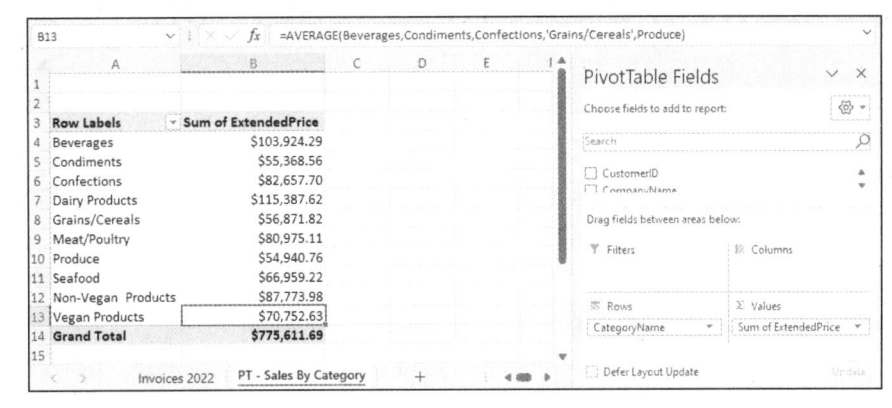

FIGURE 3-15:
Two custom calculated items added to the row area.

Editing a Custom Calculation

Sometimes you may need to edit a custom calculation to correct an error or to make the calculation deliver different information to your data analysis. Here's how to edit a custom calculation:

1. **To edit a calculated field, select any cell in the PivotTable's data area.**

   To edit a calculated item, select any cell in the field that contains the calculated item.

2. **On the PivotTable Analyze tab of the ribbon, click Fields, Items, & Sets and then click Calculated Field.**

   The Insert Calculated Field dialog box opens.

   To edit a calculated item instead, click the PivotTable Analyze tab of the ribbon, click Fields, Items, & Sets, and then click Calculated Item to open the Insert Calculated Item dialog box.

CHAPTER 3 **Performing PivotTable Calculations** 433

3. **In the Name list, select the calculation that you want to edit.**
4. **Edit the formula.**
5. **Click Modify.**
6. **Click OK.**

   Excel updates the custom calculation's results.

   > **TIP:** You can also edit a calculated item by selecting the item's result. The formula appears in Excel's Formula Bar, and you can edit it from there.

Deleting a Custom Calculation

To delete a calculated field or calculated item you no longer need, follow these steps:

1. **Select any cell in the PivotTable.**
2. **To delete a calculated field, click the PivotTable Analyze tab of the ribbon, click Fields, Items, & Sets, and then click Calculated Field.**

   The Insert Calculated Field dialog box opens.

   To delete a calculated item instead, click the PivotTable Analyze tab of the ribbon, click Fields, Items, & Sets, and then click Calculated Item to open the Insert Calculated Item dialog box.

3. **In the Name list, select the calculation that you want to delete.**
4. **Click Delete.**
5. **Click OK.**

   Excel removes the custom calculation.

IN THIS CHAPTER

» Shaking hands with the PivotChart

» Discovering the difference between a PivotTable and a PivotChart

» Messing around with PivotCharts

» Making your PivotCharts look good

Chapter 4
Building PivotCharts

If a PivotTable appeals to the left side of your brain — the analytical side that likes numbers — the PivotChart will likely appeal to the right side of your brain — the visual side that likes patterns. That's because a PivotChart is to a PivotTable what a regular chart is to a range. That is, the PivotChart is a graphical representation of the PivotTable. The PivotChart enables you to visualize the PivotTable report by displaying the value area results in chart form.

However, you can also say that a PivotChart is to a regular chart what a PivotTable is to a regular range. In other words, the PivotChart goes far beyond the capabilities of a simple chart because the PivotChart comes with most of the same features that make PivotTables so powerful: You can filter the results to see just the data you need, and you can pivot fields from one area of the PivotChart to another to get the layout you want.

In this chapter, you discover what PivotCharts are all about, find out how to build PivotCharts, and explore ways to get the most out of your PivotCharts.

Introducing the PivotChart

As you may expect, PivotCharts have a number of elements in common with PivotTables, but some key differences also exist. The following list explains these differences and introduces you to some important PivotChart concepts:

» **Chart categories (*x*-axis):** As does a PivotTable, a PivotChart automatically groups large amounts of data into smaller, more manageable groups. For example, if you have data with a Category field containing values such as Beverages, Condiments, Confections, and so on and you build your PivotChart using the Category field, the resulting chart will display one chart category (*x*-axis value) for each unique Category field value. The chart *x*-axis is the equivalent of a row field in a PivotTable.

» **Chart data series:** Also, as with a PivotTable, you can break down your data in terms of a second field. For example, your data may have an Order Date field. If you add that field to the PivotChart, Excel creates one data series for each unique value in that field. The chart data series is the equivalent of a column field in a PivotTable.

» **Chart values (*y*-axis):** You can't have a PivotTable without a value field, and the same is true of a PivotChart. When you add a numeric field for the summary calculation, Excel displays the results as chart values (*y*-axis). The chart *y*-axis is the equivalent of a value field in a PivotTable.

» **Dynamic PivotCharts:** Perhaps the biggest difference between a PivotChart and a regular chart is that each PivotChart is a dynamic object that you can reconfigure as needed, just as you can with a PivotTable. You can add fields to different chart areas and you can place multiple fields in any chart area.

» **Filtering:** As with a PivotTable, you can use the unique values in another field to filter the results that appear in the PivotChart. For example, if your source data has a Country field, you can add it to the PivotChart and use it to filter the chart results to show just those from a specific country. The chart filter is the equivalent of a filter field in a PivotTable.

Understanding PivotChart pros and cons

PivotCharts have advantages and disadvantages, and understanding their strengths and weaknesses can help you decide when and if you should use them.

On the positive side, a PivotChart is a powerful data analysis tool because it combines the strengths of Excel's charting capabilities — including most of the options available with regular charts — with the features of a PivotTable. Also, creating a basic PivotChart is just as straightforward as creating a PivotTable. In fact, if you already have a PivotTable, you can create the equivalent PivotChart by pressing a single key.

On the negative side, PivotCharts share the same caveats that come with regular charts, particularly the fact that if you don't choose the proper chart type or layout, your data will not be readily understood. Moreover, a PivotChart can quickly become extremely confusing when you have multiple Category fields or Data Series fields. Finally, PivotCharts have inherent limitations that restrict the options and formatting that you can apply. We talk about these limitations a bit later in this chapter.

Taking a PivotChart tour

PivotCharts carry over some of the same terminology that we discuss in Chapter 2 of this minibook for PivotTables, including the concepts of the *report filter, value area,* and *field button*. However, PivotCharts also use several unique terms that you need to understand to get the most out of PivotCharts (see Figure 4-1):

- **Category items:** The unique field values that define the chart's categories.
- **Category axis:** The chart's *x*-axis (that is, the horizontal axis) that displays the category items.
- **Data series items:** The unique field values that define the chart's data series. The item names appear in the chart legend.
- **Data series axis:** The chart's *y*-axis (that is, the vertical axis) that displays the values of the data series items.
- **Value area:** Displays the charted results of the calculation that Excel applied to a numeric field in your data.

REMEMBER

One of the main sources of PivotChart confusion is the fact that Excel uses different terminology with PivotCharts and PivotTables. In both, you have a value area that contains the numeric results, and you have a report filter that you can use to filter the data. However, understanding how Excel maps the PivotTable's row and column areas to the PivotChart is important:

- **Row area versus category axis:** In a PivotTable, the row area contains the unique values that Excel has extracted from a field in the source data. The PivotChart equivalent is the category axis, which corresponds to the chart's *x*-axis. That is, each unique value from the source field has a corresponding category axis value.

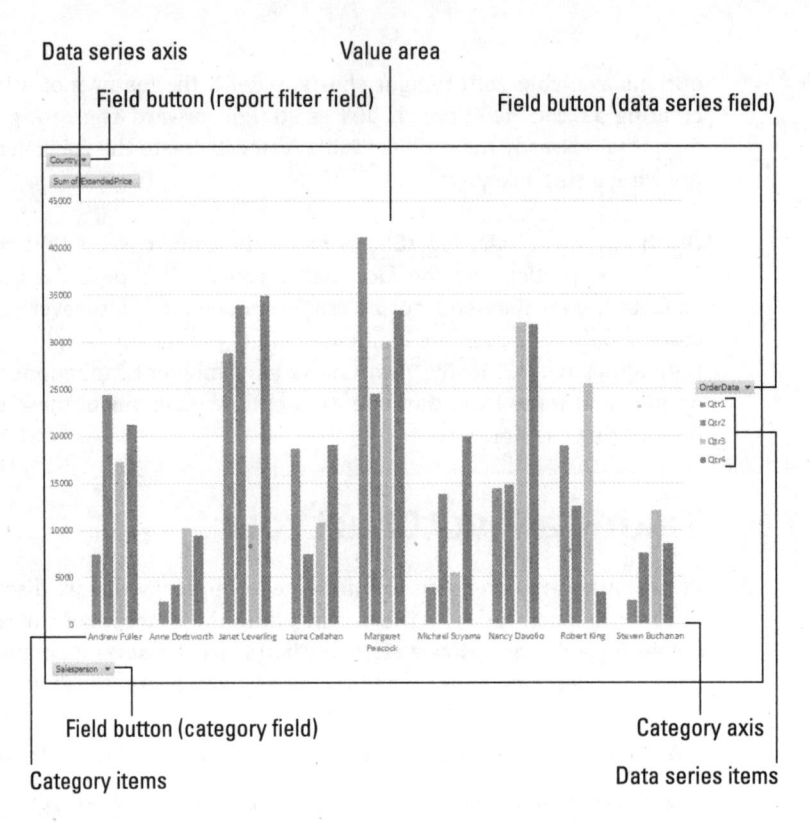

FIGURE 4-1: The major sights to see in the PivotChart landscape.

» **Column area versus series axis:** In a PivotTable, the column area contains the unique values that Excel has extracted from a field in the source data. The PivotChart equivalent is the series axis, which corresponds to the chart's y-axis. That is, each unique value from the source field has a corresponding data series.

Understanding PivotChart limitations

PivotCharts are a powerful addition to your data analysis toolkit, but they aren't always the ideal solution. Excel has rigid rules for which parts of a PivotTable report correspond to which parts of the PivotChart layout. Moving a field from one part of the PivotChart to another can easily result in a PivotChart layout that either is difficult to understand or doesn't make sense.

You also face a number of limitations that control the types of charts you can build and the formatting options you can apply:

- » **Chart types:** Excel offers a large number of chart types, and you can change the default PivotChart type to another that more closely suits your needs (see the section "Changing the PivotChart type," later in this chapter). However, there are three chart types that you can't apply to a PivotChart: Bubble, XY (Scatter), and Stock.
- » **Adding and removing fields:** After you create the PivotChart, as long as you're working with the chart itself, you can't add or remove fields. If you want to reconfigure the PivotChart's fields, you have to add or remove the fields using the underlying PivotTable.
- » **Pivoting fields:** You can't pivot the fields from one part of the PivotChart to another. If you want to pivot a field, you have to use the underlying PivotTable.

Fortunately, these PivotChart limitations aren't onerous in most situations, so they should in no way dissuade you from taking advantage of the analytical and visualization power of the PivotChart.

Creating a PivotChart

Excel gives you three ways to create a PivotChart. That seems like a lot, but is that significant? Probably not, but you should at least be familiar with all three methods, which we outline in the sections that follow.

Creating a PivotChart from a PivotTable

If you already have a PivotTable, you can create a PivotChart from it in moments:

1. **Select any cell in the PivotTable.**
2. **Press F11.**

Yep, that's all there is to it. Excel creates a new chart sheet and displays the PivotChart and the PivotChart Fields task pane.

Embedding a PivotChart on a PivotTable's worksheet

When you create a PivotChart directly from an existing PivotTable by pressing F11, as described in the preceding section, Excel places the chart in a new chart sheet. This is usually the best solution because it gives you the most room to view and manipulate the PivotChart. However, viewing the PivotChart together with its associated PivotTable is often useful. For example, when you change the PivotTable view, Excel automatically changes the PivotChart view in the same way. Rather than switching from one sheet to another to compare the results, having the PivotChart on the same worksheet lets you compare the PivotChart and PivotTable immediately. Nice.

Creating a new PivotChart on the same worksheet as an existing PivotTable is called *embedding* the PivotChart. Here are the steps to follow to embed a PivotChart:

1. **Select any cell in the PivotTable.**
2. **On the PivotTable Analyze tab of the ribbon, click PivotChart.**

   The Insert Chart dialog box opens.
3. **In the list of chart types on the left side of the Insert Chart dialog box, select the chart type you want.**

   You can't use the XY (Scatter), Bubble, or Stock chart type with a PivotChart.

   Excel displays one or more chart subtypes for the chart type you selected.
4. **On the right side of the Insert Chart dialog box, select the chart subtype you want.**
5. **Click OK.**

   Excel embeds the PivotChart on the PivotTable's worksheet.

Excel embeds the PivotChart in the center of the visible worksheet area. In most cases, this location means that the new PivotChart overlaps your existing Pivot-Table, which makes comparing them difficult. To fix this problem, you can move or resize the PivotChart:

- >> To move the PivotChart, move the mouse pointer over an empty part of the chart area and then drag the chart object to the new position.
- >> To resize the PivotChart, select the chart and then move the mouse pointer over any one of the selection handles that appear on the chart area's corners and sides. Drag a handle to the size you require.

If you already have a PivotChart in a separate chart sheet, you can embed it in the PivotTable's worksheet. We describe how this works later in this chapter, in the section "Moving a PivotChart to another sheet."

Creating a PivotChart from an Excel range or table

If the data you want to summarize and visualize exists as an Excel range or table, you can build a PivotChart (and its underlying PivotTable) directly from that data. Here are the steps to follow:

1. **Select a cell in the table that you want to use as the source data.**

    If you're using a range, select any cell in the range instead.

2. **On the Insert tab of the ribbon, click PivotChart.**

    The Create PivotChart dialog box appears, with the Select a Table or Range radio button selected. The Table/Range box should show the name of your table (or the address of your range). If not, adjust the name or address as needed before moving on.

3. **Select the New Worksheet radio button.**

    Alternatively, if you want to add the PivotTable to an existing location, select the Existing Worksheet radio button and then, in the Location range box, select the worksheet and cell where you want the PivotTable to appear.

4. **Click OK.**

    Excel creates a blank PivotTable and a blank, embedded PivotChart, and it displays the PivotChart Fields task pane, as shown in Figure 4-2. This pane contains two main areas:

    - A list of the column headers from your table, each of which has a check box to its left. These are your PivotChart (and PivotTable) fields.

    - Four boxes representing the four areas of the PivotChart: Filters, Legend (Series), Axis (Categories), and Values. To complete the PivotChart, add one or more fields to some or all of these areas.

5. **Drag a text field and drop it in the Axis (Categories) area.**

    Excel adds a button for the field to the PivotChart's category (x) axis.

6. **Drag a numeric field and drop it in the Values area.**

    Excel sums the numeric values based on the row values.

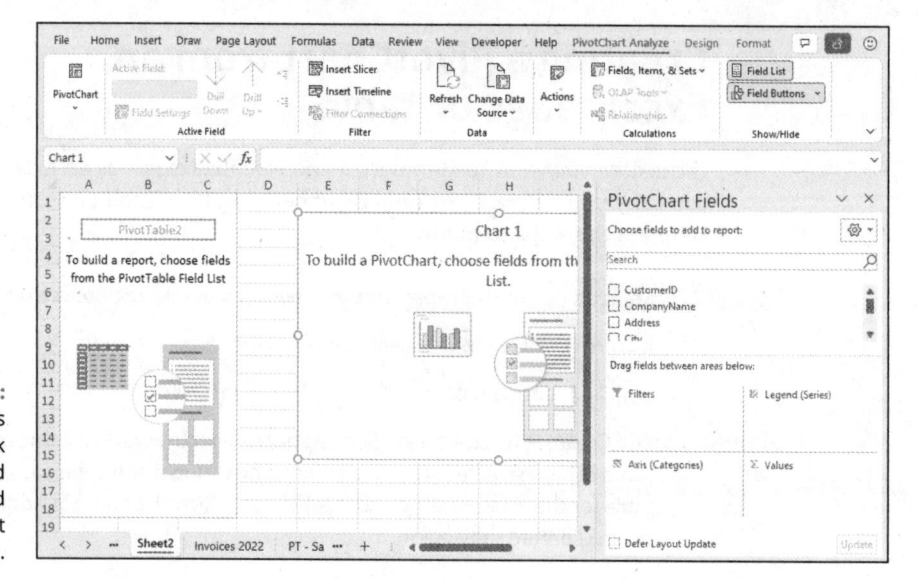

FIGURE 4-2:
Excel kicks things off with a blank PivotTable and PivotChart, and the PivotChart Fields task pane.

7. **If desired, drag fields and drop them in the Legend (Series) area and the Filters area.**

    Each time you drop a field into an area, Excel updates the PivotChart (and its associated PivotTable) to include the new data. Figure 4-3 shows a completed PivotChart (and PivotTable), with fields in just the Axis (Categories), Values, and Filters boxes. Note, too, that when you select the PivotChart, Excel displays three contextual tabs — PivotChart Analyze, Design, and Format — that are bursting with options for manipulating and formatting your PivotChart.

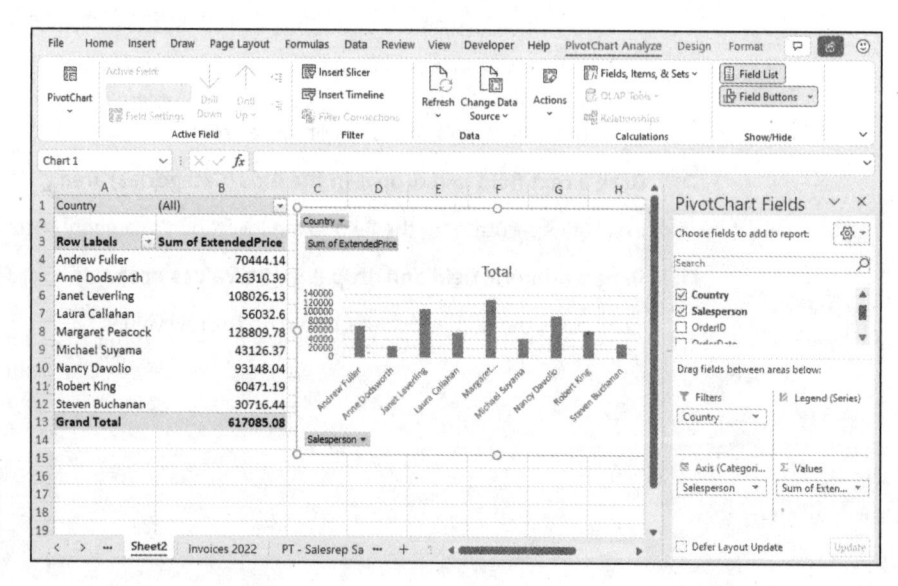

FIGURE 4-3:
An embedded PivotChart and its PivotTable.

442 BOOK 5 Summarizing, Visualizing, and Illustrating Data

If your PivotChart includes just a Category field, Excel displays the results using a standard bar chart. If the PivotChart includes both a Category field and a series field, Excel displays the results using a clustered column chart. We talk about how to view the PivotChart using a different type of chart in the section "Changing the PivotChart type," later in this chapter.

TECHNICAL STUFF

The clustered column chart is a great way to visualize two-dimensional Pivot-Table results, but deciphering the chart isn't always easy — especially if you have a large number of data series, which usually means that most of the columns in each category are quite small. To get a better understanding of the chart, you may want to know what data is represented by specific columns.

You can find the specifics related to each column by moving the mouse pointer over the column in the plot area. Excel then displays a banner with data in the following format:

Series *"Series Item"* Point *"Category Item"* Value: *Value*

Here, *Series Item* is an item from the series field, *Category Item* is an item from the Category field, and *Value* is the value of the data point. For example, if the Shipper field has an item named United Package, the Salesperson field has an item named Steven Buchanan, and the value is 488, the banner shows the following:

Series "United Package" Point "Steven Buchanan" Value: 488

Working with PivotCharts

After you have a PivotChart up and charting, you may want to leave it as is. That's perfectly fine, but you're more likely to want to take advantage of the many ways Excel offers to manipulate and format a PivotChart. In the rest of this chapter, we run through a fistful of techniques for messing around with PivotCharts.

Moving a PivotChart to another sheet

In the section "Creating a PivotChart from a PivotTable," earlier in this chapter, I talk about creating a new PivotChart on a separate chart sheet. However, in some situations, this separate chart sheet may not be convenient. For example, if you want to compare the PivotChart and its associated PivotTable, that comparison is more difficult if the PivotChart and PivotTable reside in separate sheets. Similarly, you may prefer to place all your PivotCharts on a single sheet so that you can compare them or they're easy to find. Finally, if you plan on creating several PivotCharts, you may not want to clutter your workbook with separate chart sheets.

The solution in all these cases is to move your PivotChart to the worksheet you prefer. To that worthy end, follow these steps to move a PivotChart to a new location:

1. **Select the PivotChart you want to move.**
2. **On the Design tab of the ribbon, click Move Chart.**

   The Move Chart dialog box opens.
3. **Select the Object In radio button and open its drop-down list to select the sheet where you want the PivotChart moved (see Figure 4-4).**
4. **Click OK.**

   Excel moves the PivotChart to the location you specified.

FIGURE 4-4:
Use the Move Chart dialog box to move a PivotChart to another worksheet.

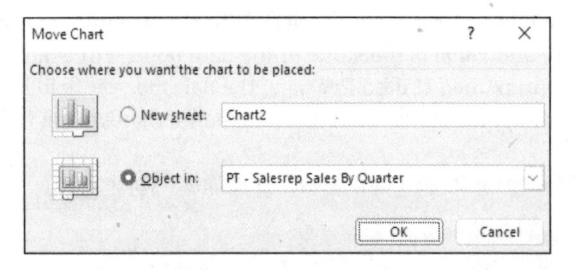

The steps in this section apply both to PivotCharts embedded in separate chart sheets and to PivotChart objects embedded in worksheets. For the latter, however, you can use a second technique. Select the PivotChart, click the Home tab of the ribbon, and click Cut (or press Ctrl+X) to remove the PivotChart and store it in the Windows Clipboard. Switch to the sheet where you want the PivotChart moved. If you're moving the PivotChart to a worksheet, select the cell where you want the upper-left corner of the chart to appear. On the Home tab of the ribbon, click Paste (or press Ctrl+V). Excel pastes the PivotChart object to the sheet. Move and resize the PivotChart object to taste.

Filtering a PivotChart

By default, each PivotChart report displays a summary for all the records in your source data, which is usually what you want to see. However, you may have situations that require you to focus more closely on some aspect of the data. You can focus on a specific item from one of the source data fields by taking advantage of the PivotChart's report filter.

For example, suppose you're dealing with a PivotChart that summarizes data from thousands of customer invoices over some period of time. A basic PivotChart may tell you the total units sold for each product category. However, what if you want to see the units sold for each product in a specific country? If the Product field is in the PivotChart's Axis (Categories) area, you can add the Country field to the Legend (Series) area. However, dozens of countries may be involved, so that isn't an efficient way to go. Instead, you can add the Country field to the Report Filter area. You can then tell Excel to display the total sold for each product for the specific country in which you're interested.

As another example, suppose you ran a marketing campaign in the previous quarter and set up an incentive plan for your salespeople whereby they could earn bonuses for selling at least a specified number of units. Suppose, as well, that you have a PivotChart showing the sum of the units sold for each product. To see the numbers for a particular employee, you can add the Salesperson field to the Report Filter area and then select the employee you want to work with.

Here are the steps to follow to filter a PivotChart:

1. **Click the PivotChart's Report Filter button.**

   Excel displays a list of the Report Filter field items.

2. **Select the item you want to view, as shown in Figure 4-5.**

   If you want to display data for two or more items, select the Select Multiple Items check box and then repeat Step 2 to select the other items.

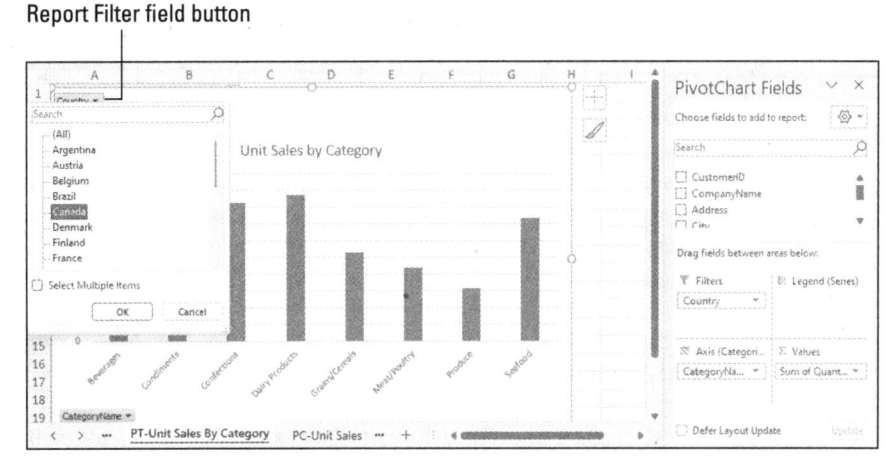

FIGURE 4-5: Pull down the Report Filter Field List and then select an item.

CHAPTER 4 **Building PivotCharts** 445

3. **Click OK.**

    Excel filters the PivotChart to show only the data for the item(s) you selected.

If you want to return to seeing all the items, click the Report Filter field button, select (All), and then click OK.

You can also filter the items in the Axis (Categories) area. For example, in a PivotChart that includes items from the ProductName field in the row area, you may want to see only those products with names that begin with the letter *G* or contain the word *tofu*. You can do that by applying a filter to a Category field. Excel offers several text filters, including Equals, Doesn't Equal, Begins With, Ends With, Contains, Greater Than, and Less Than. If the field uses dates, you can apply a date filter such as Before, Yesterday, Last Month, and This Year.

In the PivotChart, click the button for the field you want to work with and then choose either the Label Filters or the Date Filters command. In the list that appears, select the filter type you want to apply, such as Begins With; then type your filter criteria and click OK.

Changing the PivotChart type

If you don't include a series field in the PivotChart, Excel displays the report using regular columns, which is useful for comparing the values across the Category field's items. If you include a series field in the PivotChart, Excel displays the report using clustered columns, where each category shows several different-colored columns grouped beside one another, one for each item in the series field. These clustered columns are useful for comparing the series values for each item in the category.

Although these default chart types are fine for many applications, they're not always the best choice. For example, if you don't have a series field and you want to see the relative contribution of each category item to the total, a pie chart would be a better choice. If you're more interested in showing how the results trend over time, a line chart is usually the ideal type.

Whatever your needs, Excel enables you to change the default PivotChart type to any of the following types: Column, Bar, Line, Pie, Area, Doughnut, Radar, Surface, Cylinder, Cone, or Pyramid.

REMEMBER

Excel doesn't allow you to use a PivotChart with the following chart types: XY (Scatter), Bubble, or Stock.

Follow these steps to change your PivotChart's type:

1. **Select the PivotChart.**
2. **On the Design tab of the ribbon, click Change Chart Type.**

   The Change Chart Type dialog box appears.
3. **In the list of chart types on the left, select the chart type you want to use.**

   Excel displays the available chart subtypes.
4. **On the right side of the dialog box, select the Chart subtype you want to use.**
5. **Click OK.**

   Excel redisplays the PivotChart with the new chart type. For example, Figure 4-6 shows the PivotChart from Figure 4-5 displayed using the pie chart type.

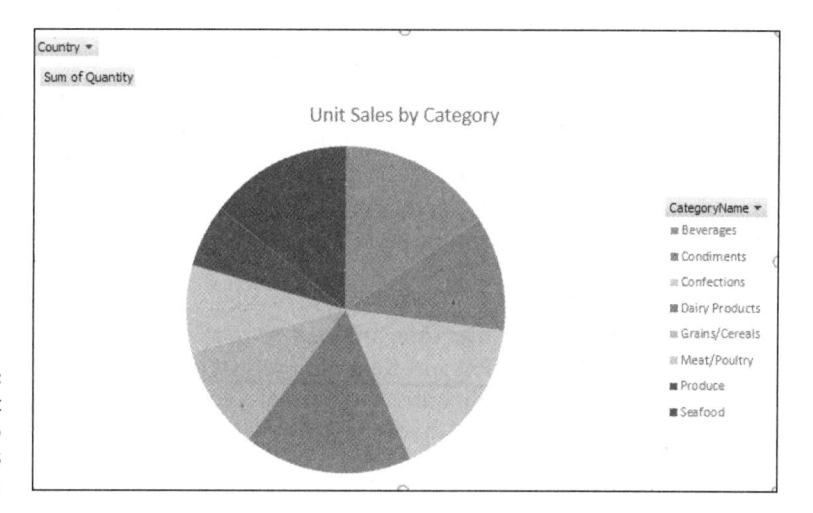

FIGURE 4-6: The PivotChart from Figure 4-5 now displayed as a pie chart.

Adding data labels to your PivotChart

Depending on the chart type you choose, augmenting the chart with the values from the report is often useful. For example, with a pie chart, you can add to each slice the value as well as the percentage the value represents of the grand total. In most cases, you can also add the series name and the category name.

To add these data labels to your PivotChart, follow these steps:

1. **Select the chart.**
2. **On the Design tab of the ribbon, click Add Chart Element and then click Data Labels.**

   Excel displays a menu of data label types.

3. **Select the data label position you want to use.**

   The choices you see depend on the chart type.

   You can also select More Data Label Options to open the Format Data Labels task pane and then select the Value check box. Depending on the data, you may also be able to select the Series Name, Category Name, and Percentage check boxes.

Sorting the PivotChart

When you create a PivotChart and include a series field, Excel displays the data series based on the order of the field's items as they appear in the PivotTable. That is, as you move left to right through the items in the PivotTable's column field, the data series moves left to right in the PivotChart's series field (or top to bottom if you're looking at the PivotChart legend). This default series order is fine in most applications, but you may prefer to change the order. In the default clustered column chart, for example, you may prefer to reverse the data series so that they appear from right to left.

Similarly, the PivotChart categories appear in the same order as they appear in the underlying PivotTable's row field. In this case, you may prefer to display the categories in some custom order. For example, you may want to rearrange employee names so that those who have the same supervisor or who work in the same division appear together.

First, here are the steps to follow to sort the data series items:

1. **Select the PivotChart.**
2. **Select the field button for the PivotChart's Data Series field.**

   Excel displays a list of sort options for the field. The sort options you see vary depending on the field's data type:

   - **For a text field:** Sort A to Z (ascending) and Sort Z to A (descending).
   - **For a date field:** Sort Oldest to Newest (ascending) and Sort Newest to Oldest (descending).

- **For a numeric field:** Sort Smallest to Largest (ascending) and Sort Largest to Smallest (descending).

3. **Select the sort order you want to use.**

   Excel redisplays the PivotChart using the new series order.

Follow these steps to sort the category items:

1. **Select the PivotChart.**
2. **Select the field button for the PivotChart's Category field.**

   Excel displays a list of sort options for the field.

   The sort options you see vary depending on the field's data type, and the possible options are the same as those in Step 2 of the preceding steps.

3. **Select the sort order you want to use.**

   Excel redisplays the PivotChart using the new field order.

Adding PivotChart titles

By default, Excel doesn't add titles to your PivotChart. This absence of titles isn't a big deal for most PivotCharts because the field names and item labels often provide enough context to understand the report. However, the data you use may have cryptic field names or coded item names, so the default PivotChart may be difficult to decipher. In that case, you may want to add titles to the PivotChart that make the report more comprehensible.

Excel offers three PivotChart titles:

» An overall chart title that sits above the chart's plot area or is overlaid on the plot area

» A category (*x*) axis title that sits below the category items

» A data series (*y*) axis title that sits to the left of the data series axis labels

You can add one or more of these titles to your PivotChart. And although Excel doesn't allow you to move these titles to a different location, you can play around with the font, border, background, and text alignment.

WARNING The downside to adding PivotChart titles is that most of them take up space in the chart area, which means you have less space to display the PivotChart itself. (The exception is an overall chart title overlaid on the plot area.) This reduced space isn't usually a problem with a simple PivotChart, but if you have a complex chart — particularly if you have a large number of category items — you may prefer not to display titles at all, or you may prefer to display only one or two.

To get the PivotChart title ball rolling, here's how you add an overall chart title:

1. **Select the PivotChart.**
2. **On the Design tab of the ribbon, click Add Chart Element and then click Chart Title.**
3. **Select the type of chart title you want to add.**

    Besides None, you have two choices:

    - **Above Chart:** Places the title above the PivotChart's plot area, centered on the PivotChart
    - **Centered Overlay:** Places the title centered in the PivotChart's plot area

    Excel adds a default title to the PivotChart. The title that Excel adds depends on your data, but it's usually something generic such as "Chart Title" or "Total."

4. **Select the chart title.**
5. **Enter the title you want to use.**
6. **Click outside the chart title to set it.**

Here are the steps to follow to add an axis title:

1. **Select the PivotChart.**
2. **On the Design tab of the ribbon, click Add Chart Element and then click Axis Titles.**
3. **Select the type of chart title you want to add.**

    You have two choices:

    - **Primary Horizontal:** Adds a category (*x*) axis title
    - **Primary Vertical:** Adds a data series (*y*) axis title

    Excel adds a default axis title to the PivotChart. The title that Excel adds is usually something generic, such as "Axis Title."

4. **Select the title.**
5. **Enter the title you want to use.**
6. **Click outside the chart title to set it.**

To format a chart title, select the title, click the Format tab on the ribbon, and then click Format Selection. The task pane that appears offers two tabs:

- **Title Options:** This tab comes with three subtabs: Fill & Line (use the Fill and Border sections to format the title's background and borders), Effects (use the Shadow, Glow, Soft Edges, and 3-D Format sections to apply these effects to the title), and Size & Properties (use the Alignment options to align the title).

- **Text Options:** This tab comes with three subtabs: Text Fill & Outline (use the Text Fill and Text Outline sections to format the title text background and outline), Text Effects (use the Shadow, Reflection, Glow, Soft Edges, 3-D Format, and 3-D Rotation sections to apply these effects to the title text), and Textbox (use the Text Box options to align the title text).

To edit a title, either double-click the title or right-click the title and then select Edit Text.

Excel gives you three methods for removing a title from a PivotChart:

- Follow the steps in this section, and in the menu of title options, select None.
- Right-click the title you want to remove and choose the Delete command.
- Select the title you want to remove and then press the Delete key.

Moving the PivotChart legend

The PivotChart legend displays the series field items along with a colored box that tells you which series belongs to which item. By default, Excel displays the legend to the right of the plot area. This position is usually the best because it doesn't interfere with other chart elements such as titles (which we describe in the preceding section, "Adding PivotChart titles") or the axis labels.

However, displaying the legend on the right does mean that it takes up space that would otherwise be used by your PivotChart. If you have a number of category items in your PivotChart report, you may prefer to display the legend above or below the plot area to give the PivotChart more horizontal room.

Excel enables you to move the legend to one of five positions with respect to the plot area: right, left, bottom, top, and upper-right corner. Excel also gives you the option of having the legend overlapping the chart, which means that Excel doesn't resize the plot area to accommodate the legend. This position is useful if you have some white space on the chart (for example, at the top) where you can place the legend so it doesn't hide any chart data.

CHAPTER 4 **Building PivotCharts** 451

Follow these steps to set the position of the PivotChart legend:

1. **Select the PivotChart.**

2. **On the Design tab of the ribbon, click Add Chart Element and then click Legend.**

   If you want, you can select a predefined legend position: Right, Top, Left, or Bottom.

3. **Select More Legend Options.**

   The Format Legend task pane appears and displays the Legend Options tab.

4. **Click the Legend Options subtab; expand the Legend Options section, if necessary; and then select the radio button for the legend position you want.**

   To display the legend overlapping the chart, deselect the Show the Legend without Overlapping the Chart check box.

   Excel moves the legend to the new position.

In some cases, you may prefer to not display the legend. For example, if your PivotChart doesn't have a series field, Excel still displays a legend for the default "series" named Total. This legend isn't particularly useful, so you can gain some extra chart space by hiding the legend. To do this, follow the preceding Steps 1 and 2 to display the Legend menu and then select None, or right-click the legend and choose Delete.

Displaying a data table with the PivotChart

The point of a PivotChart is to combine the visualization effects of an Excel chart with the pivoting and filtering capabilities of a PivotTable. The visualization part helps your data analysis because it enables you to make at-a-glance comparisons among series and categories, and it enables you to view data points relative to other parts of the report.

If you want to see the underlying data, you can display a data table along with the PivotChart. A *PivotChart data table* displays the chart's categories as columns and its data series as rows, with the cells filled with the actual data values. Because these values appear directly below the chart, the data table gives you an easy way to combine a visual report with the specifics of the underlying data. To display a data table with the PivotChart, follow these steps:

1. **Select the PivotChart.**
2. **On the Design tab of the ribbon, click Add Chart Element and then click Data Table.**

   Select a predefined data table:

   - **With Legend Keys:** Displays the data table with the same colored squares that appear in the legend to identify each series
   - **No Legend Keys:** Displays the data table without the colored squares

   Excel displays the data table below the PivotChart. Figure 4-7 shows an example.

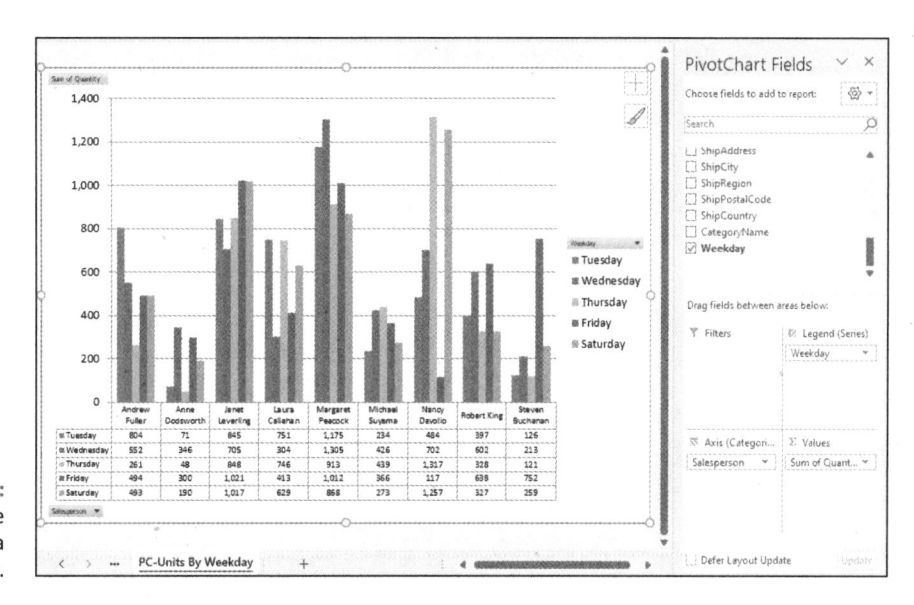

FIGURE 4-7: A data table shown below a PivotChart.

CHAPTER 4 Building PivotCharts 453

6 Reporting and Querying Data

Contents at a Glance

CHAPTER 1: Introducing Power Pivot 457
  Understanding the Power Pivot Internal Data Model 458
  Linking Excel Tables to Power Pivot 460

CHAPTER 2: Advanced Moves with PivotTables 469
  Creating a PivotTable 470
  Customizing PivotTable Reports 476
  Understanding Slicers 488
  Creating a Standard Slicer 490
  Getting Fancy with Slicer Customizations 492
  Controlling Multiple PivotTables with One Slicer 494
  Creating a Timeline Slicer 495

CHAPTER 3: Working Directly with the Internal Data Model 499
  Directly Feeding the Internal Data Model 499
  Managing Relationships in the Internal Data Model 505
  Managing Queries and Connections 506
  Creating a New PivotTable Using the Internal Data Model 506
  Filling the Internal Data Model with Multiple External Data Tables 508

CHAPTER 4: Adding Formulas to Power Pivot 513
  Enhancing Power Pivot Data with Calculated Columns 513
  Utilizing DAX to Create Calculated Columns 518
  Understanding Calculated Measures 526

CHAPTER 5: Meeting Power Query and Its Connection Types 531
  Power Query Basics 532
  Understanding Column-Level Actions 542
  Understanding Table Actions 544
  Importing Data from Files 545
  Importing Data from Database Systems 550
  Managing Data Source Settings 553
  Data Profiling with Power Query 555

> **IN THIS CHAPTER**
> - **Getting to know the internal data model**
> - **Activating the Power Pivot add-in**
> - **Linking to Excel data**
> - **Managing relationships**

Chapter 1
Introducing Power Pivot

Over the past decade or so, corporate managers, eager to turn impossible amounts of data into useful information, drove the business intelligence (BI) industry to innovate new ways of synthesizing data into meaningful insights. During this period, organizations spent lots of time and money implementing big enterprise reporting systems to help keep up with the hunger for data analytics and dashboards.

Recognizing the importance of the BI revolution and the place that Excel holds within it, Microsoft made substantial investments in improving Excel's BI capabilities. It specifically focused on Excel's *self-service* BI capabilities and ability to better manage and analyze information from the increasing number of available data sources.

The key product of that endeavor was Power Pivot (introduced in Excel 2010 as an add-in). With Power Pivot came the ability to set up relationships between large, disparate data sources. For the first time, Excel analysts were able to add a relational view to their reporting without the use of problematic functions such as VLOOKUPS. The ability to merge data sources with hundreds of thousands of rows into one analytical engine within Excel was groundbreaking.

With the release of Excel 2016, Microsoft incorporated Power Pivot directly into Excel. The powerful capabilities of Power Pivot are now available out of the box.

In this chapter, you get an overview of those capabilities by exploring the key features, benefits, and capabilities of Power Pivot.

Understanding the Power Pivot Internal Data Model

At its core, Power Pivot is essentially a SQL Server Analysis Services engine made available by way of an in-memory process that runs directly within Excel. However, in Excel, it's referred to as the internal data model.

Every Excel workbook contains an *internal data model,* a single instance of the Power Pivot in-memory engine. The most effective way to interact with the internal data model is to use the Power Pivot ribbon interface (see Figure 1-1).

FIGURE 1-1:
The Power Pivot ribbon interface.

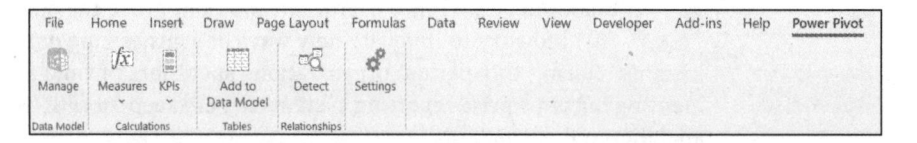

WHERE'S THE POWER PIVOT TAB?

Organizations often install Excel in accordance with their own installation policies. In some organizations, Excel is installed without the Power Pivot add-in activated, so the Power Pivot tab won't be visible. If you don't see the Power Pivot tab shown in Figure 1-1, you can follow these steps to activate it:

1. **On the File tab of the ribbon, click Options.**
2. **Select the Add-Ins option on the left.**
3. **From the Manage drop-down list, select COM Add-Ins and click Go.**

   The COM Add-Ins dialog box opens.

4. **In the list of available COM Add-Ins, check the box next to Microsoft Power Pivot for Excel and click OK.**
5. **If the Power Pivot tab doesn't appear on the ribbon, quit and restart Excel.**

458 BOOK 6 Reporting and Querying Data

The Power Pivot ribbon interface exposes the full set of functionalities you don't get with the standard Excel Data tab. Here are a few examples of functionality available with the Power Pivot interface:

» Browsing, editing, filtering, and applying custom sorting to data
» Creating custom calculated columns that apply to all rows in the data import
» Defining a default number format to use when the field appears in a PivotTable
» Configuring relationships via the handy Graphical Diagram view
» Preventing certain fields from appearing in the PivotTable Field List

As with everything else in Excel, the internal data model does have limitations. Most Excel users won't likely hit these limitations, because Power Pivot's compression algorithm is typically able to shrink imported data to about one-tenth its original size. For example, a 100MB text file would take up only approximately 10MB in the internal data model.

Nevertheless, it's important to understand the maximum and configurable limits for Power Pivot Data Models. Table 1-1 highlights them.

TABLE 1-1 **Limitations of the Internal Data Model**

Object	Specification
Data model size	In 32-bit environments, Excel workbooks are subject to a 2GB limit. This includes the in-memory space shared by Excel, the internal data model, and add-ins that run in the same process.
	In 64-bit environments, there are no hard limits on file size. Workbook size is limited only by available memory and system resources.
Number of tables in the data model	No hard limits exist on the count of tables. However, all tables in the data model can't exceed 2,147,483,647 bytes.
Number of rows in each table in the data model	1,999,999,997
Number of columns and calculated columns in each table in the data model	The number can't exceed 2,147,483,647 bytes.
Number of distinct values in a column	1,999,999,997
Characters in a column name	100 characters
String length in each field	It's limited to 536,870,912 bytes (512MB), which is equivalent to 268,435,456 Unicode characters (256 mega-characters).

A WORD ON COMPATIBILITY

Microsoft has made several versions of Power Pivot available over the years. Different versions of Power Pivot are being used, depending on the version of Excel. Be careful when sharing Power Pivot workbooks in environments where some people are using earlier versions of Excel while others are using more recent versions of Excel. Opening and refreshing a workbook that contains a Power Pivot model created with an older version of the Power Pivot add-in will trigger an automatic upgrade of the underlying model. When this happens, users with older versions of Excel will no longer be able to use the Power Pivot model in the workbook.

Power Pivot workbooks created in a version of Excel that is older than your version should give you no problems. However, you won't be able use Power Pivot workbooks created in a version of Excel newer than your version.

Linking Excel Tables to Power Pivot

The first step in using Power Pivot is to fill it with data. You can either import data from external data sources or link to Excel tables in your current workbook. For now, let's start this walkthrough by looking at how to link three Excel tables to Power Pivot.

TIP The sample file for this chapter is named 6.1.1 Chapter 1 Samples.xlsx. To download this file, go to www.dummies.com/go/microsoft365excelaiofd.

In this scenario, you have three datasets in three different worksheets (see Figure 1-2):

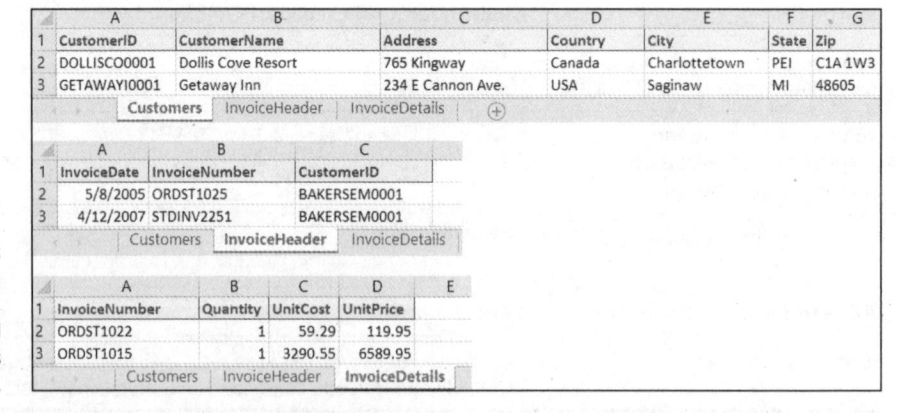

FIGURE 1-2: The Customers, InvoiceHeader, and InvoiceDetails worksheets.

460 BOOK 6 Reporting and Querying Data

- » **Customers:** The Customers dataset contains basic information, such as CustomerID, Customer Name, and Address.
- » **InvoiceHeader:** The InvoiceHeader dataset contains data that points specific invoices to specific customers.
- » **InvoiceDetails:** The InvoiceDetails dataset contains the specifics of each invoice.

To analyze revenue by customer and month, it's clear that you first need to somehow join these three tables together. In the past, you would have to go through a series of gyrations involving VLOOKUP or other clever formulas. But with Power Pivot, you can build these relationships in just a few clicks.

Preparing Excel tables

When linking Excel data to Power Pivot, the best practice is to first convert the Excel data to explicitly named tables. Although not technically necessary, giving tables friendly names will help you track and manage your data in the Power Pivot data model. If you don't convert your data to tables first, Excel does it for you and gives your tables uninformative names like Table1, Table2, and so on.

Follow these steps to convert each dataset into an Excel table:

1. **Click the Customers worksheet and click anywhere inside the data range.**
2. **Press Ctrl+T.**

   The Create Table dialog box, shown in Figure 1-3, opens.

FIGURE 1-3: Converting the data range into an Excel table.

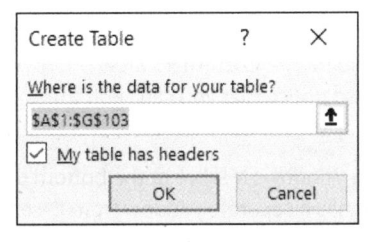

3. **In the Create Table dialog box, make sure that the range for the table is correct and that the My Table Has Headers check box is selected; then click OK.**

   You should now see the Table Design tab on the ribbon.

CHAPTER 1 **Introducing Power Pivot** 461

4. **Click the Table Design tab, and use the Table Name input to give your table a friendly name, as shown in Figure 1-4.**

   This step ensures that you can recognize the table when adding it to the internal data model.

FIGURE 1-4: Giving your newly created Excel table a friendly name.

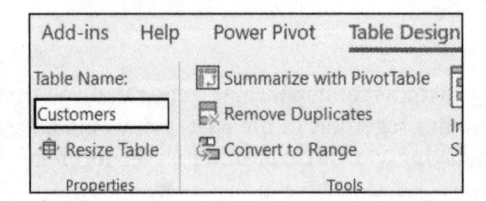

5. **Repeat Steps 1 through 4 for the InvoiceHeader and InvoiceDetails worksheets.**

Adding Excel tables to the data model

After you convert your data to Excel tables, you're ready to add them to the Power Pivot data model. Follow these steps to add the newly created Excel tables to the data model using the Power Pivot tab on the ribbon:

1. **Place the cursor anywhere inside the Customers Excel table.**

2. **Click the Power Pivot tab on the ribbon and click the Add to Data Model command.**

   Power Pivot creates a copy of the table and opens the Power Pivot window, shown in Figure 1-5.

   Although the Power Pivot window looks like Excel, it's a separate program altogether. Notice that the grid for the Customers table offers row numbers but no column references. Also notice that you can't edit the data within the table. This data is simply a snapshot of the Excel table you imported.

   Additionally, if you look at the Windows taskbar at the bottom of the screen, you can see that Power Pivot has a separate window from Excel. You can switch between Excel and the Power Pivot window by clicking each respective program on the taskbar.

   TIP If your Windows taskbar combines taskbar buttons, the Power Pivot button may be hidden with the Excel group of buttons. Click or mouse over the Excel icon on the taskbar to reach the Power Pivot button.

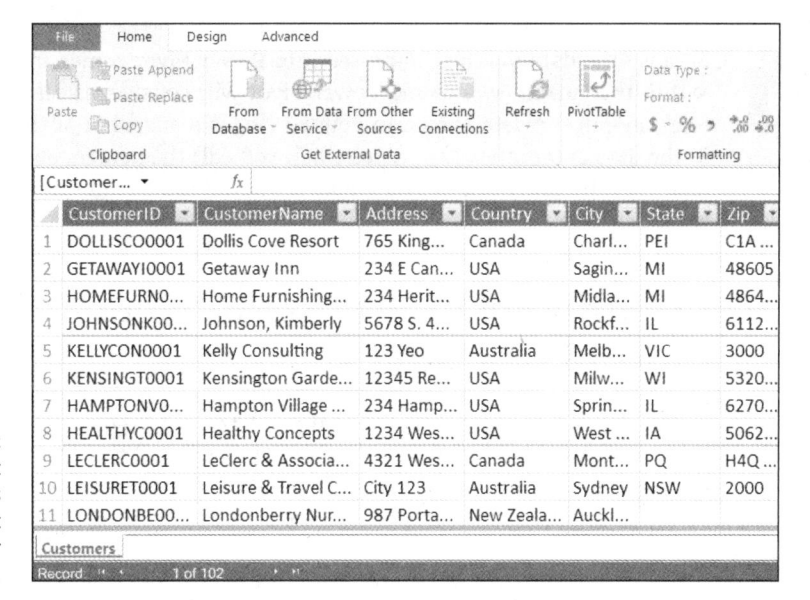

FIGURE 1-5: The Power Pivot window shows all the data that exists in your data model.

3. **Repeat Steps 1 and 2 in the preceding list for your other Excel tables: InvoiceHeader and InvoiceDetails.**

   After you've imported all your Excel tables into the data model, the Power Pivot window shows each dataset on its own tab, as shown in Figure 1-6.

FIGURE 1-6: Each table you add to the data model is placed on its own tab in Power Pivot.

CHAPTER 1 Introducing Power Pivot 463

REMEMBER: Because the data you just imported into Power Pivot comes from an Excel table within the current workbook, Power Pivot will consider these linked tables. So, even though the data shown in Power Pivot is a snapshot at the time you added it, the data automatically updates when you edit the source table in Excel. Linked tables are the only kind of data source that automatically refreshes as the data within changes.

Creating relationships between Power Pivot tables

At this point, Power Pivot knows that you have three tables in the data model but it has no idea how the tables relate to one another. You connect these tables by defining relationships between the Customers, InvoiceDetails, and InvoiceHeader tables. You can do so directly within the Power Pivot window.

TIP: If you've inadvertently closed the Power Pivot window, you can easily reopen it by clicking the Manage command button on the Power Pivot tab of the ribbon.

Follow these steps to create relationships between your tables:

1. **Activate the Power Pivot window and click the Diagram View command button on the Home tab of the Power Pivot window's ribbon.**

   The Power Pivot screen you see shows a visual representation of all tables in the data model, as shown in Figure 1-7.

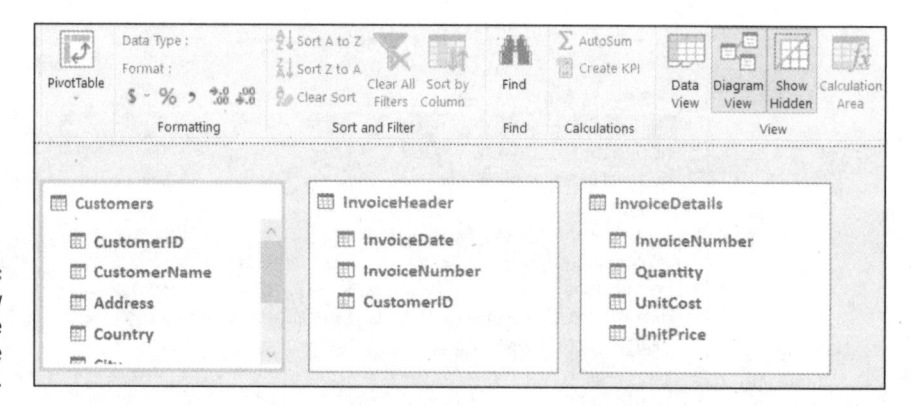

FIGURE 1-7: Diagram view allows you to see all tables in the data model.

You can move the tables in Diagram view simply by clicking and dragging them.

The idea is to identify the primary index keys in each table and connect them. In this scenario, the Customers table and the InvoiceHeader table can be connected using the CustomerID field. The InvoiceHeader and InvoiceDetails tables can be connected using the InvoiceNumber field.

2. **Click and drag a line from the CustomerID field in the Customers table to the CustomerID field in the InvoiceHeader table, as demonstrated in Figure 1-8.**

FIGURE 1-8: To create a relationship, you simply click and drag a line between the fields in your tables.

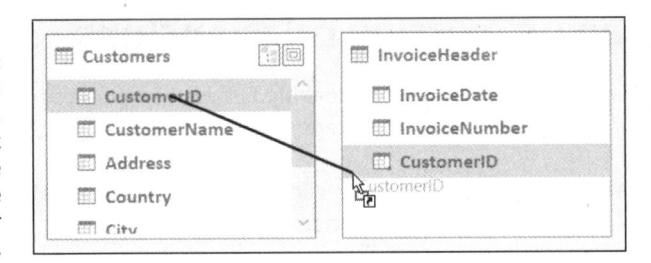

3. **Click and drag a line from the InvoiceNumber field in the InvoiceHeader table to the InvoiceNumber field in the InvoiceDetails table.**

At this point, your diagram will look similar to Figure 1-9. Notice that Power Pivot shows a line between the tables you just connected. In database terms, these are referred to as *joins*.

FIGURE 1-9: When you create relationships, the Power Pivot diagram shows join lines between tables.

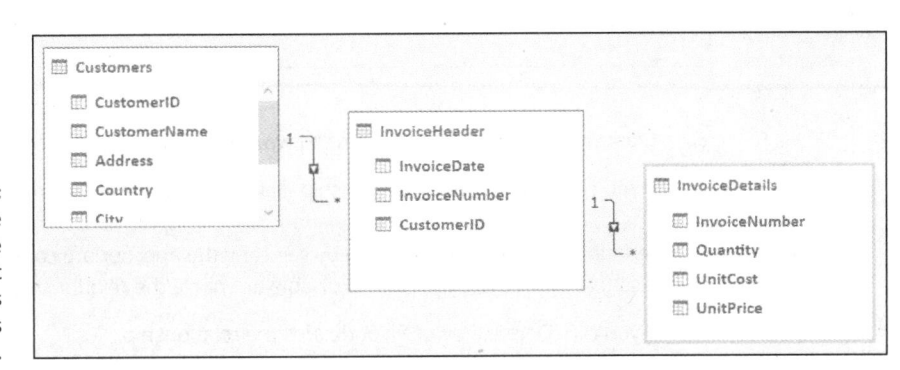

The joins in Power Pivot are always one-to-many joins. This means that when one table is joined to another, one of the tables has unique records with unique index numbers (CustomerID for example), while the other table can have many records where index numbers are duplicated.

CHAPTER 1 Introducing Power Pivot   465

Notice in Figure 1-9 that the join lines have arrows pointing from one table to another table. The arrows in these join lines will always point to the table that has the duplicated index. In this case, the Customers table contains a unique list of customers, each with its own unique identifier. No CustomerID in that table is duplicated. The InvoiceHeader table has many rows for each CustomerID; each customer can have many invoices.

TIP To close the diagram and return to seeing the data tables, click the Data View command in the Power Pivot window.

Managing existing relationships

If you need to edit or delete a relationship between two tables in your data model, you can do so by following these steps:

1. **Open the Power Pivot window, click the Design tab, and select the Manage Relationships command.**

   The Manage Relationships dialog box, shown in Figure 1-10, opens.

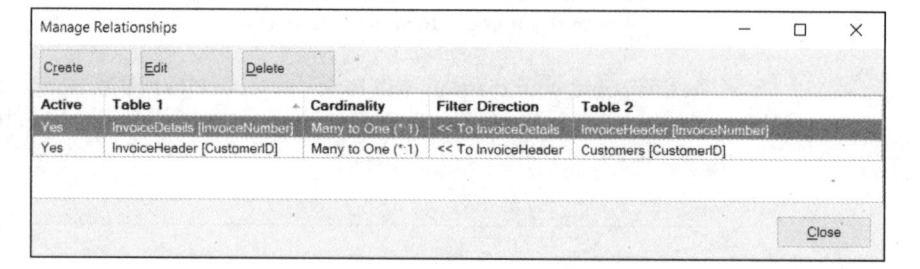

   FIGURE 1-10: Use the Manage Relationships dialog box to edit or delete existing relationships.

2. **Click the relationship you want to work with and click Edit or Delete.**

   If you click Edit, the Edit Relationship dialog box (shown in Figure 1-11) appears. The columns used to form the relationship are highlighted. Here, you can redefine the relationship simply by selecting the appropriate columns. You can also use the Active check box to disable or enable the relationship.

   If you click Delete, Power Pivot deletes the relationship.

REMEMBER In Figure 1-9, you see a graphic of an arrow between the list boxes. The graphic has an asterisk next to the list box on the left, and a number 1 next to the list box on the right. The number 1 basically indicates that the model will use the table listed on the right as the source for a unique primary key.

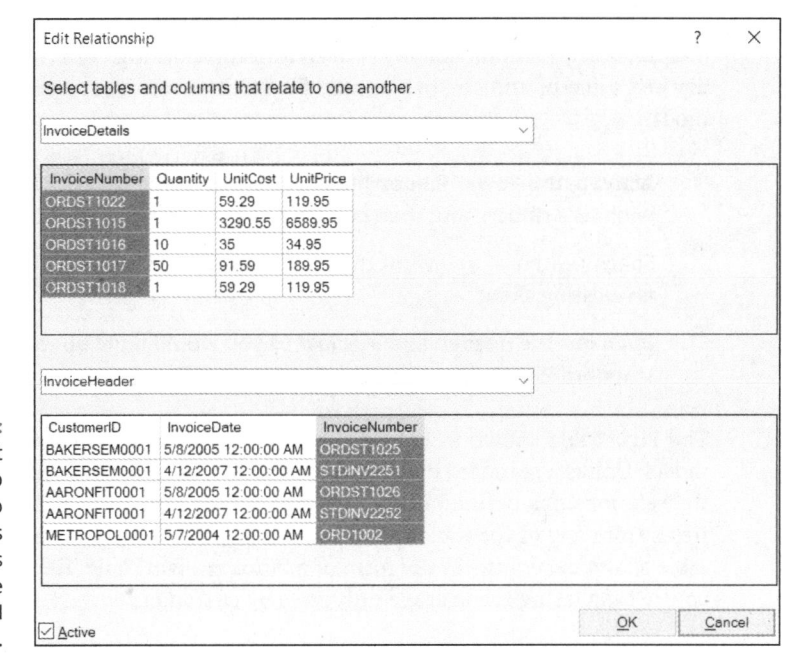

FIGURE 1-11: Use the Edit Relationship dialog box to adjust the tables and field names that define the selected relationship.

Every relationship must have a field that you designate as the primary key. Primary key fields are necessary in the data model to prevent aggregation errors and duplications. In that light, the Excel data model must impose some strict rules around the primary key.

You can't have any duplicates or null values in a field being used as the primary key. So, the Customers table (refer to Figure 1-9) must have all unique values in the CustomerID field, with no blanks or null values. This is the only way that Excel can ensure data integrity when joining multiple tables.

At least one of your tables must contain a field that serves as a primary key — that is, a field that contains only unique values and no blanks.

Using the Power Pivot data model in reporting

After you define the relationships in your Power Pivot data model, the data model is essentially ready for action. In terms of Power Pivot, *action* means analysis with a PivotTable. In fact, all Power Pivot data is presented through the framework of PivotTables.

Chapter 2 of this minibook dives deep into the workings of PivotTables. For now, dip just a toe in and create a simple PivotTable from your new Power Pivot data model:

1. **Activate the Power Pivot window, click the Home tab of the Power Pivot window's ribbon, and then click the PivotTable command button.**

2. **Specify whether you want the PivotTable placed on a new worksheet or an existing sheet.**

3. **Build out the needed analysis just as you would build out any other standard PivotTable, using the Pivot Field List.**

The PivotTable shown in Figure 1-12 contains all tables in the Power Pivot data model. Unlike a standard PivotTable, where you can use fields from only one table, the relationships defined in the internal data model allow you to use any of the fields from any of the tables. With this configuration, you have a powerful cross-table analytical engine in the form of a familiar PivotTable. Here, you can see that you're calculating the average unit price by customer.

FIGURE 1-12:
You now have a Power Pivot–driven PivotTable that aggregates across multiple tables.

CustomerName	Average of UnitPrice
Aaron Fitz Electrical	$272
Adam Park Resort	$640
Advanced Paper Co.	$192
Advanced Tech Satellite System	$63
American Science Museum	$157
Associated Insurance Company	$325
Astor Suites	$1,583
Atmore Retirement Center	$40
Baker's Emporium Inc.	$601
Blue Yonder Airlines	$856
Boyle's Country Inns	$610
Breakthrough Telemarketing	$864
Castle Inn Resort	$120
Central Communications LTD	$769
Central Distributing	$125
Central Illinois Hospital	$1,705
Communication Connections	$127
Computerized Phone Systems	$120
Contoso, Ltd.	$8,912
Country View Estates	$129

In the days before Power Pivot, this analysis would've been a bear to create. You would've had to build VLOOKUP formulas to get from CustomerNumber to InvoiceNumber, and then another set of VLOOKUP formulas to get from Invoice-Number to InvoiceDetails. And after all that formula building, you still would've had to find a way to aggregate the data to the average unit price per customer.

IN THIS CHAPTER

» **Building a PivotTable**

» **Creating top and bottom reports**

» **Understanding, creating, and formatting slicers**

» **Sprucing up slicers with customization**

» **Controlling multiple PivotTables with slicers**

» **Using timeline slicers**

Chapter **2**

Advanced Moves with PivotTables

When creating Power Pivot data models, you have to use some form of PivotTable structure to expose the data in those models available to your audience. As we explain in Book 5, Chapter 2, a PivotTable is a powerful tool that enables you to create a PivotTable report, an interactive view of a dataset. The PivotTable report enables you to quickly and easily categorize your data into groups, summarize large amounts of data into meaningful analyses, and interactively perform a wide variety of calculations.

This chapter gives you the fundamental understanding you need in order to analyze and report on the data in your Power Pivot data model.

> **TIP** This chapter uses two sample files, a workbook named 6.2.1 Chapter 2 Samples.xlsx and a workbook named 6.2.2 Chapter 2 Slicers.xlsx. To download these files, go to www.dummies.com/go/microsoft365excelaiofd.

CHAPTER 2 Advanced Moves with PivotTables   469

Creating a PivotTable

To get started, open `6.2.1 Chapter 2 Samples.xlsx` and create a PivotTable in it. Then follow these steps:

1. **Click any single cell inside the data source, the table you use to feed the PivotTable.**

   If you're following along, the data source is the table found on the Sample Data tab.

2. **Click the Insert tab of the ribbon.**

3. **Click the PivotTable button in the Tables group.**

   TIP It's easiest to click the icon at the top of the button, but you can also click the drop-down arrow and then click From Table/Range on the drop-down list.

   The PivotTable from Table or Range dialog box, shown in Figure 2-1, opens. As you can see, this dialog box asks you to specify the location of the source data and the place where you want to put the PivotTable.

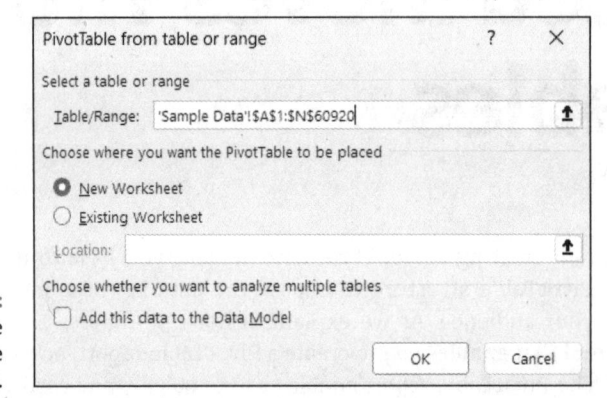

FIGURE 2-1:
The Create PivotTable dialog box.

REMEMBER Notice that in the PivotTable from Table or Range dialog box, Excel tries to fill in the range of your data for you. In most cases, Excel gets this right. However, always make sure that the correct range is selected.

Also note in Figure 2-1 that the default location for a new PivotTable is New Worksheet. This means your PivotTable is placed in a new worksheet within the current workbook. You can change this by selecting the Existing Worksheet option and specifying the worksheet where you want the PivotTable placed.

4. **Click OK.**

   At this point, you have an empty PivotTable report on a new worksheet. Next to the empty PivotTable, you see the PivotTable Fields task pane, shown in Figure 2-2.

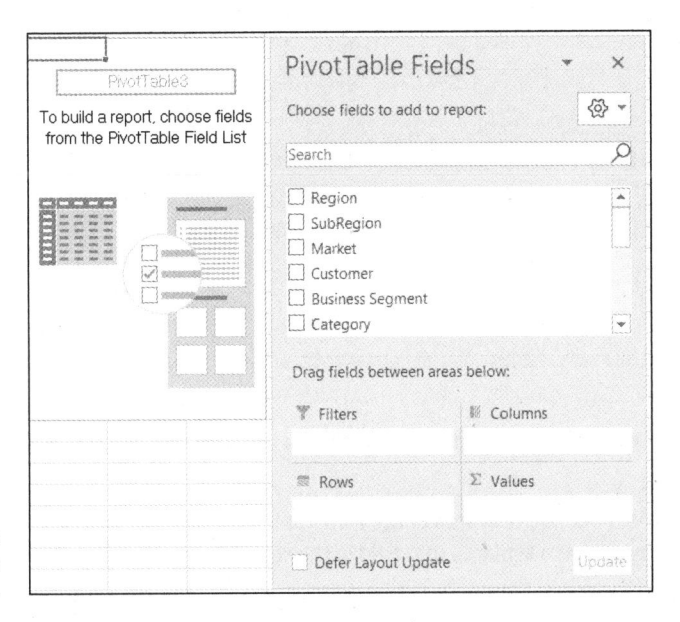

FIGURE 2-2: The PivotTable Fields task pane.

The idea here is to add the fields you need into the PivotTable by using the four drop zones found in the PivotTable Fields task pane — Filters, Columns, Rows, and Values — thus adding the fields to the four areas of the PivotTable.

TIP

If clicking the PivotTable doesn't open the PivotTable Fields task pane, you can manually open it by right-clicking anywhere inside the PivotTable and selecting Show Field List.

Now, before you go wild and start dropping fields into the various drop zones, ask yourself two questions: "What am I measuring?" and "How do I want to see it?" The answers to these questions will give you some guidance when determining which fields go where.

For the sample PivotTable report, measure the dollar sales by market. This automatically tells you that you need to work with the Sales Amount field and the Market field.

How do you want to see that? You want markets to be listed down the left side of the report and the sales amount to be calculated next to each market. Remembering the four areas of the PivotTable, you need to add the Market field to the Rows drop zone and add the Sales Amount field to the Values drop zone.

CHAPTER 2 **Advanced Moves with PivotTables** 471

5. **Select the Market check box in the list, as shown in Figure 2-3.**

   Now that you have regions in the PivotTable, it's time to add the dollar sales.

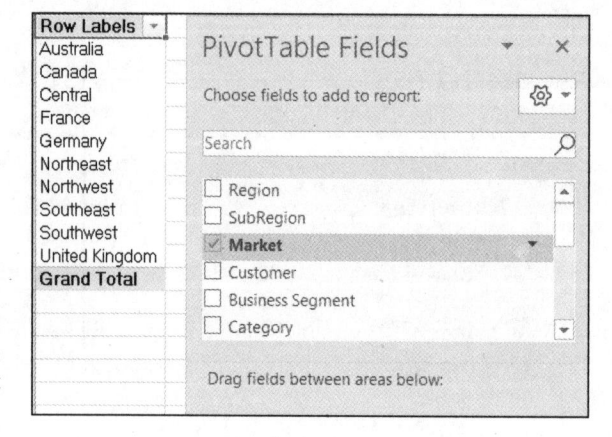

   FIGURE 2-3: Select the Market check box.

6. **Select the Sales Amount check box in the list, as shown in Figure 2-4.**

   TIP

   Selecting a check box that is *nonnumeric* (text or date) automatically places that field into the row area of the PivotTable. Selecting a check box that is *numeric* automatically places that field in the values area of the PivotTable.

   What happens if you need fields in the other areas of the PivotTable? Well, instead of selecting the field's check box, you can drag any field directly to the different drop zones.

   One more thing: When you add fields to the drop zones, you may find it difficult to see all the fields in each drop zone. You can expand the PivotTable Fields dialog box by clicking and dragging the borders of the dialog box.

   FIGURE 2-4: Add the Sales Amount field by selecting its check box.

472 BOOK 6 **Reporting and Querying Data**

As you can see, you've analyzed the sales for each market in just five steps! That's an amazing feat, considering that you started with more than 60,000 rows of data. With a little formatting, this modest PivotTable can become the starting point for a management report.

Changing and rearranging a PivotTable

Now, here's the wonderful thing about PivotTables: You can add as many layers of analysis as made possible by the fields in the source data table. Say you want to show the dollar sales that each market earned by business segment. Because the PivotTable already contains the Market and Sales Amount fields, all you have to add is the Business Segment field.

So, simply click anywhere on the PivotTable to reopen the PivotTable Fields task pane, and then select the Business Segment check box. Figure 2-5 illustrates what the PivotTable should look like now.

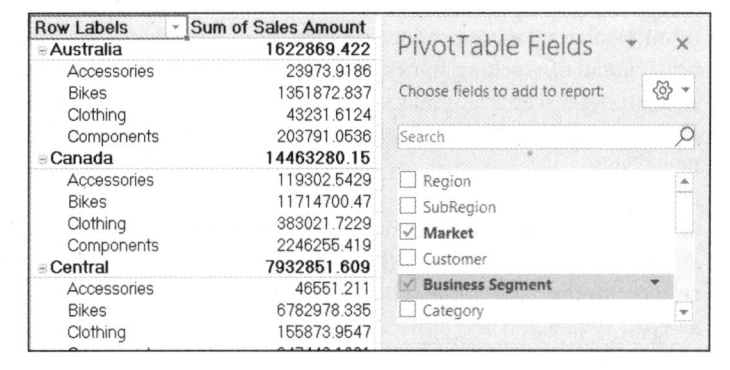

FIGURE 2-5:
Adding a layer of analysis is as easy as bringing in another field.

TIP If clicking the PivotTable doesn't open the PivotTable Fields task pane, you can manually open it by right-clicking anywhere inside the PivotTable and selecting Show Field List.

Imagine that your manager says that this layout doesn't work for them. They want to see business segments displayed across the top of the PivotTable report. No problem: Simply drag the Business Segment field from the Rows drop zone to the Columns drop zone. As you can see in Figure 2-6, this instantly restructures the PivotTable to your manager's specifications.

CHAPTER 2 Advanced Moves with PivotTables   473

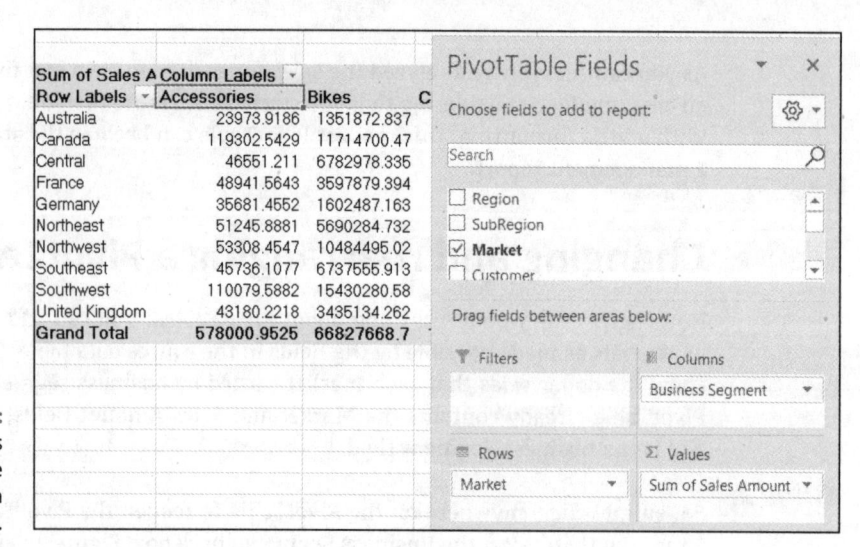

FIGURE 2-6: Your business segments are now column oriented.

Adding a report filter

Often, you're asked to produce reports for one particular region, market, or product. Instead of working hours and hours building separate reports for every possible analysis scenario, you can leverage PivotTables to help create multiple views of the same data. For example, you can do so by creating a region filter in the PivotTable.

Click anywhere inside the PivotTable to reopen the PivotTable Fields task pane, and then drag the Region field to the Filters drop zone. This adds a drop-down selector to the PivotTable, shown in cell B1 in Figure 2-7. You can then use this selector to analyze one particular region at a time.

Keeping the PivotTable fresh

In Hollywood, it's important to stay fresh and relevant. As boring as the Pivot-Tables may seem, they'll eventually become the stars of your reports. So, it's just as important to keep your PivotTables fresh and relevant.

As time goes by, your data may change and grow with newly added rows and columns. The action of updating your PivotTable with these changes is *refreshing* your data.

The PivotTable report can be refreshed simply by right-clicking inside the Pivot-Table report and selecting Refresh, as shown in Figure 2-8.

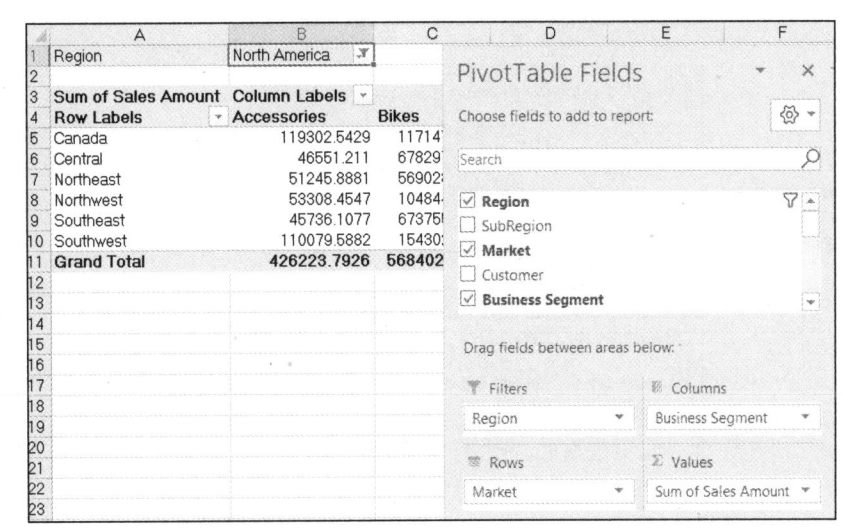

FIGURE 2-7:
Adding Region to the Filters drop zone displays a Region drop-down list in cell B2.

FIGURE 2-8:
Refreshing the PivotTable captures changes made to your data.

Sometimes, *you're* the data source that feeds your PivotTable changes in structure. For example, you may have added or deleted rows or columns from the data table. These types of changes affect the range of the data source, not just a few data items in the table.

In these cases, performing a simple Refresh of the PivotTable won't do. You have to update the range being captured by the PivotTable. Here's how:

1. **Click anywhere inside the PivotTable to select the PivotTable Analyze tab of the ribbon.**
2. **Click Change Data Source, as shown in Figure 2-9.**

    The Change PivotTable Data Source dialog box opens.

3. **Change the range selection to include any new rows or columns (see Figure 2-10).**
4. **Click OK.**

CHAPTER 2 Advanced Moves with PivotTables   475

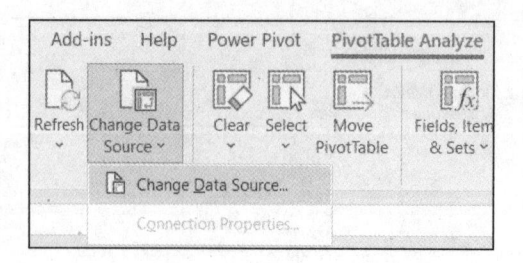

FIGURE 2-9: Changing the range that feeds the PivotTable.

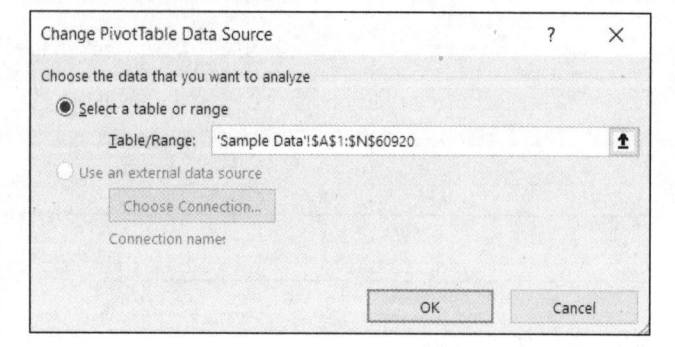

FIGURE 2-10: Select the new range that feeds the PivotTable.

Customizing PivotTable Reports

The PivotTables you create often need to be tweaked to get the look and feel you're looking for. In this section, we cover some of the options you can adjust to customize your PivotTables to suit your reporting needs.

Changing the PivotTable layout

Excel gives you a choice in the layout of the data in a PivotTable. The three layouts, shown side by side in Figure 2-11, are the Compact Form, Outline Form, and Tabular Form. Although no layout stands out as better than the others, we prefer using the Tabular Form layout because it seems easiest to read and it's the layout that most people who have seen PivotTables are used to.

The layout you choose affects not only the look and feel of your reporting mechanisms but also, possibly, the way you build and interact with any reporting models based on your PivotTables.

FIGURE 2-11:
The three layouts for a PivotTable report.

Compact Form Layout		Outline Form Layout			Tabular Form Layout		
Row Labels	Sales	Market	Segment	Sales	Market	Segment	Sales
⊟Australia	1622869.422	⊟Australia		1622869.422	⊟Australia	Accessories	23973.9186
Accessories	23973.9186		Accessories	23973.9186		Bikes	1351872.837
Bikes	1351872.837		Bikes	1351872.837		Clothing	43231.6124
Clothing	43231.6124		Clothing	43231.6124		Components	203791.0536
Components	203791.0536		Components	203791.0536	Australia Total		1622869.422
⊟Canada	14463280.15	⊟Canada		14463280.15	⊟Canada	Accessories	119302.5429
Accessories	119302.5429		Accessories	119302.5429		Bikes	11714700.47
Bikes	11714700.47		Bikes	11714700.47		Clothing	383021.7229
Clothing	383021.7229		Clothing	383021.7229		Components	2246255.419
Components	2246255.419		Components	2246255.419	Canada Total		14463280.15
⊟Central	7932851.609	⊟Central		7932851.609	⊟Central	Accessories	46551.211
Accessories	46551.211		Accessories	46551.211		Bikes	6782978.335
Bikes	6782978.335		Bikes	6782978.335		Clothing	155873.9547
Clothing	155873.9547		Clothing	155873.9547		Components	947448.1091
Components	947448.1091		Components	947448.1091	Central Total		7932851.609
⊟France	4647454.207	⊟France		4647454.207	⊟France	Accessories	48941.5643
Accessories	48941.5643		Accessories	48941.5643		Bikes	3597879.394
Bikes	3597879.394		Bikes	3597879.394		Clothing	129508.0548
Clothing	129508.0548		Clothing	129508.0548		Components	871125.1938
Components	871125.1938		Components	871125.1938	France Total		4647454.207
⊟Germany	2051547.729	⊟Germany		2051547.729	⊟Germany	Accessories	35681.4552
Accessories	35681.4552		Accessories	35681.4552		Bikes	1602487.163
Bikes	1602487.163		Bikes	1602487.163		Clothing	75592.5945
Clothing	75592.5945		Clothing	75592.5945		Components	337786.516
Components	337786.516		Components	337786.516	Germany Total		2051547.729

Changing the layout of a PivotTable is easy. Follow these steps:

1. **Click anywhere inside the PivotTable.**
2. **Click the Design tab of the ribbon.**
3. **Click the Report Layout icon and choose the layout you like (see Figure 2-12).**

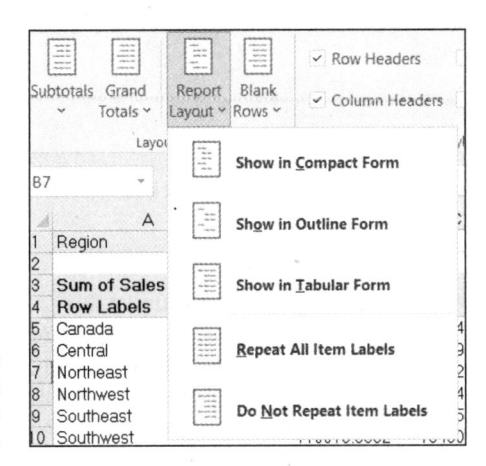

FIGURE 2-12: Changing the layout of the PivotTable.

CHAPTER 2 **Advanced Moves with PivotTables** 477

Customizing field names

Notice that every field in the PivotTable has a name. The fields in the row, column, and filter areas inherit their names from the data labels in the source table. The fields in the values area are given a name, such as Sum of Sales Amount.

Sometimes you may prefer the name Total Sales instead of the unattractive default name, such as Sum of Sales Amount. In these situations, the ability to change your field names comes in handy. To change a field name, follow these steps:

1. **Right-click any value within the target field.**

   For example, if you want to change the name of the field Sum of Sales Amount, right-click the field name, or any value under that field.

2. **Select Value Field Settings, as shown in Figure 2-13.**

   The Value Field Settings dialog box opens.

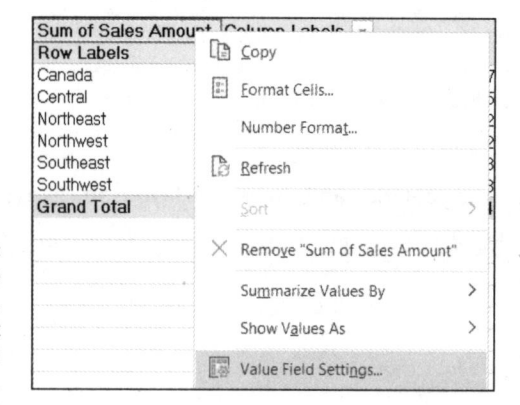

FIGURE 2-13: Right-click the target field, and then select the Value Field Settings option.

3. **Enter the new name in the Custom Name text box, shown in Figure 2-14.**
4. **Click OK.**

TIP If you use the name of the data label used in the source table, you receive an error. For example, if you rename Sum of Sales Amount as Sales Amount, you see an error message because there's already a Sales Amount field in the source data table. Well, this is kind of lame, especially if Sales Amount is exactly what you want to name the field in your PivotTable.

To get around this, you can name the field and add a space to the end of the name. Excel considers Sales Amount (followed by a space) to be different from Sales Amount. This way, you can use the name you want, and no one will notice that it's any different.

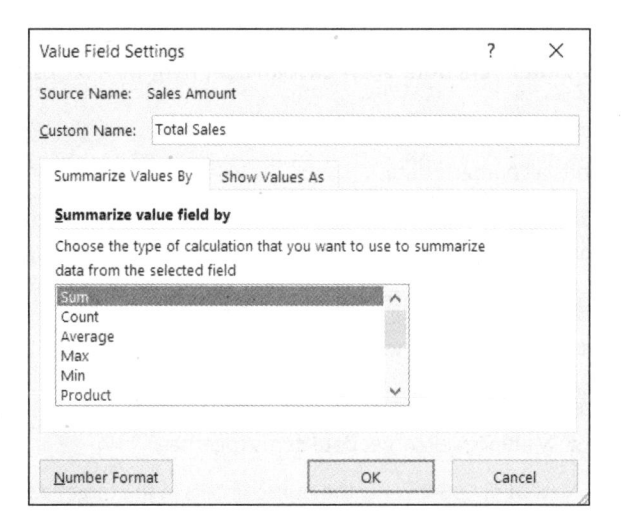

FIGURE 2-14: Type the new name of the field in the Custom Name text box.

Applying numeric formats to data fields

Numbers in PivotTables can be formatted to fit your needs (that is, formatted as currency, percentage, or number). You can easily control the numeric formatting of a field using the Value Field Settings dialog box. Here's how:

1. **Right-click the target field's name or any value within the target field.**

   For example, if you want to change the format of the values in the Sales Amount field, right-click the field name or any value under that field.

2. **Select Value Field Settings.**

   The Value Field Settings dialog box opens.

3. **Click the Number Format button.**

   The Format Cells dialog box opens.

4. **Apply the number format you desire, just as you typically would on your spreadsheet.**

5. **Click OK.**

   After you set the formatting for a field, the applied formatting persists, even if you refresh or rearrange the PivotTable.

Changing summary calculations

When creating the PivotTable report, Excel, by default, summarizes your data by counting or summing the items. Instead of choosing Sum or Count, you may want

CHAPTER 2 **Advanced Moves with PivotTables** 479

to choose another function, such as Average, Min, or Max. In all, 11 options are available:

- **Sum:** Adds all numeric data.
- **Count:** Counts all data items within a given field, including numeric-, text-, and date-formatted cells.
- **Average:** Calculates an average for the target data items.
- **Max:** Displays the largest value in the target data items.
- **Min:** Displays the smallest value in the target data items.
- **Product:** Multiplies all target data items together.
- **Count Numbers:** Counts only the numeric cells in the target data items.
- **StdDevP and StdDev:** Calculates the standard deviation for the target data items. Use StdDevP if your dataset contains the complete population. Use StdDev if your dataset contains a sample of the population.
- **VarP and Var:** Calculates the statistical variance for the target data items. Use VarP if your data contains a complete population. If your data contains only a sampling of the complete population, use Var to estimate the variance.

You can easily change the summary calculation for any given field by taking the following actions:

1. **Right-click any value within the target field.**
2. **Select Value Field Settings.**

   The Value Field Settings dialog box opens.
3. **Choose the type of calculation you want to use from the list of calculations (see Figure 2-15).**
4. **Click OK.**

REMEMBER: Did you know that a single blank cell causes Excel to count instead of sum? That's right: If all cells in a column contain numeric data, Excel chooses Sum. If only one cell is either blank or contains text, Excel chooses Count.

Pay attention to the fields that you place into the values area of the PivotTable. If the field name starts with *Count Of*, Excel is counting the items in the field instead of summing the values.

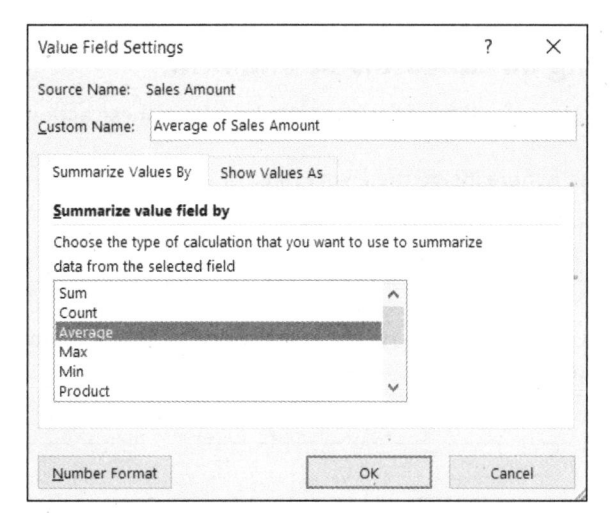

FIGURE 2-15: Changing the type of summary calculation used in a field.

Suppressing subtotals

Notice that every time you add a field to the PivotTable, Excel adds a subtotal for that field. At times, however, the inclusion of subtotals either doesn't make sense or simply hinders a clear view of the PivotTable report. For example, Figure 2-16 shows a PivotTable in which the subtotals inundate the report with totals that hide the real data you're trying to report.

FIGURE 2-16: Subtotals sometimes muddle the data you're trying to show.

	A	B	C	D	E
1	Region	SubRegion	Market	Business Segment	Sum of Sales Amount
2	⊟North America	⊟United States	⊟Central	Accessories	46,551
3				Bikes	6,782,978
4				Clothing	155,874
5				Components	947,448
6			Central Total		7,932,852
7			⊟Northeast	Accessories	51,246
8				Bikes	5,690,285
9				Clothing	163,442
10				Components	1,051,702
11			Northeast Total		6,956,674
12			⊟Northwest	Accessories	53,308
13				Bikes	10,484,495
14				Clothing	201,052
15				Components	1,784,207
16			Northwest Total		12,523,063
17			⊟Southeast	Accessories	45,736
18				Bikes	6,737,556
19				Clothing	165,689
20				Components	959,337
21			Southeast Total		7,908,318
22			⊟Southwest	Accessories	110,080
23				Bikes	15,430,281
24				Clothing	364,099
25				Components	2,693,568
26			Southwest Total		18,598,027
27		United States Total			53,918,934
28	North America Total				53,918,934

CHAPTER 2 **Advanced Moves with PivotTables** 481

Removing all subtotals at one time

You can remove all subtotals at one time by taking these actions:

1. **Click anywhere inside the PivotTable.**
2. **Click the Design tab of the ribbon.**
3. **Click the Subtotals icon and select Do Not Show Subtotals.**

As you can see in Figure 2-17, the same report without subtotals is much more pleasant to review.

	A	B	C	D	E
1	Region	SubRegion	Market	Business Segment	Sum of Sales Amount
2	North America	United States	Central	Accessories	46,551
3				Bikes	6,782,978
4				Clothing	155,874
5				Components	947,448
6			Northeast	Accessories	51,246
7				Bikes	5,690,285
8				Clothing	163,442
9				Components	1,051,702
10			Northwest	Accessories	53,308
11				Bikes	10,484,495
12				Clothing	201,052
13				Components	1,784,207
14			Southeast	Accessories	45,736
15				Bikes	6,737,556
16				Clothing	165,689
17				Components	959,337
18			Southwest	Accessories	110,080
19				Bikes	15,430,281
20				Clothing	364,099
21				Components	2,693,568
22	Grand Total				53,918,934

FIGURE 2-17: The report shown in Figure 2-16, without subtotals.

Removing the subtotals for only one field

Maybe you want to remove the subtotals for only one field? In such a case, you can take the following actions:

1. **Right-click any value within the target field.**
2. **Select Field Settings.**

    The Field Settings dialog box opens.

3. **Select the None radio button under Subtotals, as shown in Figure 2-18.**
4. **Click OK.**

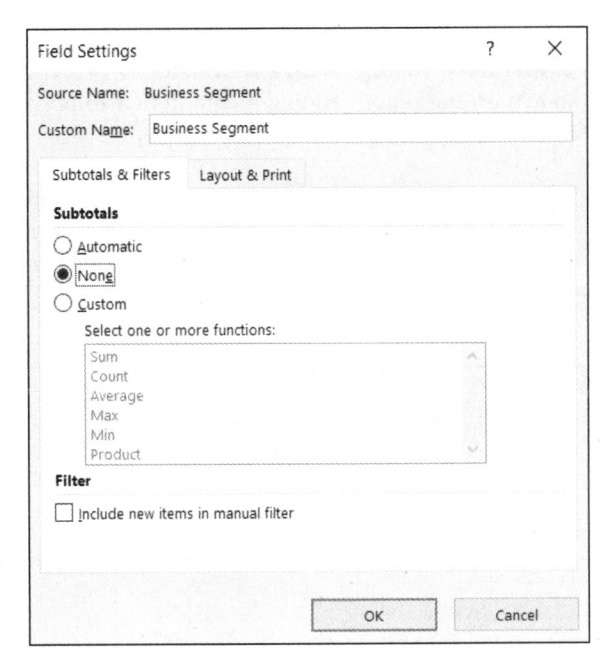

FIGURE 2-18: Select the None radio button in the Field Settings dialog box to remove subtotals for one field.

Removing grand totals

In certain instances, you may want to remove the grand totals from the PivotTable. Follow these steps:

1. **Right-click anywhere on the PivotTable.**
2. **Select PivotTable Options.**

   The PivotTable Options dialog box opens.

3. **Click the Totals & Filters tab.**
4. **Deselect the Show Grand Totals for Rows check box.**
5. **Deselect the Show Grand Totals for Columns check box.**
6. **Click OK.**

Showing and hiding data items

A PivotTable summarizes and displays all records in a source data table. In certain situations, however, you may want to prevent certain data items from being included in the PivotTable summary. In these situations, you can choose to hide a data item.

CHAPTER 2 **Advanced Moves with PivotTables** 483

In terms of PivotTables, hiding doesn't mean simply preventing the data item from being shown on the report. Hiding a data item also prevents it from being factored into the summary calculations.

In the PivotTable shown in Figure 2-19, we show sales amounts for all business segments by market. In this example, we want to show totals without taking sales from the Bikes segment into consideration. In other words, we want to hide the Bikes segment.

	A	B	C
1	Market	Business Segment	Sum of Sales Amount
2	⊟Australia	Accessories	$23,974
3		Bikes	$1,351,873
4		Clothing	$43,232
5		Components	$203,791
6	Australia Total		$1,622,869
7	⊟Canada	Accessories	$119,303
8		Bikes	$11,714,700
9		Clothing	$383,022
10		Components	$2,246,255
11	Canada Total		$14,463,280
12	⊟Central	Accessories	$46,551
13		Bikes	$6,782,978
14		Clothing	$155,874
15		Components	$947,448
16	Central Total		$7,932,852
17	⊟France	Accessories	$48,942

FIGURE 2-19: To remove Bikes from this analysis . . .

You can hide the Bikes Business Segment by clicking the Business Segment drop-down arrow and deselecting the Bikes check box, as shown in Figure 2-20.

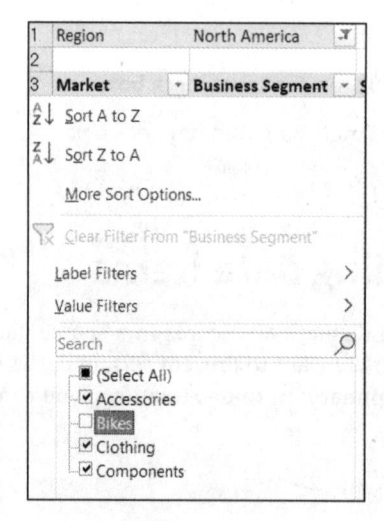

FIGURE 2-20: . . . deselect the Bikes check box.

484   BOOK 6 **Reporting and Querying Data**

After you click OK to close the selection box, the PivotTable instantly recalculates, leaving out the Bikes segment. As you can see in Figure 2-21, the Market total sales now reflect the sales without Bikes.

	A	B	C
1	Market	Business Segment	Sum of Sales Amount
2	⊟Australia	Accessories	$23,974
3		Clothing	$43,232
4		Components	$203,791
5	Australia Total		$270,997
6	⊟Canada	Accessories	$119,303
7		Clothing	$383,022
8		Components	$2,246,255
9	Canada Total		$2,748,580
10	⊟Central	Accessories	$46,551
11		Clothing	$155,874
12		Components	$947,448
13	Central Total		$1,149,873
14	⊟France	Accessories	$48,942

FIGURE 2-21: The analysis from Figure 2-19, without the Bikes segment.

You can just as quickly reinstate all hidden data items for the field. Just click the Business Segment drop-down arrow and select the Select All check box.

Hiding or showing items without data

By default, the PivotTable shows only data items that have data. This inherent behavior may cause unintended problems for your data analysis.

Look at Figure 2-22, which shows a PivotTable with the SalesPeriod field in the row area and the Region field in the filter area. Note that the Region field is set to (All) and that every sales period appears in the report.

	A	B
1	Region	(All)
2		
3	SalesPeriod	Sum of Sales Amount
4	01/01/08	$713,230
5	02/01/08	$1,900,797
6	03/01/08	$1,455,282
7	04/01/08	$883,011
8	05/01/08	$2,269,722
9	06/01/08	$1,137,250
10	07/01/08	$2,411,569
11	08/01/08	$3,615,926

FIGURE 2-22: All sales periods are showing.

If you choose Europe in the filter area, only a portion of all the sales periods is shown (see Figure 2-23). The PivotTable shows only those sales periods that have data for the Europe region.

	A	B
1	Region	Europe
2		
3	SalesPeriod	Sum of Sales Amount
4	07/01/08	$180,241
5	08/01/08	$448,373
6	09/01/08	$373,122
7	10/01/08	$119,384
8	11/01/08	$330,026
9	12/01/08	$254,011
10	01/01/09	$71,313

FIGURE 2-23: Filtering for the Europe region causes certain sales periods to disappear.

From a reporting perspective, it isn't ideal if half the year's data disappears every time customers select Europe.

Here's how you can prevent Excel from hiding pivot items without data:

1. **Right-click any value within the target field.**

   In this example, the target field is the SalesPeriod field.

2. **Select Field Settings.**

   The Field Settings dialog box opens.

3. **Select the Layout & Print tab in the Field Settings dialog box.**
4. **Select the Show Items with No Data radio button, as shown in Figure 2-24.**
5. **Click OK.**

As you can see in Figure 2-25, after you select the Show Items with No Data radio button, all sales periods appear whether the selected region had sales that period or not.

Now that you're confident that the structure of the PivotTable is locked, you can use it to feed charts and other components on your report.

Sorting the PivotTable

By default, items in each pivot field are sorted in ascending sequence based on the item name. Excel gives you the freedom to change the sort order of the items in the PivotTable.

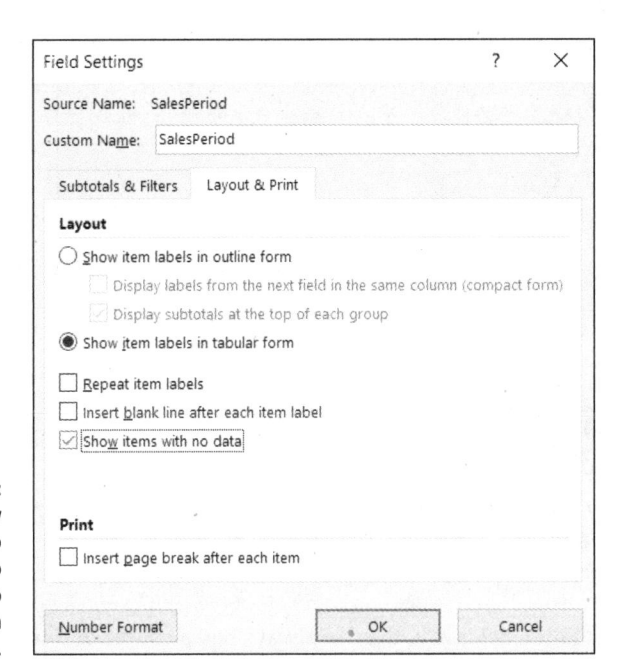

FIGURE 2-24: Select the Show Items with No Data option to force Excel to display all data items.

FIGURE 2-25: All sales periods are now displayed, even if there is no data to be shown.

Like many actions you can perform in Excel, you have lots of different ways to sort data within a PivotTable. The easiest way is to apply the sort directly in the PivotTable. Here's how:

1. **Right-click any value within the target field, the field you need to sort.**

   In the example shown in Figure 2-26, you want to sort by Sales Amount.

2. **Select Sort and then select the sort direction.**

   The changes take effect immediately and persist while you work with the PivotTable.

CHAPTER 2 Advanced Moves with PivotTables   487

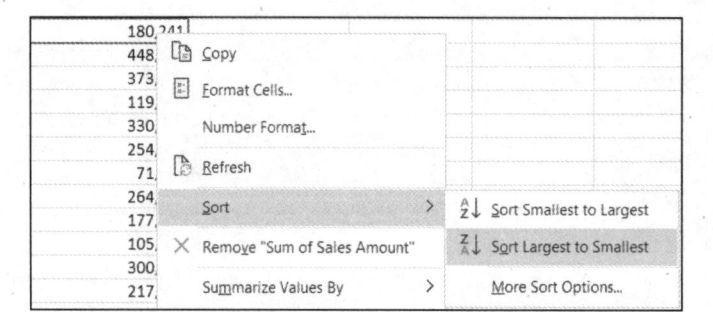

FIGURE 2-26: Applying a sort to a PivotTable field.

Understanding Slicers

Slicers allow you to filter your PivotTable in a way that's similar to the way Filter fields filter a PivotTable. The difference is that slicers offer a user-friendly interface, enabling you to better manage the filter state of your PivotTable reports.

As useful as Filter fields are, they've always had a couple of drawbacks:

» **Filter fields are not cascading filters — the filters don't work together to limit selections when needed.** For example, in Figure 2-27, you can see that the Region filter is set to the North America region. However, the Market filter still allows you to select markets that are clearly not in the North America region (Germany, for example). Because the Market filter is not in any way limited based on the Region Filter field, you have the annoying possibility of selecting a market that could yield no data because it's not in the North America region.

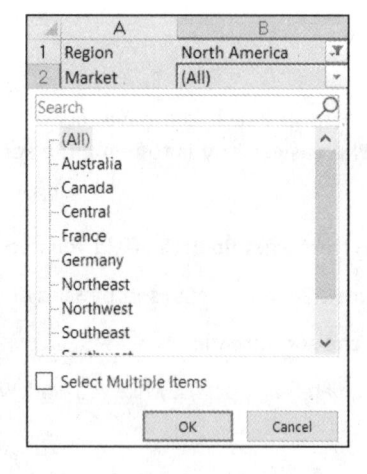

FIGURE 2-27: Default PivotTable Filter fields do not work together to limit filter selections.

488 BOOK 6 **Reporting and Querying Data**

» **Filter fields don't provide an easy way to tell what exactly is being filtered when you select multiple items.** In Figure 2-28, you can see an example. The Market filter has been limited to four markets. However, notice that the Market filter value shows (Multiple Items). By default, Filter fields show (Multiple Items) when you select more than one item. The only way to tell what has been selected is to click the drop-down list. You can imagine the confusion on a printed version of this report, in which you can't click down to see which data items make up the numbers on the page.

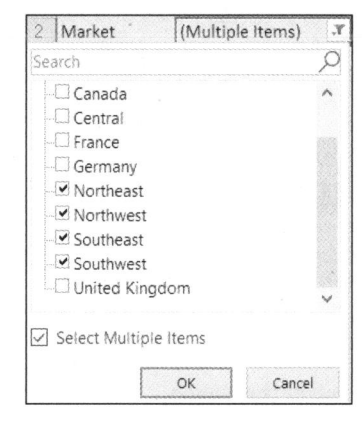

FIGURE 2-28: Filter fields show the phrase (Multiple Items) whenever multiple selections are made.

By contrast, slicers don't have these issues. Slicers respond to one another. As you can see in Figure 2-29, the Market slicer visibly highlights the relevant markets when the North America region is selected. The rest of the markets are dimmed, signaling that they aren't part of the selected region.

FIGURE 2-29: Slicers work together to show you relevant data items based on your selection.

CHAPTER 2 **Advanced Moves with PivotTables** 489

When selecting multiple items in a slicer, you can easily see that multiple items have been chosen. In Figure 2-30, you can see that the PivotTable is being filtered by the Northeast and Southwest markets.

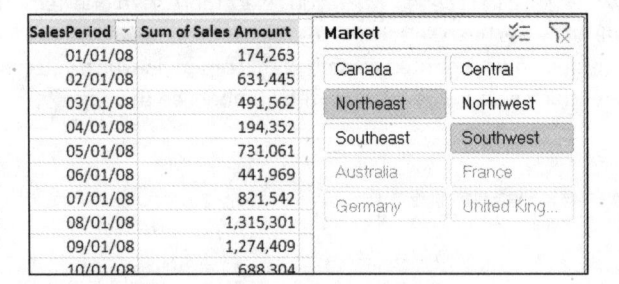

FIGURE 2-30: Slicers do a better job at displaying multiple item selections.

Creating a Standard Slicer

Enough talk. Try creating a standard slicer. Just follow these steps:

1. **Click anywhere inside the PivotTable.**
2. **Click the PivotTable Analyze tab of the ribbon.**
3. **Click the Insert Slicer icon, shown in Figure 2-31.**

    This step opens the Insert Slicers dialog box, shown in Figure 2-32. Select the fields you want to filter. In this example, the Region and Market slicers are created.

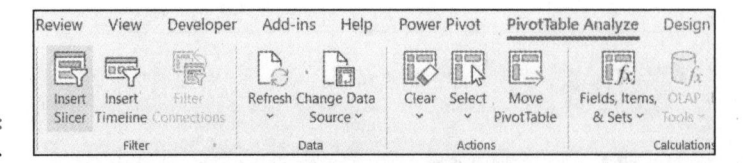

FIGURE 2-31: Inserting a slicer.

4. **After the slicers are created, simply click the filter values to filter the PivotTable.**

    As you can see in Figure 2-33, not only does clicking Midwest in the Region slicer filter the PivotTable, but the Market slicer also responds by highlighting the markets that belong to the Midwest region.

FIGURE 2-32:
Select the fields for which you want slicers created.

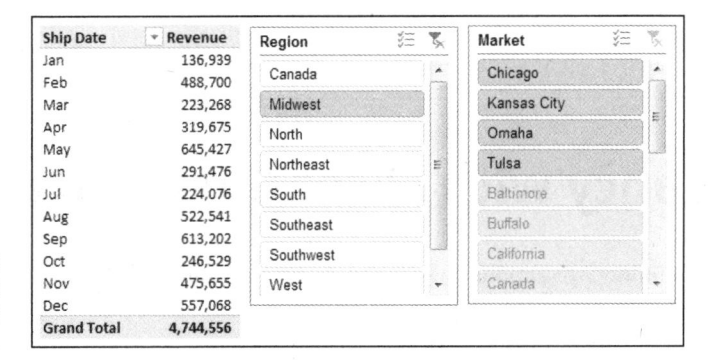

FIGURE 2-33: Select the fields you want filtered using slicers.

You can also select multiple values by holding down the Ctrl key on the keyboard while selecting the needed filters. In Figure 2-34, we held down the Ctrl key while selecting Baltimore, California, Charlotte, and Chicago. This highlights not only the selected markets in the Market slicer but also their associated regions in the Region slicer.

TIP To clear the filtering on a slicer, simply click the Clear Filter icon on the target slicer, as shown in Figure 2-35.

CHAPTER 2 Advanced Moves with PivotTables   491

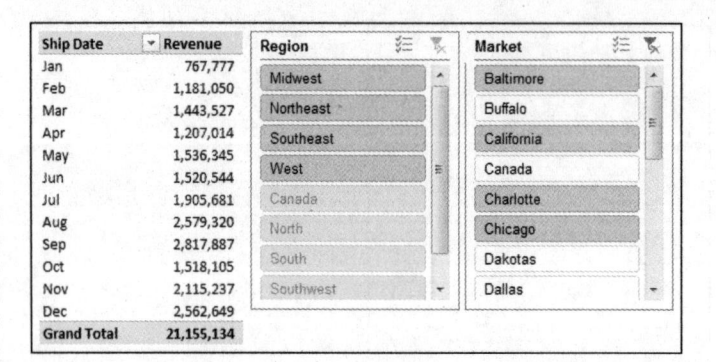

FIGURE 2-34:
The fact that you can see the current filter state gives slicers a unique advantage over Filter fields.

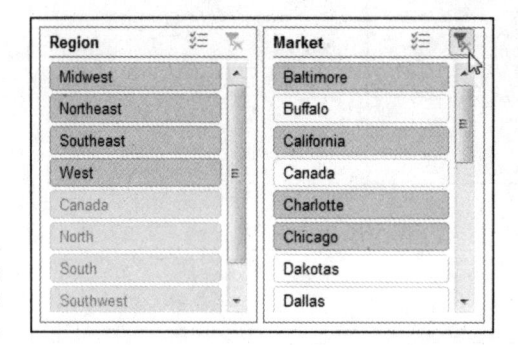

FIGURE 2-35:
Clearing the filters on a slicer.

Getting Fancy with Slicer Customizations

The following sections cover a few formatting adjustments you can make to your slicers.

Size and placement

A slicer behaves like a standard Excel shape object in that you can move it around and adjust its size by clicking it and dragging its position points (see Figure 2-36).

You can also right-click the slicer and select Size and Properties. This brings up the Format Slicer pane (see Figure 2-37), allowing you to adjust the size of the slicer, how the slicer should behave when cells are shifted, and whether the slicer should appear on a printed copy of your report.

492   BOOK 6 **Reporting and Querying Data**

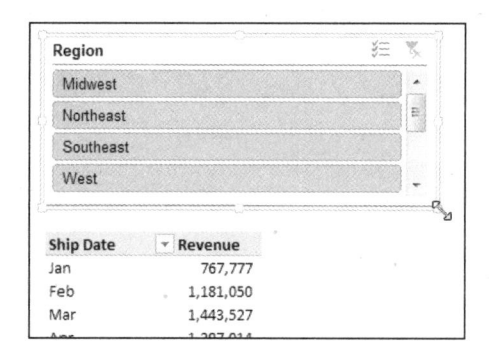

FIGURE 2-36:
Adjust the slicer size and placement by dragging its position points.

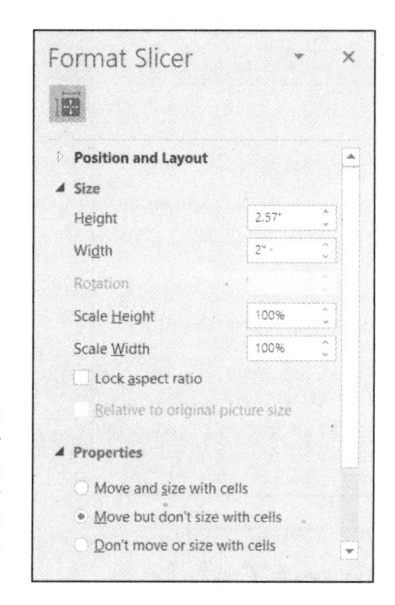

FIGURE 2-37:
The Format Slicer pane offers more control over how the slicer behaves in relation to the worksheet it's on.

Data item columns

By default, all slicers are created with one column of data items. You can change this number by right-clicking the slicer and selecting Size and Properties. This opens the Format Slicer pane. Under the Position and Layout section, you can specify the number of columns in the slicer. Adjusting the number to 2, as shown in Figure 2-38, forces the data items to be displayed in two columns, adjusting the number to 3 forces the data items to be displayed in three columns, and so on.

Miscellaneous slicer settings

Right-clicking the slicer and selecting Slicer Settings opens the Slicer Settings dialog box, shown in Figure 2-39. Using this dialog box, you can control the look of the slicer's header, how the slicer is sorted, and how filtered items are handled.

CHAPTER 2 Advanced Moves with PivotTables   493

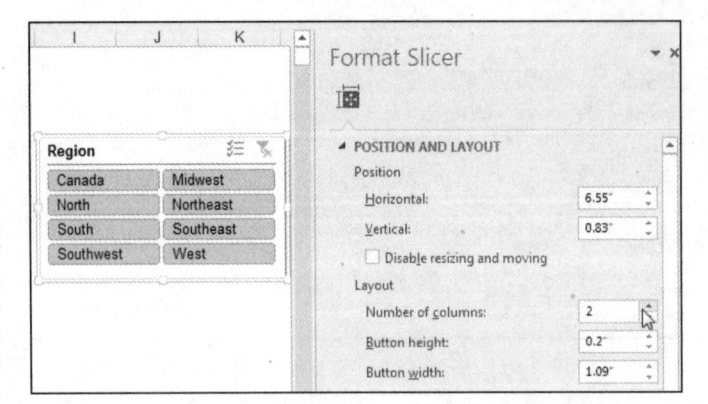

FIGURE 2-38: Adjust the Number of Columns property to display the slicer data items in more than one column.

FIGURE 2-39: The Slicer Settings dialog box.

Controlling Multiple PivotTables with One Slicer

Another advantage you gain with slicers is that each slicer can be tied to more than one PivotTable; that is to say, any filter you apply to your slicer can be applied to multiple PivotTables.

To connect the slicer to more than one PivotTable, simply right-click the slicer and select Report Connections. This opens the Report Connections dialog box, shown in Figure 2-40. Place a check mark next to any PivotTable that you want to filter using the current slicer.

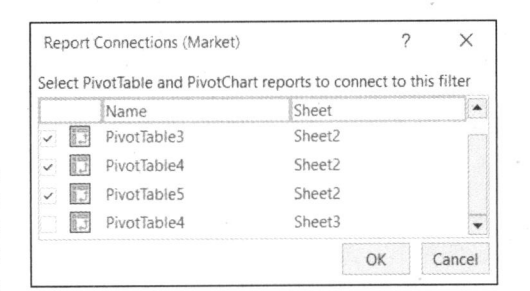

FIGURE 2-40: Choose the PivotTables to be filtered by this slicer.

At this point, any filter you apply to the slicer is applied to all connected PivotTables. Controlling the filter state of multiple PivotTables is a powerful feature, especially in reports that run on multiple PivotTables.

Creating a Timeline Slicer

The Timeline slicer works in the same way a standard slicer does — it lets you filter a PivotTable using a visual selection mechanism rather than the old Filter fields. The difference is that the Timeline slicer is designed to work exclusively with date fields, providing an excellent visual method to filter and group the dates in the PivotTable.

To create a Timeline slicer, the PivotTable must contain a field where *all* data is formatted as a date. It's not enough to have a column of data that contains a few dates. Each value in the date field must be a valid date and formatted as such.

To create a Timeline slicer, follow these steps:

1. **Click anywhere inside the PivotTable.**
2. **Click the PivotTable Analyze tab of the ribbon.**
3. **Click the Insert Timeline command.**

   The Insert Timelines dialog box, shown in Figure 2-41, appears, showing you all available date fields in the chosen PivotTable.

4. **Select the date fields for which you want to create the timeline.**

After the Timeline slicer is created, you can filter the data in the PivotTable and PivotChart, using this dynamic data selection mechanism. Figure 2-42 demonstrates how selecting Mar, Apr, and May in the Timeline slicer automatically filters the PivotChart.

CHAPTER 2 **Advanced Moves with PivotTables** 495

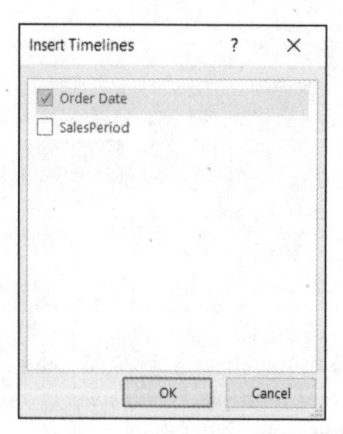

FIGURE 2-41: Select the date fields for which you want slicers created.

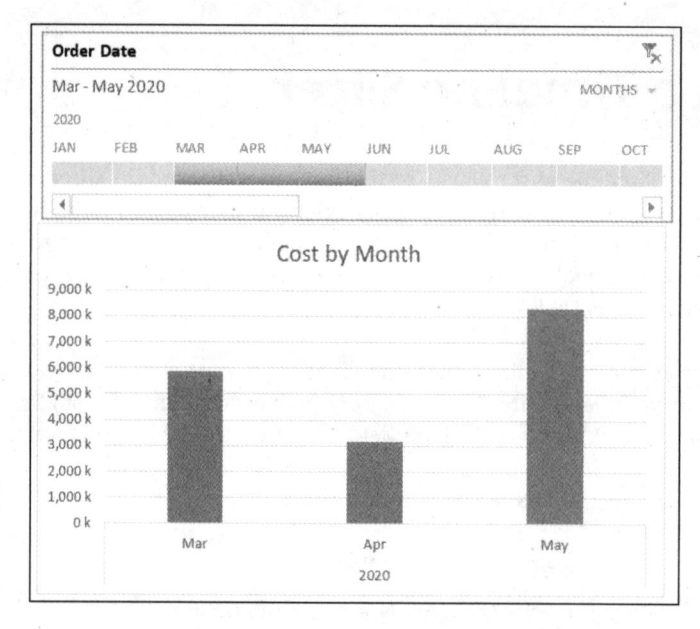

FIGURE 2-42: Click a date selection to filter the PivotTable or PivotChart.

Figure 2-43 illustrates how you can expand the slicer range with the mouse to include a wider range of dates in your filtered numbers.

Want to quickly filter the PivotTable by quarters? Well, that's easy with a Timeline slicer. Simply click the time period drop-down list in the upper-right corner and select Quarters. As you can see in Figure 2-44, you can also switch to Years or Days, if needed.

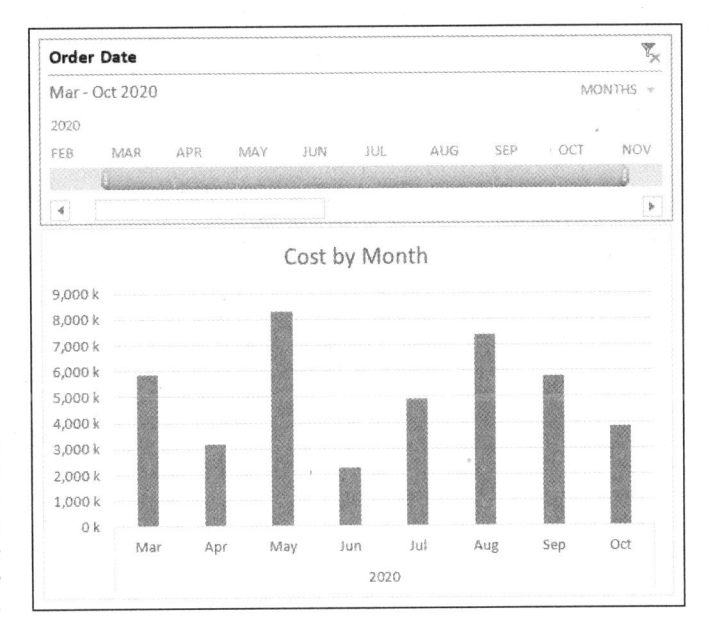

FIGURE 2-43:
You can expand the range on the Timeline slicer to include more data in the filtered numbers.

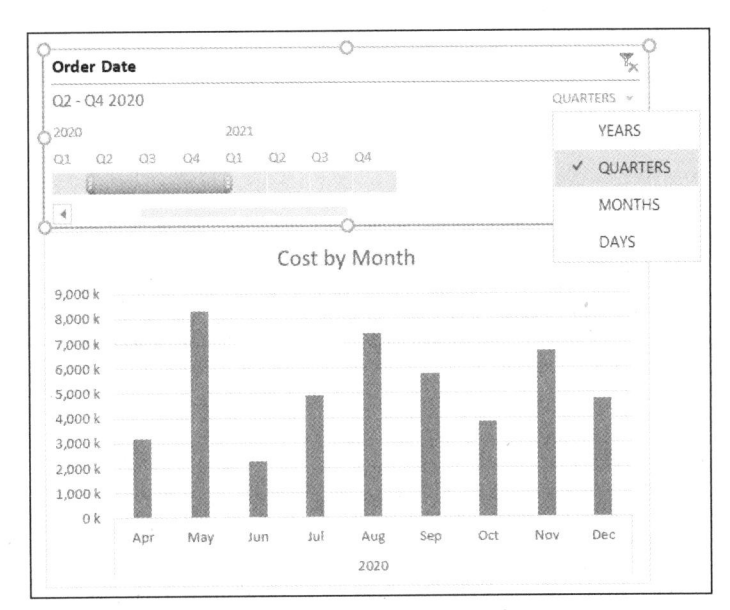

FIGURE 2-44:
Quickly switch among Quarters, Years, Months, and Days.

CHAPTER 2 **Advanced Moves with PivotTables** 497

IN THIS CHAPTER

» Interacting with the internal data model directly

» Starting a PivotTable from the internal data model

» Using multiple tables with the internal data model

Chapter 3
Working Directly with the Internal Data Model

In the preceding chapters of this minibook, you use the Power Pivot add-in to work with the internal data model. But as you'll see in this chapter, you can use a combination of PivotTables and Excel data connections to directly interact with the internal data model, without using the Power Pivot add-in.

> **TIP** This chapter uses two sample files, an Excel workbook named `6.3.1 Chapter 3 Sample File.xlsx` and an Access database named `6.3.2 Facility Services.accdb`. To download these files, go to www.dummies.com/go/microsoft365excelaiofd.

Directly Feeding the Internal Data Model

Imagine that you have the Transactions table you see in Figure 3-1, and on another worksheet you have an Employees table (see Figure 3-2) that contains information about the employees.

	A	B	C	D
1	Sales_Rep	Invoice_Date	Sales_Amount	Contracted Hours
2	4416	1/5/2021	111.79	2
3	4416	1/5/2021	111.79	2
4	160006	1/5/2021	112.13	2
5	6444	1/5/2021	112.13	2
6	160006	1/5/2021	145.02	3
7	52661	1/5/2021	196.58	4
8	6444	1/5/2021	204.20	4
9	51552	1/5/2021	225.24	3
10	55662	1/6/2021	86.31	2
11	1336	1/6/2021	86.31	2
12	60224	1/6/2021	86.31	2
13	54564	1/6/2021	86.31	2

FIGURE 3-1: This table shows transactions by employee number.

	A	B	C	D
1	Employee_Number	Last_Name	First_Name	Job_Title
2	21	SIOCAT	ROBERT	SERVICE REPRESENTATIVE 3
3	42	BREWN	DONNA	SERVICE REPRESENTATIVE 3
4	45	VAN HUILE	KENNETH	SERVICE REPRESENTATIVE 2
5	104	WIBB	MAURICE	SERVICE REPRESENTATIVE 2
6	106	CESTENGIAY	LUC	SERVICE REPRESENTATIVE 2
7	113	TRIDIL	ROCH	SERVICE REPRESENTATIVE 2
8	142	CETE	GUY	SERVICE REPRESENTATIVE 3
9	145	ERSINEILT	MIKE	SERVICE REPRESENTATIVE 2
10	162	GEBLE	MICHAEL	SERVICE REPRESENTATIVE 2
11	165	CERDANAL	ALAIN	SERVICE REPRESENTATIVE 3
12	201	GEIDRIOU	DOMINIC	TEAMLEAD 1
13	213	MERAN	DENIS	SERVICE REPRESENTATIVE 2

FIGURE 3-2: This table provides information on employees: first name, last name, and job title.

You need to create an analysis that shows sales by job title. This would normally be difficult given the fact that sales and job title are in two separate tables. But with the internal data model, you can follow these simple steps:

1. **Click inside the Transactions data table and start a new PivotTable by clicking the Insert tab of the ribbon and clicking PivotTable.**

   Click the top part of the PivotTable button, not the drop-down arrow.

   The PivotTable from Table or Range dialog box opens.

2. **Select the Add This Data to the Data Model check box (see Figure 3-3) and then click OK.**

3. **Click inside the Employees data table and start a new PivotTable by clicking the Insert tab of the ribbon and clicking PivotTable.**

   Again, click the top part of the PivotTable button, not the drop-down arrow. And this time too, select the Add This Data to the Data Model check box, as shown in Figure 3-4.

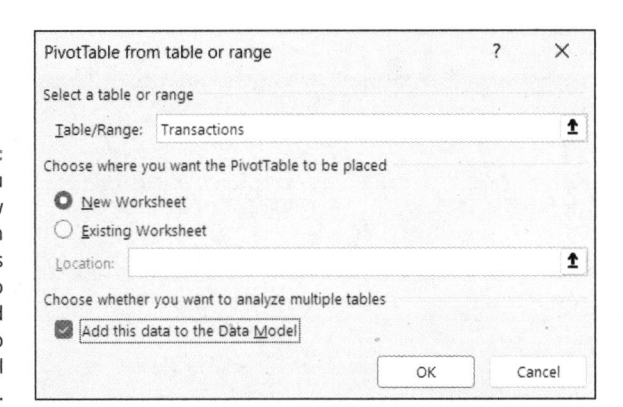

FIGURE 3-3:
When you create a new PivotTable from the Transactions table, be sure to select the Add This Data to the Data Model check box.

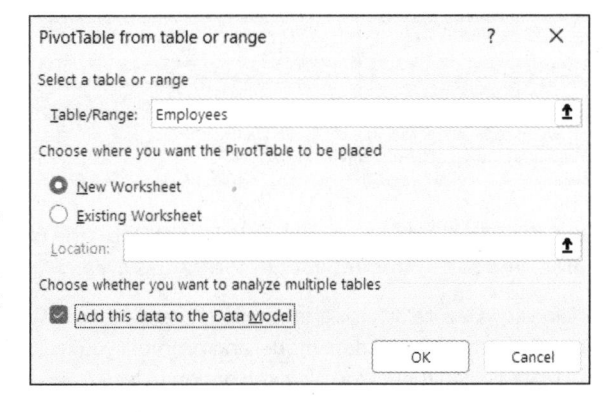

FIGURE 3-4:
Create a new PivotTable from the Employees table, and select the Add This Data to the Data Model check box.

TIP — Notice that in Figures 3-3 and 3-4, the PivotTable from Table or Range dialog box is referencing named ranges — in other words, each table was given a specific name. When you're adding data to the internal data model, you should name the data tables. That way, you can easily recognize your tables in the internal data model.

If you don't name your tables, the internal data model shows them as Range1, Range2, and so on.

4. **To give the data table a name, highlight all data in the table, click the Formulas tab of the ribbon, click Define Name, and enter a name for the table in the New Name dialog box.**

   Repeat for all other tables.

5. **After both tables have been added to the internal data model, open the PivotTable Fields. List and choose the All selector, as shown in Figure 3-5.**

   This step shows both ranges in the Fields.

CHAPTER 3 Working Directly with the Internal Data Model   501

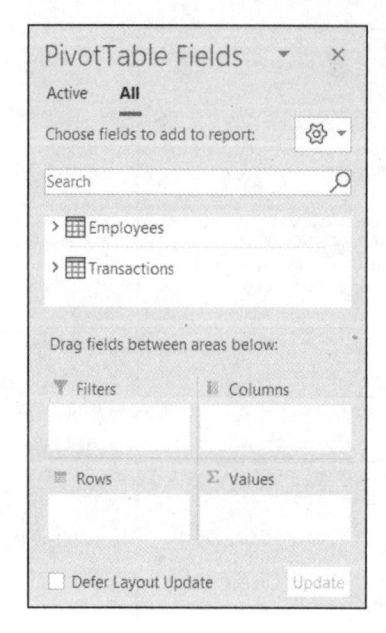

FIGURE 3-5:
Select All in the PivotTable Fields List to see both tables in the internal data model.

6. **Build out the PivotTable as normal; in this case, Job_Title is placed in the Rows area, and Sales_Amount goes in the Values area.**

    As you can see in Figure 3-6, Excel immediately recognizes that you're using two tables from the internal data model and prompts you to create a relationship between them. You have the option to let Excel autodetect the relationships between your tables or to click the Create button. Always create the relationships yourself, to avoid any possibility of Excel getting it wrong.

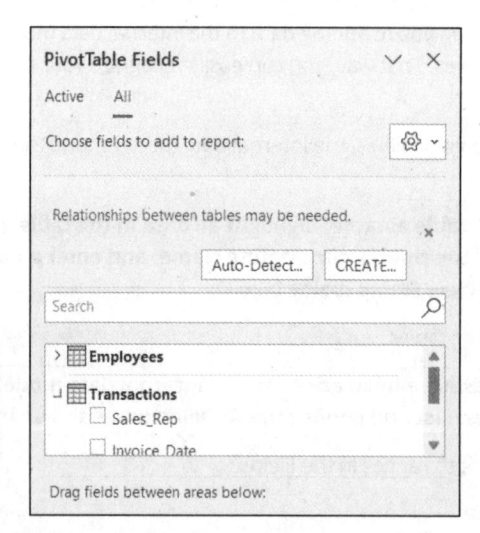

FIGURE 3-6:
When Excel prompts you, choose to create the relationship between the two tables.

502 BOOK 6 **Reporting and Querying Data**

7. **Click the Create button.**

   The Create Relationship dialog box, shown in Figure 3-7, opens. There, you select the tables and fields that define the relationship. In Figure 3-7, you can see that the Transactions table has a Sales_Rep field, which is related to the Employees table via the Employee_Number field.

FIGURE 3-7: Build the appropriate relationship using the Table and Column drop-down lists.

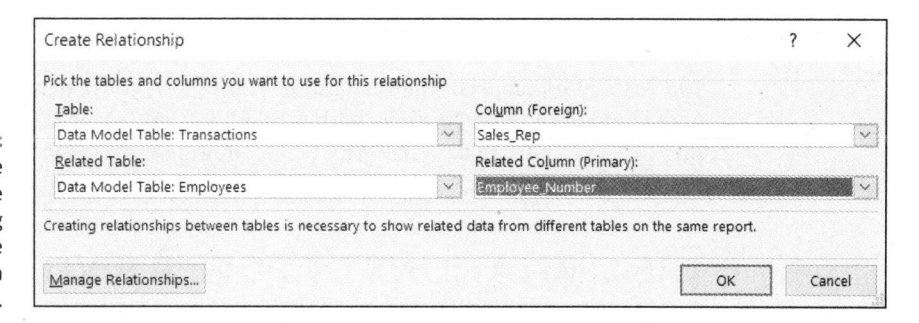

After you create the relationship, you have a single PivotTable that effectively uses data from both tables to create the analysis you need. Figure 3-8 illustrates that, by using the Excel internal data model, you've achieved the goal of showing sales by job title.

FIGURE 3-8: You've achieved your goal of showing sales by job title.

CHAPTER 3 **Working Directly with the Internal Data Model**

REMEMBER: In Figure 3-7, you see that the lower-right drop-down is named Related Column (Primary). The term *primary* means that the internal data model uses this field from the associated table as the primary key.

A *primary key* is a field that contains only unique non-null values (no duplicates or blanks). Primary key fields are necessary in the data model to prevent aggregation errors and duplications. Every relationship you create must have a field designated as the primary key.

The Employees table (in the scenario in Figure 3-7) must have all unique values in the Employee_Number field, with no blanks or null values. This is the only way that Excel can ensure data integrity when joining multiple tables.

THE LIMITATIONS OF POWER PIVOT-DRIVEN PIVOTTABLES

PivotTables built on top of Power Pivot or the internal data model come with limitations that could be showstoppers in terms of your reporting needs. Here's a quick rundown of the limitations you should consider before deciding to base your PivotTable reporting on Power Pivot or the internal data model:

- The Group feature is disabled for Power Pivot-driven PivotTables. You can't roll dates into months, quarters, or years, for example.
- In a standard PivotTable, you can double-click a cell in the pivot to drill into the rows that make up the figure in that cell. In Power Pivot-driven PivotTables, however, you see only the first 1,000 rows.
- Power Pivot-driven PivotTables don't allow you to create the traditional Calculated Fields and Calculated Items found in standard Excel PivotTables.
- You can't refresh or configure workbooks that use the Power Pivot data model if you open them in a version of Excel earlier than Excel 2013.
- You can't use custom lists to automatically sort the data in your Power Pivot-driven PivotTables.
- Neither the Product nor Count Numbers summary calculations are available in Power Pivot-driven PivotTables.

Managing Relationships in the Internal Data Model

After you assign tables to the internal data model, you may need to adjust the relationships between the tables. To make changes to the relationships in an internal data model, click the Data tab on the ribbon and click Relationships. The Manage Relationships dialog box, shown in Figure 3-9, opens.

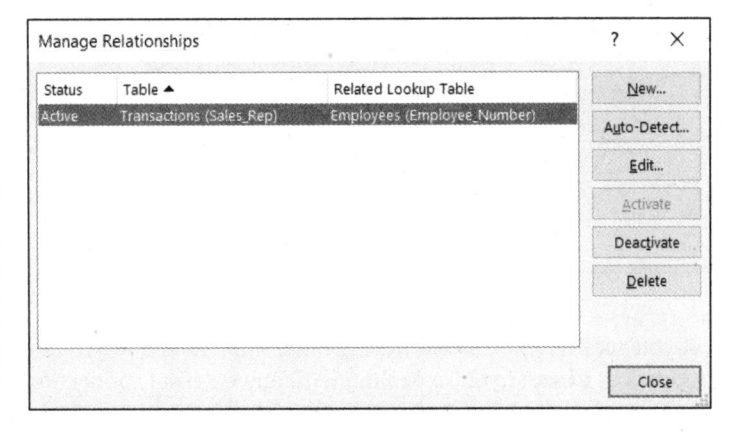

FIGURE 3-9: The Manage Relationships dialog box enables you to make changes to the relationships in the internal data model.

Here, you'll find the following commands:

- **New:** Create a new relationship between two tables in the internal data model.
- **Auto-Detect:** Ask Power Pivot to automatically detect and create relationships.
- **Edit:** Alter the selected relationship.
- **Activate:** Enforce the selected relationship, telling Excel to consider the relationship when aggregating and analyzing the data in the internal data model.
- **Deactivate:** Turn off the selected relationship, telling Excel to ignore the relationship when aggregating and analyzing the data in the internal data model.
- **Delete:** Remove the selected relationship.

Managing Queries and Connections

Click the Data tab on the ribbon and then click Queries & Connections. Excel activates the Queries & Connections task pane (see Figure 3-10). At the top of the task pane, you'll see two tabs: Queries and Connections. The Queries tab lets you view and manage the queries within the current workbook. The Connections tab lets you manage the connection information stored in your workbook.

FIGURE 3-10: Use the Queries & Connections task pane to manage the queries and connections in the internal data model.

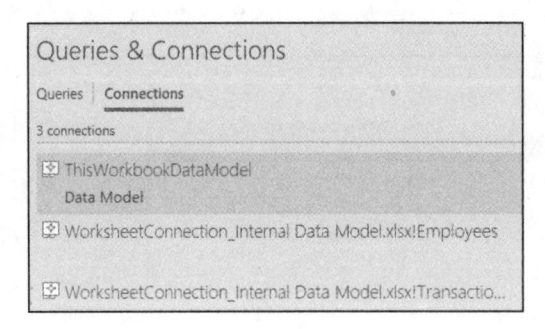

> **TIP** If you receive a workbook that is unfamiliar to you, activate Queries & Connections just to see if you're dealing with any external connections or queries in the internal data model of the workbook.

Right-click any of the entries on the Connections tab to expose a shortcut menu for that entry, allowing you to refresh the connection, delete the connection, or edit the connection properties.

> **TIP** The connection name for the internal data model will always be ThisWorkbookDataModel. Excel won't allow you to delete the ThisWorkbookDataModel connection.

Creating a New PivotTable Using the Internal Data Model

In certain instances, you may want to create a PivotTable from scratch using the existing internal data model as the source data. Here are the steps to do so:

1. **On the Insert tab of the ribbon, click the drop-down arrow on the PivotTable button and select From External Data Source.**

    The PivotTable from an External Data Source dialog box opens (see Figure 3-11).

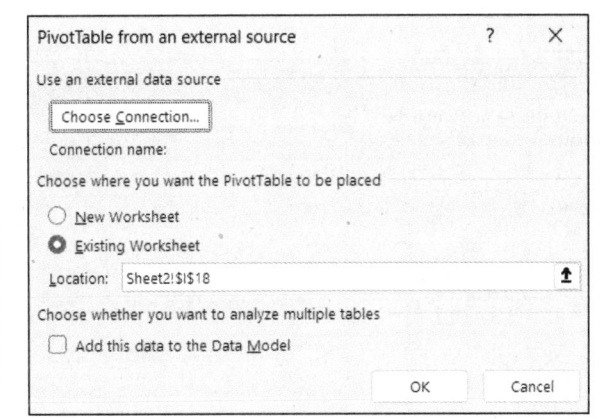

FIGURE 3-11:
In the PivotTable from an External Data Source dialog box, click the Choose Connection button.

2. **Click the Choose Connection button.**

   The Existing Connections dialog box, shown in Figure 3-12, opens.

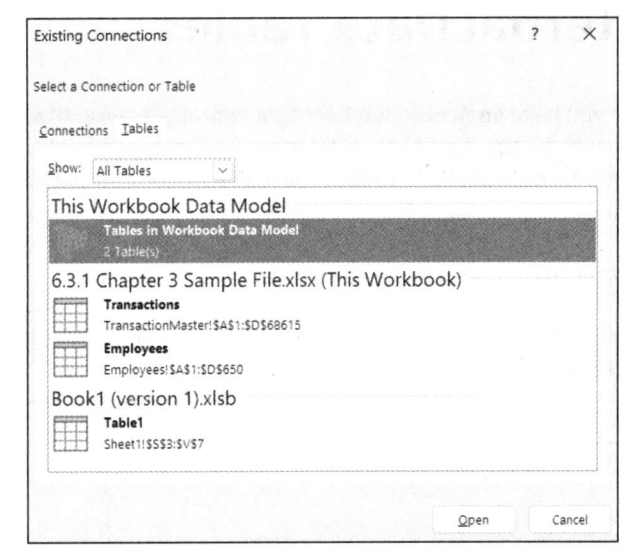

FIGURE 3-12:
Use the Existing Connections dialog box to select the Data Model as the data source for your PivotTable.

3. **On the Tables tab, select Tables in Workbook Data Model, and then click the Open button.**

   You return to the PivotTable from an External Source dialog box.

4. **Click the OK button to create the PivotTable.**

   If all goes well, you see the PivotTable Fields dialog box with all tables that are included in the internal data model, as shown in Figure 3-13.

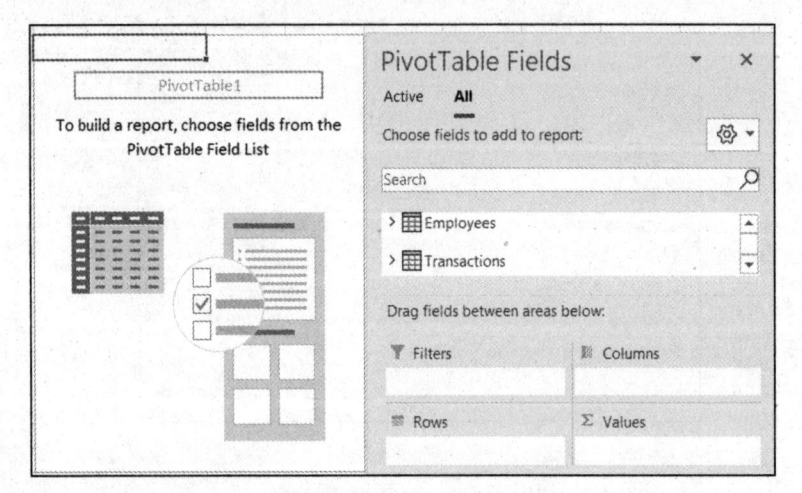

FIGURE 3-13: The newly created PivotTable shows all tables in the internal data model.

Filling the Internal Data Model with Multiple External Data Tables

Suppose you have an Access database that contains a normalized set of tables. You want to analyze the data in that database in Excel, so you decide to use the new Excel internal data model to expose the data you need through a PivotTable. To try this, you can use the sample file named `6.3.2 Facility Services.accdb`.

To accomplish this task, follow these steps:

1. **On the Data tab of the ribbon, click Get Data, select From Database, and select From Microsoft Access Database (see Figure 3-14).**

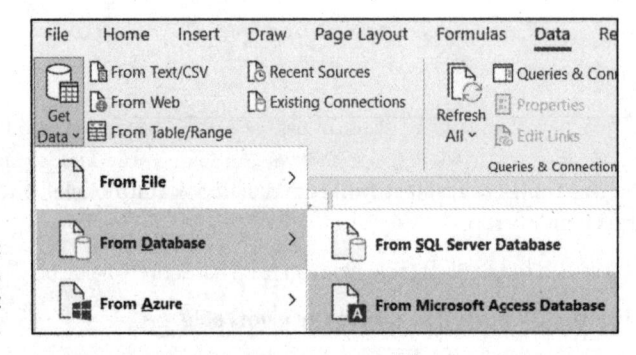

FIGURE 3-14: Getting data from a Microsoft Access database.

508 BOOK 6 **Reporting and Querying Data**

2. **Browse to your target Access database and open it.**

   The Navigator dialog box opens.

3. **Select the Select Multiple Items check box (see Figure 3-15).**

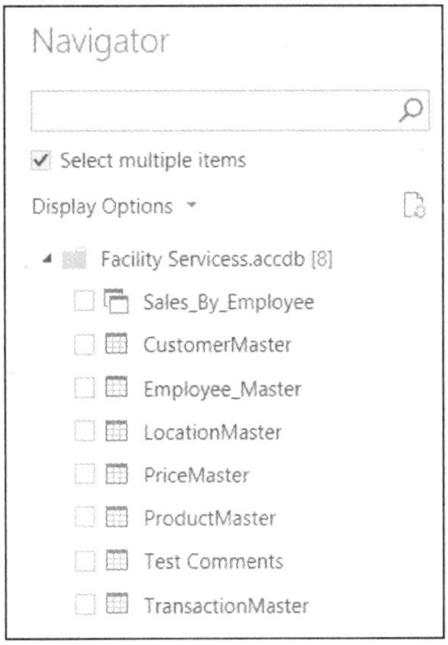

FIGURE 3-15: Enable the selection of multiple tables.

4. **Select the check box next to each table that you want to import into the internal data model.**

5. **Click the drop-down arrow next to the Load button and select the Load To command (see Figure 3-16).**

   The Import Data dialog box opens (see Figure 3-17).

6. **Choose the PivotTable Report radio button and click OK to create the base pivot.**

You now have a PivotTable based on external data imported into the internal data model (see Figure 3-18). A quick look at the PivotTable Fields. List shows all the external data sources imported into the internal data model.

CHAPTER 3 Working Directly with the Internal Data Model   509

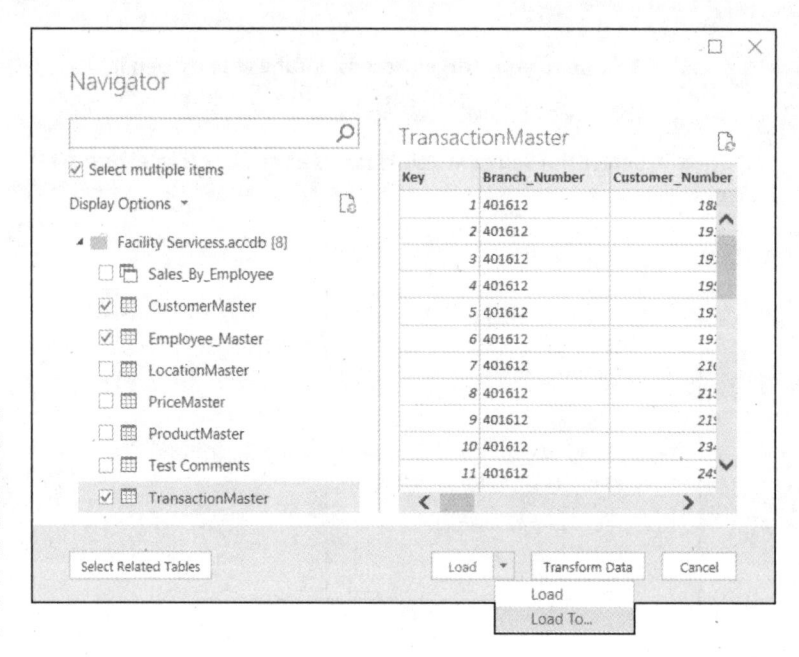

FIGURE 3-16: Place a check mark next to each table you want import to the internal data model, and then give the Load To command.

FIGURE 3-17: Create a PivotTable Report from the Import Data dialog box.

In just a few clicks, you've created a powerful platform to build and maintain PivotTable analysis based on data in an Access database!

TIP

When you import tables from multiple data sources, Excel tries to detect and create relationships between the tables. It typically does a good job at recognizing the appropriate relationships, especially when your tables contain common column names such as EmployeeID and SalesRep. Though Excel gets the relationships right in most cases, it's always best to confirm that the right relationships were created before using your PivotTable. Use the Manage Relationships dialog box (shown in Figure 3-9) to double-check the relationships. To open the Manage Relationships dialog box, click inside your PivotTable, click the PivotTable Analyze tab of the ribbon, and then click Relationships.

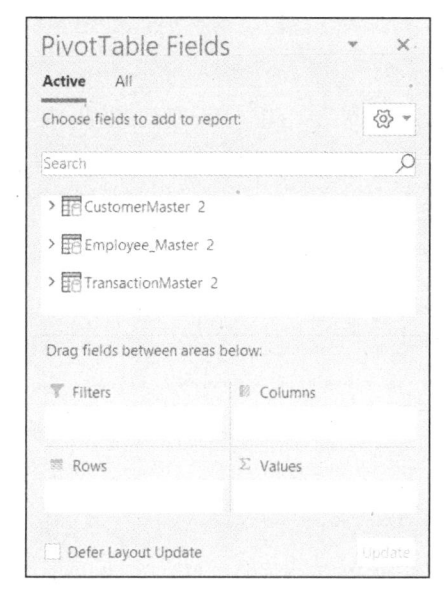

FIGURE 3-18: You're ready to build your PivotTable analysis based on multiple external data tables!

CHAPTER 3 Working Directly with the Internal Data Model 511

IN THIS CHAPTER

» Creating, formatting, and hiding your own calculated columns

» Creating calculated columns by using DAX

» Creating calculated measures

Chapter 4
Adding Formulas to Power Pivot

When analyzing data with Power Pivot, you often find the need to expand your analysis to include data based on calculations that are not in the original dataset. Power Pivot has a robust set of functions (called Data Analysis Expressions, or DAX) that allow you to perform mathematical operations, recursive calculations, data lookups, and much more.

TIP This chapter introduces you to DAX functions and provides the ground rules for building your own calculations in Power Pivot data models. To work through this chapter, download the sample workbook named `6.4.1 Power Pivot Formulas.xlsx` at www.dummies.com/go/microsoft365excelaiofd.

Enhancing Power Pivot Data with Calculated Columns

Calculated columns are columns you create to enhance a Power PivotTable with your own formulas. When you enter calculated columns directly in the Power Pivot window, they become part of the source data you use to feed your PivotTable.

Calculated columns work at the row level. That is to say, the formulas you create in a calculated column perform their operations based on the data in each individual row. For example, if you have a Revenue column and a Cost column in your Power PivotTable, you could create a new column that calculates [Revenue] minus [Cost]. Excel performs the same calculation for each row in the dataset.

Calculated measures are used to perform more complex calculations that work on an aggregation of data. These calculations are applied directly to a PivotTable, creating a sort of virtual column that can't be seen in the Power Pivot window. Calculated measures are needed whenever you need to calculate based on an aggregated grouping of rows — for example, the sum of [Year2] minus the sum of [Year1]. See the "Understanding Calculated Measures" section, later in this chapter, for the lowdown on calculated measures.

Creating your first calculated column

Creating a calculated column works much like building formulas in an Excel table. Follow these steps to create a calculated column:

1. **Open the sample file named** 6.4.1 Power Pivot Formulas.xlsx.
2. **Click the Power Pivot tab on the ribbon.**
3. **Click the Manage button in the Data Model group.**

    The Power Pivot window opens.

4. **Click the InvoiceDetails tab to display its contents.**

    In the table, you see an empty column on the far right, labeled Add Column.

5. **Click the first blank cell in that column.**
6. **In the Formula Bar, enter the following formula (as shown in Figure 4-1):**

    ```
    =[UnitPrice]*[Quantity]
    ```

7. **Press Enter.**

    The formula populates the entire column, and Power Pivot automatically renames the column to Calculated Column 1.

8. **Double-click the column label, type the new name** — Total Revenue — **and then press Enter.**

    You can rename any column in the Power Pivot window by double-clicking the column name and entering a new name. Alternatively, you can right-click any column and click Rename.

FIGURE 4-1:
Start the calculated column by entering an operation on the Formula Bar.

	InvoiceN...	Quantity	UnitCost	UnitPrice	Total Revenue
1	ORDST1022	1	59.29	119.95	119.95
2	ORDST1015	1	3290.55	6589.95	6589.95
3	ORDST1016	10	35	34.95	349.5
4	ORDST1017	50	91.59	189.95	9497.5
5	ORDST1018	1	59.29	119.95	119.95
6	INV1010	1	674.5	1349.95	1349.95
7	INV1011	1	91.25	189.95	189.95
8	INV1012	1	303.85	609.95	609.95
9	ORDST1020	1	59.29	119.95	119.95

Formula Bar: [Total Revenue], fx =[UnitPrice]*[Quantity]

> **TIP** You can build calculated columns by clicking instead of typing. For example, instead of manually entering =**[UnitPrice]*[Quantity]**, you can enter the equal sign (=), click the UnitPrice column, type the asterisk (*), and then click the Quantity column. You can also enter your own static data. For example, you can enter a formula to calculate a 10 percent tax rate by entering =**[UnitPrice]*1.10**.

Each calculated column you create is automatically available in any PivotTable connected to the Power Pivot data model. You don't have to take any action to get your calculated columns into the PivotTable. Figure 4-2 shows the Total Revenue calculated column in the PivotTable Fields List. These calculated columns can be used just as you would use any other field in the PivotTable.

FIGURE 4-2:
Calculated columns automatically show up in the PivotTable Fields List.

Row Labels	Sum of Total Revenue
Aaron Fitz Electrical	45668.4
Adam Park Resort	6238.5
Advanced Paper Co.	131930.45
Advanced Tech Satellite System	2278.7
American Science Museum	6357.8
Associated Insurance Company	1299.8
Astor Suites	174604.55
Atmore Retirement Center	39.95
Baker's Emporium Inc.	18418
Blue Yonder Airlines	26138.3
Boyle's Country Inns	1829.85
Breakthrough Telemarketing	91437
Castle Inn Resort	239.9
Central Communications LTD	36816.2

PivotTable Fields — Active / All — Choose fields to add to report:
- InvoiceDetails
  - ☐ InvoiceNumber
  - ☐ Quantity
  - ☐ UnitCost
  - ☐ UnitPrice
  - ☑ Total Revenue

> **TIP** If you need to edit the formula in a calculated column, find the calculated column in the Power Pivot window, click the column, and then make changes directly on the Formula Bar.

See Chapter 2 of this minibook for a refresher on how to create a PivotTable from Power Pivot.

Formatting calculated columns

You often need to change the formatting of Power Pivot columns to appropriately match the data within them. For example, you may want to show numbers as currency, remove decimal places, or display dates in a certain way.

You're by no means limited to formatting only calculated columns. Follow these steps to format any column you see in the Power Pivot window:

1. **In the Power Pivot window, click the column you want to format.**
2. **Click the Home tab of the Power Pivot window and find the Formatting group (see Figure 4-3).**
3. **Use the options to alter the formatting of the column as you see fit.**

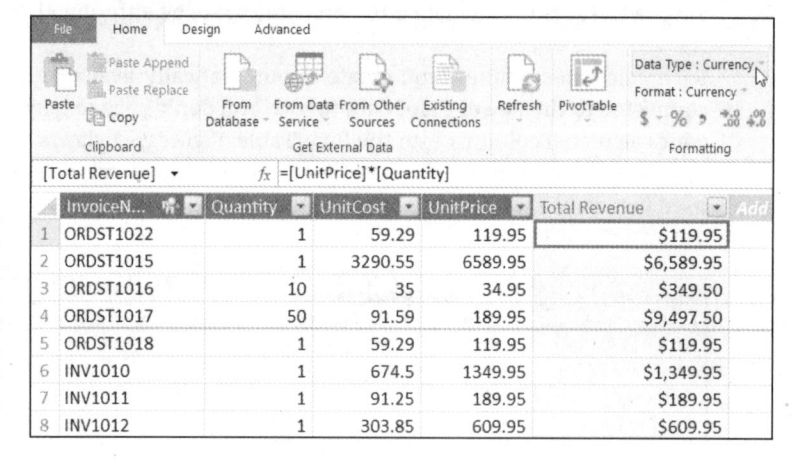

FIGURE 4-3:
You can use the formatting tools found on the Power Pivot window's Home tab to format any column in the data model.

TIP Any format you apply to the columns in the Power Pivot window is automatically applied to all PivotTables connected to the data model. This means you can save time and effort by applying formatting in Power Pivot instead of applying PivotTable number formats one data field at a time.

Referencing calculated columns in other calculations

As with all calculations in Excel, Power Pivot allows you to reference a calculated column as a variable in another calculated column. Figure 4-4 illustrates this concept with a new calculated column named Gross Margin. Notice that on the Formula Bar, the calculation is using the following formula:

```
=[Total Revenue]-([UnitCost]*[Quantity])
```

FIGURE 4-4:
The new Gross Margin calculation is using the previously created calculated column named [Total Revenue].

Hiding calculated columns from end users

Because calculated columns can reference each other, you can imagine creating columns simply as helper columns for other calculations. You may not want your end users to see these columns in your PivotTables, dashboards, or other client tools.

Similar to hiding columns on an Excel worksheet, Power Pivot allows you to hide any column. (It doesn't have to be a calculated column.) To hide columns, select the columns you want hidden, right-click the selection, and then choose the Hide from Client Tools option (as shown in Figure 4-5).

FIGURE 4-5:
Right-click and select Hide from Client Tools.

REMEMBER

When a column is hidden, it doesn't show as an available selection in the Pivot-Table Fields List. However, if the column you're hiding is already part of the pivot report (meaning you've already dragged it onto the PivotTable), hiding the column doesn't automatically remove it from the report. Hiding merely affects the ability to see the column in the PivotTable Fields List.

Note in Figure 4-6 that Power Pivot recolors columns based on their attributes. Hidden columns are subdued and grayed out, whereas calculated columns that are not hidden have a darker (black) header.

CHAPTER 4 **Adding Formulas to Power Pivot** 517

	InvoiceN...	Quantity	UnitCost	UnitPrice	Total Revenue	Gross Margin
1	ORDST1022	1	59.29	119.95	$119.95	60.66
2	ORDST1015	1	3290.55	6589.95	$6,589.95	3299.4
3	ORDST1016	10	35	34.95	$349.50	-0.5
4	ORDST1017	50	91.59	189.95	$9,497.50	4918
5	ORDST1018	1	59.29	119.95	$119.95	60.66
6	INV1010	1	674.5	1349.95	$1,349.95	675.45
7	INV1011	1	91.25	189.95	$189.95	98.7
8	INV1012	1	303.85	609.95	$609.95	306.1

FIGURE 4-6: Hidden columns are grayed out, and calculated columns have darker headings.

> **TIP** To unhide columns, select the hidden columns in the Power Pivot window, right-click the selection, and then click Unhide from Client Tools.

Utilizing DAX to Create Calculated Columns

DAX is essentially the formula language that Power Pivot uses to perform calculations within its own construct of tables and columns. The DAX formula language comes supplied with its own set of functions. Some of these functions can be used in calculated columns for row-level calculations, and others are designed to be used in calculated measures to aggregate operations.

In this section, I touch on some of the DAX functions that you can leverage in calculated columns.

Identifying DAX functions that are safe for calculated columns

Earlier in this chapter, you use the Formula Bar within the Power Pivot window to enter calculations. Next to the Formula Bar, you may have noticed the Insert Function button (the button labeled *fx*). It's similar to the Insert Function button in Excel. Clicking this button opens the Insert Function dialog box, shown in Figure 4-7, which enables you to browse, search for, and insert the available DAX functions.

As you look through the list of DAX functions, notice that many of them look like the common Excel functions that most people are familiar with. But make no mistake: They aren't Excel functions. Whereas Excel functions work with cells and ranges, these DAX functions are designed to work at the table and column levels.

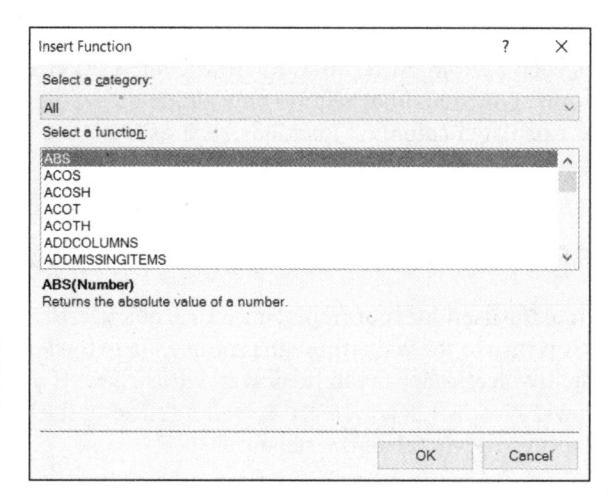

FIGURE 4-7:
The Insert Function dialog box shows you all available DAX functions.

To understand what we mean, start a new calculated column on the Invoice Details tab. Click in the Formula Bar and type a good old SUM function: **SUM([Gross Margin])**. The result is shown in Figure 4-8.

FIGURE 4-8:
The DAX SUM function can only sum the column as a whole.

ntity	UnitCost	UnitPrice	Total Revenue	Gross Margin	Calculated Column 1
1	59.29	119.95	$119.95	60.66	928378.069999998
1	3290.55	6589.95	$6,589.95	3299.4	928378.069999998
10	35	34.95	$349.50	-0.5	928378.069999998
50	91.59	189.95	$9,497.50	4918	928378.069999998
1	59.29	119.95	$119.95	60.66	928378.069999998
1	674.5	1349.95	$1,349.95	675.45	928378.069999998
1	91.25	189.95	$189.95	98.7	928378.069999998
1	303.85	609.95	$609.95	306.1	928378.069999998

Formula bar: fx =sum([Gross Margin])

As you can see, the SUM function sums the entire column. This is because Power Pivot and DAX are designed to work with tables and columns. Power Pivot has no construct for cells and ranges. It doesn't even have column letters and row numbers on its grid. Where an Excel function (such as SUM) would normally reference a range, DAX basically takes the entire column.

The bottom line is that not all DAX functions can be used with calculated columns. Because a calculated column evaluates at the row level, only DAX functions that evaluate single data points can be used in a calculated column.

> **TIP** Here's a good rule of thumb: If the function requires an array or a range of cells as an argument, it isn't viable in a calculated column.

CHAPTER 4 **Adding Formulas to Power Pivot**

So, functions such as SUM, MIN, MAX, AVERAGE, and COUNT don't work in calculated columns. Functions that require only single data-point arguments work quite well in calculated columns: functions such as YEAR, MONTH, MID, LEFT, RIGHT, IF, and IFERROR.

Building DAX-driven calculated columns

To demonstrate the usefulness of employing a DAX function to enhance calculated columns, let's return to the walk-through example. Go to the Power Pivot window and select the InvoiceHeader tab in the lower-left corner. (If you've accidentally closed the Power Pivot window, you can open it by clicking the Manage command button on the Power Pivot tab of the ribbon.)

The InvoiceHeader tab, shown in Figure 4-9, contains an InvoiceDate column. Although this column is valuable in the raw table, the individual dates aren't convenient when analyzing the data with a PivotTable. It would be beneficial to have a column for Month and a column for Year. This way, you could aggregate and analyze the data by month and year.

FIGURE 4-9: DAX functions can help enhance the invoice header data with Year and Month time dimensions.

	InvoiceDate	InvoiceNu...	Custom...	Add Column
1	5/8/2018 12:00:00 AM	ORDST1025	BAKERSEM0001	
2	4/12/2020 12:00:00 AM	STDINV2251	BAKERSEM0001	
3	5/8/2018 12:00:00 AM	ORDST1026	AARONFIT0001	
4	4/12/2020 12:00:00 AM	STDINV2252	AARONFIT0001	
5	5/7/2017 12:00:00 AM	ORD1002	METROPOL0001	
6	2/10/2017 12:00:00 AM	INV1024	AARONFIT0001	
7	2/15/2017 12:00:00 AM	INV1025	AARONFIT0001	
8	5/10/2017 12:00:00 AM	ORDPH1005	LECLERC0001	

For this endeavor, you use the DAX functions YEAR, MONTH, and FORMAT to add some time dimensions to the data model. Follow these steps:

1. **In the InvoiceHeader table, click the first blank cell in the empty column labeled Add Column, on the far right.**

2. **In the Formula Bar, type** =YEAR([InvoiceDate]) **and then press Enter.**

   Power Pivot automatically renames the column to Calculated Column 1.

3. **Double-click the column label and rename the column** Year.

4. **Starting in the next column, click the first blank cell in the empty column labeled Add Column, on the far right.**

5. **In the Formula Bar, type** =MONTH([InvoiceDate]), **and then press Enter.**

   Power Pivot automatically renames the column to Calculated Column 1.

6. **Double-click the column label and rename the column** Month.

7. **Starting in the next column, click the first blank cell in the empty column labeled Add Column, on the far right.**

8. **In the Formula Bar, type** =FORMAT([InvoiceDate],"mmm") **and then press Enter.**

   Power Pivot automatically renames the column to Calculated Column 1.

9. **Double-click the column label and rename the column** Month Name.

After completing these steps, you should have three new calculated columns similar to the ones shown in Figure 4-10.

InvoiceDate	InvoiceNu...	Custom...	Year	Month	Month Name
5/8/2018 12:00:00 AM	ORDST1025	BAKERSEM0001	2018	5	May
4/12/2020 12:00:00 AM	STDINV2251	BAKERSEM0001	2020	4	Apr
5/8/2018 12:00:00 AM	ORDST1026	AARONFIT0001	2018	5	May
4/12/2020 12:00:00 AM	STDINV2252	AARONFIT0001	2020	4	Apr
5/7/2017 12:00:00 AM	ORD1002	METROPOL0001	2017	5	May
2/10/2017 12:00:00 AM	INV1024	AARONFIT0001	2017	2	Feb
2/15/2017 12:00:00 AM	INV1025	AARONFIT0001	2017	2	Feb
5/10/2017 12:00:00 AM	ORDPH1005	LECLERC0001	2017	5	May

FIGURE 4-10: Using DAX functions to supplement a table with Year, Month, and Month Name columns.

As we mention earlier in this chapter, creating calculated columns automatically makes them available through the PivotTable Fields List (see Figure 4-11).

FIGURE 4-11: DAX calculations are immediately available in any connected PivotTable.

Sorting by month in Power Pivot-driven PivotTables

One of the more annoying aspects of Power Pivot is that it doesn't inherently know how to sort months. Unlike standard Excel, Power Pivot doesn't use the built-in custom lists that define the order of month names. Whenever you create a calculated column such as [Month Name] and place it into your PivotTable, Power Pivot puts those months in alphabetical order. Figure 4-12 illustrates this in a PivotTable designed to show average revenue by month.

Row Labels	Average of Total Revenue
Aaron Fitz Electrical	
Apr	$1,121.88
Feb	$826.75
Jan	$396.49
Mar	$248.14
May	$1,829.83
Sep	$59.95
Adam Park Resort	
Apr	$839.92
Jan	$599.50
May	$59.90
Sep	$2,399.95
Advanced Paper Co.	
Apr	$13,049.13
Jan	$359.80
Advanced Tech Satellite System	
Apr	$49.95
Jul	$138.24
May	$949.75

FIGURE 4-12: Month names in Power Pivot-driven PivotTables don't automatically sort in month order.

The fix for this problem is fairly easy. Open the Power Pivot window and select the Home tab. There, click the icon part of the Sort by Column command button. The Sort by Column dialog box opens, as shown in Figure 4-13.

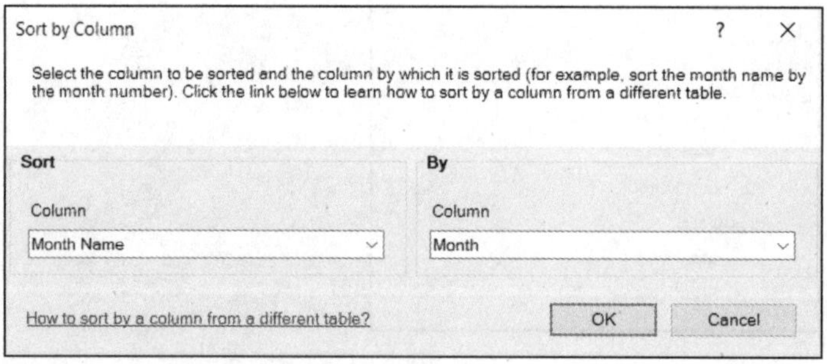

FIGURE 4-13: The Sort by Column dialog box lets you define how columns are sorted.

The idea is to select the column you want sorted and then select the column you want to sort by. In this scenario, you want to sort Month Name by month, so select Month Name in the Sort drop-down list on the left, select Month in the By drop-down list on the right, and then click OK.

After you confirm the change, it initially appears as though nothing has happened. The reason is that the sort order you defined isn't for the Power Pivot window. The sort order is applied to the PivotTable. You can switch over to Excel to see the result in the PivotTable (see Figure 4-14).

Row Labels	Average of Total Revenue
⊟ Aaron Fitz Electrical	
Jan	$396.49
Feb	$826.75
Mar	$248.14
Apr	$1,121.88
May	$1,829.83
Sep	$59.95
⊟ Adam Park Resort	
Jan	$599.50
Apr	$839.92
May	$59.90
Sep	$2,399.95
⊟ Advanced Paper Co.	
Jan	$359.80
Apr	$13,049.13
⊟ Advanced Tech Satellite System	
Apr	$49.95
May	$949.75
Jul	$138.24

FIGURE 4-14: The month names now show in the correct month order.

> **TIP** PivotTables based on your data model will first inherit the formatting and sorting explicitly applied in the data model; then they'll apply any formatting you set in the PivotTable itself. In other words, any formatting you apply in the Pivot-Table itself will supersede the formatting and sorting applied via the Power Pivot window.

Referencing fields from other tables

Sometimes the operation you're trying to perform with a calculated column requires you to utilize fields from other tables within the Power Pivot data model. For example, you may need to account for a customer-specific discount amount from the Customers table (see Figure 4-15) when creating a calculated column in the InvoiceDetails table.

CHAPTER 4 **Adding Formulas to Power Pivot** 523

FIGURE 4-15:
The discount amount in the Customers table can be used in a calculated column in another table.

	Custome...	CustomerName	Discount Amount	Address
1	DOLLISCO0001	Dollis Cove Resort	11%	765 Kingway
2	GETAWAYI0001	Getaway Inn	10%	234 E Cannon Ave.
3	HOMEFURN0001	Home Furnishings Limited	25%	234 Heritage Ave.
4	JOHNSONK0001	Johnson, Kimberly	12%	5678 S. 42nd Ave.
5	KELLYCON0001	Kelly Consulting	5%	123 Yeo
6	KENSINGT0001	Kensington Gardens Resort	13%	12345 Redmond Rd
7	HAMPTONV0001	Hampton Village Eatery	20%	234 Hampton Village
8	HEALTHYC0001	Healthy Concepts	11%	1234 Westown Road

To accomplish this, you can use a DAX function named RELATED. Similar to VLOOKUP in standard Excel, the RELATED function allows you to look up values from one table in order to use them in another.

Follow these steps to create a new calculated column that displays a discounted amount for each transaction in the InvoiceDetails table:

1. **In the InvoiceDetails table, click the first blank cell in the empty column labeled Add Column, on the far right.**

2. **In the Formula Bar, type** =RELATED(.

   As soon as you enter the open parenthesis, a menu of available fields (shown in Figure 4-16) is displayed. Note that the items in the list represent the table name followed by the field name in brackets. In this case, you're interested in the Customers[Discount Amount] field.

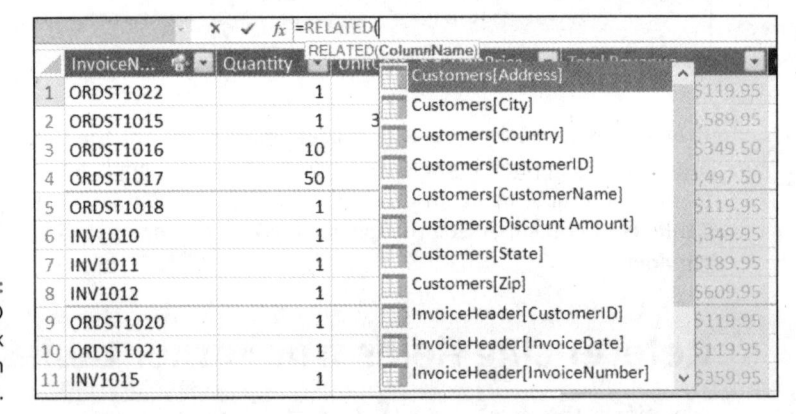

FIGURE 4-16:
Use the RELATED function to look up a field from another table.

3. **Double-click the Customers[Discount Amount] field and then press Enter.**

   Power Pivot automatically renames the column to Calculated Column 1.

4. **Double-click the column label and rename the column** Discount%.

524 BOOK 6 **Reporting and Querying Data**

5. **Starting in the next column, click the first blank cell in the empty column labeled Add Column, on the far right.**

6. **In the Formula Bar, type** =[UnitPrice]*[Quantity]*(1-[Discount%]) **and then press Enter.**

   Power Pivot automatically renames the column to Calculated Column 1.

7. **Double-click the column label and rename the column** Discounted Revenue.

The reward for your efforts is a new column that uses the discount percent from the Customers table to calculate discounted revenue for each transaction. Figure 4-17 illustrates the new calculated column.

FIGURE 4-17: The final discount amount calculated column using the Discount% column from the Customers table.

UnitCost	UnitPrice	Total Revenue	Discount%	Discounted Revenue
1	59.29	119.95	$119.95	13.00%	$104.36
1	3290.55	6589.95	$6,589.95	11.00%	$5,865.06
10	35	34.95	$349.50	9.00%	$318.05
50	91.59	189.95	$9,497.50	6.00%	$8,927.65
1	59.29	119.95	$119.95	9.00%	$109.15
1	674.5	1349.95	$1,349.95	15.00%	$1,147.46
1	91.25	189.95	$189.95	17.00%	$157.66
1	303.85	609.95	$609.95	5.00%	$579.45

=RELATED(Customers[Discount Amount])

REMEMBER The RELATED function leverages the relationships you defined when creating the data model to perform the lookup. So, this list of choices contains only the fields that are available based on the relationships you defined.

Nesting functions

In the example from the preceding section, you first create a Discount% column using the RELATED function; then you use that column in another calculated column to calculate the discount amount.

You don't necessarily have to create multiple calculated columns to accomplish a task like this one. You could instead nest the RELATED function into the discount amount calculation. The following line shows the syntax for the nested calculation:

```
=[UnitPrice]*[Quantity]*(1-RELATED(Customers[Discount Amount]))
```

CHAPTER 4 Adding Formulas to Power Pivot   525

As you can see, *nesting* simply means to embed functions within a calculation. In this case, rather than use the RELATED function in a separate Discount% field, you can embed it directly into the discounted revenue calculation.

Nesting functions can definitely save time and even improve performance in larger data models. On the other hand, complicated nested functions can be harder to read and understand.

Understanding Calculated Measures

You can enhance the functionality of your Power Pivot reports by using a kind of calculation called a *calculated measure*. Calculated measures are not applied to the Power Pivot window like calculated columns. Instead, they're applied directly to the PivotTable, creating a sort of virtual column that isn't visible in the Power Pivot window. You use calculated measures when you need to calculate based on an aggregated grouping of rows.

Creating a calculated measure

Imagine that you want to show the difference in unit costs between the years 2020 and 2019 for each of your customers. Think about what technically has to be done to achieve this calculation: You have to figure out the sum of unit costs for 2020, determine the sum of unit costs for 2019, and then subtract the sum of 2020 from the sum of 2019. This calculation simply can't be completed using calculated columns. Using calculated measures is the only way to calculate the cost variance between 2020 and 2019.

Follow these steps to create a calculated measure:

1. **Start with a PivotTable created from a Power Pivot data model.**

   The 6.4.1 Power Pivot Formulas.xlsx workbook contains the Calculated Measures worksheet with a PivotTable already created.

2. **Click the Power Pivot tab on the ribbon, and choose Measures⇨New Measure.**

   The Measure dialog box, shown in Figure 4-18, opens.

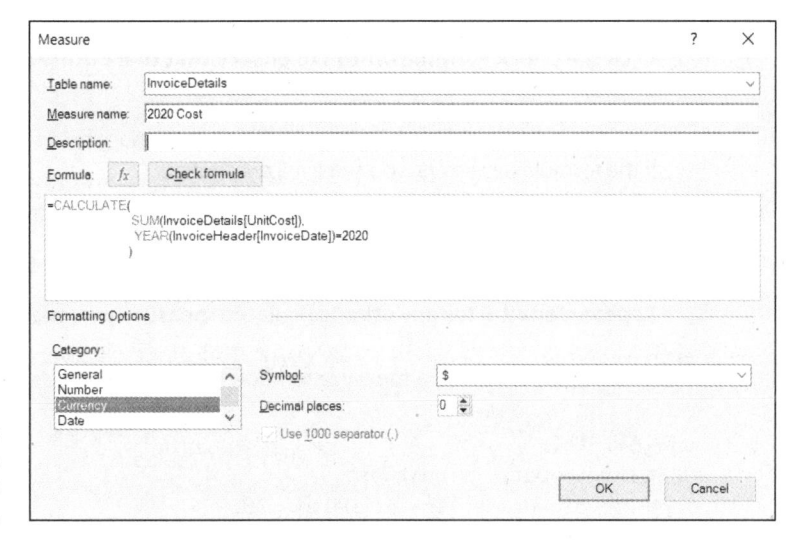

FIGURE 4-18:
Creating a new calculated measure.

3. **In the Measure dialog box, set the following inputs:**

   - *Table name:* Choose the table you want to contain the calculated measure when looking at the PivotTable Fields List. Don't sweat this decision too much. The table you select has no bearing on how the calculation works. It's simply a preference on where you want to see the new calculation within the PivotTable Fields List.

   - *Measure name:* Give the calculated measure a descriptive name.

   - *Description:* Enter a friendly description to document what the calculation does.

   - *Formula:* Enter the DAX formula that will calculate the results of the new field.

     In this example, you use the following DAX formula:

     ```
     =CALCULATE(
     SUM( InvoiceDetails[UnitCost] ),
     YEAR( InvoiceHeader[InvoiceDate] )=2020
     )
     ```

     This formula uses the CALCULATE function to sum the Total Revenue column from the InvoiceDetails table, where the Year column in the InvoiceHeader is equal to 2020.

   - *Formatting Options:* Specify the formatting for the calculated measure results.

CHAPTER 4 **Adding Formulas to Power Pivot** 527

4. **Click the Check Formula button to ensure that there are no syntax errors.**

   If your formula is well formed, you see the message No errors in formula. If the formula has errors, you see a full description.

5. **Click OK.**

   You see your newly created calculated measure in the PivotTable.

6. **Repeat steps 2–5 for any other calculated measure you need to create.**

In this example, you need a measure to show the 2019 cost:

```
=CALCULATE(
SUM(InvoiceDetails[UnitCost]),
YEAR(InvoiceHeader[InvoiceDate])=2019
)
```

You also need a measure to calculate the variance:

```
=[2020 Revenue]-[2019 Revenue]
```

Figure 4-19 illustrates the newly created calculated measures. The calculated measures are applied to each customer, displaying the variance between their 2020 and 2019 costs. As you can see, each calculated measure is available for selection in the PivotTable Fields List.

FIGURE 4-19: Calculated measures can be seen in the PivotTable Fields List.

2020 Cost	2019 Cost	2020 vs 2019
$3,239	$7,922	($4,683)
$1,244	$1,308	($64)
$56	$56	$0
$225	$186	$39
$324		$324
$14,060	$16,791	($2,731)
$1,859		$1,859
$2,525	$6,781	($4,256)
$3,436	$3,020	$416
$2,906	$9,069	($6,163)
$8		$8
$59		$59
$35,461	$2,233	$33,228

TIP Always try to achieve readability by using carriage returns and spaces. In Figure 4-18, the DAX calculation is entered with carriage returns and spaces. This is purely for readability purposes. DAX ignores white spaces and isn't case sensitive, so it's quite forgiving on how you structure the calculation.

Editing and deleting calculated measures

You may find that you need to either edit or delete a calculated measure. You can do so by following these steps:

1. **Click anywhere inside the PivotTable, click the Power Pivot tab on the ribbon, and choose Measures➪Manage Measures.**

   The Manage Measures dialog box opens.

2. **Select the target calculated measure, and click one of these two buttons:**

   - *Edit:* Opens the Measure dialog box, where you can make changes to the calculation setting.

   - *Delete:* Opens a message box asking you to confirm that you want to remove the measure. After you confirm, the calculated measure is removed.

CHAPTER 4 **Adding Formulas to Power Pivot** 529

IN THIS CHAPTER

» Spelling out Power Query basics

» Managing existing queries

» Overviewing query actions

» Extracting data from files

» Getting data from external databases

» Importing from other nonstandard data systems

» Understanding the Data Profiling feature

Chapter **5**

Meeting Power Query and Its Connection Types

In information management, the term *ETL* describes the three separate functions typically required to integrate disparate data sources: Extract, Transform, and Load. Extraction involves reading the data from the specified source and retrieving the desired subset of data. Transformation means cleaning, shaping, and aggregating the data to convert it to the desired structure. Loading is the actual importing or writing of the resulting data to the target location.

Excel analysts have been manually performing ETL processes for years — although they rarely call it ETL. Every day, millions of Excel users manually pull data from a source location, manipulate that data, and integrate it into their reporting. This process requires lots of manual effort. Power Query greatly improves each part of the ETL experience:

» It provides an intuitive mechanism for extracting data from a wide variety of sources.

» It enables you to perform complex transformations on the extracted data.

» It enables you to load the transformed data into a workbook or into the internal data model.

This chapter covers the basics of the Power Query Add-in. Then it fills you in on the various connection types you can leverage to import external data.

Power Query Basics

In this section, we walk you through a simple example of using Power Query. Imagine that you need to import Microsoft Corporation stock prices from the past 30 days by using Yahoo Finance. For this scenario, you need to perform a web query to pull the data you need from Yahoo Finance.

Starting the query

To start the query, follow these steps:

1. **On the Data tab of the Excel ribbon, go to the Get & Transform Data group, select the Get Data command, click From Other Sources, and then click From Web (see Figure 5-1).**

   WARNING: Don't be tempted to click the From Web button in the Get & Transform Data group on the Data tab of the ribbon. This unfortunate duplicate command is the legacy web-scraping capability found in all Excel versions since Excel 2000. The Power Query version of the From Web command (found in the Get Data drop-down list) goes beyond simple web scraping. Power Query can pull data from advanced web pages and manipulate the data. Make sure you're using the correct feature when pulling data from the web.

2. **In the dialog box that appears, enter the URL for the data you need, as shown in Figure 5-2.**

   In this example, you type `http://finance.yahoo.com/q/hp?s=MSFT`.

   After Excel establishes the connection, the Navigator dialog box shown in Figure 5-3 appears. You can select the data source that you want to extract. Click each table to see a preview of the data.

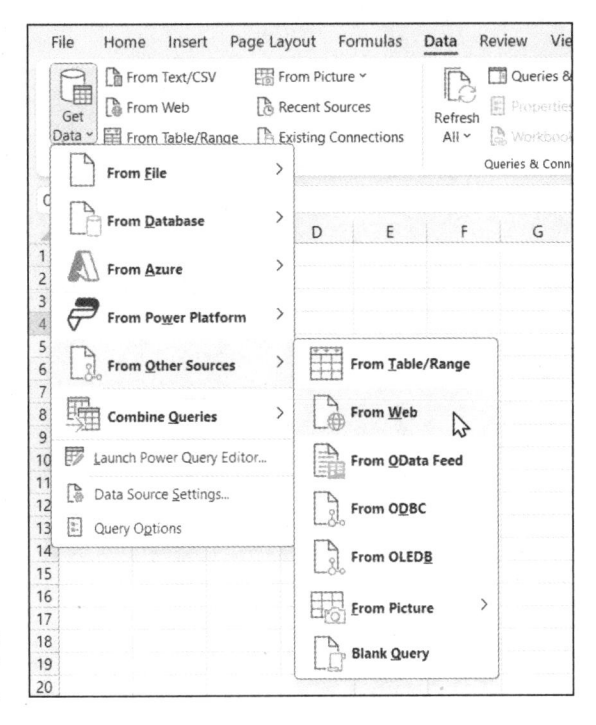

FIGURE 5-1:
Starting a Power Query web query.

FIGURE 5-2:
Enter the target URL containing the data you need.

3. **In this case, Table 0 holds the historical stock data you need, so click Table 0 in the list box on the left and then click the Transform Data button.**

   You may have noticed that the Navigator dialog box, shown in Figure 5-3, offers a Load button (next to the Transform Data button). You can use this button to skip any editing and import your targeted data as is. If you're sure that you won't need to transform or shape your data in any way, click the Load button to import the data directly into the data model or a spreadsheet in your workbook.

CHAPTER 5 Meeting Power Query and Its Connection Types   533

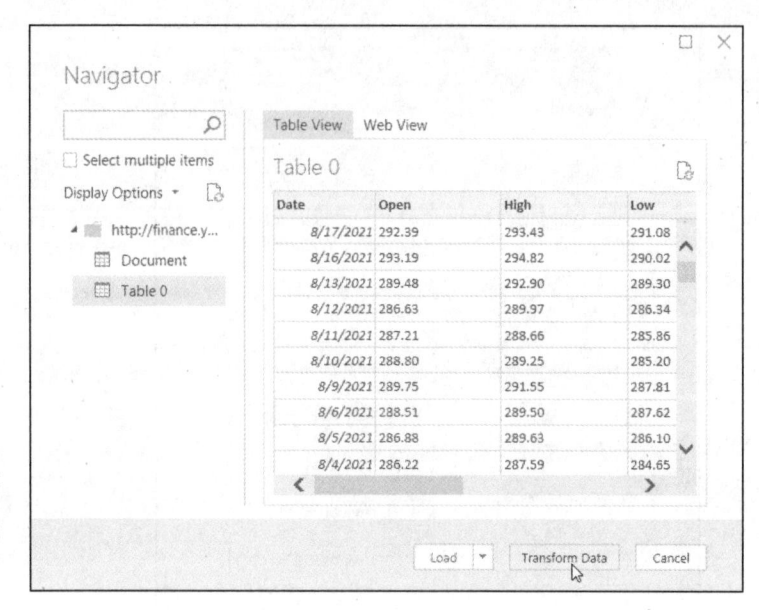

FIGURE 5-3:
Select the correct data source and then click the Transform Data button.

When you click the Transform Data button, Power Query activates a new Query Editor window, which contains its own ribbon and a preview pane that shows a preview of the data (see Figure 5-4). You can apply certain actions to shape, clean, and transform the data before importing.

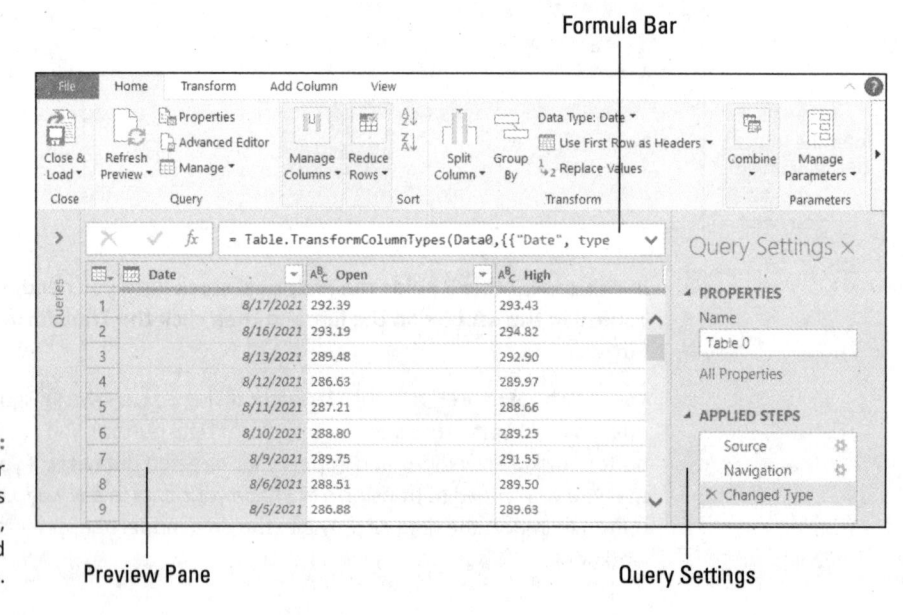

FIGURE 5-4:
The Query Editor window allows you to shape, clean, and transform data.

534 BOOK 6 **Reporting and Querying Data**

The idea is to work with each column shown in the Query Editor, applying the necessary actions that will give you the data and structure you need. You can dive deeper into column actions later in this chapter. For now, continue toward the goal of getting the last 30 days of stock prices for Microsoft Corporation.

4. **Click the High field and then hold down the Ctrl key on your keyboard while you click the Low field and the Close field.**

5. **Right-click and choose Change Type➪Currency, as shown in Figure 5-5.**

   This ensures that the Date field is formatted as a proper date. Power Query will ask if you want to replace the current step or add a new step.

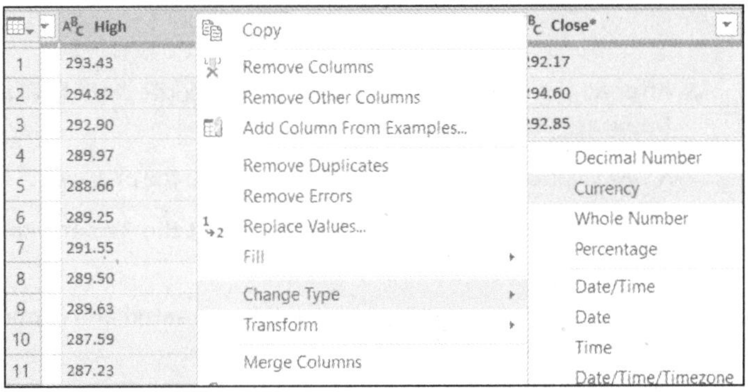

FIGURE 5-5: Change the data type of the High, Low, and Close fields to currency format.

6. **Choose Add a New Step.**

7. **Remove all unnecessary columns by right-clicking each one and selecting Remove.**

   Besides the Date field, the only other columns you need are the High, Low, and Close fields.

   Alternatively, you can hold down the Ctrl key on the keyboard, select the columns you want to keep, right-click any selected column, and then choose Remove Other Columns.

   You may notice that some of the rows show the word *Error*. These rows contained text values that couldn't be converted.

8. **Remove the Error rows by right-clicking the High field and selecting Remove Errors, as shown in Figure 5-6.**

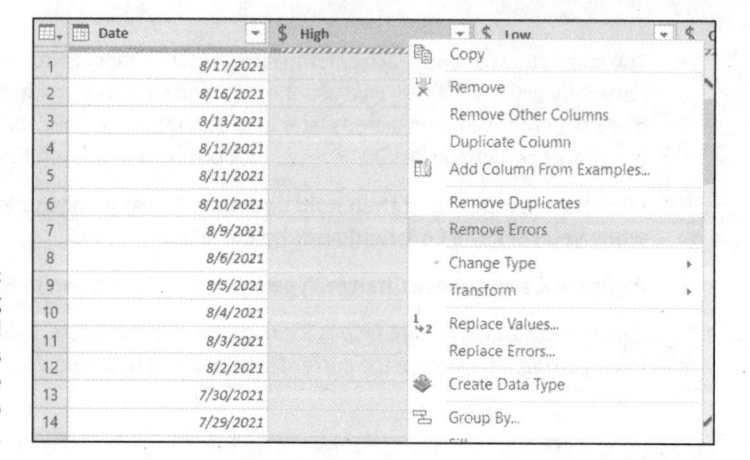

FIGURE 5-6: Removing errors caused by text values that couldn't be converted to currency.

9. **After all the errors are removed, right-click the Date field and select the Duplicate Column command.**

   A new column (named Date-Copy) is added to the preview.

10. **Right-click the newly added column, select the Rename command, and then rename the column Week Of.**

11. **Right-click the Week Of column you just created and choose Transform⇨Week⇨Start of Week.**

    Excel transforms the date to display the start of the week for a given date.

12. **When you've finished configuring your Power Query feed, click the Close & Load drop-down found on the Home tab of the Power Query Editor to reveal the two following commands:**

    - *Close & Load:* Saves your query and outputs the results to a new worksheet in your workbook as an Excel table. You can choose the Close & Load To command to activate the Import Data dialog box (see Figure 5-7). There, you can choose to output the results to a specific worksheet or to the internal data model.

    - *Close & Load To:* Activates the Import Data dialog box (see Figure 5-7). There, you can choose to output the results to a specific worksheet. The Import Data dialog box also enables you to save the query as a query connection only, which means you'll be able to use the query in various processes without needing to output the results anywhere.

13. **Select the New Worksheet radio button to output your results as a table on a new worksheet in the active workbook.**

14. **Click OK.**

536   BOOK 6 Reporting and Querying Data

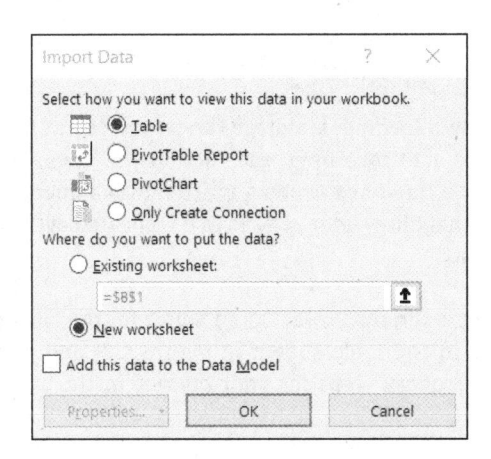

FIGURE 5-7:
The Import Data dialog box gives you more control over how the results of queries are used.

FIGURE 5-8:
Your final query pulled from the internet: transformed, put into an Excel table, and ready to use in a PivotTable.

	A	B	C	D	E
1	Date	High	Low	Close*	Week Of
2	8/17/2021	293.43	291.08	292.86	8/15/2021
3	8/16/2021	294.82	290.02	294.6	8/15/2021
4	8/13/2021	292.9	289.3	292.85	8/8/2021
5	8/12/2021	289.97	286.34	289.81	8/8/2021
6	8/11/2021	288.66	285.86	286.95	8/8/2021
7	8/10/2021	289.25	285.2	286.44	8/8/2021
8	8/9/2021	291.55	287.81	288.33	8/8/2021
9	8/6/2021	289.5	287.62	289.46	8/1/2021
10	8/5/2021	289.63	286.1	289.52	8/1/2021
11	8/4/2021	287.59	284.65	286.51	8/1/2021
12	8/3/2021	287.23	284	287.12	8/1/2021
13	8/2/2021	286.77	283.74	284.82	8/1/2021
14	7/30/2021	286.66	283.91	284.91	7/25/2021
15	7/29/2021	288.62	286.08	286.5	7/25/2021
16	7/28/2021	290.15	283.83	286.22	7/25/2021
17	7/27/2021	289.58	282.95	286.54	7/25/2021

At this point, you have a table similar to the one shown in Figure 5-8, which can be used to produce the PivotTable you need.

Take a moment to appreciate what Power Query allowed you to do just now. With a few clicks, you searched the internet, found some base data, shaped the data to keep only the columns you needed, and even manipulated that data to add an extra Week Of dimension to the base data. This is what Power Query is about: enabling you to easily extract, filter, and reshape data without the need for any programmatic coding skills.

> **TIP**
> You can get back to the Power Query Editor window for any query by activating the Queries & Connections task pane. On the Data tab of the ribbon, go to the Queries & Connections group and click the Queries & Connections button to activate the Queries & Connections task pane. From here, you can simply right-click a query and select Edit.

CHAPTER 5 **Meeting Power Query and Its Connection Types** 537

Understanding query steps

Power Query uses its own formula language (known as the M language) to codify your queries. As with macro recording, each action you take when working with Power Query results in a line of code being written into a query step. Query steps are embedded M code that allow your actions to be repeated every time you refresh your Power Query data.

To explore this concept, open the Power Query Editor for the table you just created. Right-click anywhere in the table shown in Figure 5-8 and choose Table ⇨ Edit Query. You can see the query steps for your queries in the Query Settings pane (see Figure 5-9).

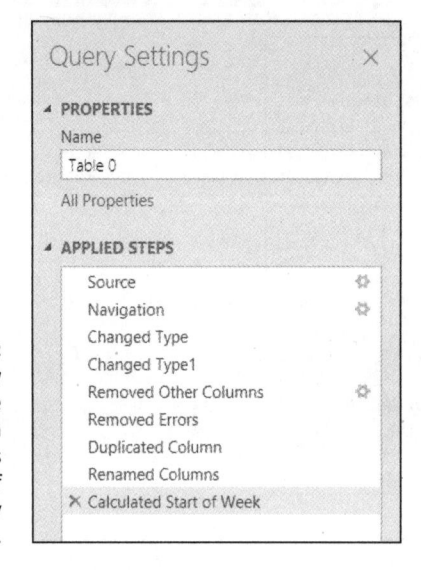

FIGURE 5-9:
You can view and manage query steps in the Applied Steps section of the Query Settings pane.

Each query step represents an action you took to get to a data table. You can click any step to see the underlying M code in the Power Query Formula Bar. For example, clicking the step called Removed Errors reveals the code for that step in the Formula Bar.

TIP If you don't see the Query Settings pane, click the Query Settings command on the View tab of the Power Query Editor ribbon. The View tab also contains the Formula Bar check box, allowing you to display the Formula Bar, which displays the M syntax for each given step.

When you click a query step, the data shown in the preview pane shows you what the data looked like up to and including the step you clicked. For example, in Figure 5-9, clicking the step before the Removed Other Columns step lets you see what the data looked like before you removed the nonessential columns.

You can right-click any step to see a menu of commands for managing your query steps. Figure 5-10 illustrates the following commands:

» **Edit Settings:** Edit the arguments or parameters for the selected step.

» **Rename:** Give the selected step a meaningful name.

» **Delete:** Remove the selected step. Be aware that removing a step can cause errors if subsequent steps depend on the deleted step.

» **Delete Until End:** Remove the selected step and all following steps.

» **Insert Step After:** Insert a step after the selected step.

» **Move Up:** Move the selected step up in the order of steps.

» **Move Down:** Move the selected step down in the order of steps.

» **Extract Previous:** Create a new query using the steps prior to the selected step.

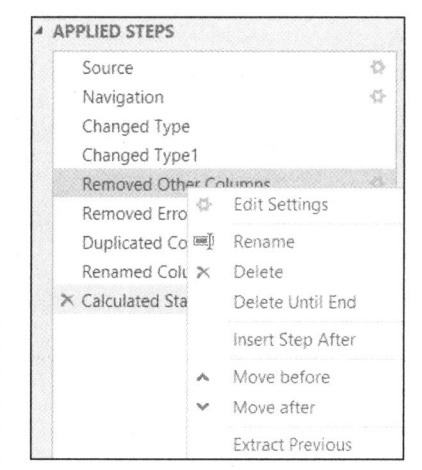

FIGURE 5-10: Right-click any query step to edit, rename, delete, or move the step.

Refreshing Power Query data

Power Query data is in no way connected to the source data used to extract it. A Power Query data table is merely a snapshot. In other words, as the source data changes, Power Query doesn't automatically keep up with the changes; you need to intentionally refresh your query.

If you chose to load your Power Query results to an Excel table in the existing workbook, you can manually refresh by right-clicking the table and clicking Refresh.

If you chose to load your Power Query data to the internal data model, click the Data tab, go to the Queries & Connections group, and then click Queries & Connections to display the Queries & Connections task pane. You can right-click the target query and click Refresh.

To get a bit more automated with the refreshing of queries, you can configure your data sources to automatically refresh the Power Query data. To do so, follow these steps:

1. **On the Data tab of the Excel ribbon, go to the Queries & Connections group and click the Queries & Connections command.**

   The Queries & Connections task pane appears.

2. **Right-click the Power Query data connection you want to refresh and click Properties.**

   The Properties dialog box opens.

3. **Select the Usage tab.**

4. **Set the options to refresh the chosen data connection:**

   - *Refresh Every X Minutes:* Tells Excel to automatically refresh the chosen data every specified number of minutes. Excel refreshes all tables associated with that connection.

   - *Refresh Data When Opening the File:* Tells Excel to automatically refresh the chosen data connection after opening the workbook. Excel refreshes all tables associated with that connection as soon as the workbook is opened.

These refresh options are useful when you want to ensure that your customers are working with the latest data. You or your customers can still manually refresh the data using the Refresh command on the Data tab of the ribbon.

Managing existing queries

As you add various queries to a workbook, you need a way to manage them. Excel accommodates this need by offering the Queries & Connections task pane, which enables you to edit, duplicate, refresh, and generally manage all existing queries in the workbook.

Open the Queries & Connections task pane by clicking the Queries & Connections button in the Queries & Connections group on the Data tab of the Excel ribbon. Find the query you want to work with, and right-click it to take any one of the actions described in the following list:

- **Edit:** Open the Query Editor, where you can modify the query steps.
- **Delete:** Delete the selected query.
- **Refresh:** Refresh the data in the selected query.
- **Load To:** Activate the Import Data dialog box, where you can redefine where the selected query's results are used.
- **Duplicate:** Create a copy of the query.
- **Reference:** Create a new query that references the output of the original query.
- **Merge:** Merge the selected query with another query in the workbook by matching specified columns.
- **Append:** Append the results of another query in the workbook to the selected query.
- **Send to Data Catalog:** Publish and share the selected query via a Microsoft Power BI server that your IT department sets up and manages.
- **Export Connection File:** Save an Office Data Connection (.odc) file with the connection credentials for the query's source data.
- **Move to Group:** Move the selected query into a logical group that you create for better organization.
- **Move Up:** Move the selected query up in the Queries & Connections pane.
- **Move Down:** Move the selected query down in the Queries & Connections pane.
- **Show the Peek:** Show a preview of the query results for the selected query.
- **Properties:** Rename the query and add a friendly description.

> **TIP** The Queries & Connections pane is especially useful when your workbook contains several queries. Think of this pane as a kind of table of contents that allows you to easily find and interact with the queries in your workbook.

Understanding Column-Level Actions

Right-clicking a column in the Power Query Editor activates a shortcut menu that shows a full list of the actions you can take. You can also apply certain actions to multiple columns at one time by selecting two or more columns before right-clicking. Table 5-1 explains the commands you see when right-clicking a column within the Power Query Editor.

TABLE 5-1 Column-Level Actions

Action	Purpose	Available with Multiple Columns?
Remove	Remove the selected column from the Power Query data.	Yes
Remove Other Columns	Remove all nonselected columns from the Power Query data.	Yes
Duplicate Column	Create a duplicate of the selected column as a new column placed on the far right end of the table. The name given to the new column is Copy of X, where X is the name of the original column.	No
Add Column from Examples	Similar to Excel's Flash Fill feature, this command creates data in a new column from examples you provide. Power Pivot automatically fills in data when it senses a pattern.	Yes
Remove Duplicates	Remove all rows from the selected column where the values duplicate earlier values. The row with the first occurrence of a value isn't removed.	Yes
Remove Errors	Remove rows containing errors in the selected column.	Yes
Change Type	Change the data type of the selected column to any of these types: Binary, Date, Date/Time, Date/Time/Timezone, Duration, Number, Currency, Decimal Number, Whole Number, Percentage, Text, Time, or Using Locale (which localizes data types to the country you specify).	Yes
Transform	Change the way values in the column are rendered. You can choose from the following commands: Lowercase, Uppercase, Capitalize Each Word, Left, Trim, Clean, and Length. If the values in the column are date/time values, the commands are Date, Time, Day, Month, Year, or Day of Week. If the values in the column are number values, the commands are Round, Absolute Value, Factorial, Base-10 Logarithm, Natural Logarithm, Power, and Square Root.	Yes
Replace Values	Replace one value in the selected column with another specified value.	Yes

Action	Purpose	Available with Multiple Columns?
Replace Errors	Replace unsightly error values with your own, friendlier text.	Yes
Create Data Type	Stores multiple columns of data in one column as metadata, allowing you to expose all the data you need without taking up space in your worksheet. Excel formulas can interact with these rich data types to expose the stored data within.	Yes
Group By	Aggregate data by row values. For example, you can group by state and either count the number of cities in each state or sum the population of each state.	Yes
Fill	Fill empty cells in the column with the value of the first non-empty cell. You have the option to fill up or fill down.	Yes
Unpivot Other Columns	Transpose the unselected columns from column-oriented to row-oriented or vice versa.	Yes
Unpivot Selected Columns	Transpose the selected columns from column-oriented to row-oriented or vice versa.	Yes
Rename	Rename the selected column to a name you specify.	No
Move	Move the selected column to a different location in the table. You have these choices for moving the column: Left, Right, To Beginning, and To End.	Yes
Drill Down	Navigate to the contents of the column. This command is used with tables that contain metadata representing embedded information.	No
Add as New Query	Create a new query with the content of the column, by referencing the original query in the new one. The name of the new query is the same as the column header of the selected column.	No
Split Column (ribbon only)	Split the value of a single column into two or more columns, based on a number of characters or a given delimiter, such as a comma, semicolon, or tab.	No
Merge Column (ribbon only)	Merge the values of two or more columns into a single column that contains a specified delimiter, such as a comma, semicolon, or tab.	Yes

> **TIP** All column-level actions available in Power Query are also available on the Query Editor ribbon, so you can either choose the convenience of right-clicking to quickly select an action or use the more visual ribbon list. A few useful column-level actions are found only on the ribbon, as described in Table 5-1.

Understanding Table Actions

While you're in the Query Editor, Power Query lets you apply certain actions to an entire data table. You can see the available table-level actions by clicking the Table Actions icon.

Table 5-2 lists the more commonly used table-level actions and describes the primary purpose of each one.

TABLE 5-2 **Table-Level Actions**

Action	Purpose
Use First Row as Headers	Replace each table header name with the values in the first row of each column.
Add Custom Column	Insert a new column after the last column of the table. The values in the new column are determined by the value or formula you define.
Add Column from Example	Similar to Excel's Flash Fill feature, this command creates data in a new column from examples you provide. Power Pivot automatically fills in data when it senses a pattern.
Add Conditional Column	Insert a new column that contains the results of a specified IF . . . THEN . . . ELSE statement.
Add Index Column	Insert a new column containing a sequential list of numbers starting from 1, 0, or another specified value you define.
Choose Columns	Choose the columns you want to keep in the query results.
Keep Top Rows	Remove all but the top *n* number of rows. You specify the number threshold.
Keep Bottom Rows	Remove all but the bottom *n* number of rows. You specify the number threshold.
Keep Range of Rows	Remove all rows except the ones that fall within a range you specify.
Keep Duplicates	Remove all but duplicated rows.
Keep Errors	Remove all but duplicated rows with error values.
Remove Top Rows	Remove the top *n* rows from the table.
Remove Bottom Rows	Remove the bottom *n* rows from the table.
Remove Alternate Rows	Remove alternate rows from the table, starting at the first row to remove and specifying the number of rows to remove and the number of rows to keep.
Remove Duplicates	Remove all rows where the values in the selected columns duplicate earlier values. The row with the first occurrence of a value set isn't removed.

Action	Purpose
Remove Errors	Remove rows containing errors in the selected columns.
Merge Queries	Create a new query that merges the current table with another query in the workbook by matching specified columns.
Append Queries	Create a new query that appends the results of another query in the workbook to the current table.

TIP All table-level actions available in Power Query are also available on the Power Query Editor ribbon, so you can either choose the convenience of right-clicking to quickly select an action or use the more visual ribbon.

Importing Data from Files

Organizational data is often stored in files such as text files, comma-separated values (CSV) files, and even other Excel workbooks. It's not uncommon to use these kinds of files as data sources for data analysis. Power Query offers several connection types that enable the importing of data from external files.

TECHNICAL STUFF A *CSV* file is a kind of text file that contains commas to delimit (separate) values into columns of data.

REMEMBER The files you import don't necessarily have to be on your own PC. You can import files on network drives, as well as in cloud repositories such as Google Drive and Microsoft OneDrive.

Getting data from Excel workbooks

You can import data from other Excel workbooks by clicking the Data tab of the ribbon, clicking Get Data, clicking From File, and then clicking From Excel Workbook. The Import Data dialog box opens. There you can browse for the Excel file you want to work with. Note that you can import any kind of Excel file, including macro-enabled workbooks and template workbooks.

After you've selected a file, the Navigator pane activates (see Figure 5-11), showing you all the data sources available in the workbook.

CHAPTER 5 **Meeting Power Query and Its Connection Types** 545

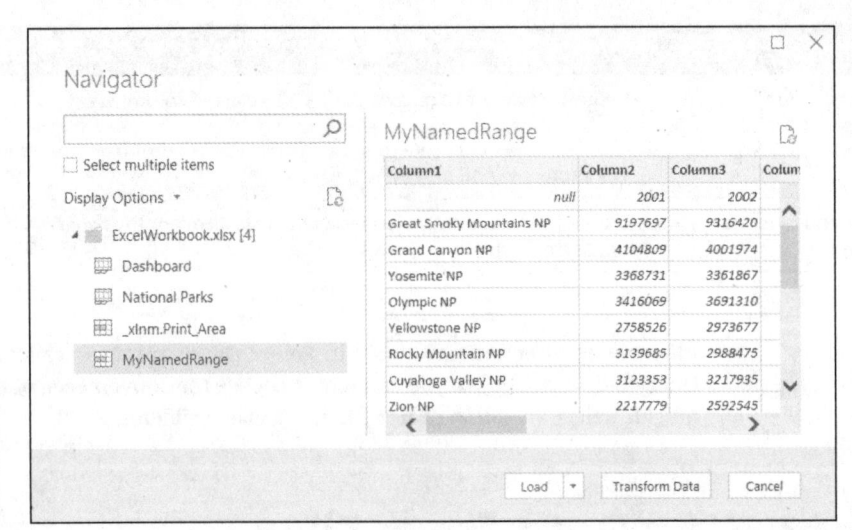

FIGURE 5-11:
Select the data sources you want to work with, and then click the Load button.

The idea here is to select the data source you want and then either load or transform the data using the buttons at the bottom of the Navigator pane. Click the Load button to skip any editing and import your targeted data as is. Click the Transform Data button if you want to transform or shape the data before completing the import.

In terms of Excel workbooks, a *data source* is either a worksheet or a defined named range. The icons next to each data source let you distinguish which sources are worksheets and which are named ranges. In Figure 5-11, the source named MyNamedRange is a defined named range, and the source named National Parks is a worksheet.

You can import multiple sources at a time by selecting the Select Multiple Items check box and then placing a check mark next to each worksheet and named range that you want to import.

REMEMBER

Power Query won't bring in charts, PivotTables, shapes, Visual Basic for Applications (VBA) code, or any other objects that may exist within a workbook. Power Query simply imports the data found in the used cell ranges of the workbook.

Getting data from CSV and text files

Text files are commonly used to store and distribute data because of their inherent ability to hold many thousands of bytes of data without having an inflated file size. Text files can do this by forgoing all the fancy formatting, leaving only the text.

To import a text file, click the Data tab of the ribbon, click Get Data, click From File, and then click From Text/CSV. The Import Data dialog box opens. There you can browse for and select a text or CSV file.

Power Query then opens the dialog box shown in Figure 5-12. Here, you can preview the contents and specify how the file should be imported. Note the drop-down lists at the top of the dialog box:

- **File Origin:** Define what encoding standards to use. This list is useful when you're handling data that comes from different regions of the world.

- **Delimiter:** Specify how the contents are delimited. Some text files are tab delimited, meaning they contain tab characters that separate text values into columns of data. Other text files are comma delimited, while others still are delimited by another character such as a space or a colon. Use the Delimiter drop-down list to tell Power Query which delimiter to look for when separating values into columns.

- **Data Type Detection:** When you import text files, Power Query uses the first 200 rows to guess the data types for each of the columns in the data. For instance, if the first 200 rows of a particular column are made up of numbers, Power Query will automatically change the data type of that column to numeric after importing the file. The Data Type Detection drop-down list allows you to tell Power Query to analyze the entire file (as opposed to the first 200 rows) when guessing the data types. You also have the option of telling Power Query not to change any data types.

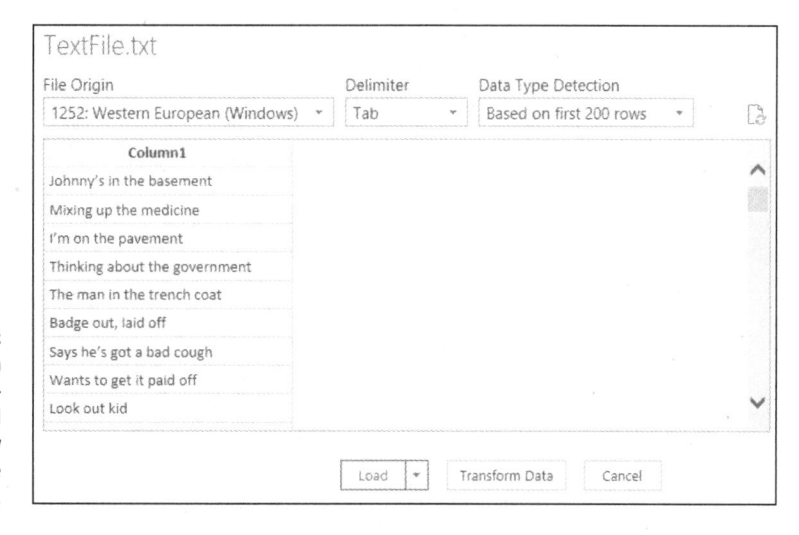

FIGURE 5-12: Preview the data and use the drop-down lists to tell Power Query how to import the data.

Click the Load button to import the data directly into your workbook. Click the Transform Data button to bring the data source into the Query Editor, where you can apply your edits and then click the Close & Load command to complete the import.

Getting data from PDF files

Power Query enables you to import data from PDFs. You can access PDF data by clicking the Data tab of the ribbon, clicking Get Data, clicking From File, and then clicking From PDF. The Import Data dialog box opens, allowing you to browse for your target PDF. After a few seconds, the Navigator dialog box, shown in Figure 5-13, opens, showing you the available tables and pages found in your chosen file.

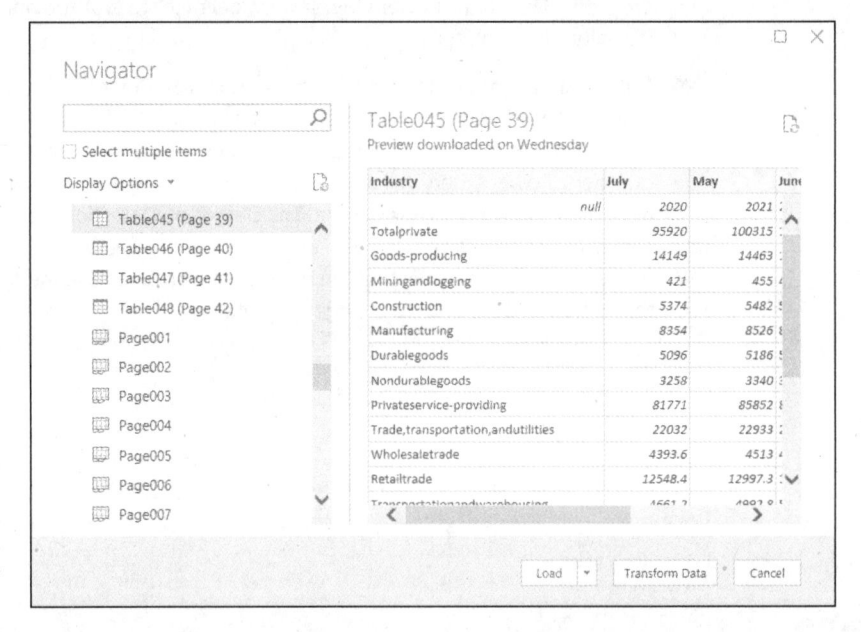

FIGURE 5-13: The available tables and pages in the PDF are shown in the Navigator dialog box.

Notice that both structured tables and pages are shown, allowing you the option of importing a specific table or an entire page from the PDF. Simply click the item you want to import and then click the Load button to import directly into your workbook or click the Transform Data button to clean the source data before importing.

You can even import multiple items from your PDFs by selecting the Select Multiple Items check box (see Figure 5-13).

TIP — Rarely does the data from a PDF come in clean. You'll almost always need to click the Transform Data button in order to clean up column names, remove empty spaces, and generally remove unwanted data elements.

Getting data from folders

Power Query has the ability to use the Windows file system as a data source, enabling you to import a list of folder contents for a specified directory. This feature comes in handy when you need to create a list of all the files in a particular folder.

Click the Data tab of the ribbon, click Get Data, click From File, and then click From Folder. After you browse for the folder (directory) you want to use, the dialog box shown in Figure 5-14 opens.

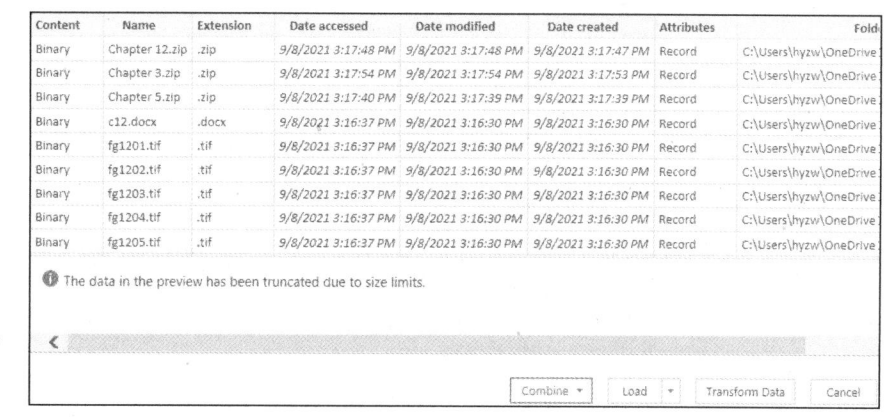

FIGURE 5-14: Data preview of the files in the target folder.

The incoming data contains a row for each file contained inside the folder, including any files in subfolders. Click the Load button to import the data directly into your workbook. Click the Transform Data button to bring the data into the Query Editor.

In the Power Query Editor (see Figure 5-15), you'll see that the imported table shows the key attributes for each file, such as filename, file extension, date created, and date modified. You can even click the Expand icon in the Attributes field and choose to display some of the more advanced attributes for each file.

After you have all the attributes you need, you can click the Close & Load button on the Home tab of the ribbon to complete the import.

CHAPTER 5 **Meeting Power Query and Its Connection Types** 549

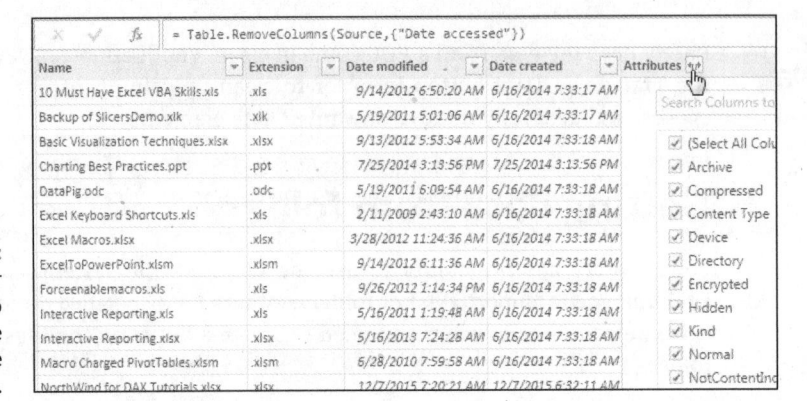

FIGURE 5-15: Use the Power Query Editor to add more file attributes to the import.

> **TIP** The files that are listed include all files contained in subfolders inside the folder you specified. Unfortunately, the resulting output is not hyperlinked back to the actual folder contents. In other words, you can't open the individual files from the query table.

Importing Data from Database Systems

In smart organizations, the task of data management is not performed by Excel; instead, it's performed primarily by database systems such as Microsoft Access and SQL Server. Databases like these not only store millions of rows of data, but also ensure data integrity and allow for the rapid search and retrieval of data by way of queries and views.

A connection for every database type

Power Query offers commands to connect to a wide array of database types. Microsoft has been keen to add connection types for as many commonly used databases as it can.

Relational and OLAP databases

On the Data tab of the ribbon, click Get Data and then click From Database to display the list of accessible databases types. Power Query has the ability to connect to virtually any database commonly used today: Microsoft Access, MySQL, Oracle, SQL Server, and so forth.

Azure databases

If your organization has a Microsoft Azure cloud database or a subscription to Microsoft Azure Marketplace, you can use the connection types designed to import data from Azure databases. On the Data tab of the ribbon, click Get Data, click From Azure, and then click the appropriate connection type on the continuation menu.

ODBC connections to nonstandard databases

If you're using a unique, nonstandard database system that isn't listed on the From Database continuation menu or the From Azure continuation menu, not to worry: As long as your database system can be connected to via an ODBC connection string, Power Query can connect to it.

On the Data tab of the ribbon, click Get Data and then click From Other Data Sources to see a list of other connection types. Click the From ODBC command to start a connection to your unique database via an ODBC connection string.

Getting data from other data systems

In addition to ODBC, Power Query can access various other kinds of data systems.

Some of these data systems (such as Microsoft Exchange and SharePoint) are popular systems that are used in many organizations to store data and manage emails. Other systems (such as Hadoop and OData Feeds) are less-common services used to work with very large volumes of data. These services are often mentioned in conversations about big data. And of course, the From Web command (demonstrated earlier in this chapter) is an integral connection type for any analyst who leverages data from the internet.

Clicking any of these connections opens a set of dialog boxes customized for the selected connection. These dialog boxes ask for the basic parameters that Power Query needs in order to connect to the specified data source (parameters such as file path, URL, server name, and credentials).

Each connection type requires its own, unique set of parameters, so each of the dialog boxes is different. Luckily, Power Query rarely needs more than a handful of parameters to connect to any single data source, so the dialog boxes are relatively intuitive and hassle-free.

Walk-through: Getting data from a database

Walking through the connection process for every type of database available would be redundant. However, it would be useful to walk through the basic steps of connecting to a database.

Here are the steps for connecting an Excel workbook to one of the more ubiquitous database systems, Microsoft Access:

1. **On the Data tab of the ribbon, click Get Data, click From Database, and then click From Microsoft Access Database.**

2. **Browse for your target database.**

   TIP: You can use the 6.3.2 Facility Services.accdb database, found in the sample files for Book 6, Chapter 3.

   After Power Query connects to the database, the Navigator pane, shown in Figure 5-16, activates. There, you see all database objects available to you, including tables and views (or *queries,* in Access lingo).

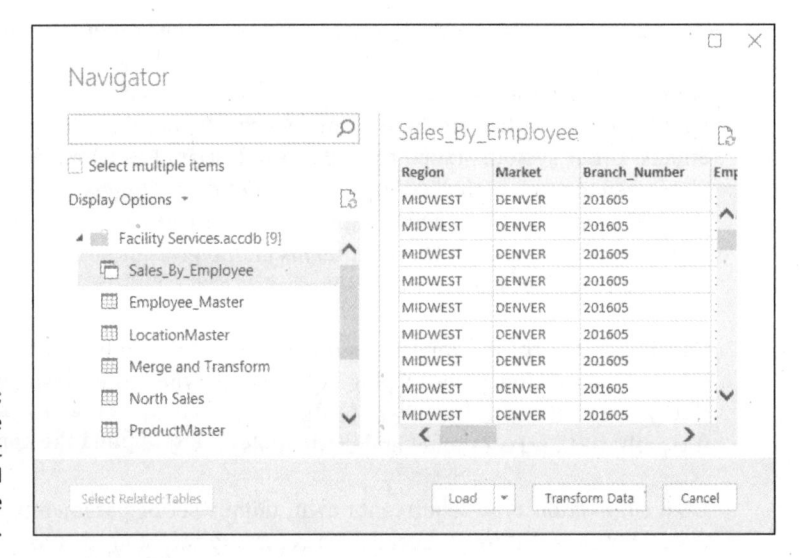

   FIGURE 5-16: Select the view you want imported, and then click the Load button.

3. **Click the Sales_By_Employee view.**

   The Navigator pane displays a preview of the Sales_By_Employee data. If you want to transform or shape this data, click the Transform Data button. In this case, the data looks fine as is.

4. **Click the Load button to complete the import.**

   After a bit of processing, Power Query loads the data to a new Excel worksheet and adds the new query to the Workbook Queries pane, as shown in Figure 5-17.

FIGURE 5-17:
The final imported database data.

> **REMEMBER**
> You can select multiple tables and views by selecting the Select Multiple Items check box and then placing a check mark next to each database object you want imported.

> **REMEMBER**
> The icon next to each database object distinguishes whether that object is a table or a view. Views have an icon that looks like two overlapping grids. See the icon for the Sales_By_Employee view, shown in Figure 5-16, for an example.

It's a best practice to use views whenever possible. Views are often cleaner datasets because they're already optimized to include only the columns and data that are necessary. (This optimization improves query performance and helps minimize the workbook's file size.) In addition, you don't need to have an intimate knowledge of the database architecture. Someone with that knowledge has already done the work for you — joined the correct tables, applied the appropriate business rules, and optimized output, for example.

Managing Data Source Settings

Every time you connect to any web-based data source or data source that requires some level of credentials, Power Query *caches* (stores) the settings for that data source.

Suppose that you connect to a SQL Server database, enter all your credentials, and import the data you need. At the moment of successful connection, Power Query caches information about that connection in a file located on your local PC. It includes the connection string, username, password, and privacy settings, for example.

The purpose of all this caching is so that you don't have to reenter credentials every time you need to refresh your queries. That's nifty, but what happens when your credentials are changed? Well, the short answer is those queries will fail until the data source settings are updated.

You can edit data source settings by activating the Data Source Settings dialog box. To do so, click the Data tab of the ribbon, click Get Data, and then click Data Source Settings. The Data Source Settings dialog box, shown in Figure 5-18, contains a list of all credentials-based data sources previously used in queries. Select the data source you need to change, and then click the Edit Permissions button.

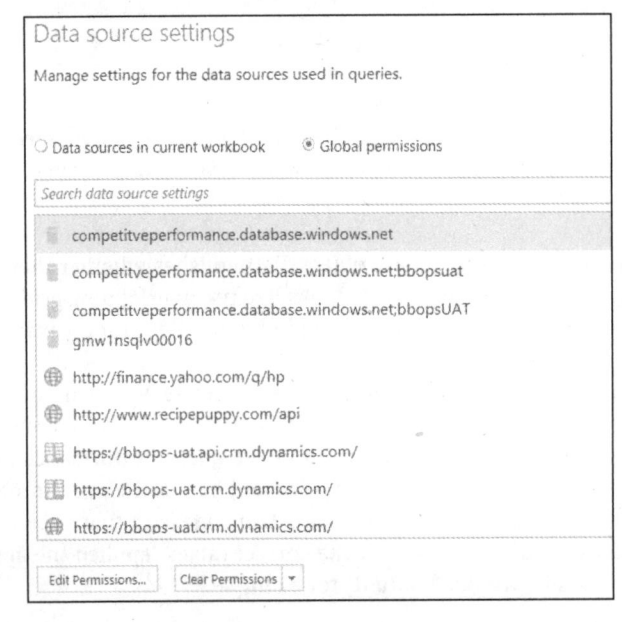

FIGURE 5-18: Edit a data source by selecting it and clicking the Edit Permissions button.

Another dialog box opens — this time, specific to the data source you selected (see Figure 5-19). This dialog box enables you to edit credentials and other data privacy settings.

554   BOOK 6 **Reporting and Querying Data**

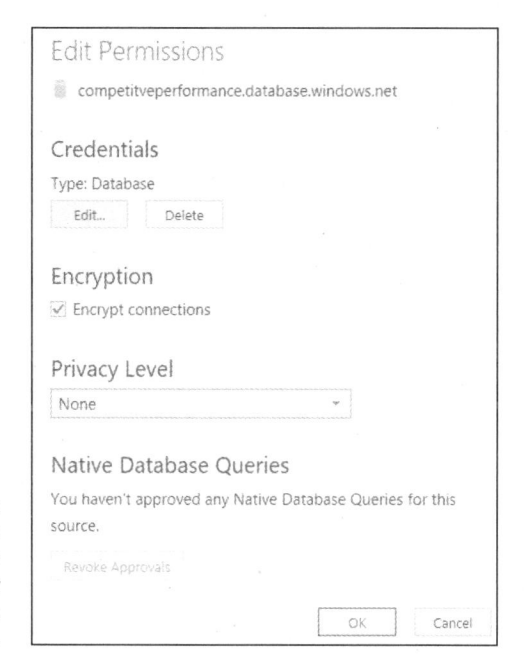

FIGURE 5-19:
Edit the credentials for a data source by clicking the Edit button.

Click the Edit button to make changes to the credentials for the data source. The credentials editing screen will differ based on the data source you're working with, but again, the input dialog boxes are relatively intuitive and easy to update.

Power Query caches data source settings in a file located on your local PC. Even though you may have deleted a particular query, the data source setting is retained for possible future use. This can lead to a cluttered list of old and current data sources. You can clean out old items by selecting the data source in the Data Source Settings dialog box and clicking the Clear Permissions button.

Data Profiling with Power Query

When you're importing a new data source, it's often useful to understand the intricacies and pitfalls of the data before you start working with it. For instance, how many records are empty? How many unique values are there in a given column? What are the minimum and maximum values? Power Query's data profiling capabilities allow you to know your data and identify potential issues before using it.

In this section, we fill you in on some of the ways you can leverage data profiling in Power Query to get a better understanding of your data and address problem areas before they become a problem later in your reporting processes.

Data Profiling options

While in the Power Query Editor window, click the View tab to see options for data profiling in the Data Preview group (see Figure 5-20).

FIGURE 5-20: Data Profiling options are found in the Data Preview group under the View tab.

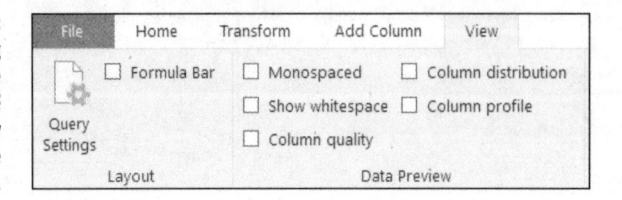

Take a moment to review the purpose of each option.

- **Monospaced:** Converts the font in the Data Preview window to monospaced, making it easier to see differences in data.

- **Show Whitespace:** Useful for calling out inline carriage returns and other invisible space characters.

- **Column Quality:** Displays the percentage of column values that are empty, the percentage that are rendered as errors, and the percentage that are considered valid values. This option is the most powerful in terms of providing an at-a-glance view of your data.

- **Column Distribution:** Provides a histogram visual displaying how many distinct and unique records are found in the values in each of the columns.

- **Column Profile:** Provides a useful way to see detailed descriptive statistics on a chosen column, such as the number of records with a 0 value, the minimum value in the column, the maximum value, the average value, and the standard deviation of all values in the column.

Be aware that the data profiler in Power Query, by default, profiles only the first 1,000 records. You can tell the profile to use the entire dataset to get a more complete picture of your data. Figure 5-21 illustrates how to change the scope of data profiling to the entire dataset.

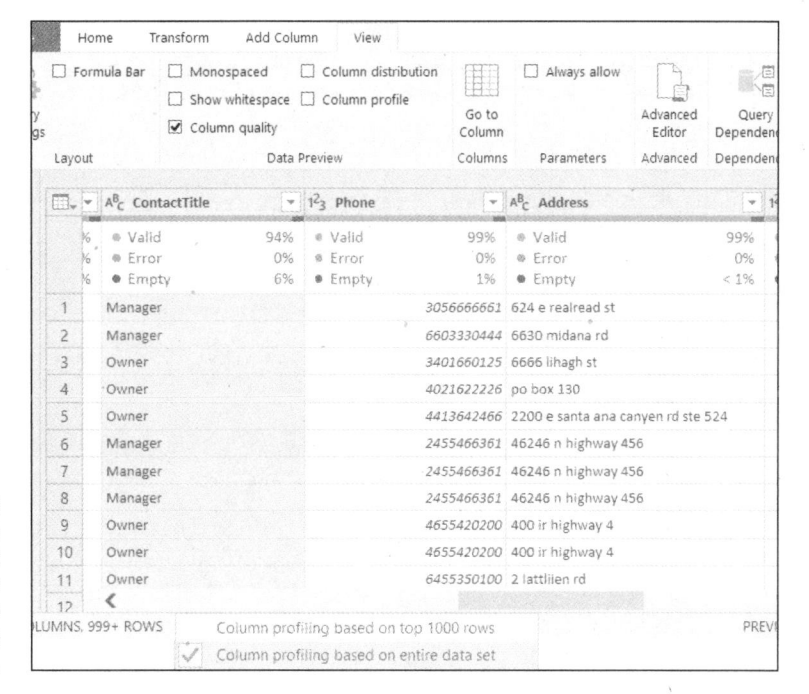

FIGURE 5-21:
Choose Column Profiling Based on Entire Data Set to get a more complete picture of your data.

Data Profiling quick actions

When you select the Column Quality check box in the Data Preview group on the File tab of the ribbon, you'll see a set of figures that represent the percentages of values in a column that are valid, that contain empty records, and that are rendered as an error. Hovering over these percentages exposes a pop-up containing an ellipsis. Clicking the ellipsis activates a shortcut menu allowing you to apply quick actions such as Remove Errors, Remove Empty, and Remove Duplicates.

When you select the Column Profile check box, you'll see two new panes below the data preview window: Column Statistics and Value Distribution. As you can see in Figure 5-22, the Value Distribution pane contains a histogram visual displaying the distribution of values. Right-clicking any of the bars reveals a quick action menu allowing you to apply transformations based on the type of data in that column. In this case, right-clicking the bar for zero reveals the Number Filters continuation menu and the Replace Values command.

> **TIP** The quick actions exposed via the data profiler are simply an easy way to find and apply needed transformations. They aren't any different from those found in the Power Query Editor ribbon and those exposed by simply right-clicking a value in the data preview window.

CHAPTER 5 Meeting Power Query and Its Connection Types   557

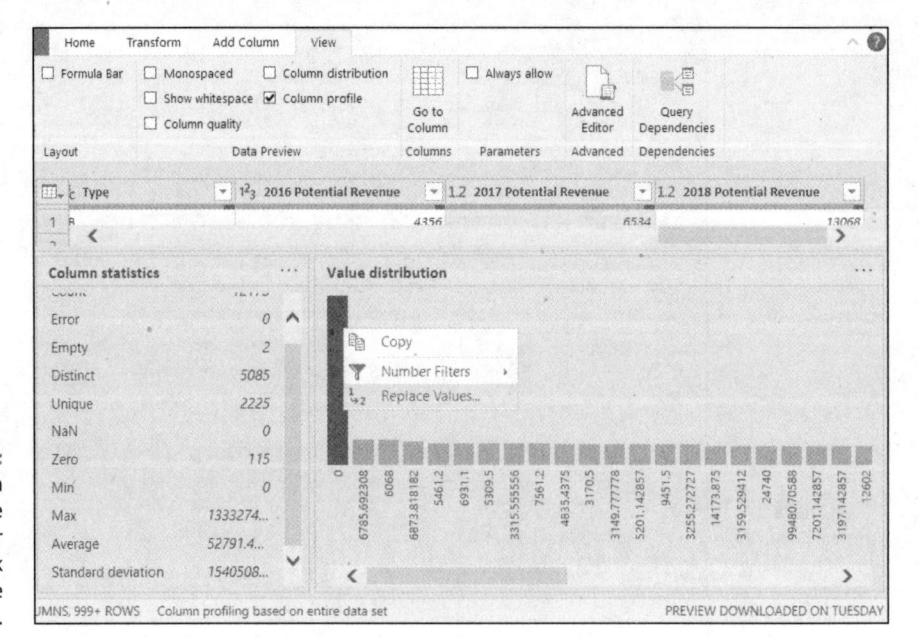

FIGURE 5-22: Right-clicking a column profile histogram bar exposes the quick actions for the associated value.

7
Creating Dashboards and Reports

Contents at a Glance

CHAPTER 1: Getting in the Dashboard State of Mind 561
- Defining Dashboards and Reports 561
- Preparing for Greatness.................................. 564
- A Quick Look at Dashboard Design Principles 568

CHAPTER 2: Building a Super Model............................ 575
- Understanding Data Modeling Best Practices.................. 576
- Finding Excel Functions That Really Deliver.................. 586
- Using Smart Tables That Expand with Data 598
- Introducing Dynamic Arrays 602
- Exploring Dynamic Array Functions 607

CHAPTER 3: Dressing Up Your Data Tables 619
- Table Design Principles................................... 620
- Getting Fancy with Custom Number Formatting 627

CHAPTER 4: Formatting Your Way to Visualizations 635
- Enhancing Reports with Conditional Formatting 635
- Using Symbols to Enhance Reporting 652
- Wielding the Magical Camera Tool 655
- Enhancing Excel Reports with Shapes 659

CHAPTER 5: Displaying Performance against a Target 663
- Showing Performance with Variances 663
- Showing Performance against Organizational Trends.......... 665
- Using a Thermometer-Style Chart 666
- Using a Bullet Graph...................................... 667
- Showing Performance against a Target Range 675

IN THIS CHAPTER

» Comparing dashboards to reports

» Getting started on the right foot

» Finding dashboard best practices

Chapter **1**

Getting in the Dashboard State of Mind

In Excel, there are great differences between building a dashboard and creating standard table-driven analyses. To approach a dashboarding project, you truly have to get into the dashboard state of mind. As you see in this minibook, dashboarding requires far more preparation than standard Excel analyses. It calls for closer communication with business leaders, stricter data modeling techniques, and the following of certain best practices. Being familiar with fundamental dashboarding concepts before venturing off into the mechanics of building a dashboard is a good idea.

In this chapter, you get a solid understanding of these basic dashboard concepts and design principles, as well as what it takes to prepare for a dashboarding project.

Defining Dashboards and Reports

Many people use the terms *report* and *dashboard* interchangeably, blurring the line between reports and dashboards. We've seen countless reports referred to as dashboards just because they included a few charts. Likewise, we've seen many examples of what could be considered dashboards but have been called reports.

Now, this may all seem like semantics to you, but it's helpful to clear the air and understand the core attributes of what are considered to be reports and dashboards.

Defining reports

The report is probably the most common application of business intelligence. A *report* can be described as a document that contains data used for reading or viewing. It can be as simple as a data table or as complex as a subtotaled view with interactive drill-downs, similar to Excel's Subtotal or Pivot Table functionality.

The key attribute of a report is that it doesn't lead a reader to a predefined conclusion. Although reports can include analysis, aggregations, and even charts, reports often allow for the end users to apply their own judgment and analysis to the data.

To clarify this concept, Figure 1-1 shows an example of a report. This report shows the National Park overnight visitor statistics by period. Although this data can be useful, this report clearly isn't steering the reader toward any predefined judgment or analysis; it's simply presenting the aggregated data.

	A	B	C	D	E	F
4		Number of Visitors (thousands)				
5		2009	2010	2011	2012	2013
6	Great Smoky Mountains NP	9,198	9,316	9,367	9,167	9,192
7	Grand Canyon NP	4,105	4,002	4,125	4,326	4,402
8	Yosemite NP	3,369	3,362	3,379	3,281	3,304
9	Olympic NP	3,416	3,691	3,225	3,074	3,143
10	Yellowstone NP	2,759	2,974	3,019	2,868	2,836
11	Rocky Mountain NP	3,140	2,988	3,067	2,782	2,798
12	Cuyahoga Valley NP	3,123	3,218	2,880	3,306	2,534
13	Zion NP	2,218	2,593	2,459	2,677	2,587
14	Grand Teton NP	2,535	2,613	2,356	2,360	2,463
15	Acadia NP	2,517	2,559	2,431	2,208	2,051
16	Glacier NP	1,681	1,906	1,664	2,034	1,925
17	Hot Springs NP	1,297	1,440	1,561	1,419	1,340
18	Hawaii Volcanoes NP	1,343	1,111	992	1,307	1,661

FIGURE 1-1: Reports present data for viewing but don't lead readers to conclusions.

Defining dashboards

A *dashboard* is a visual interface that provides at-a-glance views into key measures relevant to a particular objective or business process. Dashboards have three main attributes:

» Dashboards are typically graphical in nature, providing visualizations that help focus attention on key trends, comparisons, and exceptions.

» Dashboards often display only data that are relevant to the goal of the dashboard.

» Because dashboards are designed with a specific purpose or goal, they inherently contain predefined conclusions that relieve the end user from performing their own analysis.

Figure 1-2 illustrates a dashboard that uses the same data shown in Figure 1-1. This dashboard displays key information about the National Park overnight-visitor stats. As you can see, this presentation has all the main attributes that define a dashboard:

» It's a visual display that allows you to quickly recognize the overall trend of the overnight-visitor stats.

» Not all the detailed data is shown here — you see only the key pieces of information relevant to support the goal of this dashboard, which in this case would be to get some insights on which parks would need some additional resources to increase visitor rates.

» By virtue of its objective, this dashboard effectively presents you with analysis and conclusions about the trend of overnight visitors.

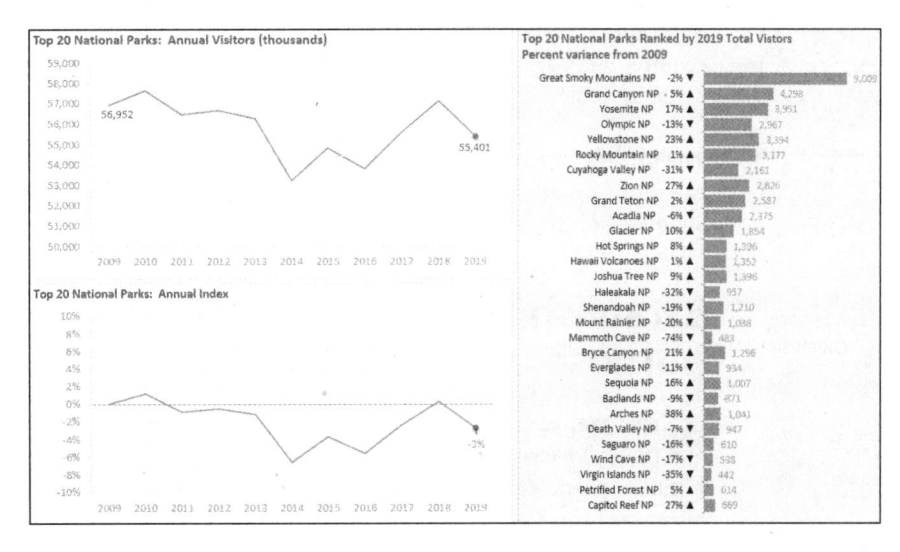

FIGURE 1-2: Dashboards provide at-a-glance views into key measures relevant to a particular objective or business process.

CHAPTER 1 **Getting in the Dashboard State of Mind** 563

Preparing for Greatness

Imagine that your manager asks you to create a dashboard that tells them everything they should know about monthly service subscriptions. Do you jump to action and slap together whatever comes to mind? Do you take a guess at what they want to see and hope it's useful? These questions sound ridiculous, but these types of situations happen more than you think. We're continually called to create the next great reporting tool, but we're rarely provided the time to gather the true requirements for it. Between limited data and unrealistic deadlines, the end product often ends up being unused or having little value.

This brings us to one of the key steps in preparing for dashboarding: collecting user requirements.

In the non-IT world of the Excel analyst, user requirements are practically useless because of sudden changes in project scope, constantly changing priorities, and shifting deadlines. The gathering of user requirements is viewed to be a lot of work and a waste of valuable time in the ever-changing business environment. But as we mention at the start of this chapter, it's time to get into the dashboard state of mind.

Consider how many times a manager has asked you for an analysis and then said, "No, I meant this" or "Now that I see it, I realize I need this." As frustrating as this can be for a single analysis, imagine running into it again and again during the creation of a complex dashboard with several data integration processes. The question is, would you rather spend your time on the front end gathering user requirements or spend time painstakingly redesigning the dashboard you'll surely come to hate?

The process of gathering user requirements doesn't have to be an overly complicated or formal one. Here are six simple things you can do to ensure you have a solid idea of the purpose of the dashboard.

Establish the audience for, and purpose of, the dashboard

Chances are, your manager has been asked to create the reporting mechanism, and they've passed the task to you. Don't be afraid to ask about the source of the initial request. Talk to the requesters about what they're asking for. Discuss the purpose of the dashboard and the triggers that caused them to ask for a dashboard in the first place. You may find, after discussing the matter, that a simple Excel report meets their needs, forgoing the need for a full-on dashboard.

If a dashboard is, indeed, warranted, talk about who the end users are. Take some time to meet with a few of the end users to talk about how they'd use the dashboard. Will the dashboard be used as a performance tool for regional managers? Will the dashboard be used to share data with external customers? Talking through these fundamentals with the right people helps align your thoughts and avoids the creation of a dashboard that doesn't fulfill the necessary requirements.

Delineate the measures for the dashboard

Most dashboards are designed around a set of measures, or *key performance indicators* (KPIs). A KPI is an indicator of the performance of a task deemed to be essential to daily operations or processes. The idea is that a KPI reveals performance that is outside the normal range for a particular measure, so it often signals the need for attention and intervention. Although the measures you place into your dashboards may not officially be called KPIs, they undoubtedly serve the same purpose: to draw attention to problem areas.

REMEMBER The topic of creating effective KPIs for your organization is a subject worthy of its own book and is out of the scope of this endeavor. For a detailed guide on KPI development strategies, pick up David Parmenter's *Key Performance Indicators: Developing, Implementing, and Using Winning KPIs* (published by Wiley). That book provides an excellent step-by-step approach to developing and implementing KPIs.

The measures used on a dashboard should absolutely support the initial purpose of that dashboard. For example, if you're creating a dashboard focused on supply chain processes, it may not make sense to incorporate human resources (HR) head-count data. It's generally good practice to avoid nice-to-know data in your dashboards simply to fill white space or because the data is available. If the data doesn't support the core purpose of the dashboard, leave it out.

TIP Here's another tip: When gathering the measures required for the dashboard, it often helps to write a sentence to describe the measure needed. For example, instead of simply adding the word *Revenue* into our user requirements, we write what we call a *component question,* such as "What is the overall revenue trend for the past two years?" We call it a *component question* because we intend to create a single component, such as a chart or a table, to answer the question. For instance, if the component question is "What is the overall revenue trend for the past two years?" you can imagine a chart component answering this question by showing the two-year revenue trend.

We sometimes take this a step further and actually incorporate the component questions into a mock layout of the dashboard to get a high-level sense of the data the dashboard will require. Figure 1-3 illustrates an example.

CHAPTER 1 **Getting in the Dashboard State of Mind** 565

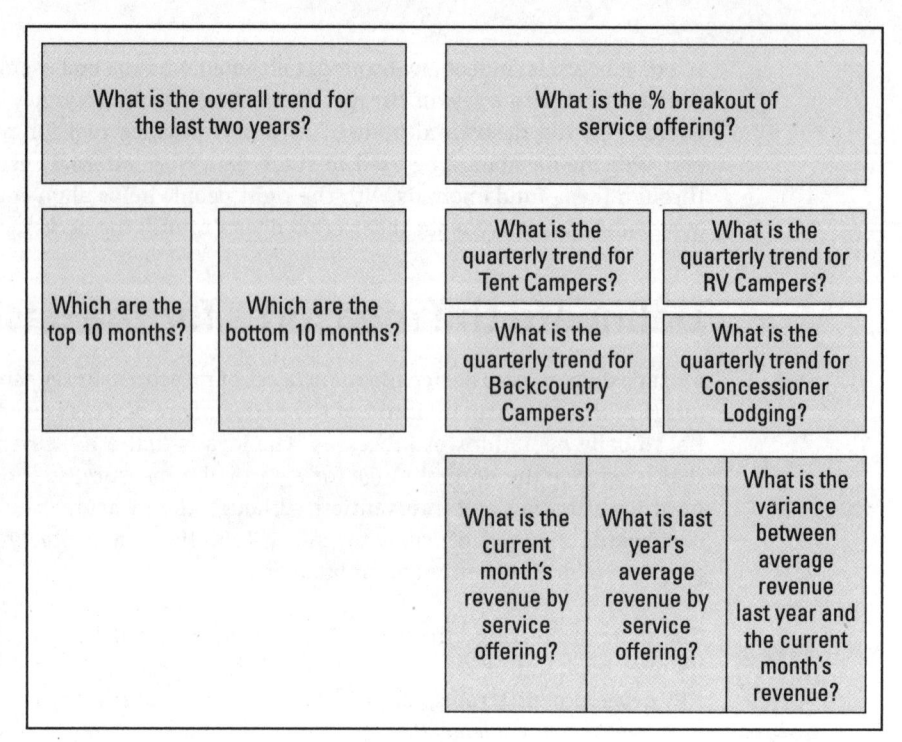

FIGURE 1-3: Each box in this dashboard layout mockup represents a component and the type of data required to create the measures.

What is the overall trend for the last two years?	What is the % breakout of service offering?

Which are the top 10 months?	Which are the bottom 10 months?	What is the quarterly trend for Tent Campers?	What is the quarterly trend for RV Campers?
		What is the quarterly trend for Backcountry Campers?	What is the quarterly trend for Concessioner Lodging?

What is the current month's revenue by service offering?	What is last year's average revenue by service offering?	What is the variance between average revenue last year and the current month's revenue?

Each box in this dashboard layout mockup represents a component on the dashboard and its approximate position. The questions within each box provide a sense of the types of data required to create the measures for the dashboard.

Catalog the required data sources

When you have the list of measures that need to be included on the dashboard, it's important to take a tally of the available systems to determine whether the data required to produce those measures is available. Ask yourself the following questions:

» Do you have access to the data sources necessary?

» How often are those data sources refreshed?

» Who owns and maintains those data sources?

» What are the processes to get the data from those sources?

» Does the data even exist?

TIP — Conventional wisdom says that the measures on your dashboard shouldn't be governed by the availability of data. Instead, you should let dashboard KPIs and measures govern the data sources in your organization. Although we agree with the spirit of that statement, we've been involved in too many dashboard projects that have fallen apart because of lack of data. Real-world experience has taught us the difference between the *ideal* and the *ordeal*.

If your organizational strategy requires you to collect and measure data that is nonexistent or not available, press pause on the dashboard project and turn your attention to creating a data collection mechanism that will get the data you need.

Define the dimensions and filters for the dashboard

In the context of reporting, a *dimension* is a data category used to organize business data. Examples of dimensions are Region, Market, Branch, Manager, or Employee. When you define a dimension in the user requirements stage of development, you're determining how the measures should be grouped or distributed. For example, if your dashboard should report data by employee, you need to ensure that your data collection and aggregation processes include employee detail. As you can imagine, adding a new dimension after the dashboard is built can get complicated, especially when your processes require many aggregations across multiple data sources. The bottom line is that locking down the dimensions for a dashboard early in the process definitely saves you headaches.

Along those same lines, you want to get a clear sense of the types of filters that are required. In the context of dashboards, *filters* are mechanisms that allow you to narrow the scope of the data to a single dimension. For example, you can filter on Year, Employee, or Region. Again, if you don't account for a particular filter while building your dashboarding process, you'll likely be forced into an unpleasant redesign of both your data collection processes and your dashboard.

If you're confused by the difference between dimensions and filters, think about a simple Excel table. A dimension is like a column of data (such as a column containing employee names) in an Excel table. A filter, then, is the mechanism that allows you to narrow your table to show only the data for a particular employee. For example, if you apply Excel's AutoFilter to the Employee column, you're building a filter mechanism into your table.

Determine the need for drill-down features

Many dashboards provide *drill-down features* that allow users to "drill" into the details of a specific measure. You want to get a clear understanding of the types of drill-downs your users have in mind.

To most users, *drill-down feature* means the ability to get a raw data table supporting the measures shown on the dashboard. Although getting raw data isn't always practical or possible, discussing these requests will, at minimum, allow you to talk to your users about additional reporting, links to other data sources, and other solutions that may help them get the data they need.

Establish the refresh schedule

A *refresh schedule* refers to the schedule by which a dashboard is updated to show the latest information available. Because you're the one responsible for building and maintaining the dashboard, you should have a say in the refresh schedules — your manager may not know what it takes to refresh the dashboard in question.

While you're determining the refresh schedule, keep in mind the refresh rates of the different data sources whose measures you need to get. You can't refresh your dashboard any faster than your data sources. Also, negotiate enough development time to build macros that aid in automation of redundant and time-consuming refresh tasks.

A Quick Look at Dashboard Design Principles

When collecting user requirements for your dashboarding project, there's a heavy focus on the data aspects of the dashboard: the types of data needed, the dimensions of data required, the data sources to be used, and so on. This is a good thing — without solid data processes, your dashboards won't be effective or maintainable. That said, here's another aspect to your dashboarding project that calls for the same fervor in preparation: the design aspect.

Excel users live in a world of numbers and tables, not visualization and design. Your typical Excel analysts have no background in visual design and are often left to rely on their own visual instincts to design their dashboards. As a result, most people give little thought to effective design in Excel-based dashboards, often resulting in overly cluttered and ineffective user interfaces.

The good news is that dashboarding has been around for such a long time that there's a vast knowledge base of prescribed visualization and dashboard design principles. Many of these principles seem like common sense; even so, these are concepts that Excel users don't often find themselves thinking about. Because this chapter is about getting into the dashboard state of mind, we break that trend and review a few dashboard design principles that improve the look and feel of your Excel dashboards.

> **TIP** Many of the concepts in this section come from the work of Stephen Few, a visualization expert and the author of several books and articles on dashboard design principles. This minibook is primarily focused on the technical aspects of building reporting components in Excel, but this section offers a high-level look at dashboard design. If you find that you're captivated by the subject, visit Stephen Few's website at www.perceptualedge.com.

Rule number 1: Keep it simple

Stephen Few has the mantra, "Simplify, simplify, simplify." The basic idea is that dashboards cluttered with too many measures or too much eye candy can dilute the significant information you're trying to present. How many times has someone told you that your reports look "busy"? In essence, this complaint means that too much is happening on the page or screen, making it hard to see the actual data.

Here are a few actions you can take to ensure simpler and more effective dashboard designs.

Don't turn your dashboard into a data repository

Admit it: You include as much information in a report as possible, primarily to avoid being asked for additional information. We all do it. But in the dashboard state of mind, you have to fight the urge to force every piece of data available onto your dashboards.

Overwhelming users with too much data can cause them to lose sight of the primary goal of the dashboard and focus on inconsequential data. The measures used on a dashboard should support the initial purpose of that dashboard. Avoid the urge to fill white space for the sake of symmetry and appearances. Don't include nice-to-know data just because the data is available. If the data doesn't support the core purpose of the dashboard, leave it out.

CHAPTER 1 **Getting in the Dashboard State of Mind** 569

Avoid the fancy formatting

The key to communicating effectively with your dashboards is to present your data as simply as possible. There's no need to wrap it in eye candy to make it more interesting. It's okay to have a dashboard with little to no color or formatting. You'll find that the lack of fancy formatting only serves to call attention to the actual data. Focus on the data and not the shiny happy graphics.

Here are a few guidelines:

- » **Avoid using colors or background fills to partition your dashboards.** Colors, in general, should be used sparingly, reserved for providing information about key data points. For example, assigning the colors red, yellow, and green to measures traditionally indicates performance level. Adding these colors to other sections of your dashboard serves only to distract your audience.

- » **De-emphasize borders, backgrounds, and other elements that define dashboard areas.** Try to use the natural white space between components to partition the dashboard. If borders are necessary, format them to hues lighter than the ones you've used for your data. Light grays are typically ideal for borders. The idea is to indicate sections without distracting from the information displayed.

- » **Avoid applying fancy effects such as gradients, pattern fills, shadows, glows, soft edges, and other formatting.** Excel makes it easy to apply effects that make everything look shiny, glittery, and generally happy. Although these formatting features make for great marketing tools, they don't do your reporting mechanisms any favors.

- » **Don't try to enhance your dashboards with clip art or pictures.** Not only do they do nothing to further data presentation, but also they often just look tacky.

Limit each dashboard to one printable page

Dashboards, in general, should provide at-a-glance views into key measures relevant to particular objectives or business processes. This implies that all the data is immediately viewable on the one page. Although including all your data on one page isn't always the easiest thing to do, there's much benefit to being able to see everything on one page or screen. You can compare sections more easily, you can process cause-and-effect relationships more effectively, and you rely less on short-term memory. When a user has to scroll left, right, or down, these benefits are diminished. Furthermore, users tend to believe that when information is placed out of normal view (in areas that require scrolling), it's somehow less important.

But what if you can't fit all the data on one sheet? First, review the measures on your dashboard and determine whether they really need to be there. Next, format your dashboard to use less space (format fonts, reduce white space, and adjust column and row widths). Finally, try adding interactivity to your dashboard, allowing users to dynamically change views to show only those measures that are relevant to them.

Use layout and placement to draw focus

As we discuss earlier in this chapter, only measures that support the dashboard's utility and purpose should be on the dashboard. However, just because all measures on your dashboard are significant doesn't mean they have the same level of importance. In other words, you'll frequently want one component of your dashboard to stand out from the others.

Instead of using bright colors or exaggerated sizing differences, you can leverage location and placement to draw focus to the most important components on your dashboard.

Various studies have shown that readers have a natural tendency to focus on particular regions of a document. For example, researchers at the Poynter Institute's Eyetrack III project have found that readers view various regions on a screen in a certain order, paying particular attention to specific regions onscreen. The researchers use the diagram in Figure 1-4 to illustrate what they call *priority zones.* Regions with the number 1 in the diagram seem to have high prominence, attracting the most attention for longer periods. Meanwhile, number 3 regions seem to have low prominence.

1	1	2	3
1	1	2	2
2	2	2	3
3	3	3	3

FIGURE 1-4: Studies show that users pay particular attention to the upper left and middle left of a document.

You can leverage these priority zones to promote or demote certain components based on significance. If one of the charts on your dashboard warrants special focus, you can simply place that chart in a region of prominence.

TIP: Note that surrounding colors, borders, fonts, and other formatting can affect the viewing patterns of your readers, de-emphasizing a previously high-prominence region.

Format numbers effectively

There will undoubtedly be lots of numbers on your dashboards. Some of them will be in charts; others will be in tables. Remember that every piece of information on your dashboard should have a reason for being there. It's important that you format your numbers effectively to allow your users to understand the information they represent without confusion or hindrance.

TIP: Here are some guidelines to keep in mind when formatting the numbers on your dashboards and reports:

- » **Always use commas to make numbers easier to read.** For example, instead of 2345, show 2,345.

- » **Use decimal places only if that level of precision is required.** For instance, there's rarely a benefit to showing the decimal places in a dollar amount, such as $123.45. In most cases, the $123 will suffice. Likewise in percentages, use only the minimum number of decimals required to represent the data effectively. For example, instead of 43.21%, you may be able to get away with 43%.

- » **Use the dollar symbol only when you need to clarify that you're referring to monetary values.** If you have a chart or table that contains all revenue values, and there's a label clearly stating this, you can save room and pixels by leaving out the dollar symbol.

- » **Format very large numbers to the thousands or millions place.** For instance, instead of displaying 16,906,714, you can format the number to read 17M.

TIP: Chapter 3 of this minibook explores how to leverage number-formatting tricks to enhance the readability of your dashboards and reports.

Use titles and labels effectively

It's common sense, but many people often fail to label items on dashboards effectively. If your manager looks at your dashboard and asks you, "What is this telling me?" you likely have labeling issues.

TIP Here are a few guidelines for effective labeling on your dashboards and reports:

- **Always include a time stamp on your reporting mechanisms.** This minimizes confusion when distributing the same dashboard or report in monthly or weekly installments.
- **Always include some text indicating when the data for the measures was retrieved.** In many cases, the timing of the data is a critical piece of information when analyzing a measure.
- **Use descriptive titles for each component on your dashboard.** This allows users to clearly identify what they're looking at. Be sure to avoid cryptic titles with lots of acronyms and symbols.
- **Although it may seem counterintuitive, it's generally good practice to de-emphasize labels by formatting them with hues lighter than the ones used for your data.** Lightly colored labels give your users the information they need without distracting them from the information displayed. Ideal colors for labels are colors commonly found in nature: soft grays, browns, blues, and greens.

> **IN THIS CHAPTER**
>
> » Understanding the best data modeling practices
>
> » Leveraging Excel functions to deliver data
>
> » Creating smart tables that expand with data
>
> » Introducing dynamic arrays
>
> » Exploring dynamic array functions

Chapter 2
Building a Super Model

One of Excel's most attractive features is its flexibility. You can create an intricate system of interlocking calculations, linked cells, and formatted summaries that work together to create a final analysis. However, years of experience have brought us face-to-face with an ugly truth: Excel is like the cool gym teacher who lets you do anything you want — the freedom can be fun, but a lack of structure in your data models can lead to some serious headaches in the long run.

What's a data model? A *data model* provides the foundation upon which your reporting mechanism is built. When you build a spreadsheet that imports, aggregates, and shapes data, you're essentially building a data model that feeds your dashboards and reports.

Creating a poorly designed data model can mean hours of manual labor maintaining and refreshing your reporting mechanisms. On the other hand, creating an effective model allows you to easily repeat monthly reporting processes without damaging your reports or your sanity.

The goal of this chapter is to show you the concepts and techniques that help you build effective data models. In this chapter, you discover that creating a successful reporting mechanism requires more than slapping data onto a spreadsheet. Although you see how to build cool dashboard components in later chapters, those components won't do you any good if you can't effectively manage your data models. On that note, let's get started.

Understanding Data Modeling Best Practices

Building an effective model isn't as complicated as you may think. It's primarily a matter of thinking about your reporting processes differently. Most people spend very little time thinking about the supporting data model behind a reporting process. If they think about it at all, they usually start by imagining a mockup of the finished dashboard and work backward from there.

Instead of seeing only the finished dashboard in your head, try to think of the end-to-end process. Where will you get the data? How should the data be structured? What analysis will need to be performed? How will the data be fed to the dashboard? How will the dashboard be refreshed?

Obviously, the answers to these questions are highly situation-specific. However, some data modeling best practices will guide you to a new way of thinking about your reporting process. We discuss practices in the next few sections.

Separating data, analysis, and presentation

One of the most important concepts in a data model is the separation of data, analysis, and presentation. The fundamental idea is that you don't want your data to become too tied into any one particular way of presenting that data.

To wrap your mind around this concept, think about an invoice. When you receive an invoice, you don't assume that the financial data on the invoice is the true source of your data. It's merely a presentation of data that's actually stored in a database. That data can be analyzed and presented to you in many other manners: in charts, in tables, or even on websites. This sounds obvious, but Excel users often fuse data, analysis, and presentation.

For instance, we've seen Excel workbooks that contain 12 tabs, each representing a month. On each tab, data for that month is listed along with formulas, PivotTables, and summaries. Now what happens when you're asked to provide a summary by quarter? Do you add more formulas and tabs to consolidate the data on each of the month tabs? The fundamental problem in this scenario is that the tabs actually represent data values that are fused into the presentation of your analysis.

For an example more in line with reporting, take a look at Figure 2-1. Hard-coded tables like this one are common. This table is an amalgamation of data, analysis, and presentation. Not only does this table tie you to a specific analysis, but there's little to no transparency into what exactly the analysis consists of. Also, what happens when you need to report by quarter or when you need another dimension of analysis? Do you import a table that consists of more columns and rows? How does that affect your model?

FIGURE 2-1: Avoid hard-coded tables that fuse data, analysis, and presentation.

	Jan	Feb	Mar	Apr	May	Jun	Jul
Sales	3.69 M	6.99 M	5.77 M	4.96 M	8.48 M	4.71 M	7.48 M
% Distribution	5%	9%	7%	6%	10%	6%	9%

The alternative is to create three layers in your data model: a data layer, an analysis layer, and a presentation layer. You can think of these layers as three different worksheets in an Excel workbook: one sheet to hold the raw data that feeds your report, one sheet to serve as a staging area where the data is analyzed and shaped, and one sheet to serve as the presentation layer. Figure 2-2 illustrates the three layers of an effective data model.

As you can see in Figure 2-2, the raw dataset is located on its own sheet. Although the dataset has some level of aggregation applied to keep it manageably small, no further analysis is done on the Data sheet.

The analysis layer consists primarily of formulas that analyze and pull data from the data layer into formatted tables commonly referred to as *staging tables.* These staging tables ultimately feed the reporting components in your presentation layer. In short, the sheet that contains the analysis layer becomes the staging area where data is summarized and shaped to feed the reporting components.

CHAPTER 2 **Building a Super Model**

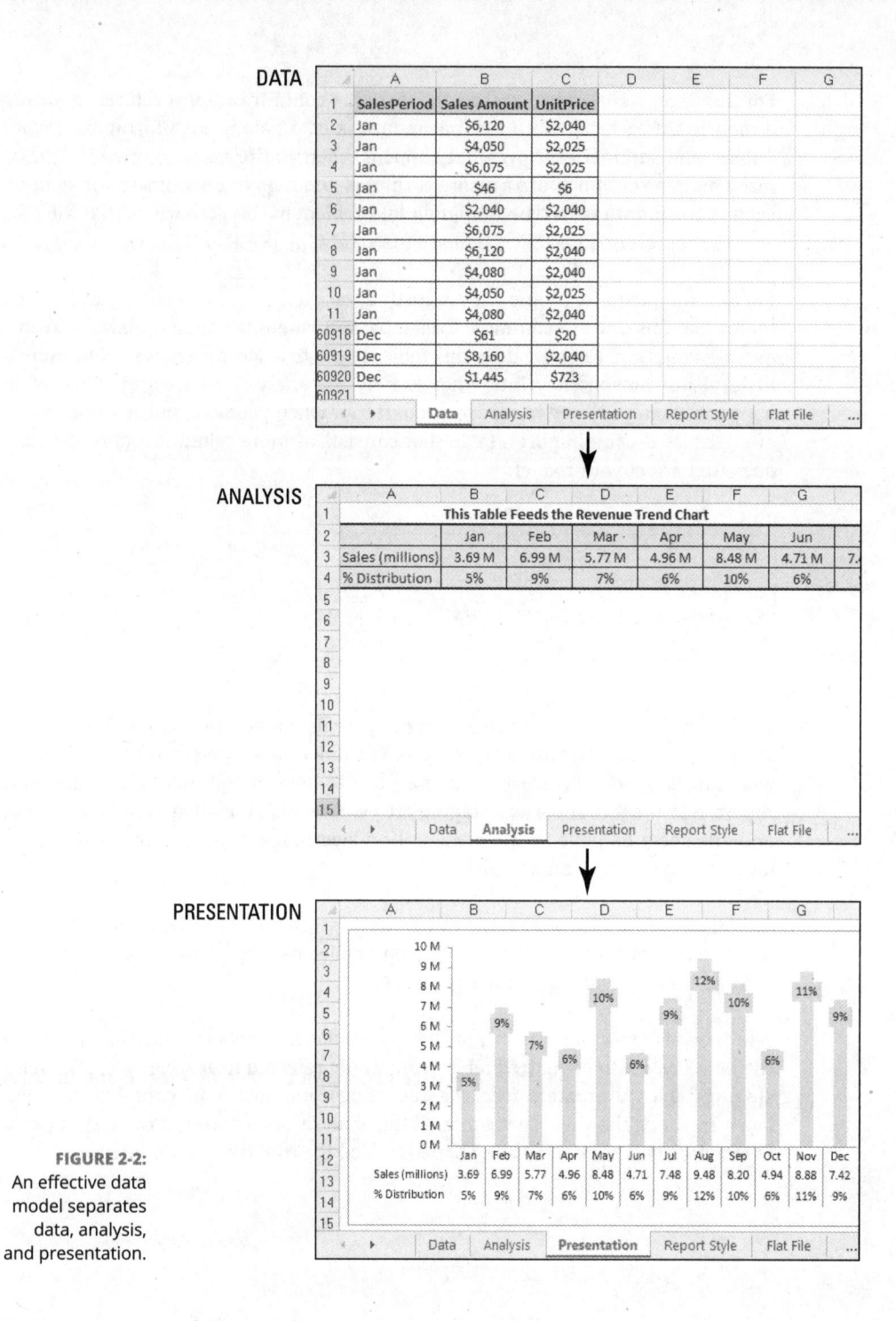

DATA

	A	B	C	D	E	F	G
1	SalesPeriod	Sales Amount	UnitPrice				
2	Jan	$6,120	$2,040				
3	Jan	$4,050	$2,025				
4	Jan	$6,075	$2,025				
5	Jan	$46	$6				
6	Jan	$2,040	$2,040				
7	Jan	$6,075	$2,025				
8	Jan	$6,120	$2,040				
9	Jan	$4,080	$2,040				
10	Jan	$4,050	$2,025				
11	Jan	$4,080	$2,040				
60918	Dec	$61	$20				
60919	Dec	$8,160	$2,040				
60920	Dec	$1,445	$723				
60921							

Data | Analysis | Presentation | Report Style | Flat File

ANALYSIS

	A	B	C	D	E	F	G
1		This Table Feeds the Revenue Trend Chart					
2		Jan	Feb	Mar	Apr	May	Jun
3	Sales (millions)	3.69 M	6.99 M	5.77 M	4.96 M	8.48 M	4.71 M	7.
4	% Distribution	5%	9%	7%	6%	10%	6%

Data | Analysis | Presentation | Report Style | Flat File

PRESENTATION

	Jan	Feb	Mar	Apr	May	Jun	Jul	Aug	Sep	Oct	Nov	Dec
Sales (millions)	3.69	6.99	5.77	4.96	8.48	4.71	7.48	9.48	8.20	4.94	8.88	7.42
% Distribution	5%	9%	7%	6%	10%	6%	9%	12%	10%	6%	11%	9%

Data | Analysis | Presentation | Report Style | Flat File

FIGURE 2-2: An effective data model separates data, analysis, and presentation.

This setup offers a couple of benefits:

- **The entire reporting model can be refreshed easily simply by replacing the raw data with an updated dataset.** The formulas on the Analysis tab continue to work with the latest data.

- **Any additional analysis can be created easily by using different combinations of formulas on the Analysis tab.** If you need data that doesn't exist in the Data sheet, you can easily append a column to the end of the raw dataset without disturbing the Analysis or Presentation sheets.

TIP

You don't necessarily have to place your data, analysis, and presentation layers on different worksheets. In small data models, you may find it easier to place your data in one area of a worksheet while building staging tables in another area of the same worksheet.

Along those same lines, remember that you're not limited to three worksheets. You can have several sheets that provide the raw data, several sheets that analyze, and several sheets that serve as the presentation layer.

Wherever you choose to place the different layers, keep in mind that the idea remains the same: The analysis layer should primarily consist of formulas that pull data from the Data sheets into staging tables used to feed your presentation. Later in this chapter, you explore some of the formulas that you can use in your analysis sheets.

Starting with appropriately structured data

Not all datasets are created equal. Although some datasets work in a standard Excel environment, they may not work for data modeling purposes. Before building your data model, ensure that your source data is appropriately structured for dashboarding purposes.

At the risk of oversimplification, datasets typically used in Excel come in three fundamental forms:

- The spreadsheet report
- The flat data file
- The tabular dataset

The punch line is that only flat data files and tabular datasets make for effective data models. We review and discuss each of these different forms in the next few sections.

Spreadsheet reports make for ineffective data models

Spreadsheet reports display highly formatted, summarized data and are often designed as presentation tools for management or executive users. A typical spreadsheet report makes judicious use of empty space for formatting, repeats data for aesthetic purposes, and presents only high-level analysis. Figure 2-3 illustrates a spreadsheet report.

	A	B	C	D	E	F	G
1							
2		Europe				North America	
3	**France**				**Canada**		
4	Segment	Sales Amount	Unit Price		Segment	Sales Amount	Unit Price
5	Accessories	$48,942	$7,045		Accessories	$119,303	$22,381
6	Bikes	$3,597,879	$991,098		Bikes	$11,714,700	$3,908,691
7	Clothing	$129,508	$23,912		Clothing	$383,022	$72,524
8	Components	$871,125	$293,854		Components	$2,246,255	$865,410
9							
10	**Germany**				**Northeast**		
11	Segment	Sales Amount	Unit Price		Segment	Sales Amount	Unit Price
12	Accessories	$35,681	$5,798		Accessories	$51,246	$9,666
13	Bikes	$1,602,487	$545,175		Bikes	$5,690,285	$1,992,517
14	Clothing	$75,593	$12,474		Clothing	$163,442	$30,969
15	Components	$337,787	$138,513		Components	$1,051,702	$442,598
16							
17	**United Kingdom**				**Northwest**		
18	Segment	Sales Amount	Unit Price		Segment	Sales Amount	Unit Price
19	Accessories	$43,180	$7,419		Accessories	$53,308	$11,417
20	Bikes	$3,435,134	$1,094,354		Bikes	$10,484,495	$3,182,041
21	Clothing	$120,225	$21,981		Clothing	$201,052	$40,055
22	Components	$712,588	$253,458		Components	$1,784,207	$695,876

FIGURE 2-3: A spreadsheet report.

Although a spreadsheet report may look nice, it doesn't make for an effective data model. Why? The primary reason is that these reports offer you no separation of data, analysis, and presentation. You're essentially locked into one analysis.

Although you could make charts from the report shown in Figure 2-3, it'd be impractical to apply any analysis outside what's already there. For instance, how would you calculate and present the average of all bike sales using this particular report? How would you calculate a list of the top ten best-performing markets?

With this setup, you're forced into very manual processes that are difficult to maintain month after month. Any analysis outside the high-level ones already in the report is basic at best — even with fancy formulas. Furthermore, what happens when you're required to show bike sales by month? When your data model requires analysis with data that isn't in the spreadsheet report, you're forced to search for another dataset.

Flat data files lend themselves nicely to data models

Another type of file format is a flat file. *Flat files* are data repositories organized by row and column. Each row corresponds to a set of data elements, or a *record*. Each column is a *field*. A field corresponds to a unique data element in a record. Figure 2-4 contains the same data as the report in Figure 2-3 but expressed in a flat data file format.

	A	B	C	D	E	F
1	Region	Market	Business Segment	Jan Sales Amount	Feb Sales Amount	Mar Sales Amount
2	Europe	France	Accessories	2,628	8,015	3,895
3	Europe	France	Bikes	26,588	524,445	136,773
4	Europe	France	Clothing	6,075	17,172	6,043
5	Europe	France	Components	20,485	179,279	54,262
6	Europe	Germany	Accessories	2,769	6,638	2,615
7	Europe	Germany	Bikes	136,161	196,125	94,840
8	Europe	Germany	Clothing	7,150	12,374	7,159
9	Europe	Germany	Components	46,885	56,611	29,216
10	Europe	United Kingdom	Accessories	4,205	2,579	5,745
11	Europe	United Kingdom	Bikes	111,830	175,522	364,844
12	Europe	United Kingdom	Clothing	7,888	6,763	12,884
13	Europe	United Kingdom	Components	31,331	39,005	124,030
14	North America	Canada	Accessories	3,500	12,350	9,768

FIGURE 2-4: A flat data file.

Notice that every data field has a column, and every column corresponds to one data element. Furthermore, there's no extra spacing, and each row (or record) corresponds to a unique set of information. But the key attribute that makes this a flat file is that no single field uniquely identifies a record. In fact, you'd have to specify four separate fields (Region, Market, Business Segment, and a month's sales amount) before you could uniquely identify the record.

Flat files lend themselves nicely to data modeling in Excel because they can be detailed enough to hold the data you need and still be conducive to a wide array of analysis with simple formulas — SUM, AVERAGE, VLOOKUP, and SUMIF, just to name a few. Later in this chapter, we cover formulas that come in handy in a reporting data model.

Tabular datasets are perfect for PivotTable-driven data models

Many effective data models are driven primarily by PivotTables. PivotTables (covered in Book 5, Chapter 2 and Book 6, Chapter 2) are Excel's premier analysis tools. If you've used PivotTables, you know they offer an excellent way to summarize and shape data for use by reporting components, such as charts and tables.

Tabular datasets are ideal for PivotTable-driven data models. Figure 2-5 illustrates a tabular dataset. Note that the primary difference between a tabular dataset and a flat data file is that, in tabular datasets, the column labels don't double as actual data. For instance, in Figure 2-4, the month identifiers are integrated into the column labels. In Figure 2-5, the Sales Period column contains the month identifier. This subtle difference in structure is what makes tabular datasets optimal data sources for PivotTables. This structure ensures that key PivotTable functions, such as sorting and grouping, work the way they should.

	A	B	C	D	E
1	Region	Market	Business Segment	Sales Period	Sales Amount
2	Europe	France	Accessories	Jan	1,706
3	Europe	France	Accessories	Feb	3,767
4	Europe	France	Accessories	Mar	1,219
5	Europe	France	Accessories	Apr	3,091
6	Europe	France	Accessories	May	7,057
7	Europe	France	Accessories	Jul	5,930
8	Europe	France	Accessories	Aug	9,628
9	Europe	France	Accessories	Sep	4,279
10	Europe	France	Accessories	Oct	2,504
11	Europe	France	Accessories	Nov	7,493
12	Europe	France	Accessories	Dec	2,268
13	Europe	France	Bikes	Jan	64,895
14	Europe	France	Bikes	Feb	510,102
15	Europe	France	Bikes	Mar	128,806
16	Europe	France	Bikes	Apr	81,301

FIGURE 2-5: A tabular dataset.

The attributes of a tabular dataset are as follows:

» The first row of the dataset contains field labels that describe the information in each column.

» The column labels don't pull double duty as data items that can be used as filters or query criteria (such as months, dates, years, regions, or markets).

» There are no blank rows or columns — every column has a heading, and a value is in every row.

» Each column represents a unique category of data.

» Each row represents individual items in each column.

Avoiding turning your data model into a database

In Chapter 1 of this minibook, we mention that measures used on a dashboard should absolutely support the initial purpose of that dashboard. The same concept applies to the back-end data model. You should only import data that's necessary to fulfill the purpose of your dashboard or report.

In an effort to have as much data as possible at their fingertips, many Excel users bring into their spreadsheets every piece of data they can get their hands on. You can spot these people by the 40MB files they send through email. You've seen these spreadsheets — two tabs that contain some reporting or dashboard interface and then six hidden tabs that contain thousands of lines of data (most of which isn't used). They essentially build a database in their spreadsheet.

What's wrong with utilizing as much data as possible? Well, here are a few issues:

- **Aggregating data within Excel increases the number of formulas.** If you're bringing in all raw data, you have to aggregate that data in Excel. This inevitably causes you to exponentially increase the number of formulas you have to employ and maintain. Remember that your data model is a vehicle for presenting analyses, not processing raw data. The data that works best in reporting mechanisms is what's already been aggregated and summarized into useful views that can be navigated and fed to dashboard components. Importing data that's already been aggregated as much as possible is far better. For example, if you need to report on Revenue by Region and Month, there's no need to import sales transactions into your data model. Instead, use an aggregated table consisting of Region, Month, and Sum of Revenue.

- **Your data model will be distributed with your dashboard.** In other words, because your dashboard is fed by your data model, you need to maintain the model behind the scenes (likely in hidden tabs) when distributing the dashboard. Besides the fact that it causes the file size to be unwieldy, including too much data in your data model can actually degrade the performance of your dashboard. Why? When you open an Excel file, the entire file is loaded into memory to ensure quick data processing and access. The drawback to this behavior is that Excel requires a great deal of RAM to process even the smallest change in your spreadsheet. You may have noticed that when you try to perform an action on a large, formula-intensive dataset, Excel is slow to respond, giving you a Calculating indicator on the status bar. The larger your dataset is, the less efficient the data crunching in Excel is.

- **Large datasets can cause difficulty in scalability.** Imagine that you're working in a small company and you're using monthly transactions in your data model. Each month holds 80,000 lines of data. As time goes on, you build a robust process complete with all the formulas, PivotTables, and macros you need to analyze the data that's stored on your neatly maintained tab. Now what happens after one year? Do you start a new tab? How do you analyze two datasets on two different tabs as one entity? Are your formulas still good? Do you have to write new macros?

All these issues can be avoided by importing only aggregated and summarized data that's useful to the core purpose of your reporting needs.

Using tabs to document and organize your data model

Wanting to keep your data model limited to one worksheet tab is natural. In my mind, keeping track of one tab is much simpler than using different tabs. However, limiting your data model to one tab has its drawbacks, including the following:

- **Using one tab typically places limits on your analysis.** Because only so many datasets can fit on a tab, using one tab limits the number of analyses that can be represented in your data model. This in turn limits the analysis that your dashboard can offer. Consider adding tabs to your data model to provide additional data and analysis that may not fit on just one tab.

- **Too much on one tab makes for a confusing data model.** When working with large datasets, you need plenty of staging tables to aggregate and shape the raw data so that it can be fed to your reporting components. If you use only one tab, you're forced to position these staging tables below or to the right of your datasets. Although this may provide all the elements needed to feed your presentation layer, a good deal of scrolling is necessary to view all the elements positioned in a wide range of areas. This makes the data model difficult to understand and maintain. Use separate tabs to hold your analysis and staging tables, particularly in data models that contain large datasets occupying a lot of real estate.

- **Using one tab limits the amount of documentation you can include.** You'll find that your data models easily become a complex system of intertwining links among components, input ranges, output ranges, and formulas. Sure, it all makes sense while you're building your data model, but try coming back to it after a few months. You'll find you've forgotten what each data range does and how each range interacts with the final presentation layer.

    To avoid this problem, consider adding a Model Map tab to your data model; the Model Map tab essentially summarizes the key ranges in the data model and allows you to document how each range interacts with the reporting components in the final presentation layer. As you can see in Figure 2-6, a model map is nothing fancy — just a table that lists key information about each range in the model.

You can include any information you think appropriate in your model map. The idea is to give yourself a handy reference that guides you through the elements in your data model.

SPEAKING OF DOCUMENTING YOUR DATA MODEL . . .

Another way to document the logic in your data model is to use notes and labels liberally. It's amazing how a few explanatory notes and labels can help clarify your spreadsheets. The general idea here is that the logic in your model should be clear to you even after you've been away from your data model for a long time.

Also, consider using colors to identify the ranges in your data model. Using colors in your data model enables you to quickly look at a range of cells and get a basic indication of what that range does. The general concept behind this best practice is that each color represents a range type. For example, you could use yellow to represent staging tables used to feed the charts and the tables in your presentation layer. You could use gray to represent formulas that aren't to be altered or touched, or purple to represent reference tables used for lookups and drop-down lists.

You can use any color you want; it's up to you to give these colors meaning. The important thing is that you have a visual distinction between the various ranges being used in your data model.

Tab	Range	Purpose	Linked Component/s
Analysis 1	A2:A11	Provides the data source for the trend graph component.	United States trend 1
Analysis 2	A3:A11	Data source for the List Box component.	List Box 1
Analysis 2	C1	Output range for the selected item in the List Box component.	Conditional trend icon
Analysis 2	D1:R1	Vlookup formulas that reference cell C1. This range also serves as the source data for the Combination Chart component.	Combination Chart 1
Data	C4:R48	Main data set for this data model.	

FIGURE 2-6: A model map allows you to document how each range interacts with your data model.

Testing your data model before building reporting components on top of it

This best practice is simple. Make sure your data model does what it's supposed to do before building dashboard components on top of it. In that vein, here are a few things to watch for:

» **Test your formulas to ensure they're working properly.** Make sure your formulas don't produce errors and that each formula outputs expected results.

CHAPTER 2 **Building a Super Model** 585

» **Double-check your main dataset to ensure it's complete.** Check that your data table wasn't truncated when transferring to Excel. Also, be sure that each column of data is present with appropriate data labels.

» **Make sure all numeric formatting is appropriate.** Be sure that the formatting of your data is appropriate for the field. For example, check to see that dates are formatted as dates, currency values are formatted properly, and the correct number of decimal places is displayed where needed.

The obvious goal here is to eliminate easily avoidable errors that may cause complications later.

Finding Excel Functions That Really Deliver

As you discover in this chapter, the optimal data model for any reporting mechanism is one in which data, analysis, and presentation are separated into three layers. Although all three layers are important, the analysis layer is where the real art comes into play. The fundamental task of the analysis layer is to pull information from the data layer and then create staging tables that feed your charts, tables, and other reporting components. To do this effectively, you need to employ formulas that serve as data delivery mechanisms — formulas that deliver data to a destination range.

You see, the information you need lives in the data layer (typically, a table containing aggregated data). *Data delivery formulas* are designed to get that data and deliver it to the analysis layer so it can be analyzed and shaped. The cool thing is that after you've set up the data delivery formulas, the analysis layer automatically updates each time the data layer is refreshed.

Confused? Don't worry — in this section, we show you a few Excel functions that work particularly well in data delivery formulas. As you complete the examples here, you'll start to see how these concepts come together.

The VLOOKUP function

The VLOOKUP function is the king of all lookup functions in Excel. We'd be willing to bet you've at least heard of VLOOKUP, if not used it a few times yourself. The purpose of VLOOKUP is to find a specific value from a column of data where the leftmost row value matches a given criterion.

VLOOKUP basics

Take a look at Figure 2-7 to get the general idea. The table on the left shows sales by month and product number. The bottom table translates those product numbers to actual product names. The VLOOKUP function can help in associating the appropriate name to each respective product number.

FIGURE 2-7: In this example, the VLOOKUP function helps to look up the appropriate product name for each product number.

	A	B	C	D	E	F	G
1							
2		Month	Product Number	Sales	Product Name		
3		Feb	5	$ 396	Pinapples		#VLOOKUP(C3,$D$16:$E$22,2,FALSE)
4		Feb	2	$ 388	Oranges		#VLOOKUP(C4,$D$16:$E$22,2,FALSE)
5		Feb	1	$ 377	Apples		#VLOOKUP(C5,$D$16:$E$22,2,FALSE)
6		Feb	3	$ 204	Bananas		#VLOOKUP(C6,$D$16:$E$22,2,FALSE)
7		Feb	4	$ 200	Pears		#VLOOKUP(C7,$D$16:$E$22,2,FALSE)
8		Feb	6	$ 161	Mangos		#VLOOKUP(C8,$D$16:$E$22,2,FALSE)
9		Jan	3	$ 489	Bananas		#VLOOKUP(C9,$D$16:$E$22,2,FALSE)
10		Jan	6	$ 465	Mangos		#VLOOKUP(C10,$D$16:$E$22,2,FALSE)
11		Jan	1	$ 382	Apples		#VLOOKUP(C11,$D$16:$E$22,2,FALSE)
12		Jan	2	$ 285	Oranges		#VLOOKUP(C12,$D$16:$E$22,2,FALSE)
13		Jan	4	$ 200	Pears		#VLOOKUP(C13,$D$16:$E$22,2,FALSE)
14		Jan	5	$ 113	Pinapples		#VLOOKUP(C14,$D$16:$E$22,2,FALSE)
15							
16				Product Number	Product Name		
17				1	Apples		
18				2	Oranges		
19				3	Bananas		
20				4	Pears		
21				5	Pinapples		
22				6	Mangos		

To understand how VLOOKUP formulas work, take a moment to review the basic syntax. A VLOOKUP formula requires four arguments:

```
VLOOKUP(Lookup_value, Table_array, Col_index_num, Range_lookup)
```

Here's what these arguments do:

» *Lookup_value:* Identifies the value being looked up. This is the value that needs to be matched to the lookup table. In the example in Figure 2-7, *Lookup_value* is the product number. Therefore, the first argument for all the formulas shown in Figure 2-7 references column C (the column that contains the product number).

- » *Table_array:* Specifies the range that contains the lookup values. In Figure 2-7, that range is D16:E22. Here are a couple of points to keep in mind with this argument:
  - For a VLOOKUP to work, the leftmost column of the table must be the matching value. For instance, if you're trying to match product numbers, the leftmost column of the lookup table must contain product numbers.
  - Notice that the reference used for this argument is an absolute reference. This means the column and row references are prefixed with dollar signs ($) — as in $D$16:$E$22. This ensures that the references don't shift while you copy the formulas down or across.

- » *Col_index_num:* Identifies the column number in the lookup table that contains the value to be returned. In the example in Figure 2-7, the second column contains the product name (the value being looked up), so the formula uses the number 2. If the product name column were the fourth column in the lookup table, the number 4 would be used.

- » *Range_lookup:* Specifies whether you're looking for an exact match or an approximate match. If an exact match is needed, you'd enter **FALSE** for this argument. If the closest match will do, you'd enter **TRUE** or leave the argument blank.

Applying VLOOKUP formulas in a data model

As you can imagine, there are countless ways to apply a VLOOKUP in all kinds of analyses. Let's take a moment to walk through a scenario where using a VLOOKUP can help enhance your dashboard model.

With a few VLOOKUP formulas and a simple drop-down list, you can create a data model that not only delivers data to the appropriate staging table, but also allows you to dynamically change data views based on a selection you make. Figure 2-8 illustrates the setup.

TIP

To see this effect in action, download the 7.2.1 Chapter 2 Samples.xlsx workbook at www.dummies.com/go/microsoft365excelaiofd. Open that workbook and click the VLOOKUP tab.

The data layer in the model shown in Figure 2-8 resides in the range A9:F209. The analysis layer is held in range E2:F6. The data layer consists of all formulas that extract and shape the data as needed. As you can see, the VLOOKUP formulas use the Customer Name value in cell C3 to look up the appropriate data from the data layer. So, if you entered **Chevron** in cell C3, the VLOOKUP formulas would extract the data for Chevron.

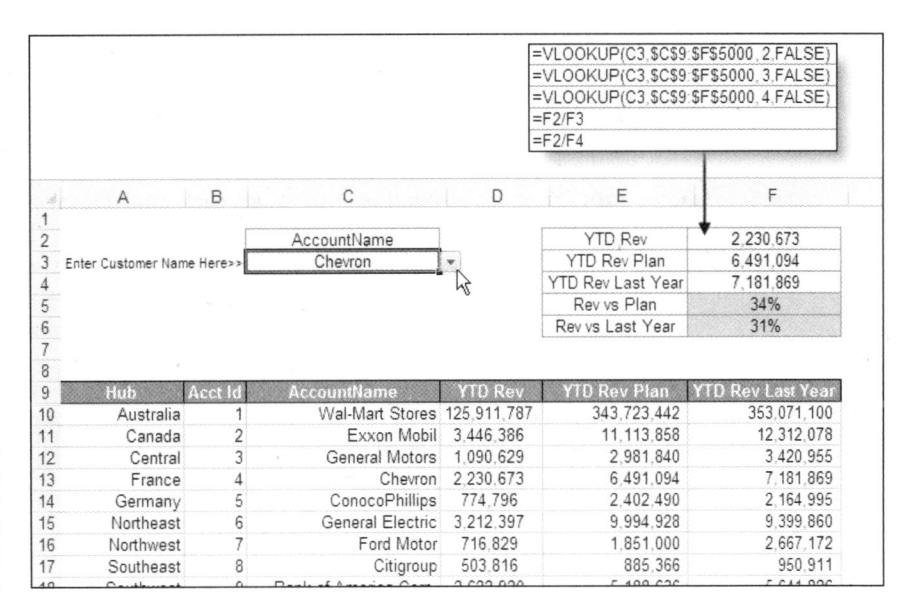

FIGURE 2-8: Using the VLOOKUP function to extract and shape data.

	A	B	C	D	E	F
1						
2			AccountName		YTD Rev	2,230,673
3	Enter Customer Name Here>>		Chevron		YTD Rev Plan	6,491,094
4					YTD Rev Last Year	7,181,869
5					Rev vs Plan	34%
6					Rev vs Last Year	31%
7						
8						
9	Hub	Acct Id	AccountName	YTD Rev	YTD Rev Plan	YTD Rev Last Year
10	Australia	1	Wal-Mart Stores	125,911,787	343,723,442	353,071,100
11	Canada	2	Exxon Mobil	3,446,386	11,113,858	12,312,078
12	Central	3	General Motors	1,090,629	2,981,840	3,420,955
13	France	4	Chevron	2,230,673	6,491,094	7,181,869
14	Germany	5	ConocoPhillips	774,796	2,402,490	2,164,995
15	Northeast	6	General Electric	3,212,397	9,994,928	9,399,860
16	Northwest	7	Ford Motor	716,829	1,851,000	2,667,172
17	Southeast	8	Citigroup	503,816	885,366	950,911

Formulas shown:
=VLOOKUP(C3,$C$9:$F$5000,2,FALSE)
=VLOOKUP(C3,$C$9:$F$5000,3,FALSE)
=VLOOKUP(C3,$C$9:$F$5000,4,FALSE)
=F2/F3
=F2/F4

TECHNICAL STUFF

You may have noticed that the VLOOKUP formulas in Figure 2-8 specify a `Table_array` argument of $C$9:$F$5000. This means that the lookup table they're pointing to stretches from C9 to F5000. That seems strange because the table ends at F209. Why would you force your VLOOKUP formulas to look at a range far past the end of the data table?

Well, remember that the idea behind separating the data layer and the analysis layer is so that the analysis layer can be automatically updated when the data is refreshed. When you get new data next month, you should be able to simply replace the data layer in the model without having to rework the analysis layer. Allowing for more rows than necessary in your VLOOKUP formulas ensures that if the data layer grows, records won't fall outside the lookup range of the formulas.

Later in this chapter, we show you how to automatically keep up with growing data tables by using smart tables.

Using data validation drop-down lists in the data model

In the example in Figure 2-8, the data model allows you to select customer names from a drop-down list when you click cell C3. The customer name serves as the lookup value for the VLOOKUP formulas. Changing the customer name extracts a new set of data from the data layer. This allows you to quickly switch from one customer to another without having to remember and type the customer name.

Now, as cool as this seems, the reasons for this setup aren't all cosmetic. There are practical reasons for adding drop-down lists to your data models.

Many of your models consist of multiple analytical layers in which each layer shows a different set of analyses. Although each analysis layer is different, they often need to revolve around a shared dimension, such as the same customer name, the same market, or the same region. For instance, when you have a data model that reports on Financials, Labor Statistics, and Operational Volumes, you want to make certain that when the model is reporting Financials for the South region, the Labor Statistics are for the South region as well.

An effective way to ensure this happens is to force your formulas to use the same dimension references. If cell C3 is where you switch customers, every analysis that is customer dependent should reference cell C3. Drop-down lists allow you to have a predefined list of valid variables located in a single cell. With a drop-down list, you can easily switch dimensions while building and testing multiple analysis layers.

Adding a drop-down list is relatively easy with Excel's Data Validation functionality. To add a drop-down list, follow these steps:

1. **Select the Data tab on the ribbon.**
2. **In the Data Tools group, click the icon part of the Data Validation button (not the drop-down arrow).**

   The Data Validation dialog box opens.

3. **Select the Settings tab (see Figure 2-9).**

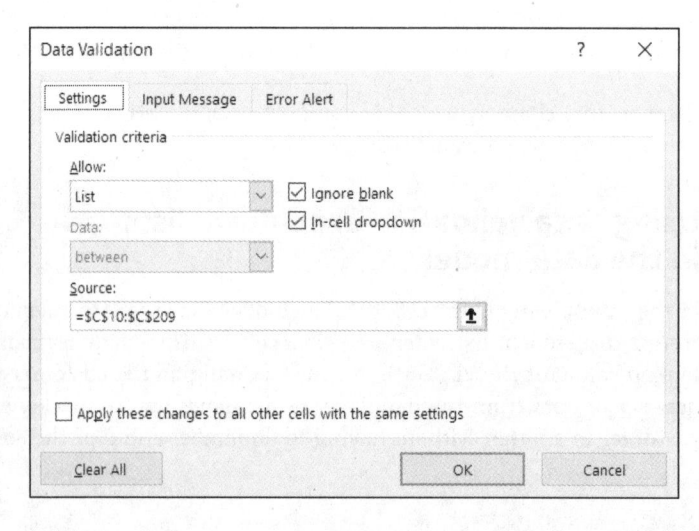

FIGURE 2-9: You can use data validation to create a predefined list of valid variables for your data model.

4. **From the Allow drop-down list, choose List.**
5. **In the Source input box, reference the range of cells that contain your predefined selection list.**

   In our example, this would be the list of customers you want exposed through the dashboard.
6. **Click OK.**

The HLOOKUP function

The HLOOKUP function is the less popular cousin of the VLOOKUP function. The H in HLOOKUP stands for *horizontal.* Because Excel data is typically vertically oriented, most situations require a vertical lookup, or VLOOKUP. However, some data structures are horizontally oriented, requiring a horizontal lookup; thus, the HLOOKUP function comes in handy. The HLOOKUP searches a lookup table to find a single value from a row of data where the column label matches a given criterion.

HLOOKUP basics

Figure 2-10 demonstrates a typical scenario in which HLOOKUP formulas are used. The table in C5 requires quarter-end numbers (March and June) for 2021. The HLOOKUP formulas use the column labels to find the correct month columns and then locate the 2021 data by moving down to the specified row. In this case, 2021 data is in row 4, so the number 4 is used in the formulas.

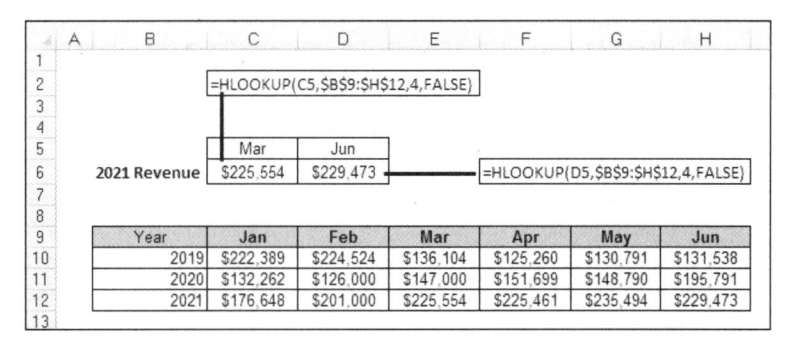

FIGURE 2-10: HLOOKUP formulas help to find March and June numbers from the lookup table.

To get your mind around how this works, take a look at the basic syntax of the HLOOKUP function.

```
HLOOKUP(Lookup_value, Table_array, Row_index_num, Range_lookup)
```

Here's what these arguments do:

- *Lookup_value:* Identifies the value being looked up. In most cases, these values are column names. In the example in Figure 2-10, the column labels are being referenced for the *Lookup_value*. This points the HLOOKUP function to the appropriate column in the lookup table.

- *Table_array:* Identifies the range that contains the lookup table. In Figure 2-10, that range is B9:H12. Like the VLOOKUP examples earlier in this chapter, notice that the references used for this argument are absolute. This means the column and row references are prefixed with dollar signs ($) — as in $B$9:$H$12. This ensures that the reference doesn't shift while you copy the formula down or across.

- *Row_index_num:* Identifies the row number that contains the value you're looking for. In the example in Figure 2-10, the 2021 data is located in row 4 of the lookup table. Therefore, the formulas use the number 4.

- *Range_lookup:* Specifies whether you're looking for an exact match or an approximate match. If an exact match is needed, you'd enter **FALSE** for this argument. If the closest match will do, you'd enter **TRUE** or leave the argument blank.

Applying HLOOKUP formulas in a data model

HLOOKUPs are especially handy for shaping data into structures appropriate for charting or other types of reporting. A simple example is demonstrated in Figure 2-11. With HLOOKUPs, the data shown in the raw data table at the bottom of the figure is reoriented in a staging table at the top. When the raw data is changed or refreshed, the staging table captures the changes.

The SUMPRODUCT function

The SUMPRODUCT function is actually listed under the math and trigonometry category of Excel functions. Because the primary purpose of SUMPRODUCT is to calculate the sum product, most people don't know you can actually use it to look up values. In fact, you can use this versatile function quite effectively in most data models.

SUMPRODUCT basics

The SUMPRODUCT function is designed to multiply values from two or more ranges of data and then add the results together to return the sum of the products. Take a look at Figure 2-12 to see a typical scenario in which the SUMPRODUCT function is useful.

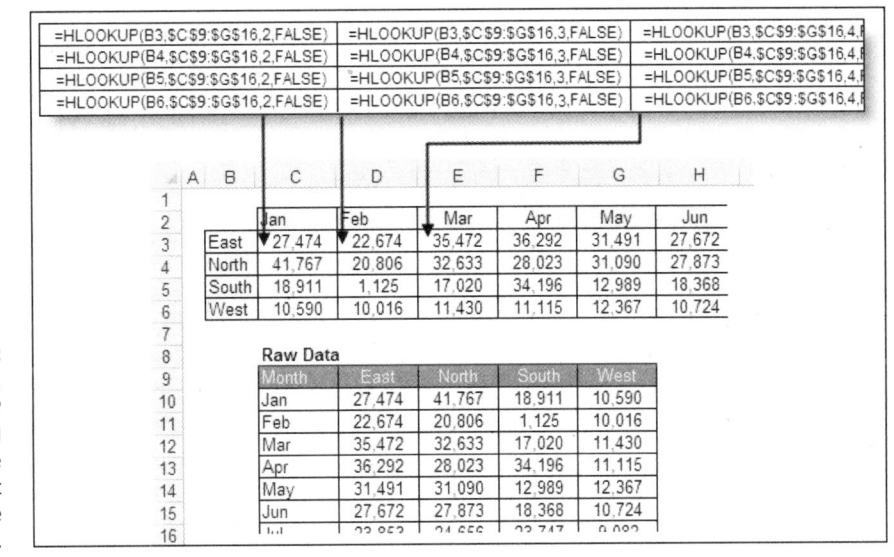

```
=HLOOKUP(B3,$C$9:$G$16,2,FALSE)    =HLOOKUP(B3,$C$9:$G$16,3,FALSE)    =HLOOKUP(B3,$C$9:$G$16,4,
=HLOOKUP(B4,$C$9:$G$16,2,FALSE)    =HLOOKUP(B4,$C$9:$G$16,3,FALSE)    =HLOOKUP(B4,$C$9:$G$16,4,
=HLOOKUP(B5,$C$9:$G$16,2,FALSE)    =HLOOKUP(B5,$C$9:$G$16,3,FALSE)    =HLOOKUP(B5,$C$9:$G$16,4,
=HLOOKUP(B6,$C$9:$G$16,2,FALSE)    =HLOOKUP(B6,$C$9:$G$16,3,FALSE)    =HLOOKUP(B6,$C$9:$G$16,4,
```

	A	B	C	D	E	F	G	H
1								
2			Jan	Feb	Mar	Apr	May	Jun
3		East	27,474	22,674	35,472	36,292	31,491	27,672
4		North	41,767	20,806	32,633	28,023	31,090	27,873
5		South	18,911	1,125	17,020	34,196	12,989	18,368
6		West	10,590	10,016	11,430	11,115	12,367	10,724
7								
8			Raw Data					
9			Month	East	North	South	West	
10			Jan	27,474	41,767	18,911	10,590	
11			Feb	22,674	20,806	1,125	10,016	
12			Mar	35,472	32,633	17,020	11,430	
13			Apr	36,292	28,023	34,196	11,115	
14			May	31,491	31,090	12,989	12,367	
15			Jun	27,672	27,873	18,368	10,724	
16			Jul	22,853	24,656	22,747	9,082	

FIGURE 2-11: In this example, HLOOKUP formulas pull and reshape data without disturbing the raw data table.

	A	B	C	D	E	F	G	H
1								
2		Year	Region	Price	Units			
3		2022	North	$40	751	$30,040		=D3*E3
4		2022	South	$35	483	$16,905		=D4*E4
5		2022	East	$32	789	$25,248		=D5*E5
6		2022	West	$41	932	$38,212		=D6*E6
7		2021	North	$40	877	$35,080		=D7*E7
8		2021	South	$35	162	$5,670		=D8*E8
9		2021	East	$32	258	$8,256		=D9*E9
10		2021	West	$41	517	$21,197		=D10*E10
11								
12					2022 total	$110,405		=SUM(F3:F6)
13					2021 total	$70,203		=SUM(F7:F10)
14					Variance	$40,202		=F12-F13

FIGURE 2-12: Without the SUMPRODUCT function, getting the total sales involves multiplying price by units and then summing the results.

In Figure 2-12, you see a common analysis in which you need the total sales for the years 2021 and 2022. As you can see, to get the total sales for each year, you first have to multiply Price by the number of Units to get the total for each Region. Then you have to sum those results to get the total sales for each year.

With the SUMPRODUCT function, you can perform the two-step analysis with just one formula. Figure 2-13 shows the same analysis with SUMPRODUCT formulas. Rather than use 11 formulas, you can accomplish the same analysis with just 3!

The syntax of the SUMPRODUCT function is fairly simple:

```
SUMPRODUCT(Array1, Array2, ...)
```

FIGURE 2-13:
The SUMPRODUCT function allows you to perform the same analysis with just 3 formulas instead of 11.

	A	B	C	D	E	F	G
1							
2		Year	Region	Price	Units		
3		2012	North	$40	751		
4		2012	South	$35	483		
5		2012	East	$32	789		
6		2012	West	$41	932		
7		2011	North	$40	877		
8		2011	South	$35	162		
9		2011	East	$32	258		
10		2011	West	$41	517		
11							
12				2012 total	$110,405		=SUMPRODUCT(D3:D6,E3:E6)
13				2011 total	$70,203		=SUMPRODUCT(D7:D10, E7:E10)
14				Variance	$40,202		=E12-E13
15							

Array represents a range of data. You can use anywhere from 2 to 255 arrays in a SUMPRODUCT formula. The arrays are multiplied together and then added. The only hard-and-fast rule you have to remember is that all arrays must have the same number of values. In other words, you can't use the SUMPRODUCT if range X has 10 values and range Y has 11 values. Otherwise, you get the #VALUE! error.

A twist on the SUMPRODUCT function

The interesting thing about the SUMPRODUCT function is that you can use it to filter out values. Take a look at Figure 2-14 to see what we mean.

	A	B	C	D	E	F	G
1							
2		Year	Region	Price	Units		
3		2022	North	$40	751		
4		2022	South	$35	483		
5		2022	East	$32	789		
6		2022	West	$41	932		
7		2021	North	$40	877		
8		2021	South	$35	162		
9		2021	East	$32	258		
10		2021	West	$41	517		
11							
12			North Units		1,628		=SUMPRODUCT((C3:C10="North")*(E3:E10))
13			2021 North Units		877		
14							
15							
16					=SUMPRODUCT((C3:C10="North")*(B3:B10=2011)*(E3:E10))		

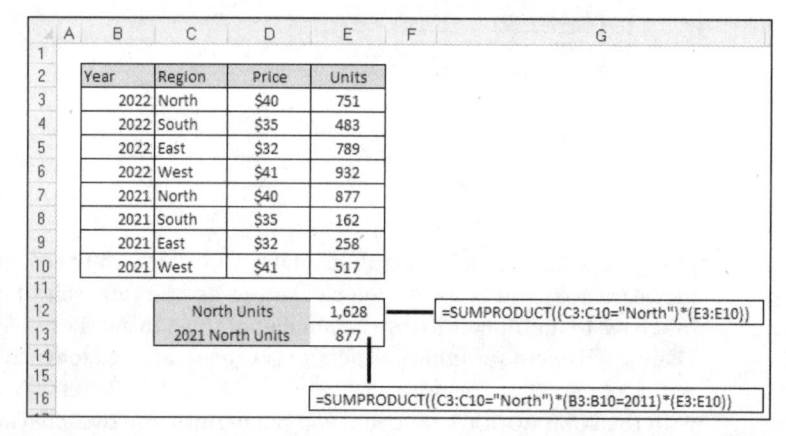

FIGURE 2-14:
The SUMPRODUCT function can be used to filter data based on criteria.

The formula in cell E12 is pulling the sum of total units for just the North region. Meanwhile, cell E13 is pulling the units logged for the North region in the year 2021.

To understand how this works, take a look at the formula in cell E12, shown in Figure 2-14. That formula reads SUMPRODUCT((C3:C10="North")*(E3:E10)).

In Excel, TRUE evaluates to 1 and FALSE evaluates to 0. Every value in column C that equals North evaluates to TRUE or 1. Where the value is not North, it evaluates to FALSE or 0. The part of the formula that reads (C3:C10="North") enumerates through each value in the range C3:C10, assigning a 1 or 0 to each value. Then internally, the SUMPRODUCT formula translates to

```
(1*E3)+(0*E4)+(0*E5)+(0*E6)+(1*E7)+(0*E8)+(0*E9)+(0*E10)
```

This gives you the answer of 1628 because

```
(1*751)+(0*483)+(0*789)+(0*932)+(1*877)+(0*162)+(0*258)+(0*517)
```

equals 1628.

Applying SUMPRODUCT formulas in a data model

As always in Excel, you don't have to hard-code the criteria in your formulas. Instead of explicitly using "North" in the SUMPRODUCT formula, you could reference a cell that contains the filter value. You can imagine that cell A3 contains the word North, in which case you can use (C3:C10=A3) instead of (C3:C10="North"). This way, you can dynamically change your filter criteria, and your formula keeps up.

Figure 2-15 demonstrates how you can use this concept to pull data into a staging table based on multiple criteria. Note that each of the SUMPRODUCT formulas shown here references cells B3 and C3 to filter on Account and Product Line. Again, you can add data validation drop-down lists to cells B3 and C3, allowing you to easily change criteria.

The CHOOSE function

The CHOOSE function returns a value from a specified list of values based on a specified position number. For instance, if you enter the formulas CHOOSE(3, "Red", "Yellow", "Green", "Blue") into a cell, Excel returns Green because Green is the third item in the list of values. The formula CHOOSE(1, "Red", "Yellow", "Green", "Blue") would return Red. Although this may not look useful on the surface, the CHOOSE function can dramatically enhance your data models.

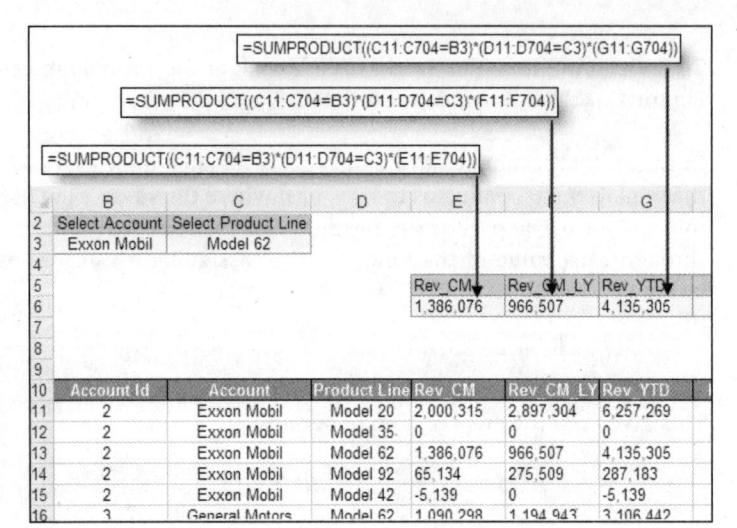

FIGURE 2-15: The SUMPRODUCT function can be used to pull summarized numbers from the data layer into staging tables.

CHOOSE basics

Figure 2-16 illustrates how CHOOSE formulas can help pinpoint and extract numbers from a range of cells. Note that instead of using hard-coded values, like Red, Green, and so on, you can use cell references to list the choices.

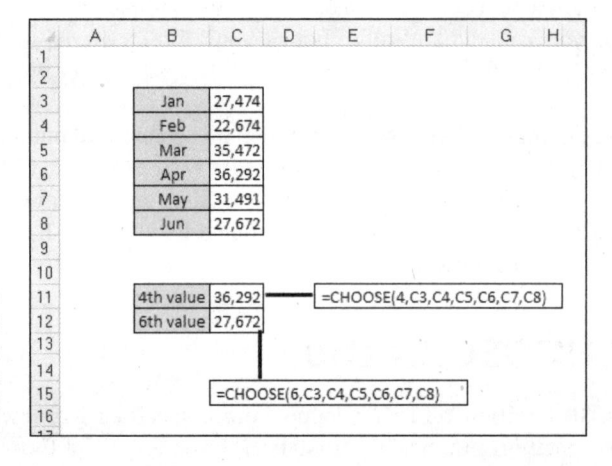

FIGURE 2-16: The CHOOSE function allows you to find values from a defined set of choices.

Take a moment to review the basic syntax of the CHOOSE function:

```
CHOOSE(Index_num, Value1, Value2, ...)
```

596   BOOK 7   Creating Dashboards and Reports

Here's what these arguments do:

- *Index_num:* Specifies the position number of the chosen value in the list of values. If the third value in the list is needed, the *Index_num* is 3. The *Index_num* argument must be an integer between one and the maximum number of values in the defined list of values. That is to say, if there are ten choices defined in the CHOOSE formula, the *Index_num* argument can't be more than ten.

- *Value:* Each *Value* argument represents a choice in the defined list of choices for that CHOOSE formula. The *Value* arguments can be hard-coded values, cell references, defined names, formulas, or functions. You can have up to 255 choices listed in your CHOOSE formulas.

Applying CHOOSE formulas in a data model

The CHOOSE function is especially valuable in data models in which multiple layers of data need to be brought together. Figure 2-17 illustrates an example in which CHOOSE formulas help pull data together.

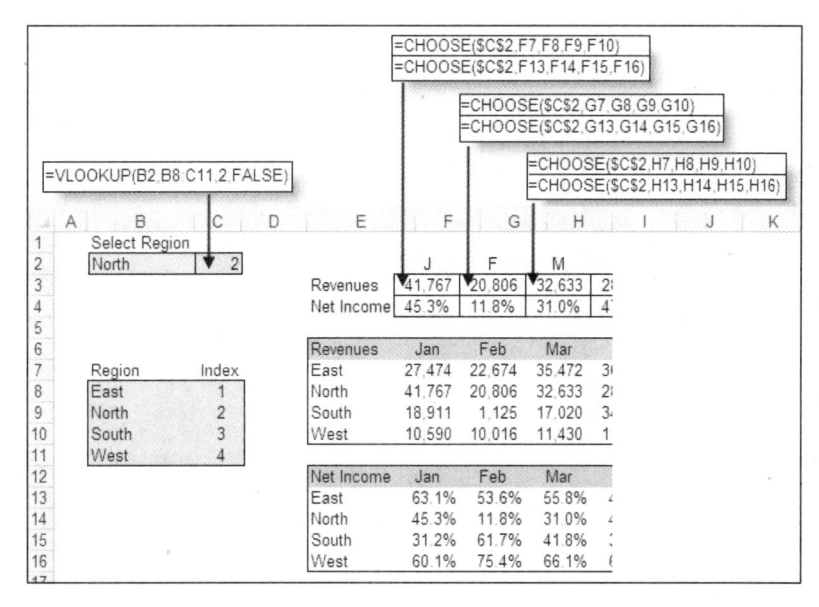

FIGURE 2-17: The CHOOSE formulas ensure that the appropriate data is synchronously pulled from multiple data feeds.

In this example, you have two data tables: one for Revenues and one for Net Income. Each table contains numbers for separate regions. The idea is to create a staging table that pulls data from both tables so that the data corresponds to a selected region.

CHAPTER 2 **Building a Super Model** 597

To understand what's going on, focus on the formula in cell F3, shown in Figure 2-17. The formula is CHOOSE($C$2,F7,F8,F9,F10). The *Index_num* argument is actually a cell reference that looks at the value in cell C2, which happens to be the number 2. As you can see, cell C2 is actually a VLOOKUP formula that pulls the appropriate index number for the selected region. The list of defined choices in the CHOOSE formula is essentially the cell references that make up the revenue values for each region: F7, F8, F9, and F10. So, the formula in cell F3 translates to CHOOSE(2, 27474, 41767, 18911, 10590). The answer is 41,767.

Using Smart Tables That Expand with Data

One of the challenges you can encounter when building data models is a data table that expands over time. That is to say, the table grows in the number of records it holds due to new data being added. To get a basic understanding of this challenge, take a look at Figure 2-18. In this figure, you see a simple table that serves as the source for the chart. Notice that the table lists data for January through June.

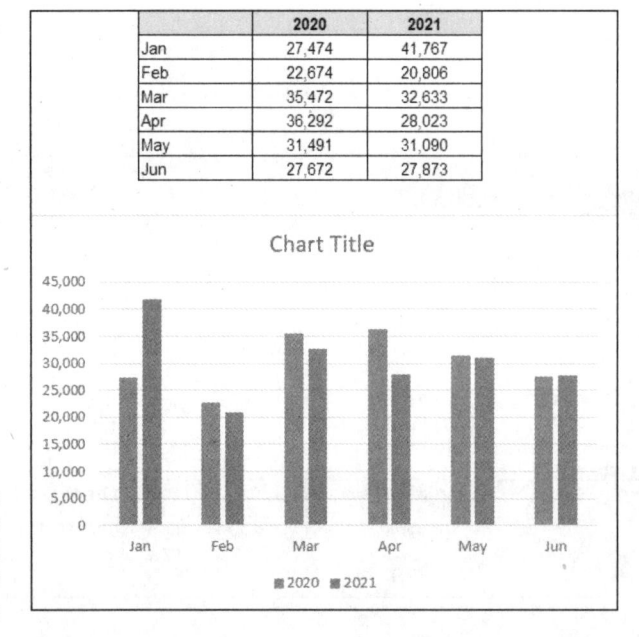

FIGURE 2-18: The date in both the table and chart ends in June.

Imagine that next month, this table expands to include July data. You'll have to manually update your chart to include July data. Now imagine you had this same

598 BOOK 7 Creating Dashboards and Reports

issue across your data model, with multiple data tables that link to multiple staging tables and dashboard components. You can imagine it'd be an extremely painful task to keep up with changes each month.

To solve this issue, you can use Excel's Table feature (you can tell they spent all night coming up with that name). The *Table feature* allows you to convert a range of data into a defined table that's treated independently of other rows and columns on the worksheet. After a range is converted to a table, Excel views the individual cells in the table as a single object with functionality that a typical data range doesn't have.

For instance, Excel tables offer the following features:

- Tables are automatically enabled with Filter drop-down headers so that you can filter and sort easily.
- Tables come with the ability to quickly add a Total row with various aggregate functions.
- You can apply special formatting to Excel tables independent of the rest of the spreadsheet.
- Most important for data modeling purposes, tables automatically expand to allow for new data.

Converting a range to an Excel table

To convert a range of data to an Excel table, follow these steps:

1. **Select the range of cells that contain the data you want included in your Excel table.**
2. **On the Insert tab of the ribbon, click the Table button.**

   The Create Table dialog box, shown in Figure 2-19, opens.
3. **In the Create Table dialog box, verify the range for the table and specify whether the first row of the selected range is a header row.**
4. **Click OK.**

After the conversion takes place, notice a few small changes. Excel has put autofilter drop-downs on the header rows and named any header that didn't have a value.

FIGURE 2-19: Converting a range of data to an Excel table.

You can use Excel tables as the source for charts, PivotTables, list boxes, or anything else for which you'd typically use a data range. In Figure 2-20, a chart has been linked to the Excel table.

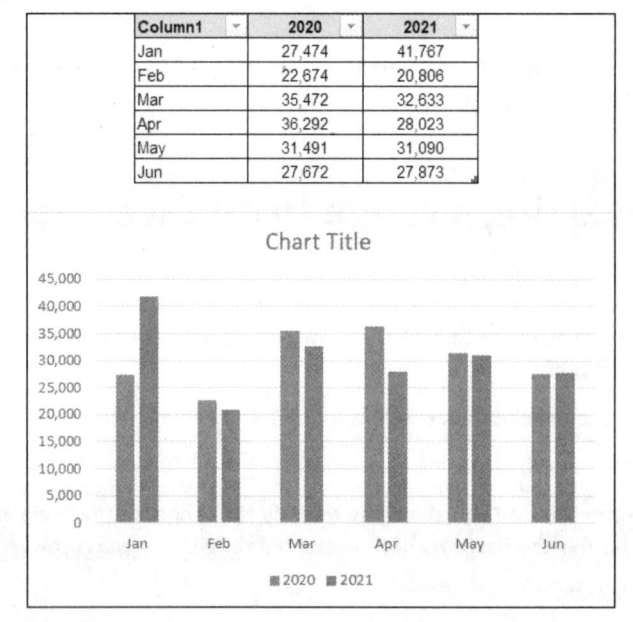

FIGURE 2-20: Excel tables can be used as the source for charts, PivotTables, named ranges, and so on.

Here's the impressive bit: When data is added to the table, Excel automatically expands the range of the table and incorporates the new range into any linked object. That's just a fancy way of saying that any chart or PivotTable tied to an Excel table automatically captures new data without manual intervention.

For example, if we add July and August data to the end of the Excel table, the chart automatically updates to capture the new data. In Figure 2-21, we added July with no data and August with data to show you that the chart captures any new records and automatically plots the data given.

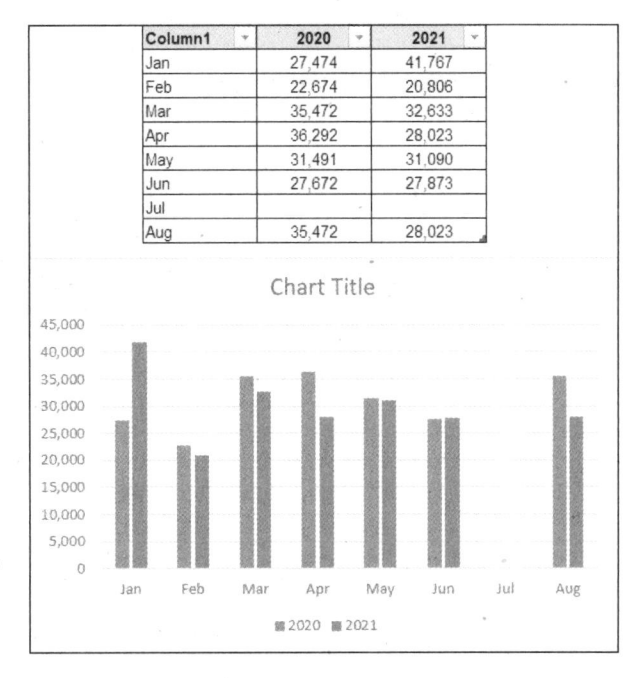

Column1	2020	2021
Jan	27,474	41,767
Feb	22,674	20,806
Mar	35,472	32,633
Apr	36,292	28,023
May	31,491	31,090
Jun	27,672	27,873
Jul		
Aug	35,472	28,023

FIGURE 2-21: Excel tables automatically expand when new data is added.

Take a moment to think about what Excel tables mean to a data model. They mean PivotTables that never have to be reconfigured, charts that automatically capture new data, and ranges that automatically keep up with changes.

Converting an Excel table back to a range

If you want to convert an Excel table back to a range, you can follow these steps:

1. **Place the cursor in any cell inside the Excel table and select the Table Design tab on the ribbon.**
2. **Click the Convert to Range button, as shown in Figure 2-22.**
3. **When asked if you're sure, click Yes.**

CHAPTER 2 Building a Super Model

FIGURE 2-22: To remove Excel table functionality, convert the table back to a range.

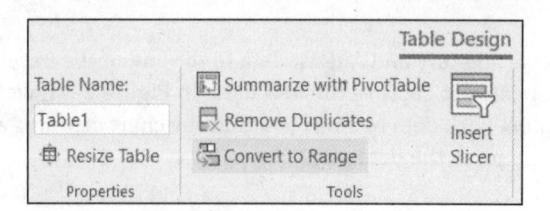

Introducing Dynamic Arrays

The easiest way to grasp the concept of arrays is to imagine a collection of rows and columns. Picture a table containing five rows and one column. On the worksheet, we call that a range of cells, but if we somehow took that range and stored it in memory, it would cease to be a range and be an array. While the array is in memory, any formula operation performed on it is performed as a collective. That is to say, all items in that array would be touched by the formula in various ways (depending on the formula you're using).

With dynamic arrays, Excel moves into a new era where you no longer need to be a formula guru to leverage the power of arrays. This section explores Excel's exciting new dynamic array functions and illustrates some of the ways these new functions can help you go far beyond the capabilities of traditional formulas.

Getting the basics of dynamic arrays

To see a simple dynamic array in action, take a gander at Figure 2-23 showing a formula that references cells A2:C7.

FIGURE 2-23: A simple formula that references a range.

Simply pressing Enter will automatically propagate the formula to the surrounding cells (see Figure 2-24). The initial formula provides the array dimensions of six rows and three columns. Excel takes that information and outputs the results into a grid equivalent to the dimensions provided.

602   BOOK 7 Creating Dashboards and Reports

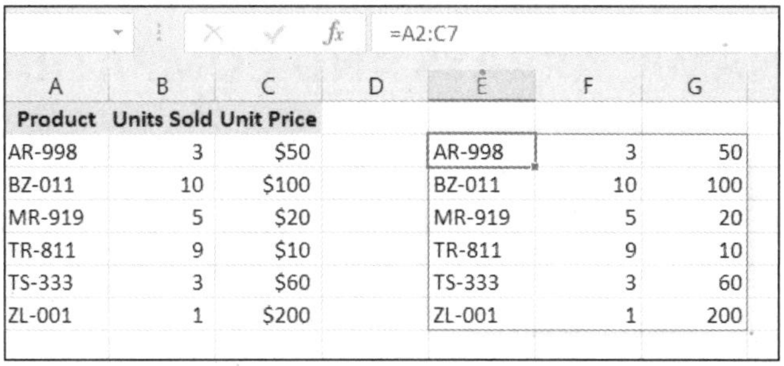

FIGURE 2-24: Excel automatically spills the results into the surrounding cells.

This behavior of automatically propagating results to surrounding cells is called *spilling*. The area around an array formula is called the *spill range*. The spill range is determined by dimensions specified in your array formula. In the example shown in Figure 2-24, the array formula references an array that is six rows by three columns. Therefore, no matter where you put the formula, the spill range will be fixed to a grid that is six rows by three columns.

It's important to note that dynamic array behavior is fundamentally part of Excel's calculation engine. When any function uses an array that returns multiple values, the results will be output to a spill range. This even includes older functions that weren't designed to output arrays. For instance, the Formula Bar in Figure 2-25 shows the following:

```
=SUM(B14:B19*C14:C19)
```

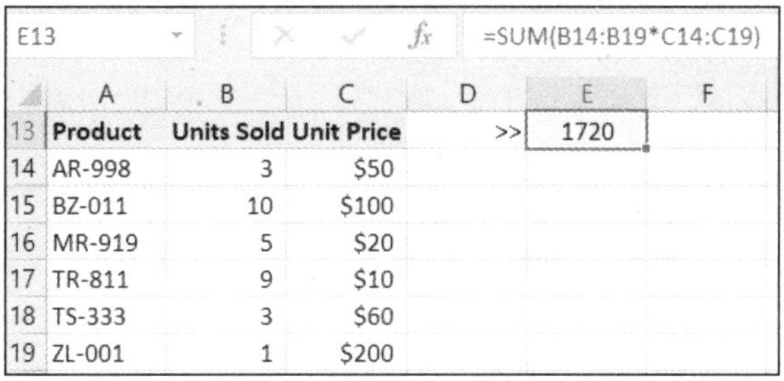

FIGURE 2-25: Dynamic arrays work with any traditional Excel function that accepts arrays as arguments.

This formula uses a simple SUM function to multiply the sum of B14:B19 by the sum of C14:C19. Because dynamic arrays are now inherent to Excel's calculation engine, the arrays are automatically processed without needing to press Ctrl+Shift+Enter as you had to do in older versions of Excel.

CHAPTER 2 Building a Super Model   603

DYNAMIC ARRAYS AND COMPATIBILITY

As of this writing, dynamic arrays are available only to those with Office 365 subscriptions and those using the stand-alone (perpetual license) version of Office/Excel 2022 or later. Dynamic arrays aren't available to those using Excel 2019 or earlier versions. If you save a worksheet with dynamic arrays and open that workbook in an older version of Excel, the dynamic arrays are converted to legacy array formulas. Excel does its best to retain fidelity, but be aware that the conversion may cause a loss of functionality or unexpected behavior. If your audience is using older versions of Excel, you'll want to fully test your dynamic formulas in their version of Excel to determine how the formulas behave when converted.

Understanding spill ranges

When you enter a dynamic array, the results spill into adjacent cells. Excel visually demarcates a spill range with a solid blue line. All cells inside the spill range are effectively disabled except for the *point of entry* (the cell containing the original formula). Figure 2-26 shows an active spill range containing the results of a dynamic array. The original formula was entered into cell E2. None of the values in the spill range, except for cell E2, can be deleted, moved, or edited in any way.

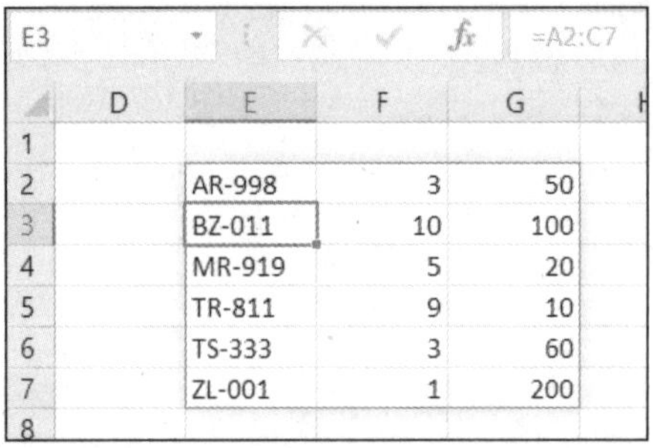

FIGURE 2-26: Spill ranges will visually show a line around them.

Attempting to enter data inside a spill range causes what's known as a #SPILL! error. Figure 2-27 demonstrates a #SPILL! error caused by entering a value in the spill range. Removing the obstructing data from the spill range immediately brings back the array values.

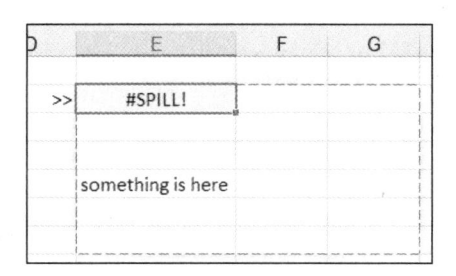

FIGURE 2-27:
A spill error caused by an obstruction in the spill range.

You may see a #SPILL! error for several reasons:

- **The spill range contains an obstruction.** This is the most common cause of a #SPILL! error. The spill range must be blank for your dynamic arrays to work. Any cell containing data will cause an error if it's in the path of the spill range.

- **The spill range extends beyond the worksheet end.** Try selecting cell A2 and entering the formula =B:B. You'll get a # SPILL! error because the spill range needs more room than the worksheet allows.

- **You're trying to use dynamic arrays in a Table object.** Excel Table objects don't allow other objects inside them. Because spill ranges are essentially a kind of auto-expanding object themselves, you can't use dynamic arrays inside tables.

- **You're out of memory.** If your dynamic array causes Excel to run out of memory, you'll get a #SPILL! error. In these cases, you'll need to rethink your formula and reference a smaller array.

- **The spill range has hit a merged cell.** Your spill range can't include merged cells.

- **The array doesn't have a fixed size.** As mentioned earlier in this chapter, dynamic arrays allow you to use any existing Excel functions within them. However, dynamic array formulas have trouble keeping up with volatile functions such as RAND and RANDBETWEEN. Dynamic arrays inherently trigger calculation refreshes until the formula is fully resolved. Meanwhile, volatile functions resize on each calculation pass, in turn causing the dynamic array to continue calculating. This causes a kind of continuous loop until Excel finally throws a #SPILL! error.

- **There is an unrecognized error.** In rare cases, Excel encounters an error it can't reconcile, so it throws a #SPILL! error. In these cases, it's best to review your formula to make sure it has all the required arguments.

Referencing spill ranges

It's often useful to reference a spill range in other formulas. However, simply pointing subsequent formulas to a single cell in the spill range won't capture the entirety of the range. You need to use the spill range operator, designated by a hashtag (#). To explore this concept, have a look at Figure 2-28. In the example shown, we want to capture the length of each string value in the spill range found in E2:E7. You can see that entering the formula LEN(E2) gives the length for only the first value in the spill range.

	D	E	F	G	H
1				String Length	
2		AR-90018		8	=Len(E2)
3		BZ-011			
4		MR-9198			
5		TR-81			
6		TS-3333			
7		ZL-001			

FIGURE 2-28: Referencing a single cell in a spill range doesn't allow you to capture all values.

In Figure 2-29, you can see in the Formula Bar that we've added the spill range operator (#) to the cell reference, telling Excel to use the entire spill range. This has the effect of carrying over the spill range and effectively creating a new spill range for the LEN function.

G2   fx =LEN(E2#)

	D	E	F	G	H
1				String Length	
2		AR-90018		8	
3		BZ-011		6	
4		MR-9198		7	
5		TR-81		5	
6		TS-3333		7	
7		ZL-001		6	
8					

FIGURE 2-29: Using the spill range operator to apply a function to the entire spill range.

In Figure 2-30, we're using the spill range operator with the COUNTA function to count all the values in the referenced spill range. Without the spill range operator, you would get a count of 1 for the first cell in the spill range.

WHY DO I SEE AN @ SIGN IN MY FORMULAS?

Traditional Excel formulas had an inherent calculation behavior called *implicit intersection,* in which a single value would be returned from an array of values. This ensured that formulas would always return just one value because, before dynamic arrays came along, a cell could only contain one value.

Now that dynamic arrays exist, Excel is no longer limited to returning single values, so if you have an Office 365 subscription and you're using the stand-alone (perpetual license) version of Office/Excel 2022 or later, you won't have implicit intersection applied.

However, if you open a workbook created in an older version of Excel, you may see an at sign (@) in the formulas. The @ is known as the *implicit intersection operator;* it's effectively a visual representation of the previously invisible implicit intersection behavior. Generally speaking, functions that return arrays (INDEX and OFFSET, for instance) will be prefixed with @ if they were authored in an older version of Excel.

If the formula containing the @ operator returns a single value, you can safely remove the @ without effect. If, however, the formula returns an array, removing the @ will cause it to spill to the neighboring cells.

If you remove the @ from a formula that returns an array and later open the workbook in an older version of Excel, the formula will be converted to a legacy array formula.

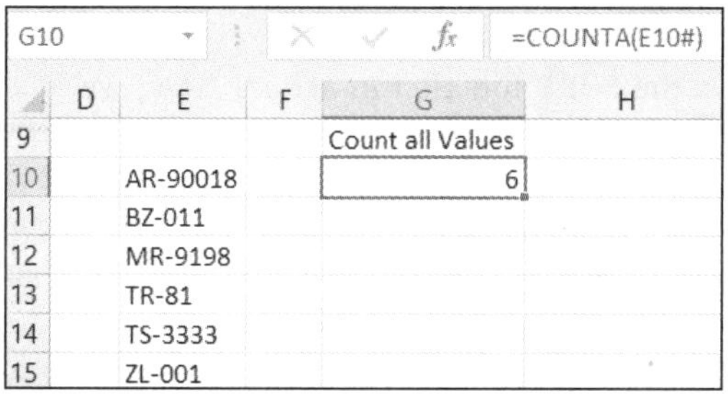

FIGURE 2-30: Using the spill range operator to count all values in the referenced spill range.

Exploring Dynamic Array Functions

With the introduction of dynamic arrays, Microsoft released new functions that leverage dynamic arrays to improve the ability to carry out complex formula operations with ease. These new functions can remove duplicates, extract unique values, filter data, dynamically sort data, and perform lookups. This section provides an overview of each of the new dynamic array functions.

The SORT function

The SORT function sorts the values in a given range in ascending or descending order with a formula. Results are output into a spill range that automatically updates when values in the source range change. The SORT function takes four arguments: *Array*, *Sort_index*, *Sort_order*, and *By_col*.

The *Array* argument defines the source range to sort and is the only required argument. The following formula will sort the values in A2:A11 in ascending order.

```
=SORT(A2:A11)
```

The *Sort_index* argument allows you to specify the column to sort by. By default, the SORT function uses the first column in the given range. You can set the *Sort_index* to a different column based on column number. The following formula will sort the values in A2:B11 by column B in ascending order.

```
=SORT(A2:B11,2)
```

The SORT function will sort ascending by default. You can sort descending by adding the *Sort_order* argument. Use -1 as *Sort_order* to sort descending. The following formula will sort the values in A2:B11 by column B in descending order.

```
=SORT(A2:B11,2,-1)
```

Figure 2-31 shows the SORT function in action. Here, we're sorting students in descending order by the change in test scores.

The SORT function will sort rows by default. The last argument of the SORT function is the *By_col* argument. You can set the *By_col* argument to 1 (see Figure 2-32) to sort by columns instead.

The SORTBY function

The SORTBY function sorts the contents of a range based on the values from other ranges. This function comes in handy when you need to apply sorting based on multiple columns. The SORTBY function takes three arguments: *Array*, *By_array*, and *Sort_order*.

FIGURE 2-31: Using the SORT function to sort students by the change in test scores.

	A	B	C	D	E	F	G	H	I
1	Student	Pre-Test	Post-Test	Change					
2	Andy	56	67	11		Linda	45	68	23
3	Beth	59	74	15		Michelle	71	92	21
4	Cindy	98	92	-6		Eddy	81	100	19
5	Duane	78	79	1		Beth	59	74	15
6	Eddy	81	100	19		Isabel	54	69	15
7	Francis	92	94	2		Andy	56	67	11
8	Georgia	100	100	0		Kent	80	88	8
9	Hilda	92	99	7		Hilda	92	99	7
10	Isabel	54	69	15		Francis	92	94	2
11	Jack	91	92	1		Duane	78	79	1
12	Kent	80	88	8		Jack	91	92	1
13	Linda	45	68	23		Georgia	100	100	0
14	Michelle	71	92	21		Cindy	98	92	-6
15	Nancy	94	83	-11		Nancy	94	83	-11

F2: `=SORT(A2:D15,4,-1)`

FIGURE 2-32: Using the SORT function to sort by columns.

`=SORT(N2:AA3,2,-1,1)`

M	N	O	P	Q	R	S	T	U	V	W	X	Y	Z	AA
Student	Andy	Beth	Cindy	Duane	Eddy	Francis	Georgia	Hilda	Isabel	Jack	Kent	Linda	Michelle	Nancy
Score	56	59	98	78	81	92	100	92	54	91	80	45	71	94

Georgia	Cindy	Nancy	Francis	Hilda	Jack	Eddy	Kent	Duane	Michelle	Beth	Andy	Isabel	Linda
100	98	94	92	92	91	81	80	78	71	59	56	54	45

The *Array* argument defines the range to sort, while the *By_array* argument specifies a range to sort by. You can sort ascending or descending using the *Sort_order* argument. Use 1 as *Sort_order* to sort ascending. Use –1 as *Sort_order* to sort descending. For instance, the following formula sorts the values in A2:C18 by the values in C2:18 in descending order.

```
=SORTBY(A2:C18, C2:C18,-1)
```

That's neat, but it's not different from using this SORT function to sort the same range by the third column (column C) in descending order:

```
=SORT(A2:C18,3,-1)
```

Well, the real power of the SORTBY function is the ability to sort by multiple columns. The formula in Figure 2-33 shows the following:

```
=SORTBY(A2:C18, A2:C18,1, C2:C18,-1, B2:B18,1)
```

CHAPTER 2 Building a Super Model   609

	A	B	C	D	E	F	G
1	Market	Quarter	Sales Amount				
2	BUFFALO	Q2	66,845		C2:C18,-1, B2:	Q3	500,297
3	BUFFALO	Q3	500,297		BUFFALO	Q1	283,337
4	BUFFALO	Q1	283,337		BUFFALO	Q2	66,845
5	CALIFORNIA	Q2	137,401		CALIFORNIA	Q1	1,138,579
6	CALIFORNIA	Q3	78,755		CALIFORNIA	Q2	137,401
7	CALIFORNIA	Q1	1,138,579		CALIFORNIA	Q3	78,755
8	CANADA	Q3	192,717		CANADA	Q1	683,529
9	CANADA	Q1	683,529		CANADA	Q3	192,717
10	CHARLOTTE	Q2	1,170,341		CHARLOTTE	Q2	1,170,341
11	CHARLOTTE	Q3	126,723		CHARLOTTE	Q1	593,458
12	CHARLOTTE	Q1	593,458		CHARLOTTE	Q3	126,723
13	DALLAS	Q2	318,807		DALLAS	Q1	352,632
14	DALLAS	Q3	295,650		DALLAS	Q2	318,807
15	DALLAS	Q1	352,632		DALLAS	Q3	295,650
16	DENVER	Q2	4,312,564		DENVER	Q2	4,312,564
17	DENVER	Q3	116,030		DENVER	Q1	516,989
18	DENVER	Q1	516,989		DENVER	Q3	116,030

Formula: =SORTBY(A2:C18, A2:A18,1, C2:C18,-1, B2:B18,1)

FIGURE 2-33: Using the SORTBY function to apply a multi-column sort.

In this formula, we're sorting the range first by Market ascending (A2:C18), then by Sales descending (C2:C18), and then by Quarter ascending (B2:B18). The result gives an output containing markets in alphabetical order, sorted by the quarters with the largest sales amount.

TIP

The SORTBY function does not require that the columns you sort by (specified by the *By_array* arguments) be part of the source data. You can sort by another range in a separate table if you want. However, the range you choose to sort by must have compatible dimensions. For instance, if your source data has 15 rows, the range by which you sort must also have 15 rows.

The UNIQUE function

The UNIQUE function extracts a list of distinct values from a range or array using just three arguments: *Array*, *By_col*, and *Exactly_once*. The *Array* argument is the only required argument. The following formula illustrates the most basic use of the UNIQUE function. This formula will extract the unique values A1:A10 to a spill range, which automatically updates when values in the source range change.

```
=UNIQUE(A1:A10)
```

The UNIQUE function works on rows by default. You can, however, tell Excel to extract unique values from columns setting the *By_col* argument to 1. In the following example, the UNIQUE function is used to extract the unique values from A1:J1 into a new spill range.

```
=UNIQUE(A1:J1,1)
```

The last argument, *Exactly_once*, tells Excel to extract values that appear only once in the given array. Figure 2-34 illustrates the difference between using a basic UNIQUE and using UNIQUE with the *Exactly_once* argument. As you can see, the values in column G show only those markets that appear one time in the source range (CANADA and TULSA).

	A	B	C	D	E	F	G
1	Market	Quarter	Sales Amount		=UNIQUE(A2:A13)		=UNIQUE(A2:A13,,1)
2	BUFFALO	Q2	66,845	>>	BUFFALO	>>	CANADA
3	BUFFALO	Q1	283,337		CALIFORNIA		TULSA
4	CALIFORNIA	Q2	137,401		CANADA		
5	CALIFORNIA	Q3	78,755		CHARLOTTE		
6	CANADA	Q3	192,717		DALLAS		
7	CHARLOTTE	Q3	126,723		DENVER		
8	CHARLOTTE	Q1	593,458		TULSA		
9	DALLAS	Q2	318,807				
10	DALLAS	Q1	352,632				
11	DENVER	Q2	4,312,564				
12	DENVER	Q3	116,030				
13	TULSA	Q1	516,989				

FIGURE 2-34: Adding the *Exactly_once* argument extracts only values that appear only once in the given range.

The FILTER function

The FILTER function extracts matching records from a dataset based on criteria specified in arguments. Results are output to a spill range and are automatically updated when the source data changes. This function becomes quite useful when building a reporting model using a subset of a larger data table. The FILTER function takes three arguments: *Array*, *Include*, and *If_empty*.

The *Array* argument points to the source data you're extracting from, the *Include* argument specifies the criteria that source records must meet in order to be extracted, and the *If_empty* argument defines what should be returned if no data matches the criteria.

Take a moment to examine Figure 2-35 to see how the FILTER function works. Looking at the Formula Bar, you'll see we're extracting all records from A2:D15 (the *Array* argument) if the value D2:D15 is greater than 10 (the *Include* argument). If no records match, then the formula will return No Matches (the *If_empty* argument).

FIGURE 2-35: Filtering records where the Change value is greater than 10.

F3			fx	=FILTER(A2:D15,D2:D15>10,"No Matches")			
A	B	C	D	E F	G	H	I

	A	B	C	D	E	F	G	H	I
1	Student	Pre-Test	Post-Test	Change					
2	Andy	56	67	11					
3	Beth	59	74	15		Andy	56	67	11
4	Cindy	98	92	-6		Beth	59	74	15
5	Duane	78	79	1		Linda P.	45	68	23
6	Linda P.	45	68	23		Michelle	71	92	21
7	Michelle	71	92	21		Linda J.	81	100	19
8	Nancy	94	83	-11		Isabel	54	69	15
9	Linda J.	81	100	19					
10	Francis	92	94	2					
11	Georgia	100	100	0					
12	Roland	91	92	1					
13	Kent	80	88	8					
14	Hilda	92	99	7					
15	Isabel	54	69	15					

TIP Although the *If_empty* argument is technically optional, it's a best practice to always specify a value to return if the FILTER function returns no matches. Leaving off the *If_empty* argument can potentially lead to a #CALC error if none of the records in your source range meets the specified criteria.

Instead of hard coding the *Include* argument, you may find it useful to reference a cell that will hold the criteria for your FILTER function. For example, the formula used in Figure 2-36 is essentially the same as the one in Figure 2-35 except we're getting the criteria from F1. With this setup, we can enter different values in F1 to see the results in the FILTER dynamically change.

FIGURE 2-36: Getting the FILTER criteria from cell F1.

=FILTER(A2:D15,D2:D15>F1,"No Matches")				
E	F	G	H	I
	15			
	Linda P.	45	68	23
	Michelle	71	92	21
	Linda J.	81	100	19

It's often useful to wrap the FILTER function inside of a SORT function to sort the filtered results. Figure 2-37 demonstrates sorting filtered results by the first column in the filtered array.

In some situations, you may need to filter a dataset based on multiple criteria. To do so, you simply need to wrap each criterion in parentheses separated by an asterisk (*). For instance, Figure 2-38 expands on the formula from Figure 2-35 by adding a second criterion for name. Note that each criterion is wrapped in its own set of parentheses.

612 BOOK 7 **Creating Dashboards and Reports**

FIGURE 2-37: Combining SORT with FILTER to sort results.

```
=SORT(FILTER(A2:D15,D2:D15>F1,"No Matches"),1)
```

E	F	G	H	I
	10			
	Andy	56	67	11
	Beth	59	74	15
	Isabel	54	69	15
	Linda J.	81	100	19
	Linda P.	45	68	23
	Michelle	71	92	21

FIGURE 2-38: Using multiple filter conditions.

```
=FILTER(A2:D15,(D2:D15>F1)*(A2:A15=H1),"No Matches")
```

E	F	G	H	I	J
	10		Beth		
	Beth	59	74	15	

So, what exactly is going on here? Well, behind the scenes, the two conditions are evaluated for each row of the dataset, resulting in a TRUE or FALSE for each respective condition. In Figure 2-39, we've broken the conditions into separate formulas to clearly illustrate the results from each.

FIGURE 2-39: Criteria evaluation behind the scenes.

	A	B	C	D	E	F	G	H
1	Student	Pre-Test	Post-Test	Change		10		Beth
2	Andy	56	67	11		=(D2:D15>F1)		=(A2:A15=H1)
3	Beth	59	74	15		TRUE		FALSE
4	Cindy	98	92	-6		TRUE		TRUE
5	Duane	78	79	1		FALSE		FALSE
6	Linda P.	45	68	23		FALSE		FALSE
7	Michelle	71	92	21		TRUE		FALSE
8	Nancy	94	83	-11		TRUE		FALSE
9	Linda J.	81	100	19		FALSE		FALSE
10	Francis	92	94	2		TRUE		FALSE
11	Georgia	100	100	0		FALSE		FALSE
12	Roland	91	92	1		FALSE		FALSE
13	Kent	80	88	8		FALSE		FALSE
14	Hilda	92	99	7		FALSE		FALSE
15	Isabel	54	69	15		FALSE		FALSE
16						TRUE		FALSE

In Excel, TRUE is equivalent to 1 and FALSE is equivalent to 0. The asterisk in the FILTER function (see Figure 2-38) will effectively multiply the TRUE and FALSE (1 and 0) results for each row, resulting in a 1 only for those records that show TRUE for both conditions. The asterisk can be thought of as an AND statement. Return results where the first condition is TRUE and the second condition is TRUE.

CHAPTER 2 Building a Super Model   613

To return results if the first condition is TRUE or the second condition is TRUE, use the plus operator (+). The formula in Figure 2-40 returns all records where the Change value is greater than 20 or the Student is Beth.

	A	B	C	D	E	F	G	H	I	J
1	Student	Pre-Test	Post-Test	Change		20		Beth		
2	Andy	56	67	11						
3	Beth	59	74	15		Beth	59	74	15	
4	Cindy	98	92	-6		Linda P.	45	68	23	
5	Duane	78	79	1		Michelle	71	92	21	
6	Linda P.	45	68	23						
7	Michelle	71	92	21						
8	Nancy	94	83	-11						
9	Linda J.	81	100	19						
10	Francis	92	94	2						
11	Georgia	100	100	0						
12	Roland	91	92	1						
13	Kent	80	88	8						
14	Hilda	92	99	7						
15	Isabel	54	69	15						

F3: =FILTER(A2:D15,(D2:D15>F1)+(A2:A15=H1),"No Matches")

FIGURE 2-40: Using the + operator to return results if the first condition is TRUE or the second condition is TRUE.

The XLOOKUP function

The XLOOKUP function is designed to be the successor to the traditional VLOOKUP and HLOOKUP functions you may be used to. With more flexible options like approximate matching and wildcard matching, this function is truly an improved version of Excel's lookup capability. XLOOKUP accepts a whopping six arguments: *Lookup_value*, *Lookup_array*, *Return_array*, *Not_found*, *Match_mode*, and *Search_mode*.

The minimum arguments you need for XLOOKUP to work is a *Lookup_value*, a *Lookup_array*, and a *Return_array*. To understand these arguments, take a gander at Figure 2-41. In this example, we're attempting to populate the Customer Type column (column C) based on the matching values in the table found in columns E and F. A quick look at the Formula Bar shows the following formula:

```
=XLOOKUP(B2:B19, E2:E5, F2:F5, "No Match")
```

This formula is telling Excel to look up the values in column B (the *Lookup_value*), match them to the values in column E (the *Lookup_array*), and return the matching value in column F (the *Return_array*). The final argument (*Not_found*) defines what should be returned if no data matches the lookup criteria. Although the *Not_found* argument is optional, it's typically best practice to include it to avoid the ugly #N/A errors you get when a value isn't found.

614 BOOK 7 **Creating Dashboards and Reports**

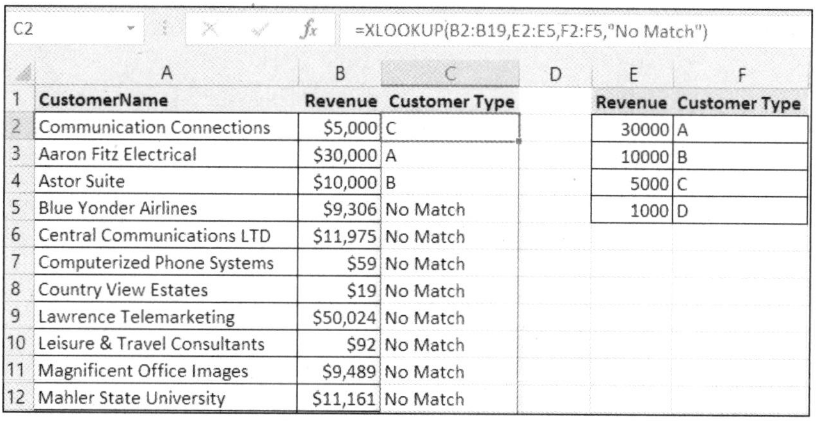

FIGURE 2-41:
A basic XLOOKUP function to find Customer Type based on revenue.

	A	B	C	D	E	F
1	CustomerName	Revenue	Customer Type		Revenue	Customer Type
2	Communication Connections	$5,000	C		30000	A
3	Aaron Fitz Electrical	$30,000	A		10000	B
4	Astor Suite	$10,000	B		5000	C
5	Blue Yonder Airlines	$9,306	No Match		1000	D
6	Central Communications LTD	$11,975	No Match			
7	Computerized Phone Systems	$59	No Match			
8	Country View Estates	$19	No Match			
9	Lawrence Telemarketing	$50,024	No Match			
10	Leisure & Travel Consultants	$92	No Match			
11	Magnificent Office Images	$9,489	No Match			
12	Mahler State University	$11,161	No Match			

Formula in C2: `=XLOOKUP(B2:B19,E2:E5,F2:F5,"No Match")`

TIP When building your XLOOKUP, keep in mind that the `Lookup_array` argument must have the same dimensions as the `Return_array` — that is, the same number of rows/columns.

As you look at Figure 2-41, you'll notice that the XLOOKUP function found a Customer Type only for those records that exactly match the revenue in the `Lookup_array` (column E). In many cases, you won't find an exact match, especially when trying to match numbers like revenue. In our example, we want to perform an approximate match on our records to catch even those revenues that don't exactly match the values in our lookup table. To do so, we can add the `Match_mode` argument.

Entering a comma after the `Not_found` argument will bring up a list of choices (see Figure 2-42). The one you choose will depend on what exactly you're trying to achieve. It's best to experiment with each option to see which option is right for you. In this case, we want to apply the option for Exact Match or Next Smaller Item. Selecting the appropriate option will immediately retrieve the valid customer types. Figure 2-43 shows the result of the applied approximate matching.

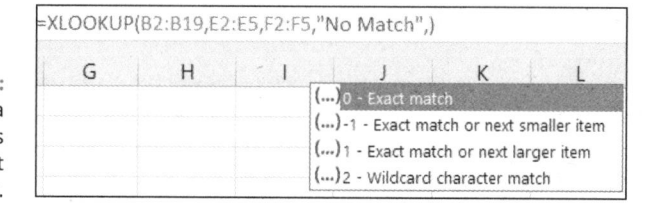

FIGURE 2-42:
Enter a comma to see choices for the next argument.

`=XLOOKUP(B2:B19,E2:E5,F2:F5,"No Match",)`

Dropdown choices:
- 0 - Exact match
- -1 - Exact match or next smaller item
- 1 - Exact match or next larger item
- 2 - Wildcard character match

CHAPTER 2 Building a Super Model   615

	A	B	C	D	E	F
1	CustomerName	Revenue	Customer Type		Revenue	Customer Type
2	Communication Connections	$5,000	C		30000	A
3	Aaron Fitz Electrical	$30,000	A		10000	B
4	Astor Suite	$10,000	B		5000	C
5	Blue Yonder Airlines	$9,306	C		1000	D
6	Central Communications LTD	$11,975	B			
7	Computerized Phone Systems	$59	No Match			
8	Country View Estates	$19	No Match			
9	Lawrence Telemarketing	$50,024	A			
10	Leisure & Travel Consultants	$92	No Match			
11	Magnificent Office Images	$9,489	C			
12	Mahler State University	$11,161	B			
13	Metropolitan Fiber Systems	$10,686	B			

Formula: =XLOOKUP(B2:B19,E2:E5,F2:F5,"No Match",-1)

FIGURE 2-43: XLOOKUP results using approximate matching.

In rare cases, you can use the *Search_mode* argument to dictate how Excel performs the search for the XLOOKUP. For this argument, you have the following options:

» **1:** This is the default search mode and will be the most appropriate in most of your lookup scenarios.

» **-1:** Search from the last value in the array up (essentially reverse order of the default behavior).

» **2:** Binary search on values that are already sorted in ascending order. This mode is used to improve performance on very large arrays. Binary searches are fast, but if your data is not sorted as prescribed, your XLOOKUP can return invalid results.

» **-2:** Binary search on values that are already sorted in descending order. Again, this mode is used to improve performance, but you'll want to ensure your data is sorted as prescribed, or your XLOOKUP will return invalid results.

TIP When using XLOOKUP to match across workbooks, both workbooks must be open, or Excel will return a #REF! error.

One of the options for the *Match_mode* argument is Wildcard character match (see Figure 2-42). Wildcards are special characters that enable complex searches using approximate matching. Excel allows the use of three different wildcard characters, each with its own purpose.

» **Asterisk (*):** The asterisk wildcard is used to tell your formula to look for a portion of text no matter what comes before or after. For example, searching for *hotel will look for any value that ends with the word *hotel,* no matter what comes before. Searching for hotel* will look for any value that starts with *hotel,* no matter what comes after. And as you may have guessed, searching for *hotel* will look for any value containing the word *hotel.*

» **Question mark (?):** The question mark wildcard is used to tell your formula to look for any one character within a text. For instance, searching for p?ace would return both *peace* and *place.* You can use multiple question mark wildcards in a search (??onder and sm?itt?n are both valid searches). In addition, you can combine the asterisk and question mark wildcards to create a more complex search. For example, searching for *vis??* would return any text string containing the word *visor* or *vision.*

» **Tilde (~):** The tilde wildcard is useful when you need to include a character that is, itself, a wildcard. For example, if you need to search for any text string that ends in a question mark, you'll need to preface the question mark with a tilde because the question mark itself is a wildcard (*~?). The same goes for the asterisk. To search for any text string that starts with an asterisk, use ~**.

Figure 2-44 demonstrates the use of wildcard characters. In column J, XLOOKUP searches for the Revenue (B2:B19) where the Customer Name contains the letters *LTD*. In column L, XLOOKUP searches for the Revenue where the Customer Name contains *f?tz*.

FIGURE 2-44: Using wildcard characters to perform complex searches.

	A	B	D	J	K	L	M
	J2		fx	=SUM(XLOOKUP(J1,A2:A19,B2:B19,"no match",2))			
1	CustomerName	Revenue		*LTD*		*f?tz*	
2	Communication Connections	$5,000		$11,975		$30,000	
3	Aaron Fitz Electrical	$30,000					
4	Astor Suite	$10,000					
5	Blue Yonder Airlines	$9,306					
6	Central Communications LTD	$11,975					
7	Computerized Phone Systems	$59					

CHAPTER 2 Building a Super Model 617

IN THIS CHAPTER

» Understanding the principles of table design

» Trying your hand at custom number formatting

» Applying custom format colors and conditions

Chapter 3
Dressing Up Your Data Tables

The Excel table is the perfect way to consolidate and relay information. Data tables are quite common — you'll find one in any Excel report. Yet the concept of making tables easier to read and more visually appealing escapes most of us.

Maybe it's because the nicely structured rows and columns of a table lull us into believing that the data is already presented in the best way possible. Maybe the options of adding color and borders make the table seem nicely packaged. Excel makes table creation easy, but even so, you can use several design principles to make your Excel table a more effective platform for conveying your data.

This chapter explores how easy it is to apply a handful of table design best practices. The tips found here ultimately help you create visually appealing tables that make the data within them easier to consume and comprehend.

Table Design Principles

Table design is one of the most underestimated endeavors in Excel reporting. How a table is designed has a direct effect on how well an audience absorbs and interprets the data in that table. Unfortunately, putting together a data table with an eye for economy and ease of consumption is an uncommon skill.

For example, the table shown in Figure 3-1 is similar to many tables found in Excel reports. The thick borders, the variety of colors, and the poorly formatted numbers are all unfortunate trademarks of tables that come from the average Excel analyst.

Top 10 Domestic Routes by Revenue							
		Revenue		Margin		Per Passenger	
From	To	Revenue Dollars	Revenue Percent	Margin Dollars	Margin Percent	Revenue per Passenger	Margin per Passenger
Atlanta	New York	$3,602,000	8.09%	$955,000	9%	245	65
Chicago	New York	$4,674,000	10.50%	$336,000	3%	222	16
Columbus (Ohio)	New York	$2,483,000	5.58%	$1,536,000	14%	202	125
New York	Detroit	$12,180,000	27.35%	$2,408,000	23%	177	35
New York	Washington	$6,355,000	14.27%	$1,230,000	12%	186	36
New York	Philadelphia	$3,582,000	8.04%	-$716,000	-7%	125	-25
New York	San Francisco	$3,221,000	7.23%	$1,856,000	18%	590	340
New York	Phoenix	$2,846,000	6.39%	$1,436,000	14%	555	280
New York	Toronto	$2,799,000	6.29%	$1,088,000	10%	450	175
New York	Seattle	$2,792,000	6.27%	$467,000	4%	448	75
Total Domestic routes		**$44,534,000**		**$10,596,000**		**272**	**53**

FIGURE 3-1: A poorly designed table.

Throughout this chapter, you improve on this table by applying these four basic design principles:

- **Use colors sparingly,** reserving them for information about key data points.
- **De-emphasize borders,** using the natural white space between the components to partition your dashboard.
- **Use effective number formatting** to avoid inundating your table with too much ink.
- **Subdue your labels and headers.**

Use colors sparingly

Color is most often used to separate the various sections of a table. The basic idea is that the colors applied to a table suggest the relationship between the rows and columns. The problem is that colors often distract and draw attention away from the important data. In addition, printed tables with dark-colored cells are notoriously difficult to read (especially on black-and-white printers). They're also hard on the toner budget, if that matters to you.

Colors in general should be used sparingly, reserved for providing information about key data points. The headers, labels, and natural structure of your table are more than enough to guide your audience. There is no real need to add a layer of color as demarcation for your rows and columns.

Figure 3-2 shows the table from Figure 3-1 with the colors removed. As you can see, it's already easier to read.

Top 10 Domestic Routes by Revenue		Revenue		Margin		Per Passenger	
		Revenue	Revenue	Margin	Margin	Revenue per	Margin per
From	To	Dollars	Percent	Dollars	Percent	Passenger	Passenger
Atlanta	New York	$3,602,000	8.09%	$955,000	9%	245	65
Chicago	New York	$4,674,000	10.50%	$336,000	3%	222	16
Columbus (Ohio)	New York	$2,483,000	5.58%	$1,536,000	14%	202	125
New York	Detroit	$12,180,000	27.35%	$2,408,000	23%	177	35
New York	Washington	$6,355,000	14.27%	$1,230,000	12%	186	36
New York	Philadelphia	$3,582,000	8.04%	-$716,000	-7%	125	-25
New York	San Francisco	$3,221,000	7.23%	$1,856,000	18%	590	340
New York	Phoenix	$2,846,000	6.39%	$1,436,000	14%	555	280
New York	Toronto	$2,799,000	6.29%	$1,088,000	10%	450	175
New York	Seattle	$2,792,000	6.27%	$467,000	4%	448	75
Total Domestic routes		$44,534,000		$10,596,000		272	53

FIGURE 3-2: Remove unnecessary cell coloring.

TIP If you're working with a table that contains colored cells, you can quickly remove the color by highlighting the cells, clicking the Home tab of the ribbon, selecting the Theme Colors drop-down list, and choosing No Fill.

De-emphasize borders

Believe it or not, borders get in the way of quickly reading the data in a table. Because borders help separate data in nicely partitioned sections, this may seem counterintuitive, but the reality is that a table's borders are the first thing your eyes see when you look at a table. Don't believe it? Stand back a bit from an Excel table and squint. The borders will come popping out at you.

TIP You should always try to de-emphasize borders and gridlines wherever you can. Try to use the natural white space between the columns to partition sections. If borders are necessary, format them to lighter hues than your data; light grays are typically ideal. The idea is to indicate sections without distracting from the information displayed.

Figure 3-3 demonstrates these concepts with the table from Figure 3-1. Notice how the numbers are no longer caged in gridlines and that headings now jump out at you with the addition of single accounting underlines.

FIGURE 3-3: Minimize the use of borders and use single accounting underlines to accent the column headers.

Top 10 Domestic Routes by Revenue

From	To	Revenue Dollars	Revenue Percent	Margin Dollars	Margin Percent	Revenue per Passenger	Margin per Passenger
Atlanta	New York	$3,602,000	8.09%	$955,000	9%	245	65
Chicago	New York	$4,674,000	10.50%	$336,000	3%	222	16
Columbus (Ohio)	New York	$2,483,000	5.58%	$1,536,000	14%	202	125
New York	Detroit	$12,180,000	27.35%	$2,408,000	23%	177	35
New York	Washington	$6,355,000	14.27%	$1,230,000	12%	186	36
New York	Philadelphia	$3,582,000	8.04%	-$716,000	-7%	125	-25
New York	San Francisco	$3,221,000	7.23%	$1,856,000	18%	590	340
New York	Phoenix	$2,846,000	6.39%	$1,436,000	14%	555	280
New York	Toronto	$2,799,000	6.29%	$1,088,000	10%	450	175
New York	Seattle	$2,792,000	6.27%	$467,000	4%	448	75
Total Domestic routes		**$44,534,000**		**$10,596,000**		272	53

TIP

Single accounting underlines are different from the standard underlining you typically apply by pressing Ctrl+U on the keyboard. Standard underlines draw a line only as far as the text goes — that is to say, if you underline the word *YES*, standard underlines give you a line under the three letters. Single accounting underlines, on the other hand, draw a line across the entire column, regardless of how big or small the word is. This makes for a minimal, but apparent, visual demarcation that calls out column headers nicely.

You can format borders by first highlighting the cells you're working with and then pressing Ctrl+1 on the keyboard. This opens the Format Cells dialog box; click the Border tab to display its controls (see Figure 3-4). From there, follow these steps:

1. **Select an appropriate line thickness.**

   Typically, you should select the line with the lightest weight.

2. **Select an appropriate color.**

   Again, lighter hues are the best options.

3. **Use the border buttons to control where the borders are placed.**

To apply the single accounting underline, right-click the column headings and select Format Cells. In the Format Cells dialog box, click the Font tab and, from the Underline drop-down list, choose Single Accounting, as shown in Figure 3-5.

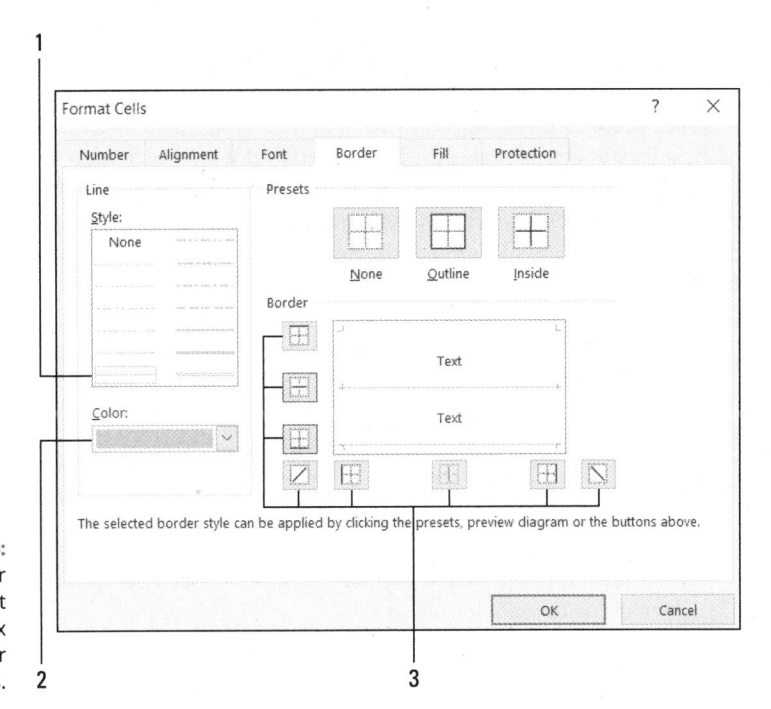

FIGURE 3-4: Use the Border tab of the Format Cells dialog box to customize your borders.

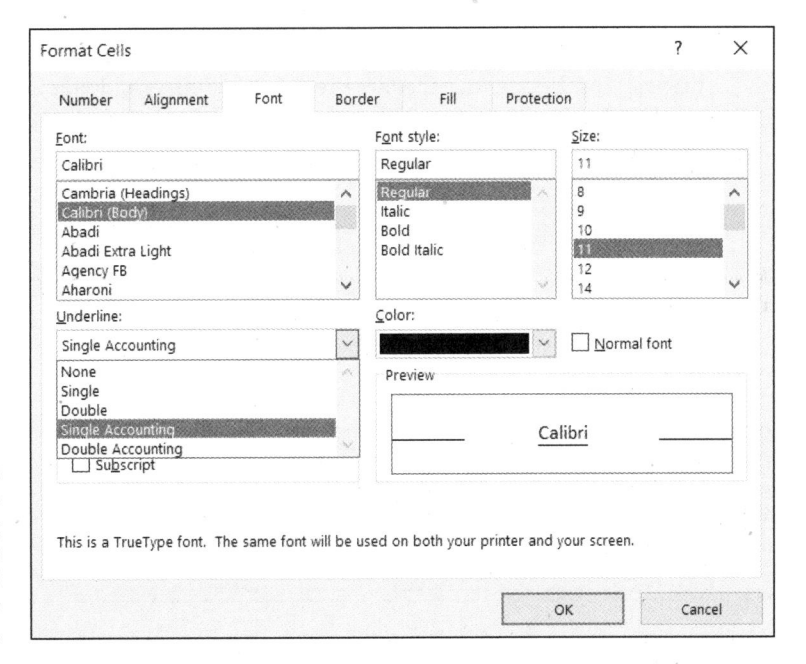

FIGURE 3-5: Single accounting underlines effectively call out your column headers.

CHAPTER 3 **Dressing Up Your Data Tables** 623

Use effective number formatting

Every piece of information in your table should have a reason for being there. In an effort to clarify, tables often inundate the audience with superfluous ink that doesn't add value to the information. For example, you'll often see tables that show a number like $145.47 when a simple 145 would be just fine. Why include the extra decimal places, which serve only to add to the mass of numbers that the audience has to plow through?

Here are some guidelines to keep in mind when applying formats to the numbers in the table:

- » Use decimal places only if that level of precision is required.
- » In percentages, use only the minimum number of decimals required to represent the data effectively.
- » Instead of using currency symbols (like $ or £), let labels clarify that you're referring to monetary values.
- » Format very large numbers to the thousands or millions place.
- » Right-align numbers so that they're easier to read and compare.

Figure 3-6 shows the table from Figure 3-1 with appropriate number formatting applied. Notice that the large revenue and margin dollar amounts have been converted to the thousands place. In addition, the labels above the numbers now clearly indicate as such.

FIGURE 3-6: Use number formatting to eliminate clutter in the table and draw attention to key metrics.

Top 10 Domestic Routes by Revenue

From	To	Revenue $ (000's)	Revenue %	Margin $ (000's)	Margin %	$ per Passenger	Margin $ per Passenger
Atlanta	New York	3,602	8%	955	9%	245	65
Chicago	New York	4,674	10%	336	3%	222	16
Columbus (Ohio)	New York	2,483	6%	1,536	14%	202	125
New York	Detroit	12,180	27%	2,408	23%	177	35
New York	Washington	6,355	14%	1,230	12%	186	36
New York	Philadelphia	3,582	8%	-716	-7%	125	-25
New York	San Francisco	3,221	7%	1,856	18%	590	340
New York	Phoenix	2,846	6%	1,436	14%	555	280
New York	Toronto	2,799	6%	1,088	10%	450	175
New York	Seattle	2,792	6%	467	4%	448	75
Total Domestic routes		**44,534**		**10,596**		**272**	**53**

The percentages have been truncated to show no decimal places. Also, the color coding draws attention to the Margin % column, the key metric in this table.

Amazingly, all these improvements have been made simply with number formatting. That's right: No formulas were used to convert large numbers to the thousands place, no conditional formatting was used to color-code the Margin % field, and there were no other peripheral tricks of any kind.

Subdue your labels and headers

No one would argue that the labels and headers of a table aren't important. On the contrary, they provide the audience with the guidance and structure needed to make sense of the data within. However, many of us have a habit of overemphasizing labels and headers to the point that they overshadow the data within the table. How many times have you seen a bold or oversized font applied to headers? The reality is that your audience will benefit more from subdued labels.

De-emphasizing labels by formatting them to lighter hues actually makes the table easier to read and draws more attention to the data *within* the table. Lightly colored labels give users the information they need without distracting them from the information being presented. Ideal colors to use for labels are soft grays, light browns, soft blues, and greens.

Font size and alignment also factor into the effective display of tables. Aligning column headers to the same alignment as the numbers beneath them helps reinforce the column structures in your table. Keeping the font size of your labels close to that of the data within the table helps keep your eyes focused on the data — not the labels.

Figure 3-7 illustrates how the original table from Figure 3-1 looks with subdued headers and labels. Note how the data now becomes the focus while the muted labels work in the background.

FIGURE 3-7: Send your labels and headers to the background by subduing their colors and keeping their font sizes in line with the data.

Top 10 Domestic Routes by Revenue

From	To	Revenue $ (000's)	Revenue %	Margin $ (000's)	Margin %	$ per Passenger	Margin $ per Passenger
New York	Detroit	12,180	27%	2,408	23%	177	35
New York	Washington	6,355	14%	1,230	12%	186	36
Chicago	New York	4,674	10%	336	3%	222	16
Atlanta	New York	3,602	8%	955	9%	245	65
New York	Philadelphia	3,582	8%	-716	-7%	125	-25
New York	San Francisco	3,221	7%	1,856	18%	590	340
New York	Phoenix	2,846	6%	1,436	14%	555	280
New York	Toronto	2,799	6%	1,088	10%	450	175
New York	Seattle	2,792	6%	467	4%	448	75
Columbus (Ohio)	New York	2,483	6%	1,536	14%	202	125
Total Domestic routes		44,534		10,596		272	53

TIP

Sorting is another key factor in the readability of your data. Many tables sort based on labels (alphabetical by route, for example). Sorting the table based on a key data point within the data helps establish a pattern the audience can use to quickly analyze the top and bottom values. Note in Figure 3-7 that the data has been sorted by the Revenue dollars. This again adds a layer of analysis, providing a quick look at the top- and bottom-generating routes.

Figure 3-8 illustrates the difference these simple improvements can make in the readability of your data tables. It's easy to see how a few table design principles can greatly enhance your ability to present table-driven data.

Top 10 Domestic Routes by Revenue

		Revenue		Margin		Per Passenger	
From	To	Revenue Dollars	Revenue Percent	Margin Dollars	Margin Percent	Revenue per Passenger	Margin per Passenger
Atlanta	New York	$3,602,000	8.09%	$955,000	9%	245	65
Chicago	New York	$4,674,000	10.50%	$336,000	3%	222	16
Columbus (Ohio)	New York	$2,483,000	5.58%	$1,536,000	14%	202	125
New York	Detroit	$12,180,000	27.35%	$2,408,000	23%	177	35
New York	Washington	$6,355,000	14.27%	$1,230,000	12%	186	36
New York	Philadelphia	$3,582,000	8.04%	-$716,000	-7%	125	-25
New York	San Francisco	$3,221,000	7.23%	$1,856,000	18%	590	340
New York	Phoenix	$2,846,000	6.39%	$1,436,000	14%	555	280
New York	Toronto	$2,799,000	6.29%	$1,088,000	10%	450	175
New York	Seattle	$2,792,000	6.27%	$467,000	4%	448	75
Total Domestic routes		**$44,534,000**		**$10,596,000**		**272**	**53**

Top 10 Domestic Routes by Revenue

		Revenue		Margin		Per Passenger	
From	To	Revenue $ (000's)	Revenue %	Margin $ (000's)	Margin %	$ per Passenger	Margin $ per Passenger
New York	Detroit	12,180	27%	2,408	23%	177	35
New York	Washington	6,355	14%	1,230	12%	186	36
Chicago	New York	4,674	10%	336	3%	222	16
Atlanta	New York	3,602	8%	955	9%	245	65
New York	Philadelphia	3,582	8%	-716	-7%	125	-25
New York	San Francisco	3,221	7%	1,856	18%	590	340
New York	Phoenix	2,846	6%	1,436	14%	555	280
New York	Toronto	2,799	6%	1,088	10%	450	175
New York	Seattle	2,792	6%	467	4%	448	75
Columbus (Ohio)	New York	2,483	6%	1,536	14%	202	125
Total Domestic routes		44,534		10,596		272	53

FIGURE 3-8: Before and after applying table design principles.

TIP

If possible, consider using modern-looking fonts such as Calibri and Segoe UI in your reports and dashboards. Fonts such as Times New Roman and Arial can make your reports look old compared with the rounded edges of the more trendy fonts used today. This change in font perception is primarily driven by popular websites that use fonts with rounded edges.

Getting Fancy with Custom Number Formatting

You can apply number formatting to cells in several ways. Most people simply use the convenient number commands found on the Home tab. By using these commands, you can quickly apply some default formatting (number, percent, currency, and so on) and just be done with it, but a better way is to use the Format Cells dialog box, in which you have the ability to create your own custom number formatting.

Number formatting basics

Follow these steps to apply basic number formatting:

1. **Right-click a range of cells and select Format Cells.**

    The Format Cells dialog box appears.

2. **Click the Number tab and choose a starting format that makes the most sense for your scenario.**

    In Figure 3-9, the format we chose is Number and the options we selected are not to use a comma separator, to include no decimal places, and to enclose negative numbers in parentheses.

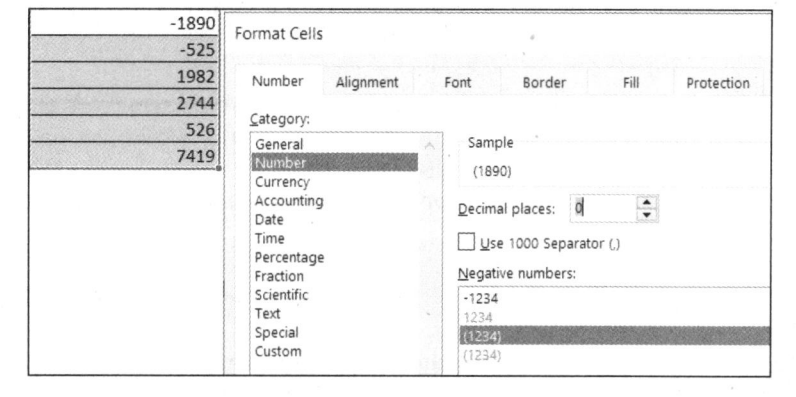

FIGURE 3-9: Choose a base format.

3. **Click the Custom option, as shown in Figure 3-10.**

    Excel takes you to a screen that exposes the syntax that makes up the format you selected. Here, you can edit the syntax in the Type input box to customize the number format.

CHAPTER 3 Dressing Up Your Data Tables   627

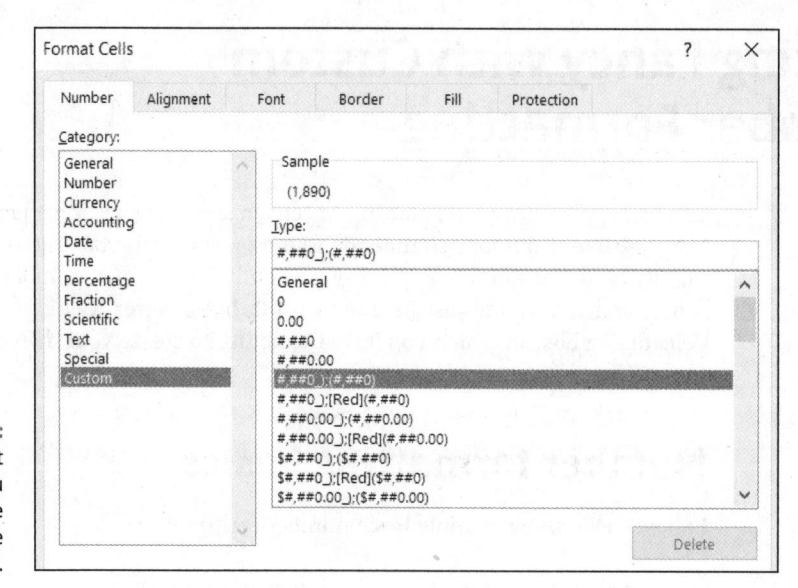

FIGURE 3-10: The Type input box allows you to customize the syntax for the number format.

The number formatting syntax tells Excel how a number should look in various scenarios. Number formatting syntax consists of different individual number formats separated by semicolons.

In this case, you see

```
#,##0_);(#,##0)
```

Here, you see two different formats: the format to the left of the semicolon and the format to the right of the semicolon.

By default, any formatting to the left of the first semicolon is applied to positive numbers and any formatting to the right of the first semicolon is applied to negative numbers. So, with this choice, positive numbers will be formatted as a simple number, whereas negative numbers will be formatted with parentheses, like this:

```
(1,890)
1,982
```

REMEMBER Note that the syntax for the positive formatting in the previous example ends with an underscore and a closing parenthesis: _). This tells Excel to leave a space the width of a parenthesis character at the end of positive numbers, which ensures that positive and negative numbers align nicely when negative numbers are wrapped in parentheses.

You can edit the syntax in the Type input box so the numbers are formatted differently. For example, try changing the syntax to

```
+#,##0;-#,##0
```

When this syntax is applied, positive numbers will start with the + symbol and negative numbers will start with the − symbol, like this:

```
+1,200
-15,000
```

This comes in handy when formatting percentages. For instance, you can apply a custom percent format by entering the following syntax into the Type input box:

```
+0%;-0%
```

This syntax gives you percentages that look like this:

```
+43%
-54%
```

You can get fancy and wrap your negative percentages with parentheses with this syntax:

```
0%_);(0%)
```

This syntax gives you percentages that look like this:

```
43%
(54%)
```

REMEMBER: If you include only one format syntax (meaning you don't add a second formatting option with the use of a semicolon separator), that single format will be applied to all numbers — negative or positive.

Formatting numbers in thousands and millions

Earlier in this chapter, you format your revenue numbers to appear in thousands. This allows you to present cleaner numbers and avoid inundating the audience with overlarge numbers. To show your numbers in thousands, highlight them, right-click, and select Format Cells from the menu that appears.

CHAPTER 3 **Dressing Up Your Data Tables** 629

In the Format Cells dialog box, click the Custom option on the Number tab. Then, in the Type input box, add a comma after the format syntax:

```
#,##0,
```

After confirming your changes, your numbers will automatically appear in the thousands place!

The beautiful thing here is that this technique doesn't change the integrity or truncate the numeric values in any way. Excel is simply applying a cosmetic effect to the number. To see what this means, take a look at Figure 3-11.

FIGURE 3-11: Formatting numbers applies only a cosmetic look. Look at the Formula Bar to see the real, unformatted number.

	A	B	C	D	E
				fx	117943.605787004
6		North	118	380k	463k
7		Northeast	24k	803k	328k
8		East	313k	780k	904k
9		Southeast	397k	466k	832k
10		South	840k	118k	800k
11		Southwest	623k	977k	808k
12		West	474k	79k	876k

The selected cell has been formatted to show in thousands; you see 118. But if you look at the Formula Bar above it, you'll see the real unformatted number (117943.605787004). The 118 you're seeing in the cell is a cosmetically formatted version of the real number shown on the Formula Bar.

REMEMBER

Custom number formatting has obvious advantages over using other techniques to format numbers to thousands. For instance, many beginning analysts would convert numbers to thousands by dividing them by 1,000 in a formula. But that changes the integrity of the number dramatically. When you perform a mathematical operation in a cell, you're literally changing the value represented in that cell. This forces you to carefully keep track of and maintain the formulas you introduced to simply achieve a cosmetic effect. Using custom number formatting avoids that by changing only how the number looks, keeping the actual number intact.

If needed, you can even indicate that the number is in thousands by adding "k" to the number syntax:

```
#,##0,"k"
```

This would show your numbers like this:

```
118k
318k
```

You can use this technique on both positive and negative numbers:

```
#,##0,"k"; (#,##0,"k")
```

After applying this syntax, your negative numbers also appear in thousands:

```
118k
(318k)
```

Need to show numbers in millions? Easy. Simply add two commas to the number format syntax in the Type input box:

```
#,##0.00,, "m"
```

Note the use of the extra decimal places (.00). When converting numbers to millions, it's often useful to show additional precision points, as in

```
24.65 m
```

Hiding and suppressing zeroes

In addition to formatting positive and negative numbers, Excel allows you to provide a format for zeroes. You do this by adding another semicolon to your custom number syntax. By default, any format syntax placed after the second semicolon is applied to any number that evaluates to zero.

For example, the following syntax applies a format that shows n/a for any cells that contain zeroes:

```
#,##0_);(#,##0);"n/a"
```

You can also use a custom format to suppress zeroes entirely. If you add the second semicolon but don't follow it with any syntax, cells containing zeroes will appear blank:

```
#,##0_);(#,##0);
```

Again, custom number formatting affects only the cosmetic look of the cell. The actual *data* in the cell is not affected. Figure 3-12 demonstrates this. The selected cell is formatted so that zeroes appear as n/a, but if you look at the Formula Bar, you can see the actual unformatted cell contents.

FIGURE 3-12: Custom number formatting that shows zeroes as n/a.

	C	D	E
Printers	37,000	64,000	24,000
Copiers	18,000	29,000	58,000
Scanners	n/a	77,000	88,000
Service Contr	16,000	12,000	n/a
Warranties	65,000	88,000	16,000

Applying custom format colors

Have you ever set the formatting on a cell so that negative numbers appear in red? If you have, you essentially applied a custom format color. In addition to controlling the look of your numbers with custom number formatting, you can control their color.

In this example, you format the percentages so positive percentages appear blue with a plus (+) symbol, whereas negative percentages appear red with a minus (–) symbol. Enter this syntax in the Type input box on the Number tab of the Format Cells dialog box:

```
[Blue]+0%;[Red]-0%
```

Notice that all it takes to apply a color is to enter the color name wrapped in square brackets [ ].

Now, you can call out by name only certain colors — the eight Visual Basic colors. These colors make up the first eight colors of the default Excel color palette:

[Black]	[Magenta]
[Blue]	[Red]
[Cyan]	[White]
[Green]	[Yellow]

Formatting dates and times

Custom number formatting isn't just for numbers. You can also format dates and times. As you can see in Figure 3-13, you use the same dialog box to apply date and time formats using the Type input box.

Figure 3-13 demonstrates that date and time formatting involves little more than stringing together date-specific or time-specific syntax. The syntax used is fairly intuitive. For example, ddd is the syntax for the three-letter day, mmm is the syntax for the three-letter month, and yyyy is the syntax for the four-digit year.

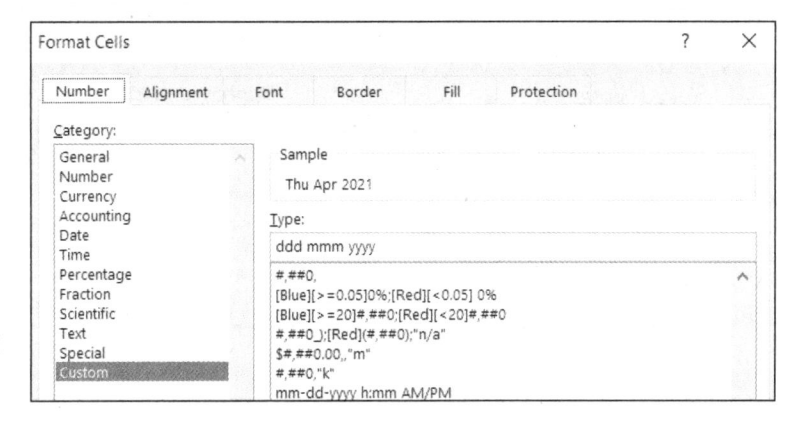

FIGURE 3-13: Dates and times can also be formatted using the Format Cells dialog box.

There are several variations on the format for days, months, years, hours, and minutes. It's worthwhile to take some time and experiment with different combinations of syntax strings.

Table 3-1 lists some common date and time format codes you can use as starter syntax for your reports and dashboards.

TABLE 3-1 ## Common Date and Time Format Codes

Format Code	1/31/2021 7:42:53 PM Displays As
m	1
mm	01
mmm	Jan
mmmm	January
mmmmm	J

(continued)

TABLE 3-1 *(continued)*

Format Code	1/31/2021 7:42:53 PM Displays As
dd	31
ddd	Sun
dddd	Sunday
yy	21
yyyy	2021
mmm-yy	Jan-21
dd/mm/yyyy	31/01/2021
dddd mmm yyyy	Sunday Jan 2021
mm-dd-yyyy h:mm AM/PM	01-31-2021 7:42 PM
h AM/PM	7 PM
h:mm AM/PM	7:42 PM
h:mm:ss AM/PM	7:42:53 PM

> **IN THIS CHAPTER**
> » Using conditional formatting
> » Working with symbols in formulas
> » Using the Camera tool
> » Using shapes to enhance Excel reports

Chapter 4
Formatting Your Way to Visualizations

Visualization is the presentation of abstract concepts or data in visual terms through some sort of graphical imagery. A traffic light, for example, is a visualization of the abstract concepts of stop and go.

In the business world, visualizations help us communicate and process the meaning of data faster than simple tables of numbers. Excel offers business analysts a wide array of features that can be used to add visualizations to dashboards and reports.

In this chapter, you explore some of the formatting techniques you can leverage to add layers of visualizations that can turn your data into meaningful views.

Enhancing Reports with Conditional Formatting

Conditional formatting is the term given to Excel's capability to dynamically change the formatting of a value, cell, or range of cells based on a set of conditions you define. Conditional formatting adds a level of visualization that allows you to look at your Excel reports and make split-second determinations on which values are "good" and which are "bad," simply based on formatting.

In this section, you enter the world of conditional formatting as you see how to leverage this functionality to enhance your reports and dashboards.

Applying basic conditional formatting

Thanks to the many predefined scenarios that Excel offers, you can apply some basic conditional formatting with a few clicks of the mouse. To get a first taste of what you can do, click the Conditional Formatting button found on the Home tab of the ribbon, as shown in Figure 4-1.

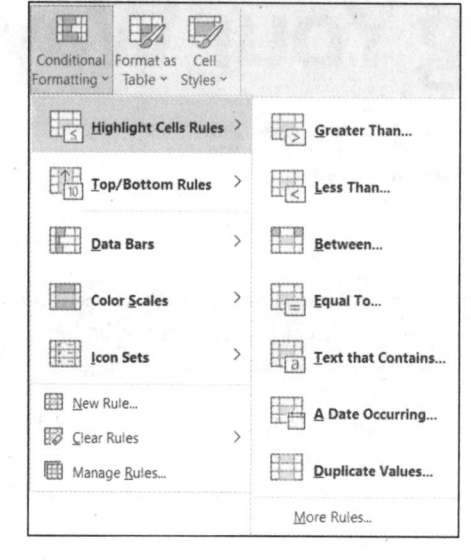

FIGURE 4-1: Excel's predefined conditional formatting scenarios include Highlight Cells Rules, which apply formatting if specific conditions are met.

As you can see, Excel has five categories of predefined scenarios: Highlight Cells Rules, Top/Bottom Rules, Data Bars, Color Scales, and Icon Sets.

Take a moment to review what you can do by using each category of predefined scenario.

Using the Highlight Cells Rules

The formatting scenarios under the Highlight Cells Rules category, also shown in Figure 4-1, allow you to highlight those cells whose values meet a specific condition.

The thing to remember about these scenarios is that they work much like an `if...then...else` statement. That is to say, if the condition is met, the cell is formatted, and if the condition is not met, the cell remains untouched.

The scenarios under the Highlight Cells Rules category are self-explanatory. Here's a breakdown of what you can conditionally format with each scenario:

- **Greater Than:** A cell whose value is greater than a specified amount. For instance, you can tell Excel to format those cells that contain a value greater than 50.

- **Less Than:** A cell whose value is less than a specified amount. For instance, you can tell Excel to format those cells that contain a value less than 100.

- **Between:** A cell whose value is between two given amounts. For example, you can tell Excel to format those cells that contain a value between 50 and 100.

- **Equal To:** A cell whose value is equal to a given amount. For example, you can tell Excel to format those cells that contain a value that is exactly 50.

- **Text That Contains:** A cell whose contents contain any form of a given text you specify as a criterion. For example, you can tell Excel to format those cells that contain the text *North*.

- **A Date Occurring:** A cell whose contents contain a date occurring in a specified period relative to today's date. For example, Yesterday, Last Week, Last Month, Next Month, or Next Week.

- **Duplicate Values:** Both duplicate values and unique values in a given range of cells. This rule was designed more for data cleanup than for dashboarding, enabling you to quickly identify either duplicates or unique values in your dataset.

Take a moment to work the following example of how to apply one of these scenarios. In this simple example, you highlight all values greater than a certain amount.

1. **Start by selecting the range of cells to which you need to apply the conditional formatting.**

2. **On the Home tab of the ribbon, go to the Styles group, click Conditional Formatting, click Highlight Cell Rules, and then click Greater Than.**

   The dialog box shown in Figure 4-2 opens. In this dialog box, the idea is to define a value that will trigger the conditional formatting.

FIGURE 4-2:
Each scenario has its own dialog box for defining the rule's trigger values and format.

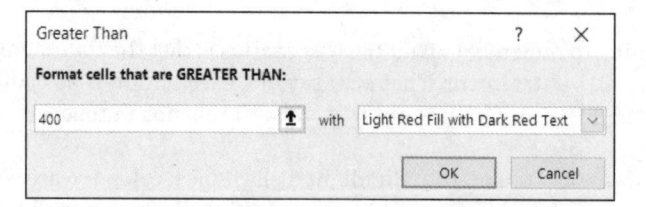

3. **Either type the value (400 in this example) or reference a cell that contains the trigger value, and then use the box's drop-down list to specify the format you want applied.**

4. **Click OK.**

   Immediately, Excel applies the formatting rule to the selected cells (see Figure 4-3).

FIGURE 4-3:
Cells greater than 400 are formatted.

	Greater Than 400
Jan	100
Feb	-100
Mar	200
Apr	250
May	-50
Jun	350
Jul	400
Aug	450
Sep	500
Oct	550
Nov	600
Dec	650

The benefit of a conditional formatting rule is that Excel automatically reevaluates the rule every time a cell is changed (as long as that cell has a conditional formatting rule applied to it). For instance, if you were to change any of the low values to 450, the formatting for that value would automatically change because all cells in the dataset have the formatting applied to them.

Applying Top/Bottom Rules

The formatting scenarios under the Top/Bottom Rules category on the Conditional Formatting drop-down list allow you to highlight those cells whose values meet a given threshold.

Like the Highlight Cells Rules, these scenarios work like if...then...else statements: If the condition is met, the cell is formatted; if the condition is not met, the cell remains untouched.

Here's a breakdown of each scenario under the Top/Bottom Rules category:

- **Top 10 Items:** Although the name doesn't suggest it, this scenario allows you to specify any number of cells to highlight based on individual cell values (not just ten). For example, you can highlight the top five cells whose values are among the five largest numbers of all selected cells.

- **Top 10 %:** This scenario is similar to the Top 10 Items scenario: Only the selected cells are evaluated on a percentage basis. Again, don't let the name fool you: The percent selection does not have to be ten. For instance, you can highlight the cells whose values make up the top 20 percent of the total values of all selected cells.

- **Bottom 10 Items:** You can use this scenario to specify the number of cells to highlight based on the lowest individual cell values. Here, too, you can specify any number of cells to highlight — not just 10. For example, you can highlight the bottom 15 cells whose values are within the 15 smallest numbers among all selected cells.

- **Bottom 10 %:** Though this scenario is similar to the Bottom 10 Items scenario, in this one, only selected cells are evaluated on a percentage basis. For instance, you can highlight the cells whose values make up the bottom 15 percent of the total values of all the selected cells.

- **Above Average:** This scenario allows you to conditionally format each cell whose value is above the average of all cells selected.

- **Below Average:** Allows you to conditionally format each cell whose value is below the average of all cells selected.

REMEMBER To avoid overlapping different conditional formatting scenarios, you may want to clear any conditional formatting you've previously applied before applying a new scenario. To clear the conditional formatting for a given range of cells, select the cells and select Conditional Formatting from the Home tab of the ribbon. There, you find the Clear Rules selection. Click Clear Rules and then click either Clear Rules from Selected Cells or Clear Rules from Entire Sheet.

In the following example, you conditionally format all cells whose values are within the top 40 percent of the total values of all cells.

1. **Start by selecting the range of cells to which you need to apply the conditional formatting.**

2. **On the Home tab of the ribbon, go to the Styles group, click Conditional Formatting, click Top/Bottom Rules, and then click Top 10 %.**

   This step opens the Top 10 % dialog box shown in Figure 4-4. The idea here is to define the threshold that that will trigger the conditional formatting.

CHAPTER 4 **Formatting Your Way to Visualizations**   639

FIGURE 4-4: Each scenario has its own dialog box you can use to define the trigger values and the format for each scenario.

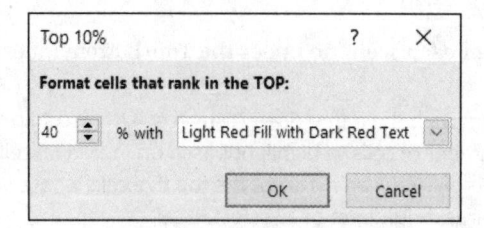

3. **In this example, enter 40 and then use the box's drop-down list to specify the format you want applied.**

4. **Click OK.**

    Immediately, Excel applies the formatting scenario to the selected cells (see Figure 4-5).

FIGURE 4-5: With conditional formatting, you can easily see that September through December makes up 40 percent of the total value in this dataset.

	Within Top 40%
Jan	100
Feb	-100
Mar	200
Apr	250
May	-50
Jun	350
Jul	400
Aug	450
Sep	500
Oct	550
Nov	600
Dec	650

Creating Data Bars

Data Bars fill each cell you're formatting with mini-bars in varying length, indicating the value in each cell relative to other formatted cells. Excel essentially takes the largest and smallest values in the selected range and calculates the length of each bar. To apply Data Bars to a range, do the following:

1. **Select the target range of cells to which you need to apply the conditional formatting.**

2. **On the Home tab of the ribbon, go to the Styles group, click Conditional Formatting, click Data Bars, and then click the style of Data Bars you want.**

    As you can see in Figure 4-6, the result is essentially a mini chart within the cells you selected. Also note that, by default, the Data Bars scenario accounts for negative numbers nicely by changing the direction of the bar and inverting the color to red.

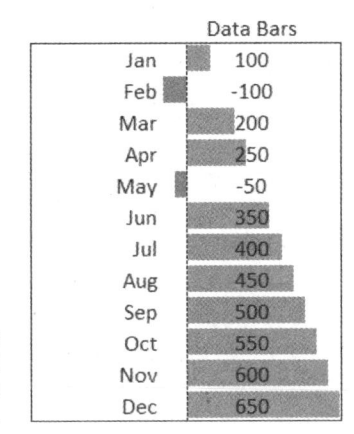

FIGURE 4-6: Conditional formatting with Data Bars.

Data Bars	
Jan	100
Feb	-100
Mar	200
Apr	250
May	-50
Jun	350
Jul	400
Aug	450
Sep	500
Oct	550
Nov	600
Dec	650

Applying Color Scales

Color Scales fill each cell you're formatting with a color varying in scale based on the value in each cell relative to other formatted cells. Excel essentially takes the largest and smallest values in the selected range and determines the color for each cell. To apply Color Scales to a range, do the following:

1. **Select the target range of cells to which you need to apply the conditional formatting.**

2. **On the Home tab of the ribbon, go to the Styles group, click Conditional Formatting, click Color Scales, and then click the style of Color Scales you want.**

   As you can see in Figure 4-7, the result is a kind of heat map within the cells you selected.

FIGURE 4-7: Conditional formatting with Color Scales.

Color Scales	
Jan	100
Feb	-100
Mar	200
Apr	250
May	-50
Jun	350
Jul	400
Aug	450
Sep	500
Oct	550
Nov	600
Dec	650

CHAPTER 4 **Formatting Your Way to Visualizations**

Using Icon Sets

Icon Sets are sets of symbols that are inserted in each cell you're formatting. Excel determines which symbol to use based on the value in each cell relative to other formatted cells. To apply an Icon Set to a range, do the following:

1. **Select the target range of cells to which you need to apply the conditional formatting.**

2. **On the Home tab of the ribbon, go to the Styles group, click Conditional Formatting, click Icon Sets, and then click the style of Icon Set you want in the Directional group, the Shapes group, or the Indicators group (see Figure 4-8).**

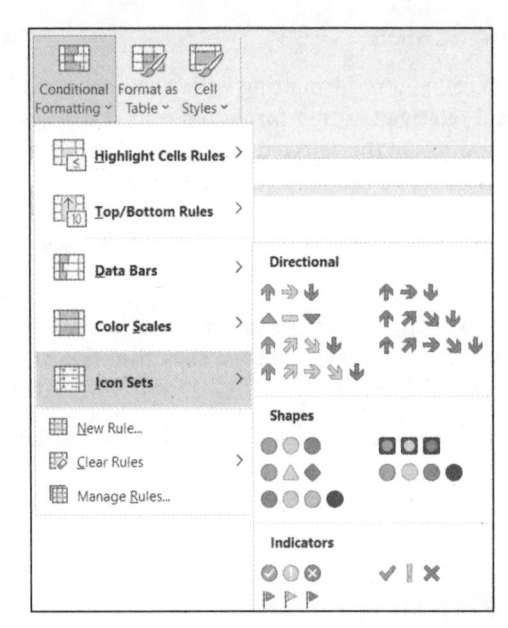

FIGURE 4-8: Applying Icon Sets.

Figure 4-9 illustrates how each cell is formatted with a symbol indicating each cell's value based on the other cells.

Adding your own formatting rules manually

You don't have to use one of the predefined scenarios offered by Excel. Excel gives you the flexibility to create your own formatting rules manually. Creating your own formatting rules helps you better control how cells are formatted and allows you to do things you wouldn't be able to do with the predefined scenarios.

642 BOOK 7 Creating Dashboards and Reports

FIGURE 4-9: Conditional formatting with Icon Sets.

For example, a useful conditional formatting rule is to tag all above-average values with a check-mark icon and all below-average values with an X icon. Figure 4-10 demonstrates this rule.

FIGURE 4-10: With a custom formatting rule, you can tag the above-average values with a check mark and the below-average values with an X.

REMEMBER

Although the Above Average and Below Average scenarios built into Excel allow you to format cell and font attributes, they don't enable the use of Icon Sets. You can imagine why Icon Sets would be better on a dashboard than simply color variances. Icons and shapes do a much better job of conveying your message, especially when the dashboard is printed in black and white.

TIP

To get started in creating your first custom formatting rule, open the 7.4.1 Chapter 4 Samples.xlsx workbook found among the sample files at www.dummies.com/go/microsoft365excelaiofd. With this workbook active, click the Create Rule by Hand tab, and then follow these steps:

1. **Select the target range of cells to which you need to apply the conditional formatting.**

CHAPTER 4 **Formatting Your Way to Visualizations**   643

2. **On the Home tab of the ribbon, go to the Styles group, click Conditional Formatting, and then click New Rule.**

   This step opens the New Formatting Rule dialog box shown in Figure 4-11. As you look at the rule types at the top of the dialog box, you may recognize some of them from the predefined scenario choices discussed earlier in this chapter. Here's what each type does:

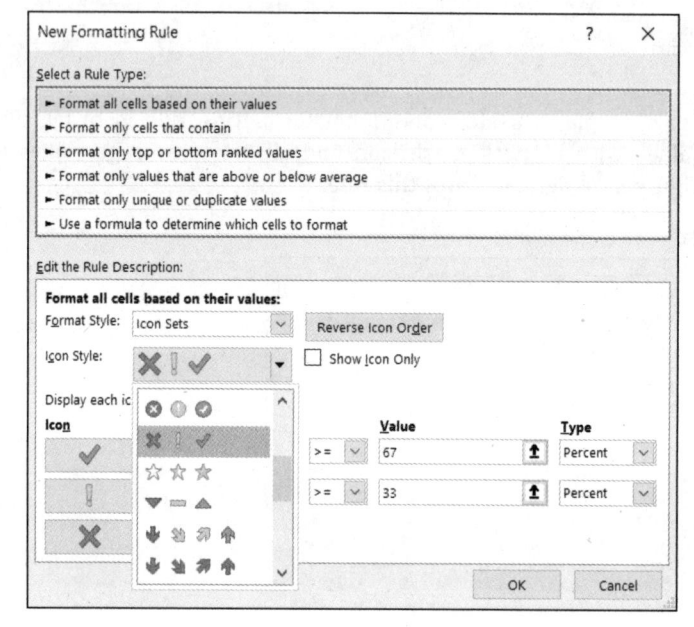

FIGURE 4-11: Select the Format All Cells Based on Their Values rule and then use the Format Style drop-down list to switch to Icon Sets.

- *Format All Cells Based on Their Values:* Measures the values in the selected range against each other. This selection is handy for finding general anomalies in your dataset.

- *Format Only Cells That Contain:* Applies conditional formatting to those cells that meet specific criteria you define. This selection is perfect for comparing values against a defined benchmark.

- *Format Only Top or Bottom Ranked Values:* Applies conditional formatting to those cells that are ranked in the top or bottom *n*th number or percent of all values in the range.

- *Format Only Values That Are Above or Below Average:* Applies conditional formatting to those values that are mathematically above or below the average of all values in the selected range.

- *Use a Formula to Determine Which Cells to Format:* Evaluates values based on a formula you specify. If a particular value evaluates to true, the conditional formatting is applied to that cell. This selection is typically used when applying conditions based on the results of an advanced formula or mathematical operation.

> **TIP** Data Bars, Color Scales, and Icon Sets can be used only with the Format All Cells Based on Their Values rule type.

3. **Ensure that the Format All Cells Based on Their Values rule type is selected.**
4. **Click the Format Style drop-down list and select Icon Sets.**
5. **Click the Icon Style drop-down list and select the Icon Set you want.**
6. **Change both Type drop-down lists to Formula.**
7. **In each Value box, enter** =Average($C$2:$C$22).

   This step tells Excel that the value in each cell must be greater than the average of the entire dataset in order to get the check-mark icon.

   At this point, the dialog box looks similar to the one in Figure 4-12.

8. **Click OK to apply your conditional formatting.**

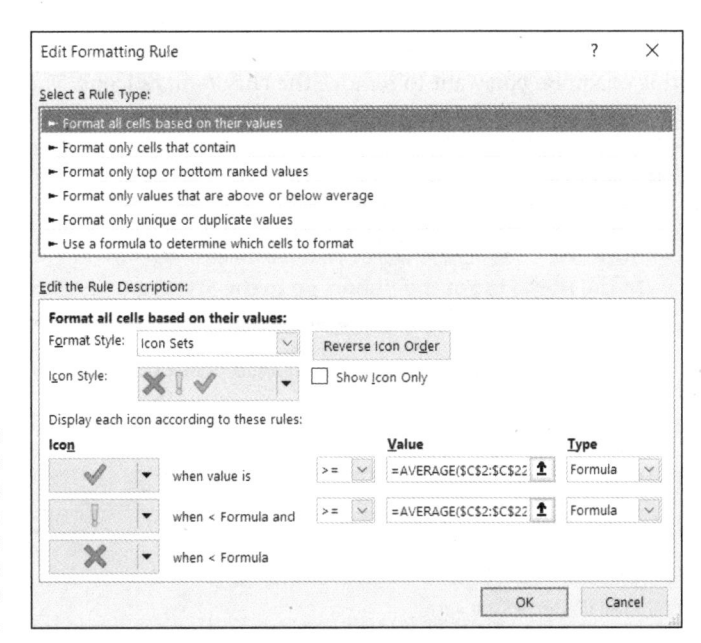

FIGURE 4-12: Change the Type drop-down boxes to Formula and enter the appropriate formulas in the Value boxes.

It's worth taking some time to understand how this conditional formatting rule works. Excel assesses every cell in the target range to see whether its contents match, in order (top box first), the logic in each Value box. As Excel evaluates the values in the target range, it will apply the specified icon for each cell that meets

CHAPTER 4 Formatting Your Way to Visualizations   645

the specified condition. Any cell that doesn't fit any of the logic placed in the Value boxes will apply the last icon.

In this example, you want a cell to get a check-mark icon only if the value of the cell is greater than (or equal to) the average of the total values. Otherwise, you want Excel to skip directly to the X icon and apply the X.

Showing only one icon

In many cases, you may not need to show all icons when applying the Icon Set. In fact, showing too many icons at one time may just obstruct the data you're trying to convey on the dashboard.

In the earlier example, you apply a check-mark icon to values above the average for the range and apply an X icon to all below-average values (see Figure 4-10). However, in the real world, you often need to bring attention to only the below-average values. This way, your eyes aren't inundated with superfluous icons.

Excel provides a clever mechanism to allow you to stop evaluating and formatting values if a condition is true.

In this example, you want to remove the check-mark icons. The cells that contain those icons all have values above the average for the range. Therefore, you first need to add a condition for all cells whose values are above average. To do so, follow these steps:

1. **Select the target range of cells.**

2. **On the Home tab of the ribbon, go to the Styles group, click Conditional Formatting, and then click Manage Rules.**

    The Conditional Formatting Rules Manager dialog box, shown in Figure 4-13, opens.

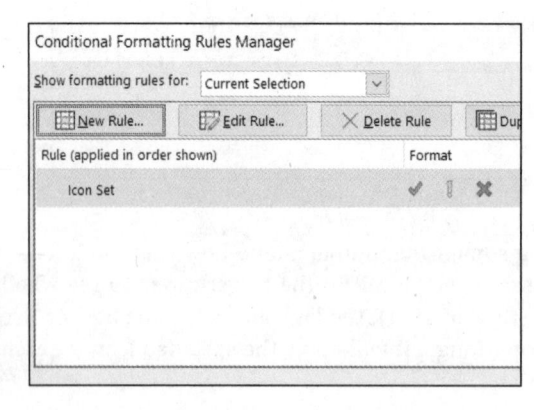

FIGURE 4-13: The Conditional Formatting Rules Manager dialog box.

3. **Click the New Rule button to start a new rule.**

   The New Formatting Rule dialog box opens.

4. **Click the Format Only Cells That Contain rule type and then configure the rule so that the format applies only to cell values greater than the average (see Figure 4-14).**

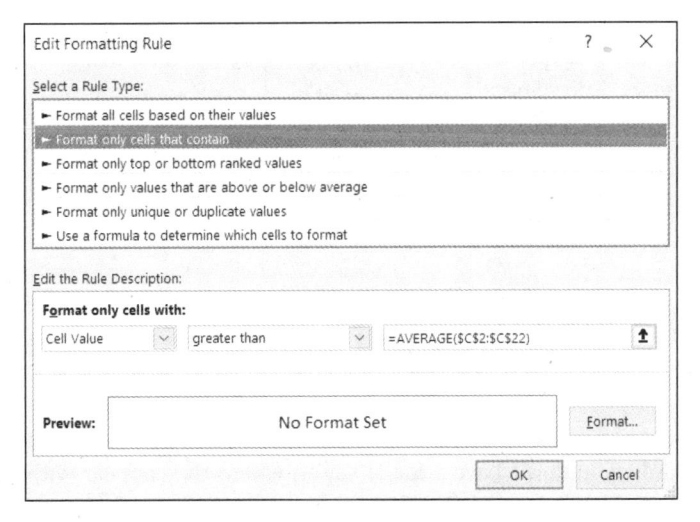

FIGURE 4-14: This new rule is meant to apply to any cell value that you don't want formatted — in this case, any value that's greater than the average of the range.

5. **Click OK without changing any of the formatting options.**

6. **Back in the Conditional Formatting Rules Manager, click to select the Stop If True check box, as shown on the right side of Figure 4-15.**

FIGURE 4-15: Click Stop If True to tell Excel to stop evaluating those cells that meet the first condition.

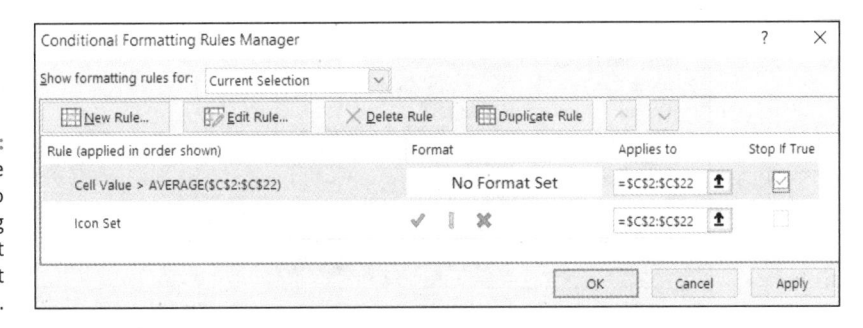

7. **Click OK to apply your changes.**

   As you can see in Figure 4-16, only the X icons are now shown. Again, this allows your audience to focus on the exceptions instead of determining which icons are good and bad.

CHAPTER 4 **Formatting Your Way to Visualizations** 647

	A	B	C
1	REGION	MARKET	Sales
2	North	Great Lakes	✖ 70,261
3	North	New England	217,858
4	North	New York North	✖ 157,774
5	North	New York South	✖ 53,670
6	North	North Carolina	✖ 124,600
7	North	Ohio	✖ 100,512
8	North	Shenandoah Valley	✖ 149,742
9	South	Florida	✖ 111,606
10	South	Gulf Coast	253,703
11	South	Illinois	✖ 129,148
12	South	Indiana	✖ 152,471
13	South	Kentucky	224,524
14	South	South Carolina	249,535
15	South	Tennessee	307,490
16	South	Texas	180,167
17	West	California	190,264
18	West	Central	✖ 133,628
19	West	Colorado	✖ 134,039
20	West	North West	✖ 120,143

FIGURE 4-16: This table is now formatted to show only one icon.

Showing Data Bars and icons outside of cells

Data Bars and Icon Sets give you a snazzy way to add visualizations to your dashboards; you don't have a lot of say in where they appear within the cell. Take a look at Figure 4-17 to see what we mean.

	A	B
1	MARKET	Sales
2	Great Lakes	70,261
3	New England	217,858
4	New York North	157,774
5	New York South	53,670
6	Ohio	100,512
7	Shenandoah Valley	149,742
8	South Carolina	249,535
9	Florida	111,606
10	Gulf Coast	253,703
11	Illinois	129,148
12	Indiana	152,471
13	Kentucky	224,524
14	North Carolina	124,600
15	Tennessee	307,490

FIGURE 4-17: Showing Data Bars inside the same cell as values can make it difficult to analyze the data.

By default, the Data Bars are placed directly inside each cell, which in this case almost obscures the data. From a dashboarding perspective, this is less than ideal, for two reasons:

» The numbers can get lost in the colors of the Data Bars, making them difficult to read — especially when printed in black and white.

» It's difficult to see the ends of each bar.

The solution to this problem is to show the Data Bars *outside* the cell that contains the value. Here's how:

1. **To the right of each cell, enter a formula that references the cell containing the data value.**

   For example, if the data is in B2, go to cell C2 and enter **=B2**.

2. **Apply the Data Bar conditional formatting to the formulas you just created.**

3. **Select the formatted range of cells.**

4. **On the Home tab of the ribbon, go to the Styles group, click Conditional Formatting, and then click Manage Rules.**

5. **In the Conditional Formatting Rules Manager dialog box, click the rule, and then click the Edit Rule button.**

6. **In the Edit Formatting Rule dialog box, select the Show Bar Only check box, as shown in Figure 4-18.**

7. **Click OK to apply the change.**

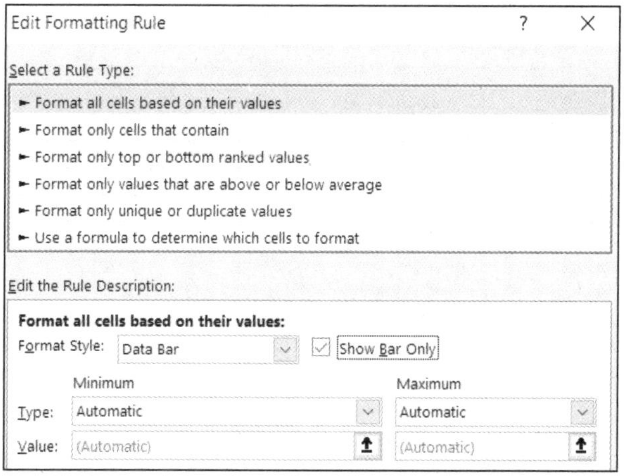

FIGURE 4-18: Edit the formatting rule to show only the Data Bars, not the data.

The reward for your efforts is a cleaner view that's much better suited for reporting in a dashboard environment. Figure 4-19 illustrates the improvement gained with this technique.

CHAPTER 4 Formatting Your Way to Visualizations 649

FIGURE 4-19: Data Bars, cleanly placed next to the data values.

	A	B	C
1	MARKET	Sales	
2	Great Lakes	70,261	
3	New England	217,858	
4	New York North	157,774	
5	New York South	53,670	
6	Ohio	100,512	
7	Shenandoah Valley	149,742	
8	South Carolina	249,535	
9	Florida	111,606	
10	Gulf Coast	253,703	
11	Illinois	129,148	
12	Indiana	152,471	
13	Kentucky	224,524	
14	North Carolina	124,600	
15	Tennessee	307,490	
16	Texas	180,167	

Using the same technique, you can separate Icon Sets from the data, allowing you to position the icons where they best suit your dashboard.

Representing trends with Icon Sets

A dashboard environment may not always have enough space available to add a chart that shows trending. In these cases, Icon Sets are ideal replacements, enabling you to visually represent the overall trending without taking up a lot of space. Figure 4-20 illustrates this concept with a table that provides a nice visual element, allowing for an at-a-glance view of which markets are up, down, or flat over the previous month.

FIGURE 4-20: The up arrow indicates an upward trend, the down arrow indicates a downward trend, and the right arrow indicates a flat trend.

	A	B	C	D	E
1	REGION	MARKET	Previous Month	Current Month	Variance
2	North	Great Lakes	70,261	72,505	⬆ 3.2%
3	North	New England	217,858	283,324	⬆ 30.0%
4	North	New York North	157,774	148,790	⬇ -5.7%
5	North	New York South	53,670	68,009	⬆ 26.7%
6	North	Ohio	100,512	98,308	➡ -2.2%
7	North	Shenandoah Valley	149,742	200,076	⬆ 33.6%
8	South	South Carolina	249,535	229,473	⬇ -8.0%
9	South	Florida	111,606	136,104	⬆ 22.0%
10	South	Gulf Coast	253,703	245,881	⬇ -3.1%
11	South	Illinois	129,148	131,538	➡ 1.9%
12	South	Indiana	152,471	151,699	➡ -0.5%
13	South	Kentucky	224,524	225,461	➡ 0.4%
14	North	North Carolina	124,600	130,791	⬆ 5.0%
15	South	Tennessee	307,490	268,010	⬇ -12.8%

You may want to do the same type of thing with your reports. The key is to create a formula that gives you a variance or trending of some sort.

To achieve this type of view, follow these steps:

1. **Select the target range of cells to which you need to apply the conditional formatting.**

   In this case, the target range will be the cells that hold your variance formulas.

2. **On the Home tab of the ribbon, go to the Styles group, click Conditional Formatting, click Icon Sets, and then click the Icon Set you want.**

   For this example, choose the first set of three arrows in the Directional group (green up arrow, yellow right arrow, and red down arrow).

   In most cases, you'll adjust the thresholds that define what up, down, and flat mean. Imagine you need any variance above 3 percent to be tagged with an up arrow, any variance below –3 percent to be tagged with a down arrow, and all others to show flat.

3. **With the target range still selected, click Conditional Formatting on the Home tab of the ribbon, and then click Manage Rules.**

4. **In the Conditional Formatting Rules Manager dialog box, click the rule and then click the Edit Rule button.**

5. **Adjust the properties in the Edit Formatting Rule dialog box, as shown in Figure 4-21.**

6. **Click OK to apply the change.**

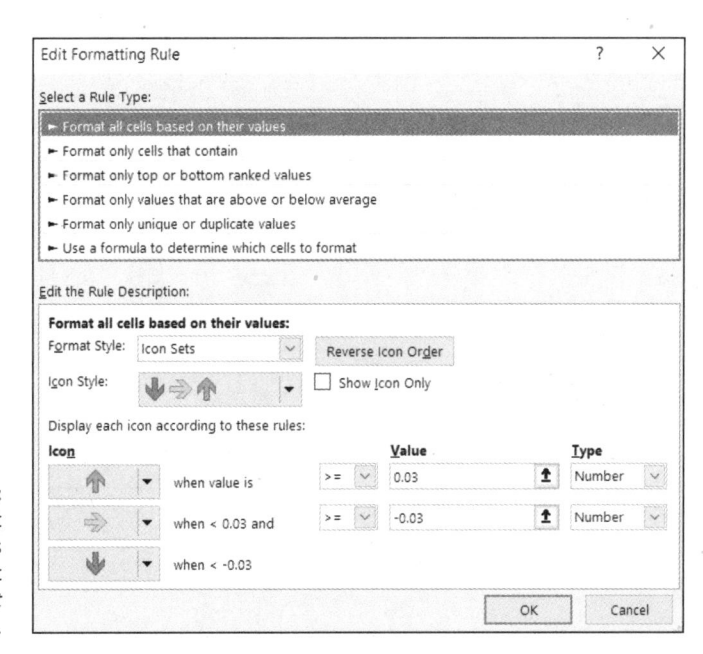

FIGURE 4-21: You can adjust the thresholds that define what *up*, *down*, and *flat* mean.

CHAPTER 4 Formatting Your Way to Visualizations   651

TIP Notice in Figure 4-21 that the Type property for the formatting rule is set to Number even though the data you're working with (the variances) is percentages. You'll find that working with the Number setting gives you more control and predictability when setting thresholds.

Using Symbols to Enhance Reporting

Symbols are essentially tiny graphics, not unlike those you see when you use Wingdings or Webdings or other fancy fonts. However, symbols are not really fonts. They're *Unicode characters* (a set of industry standard text elements designed to provide a reliable character set that remains viable on any platform regardless of international font differences).

One example of a commonly used symbol is the copyright symbol (©). This symbol is a Unicode character. You can use it on a Chinese, Turkish, French, or American PC, and it will reliably be available, with no international differences.

In terms of Excel presentations, Unicode characters (or symbols) can be used in places where conditional formatting cannot. For instance, in the chart labels you see in Figure 4-22, the x-axis shows some trending arrows that allow for an extra layer of analysis. This couldn't be done with conditional formatting.

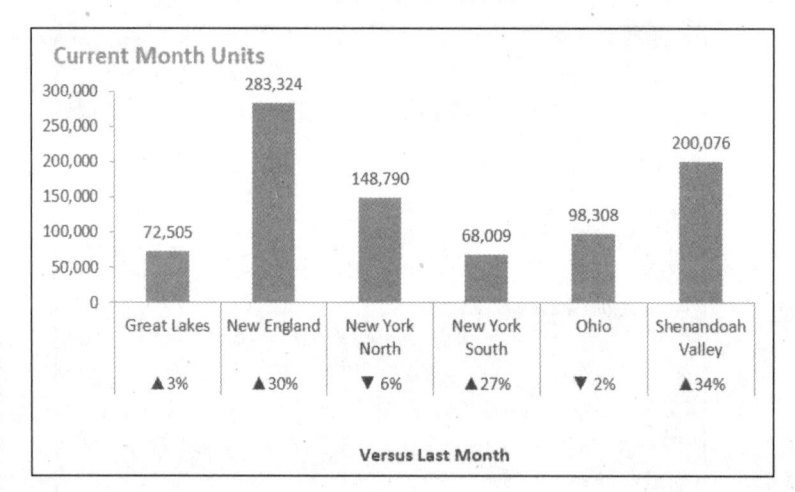

FIGURE 4-22: Use symbols to add an extra layer of analysis to charts.

We'll take some time now to review the steps that led to the chart in Figure 4-22.

Start with the data shown in Figure 4-23. Note that you have a designated cell — C1, in this case — to hold any symbols you're going to use. This cell isn't all that important. It's just a holding cell for the symbols you'll insert.

FIGURE 4-23: The starting data with a holding cell for symbols.

vs. Prior Month	Market	Current Month
3%	Great Lakes	72,505
30%	New England	283,324
6%	New York North	148,790
27%	New York South	68,009
2%	Ohio	98,308
34%	Shenandoah Valley	200,076

Now follow these steps:

1. **Click in C1 and then select the Symbol command on the Insert tab.**

   The Symbol dialog box, shown in Figure 4-24, opens.

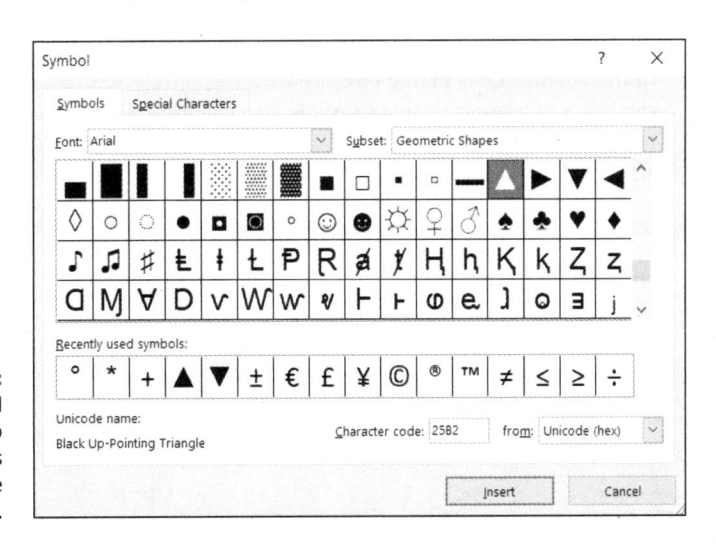

FIGURE 4-24: Use the Symbol dialog box to insert symbols into the holding cell.

CHAPTER 4 Formatting Your Way to Visualizations   653

2. **Find and select symbols by clicking the Insert button after each symbol.**

   In this scenario, select the down-pointing triangle and click Insert. Then click the up-pointing triangle and click Insert. Close the dialog box when you're done.

   At this point, you have the up-triangle and down-triangle symbols in cell C1, as shown in Figure 4-25.

   FIGURE 4-25: Copy the newly inserted symbols to the Clipboard.

3. **Click the C1 cell, go to the Formula Bar, and copy the two symbols by highlighting them and pressing Ctrl+C on the keyboard.**

4. **Go to the data table, right-click the percentages, and then select Format Cells from the list that appears.**

5. **In the Format Cells dialog box, create a new custom format by pasting the up- and down-triangle symbols into the appropriate syntax parts (see Figure 4-26).**

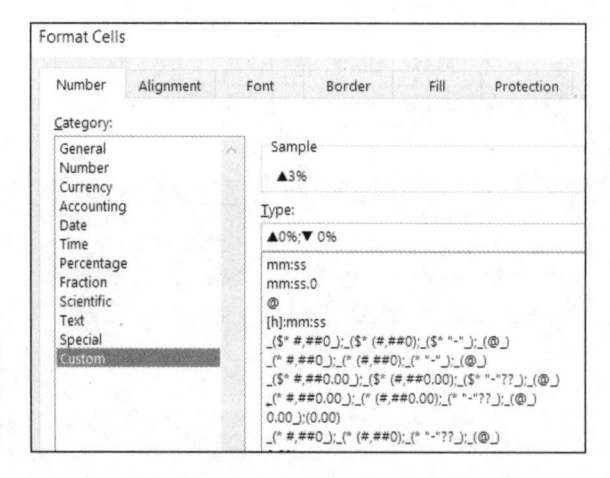

   FIGURE 4-26: Create a custom number format using the symbols.

654 BOOK 7 **Creating Dashboards and Reports**

In this case, any positive percentage will be preceded by the up-triangle symbol, and any negative percentage will be preceded by the down-triangle symbol.

TIP Not familiar with custom number formatting? Chapter 3 of this minibook covers the ins and outs of custom number formatting in detail.

6. **Click OK.**

   The symbols are now part of your number formatting! Figure 4-27 shows what the percentages look like. Change any number from positive to negative (or vice versa), and Excel automatically applies the appropriate symbol.

FIGURE 4-27: Your symbols are now part of the number formatting.

	A	B	C	D
1		Symbols>>	▲▼	
2				
3		vs. Prior Month	Market	Current Month
4		▲3%	Great Lakes	72,505
5		▲30%	New England	283,324
6		▼6%	New York North	148,790
7		▲27%	New York South	68,009
8		▼2%	Ohio	98,308
9		▲34%	Shenandoah Valley	200,076

Because charts automatically adopt number formatting, a chart created from this data shows the symbols as part of the labels. Simply use this data as the source for the chart.

This is just one way to use symbols in your reporting. With this basic technique, you can insert symbols to add visual appeal to tables, PivotTables, formulas, or any other object you can think of.

Wielding the Magical Camera Tool

Excel's Camera tool enables you to take a live picture of a range of cells that updates dynamically while the data in that range updates. If you've never heard of it, don't feel bad. This nifty tool has been hidden away in the last few versions of Excel. Although Microsoft has chosen not to include this tool on the mainstream ribbon, it's actually quite useful if you're building dashboards and reports.

CHAPTER 4 **Formatting Your Way to Visualizations** 655

Finding the Camera tool

Before you can use the Camera tool, you have to find it and add it to the Quick Access Toolbar. Follow these steps:

1. **Click the File button.**
2. **Click the Options button.**

   The Excel Options dialog box opens.
3. **Click the Quick Access Toolbar button.**
4. **In the Choose Commands From drop-down list, select Commands Not in the ribbon.**
5. **Scroll down the alphabetical list of commands and find Camera; double-click Camera to add it to the Quick Access Toolbar.**
6. **Click OK.**

   After you've taken these steps, you see the Camera tool on the Quick Access Toolbar, as shown in Figure 4-28.

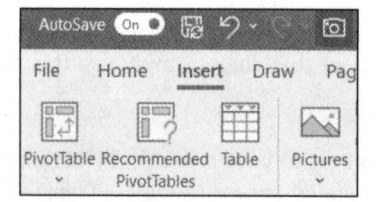

FIGURE 4-28: Not surprisingly, the icon for the Camera tool looks like a camera.

Using the Camera tool

To use the Camera tool, you simply select a range of cells and then capture everything in that range in a live picture. The cool thing about the Camera tool is that you're not limited to showing a single cell's value, as you are with a linked text box. And because the picture is live, any updates made to the source range automatically change the picture.

Take a moment to walk through this basic demonstration of the Camera tool. In Figure 4-29, you see some simple numbers and a chart based on those numbers. The goal here is to create a live picture of the range that holds both the numbers and the chart.

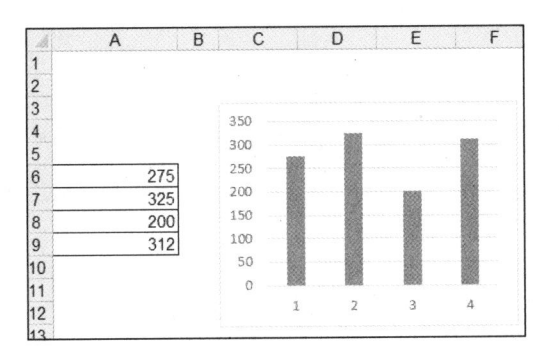

FIGURE 4-29: Enter some simple numbers in a range and create a basic chart from those numbers.

Follow these steps:

1. **Select the range that contains the information you want to capture.**

   In this scenario, you select B3:F13 to capture the area with the chart.

2. **Click the Camera tool icon on the Quick Access Toolbar.**

   You added the Camera tool to the Quick Access Toolbar in the preceding section.

3. **Click the worksheet in the location where you want to place the picture.**

   Excel immediately creates a live picture of the entire range, as shown in Figure 4-30.

   Changing any number in the original range automatically causes the picture to update.

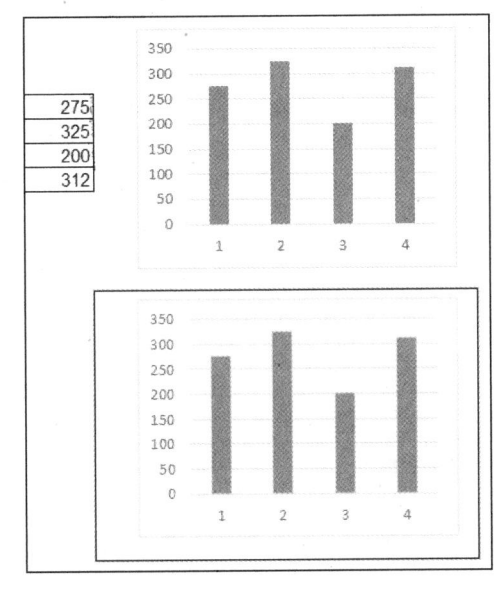

FIGURE 4-30: A live picture is created via the Camera tool.

CHAPTER 4 **Formatting Your Way to Visualizations** 657

TIP By default, the picture that's created has a border around it. To remove the border, right-click the picture and select Format Picture from the menu that appears. This opens the Format Picture task pane. On the Colors and Lines tab, you see the Line Color drop-down list. There, you can select No Color, thereby removing the border. On a similar note, to get a picture without gridlines, simply remove the gridlines from the source range.

Enhancing a dashboard with the Camera tool

Here are a few ways to go beyond the basics and use the Camera tool to enhance your dashboards and reports:

» **Consolidate disparate ranges into one print area.** Sometimes a data model gets so complex that it's difficult to keep the final data in one printable area. This often forces you to print multiple pages that are inconsistent in layout and size. Given that dashboards are most effective when contained in a compact area that can be printed in a page or two, complex data models prove to be problematic when it comes to layout and design.

You can use the Camera tool in these situations to create live pictures of various ranges that you can place on a single page. Figure 4-31 shows a workbook that contains data from various worksheets. The secret here is that these data ranges are nothing more than linked pictures created by the Camera tool.

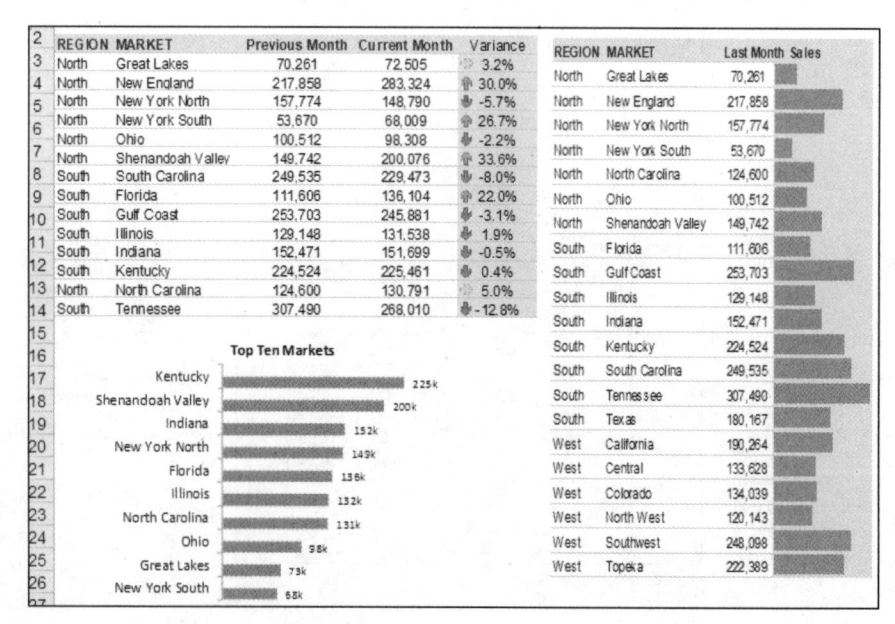

FIGURE 4-31: Use the Camera tool to get multiple source ranges into a compact area.

As you can see, you can create and manage multiple analyses on different worksheets and then bring together all your presentation pieces into a nicely formatted presentation layer.

- **Rotate objects to save time.** Again, because the Camera tool outputs pictures, you can rotate the pictures in situations in which placing the copied range on its side can help save time. A great example is a chart: Certain charts are relatively easy to create in a vertical orientation but extremely difficult to create in a horizontal orientation.

  It's the Camera tool to the rescue! When the live picture of the chart is created, all you have to do is change the alignment of the chart labels and then rotate the picture using the rotate handle to create a horizontal version.

- **Create small charts.** When you create pictures with the Camera tool, you can resize and move the pictures around freely. This gives you the freedom to test different layouts and chart sizes without the need to work around column widths, hidden rows, or other nonsense.

Enhancing Excel Reports with Shapes

Most people think of Excel shapes as mildly useful objects that can be added to a worksheet if they need to show a square, some arrows, a circle, and so forth. But if you use your imagination, you can leverage Excel shapes to create stylized interfaces that can really enhance your dashboards. Here are a few examples of how Excel shapes can spice up your dashboards and reports.

Creating visually appealing containers with shapes

A peekaboo tab lets you tag a section of your dashboard with a label that looks like it's wrapping around your dashboard components. In Figure 4-32, a peekaboo tab is used to label this group of components as belonging to the North region.

As you can see in Figure 4-33, there's no real magic here. It's just a set of shapes and text boxes that are cleverly arranged to give the impression that a label is wrapping around to show the region name.

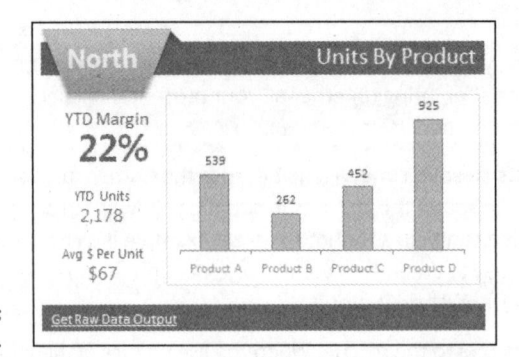

FIGURE 4-32:
A peekaboo tab.

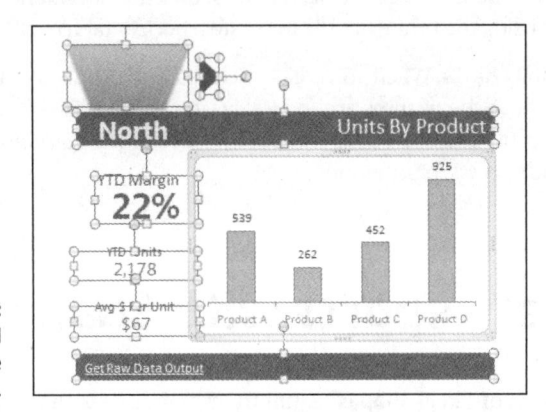

FIGURE 4-33:
A deconstructed view of the peekaboo tab.

Want to draw attention to handful of key metrics? Try wrapping your key metrics with a peekaboo banner. The banner shown in Figure 4-34 goes beyond boring text labels, allowing you to create the feeling that a banner is wrapping around your numbers. Again, this effect is achieved by layering a few Excel shapes so they fall nicely on top of each other, creating a cohesive effect.

Layering shapes to save space

Here's an idea to get the most out of your dashboard real estate. You can layer pie charts with column charts to create a unique set of views (see Figure 4-35). Each pie chart represents the percent of total revenue and a column chart showing some level of detail for the region. Simply layer your pie chart on top of a circle shape and a column chart.

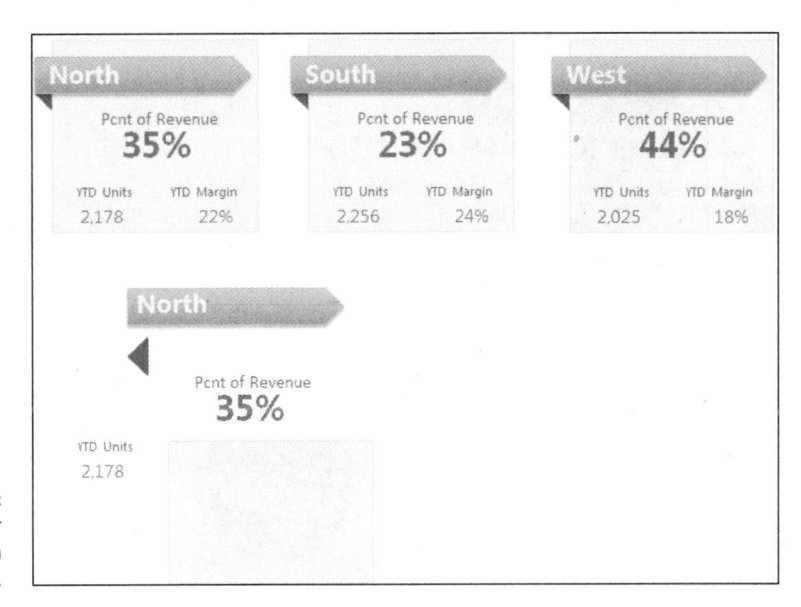

FIGURE 4-34: A visual banner made with shapes.

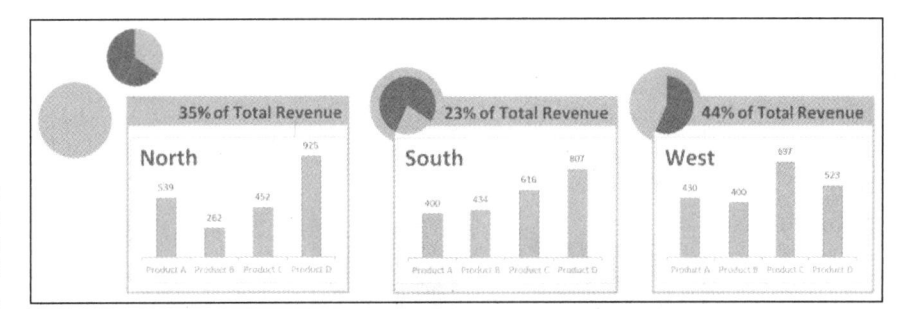

FIGURE 4-35: Combine shapes with a chart to save dashboard real estate.

Constructing your own infographic widgets with shapes

Excel offers a way to alter shapes by editing their anchor points. This opens the possibility of creating your own infographic widgets. Right-click a shape and select Edit Points. This places little points all around the shape (see Figure 4-36). You can then drag the points to reconfigure the shape.

Constructed shapes can be combined with other shapes to create interesting infographic elements that can be used in your Excel dashboards. In Figure 4-37, a newly constructed shape is combined with a standard oval and text box to create nifty infographic widgets.

CHAPTER 4 **Formatting Your Way to Visualizations**

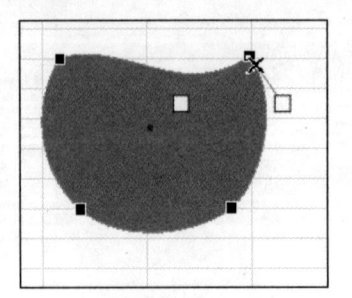

FIGURE 4-36: Use the Edit Points feature to construct your own shape.

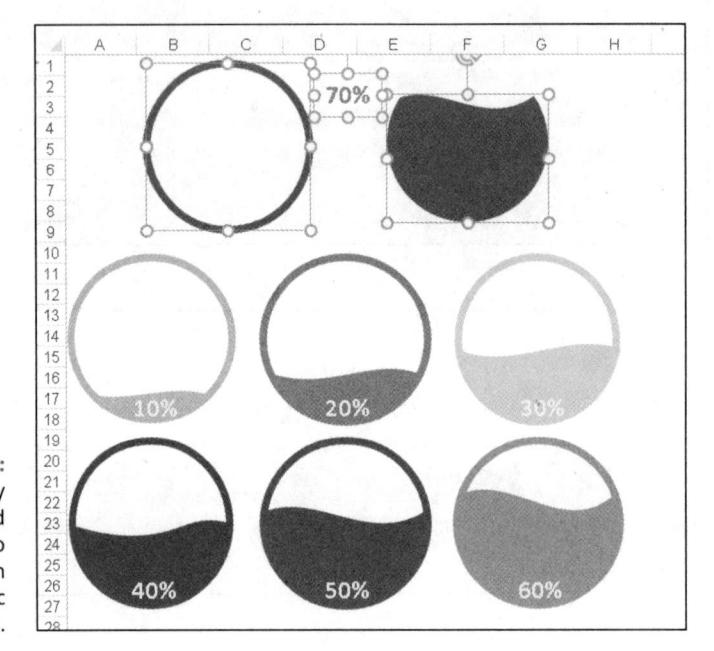

FIGURE 4-37: Using a newly constructed shape to create custom infographic elements.

662 BOOK 7 **Creating Dashboards and Reports**

IN THIS CHAPTER

» Using variance displays

» Using progress bars

» Creating bullet graphs

» Showing performance against a range

Chapter 5
Displaying Performance against a Target

The business world is full of targets and goals. Your job is to find effective ways to represent performance against those targets.

What do we mean by performance against a target? Imagine your goal is to break the land speed record, which is now 763 miles per hour. That makes the target 764 miles per hour, which will break the record. After you jump into your car and go as fast as you can, you'll have a final speed. That number is your performance against the target.

In this chapter, we explore some new and interesting ways to create components that show performance against a target.

Showing Performance with Variances

The standard way to display performance against a target is to plot the target and then plot the performance. This is usually done with a line chart or a combination chart, such as the one shown in Figure 5-1.

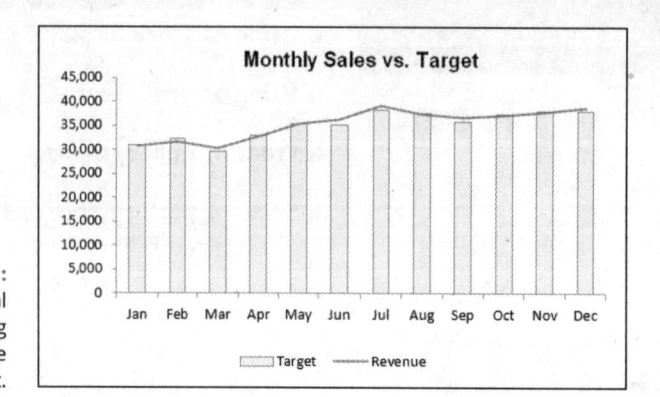

FIGURE 5-1: A typical chart showing performance against a target.

Although this chart allows you to visually pick the points where performance exceeded or fell below targets, it gives you a one-dimensional view and provides minimal information. Even if this chart offered labels that showed the actual percent of sales revenue versus target, you'd still get only a mildly informative view.

A more effective and informative way to display performance against a target is to plot the variances between the target and the performance. Figure 5-2 shows the same performance data you see in Figure 5-1, but it includes the *variances* (sales revenue minus target) under the month label. This way, you see where performance exceeded or fell below targets, but you also get an extra layer of information showing the dollar impact of each rise and fall.

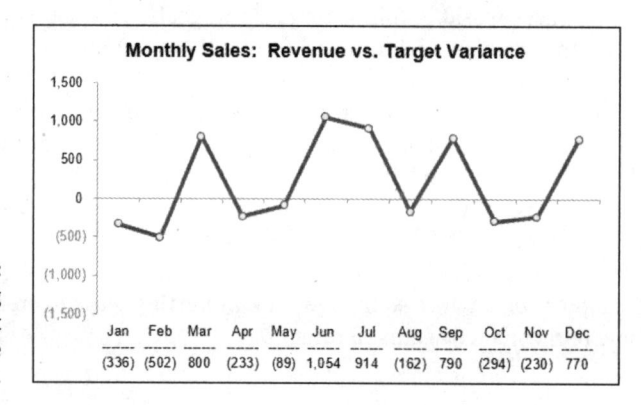

FIGURE 5-2: Consider using variances to plot performance against a target.

664 BOOK 7 Creating Dashboards and Reports

Showing Performance against Organizational Trends

The target you use to measure performance doesn't necessarily have to be set by management or organizational policy. In fact, some of the things you measure may never have a formal target or goal set for them. In situations in which you don't have a target to measure against, it's often helpful to measure performance against some organizational statistic.

For example, the component in Figure 5-3 measures the sales performance for each division against the median sales for all the divisions. You can see that divisions 1, 3, and 6 fall well below the median for the group.

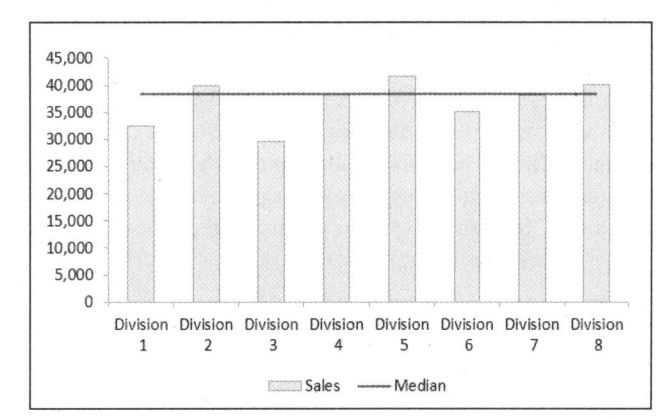

FIGURE 5-3: Measuring data when there's no target for a measure.

Here's how you'd create a median line similar to the one you see in Figure 5-3:

1. **Start a new column next to your data and type the simple MEDIAN formula, as shown in Figure 5-4.**

   Note that this formula can be any mathematical or statistical operation that works for the data you're representing. Just make sure that the values returned are the same for the entire column. This gives you a straight line.

2. **Copy the formula down to fill the table.**

   Again, all numbers in the newly created column should be the same.

3. **Plot the table into a column chart.**

4. **Right-click the Median data series and choose Change Series Chart Type from the menu that appears.**

5. **Change the chart type to a line chart.**

CHAPTER 5 Displaying Performance against a Target   665

	A	B	C
1		Sales	Median
2	Division 1	32,526	=MEDIAN($B$2:$B$9)
3	Division 2	39,939	38,291
4	Division 3	29,542	38,291
5	Division 4	38,312	38,291
6	Division 5	41,595	38,291
7	Division 6	35,089	38,291
8	Division 7	38,270	38,291
9	Division 8	40,022	38,291

FIGURE 5-4: Start a new column and enter a formula.

Using a Thermometer-Style Chart

A thermometer-style chart offers a unique way to view performance against a goal. As the name implies, the data points shown in this type of chart resemble a thermometer. The performance values and their corresponding targets are stacked on top of one another, giving an appearance similar to that of mercury rising in a thermometer. In Figure 5-5, you see an example of a thermometer-style chart.

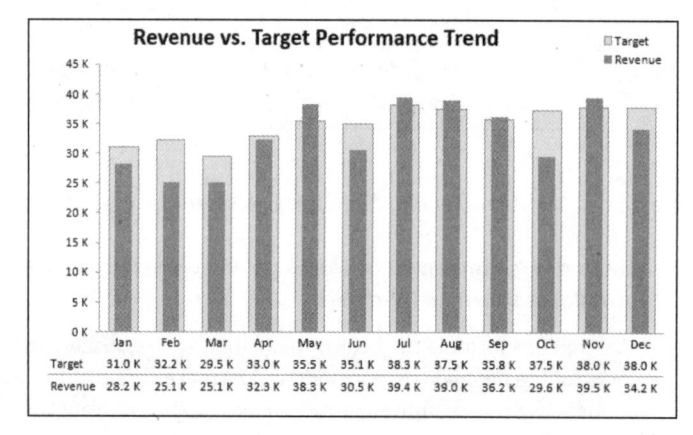

FIGURE 5-5: Thermometer-style charts offer a unique way to show performance against a goal.

To create this type of chart, follow these steps:

1. **Starting with a table that contains revenue and target data, plot the data into a new column chart.**

2. **Right-click the Revenue data series and choose Format Data Series from the menu that appears.**

BOOK 7 Creating Dashboards and Reports

3. **In the Format Data Series task pane, select Secondary Axis.**
4. **Go back to the chart and delete the new vertical axis that was added.**

   It's the vertical axis to the right of the chart.
5. **Right-click the Target series and choose Format Data Series.**
6. **In the task pane, adjust the Gap Width property so the Target series is slightly wider than the Revenue series — between 45% and 55% is typically fine.**

Using a Bullet Graph

A *bullet graph* is a type of column/bar graph developed by visualization expert Stephen Few to serve as a replacement for dashboard gauges and meters. He developed bullet graphs to allow you to clearly display multiple layers of information without occupying a lot of space on a dashboard. A bullet graph, as shown in Figure 5-6, contains a single performance measure (such as YTD [year-to-date] revenue), compares that measure with a target, and displays it in the context of qualitative ranges, such as Poor, Fair, Good, or Very Good.

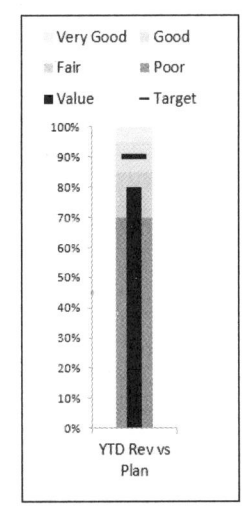

FIGURE 5-6: Bullet graphs display multiple perspectives in an incredibly compact space.

Figure 5-7 breaks down the three main parts of a bullet graph. The single bar represents the performance measure. The horizontal marker represents the comparative measure. The background color banding represents the qualitative ranges.

CHAPTER 5 **Displaying Performance against a Target** 667

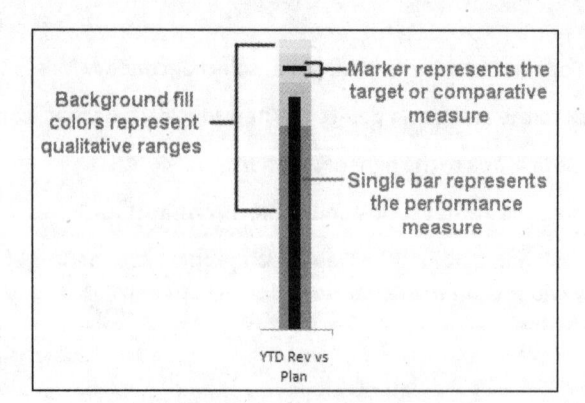

FIGURE 5-7: The parts of a bullet graph.

Creating a bullet graph

Creating a bullet graph in Excel involves quite a few steps, but the process isn't necessarily difficult. Follow these steps to create your first bullet graph:

1. **Start with a data table that gives you all the data points you need to create the three main parts of the bullet graph.**

   Figure 5-8 illustrates what that data table looks like. The first four values in the dataset (Poor, Fair, Good, and Very Good) make up the qualitative range. You don't have to have four values — you can have as many or as few as you need. In this scenario, you want the qualitative range to span from 0 to 100%. Therefore, the percentages (70%, 15%, 10%, and 5%) must add up to 100%. Again, this can be adjusted to suit your needs. The fifth value in Figure 5-8 (Value) creates the performance bar. The sixth value (Target) makes the target marker.

	A	B
1		YTD Rev vs Plan
2	Poor	70%
3	Fair	15%
4	Good	10%
5	Very Good	5%
6	Value	80%
7	Target	90%

   FIGURE 5-8: Start with data that contains the main data points of the bullet graph.

2. **Select the entire table and plot the data on a stacked column chart.**

   The chart that's created is initially plotted in the wrong direction.

3. **To fix the direction, click the chart and select the Switch Row/Column button on the Chart Design tab of the ribbon, as shown in Figure 5-9.**

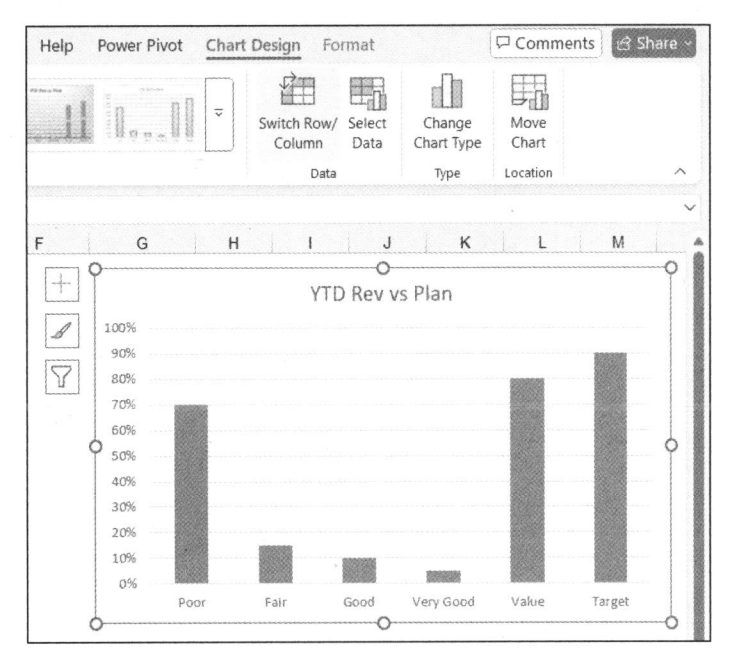

FIGURE 5-9: Switch the orientation of the chart to read from columns.

4. **Right-click the Target series and choose Change Series Chart Type from the menu that appears.**

   Doing so calls up the Change Chart Type dialog box.

5. **Use the Change Chart Type dialog box to change the Target series to Line with Markers and to place it on the secondary axis (see Figure 5-10).**

   After your change is confirmed, the Target series appears on the chart as a single dot.

6. **Right-click the Target series again and choose Format Data Series to open the Format Data Series task pane.**

7. **Click Marker to expand the Marker options, and then adjust the marker to look like a dash, as shown in Figure 5-11.**

8. **Still in the Format Data Series task pane, expand the Fill section, and in the Solid Fill property, set the color of the marker to a noticeable color, such as red.**

9. **Still in the Format Data Series task pane, expand the Border section and set the Border to No Line.**

10. **Go back to your chart and delete the new secondary axis that was added to the right of your chart (see Figure 5-12).**

    This step is an important one to ensure that the scale of the chart is correct for all data points.

CHAPTER 5 Displaying Performance against a Target   669

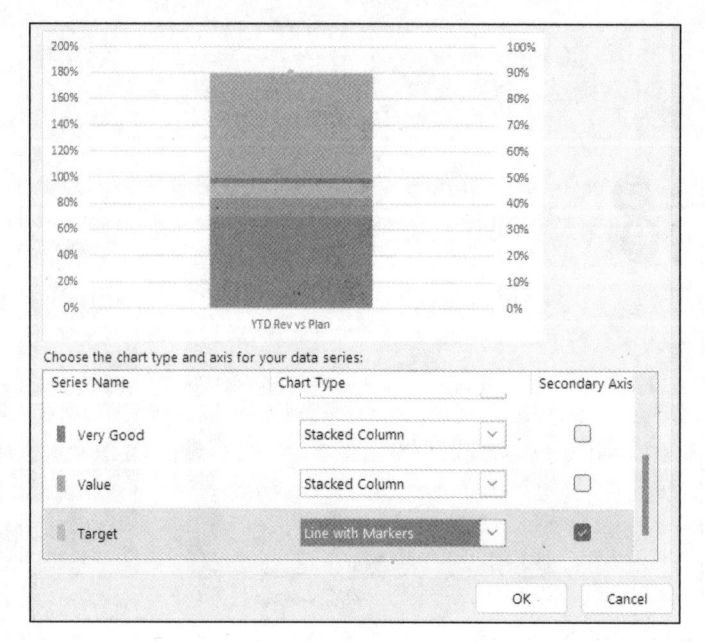

FIGURE 5-10: Use the Change Chart Type dialog box to change the Target series to Line with Markers and place it on the secondary axis.

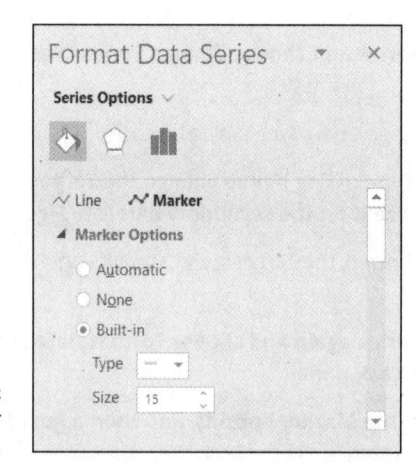

FIGURE 5-11: Adjust the marker to a dash.

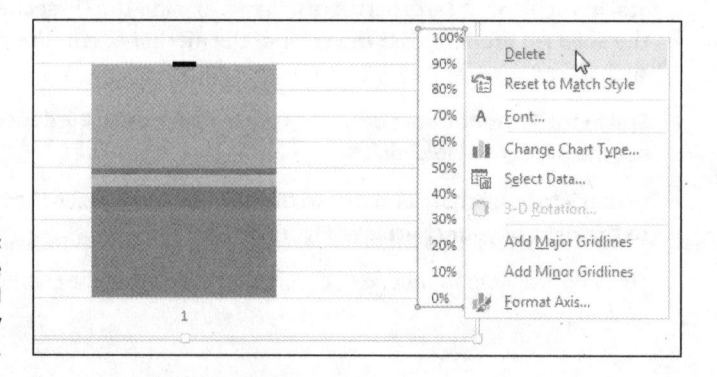

FIGURE 5-12: Be sure to delete the newly created secondary vertical axis.

670 BOOK 7 **Creating Dashboards and Reports**

11. **Right-click the Value series and choose Format Data Series from the menu that appears.**

12. **In the Format Data Series task pane, click Secondary Axis.**

13. **Still in the Format Data Series task pane, under Series Options, adjust the Gap Width property so that the Value series is slightly narrower than the other columns in the chart — between 205% and 225% is typically okay.**

14. **Still in the Format Data Series task pane, click the Fill icon (the paint bucket), expand the Fill section, and then select the Solid Fill option to set the color of the Value series to black.**

15. **All that's left to do is change the color for each qualitative range to incrementally lighter hues.**

    At this point, your bullet graph is essentially done! You can apply minor formatting adjustments to the size and shape of the chart to make it look the way you want. Figure 5-13 shows your newly created bullet graph formatted with a legend and horizontal labels.

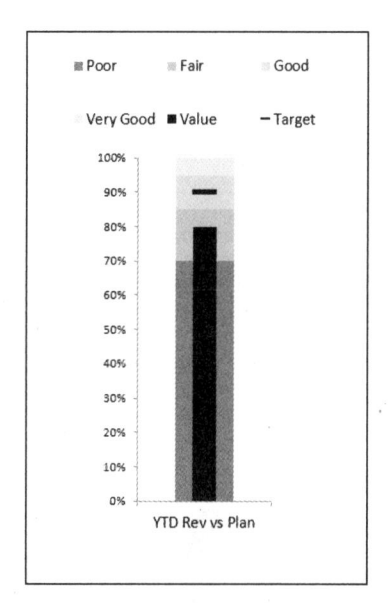

FIGURE 5-13: Your formatted bullet graph.

Adding data to your bullet graph

After you've built your chart for the first performance measure, you can use the same chart for any additional measures. Take a look at Figure 5-14.

CHAPTER 5 **Displaying Performance against a Target** 671

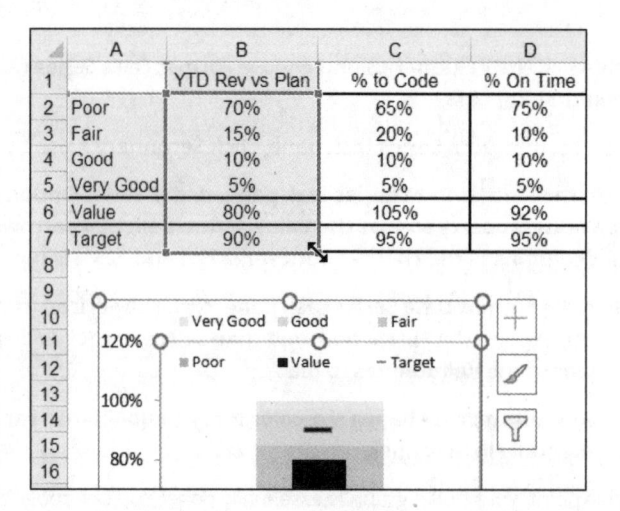

FIGURE 5-14: To add more data to your chart, manually expand the chart's data source range.

	A	B	C	D
1		YTD Rev vs Plan	% to Code	% On Time
2	Poor	70%	65%	75%
3	Fair	15%	20%	10%
4	Good	10%	10%	10%
5	Very Good	5%	5%	5%
6	Value	80%	105%	92%
7	Target	90%	95%	95%

As you can see in Figure 5-14, you've already created this bullet graph with the first performance measure. Imagine that you add two more measures and want to graph those. Here's how to do it:

1. **Click the chart so the blue outline appears around the original source data.**

2. **Hover the mouse pointer over the blue dot in the lower-right corner of the blue box (refer to Figure 5-14).**

   The cursor turns into an arrow.

3. **Click and drag the blue dot to the last column in your expanded dataset.**

   Figure 5-15 illustrates how the new data points are added without one ounce of extra work!

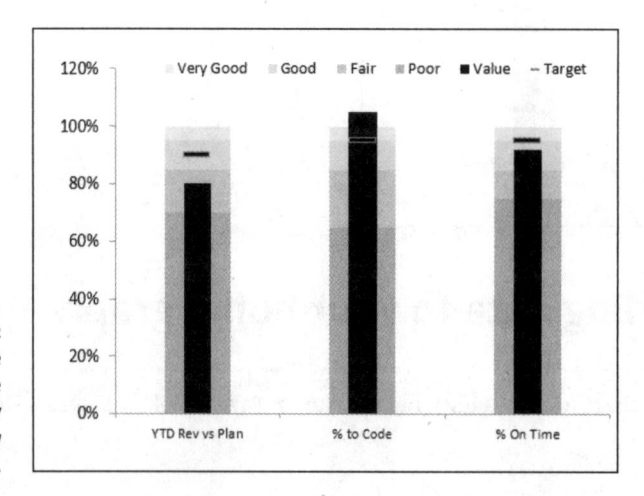

FIGURE 5-15: Expanding the data source automatically creates new bullet graphs.

672 BOOK 7 **Creating Dashboards and Reports**

Final thoughts on formatting bullet graphs

Before wrapping up this introduction to bullet graphs, we discuss two final thoughts on formatting:

» Creating qualitative bands

» Creating horizontal bullet graphs

Creating qualitative bands

First, if the qualitative ranges are the same for all performance measures in your bullet graphs, you can format the qualitative range series to have no gaps between them. For instance, Figure 5-16 shows a set of bullet graphs in which the qualitative ranges have been set to 0% Gap Width. This creates the clever effect of qualitative bands.

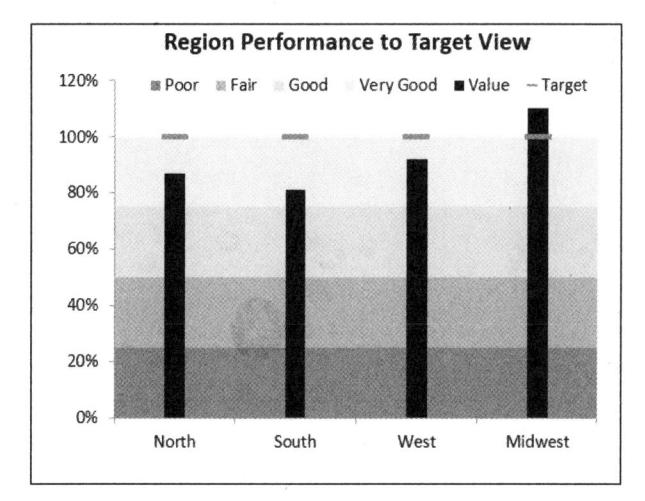

FIGURE 5-16: Try setting gap widths to zero to create clean-looking qualitative bands.

Here's how to do it:

1. **Right-click any one of the qualitative series and choose Format Data Series from the menu that appears.**

2. **In the Format Series task pane, adjust the Gap Width property to 0%.**

Creating horizontal bullet graphs

If you're waiting on the section about horizontal bullet graphs, we have good news and bad news. The bad news is that creating a horizontal bullet graph from scratch in Excel is a much more complex endeavor than creating a vertical bullet graph — and it doesn't warrant the time and effort it takes to create them.

The good news is that there is a clever way to get a horizontal bullet graph from a vertical one — and in three steps, no less. Here's how you do it:

1. **Create a vertical bullet graph.**

   For how to do this, see the "Creating a bullet graph" section, earlier in this chapter.

2. **To change the alignment for the axis and other labels on the bullet graph so that they're rotated 270 degrees, right-click the axis labels, select Format Axis, go to the Alignment settings, and then adjust the Text Direction property to rotate the axis labels as shown in Figure 5-17.**

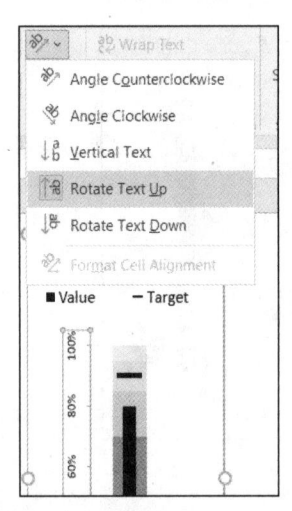

FIGURE 5-17: Rotate all labels so that they're on their sides.

3. **Use Excel's Camera tool (see Chapter 4 of this minibook) to take a picture of the bullet graph.**

   After you have a picture, you can rotate it to be horizontal. Figure 5-18 illustrates a horizontal bullet graph.

   The nifty thing about this trick is that because the picture is taken with the Camera tool, the picture automatically updates when the source table changes.

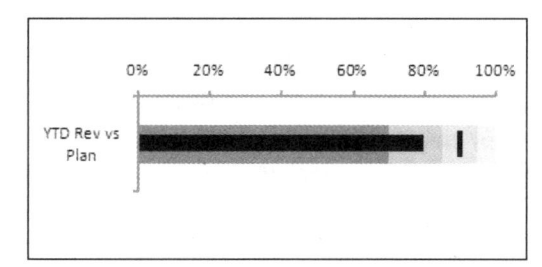

FIGURE 5-18: A horizontal bullet graph.

Showing Performance against a Target Range

In some businesses, a target isn't one value — it's a range of values. In other words, the goal is to stay within a defined target range. Imagine that you manage a small business selling boxes of meat. Part of your job is to keep the inventory stocked between 25 and 35 boxes in a month. If you have too many boxes of meat, the meat will go bad. If you have too few boxes, you'll lose money.

To track how well you do at keeping the inventory of meat between 25 and 35 boxes, you need a performance component that displays on-hand boxes against a target range. Figure 5-19 illustrates a component you can build to track performance against a target range. The gray band represents the target range you must stay within each month. The line represents the trend of on-hand meat.

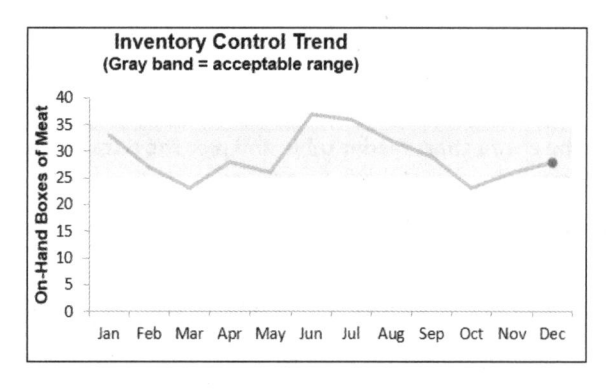

FIGURE 5-19: You can create a component that plots performance against a target range.

Obviously, the trick to this type of component is to set up the band that represents the target range. Here's how you do it:

1. **Set up a limit table in which you can define and adjust the upper and lower limits of the target range.**

    Cells B2 and B3 in Figure 5-20 serve as the place to define the limits for the range.

CHAPTER 5 **Displaying Performance against a Target** 675

2. **Build a chart feeder that's used to plot the data points for the target range.**

   This feeder consists of the formulas revealed in cells B8 and B9 in Figure 5-20. The idea is to copy these formulas across all data. The values you see in the Feb, Mar, and Apr columns are the results of these formulas.

   FIGURE 5-20: Create a chart feeder that contains formulas that define the data points for the target range.

	A	B	C	D	E
1		Limit Table			
2	Lower Limit	25			
3	Upper Limit	35			
4					
5					
6					
7		Jan	Feb	Mar	Apr
8	Lower Limit	=$B$2	25	25	25
9	Upper Limit	=$B$3-$B$2	10	10	10

3. **Add a row for the actual performance values, as shown in Figure 5-21.**

   These data points create the performance trend line.

   FIGURE 5-21: Add a row for the performance values.

	A	B	C	D	E
1		Limit Table			
2	Lower Limit	25			
3	Upper Limit	35			
4					
5					
6					
7		Jan	Feb	Mar	Apr
8	Lower Limit	25	25	25	25
9	Upper Limit	10	10	10	10
10	Values	33	27	23	28

4. **Select the entire chart feeder table and plot the data on a stacked area chart.**

5. **Right-click the Values series and choose Change Series Chart Type from the menu that appears.**

   Doing so calls up the Change Chart Type dialog box.

6. **Using the Change Chart Type dialog box, change the Values series to a line chart and place it on the secondary axis, as shown in Figure 5-22.**

   After your change is confirmed, the Values series appears on the chart as a line.

7. **Go back to your chart and delete the new vertical axis that was added.**

   It's the vertical axis to the right of the chart.

8. **Right-click the Lower Limit data series and choose Format Data Series from the menu that appears.**

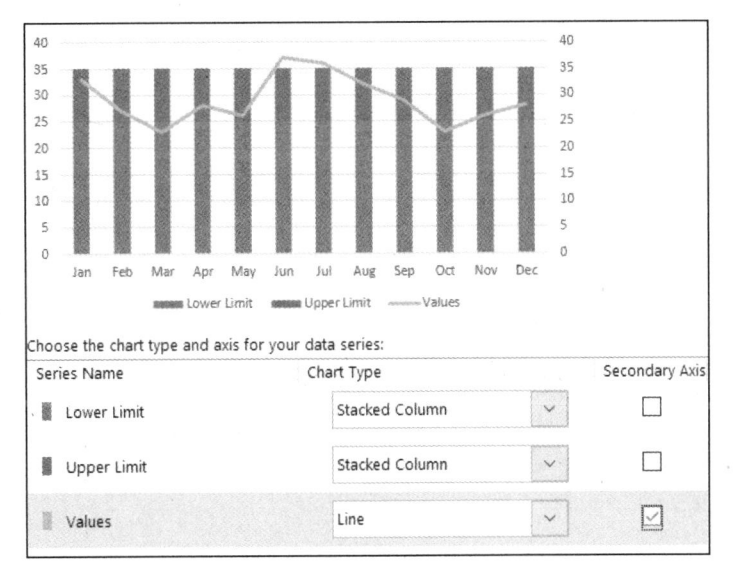

FIGURE 5-22:
Use the Change Chart Type dialog box to change the Values series to a line chart and place it on the secondary axis.

9. **In the Format Data Series task pane, click the Fill icon and then choose the No Fill option under Fill and the No Line option under Border (see Figure 5-23).**

10. **Right-click the Upper Limit series and select Format Data Series.**

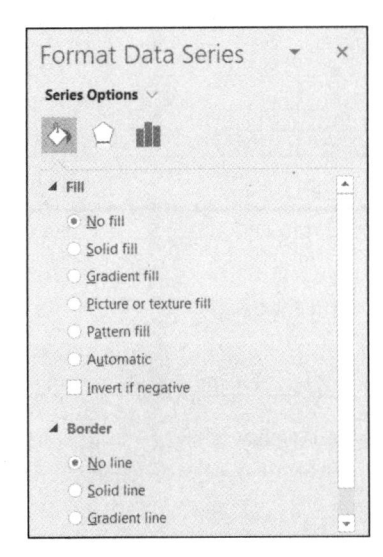

FIGURE 5-23:
Format the Lower Limit series so that it's hidden.

11. **In the Format Data Series task pane, adjust the Gap Width property to 0%.**

That's it. All that's left to do is apply the minor adjustments to colors, labels, and other formatting.

CHAPTER 5 **Displaying Performance against a Target** 677

8 Automating Excel with Macros and VBA

Contents at a Glance

CHAPTER 1: Macro Fundamentals 681
    Choosing to Use a Macro 682
    Recording a Macro 682
    Understanding Macro Security 691
    Storing and Running Macros 693
    Exploring Macro Examples 697

CHAPTER 2: Getting Cozy with the Visual Basic Editor 701
    Working in the Visual Basic Editor 701
    Working with the Project Explorer 704
    Working with a Code Pane 706
    Customizing the VBE 709

CHAPTER 3: The Anatomy of Macros 715
    A Brief Overview of the Excel Object Model 715
    A Brief Look at Variables 718
    Understanding Event Procedures 720
    Error Handling in a Nutshell 724

CHAPTER 4: Working with Workbooks 729
    Installing Macros 730
    Creating a New Workbook from Scratch 731
    Saving a Workbook When a Particular Cell Is Changed 733
    Saving a Workbook before Closing 735
    Protecting a Worksheet on Workbook Close 737
    Unprotecting a Worksheet 738
    Opening a Workbook to a Specific Tab 739
    Opening a Specific Workbook Chosen by the User 741
    Determining Whether a Workbook Is Already Open 742
    Determining Whether a Workbook Exists in a Directory 745
    Closing All Workbooks at Once 746
    Printing All Workbooks in a Directory 747
    Preventing the Workbook from Closing until a
    Cell Is Populated 749
    Creating a Backup of the Current Workbook with
    Today's Date 750

> **IN THIS CHAPTER**
>
> » Choosing macros
>
> » Recording macros
>
> » Understanding macro security
>
> » Finding out where to store and how to run macros
>
> » Exploring macro examples

Chapter 1
Macro Fundamentals

A *macro* is essentially a set of instructions or code that you create to tell Excel to execute any number of actions. In Excel, macros can be written or recorded. The key word here is *recorded*.

Recording a macro is like programming a phone number into your smartphone. First, you manually dial and save a number. Then when you want, you can redial that number with the touch of a button. With macro recording, you can record your actions in Excel while you perform them. While you record, Excel gets busy in the background, translating your keystrokes and mouse clicks to code (also known as Visual Basic for Applications, or VBA). After a macro is recorded, you can play back those actions anytime you want.

In this chapter, you explore macros and find out how you can use macros to automate your recurring processes to simplify your life.

TIP To work through the examples in this chapter and the other chapters in this minibook, download the sample files from www.dummies.com/go/microsoft365excelaiofd.

Choosing to Use a Macro

The first step in using macros is admitting you have a problem. Actually, you may have several problems:

» **Problem 1: Repetitive tasks:** As each new month rolls around, you have to make the donuts (that is, crank out those reports). You have to import that data, you have to update those PivotTables, you have to delete those columns, and so on. With a macro you could have those more redundant parts of your monthly processes done automatically.

» **Problem 2: Making mistakes:** When you go hand-to-hand combat with Excel, you're bound to make mistakes. When you're repeatedly applying formulas, sorting, and moving things around manually, there's always that risk of catastrophe. Add to that the looming deadlines and constant change requests, and your error rate goes up. Or you could calmly record a macro, ensure that everything is running correctly, and then forget it. The macro performs every action the same way every time you run it, reducing the chance of errors.

» **Problem 3: Awkward navigation:** You often create reports for an audience that probably has a limited knowledge of Excel. Making your reports more user-friendly is always helpful. Macros can be used to dynamically format and print worksheets, navigate to specific sheets in your workbook, or even save the open document in a specified location. Your audience will appreciate these little touches that help make perusal of your workbooks a bit more pleasant.

Recording a Macro

To start recording your first macro, you need to first find the Macro Recorder, which is on the Developer tab of the ribbon. Unfortunately, Excel comes out of the box with the Developer tab hidden — you may not see it on your version of Excel at first. If you plan to work with VBA macros, you'll want to make sure that the Developer tab is visible. To display this tab, follow these steps:

1. **Choose File⇨Options.**

    The Excel Options dialog box opens.

2. **Click Customize Ribbon.**

3. **In the list box on the right, place a check mark next to Developer.**

4. **Click OK.**

Now that you have the Developer tab showing in the ribbon, you can start up the Macro Recorder by clicking Record Macro on the Developer tab. This opens the Record Macro dialog box, shown in Figure 1-1.

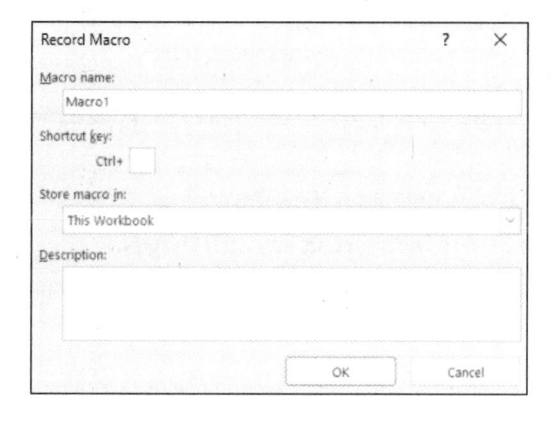

FIGURE 1-1: The Record Macro dialog box.

Here are the four parts of the Record Macro dialog box:

> » **Macro Name:** Excel gives a default name to your macro, such as Macro1, but you should give your macro a name more descriptive of what it actually does. For example, you might name a macro that formats a generic table FormatTable.
>
> **REMEMBER** You have to follow a few rules when naming a macro. The first character must be a letter. Generally, special characters other than underscores aren't allowed. And the total number of characters can't be more than 255, although hopefully you don't get close to that limit.
>
> » **Shortcut Key:** Every macro needs an *event* (something that happens) for it to run. This event can be a button being clicked, a workbook being opened, or if you use this field, a keystroke combination. When you assign a shortcut key to your macro, entering that combination of keys triggers your macro to run. This field is optional.
>
> » **Store Macro In:** The default option is This Workbook. Storing your macro in this workbook simply means that the macro is stored along with the active Excel file. The next time you open that particular workbook, the macro is available to run. Similarly, if you send the workbook to another user, that user can run the macro as well (provided the macro security is properly set by your user — more on that later in this chapter). You can also choose New Workbook to tell Excel to create a new workbook to store the macro or Personal Macro Workbook, a special workbook used to store macros you want access to all the time. See "Storing and Running Macros" later in this chapter for more on the Personal Macro Workbook.

CHAPTER 1 **Macro Fundamentals** 683

>> **Description:** This field is optional, but it can come in handy if you have numerous macros in a workbook or if you need to give a user a more detailed description about what the macro does.

With the Record Macro dialog box open, follow these steps to create a simple macro that enters your name into a worksheet cell:

1. **Enter a new single-word name for the macro to replace the default Macro1 name.**

   A good name for this example is MyName.

2. **Assign this macro to the shortcut key Ctrl+Shift+N.**

   You do this by entering uppercase N in the edit box labeled Shortcut Key.

3. **Click OK.**

   This closes the Record Macro dialog box and begins recording your actions.

4. **Select cell B3 on your worksheet, type your name into the selected cell, and press Enter.**

5. **Click the Developer tab on the ribbon, go to the Code group, and click Stop Recording (or click the Stop Recording button in the status bar).**

Examining the macro

The macro was recorded in a new module named Module1. To view the code in this module, you must activate the Visual Basic Editor (VBE). (See Chapter 2 of this minibook to find out more about the VBE.) You can activate the VBE in one of three ways:

>> Press Alt+F11.

>> Click the Developer tab of the ribbon, go to the Code group, and click Visual Basic.

>> Click the Developer tab of the ribbon, go to the Code group, click Macros, select a macro, and click Edit.

In the VBE, the Project window displays a list of all open workbooks and add-ins. If the Project Explorer isn't visible, choose View ➪ Project Explorer. This list is displayed as a tree diagram, which you can expand or collapse. The code that you recorded previously is stored in Module1 in the current workbook. When you double-click Module1, the code in the module appears in the Code window.

The macro should look something like this:

```
Sub MyName()
'
' MyName Macro
'
' Keyboard Shortcut: Ctrl+Shift+N
'
    Range("B3").Select
    ActiveCell.FormulaR1C1 = "Dick Kusleika"
    Range("B4").Select
End Sub
```

The macro recorded is a Sub procedure named MyName. The statements tell Excel what to do when the macro is executed.

Notice that Excel inserted some comments at the top of the procedure. These comments are some of the information that appeared in the Record Macro dialog box. These comment lines (which begin with a single quote) aren't really necessary, and deleting them has no effect on how the macro runs. If you ignore the comments, you'll see that this procedure has three VBA statements, the second of which is:

```
ActiveCell.FormulaR1C1 = "Dick Kusleika"
```

The first statement is selecting cell B3. The last statement is pressing Enter after you enter your name, which moves the active cell down one row. The middle statement, the one that does all the work, causes the name you typed while recording to be inserted into the active cell.

Editing the macro

After you record a macro, you can make changes to it. The macro you recorded in the previous section always inserts your name into cell B3. Edit the macro so that it enters your name in whatever cell you happen to be in when you run it. To do that, delete the first and third lines of the macro. The edited macro appears as follows:

```
Sub MyName()
'
' MyName Macro
'
' Keyboard Shortcut: Ctrl+Shift+N
'
    ActiveCell.FormulaR1C1 = "Dick Kusleika"
End Sub
```

This macro inserts text into the active cell because the first `Select` statement was removed. That same cell remains active because the second `Select` statement was removed.

Testing the macro

Before you recorded this macro, you set an option that assigned the macro to the Ctrl+Shift+N shortcut key combination. To test the macro, return to Excel by using either of the following methods:

- Press Alt+F11.
- Click the View Microsoft Excel button on the VBE's Standard toolbar.

When Excel is active, activate a worksheet. (It can be in the workbook that contains the VBA module or in any other workbook.) Select a cell and press Ctrl+Shift+N. The macro immediately enters your name into the cell.

Comparing absolute and relative macro recording

Excel has two modes for recording — absolute reference and relative reference. These modes affect what statements Excel generates when you select a cell while recording. In this section, we discuss the two modes and when to use them.

Recording macros with absolute references

In the example in the preceding section, you selected cell B3 while recording a macro and Excel dutifully recorded a statement that selects cell B3. This is an example of an absolute reference, and it's the default mode when recording macros. The term *absolute reference* is often used in the context of cell references found in formulas. When a cell reference in a formula is an absolute reference, it doesn't automatically adjust when the formula is pasted to a new location.

The best way to understand how this concept applies to macros is to try it. Open the sample file named 8.1.1 Workbook Containing Dataset.xlsm file and record a macro that counts the rows in the Branchlist worksheet (see Figure 1-2).

TIP The sample dataset used in this chapter can be found at www.dummies.com/go/microsoft365excelaiofd.

FIGURE 1-2:
Your pre-totaled worksheet containing two tables.

	A	B	C	D	E	F	G	H	I	J
1		Region	Market	Branch			Region	Market	Branch	
2		NORTH	BUFFALO	601419			SOUTH	CHARLOTTE	173901	
3		NORTH	BUFFALO	701407			SOUTH	CHARLOTTE	301301	
4		NORTH	BUFFALO	802202			SOUTH	CHARLOTTE	302301	
5		NORTH	CANADA	910181			SOUTH	CHARLOTTE	601306	
6		NORTH	CANADA	920681			SOUTH	DALLAS	202600	
7		NORTH	MICHIGAN	101419			SOUTH	DALLAS	490260	
8		NORTH	MICHIGAN	501405			SOUTH	DALLAS	490360	
9		NORTH	MICHIGAN	503405			SOUTH	DALLAS	490460	
10		NORTH	MICHIGAN	590140			SOUTH	FLORIDA	301316	
11		NORTH	NEWYORK	801211			SOUTH	FLORIDA	701309	
12		NORTH	NEWYORK	802211			SOUTH	FLORIDA	702309	
13		NORTH	NEWYORK	804211			SOUTH	NEWORLEANS	601310	
14		NORTH	NEWYORK	805211			SOUTH	NEWORLEANS	602310	
15		NORTH	NEWYORK	806211			SOUTH	NEWORLEANS	801607	
16										

Follow these steps to record the macro:

1. **Before recording, make sure cell A1 is selected.**
2. **Click Record Macro on the Developer tab of the ribbon.**
3. **Name the macro AddTotal.**
4. **Choose This Workbook for the save location.**
5. **Click OK to start recording.**

   At this point, Excel is recording your actions. While Excel is recording, perform the following steps:

   1. **Select cell A16 and type** Total **in the cell.**
   2. **Select the first empty cell in Column D (D16) and enter** = COUNTA(D2:D15)**.**

      This gives a count of branch numbers at the bottom of column D. You need to use the COUNTA function because the branch numbers are stored as text.

6. **Click Stop Recording on the Developer tab to stop recording the macro.**

The formatted worksheet should look something like the one in Figure 1-3.

To see your macro in action, delete the total row you just added and play back your macro by following these steps:

1. **Click Macros on the Developer tab of the ribbon.**
2. **Find and select the AddTotal macro you just recorded.**
3. **Click the Run button.**

CHAPTER 1 Macro Fundamentals   687

	A	B	C	D	E	F	G	H	I	J
1		Region	Market	Branch			Region	Market	Branch	
2		NORTH	BUFFALO	601419			SOUTH	CHARLOTTE	173901	
3		NORTH	BUFFALO	701407			SOUTH	CHARLOTTE	301301	
4		NORTH	BUFFALO	802202			SOUTH	CHARLOTTE	302301	
5		NORTH	CANADA	910181			SOUTH	CHARLOTTE	601306	
6		NORTH	CANADA	920681			SOUTH	DALLAS	202600	
7		NORTH	MICHIGAN	101419			SOUTH	DALLAS	490260	
8		NORTH	MICHIGAN	501405			SOUTH	DALLAS	490360	
9		NORTH	MICHIGAN	503405			SOUTH	DALLAS	490460	
10		NORTH	MICHIGAN	590140			SOUTH	FLORIDA	301316	
11		NORTH	NEWYORK	801211			SOUTH	FLORIDA	701309	
12		NORTH	NEWYORK	802211			SOUTH	FLORIDA	702309	
13		NORTH	NEWYORK	804211			SOUTH	NEWORLEANS	601310	
14		NORTH	NEWYORK	805211			SOUTH	NEWORLEANS	602310	
15		NORTH	NEWYORK	806211			SOUTH	NEWORLEANS	801607	
16	Total			14						
17										

FIGURE 1-3: Your post-totaled worksheet.

If all goes well, the macro plays back your actions to a T and gives your table a total. Now here's the thing: No matter how hard you try, you can't make the AddTotal macro work on the second table (G1:I15 in Figure 1-3). Why? Because you recorded the macro using absolute references.

To understand what this means, examine the underlying code. To examine the code, click Macros on the Developer tab to open the Macro dialog box, as shown in Figure 1-4.

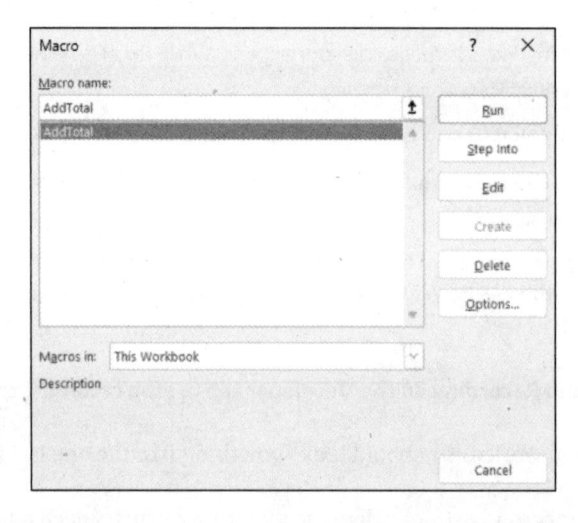

FIGURE 1-4: The Macro dialog box.

Select the AddTotal macro and click the Edit button. This opens the VBE to show you the code that was written when you recorded your macro:

```
Sub AddTotal()
    Range("A16").Select
```

```
        ActiveCell.FormulaR1C1 = "Total"
        Range("D16").Select
        ActiveCell.FormulaR1C1 = "=COUNTA(R[-14]C:R[-1]C)"
End Sub
```

Pay particular attention to lines 2 and 4 of the macro. When you asked Excel to select cell range A16 and then D16, those cells are exactly what it selected. Because the macro was recorded in absolute reference mode, Excel interpreted your range selection as absolute. In other words, if you select cell A16, that cell is what Excel gives you. In the next section, you take a look at what the same macro looks like when recorded in relative reference mode.

Recording macros with relative references

In the context of Excel macros, *relative* means relative to the currently active cell. So you should use caution with your active cell choice — both when you record the relative reference macro and when you run it.

First, make sure the file named `8.1.1 Workbook Containing Dataset.xlsm` is open. Then use the following steps to record a relative reference macro:

1. **Click Use Relative References on the Developer tab of the ribbon, as shown in Figure 1-5.**

FIGURE 1-5: Recording a macro with relative references.

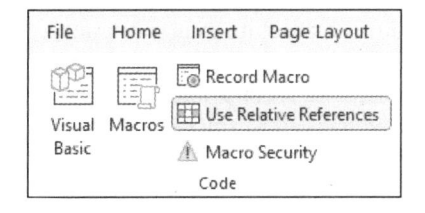

2. **Select cell A1.**
3. **Click Record Macro on the Developer tab.**
4. **Name the macro AddTotalRelative.**
5. **In the Macros In drop-down list, choose This Workbook.**
6. **Click OK to start recording.**
7. **Select cell A16 and type** Total **in the cell.**
8. **Select the first empty cell in Column D (D16) and type** = COUNTA(D2:D15).
9. **Click Stop Recording on the Developer tab to stop recording the macro.**

At this point, you've recorded two macros. Take a moment to examine the code for your newly created macro.

Click Macros on the Developer tab to open the Macro dialog box. Here, choose the AddTotalRelative macro and click Edit.

Again, this opens the VBE to show you the code that was written when you recorded your macro. This time, your code looks something like the following:

```
Sub AddTotalRelative()
    ActiveCell.Offset(15, 0).Range("A1").Select
    ActiveCell.FormulaR1C1 = "Total"
    ActiveCell.Offset(0, 3).Range("A1").Select
    ActiveCell.FormulaR1C1 = "=COUNTA(R[-14]C:R[-1]C)"
End Sub
```

Notice that there are no references to any specific cell ranges at all. Take a look at what the relevant parts of this VBA code really mean.

In line 2, Excel uses the `Offset` property of the active cell. This property tells the cursor to move a certain number of cells up or down and a certain number of cells left or right.

The `Offset` property code tells Excel to move 15 rows down and 0 columns across from the active cell (in this case, A1). Excel doesn't select a cell with a specific address as it did when recording an absolute reference macro.

Between `Offset` and `Select` on the second line is `Range("A1")`. This is Excel recording that you only selected one cell — the first cell of the range that is offset from the active cell. It's a quirk of the Macro Recorder, and it isn't necessary when you select only one cell. (The Macro Recorder records a lot of unnecessary code.) If you had selected, say A16:B17 instead of just A16, it would've recorded:

```
ActiveCell.Offset(15, 0).Range("A1:B2").Select
```

To see this macro in action, delete the total row for both tables and do the following:

1. **Select cell A1.**
2. **Click Macros on the Developer tab.**
3. **Select the AddTotalRelative macro.**
4. **Click the Run button.**
5. **Select cell F1.**

6. **Click Macros on the Developer tab.**
7. **Select the AddTotalRelative macro.**
8. **Click the Run button.**

Notice that this macro, unlike your previous macro, works on both sets of data. Because the macro applies the totals relative to the currently active cell, the totals are applied correctly.

For this macro to work, you simply need to ensure that

> You've selected the correct starting cell before running the macro.

> The block of data has the same number of rows and columns as the data on which you recorded the macro.

Understanding Macro Security

At this point, you should feel comfortable recording your own Excel macros. In the wrong hands, macros can be destructive. Because macros are so powerful, some people have used them to create macro viruses that can be harmful to your computer. For that reason, Microsoft has built some security measures around macros. This section covers some important security concepts you need to keep in mind when working with macros.

Macro-enabled file extensions

Excel's default file format, called Excel Workbook, has a .xlsx file extension. Files with the .xlsx extension can't contain macros. If your workbook contains macros and you then save that workbook as an .xlsx file, your macros are removed automatically. Excel warns you that macro content will be removed when saving a workbook with macros as an .xlsx file.

If you want to retain the macros, you must save your file as an Excel Macro-Enabled Workbook. This gives your file an .xlsm extension. The idea is that all workbooks with an .xlsx file extension are automatically known to be safe, whereas you can recognize .xlsm files as potential threats.

Trusted documents

Excel allows you to flag a document as trusted. Without getting into the technical minutiae, a trusted document is essentially a workbook you have deemed safe by enabling macros.

If you open a workbook that contains macros, you see a yellow bar message under the ribbon stating that macros (active content) have been disabled. If you have the VBE open, you'll get a dialog box instead of the yellow bar.

If you click Enable, the workbook automatically becomes a trusted document. This means you're no longer prompted to enable the content as long as you open that file on your computer. The basic idea is that if you told Excel that you "trust" a particular workbook by enabling macros, it's highly likely that you'll enable macros each time you open it. Thus, Excel remembers that you've enabled macros before and inhibits any further messages about macros for that workbook.

This is great news for you and users of your macros. After enabling your macros just one time, they won't be annoyed at the constant messages about macros, and you won't have to worry that your macro-enabled workbook will fall flat because macros have been disabled.

Trusted locations

If the thought of any macro message coming up (even one time) unnerves you, you can set up a trusted location for your files. A trusted location is a directory that is deemed a safe zone where only trusted workbooks are placed. A trusted location allows you and your clients to run a macro-enabled workbook with no security restrictions as long as the workbook is in that location.

To set up a trusted location, follow these steps:

1. **Click the Macro Security button on the Developer tab of the ribbon.**

   The Trust Center dialog box opens.

2. **Click the Trusted Locations option on the left.**

   This opens the Trusted Locations window (see Figure 1-6), which shows you all the directories that are considered trusted.

3. **Click the Add New Location button.**

4. **Click Browse to find and specify the directory that will be considered a trusted location.**

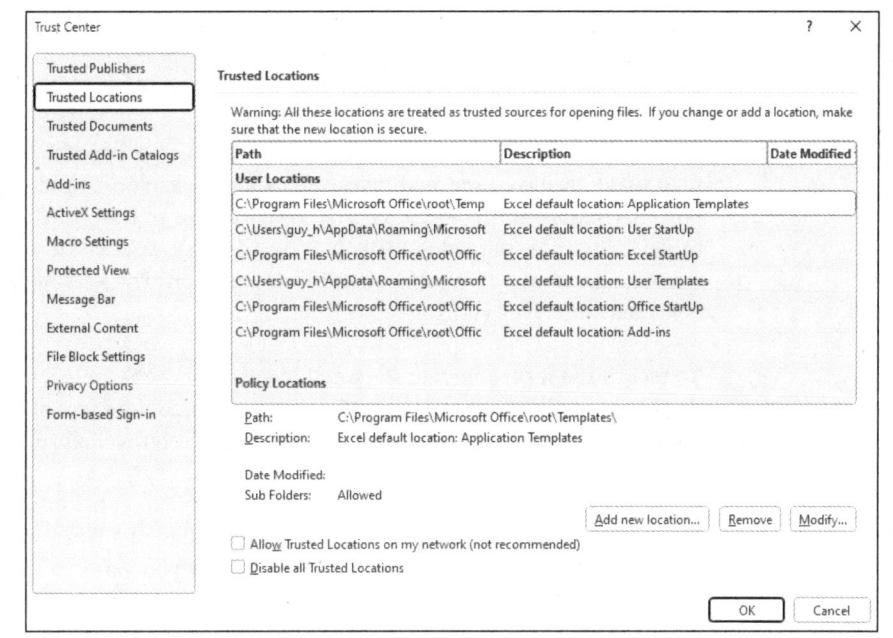

FIGURE 1-6:
The Trusted Locations window allows you to add directories that are considered trusted.

5. **Add an optional description, click OK to close the Microsoft Office Trusted Location dialog box, and then click OK again to close the Trust Center dialog box.**

After you specify a trusted location, any Excel file opened from this location will have macros automatically enabled.

Storing and Running Macros

Macros are stored in a workbook. Even though you work with macros in the VBE, the code is stored in the same file with all the worksheets, cells, shapes, or whatever else you have inside your workbook. This makes macros very easy to distribute. You simply send someone the Excel file, and the macros are included.

All macros need an event to start them running. Earlier in this chapter, we discuss assigning a shortcut key to a macro you record. Pressing the shortcut key is one type of event that can trigger a macro. In this section, we cover the Personal Macro Workbook, a special workbook for storing macros, and a few common ways to trigger macros.

Storing macros in your Personal Macro Workbook

Most user-created macros are designed for use in a specific workbook, but you may want to use some macros in all your work. You can store these general-purpose macros in the Personal Macro Workbook so that they're always available to you. This file, named PERSONAL.XLSB, doesn't exist until you record a macro using Personal Macro Workbook as the destination. The Personal Macro Workbook is loaded whenever you start Excel.

To record the macro in your Personal Macro Workbook, select the Personal Macro Workbook option in the Record Macro dialog box before you start recording. This option is in the Store Macro In drop-down list (refer to Figure 1-1).

If you store macros in the Personal Macro Workbook, you don't have to remember to open the Personal Macro Workbook when you load a workbook that uses macros. When you want to exit, Excel asks whether you want to save changes to the Personal Macro Workbook.

REMEMBER

The Personal Macro Workbook normally is in a hidden window to keep it out of the way.

Assigning a macro to a button and other form controls

When you create macros, you may want to have a clear and easy way to run each macro. A basic button can provide a simple but effective user interface.

Excel offers a set of form controls designed specifically for creating user interfaces directly on worksheets. There are several different types of form controls, from buttons (the most commonly used control) to scroll bars.

The idea behind using a form control is simple: You place a form control on a worksheet and then assign to it a macro you've already recorded. When a macro is assigned to the control, that macro is executed, or played, when the control is clicked.

Take a moment to create a button for the AddTotalRelative macro you created earlier. Here's how:

1. **On the Developer tab of the ribbon, click the Insert button (see Figure 1-7).**
2. **Select the Button Form Control from the drop-down list that appears.**

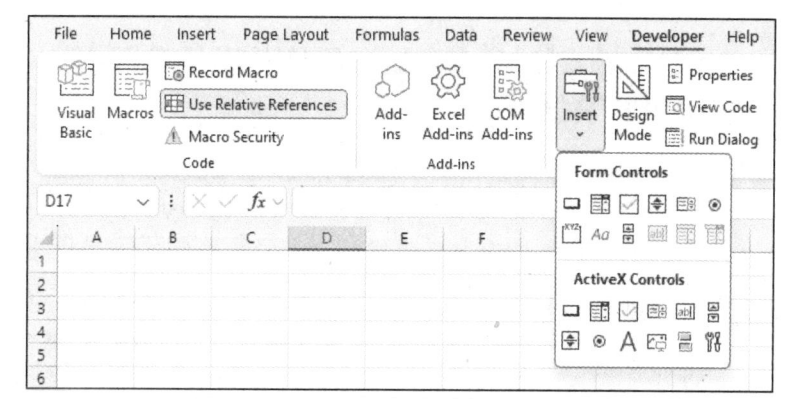

FIGURE 1-7: You can find the form controls on the Developer tab.

3. **Click the location where you want to place your button.**

   When you drop the button control onto your worksheet, the Assign Macro dialog box, shown in Figure 1-8, opens and asks you to assign a macro to this button.

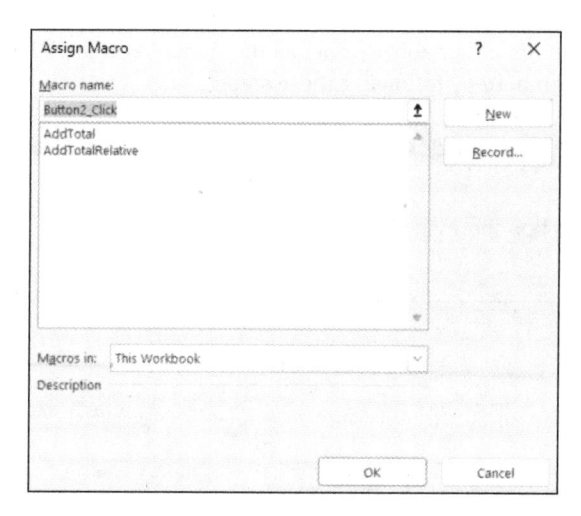

FIGURE 1-8: Assign a macro to the newly added button.

4. **Select the macro you want to assign to the button and click OK.**

   At this point, you have a button that runs your macro when you click it! Keep in mind that all the controls in the Form Controls group (shown in Figure 1-7) can work in the same way as the command button, in that you assign a macro to run when the control is selected.

CHAPTER 1 **Macro Fundamentals** 695

> ## FORM CONTROLS VERSUS ACTIVEX CONTROLS
>
> The Insert command on the Developer tab shows both form controls and ActiveX controls (refer to Figure 1-7). Although they look similar, they're quite different. Form controls are designed specifically for use on a worksheet, and ActiveX controls are typically used on Excel user forms (custom dialog boxes that are beyond the scope of this book). As a general rule, you should always use form controls when working on a worksheet unless there is a specific function that only ActiveX controls have. This is because form controls need less overhead, so they perform better, and configuring form controls is far easier than configuring their ActiveX counterparts.

Placing a macro on the Quick Access Toolbar

You can also assign a macro to a button on the Quick Access Toolbar. The Quick Access Toolbar sits either above or below the ribbon. You can add a custom button that runs your macro by following these steps:

1. **Right-click your Quick Access Toolbar and select Customize Quick Access Toolbar.**

   The dialog box shown in Figure 1-9 opens.

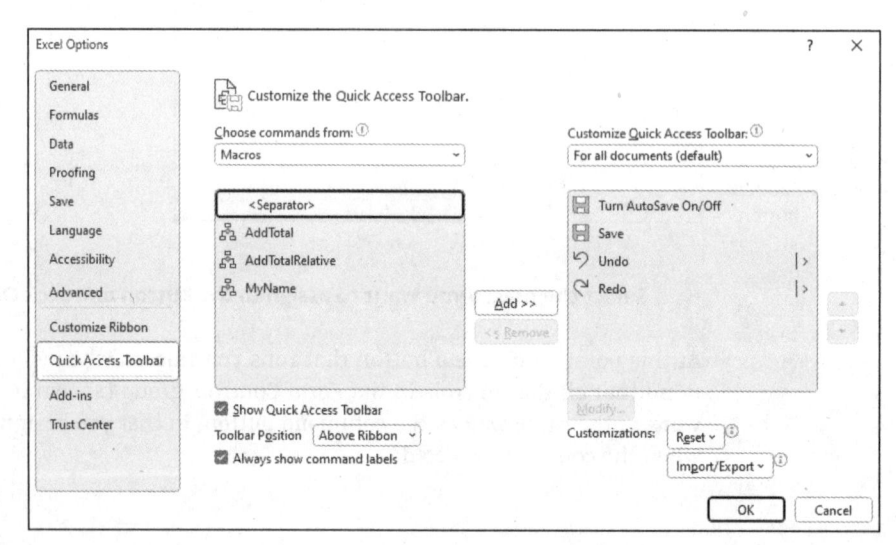

FIGURE 1-9: Adding a macro to the Quick Access Toolbar.

BOOK 8 Automating Excel with Macros and VBA

2. **Select Macros from the Choose Commands From drop-down list on the left.**

3. **Select the macro you want to add and click the Add button.**

4. **(Optional) Click the Modify button to change the icon or display name, and then click OK to close the Modify Button dialog box.**

5. **Click OK to close the Excel Options dialog box.**

Exploring Macro Examples

Covering the fundamentals of building and using macros is one thing. Coming up with good ways to incorporate them into your reporting processes is another. Take a moment to review a few examples of how macros automate simple reporting tasks.

REMEMBER

Open the file named `8.1.1 Workbook Containing Dataset.xlsm` to follow along in the next section.

Building navigation buttons

One common use of macros is navigation. Workbooks that have many worksheets or tabs can be frustrating to navigate. To help your users, you can create some sort of a switchboard, similar to the one shown in Figure 1-10. When a user clicks the Example 1 button, they're taken to the Example 1 sheet.

FIGURE 1-10: Use macros to build buttons that help users navigate your reports.

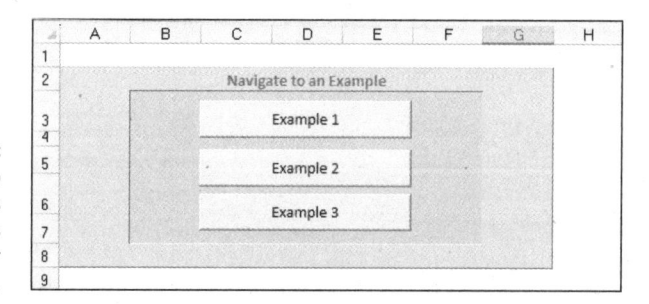

CHAPTER 1 **Macro Fundamentals** 697

Creating a macro to navigate to a sheet is quite simple.

1. **Start at the sheet that will become your switchboard or starting point.**
2. **Start recording a macro.**
3. **While recording, click the *destination sheet* (the sheet this macro will navigate to).**
4. **After you click the destination sheet, stop recording the macro.**
5. **Assign the macro to a button.**

TIP

Excel has a built-in hyperlink feature, allowing you to convert the contents of a cell into a hyperlink that links to another location. That location can be a separate Excel workbook, a website, or even another tab in the current workbook. Although using a hyperlink may be easier than setting up a macro, you can't apply a hyperlink to form controls (such as buttons). Instead of a button, you'd use text to let users know where they'll go when they click the link.

Dynamically rearranging PivotTable data

Macros can be used with any Excel object normally used in reporting. For instance, you can use a macro to give your users a way to dynamically change a PivotTable. In the example shown in Figure 1-11, macros allow a user to change the perspective of the chart simply by clicking any one of the buttons.

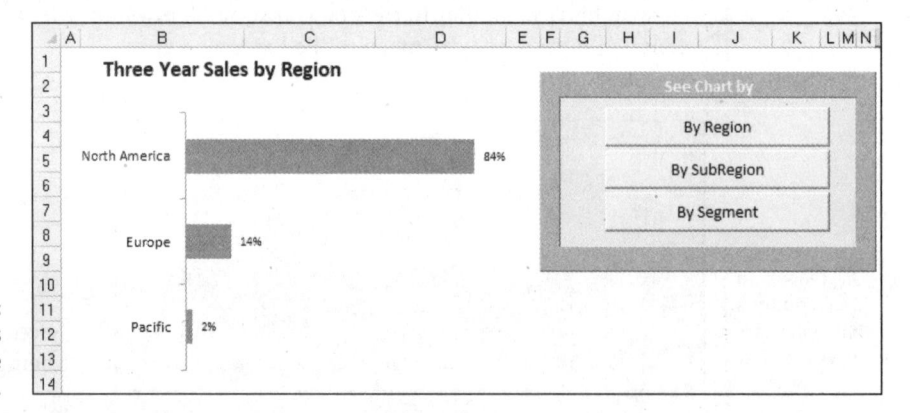

FIGURE 1-11: This report allows users to choose their perspective.

Figure 1-12 reveals that the chart is actually a PivotChart tied to a PivotTable. The recorded macros assigned to each button are doing nothing more than rearranging the PivotTable to slice the data using various pivot fields.

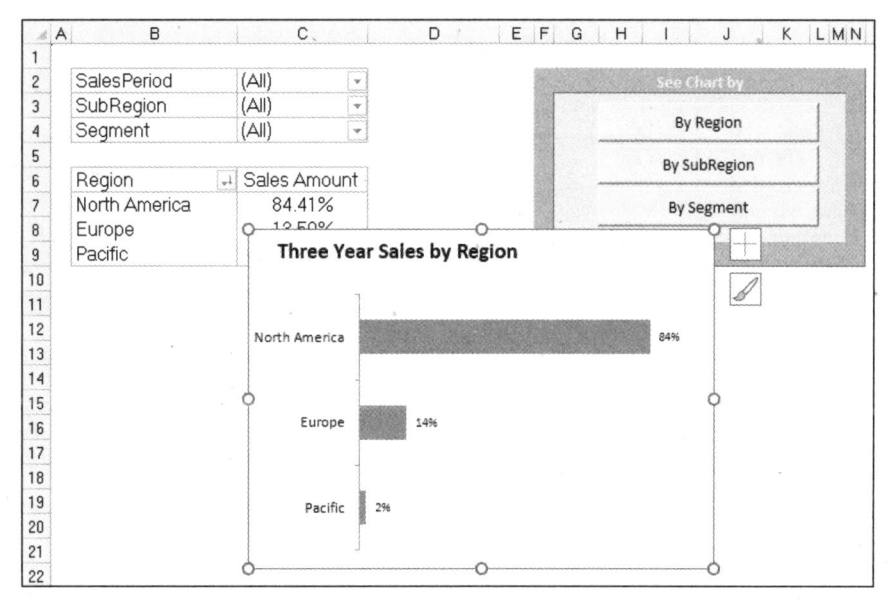

FIGURE 1-12: The macros behind these buttons rearrange the data fields in a PivotTable.

Here are the high-level steps needed to create this type of setup:

1. **Create your PivotTable and PivotChart.**
2. **Start recording a macro.**
3. **While recording, move a pivot field from one area of the PivotTable to the other; when you're done, stop recording the macro.**
4. **Record another macro to move the data field back to its original position.**
5. **After both macros are set up, assign each one to a separate button.**

You can run your new macros in turn to see your pivot field dynamically move back and forth.

Offering one-touch reporting options

The last two examples demonstrate that you can record any action that you find of value. If you think users would appreciate a certain feature being automated for them, why not record a macro to do so?

In Figure 1-13, buttons are tied to macros that filter the PivotTable for the top or bottom 20 customers. Because the steps to filter a PivotTable for the top and bottom 20 have been recorded, users can get the benefit of this functionality without knowing how to do it themselves. Also, recording a specific action allows you to manage risk a bit. In other words, your users can interact with your reports using a method that you've developed and tested.

CHAPTER 1 **Macro Fundamentals**

FIGURE 1-13: Offering prerecorded views not only saves time and effort, but also allows users who don't know how to use advanced features to benefit from them.

This not only saves them time and effort, but it also allows users that don't know how to take these actions to benefit from them.

Figure 1-14 demonstrates how you can give your audience a quick and easy way to see the same data on different charts. It's not uncommon to be asked to see the same data different ways. Instead of taking up real estate by showing both charts, just record a macro that changes the Chart Type of the chart. Your clients can switch views to their hearts' content.

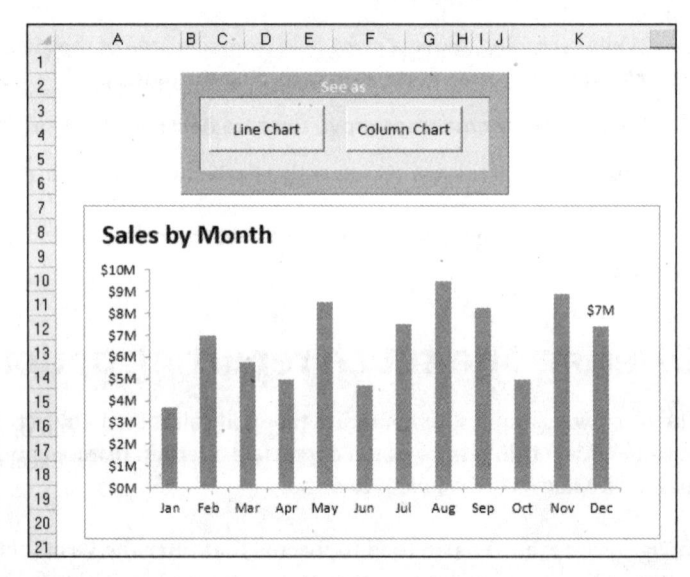

FIGURE 1-14: You can give your audience a choice in how they view data.

> **IN THIS CHAPTER**
>
> » Understanding the Visual Basic Editor components
>
> » Working with the Project Explorer
>
> » Using a Code pane
>
> » Customizing the Visual Basic Editor

Chapter 2
Getting Cozy with the Visual Basic Editor

The Visual Basic Editor (VBE) is the environment where all Excel macros are written or recorded. The VBE is included with Excel free of charge. Even if you never record one macro, the VBE is in the background waiting to be used. When you create a macro, the VBE quietly comes to life ready to process the various procedures and routines you give it.

In this chapter, you take your first look behind the curtain to explore the VBE.

Working in the Visual Basic Editor

The VBE is actually a separate application that runs when you open Excel. To see this hidden VBE environment, you need to activate it. With Excel open, do one of the following:

» Press Alt+F11.

» Click the Visual Basic button on the Developer tab of the ribbon.

To return to Excel, press Alt+F11 or click the Close button in the VBE.

Figure 2-1 shows the VBE with the key parts identified. Chances are, your VBE program window won't look exactly like what's shown in Figure 2-1. The VBE contains several windows and is highly customizable. You can hide windows, rearrange windows, dock windows to the main window, and so on.

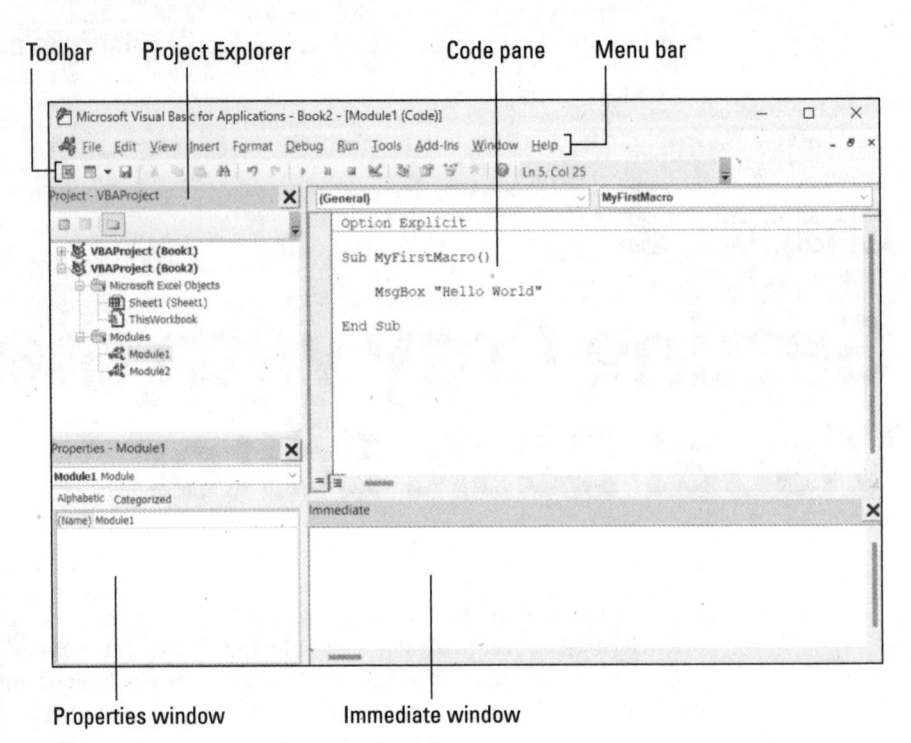

FIGURE 2-1: The VBE with significant elements identified.

VBE menu bar

The VBE menu bar works just like every other menu bar you've encountered. It contains commands that you use to do things with the various components in the VBE. Many of the menu commands also have shortcut keys associated with them, such as Ctrl+G to show the Immediate window and Ctrl+R to show the Project Explorer.

The VBE also features shortcut menus. You can right-click virtually anything in the VBE and get a shortcut menu of common commands specific to the area you clicked. For example, clicking in the Project Explorer shows a different list of commands than clicking in the Code pane.

VBE toolbars

The VBE has four toolbars: Standard, Edit, Debug, and UserForm. The Standard toolbar is the only one shown by default and is directly under the menu bar. It contains many of the most commonly used commands such as Return to Excel, Save, Cut, Copy, and Paste. You can customize the toolbars, move them around, display other toolbars, and so on. If you're so inclined, choose View➪Toolbars to toggle the display of the VBE toolbars.

Project Explorer

The Project Explorer displays a tree diagram that shows every workbook currently open in Excel (including add-ins and hidden workbooks). Double-click items to expand or contract them. You explore this window in more detail in the "Working with the Project Explorer" section later in this chapter.

If the Project Explorer isn't visible, press Ctrl+R or choose View➪Project Explorer. To hide the Project Explorer, click the Close button in its title bar. Alternatively, right-click anywhere in the Project Explorer and select Hide from the shortcut menu.

Code pane

A Code pane contains VBA code. Every object in a project has an associated Code pane. To view an object's Code pane, double-click the object in the Project Explorer. For example, to view the Code pane for the Sheet1 object, double-click Sheet1 in the Project Explorer. Unless you've added some VBA code, the Code pane is empty.

You find out more about Code panes in "Working with a Code Pane," later in this chapter.

Immediate window

The Immediate window may or may not be visible. If it isn't visible, press Ctrl+G or choose View➪Immediate Window. To close the Immediate window, click the Close button in its title bar (or right-click anywhere in the Immediate window and select Hide from the shortcut menu).

The Immediate window is most useful for executing VBA statements directly and for debugging your code. If you're just starting out with VBA, this window won't be all that useful, so feel free to hide it and free up some screen space for other things.

Working with the Project Explorer

When you're working in the VBE, each Excel workbook and add-in that's open is a project. You can think of a project as a collection of objects arranged as an outline. You can expand a project by clicking the plus sign (+) at the left of the project's name in the Project Explorer. Collapse a project by clicking the minus sign (–) to the left of a project's name. Or, you can double-click the items to expand and collapse them.

Figure 2-2 shows the Project Explorer with two projects listed: a workbook named Book1 and a workbook named Book2.

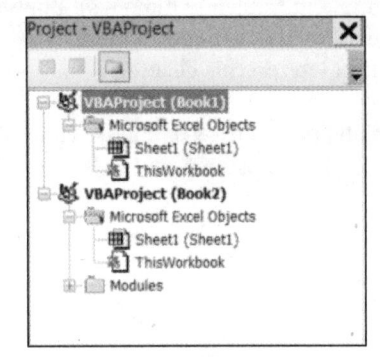

FIGURE 2-2: The Project Explorer with two projects open, expanded to show their objects.

Every project expands to show at least one folder called Microsoft Excel Objects. This folder expands to show an item for each sheet in the workbook (each sheet is considered an object) and another object called ThisWorkbook (which represents the Workbook object). If the project has any VBA modules, the project listing also shows a Modules folder.

Adding a new VBA module

When you record a macro, Excel automatically inserts a VBA module to hold the recorded code. The workbook that holds the module for the recorded macro depends on where you choose to store the recorded macro, just before you start recording.

In general, a VBA module can hold three types of code:

» **Declarations:** One or more information statements that you provide to VBA. For example, you can declare *module-level variables* (variables that apply to all procedures in the module instead of just one) or set some other module-wide options.

» **Sub procedures:** A set of programming instructions that performs some action. All recorded macros are Sub procedures.

» **Function procedures:** A set of programming instructions that returns a single value (similar in concept to a worksheet function, such as Sum).

A single VBA module can store any number of Sub procedures, Function procedures, and declarations. How you organize a VBA project is dependent on how many macros you have. If you have just a few, one module is probably all you need. If you start to get a lot of macros in a workbook, splitting them into well-named modules is best so you can easily find them later. Simply cut and paste any code from one module to another to move it.

Follow these steps to manually add a new VBA module to a project:

1. **Select the project's name in the Project Explorer.**
2. **Choose Insert⇨Module.**

Or you can

1. **Right-click the project's name.**
2. **Choose Insert⇨Module from the shortcut menu.**

The new module is added to a Modules folder in the Project Explorer (see Figure 2-3). Any modules you create in a given workbook are placed in this Modules folder.

FIGURE 2-3: Code modules are visible in the Project Explorer in a folder called Modules.

CHAPTER 2 **Getting Cozy with the Visual Basic Editor**   705

If you want to change the name of your module, select the module in the Project Explorer and press F4 to show the Properties window. Modules only have one property, Name, so it's easy to find where to change it.

Removing a VBA module

You may want to remove a code module that is no longer needed. To do so, follow these steps:

1. **Select the module's name in the Project Explorer.**
2. **Choose File ⇨ Remove *xxx*, where *xxx* is the module name.**

Or

1. **Right-click the module's name.**
2. **Choose Remove *xxx* from the shortcut menu.**

Whichever method you choose, Excel asks you if you want to export the module before removing it. Click Yes to create an export file that you can re-import into your project if you find you deleted it in error.

REMEMBER: You can remove VBA modules, but there is no way to remove the other code modules — those for the Sheet objects, or ThisWorkbook.

Working with a Code Pane

As you become proficient with VBA, you spend lots of time working in Code panes. Macros that you record are stored in a module, and you can type VBA code directly into a VBA module's Code pane.

Minimizing and maximizing windows

Code panes are much like workbook windows in Excel. You can minimize them, maximize them, resize them, hide them, rearrange them, and so on. Most people find it much easier to maximize the Code pane that they're working on. Doing so lets you see more code and keeps you from getting distracted.

To maximize a Code pane, click the maximize button in its title bar (right next to the *X*). Or, just double-click its title bar to maximize it. To restore a Code pane to its original size, click the Restore button.

706 BOOK 8 **Automating Excel with Macros and VBA**

Sometimes, you may want to have two or more Code panes visible. For example, you may want to compare the code in two modules or copy code from one module to another. You can arrange the panes manually, or choose Window➪Tile Horizontally or Window➪Tile Vertically to arrange them automatically.

You can quickly switch among Code panes by pressing Ctrl+Tab. If you repeat that key combination, you keep cycling through all the open Code panes. Pressing Ctrl+Shift+Tab cycles through the panes in reverse order.

Minimizing a Code pane gets it out of the way. You can also click the pane's Close button in the title bar to close it completely. (Closing a window just hides it — you won't lose anything.) To open it again, just double-click the appropriate object in the Project Explorer. Working with these Code panes sounds more difficult than it really is.

Getting VBA code into a module

Before you can do anything meaningful, you must have some VBA code in the VBA module. You can get VBA code into a VBA module in three ways:

- Use the Excel macro recorder to record your actions and convert them to VBA code.
- Enter the code directly.
- Copy the code from one module and paste it into another.

Chapter 1 shows you how to create code by using the Excel macro recorder. However, not all tasks can be translated to VBA by recording a macro. You often have to enter your code directly into the module. Entering code directly basically means either typing the code yourself or copying and pasting code you've found somewhere else.

Entering and editing text in a VBA module works as you might expect. You can select, copy, cut, paste, and do other things to the text.

A single line of VBA code can be as long as you like. However, you may want to use the line continuation character to break up lengthy lines of code. To continue a single line of code (also known as a *statement*) from one line to the next, end the first line with a space followed by an underscore (_). Then continue the statement on the next line. Here's an example of a single statement split into three lines:

```
Selection.Sort Key1:=Range("A1"), _
   Order1:=xlAscending, Header:=xlGuess, _
   Orientation:=xlTopToBottom
```

This statement would perform exactly the same way if it were entered on a single line (with no line continuation characters). Notice that the second and third lines of this statement are indented. Indenting is optional, but it helps clarify the fact that these lines are not separate statements.

The VBE has multiple levels of undo and redo. If you delete a statement that you shouldn't have, click the Undo button on the Standard toolbar (or press Ctrl+Z) until the statement appears again. After undoing, you can click the Redo button to perform the changes you've undone.

Ready to enter some real, live code? Try the following steps:

1. **Create a new workbook in Excel.**
2. **Press Alt+F11 to open the VBE.**
3. **Click the new workbook's name in the Project Explorer.**
4. **Choose Insert⇨Module to insert a VBA module into the project.**
5. **Type the following code into the module:**

    ```
    Sub GuessName()
        Dim Msg as String
        Dim Ans As Long
        Msg = "Is your name " & Application.UserName & "?"
        Ans = MsgBox(Msg, vbYesNo)
        If Ans = vbNo Then MsgBox "Oh, never mind."
        If Ans = vbYes Then MsgBox "I must be clairvoyant!"
    End Sub
    ```

6. **Make sure the cursor is located anywhere within the text you typed and press F5 to execute the procedure.**

TIP The VBE has its own set of shortcut keys you can use to quickly run a command using your keyboard. F5 is a shortcut for Run⇨Run Sub/UserForm.

When you enter the code listed in Step 5, you may notice that the VBE makes some adjustments to the text you enter. For example, after you type the Sub statement, the VBE automatically inserts the End Sub statement. And if you omit the space before or after an equal sign, the VBE inserts the space for you. Also, the VBE changes the color and capitalization of some text. This is all perfectly normal. It's just the VBE's way of keeping things neat and readable.

If you followed the previous steps, you just created a VBA Sub procedure, also known as a *macro*. When you press F5, Excel executes the code and follows the instructions. In other words, Excel evaluates each statement and does what you told it to do. You can execute this macro any number of times — although it tends to lose its appeal after a few dozen executions.

This simple macro uses the following concepts:

- Defining a Sub procedure (the first line)
- Declaring variables (the `Dim` statements)
- Assigning values to variables (`Msg` and `Ans`)
- Concatenating (joining) a string (using the & operator)
- Using a built-in VBA function (`MsgBox`)
- Using built-in VBA constants (`vbYesNo`, `vbNo`, and `vbYes`)
- Using an If-Then construct (twice)
- Ending a Sub procedure (the last line)

TIP As we mention earlier, you can copy and paste code into a VBA module. For example, a Sub or Function procedure that you write for one project may also be useful in another project. Instead of reentering the code, you can open the module and use the normal copy-and-paste procedures (Ctrl+C to copy and Ctrl+V to paste). After pasting the code into a VBA module, you can modify it as necessary.

Customizing the VBE

If you're serious about becoming an Excel programmer, you'll spend a lot of time with VBA modules on your screen. To help make things as comfortable as possible, the VBE provides quite a few customization options.

When the VBE is active, choose Tools➪Options. The Options dialog box has four tabs: Editor, Editor Format, General, and Docking. Take a moment to explore some of the options found on each tab.

CHAPTER 2 **Getting Cozy with the Visual Basic Editor** 709

Editor tab

Figure 2-4 shows the options accessed by clicking the Editor tab of the Options dialog box. Use the options in the Editor tab to control how certain things work in the VBE.

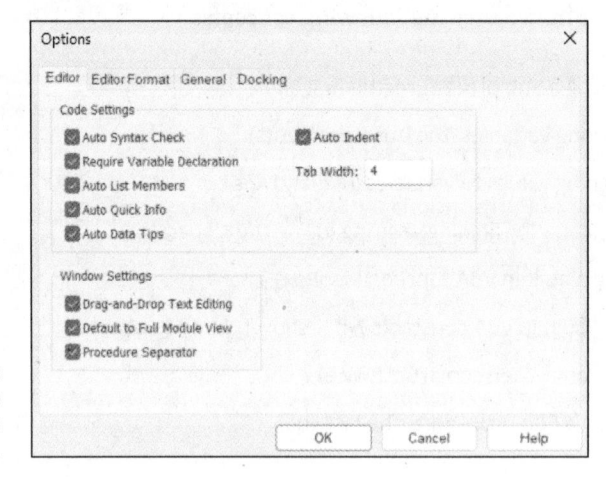

FIGURE 2-4: The Editor tab in the Options dialog box.

Auto Syntax Check

The Auto Syntax Check option determines whether the VBE opens a dialog box if it discovers a syntax error while you're entering your VBA code. The dialog box tells roughly what the problem is. If you don't choose this setting, VBE flags syntax errors by displaying them in a different color (red by default) from the rest of the code, and you don't have to deal with any onscreen dialog boxes.

Require Variable Declaration

If the Require Variable Declaration option is set, the VBE inserts the following statement at the beginning of each new VBA module you insert:

```
Option Explicit
```

Changing this setting affects only new modules, not existing modules. If this statement appears in your module, you must explicitly define each variable you use. Using a `Dim` statement is one way to declare variables.

If you don't set this option, VBA won't require you to explicitly declare your variables. If you don't declare a variable, VBA will declare it for you the first time you use it. That is, VBA will create a spot in memory with that variable's name.

That may seem like a time-saver, but the first time you mistype a variable, you'll be glad you required variable declaration. Bugs from misspelled variables can be hard to find.

Auto List Members

If the Auto List Members option is set, VBE provides some help when you're entering your VBA code. It displays a list that would logically complete the statement you're typing. This feature is very useful for saving time while coding.

Auto Quick Info

If the Auto Quick Info option is selected, VBE displays information about functions and their arguments as you type. This is similar to the way Excel lists the arguments for a function as you start typing a new formula.

Auto Data Tips

If the Auto Data Tips option is set, VBE displays the value of the variable over which your cursor is placed when you're debugging code. This is turned on by default and often quite useful — in fact, there's no reason to turn off this option.

Auto Indent

The Auto Indent setting determines whether VBE automatically indents each new line of code the same as the previous line. Most Excel developers are keen on using indentations in their code, so this option is typically kept on.

> **TIP** By the way, you should use the Tab key to indent your code, not the spacebar. Also, you can use Shift+Tab to "unindent" a line of code. If you want to indent more than just one line, select all lines you want to indent and then press the Tab key.

To show the VBE's Edit toolbar, right-click any toolbar and select Edit from the context menu. This toolbar includes two useful buttons: Indent and Outdent. These buttons let you quickly indent or "unindent" a block of code. Select the code and click one of these buttons to change the block's indenting.

Drag-and-Drop Text Editing

The Drag-and-Drop Text Editing option, when enabled, lets you copy and move text by dragging and dropping with your mouse.

Default to Full Module View

The Default to Full Module View option sets the default state for new modules. (It doesn't affect existing modules.) If set, procedures in the Code pane appear as a single scrollable list. If this option is turned off, you can see only one procedure at a time.

Procedure Separator

When the Procedure Separator option is turned on, separator bars appear between each procedure in a Code pane. Separator bars provide a nice visual line between procedures, making it easy to see where one piece of code ends and where another starts.

Editor Format tab

Figure 2-5 shows the Editor Format tab of the Options dialog box. With this tab, you can customize the way the VBE looks.

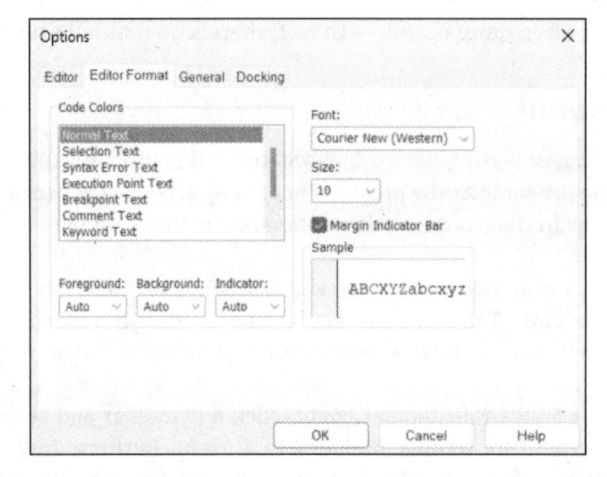

FIGURE 2-5:
Change the way the VBE looks with the Editor Format tab.

Code Colors

The Code Colors option lets you set the text color and background color displayed for various elements of VBA code. This is largely a matter of personal preference. Some Excel developers stick with the default colors. But if you like to change things up, you can play around with these settings.

Font

The Font option lets you select the font that's used in your VBA modules. For best results, stick with a fixed-width font such as Courier New. In a fixed-width font, all characters are exactly the same width. This makes your code more readable because the characters are nicely aligned vertically and you can easily distinguish multiple spaces (which is sometimes useful).

Size

The Size setting specifies the point size of the font in the VBA modules. This setting is a matter of personal preference determined by your video display resolution and how good your eyesight is.

Margin Indicator Bar

This option controls the display of the vertical margin indicator bar in your modules. You should keep this turned on; otherwise, you won't be able to see the helpful graphical indicators when you're debugging your code.

General tab

Figure 2-6 shows the options available under the General tab in the Options dialog box. In almost every case, the default settings are just fine.

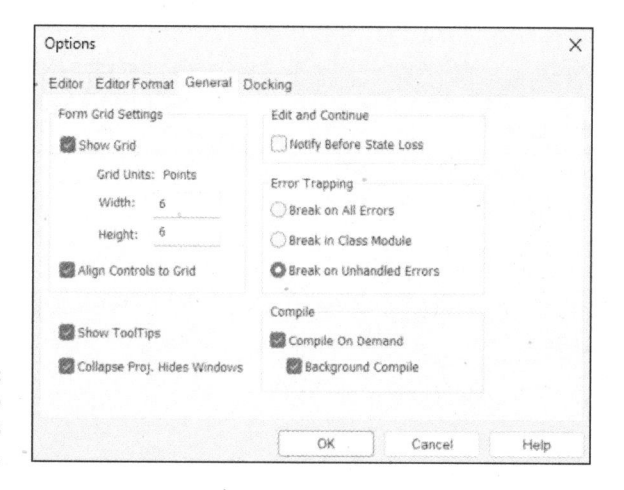

FIGURE 2-6: The General tab of the Options dialog box.

CHAPTER 2 Getting Cozy with the Visual Basic Editor   713

The most important setting on the General tab is Error Trapping. If you're just starting your Excel macro writing career, it's best to leave the Error Trapping set to Break on Unhandled Errors. That way, if Excel encounters an error, it stops executing, highlights the line that caused the error, and gives you a chance to figure out what went wrong.

Docking tab

Figure 2-7 shows the Docking tab. These options determine how the various windows in the VBE behave. When a window is docked, it's fixed in place along one of the edges of the VBE program window. This makes it much easier to identify and locate a particular window. If you turn off all docking, you have a big, confusing mess of windows. Generally, the default settings work fine.

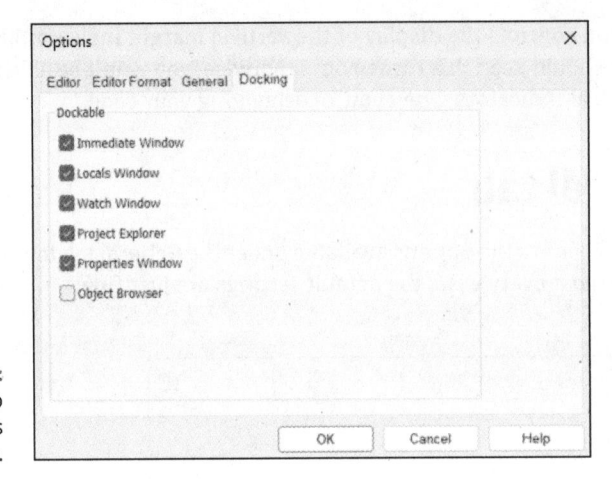

FIGURE 2-7: The Docking tab of the Options dialog box.

IN THIS CHAPTER

» Understanding the Excel object model

» Using variables

» Working with event procedures

» Handling errors

Chapter **3**

The Anatomy of Macros

The engine behind macros is Visual Basic for Applications (VBA). When you record a macro, Excel is busy writing the associated VBA behind the scenes. To fully understand macros, it's important to understand the underlying VBA typically used in Excel macros.

This chapter starts you on that journey by giving you a primer on some of the objects, variables, events, and error handlers you encounter in macros.

A Brief Overview of the Excel Object Model

VBA is an object-oriented programming language. The basic concept of object-oriented programming is that a software application (Excel, in this case) consists of various individual objects, each of which has its own set of characteristics and uses. An Excel application contains workbooks, worksheets, cells, charts, Pivot-Tables, drawing shapes — the list of Excel's objects is seemingly endless. Each object has its own set of characteristics, called *properties,* and its own set of uses, called *methods.*

You can think of this concept just as you would the objects you encounter every day, such as the computer in your office, the car in your garage, or the refrigerator in your kitchen. Each of those objects has identifying qualities, such as height, weight, and color. Each has its own distinct uses, such as your computer for working with Excel, your car to transport you over long distances, and your refrigerator to keep your food cold.

VBA objects also have their identifiable properties and methods of use. A worksheet cell is an object, and among its describable features (its properties) are its address, its height, its formatted fill color, and so on. A workbook is also a VBA object, and among its usable features (its methods) are its abilities to be opened, closed, and have a chart or PivotTable added to it.

In Excel, you deal with workbooks, worksheets, and ranges on a daily basis. You likely think of each of these "objects" as part of Excel, not really separating them in your mind. However, Excel thinks about these internally as part of a hierarchical model called the *Excel object model.* The Excel object model is a clearly defined set of objects structured according to the relationships between them.

Understanding objects

In the real world, you can describe everything you see as an object. When you look at your house, it's an object. Your house has rooms; those rooms are also separate objects. Those rooms may have closets. Those closets are likewise objects. As you think about your house, the rooms, and the closets, you may see a hierarchical relationship between them. Excel works in the same way.

In Excel, the Application object is the all-encompassing object — similar to your house. Inside the Application object, Excel has a workbook. Inside a workbook is a worksheet. Inside that is a range. These are all objects that live in a hierarchical structure.

To point to a specific object in VBA, you can traverse the object model using the dot operator. For example, to get to cell A1 on Sheet1, you can enter this code:

```
ActiveWorkbook.Sheets("Sheet1").Range("A1").Select
```

In most cases, the object model hierarchy is understood, so you don't have to type every level. Entering this code also gets you to cell A1 because Excel infers that you mean the active workbook and the active sheet:

```
Range("A1").Select
```

Indeed, if you've already selected cell A1, you can simply use the `ActiveCell` object, negating the need to actually spell out the range.

```
ActiveCell.Select
```

Understanding collections

Many of Excel's objects belong to collections. Your house sits within a neighborhood, for example, which is a collection of houses called a neighborhood. Each neighborhood sits in a collection of neighborhoods called a city. Excel considers collections to be objects themselves.

In each Workbook object, you have a collection of Worksheets. The Worksheets collection is an object that you can call upon through VBA. Each worksheet in your workbook lives in the Worksheets collection.

If you want to refer to a worksheet in the Worksheets collection, you can refer to it by its position in the collection, as an index number starting with 1, or by its name, as quoted text. If you run these two lines of code in a workbook that contains a single worksheet, called MySheet, they both do the same thing:

```
Worksheets(1).Select
Worksheets("MySheet").Select
```

If you have two worksheets in the active workbook that have the names MySheet and YourSheet, in that order, you can refer to the second worksheet by typing either of these statements:

```
Worksheets(2).Select
Worksheets("YourSheet").Select
```

If you want to refer to a worksheet called MySheet in a particular workbook that is open but not active, you must qualify the worksheet reference and the workbook reference, as follows:

```
Workbooks("MyData.xlsx").Worksheets("MySheet").Select
```

Understanding properties

Properties are essentially the characteristics of an object. Your house has a color, a square footage, an age, and so on. Some properties — such as the color of your house — can be changed. Other properties — such as the age of your house — cannot be changed. (The age of your house does change, but you physically can't change it. Only time can do that.)

Likewise, an object in Excel such as the Worksheet object has a Name property that can be changed, and a Rows.Count row property that cannot.

CHAPTER 3 The Anatomy of Macros

You refer to the property of an object by referring to the object and then the property. For example, you can change the name of your worksheet by changing its Name property.

In this example, you're renaming Sheet1 to MySheet:

```
Sheets("Sheet1").Name = "MySheet"
```

Some properties are read-only, which means that you can't assign a value to them directly — for example, the Text property of a cell. The Text property gives you the formatted appearance of value in a cell, but you can't overwrite or change it. To change the Text property, you have to change the Value property, the NumberFormat property, or both.

Understanding methods

Methods are the actions that you can perform against an object. It helps to think of methods as verbs. You can paint your house, so in VBA, that translates to something like

```
house.paint
```

A simple example of an Excel method is the Select method of the Range object:

```
Range("A1").Select
```

Another is the Copy method of the Range object:

```
Range("A1").Copy
```

Some methods have parameters that dictate how the method is applied. For example, you can use the Paste method more effectively by explicitly defining the Destination parameter:

```
ActiveSheet.Paste Destination:=Range("B1")
```

A Brief Look at Variables

Another concept you see throughout macros is the concept of *variables*. It's important to dedicate a few words to this concept, because variables play a big part in many macros.

You can think of variables as memory containers that you can use in your procedures. There are different types of variables; each is tasked with holding a specific type of data.

Some of the common types of variables you use in macros are

- **String:** Holds text
- **Long:** Holds numbers ranging from –2,147,483,648 to 2,147,483,647
- **Double:** Holds floating-point numbers
- **Variant:** Holds any kind of data
- **Boolean:** Holds True or False
- **Object:** Holds an object from the Excel object model

Creating a variable in a macro is called *declaring* a variable. You do so by entering **Dim** (which is an abbreviation for *dimension*), the name of your variable, and the type. For example:

```
Dim MyText As String

Dim MyNumber As Long

Dim MyWorksheet As Worksheet
```

After you create your variable, you can fill it with data. Here are a few simple examples of how you would create a variable and then assign values to it:

```
Dim MyText As String
MyText = Range("A1").Value

Dim MyNumber As Long
MyNumber = Range("B1").Value * 25

Dim MyObject As Worksheet
Set MyWorksheet = Sheets("Sheet1")
```

The values you assign to your variables often come from data stored in your cells. However, the values may also be information that you create. It all depends on the task at hand. As you work more with macros, values will make a lot more sense.

You can create code that doesn't use variables, but many examples of VBA code do use variables. There are two main reasons for this:

» **Excel doesn't inherently know what your data is used for.** It doesn't see numbers, symbols, or letters. It just sees data. When you declare variables with specific data types, you help Excel know how it should handle certain pieces of data so that your macros produce the results you'd expect.

» **Variables help make your code more efficient and easier to understand.** For example, suppose you have a number in cell A1 that you're repeatedly referring to in your macro. You could retrieve that number by pointing to cell A1 each time you need it, like this:

```
Sub Macro1()
    Range("B1").Value = Range("A1").Value * 5
    Range("C1").Value = Range("A1").Value * 10
    Range("D1").Value = Range("A1").Value * 15
End Sub
```

However, this would force Excel to waste cycles storing the same number into memory every time you point to cell A1. Also, if you need to change your workbook so the target number isn't in cell A1, but in, say, cell A2, you would need to edit your code by changing all the references from A1 to A2.

A better way is to store the number in cell A1 just once. For example, you can store the value in cell A1 in an Long variable called myValue:

```
Sub WithVariable()
    Dim myValue As Long
    myValue = Range("A1").Value
    Range("C3").Value = myValue * 5
    Range("D5").Value = myValue * 10
    Range("E7").Value = myValue * 15
End Sub
```

This not only improves the efficiency of your code (ensuring that Excel reads the number in cell A1 just once), but also ensures that you only have to edit one line if the design of your workbook changes.

Understanding Event Procedures

Many macros implement code as *event procedures.* To fully understand event procedures, it's important to get acquainted with events.

An *event* is nothing more than an action that takes place during a session in Excel. Everything that happens in Excel happens to an object through an event. A few examples of events are opening a workbook, adding a worksheet, changing a value in a cell, saving a workbook, double-clicking a cell, and the list goes on.

The nifty thing is that you can tell Excel to run a certain macro or piece of code when a particular event occurs. For example, you may want to ensure that your workbook automatically saves each time it closes. You can add code to the Before-Close workbook event that saves the workbook before it closes.

REMEMBER

Chapter 2 of this minibook discusses how to create a new VBA module to hold the code you write. However, event procedures are special in that they aren't stored in the standard modules. Event procedures are stored directly within each object's built-in modules, which the next few sections explain.

Worksheet events

Worksheet events occur when something happens to a particular worksheet, such as when a worksheet is selected, when a cell on the worksheet is edited, or when a formula on a worksheet is calculated. Each worksheet has its own built-in module where you can place your own event procedures.

To get to this built-in module, you can right-click the worksheet's tab and select View Code (see Figure 3-1).

FIGURE 3-1:
Getting to the built-in module for a worksheet.

The Visual Basic Editor (VBE) automatically opens to the built-in module for the worksheet. This module's Code pane has two drop-down boxes at the top.

CHAPTER 3 The Anatomy of Macros   721

Select the Worksheet option from the drop-down list on the left. This action automatically selects the `SelectionChange` event from the drop-down list on the right. Some starter code is also added where you can enter or paste your code, as shown in Figure 3-2.

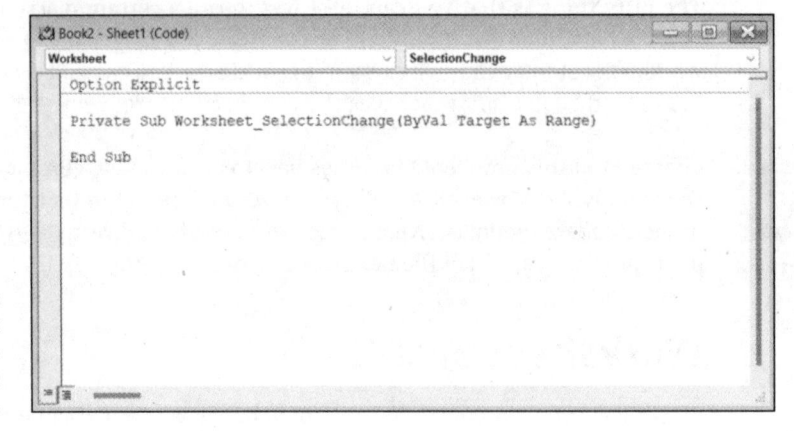

FIGURE 3-2: The default `SelectionChange` event for the Worksheet object.

The idea is to choose the most appropriate event from the Event drop-down list for the task at hand. Figure 3-3 illustrates the different events you can choose.

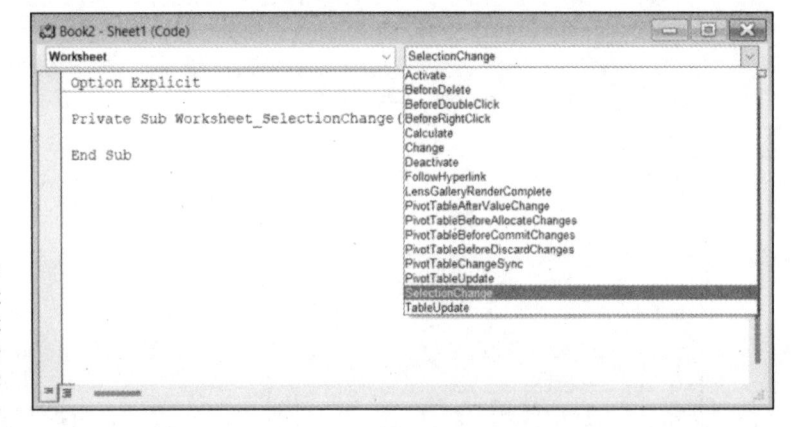

FIGURE 3-3: Click the Event drop-down list to choose the most appropriate event.

The more commonly used worksheet events are

- » `Worksheet_Change`: Triggers when any data on the worksheet is changed
- » `Worksheet_SelectionChange`: Triggers each time a new cell or object on the worksheet is selected

- **Worksheet_BeforeDoubleClick:** Triggers before Excel responds to a double-click on the worksheet
- **Worksheet_BeforeRightClick:** Triggers before Excel responds to a right-click on the worksheet
- **Worksheet_Activate:** Triggers when the user moves from another worksheet to this worksheet
- **Worksheet_Deactivate:** Triggers when the user moves from this worksheet to another worksheet
- **Worksheet_Calculate:** Triggers each time a change on the worksheet causes Excel to recalculate formulas

Workbook events

Workbook events occur when something happens to a particular workbook, such as when a workbook is opened, when a workbook is closed, when a new worksheet is added, or when a workbook is saved. Each workbook has its own built-in module where you can place your own event procedures.

To get to this built-in module, you first need to activate the VBE (press Alt+F11). Then in the Project Explorer, double-click ThisWorkbook to open its Code pane. This module's Code pane has two drop-down boxes at the top.

Select the Workbook option from the drop-down list on the left. This action automatically selects the Open event from the drop-down list on the right. Some starter code is also added where you can enter or paste your code, as shown in Figure 3-4.

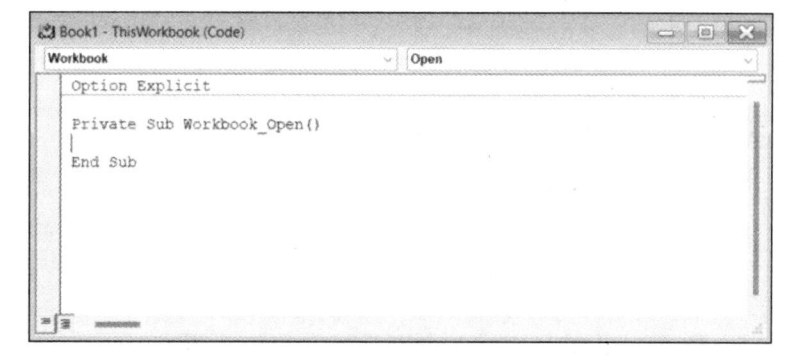

FIGURE 3-4: The default Open event for the Workbook object.

Choose the most appropriate event from the Event drop-down list for the task at hand. Figure 3-5 illustrates some of the events you can choose.

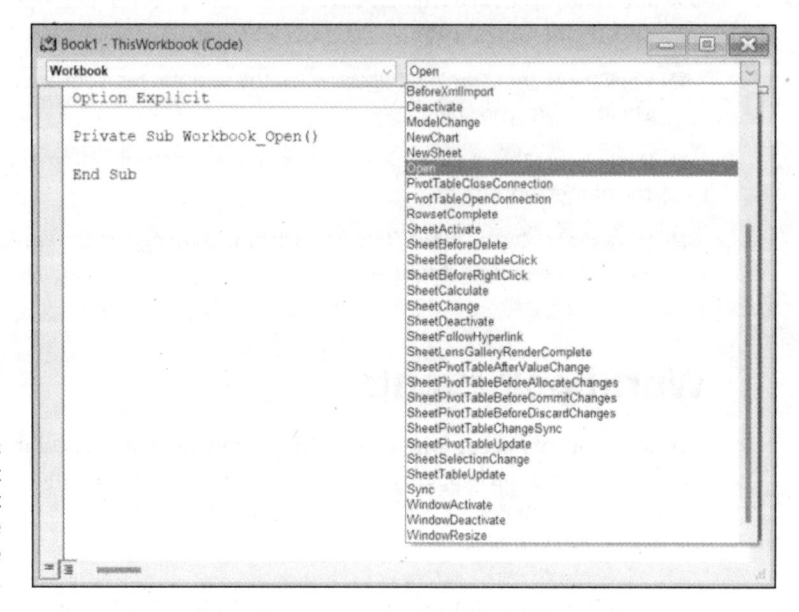

FIGURE 3-5: Click the Event drop-down list to choose the most appropriate event.

The more commonly used Workbook events are

- `Worksheet_Open`: Triggers when the workbook is opened
- `Worksheet_BeforeSave`: Triggers before the workbook is saved
- `Worksheet_BeforeClose`: Triggers before Excel closes the workbook
- `Worksheet_SheetChange`: Triggers when a user switches between sheets

Error Handling in a Nutshell

In some macros, you see a line similar to this:

```
On Error GoTo MyError
```

This is called an *error handler*. Error handlers allow you to specify what happens when an error is encountered while your code runs.

Without error handlers, any error that occurs in your code prompts Excel to display a less-than-helpful error message and throws your users into the VBE to debug it. However, with the aid of error handlers, you can choose to ignore the error or exit the code gracefully with your own message to the user.

There are three types of `On Error` statements:

- `On Error GoTo SomeLabel`: The code jumps to the specified label, a named point in the macro.
- `On Error Resume Next`: The error is ignored and the code resumes.
- `On Error GoTo 0`: VBA resets to normal error-checking behavior.

On Error GoTo SomeLabel

Sometimes an error in your code means you need to gracefully exit the procedure and give your users a clear message. In these situations, you can use the `On Error GoTo` statement to tell Excel to jump to a certain line of code.

Take this small piece of code for example. Here, it's telling Excel to divide the value in cell A1 by the value in cell A2, and then place the answer in cell A3. Easy. What could go wrong?

```
Sub CalcDivision()
    Range("A3").Value = Range("A1").Value / Range("A2").Value
End Sub
```

As it turns out, two major things can go wrong. If cell A2 contains a 0, you get a divide by 0 error. If cell A2 contains a non-numeric value, you get a type mismatch error.

To avoid a nasty error message, you can tell Excel that On Error, you want the code execution to jump to the label called `ErrExit`.

The following block of code includes the `ErrExit` label followed by a message to users that gives them friendly advice rather than a nasty error message. Also note the `Exit Sub` line before the `ErrExit` label. This line ensures that the code simply exits if no error is encountered.

```
Sub CalcDivision()
    On Error GoTo ErrExit
    Range("A3").Value = Range("A1").Value / Range("A2").Value
    Exit Sub
```

```
ErrExit:
    MsgBox "Please Use Valid Non-Zero Numbers"
End Sub
```

On Error Resume Next

Sometimes you want Excel to ignore an error and simply resume running the code. In these situations, you can use the On Error Resume Next statement.

For example, this piece of code is meant to delete a file called GhostFile.exe from the C:\Temp directory. After the file is deleted, a nice message box tells the user the file is gone.

```
Sub DeleteGhost()
    Kill "C:\Temp\GhostFile.exe"
    MsgBox "File has been deleted."
End Sub
```

It works great if there is, indeed, a file to delete. But if for some reason the file called GhostFile.exe does not exist in the C:\Temp directory, an error is thrown.

In this case, you don't care if the file isn't there. You were going to delete it anyway. So, you can simply ignore the error and move on with the code.

By using the On Error Resume Next statement, the code runs its course even if the targeted file doesn't exist.

```
Sub DeleteGhost()
    On Error Resume Next
    Kill "C:\Temp\GhostFile.exe"
    MsgBox "File has been deleted."
End Sub
```

On Error GoTo 0

When using certain error statements, it may be necessary to reset the error-checking behavior of VBA. To understand what this means, take a look at this example.

Here, you first want to delete a file called GhostFile.exe from the C:\Temp directory. To avoid errors that may stem from the fact that the targeted file doesn't exist, you use the On Error Resume Next statement. After that, you're trying to do some suspect math by dividing 100 by Mike.

```
Sub DeleteGhost()
    On Error Resume Next
        Kill "C:\Temp\GhostFile.exe"
        Range("A3").Value = 100 / "Mike"
End Sub
```

Running this piece of code should generate an error due to the fuzzy math, but it doesn't. With On Error Resume Next, you told Excel to ignore all errors, and that's what it does.

To remedy this problem, you can use the On Error GoTo 0 statement to resume the normal error-checking behavior:

```
Sub DeleteGhost()
    On Error Resume Next
        Kill "C:\Temp\GhostFile.exe"
    On Error GoTo 0
        Range("A3").Value = 100 / "Mike"
End Sub
```

This code ignores errors until the On Error GoTo 0 statement. After that statement, the code goes back to normal error checking where it triggers the expected error stemming from the fuzzy math.

IN THIS CHAPTER

» Creating a new workbook from scratch

» Saving a workbook when a particular cell is changed

» Saving a workbook before closing

» Protecting an existing workbook when closing it

» Unprotecting an existing workbook when opening it

» Opening a workbook to a specific tab

» Opening a specific workbook defined by the user

» Determining whether a workbook is already open

» Determining whether a workbook exists in a directory

Chapter 4
Working with Workbooks

A workbook isn't just an Excel file; it's also an object in Excel's object model, the programming hierarchy that exposes parts of Excel to Visual Basic for Applications (VBA; see Chapter 2 of this minibook). This means that you can reference workbooks through VBA to do cool things such as automatically create new workbooks, prevent users from closing workbooks, and automatically back up workbooks.

In this chapter, you explore a few of the more useful workbook-related macros.

Installing Macros

You can install the macros in this chapter in three places depending on what kind of macro it is and how available you want the macro to be. Event macros are put into the module of the object the event is tied to. Nonevent macros go into a standard module and can be in the workbook in which they're meant to run or in a workbook called the Personal Macro Workbook if you want to be able to run them in any workbook.

Event macros

In VBA, objects have events. VBA "listens" for these events to happen and runs special event macros when it detects an event. For example, the Workbook object has an Open event. When VBA detects that the workbook has been opened, it looks for a procedure called Workbook_Open in the ThisWorkbook module; if it's there, it runs that macro.

Most of the event macros that you'll use, and most of the examples in this chapter, are workbook or worksheet events. Workbook event macros go in the ThisWorkbook module, and worksheet event macros go in the module for the sheet you want the event code to run on.

To install an event macro, follow these steps:

1. **Press Alt+F11 to open the Visual Basic Editor (VBE).**
2. **In the Project Explorer, find your project/workbook name and click the plus sign next to it to see all the objects.**
3. **Double-click ThisWorkbook.**
4. **Select the event from the right drop-down list.**
5. **Type or paste the code in the module.**

Personal Macro Workbook

There is a special workbook called the Personal Macro Workbook named PERSONAL.XLSB. If you record a macro, you can choose this workbook as the destination of the recorded macro. The workbook doesn't exist until you first record a macro into it. After that, the Personal Macro Workbook lives in a folder called XLSTART, and Excel loads it every time it starts.

The benefit of a workbook that opens every time Excel starts is that all the macros in that workbook are always available to you. If you have a macro that works on the active sheet or whatever range is currently selected, that's a good candidate for the Personal Macro Workbook.

To install a macro in the Personal Macro Workbook, follow these steps:

1. **Press Alt+F11 to open the VBE.**
2. **Right-click** PERSONAL.XLSB **in the Project Explorer.**
3. **Choose Insert➪Module.**
4. **Type or paste the code in the newly created module.**

REMEMBER: If you don't see personal.xlsb in the Project Explorer, record a macro to the Personal Macro Workbook, and Excel will create it for you.

Standard macros

All the other macro examples in this chapter are installed in a specific workbook in a standard module. If the macro is not an event macro and it's not a macro you want in the Personal Macro Workbook, then install it using the following steps:

1. **Press Alt+F11 to open the VBE.**
2. **Right-click the project/workbook name in the Project Explorer.**
3. **Choose Insert➪Module.**
4. **Type or paste the code in the newly created module.**

Creating a New Workbook from Scratch

You may sometimes want or need to create a new workbook in an automated way. For example, you may need to copy data from a table and paste it into a newly created workbook. The following macro copies a range of cells from the active sheet and pastes the data into a new workbook. This relatively intuitive macro is in the sample file named 8.4.1 Create a New Workbook from Scratch.xlsm at www.dummies.com/go/microsoft365excelaiofd:

```
Sub CopyToNewWorkbook()

    'Step 1: Copy the data.
        Sheets("Example 1").Range("B4:C15").Copy
```

```
    'Step 2: Create a new workbook.
        Workbooks.Add

    'Step 3: Paste the data.
        ActiveSheet.Paste Destination:=Range("A1")

    'Step 4: Turn off application alerts.
        Application.DisplayAlerts = False

    'Step 5: Save the newly created workbook.
        ActiveWorkbook.SaveAs Filename:="C:\MyNewBook.xlsx"

    'Step 6: Turn application alerts back on.
        Application.DisplayAlerts = True

End Sub
```

Here's what happens in the macro:

1. The Copy method of the Range object copies the data on the Example 1 sheet ranging from cells B4 to C15. The thing to note here is that you are specifying both the sheet and the range by name. This practice is best when you are working with multiple workbooks that have multiple worksheets. Because the workbook isn't explicitly named, the macro uses the active workbook. You may wish to name the workbook so the code always uses the same one.

2. The Add method of the Workbooks collection creates a new workbook. When you add a workbook, the new workbook immediately gains focus, becoming the active workbook. This is the same behavior you would see if you were to create a workbook manually (by choosing File➪New➪Blank Workbook).

3. The Paste method sends the data you copied to cell A1 of the new workbook. Pay attention to the fact that the code refers to the ActiveSheet object.

4. The DisplayAlerts method is set to False, effectively turning off Excel's warnings. You do this because in the next step of the code, you save the newly created workbook. You may run this macro multiple times, in which case Excel attempts to save the file multiple times.

    When you try save a workbook multiple times, Excel warns you that there is already a file out there with that name and then asks if you want to overwrite the previously existing file. Because your goal is to automate the creation of the new workbook, you want to suppress that warning.

5. This statement saves the file by using the SaveAs method of the Active Workbook object. Note that you're entering the full path of the save location, including the final filename.

6. This statement turns the applications alerts on again. If you don't do this, Excel continues to suppress all warnings for the life of the current session.

Saving a Workbook When a Particular Cell Is Changed

Sometimes, you may be working on data that is so sensitive that you need to save your workbook every time a particular cell or range of cells is changed. This macro allows you to define the range of cells that, when changed, forces the workbook to save. This macro is in the sample file named `8.4.2 Save a Workbook When a Particular Cell Is Changed.xlsm` at www.dummies.com/go/microsoft365excelaiofd.

In the example shown in Figure 4-1, you want the workbook to save when an edit is made to any of the cells in the range C5:C16.

	A	B	C	D
4				
5		January	26,263	
6		February	25,343	
7		March	52,149	
8		dsff	72,579	
9		May	38,635	
10		June	60,175	
11		July	32,305	
12		August	14,288	
13		September	71,787	
14		October	48,402	
15		November	71,850	
16		December	77,798	
17				

FIGURE 4-1: Changing any cell in range C5:C16 forces the workbook to save.

The secret to this code is the `Intersect` method. Because you don't want to save the worksheet when any old cell changes, you use the `Intersect` method to determine whether the *target cell* (the cell that changed) intersects with the range you've specified to be the trigger range (C5:C16 in this case).

The `Intersect` method returns one of two things: either a `Range` object that defines the intersection between the two given ranges, or nothing. So, in essence, you need to throw the target cell against the `Intersect` method to check for a value of `Nothing`. At that point, you can decide whether to save the workbook.

```
Private Sub Worksheet_Change(ByVal Target As Range)

    'Step 1: Does the changed range intersect?
        If Not Intersect(Target, Range("C5:C16")) Is Nothing Then
    'Step 2: If there is an intersection, save the workbook.
        ActiveWorkbook.Save
    'Step 3: Close out the If statement.
        End If

End Sub
```

Here's the lowdown on what happens in the macro:

1. This statement checks to see whether the *target cell* (the cell that has changed) is in the range specified by the `Intersect` method. If it's not in the range, `Intersect` returns `Nothing` (a special keyword in VBA meaning there is no object). If it's in the range, the `Is Nothing` comparison returns `False` and the `Not` operator changes `False` to `True`.

2. If there is an intersection, VBA employs the `Save` method of the active workbook, overwriting the previous version.

3. The `End If` statement closes the `If` block. Every time you use an `If...Then` block, you must close it with `End If`.

This is an event macro, so you must install it in the worksheet's module, as shown in Figure 4-2. (See the "Installing Macros" section at the beginning of this chapter for instructions.)

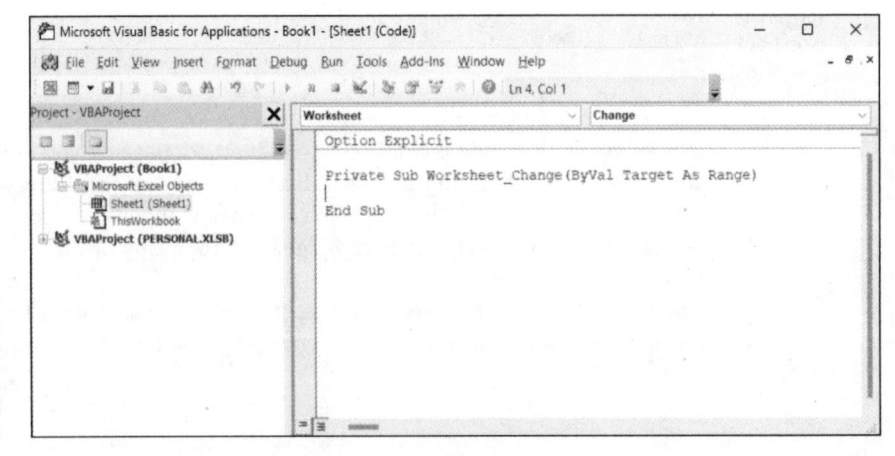

FIGURE 4-2:
Enter or paste your code in the Worksheet_Change event Code pane.

Saving a Workbook before Closing

This macro is an excellent way to protect users from inadvertently closing their file before saving. When implemented, this macro ensures that Excel automatically saves before closing the workbook. This macro is in the sample file named `8.4.3 Save a Workbook Before Closing.xlsm` at www.dummies.com/go/microsoft365excelaiofd.

REMEMBER Excel normally warns users who are attempting to close an unsaved workbook, giving them an option to save before closing. However, many users may blow past the warning and inadvertently click No, telling Excel to close without saving. With this macro, you're protecting against this by automatically saving before close.

This code is triggered by the workbook's `BeforeClose` event. When you try to close the workbook, this event fires, running the code within. The crux of the code is simple — it asks the user whether they really want to close the workbook (see Figure 4-3). The macro then evaluates whether the user clicked OK or Cancel.

FIGURE 4-3: A message box opens when you attempt to close the workbook.

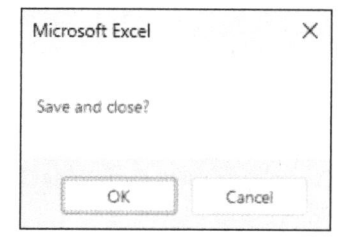

The evaluation is done with a `Select Case` statement. The `Select Case` statement is an alternative to the `If...Then...Else` statement, allowing you to perform condition checks in your macros. The basic construct of a `Select Case` statement is simple:

```
Select Case <some expression to check>
Case Is = <some value>
         <do something>
Case Is = <some other value>
         <do something else>
Case Is = <some third value>
         <do some third thing>
End Select
```

With a `Select Case` statement, you can perform many conditional checks. In this case, you're simply checking for OK or Cancel. Take a look at the code:

```
Private Sub Workbook_BeforeClose(Cancel As Boolean)

'Step 1: Activate the message box and start the check.
    Select Case MsgBox("Save and close?", vbOKCancel)

'Step 2: Cancel button pressed, cancel the close.
    Case Is = vbCancel
        Cancel = True

'Step 3: OK button pressed, save the workbook and close.
    Case Is = vbOK
        ActiveWorkbook.Save

'Step 4: Close your Select Case statement.
    End Select

End Sub
```

Here's what happens in this macro:

1. This statement displays the message box as the condition check for the `Select Case` statement. Here, the vbOKCancel argument displays an OK button and a Cancel button in the message box.

2. If the user clicks Cancel in the message box, the `Workbook_Close` event is canceled. This is done by passing `True` to the `Cancel` Boolean. (This effectively cancels the event's action, preventing the workbook from closing.)

3. If the user clicks the OK button in the message box, the workbook is saved. And because `Cancel` isn't set to `True`, Excel continues with the close.

4. Closes the `Select Case` statement. Every time you start a `Select Case`, you must close it with a corresponding `End Select`.

To install this macro, you need to copy and paste it into the `Workbook_BeforeClose` event Code pane, as shown in Figure 4-4 (see the "Installing Macros" section at the beginning of this chapter). Placing the macro there allows it to run every time you try to close the workbook.

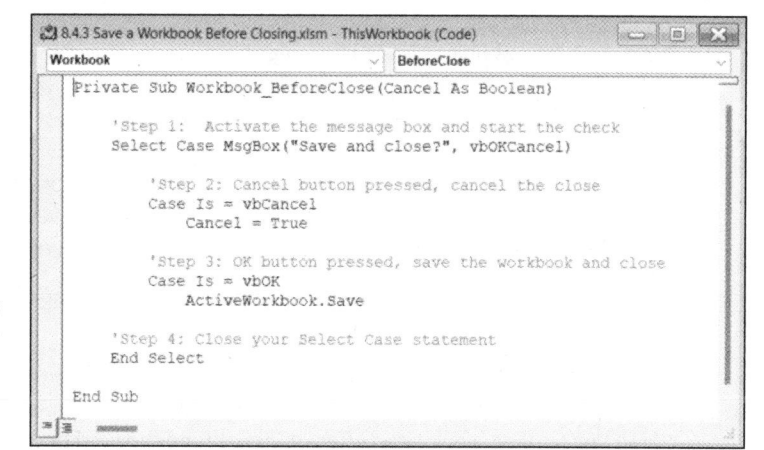

FIGURE 4-4:
Type or paste your code in the Workbook_ BeforeClose event Code pane.

```
Private Sub Workbook_BeforeClose(Cancel As Boolean)

    'Step 1:  Activate the message box and start the check
    Select Case MsgBox("Save and close?", vbOKCancel)

        'Step 2: Cancel button pressed, cancel the close
        Case Is = vbCancel
            Cancel = True

        'Step 3: OK button pressed, save the workbook and close
        Case Is = vbOK
            ActiveWorkbook.Save

    'Step 4: Close your Select Case statement
    End Select

End Sub
```

Protecting a Worksheet on Workbook Close

Sometimes you need to send your workbook into the world with specific worksheets protected. If you find that you're constantly protecting and unprotecting sheets before distributing your workbooks, this macro can help you. This macro is in the sample file named 8.4.4 Protect an Existing Workbook on Close.xlsm at www.dummies.com/go/microsoft365excelaiofd.

This code is triggered by the workbook's BeforeClose event. When you try to close the workbook, this event fires, running the code within. The macro automatically protects the specified sheet with the given password and then saves the workbook.

```
Private Sub Workbook_BeforeClose(Cancel As Boolean)

'Step 1: Protect the sheet with a password.
    Sheets("Sheet1").Protect Password:="RED"

'Step 2: Save the workbook.
    ActiveWorkbook.Save

End Sub
```

CHAPTER 4 **Working with Workbooks** 737

The following list explains what happens in this macro:

1. This statement uses the Protect method of the Sheet1 object in the Sheets collection to protect the sheet you want — Sheet1, in this case — and provides the password argument, Password:=RED. This defines the password needed to remove the protection. This password argument is optional. If you omit it, the sheet is still protected, but you won't need a password to unprotect it.

   REMEMBER Excel passwords are case-sensitive, so pay attention to the capitalization you're using.

2. This statement uses the Save method of the ActiveWorkbook object to save the workbook. If you don't save the workbook, the sheet protection you just applied won't be in effect the next time the workbook is opened.

To implement this macro, you need to copy and paste it into the Workbook_BeforeClose event Code pane, as shown in Figure 4-5 (see "Installing Macros," earlier in this chapter) Placing the macro here allows it to run each time you try to close the workbook.

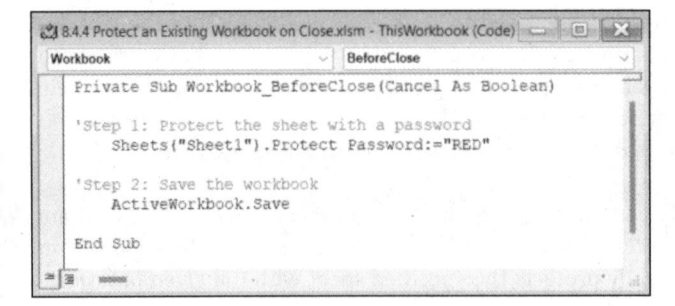

FIGURE 4-5: Type or paste your code in the Workbook_BeforeClose event Code pane.

TIP You can protect additional sheets by adding additional statements before the ActiveWorkbook.Save statement.

Unprotecting a Worksheet

If you've distributed workbooks with protected sheets, you likely get the workbooks back with the sheets still protected. You may want those sheets protected for your users, but you may need to unprotect the worksheets before continuing your portion of the work. If you find that you're continuously unprotecting worksheets, this macro may be just the ticket. You can find this macro in the sample file named 8.4.5 Unprotect an Existing Workbook.xlsm at www.dummies.com/go/microsoft365excelaiofd.

You can run this macro to automatically unprotect the specified sheet with the given password.

```
Sub UnprotectSheet()

'Step 1: Unprotect the sheet with a password.
    Sheets("Sheet1").Unprotect Password:="RED"

End Sub
```

The macro explicitly names the sheet you want to unprotect — Sheet1, in this case. Then it passes the password required to unprotect the sheet. Be aware that Excel passwords are case-sensitive, so pay attention to the exact password and capitalization that you're using.

To implement this macro, you can copy and paste it into a standard module, as shown in Figure 4-6 (see the "Installing Macros" section earlier in this chapter for details).

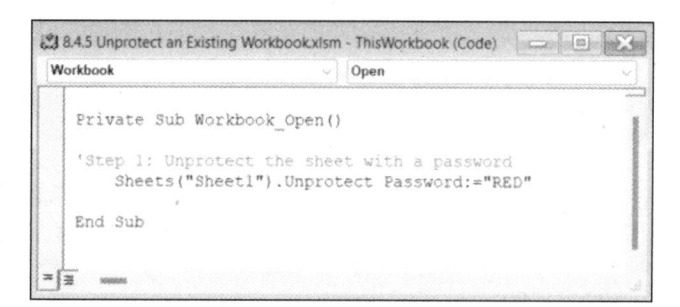

FIGURE 4-6: Type or paste your code in the Workbook_Open event Code pane.

You can unprotect additional sheets by adding additional statements.

Opening a Workbook to a Specific Tab

In some situations, you may want a specific worksheet to be visible whenever your workbook is opened. With this macro, if a user is working with your workbook, they can't go astray because the workbook starts on the exact worksheet it needs to. This macro is in the sample file named 8.4.6 Open a Workbook to a Specific Tab.xlsm at www.dummies.com/go/microsoft365excelaiofd.

In the example shown in Figure 4-7, you want the workbook to go immediately to the sheet called Start Here.

CHAPTER 4 **Working with Workbooks** 739

FIGURE 4-7:
You want your workbook to automatically open to the sheet called Start Here.

This macro uses the Open event of the Workbook object to start the workbook on the specified sheet when the workbook is opened.

```
Private Sub Workbook_Open()

'Step 1: Select the specified sheet.
    Sheets("Start Here").Select

End Sub
```

The macro explicitly names the sheet the workbook should jump to when it's opened.

To implement this macro, you need to copy and paste it into the Workbook_Open event Code pane, as shown in Figure 4-8. (See the earlier section, "Installing Macros" for more information.) Placing the macro here allows it to run each time the workbook opens.

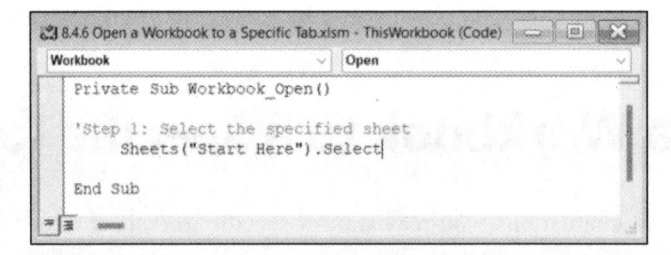

FIGURE 4-8:
Type or paste your code in the Workbook_Open event Code pane.

Opening a Specific Workbook Chosen by the User

This macro uses the `GetOpenFilename` method to open a dialog box, allowing you to browse for and open the Excel file of your choosing. This macro is in the sample file named `8.4.7 Open a Workbook Chosen by the User.xlsm` at www.dummies.com/go/microsoft365excelaiofd.

This macro opens the dialog box shown in Figure 4-9, allowing the user to browse for and open an Excel file.

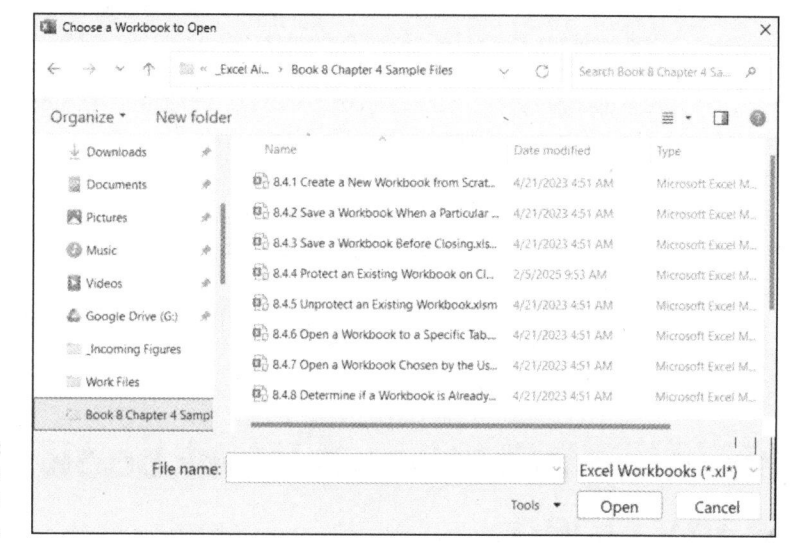

FIGURE 4-9: The macro opens the Open dialog box.

Here's how this macro works:

```
Sub OpenAWorkbook()
'Step 1: Define a variant variable.
    Dim FName As Variant

'Step 2: GetOpenFilename Method activates dialog box.
    FName = Application.GetOpenFilename( _
        FileFilter:="Excel Workbooks,*.xl*", _
        Title:="Choose a Workbook to Open", _
        MultiSelect:=False)
```

CHAPTER 4 **Working with Workbooks**   741

```
'Step 3: If a file was chosen, open it!
    If FName <> False Then
        Workbooks.Open Filename:=FName
    End If

End Sub
```

Here's what happens in this macro:

1. This statement declares a variant variable that holds the filename that the user chooses. FName is the name of the variable.

2. The GetOpenFilename method calls a dialog box that allows you to browse and select the necessary file. The GetOpenFilename method supports various parameters. The FileFilter parameter specifies the type of file you're looking for. The Title parameter changes the title that appears at the top of the dialog box. The MultiSelect parameter limits the selection to one file when False or allows multiple files when True.

3. If the user selects a file from the dialog box, the FName variable is filled with the name of the file they chose. If the user clicks Cancel, the variable is set to False. If it isn't False, the Open method of the Workbooks object opens the file.

To implement this macro, you can copy and paste it into a standard module (see the earlier section, "Installing Macros," for details).

Determining Whether a Workbook Is Already Open

The previous macro automatically opened a workbook based on the user's selection. As you think about automatically opening workbooks, you must consider what may happen if you attempt to open a book that is already open. In the non-VBA world, Excel tries to open the file again, with the message shown in Figure 4-10 warning that Excel can't have two workbooks open with the same name. You can protect against such an occurrence by checking whether a given file is already open before trying to open it again. This macro is in the sample file named 8.4.8 Determine if a Workbook is Already Open.xlsm at www.dummies.com/go/microsoft365excelaiofd.

FIGURE 4-10:
You can avoid this annoying message box when opening a workbook that is already open.

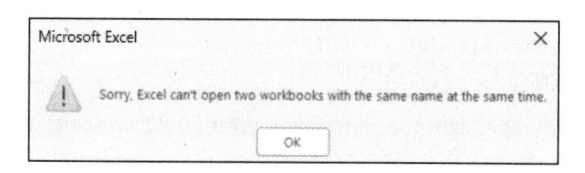

The first thing to notice about this macro is that it's a function, not a Sub procedure. With a function, you can pass a value to the procedure that calls the function. In this case, the function passes either True or False, depending on whether the workbook is open.

The gist of this code is simple: You're testing a given filename to see whether it can be assigned to an object variable. Only opened workbooks can be assigned to an object variable. When you try to assign a closed workbook to the variable, an error occurs.

So, if the given workbook can be assigned, the workbook is open; if an error occurs, the workbook is closed.

```
Function FileIsOpen(TargetWorkbook As String) As Boolean

'Step 1: Declare variables.
    Dim TestBook As Workbook

'Step 2: Tell Excel to resume on error.
    On Error Resume Next

'Step 3: Try to assign the target workbook to TestBook.
    Set TestBook = Workbooks(TargetWorkbook)

'Step 4: If no error occurred then workbook is already open.
    If Err.Number = 0 Then
        FileIsOpen = True
    Else
        FileIsOpen = False
    End If

End Function
```

The following list explains what happens in this macro:

1. This statement declares a Workbook variable to hold the open workbook if it exists. TestBook is the name of the variable.

2. This statement tells Excel what to do if an error occurs when running this code. In the event of an error, the error is ignored and the macro continues running

CHAPTER 4 **Working with Workbooks** 743

the rest of the code. Without this line, the code would simply stop when an error occurs.

3. This statement assigns the given workbook to the TestBook variable. The workbook you're trying to assign is itself a string variable called TargetWorkbook. TargetWorkbook is passed to the function in the function declarations (see the first line of the code). This structure eliminates the need to hard-code a workbook name, allowing you to pass it as a variable instead.

4. If no workbooks are open with that name, an error occurs. Excel ignores the error because of the statement in Step 2, but it does keep track of the fact that an error occurred, even if it was ignored. The Err object has a Number property that holds the error number. If it's zero, there was no error, so a workbook with that name was open. If it's anything except zero, assigning the workbook to the variable failed. The function's name is set to True or False depending on the error number.

The following macro demonstrates how to implement this function. Here, you're using the same macro you saw in the previous section, "Opening a Specific Workbook Chosen by the User," but this time, you're calling the new FileIsOpenTest function to make sure the user can't open an already opened file.

```
Sub Macro1()

'Step 1: Define a string variable.
    Dim FName As Variant
    Dim FNFileOnly As String

'Step 2: GetOpenFilename method activates dialog box.
    FName = Application.GetOpenFilename( _
        FileFilter:="Excel Workbooks,*.xl*", _
        Title:="Choose a Workbook to Open", _
        MultiSelect:=False)

'Step 3: Open the chosen file if not already opened.
    If FName <> False Then
        FNFileOnly = Dir(FName)
        If FileIsOpen(FNFileOnly) = True Then
            Workbooks(FNFileOnly).Activate
        Else
            Workbooks.Open Filename:=FName
        End If
    End If

End Sub
```

This macro uses the `GetOpenFilename` method to allow the user to browse for a file. If the user clicks Cancel, the `If` statement that starts Step 3 skips over the rest of the statements. If the user selects a file, the `Dir` function is used to get only the filename and not the path. Then the function is called to determine whether the file is open. If it is, the workbook stays closed. If not, the workbook opens.

To implement this macro, you can copy and paste both pieces of code into a standard module (see "Installing Macros," earlier in this chapter).

Determining Whether a Workbook Exists in a Directory

You may have a process that manipulates a file somewhere on your PC. For example, you may need to open an existing workbook to add new data to it on a daily basis. In these cases, you may need to test to see whether the file you need to manipulate actually exists. This macro allows you to pass a file path to evaluate whether the file is there. This macro is in the sample file named `8.4.9 Determine if a Workbook Exists in a Directory.xlsm` at www.dummies.com/go/microsoft365excelaiofd.

The first thing to notice about this macro is that it is a function, not a Sub procedure. Making this macro a function enables you to return `True` or `False` to the procedure that calls it.

The preceding example used the `Dir` function to strip away the path and leave only the filename. That was possible because you could be sure the file exists — the user just selected it. You can also use `Dir` to determine whether the file exists:

```
Function FileExists(FPath As String) As Boolean

'Step 1: Declare your variables.
    Dim FName As String

'Step 2: Use the Dir function to get the filename.
    FName = Dir(FPath)

'Step 3: If file exists, return True else False.
    If Len(FName) <> 0 Then
        FileExists = True
```

```
        Else
            FileExists = False
        End If

End Function
```

Here's what happens in this macro:

1. This statement declares a string variable to hold the filename that returned from the Dir function. FName is the name of the string variable.

2. This statement attempts to set the FName variable. Passes the FPath variable to the Dir function. This FPath variable is passed via the function declarations (see the first line of the code). This structure prevents you from having to hard-code a file path and pass it as a variable instead.

3. If the file exists, FName is the name of the file without the path. If it doesn't exist, FName is a zero-length string. Check the length of the string with the Len function to determine whether Dir found the file.

The following macro demonstrates how to use this function:

```
Sub Macro1()

    If FileExists("C:\Temp\MyNewBook.xlsx") = True Then
        MsgBox "File exists."
    Else
        MsgBox "File does not exist."
    End If

End Sub
```

To implement this macro, you can copy and paste both pieces of code into a standard module (see "Installing Macros," earlier in this chapter).

Closing All Workbooks at Once

One of the more annoying things in Excel occurs when you try to close many workbooks at once. For each open workbook, you need to reference the workbook, close it, and confirm you want to save changes. There is no easy way to close multiple workbooks at once. This little macro takes care of that annoyance. This macro is in the sample file named 8.4.10 Close All Workbooks at Once.xlsm at www.dummies.com/go/microsoft365excelaiofd.

This macro uses the Workbooks collection to loop through all the opened workbooks. As the macro loops through each workbook, it saves and closes them.

```
Sub Macro1()

'Step 1: Declare your variables.
    Dim wb As Workbook

'Step 2: Loop through workbooks, save, and close.
    For Each wb In Workbooks
        wb.Close SaveChanges:=True
    Next wb

End Sub
```

Here's what happens in this macro:

1. This statement declares a Workbook object variable. This allows you to enumerate through all the open workbooks, capturing their names as you go.

2. For Each loops through the open workbooks, saving and closing them. If you don't want to save them, change the SaveChanges argument from True to False.

The best place to store this macro is in your Personal Macro Workbook (see "Installing Macros," earlier in this chapter). This way, the macro is always available to you. The Personal Macro Workbook is loaded whenever you start Excel. In the VBE Project Explorer, it's named PERSONAL.XLSB.

Printing All Workbooks in a Directory

If you need to print from multiple workbooks in a directory, you can use this macro. This macro is in the sample file named 8.4.11 Print all Workbooks in a Directory.xlsm at www.dummies.com/go/microsoft365excelaiofd.

This code uses the `Dir` function to iterate through all the .xlsx files in a given directory, capturing each filename. Then you open each file, print it, and close the file.

```
Sub Macro1()

'Step 1: Declare your variables.
    Dim MyFiles As String

'Step 2: Specify a target directory.
    MyFiles = Dir("C:\Temp\*.xlsx")
    Do While Len(MyFiles) > 0

'Step 3: Open Workbooks one by one.
    Workbooks.Open "C:\Temp\" & MyFiles
    ActiveWorkbook.Sheets("Sheet1").PrintOut Copies:=1
    ActiveWorkbook.Close SaveChanges:=False

'Step 4: Next file in the directory.
    MyFiles = Dir

Loop

End Sub
```

The following list explains what happens in this macro:

1. This statement declares the `MyFiles` string variable that captures each filename in the enumeration.

2. The `Dir` function specifies the directory and file type you're looking for. Note that the code here is looking for *.xlsx. The asterisk means that any number of characters can be in the filename as long as the last five are .xlsx. You can use the ? wildcard to specify any single character. For example, Dir(C:\Temp\Budget2025??.xlsx) would find Budget202501.xlsx but not Budget 202406.xlsx or Budget2025Jan.xlsx.

3. This statement opens the file and prints one copy of the first sheet. You may want to change which sheet prints. You can also change the number of copies to print. Because `Dir` returns only the filename, you have to repeat the path you used from the first time you called `Dir` in Step 2.

4. When you call `Dir` with no arguments, it looks for the next file in the directory using the file mask you specified the last time you used `Dir`. In this case, it's looking for the next file ending in .xlsx. If there are no more files, `Dir` returns an empty string and the `Do While` statement exits the loop.

To implement this macro, you can copy and paste it into a standard module (see "Installing Macros," earlier in this chapter).

Preventing the Workbook from Closing until a Cell Is Populated

Sometimes you don't want a user closing a workbook without entering a specific piece of data. In these situations, it would be useful to deny the user the ability to close the workbook until the target cell is filled in (see Figure 4-11). This scenario is where this macro comes in. This macro is in the sample file named 8.4.12 Prevent the Workbook from Closing until a Cell Is Populated.xlsm at www.dummies.com/go/microsoft365excelaiofd.

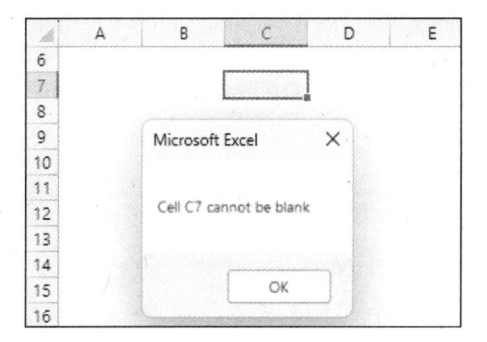

FIGURE 4-11: You can prevent your workbook from closing until a specific cell is populated.

This code is triggered by the workbook's BeforeClose event. When you try to close the workbook, this event fires, running the code within. This macro checks to see whether the target cell (cell C7, in this case) is empty. If it's empty, the close process is cancelled. If C7 is not empty, the workbook saves and closes.

```
Private Sub Workbook_BeforeClose(Cancel As Boolean)

'Step 1: Check to see if Cell C7 is blank.
    If IsEmpty(Sheets("Sheet1").Range("C7").Value) Then

'Step 2: Blank: Cancel the close and tell the user.
    Cancel = True
    MsgBox "Cell C7 cannot be blank"
```

CHAPTER 4 **Working with Workbooks** 749

```
'Step 3: Not blank; save and close.
    Else
        ActiveWorkbook.Close SaveChanges:=True
    End If

End Sub
```

Here's what happens in this macro:

1. This statement checks to see whether C7 is blank. The `IsEmpty` function returns `True` if the cell is blank.

2. If the cell is blank, the `Cancel` variable is set to `True` so Excel doesn't continue with the event's normal action (closing the workbook). Then a message box notifies the user of their stupidity (well, it's not quite that harsh).

3. If cell C7 is not blank, the workbook saves and closes.

To implement this macro, you need to copy and paste it into the `Workbook_BeforeClose` event Code pane, as shown in Figure 4-12 (see the earlier section, "Installing Macros"). Placing the macro here allows it to run every time you try to close the workbook.

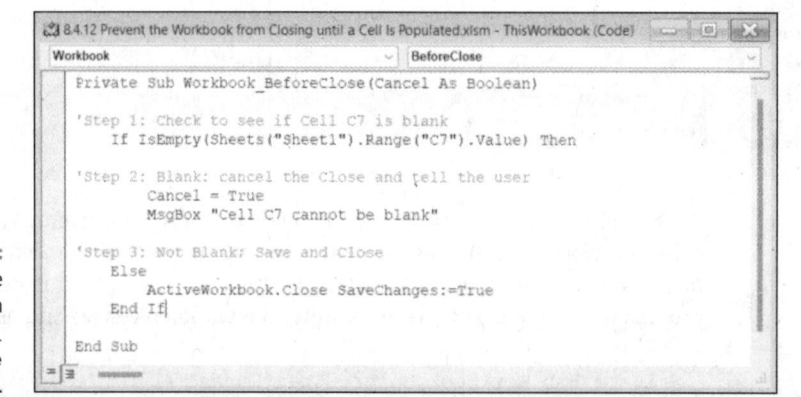

FIGURE 4-12: Type or paste your code in the Workbook_BeforeClose event Code pane.

Creating a Backup of the Current Workbook with Today's Date

Backing up your work is important. Now you can have a macro do it for you. This simple macro saves your workbook to a new file with today's date as part of the name. This macro is in the sample file named `8.4.13 Create a Backup` of the Current Workbook with Today's Date.xlsm at www.dummies.com/go/microsoft365excelaiofd.

The trick to this macro is piecing together the new filename, which has three pieces: the path, the original filename, and today's date.

The path is captured by using the Path property of the ThisWorkbook object. Use the Name property of ThisWorkbook to get the name. Today's date is provided by the Date function.

You're formatting the date: Format(Date, "yyyy-mm-dd"). This is because by default, the Date function returns mm/dd/yyyy. You need to use hyphens rather than forward slashes because the forward slashes would cause the file save to fail. (Windows doesn't allow forward slashes in filenames.) You also want to have the year first so your files sort properly.

The last piece of the new filename is the original filename. You use the Name property of the ThisWorkbook object to capture that:

```
Sub CreateBackup()

'Step 1: Save workbook with new filename.
    ThisWorkbook.SaveCopyAs _
        Filename:=ThisWorkbook.Path & "\" & _
        Format(Date, "yyyy-mm-dd") & Space(1) & _
        ThisWorkbook.Name

End Sub
```

In the one and only step, the macro builds a new filename and uses the SaveCopyAs method to save the file.

To implement this macro, you can copy and paste it into a standard module (see "Installing Macros," earlier in this chapter, for more information).

Index

Symbols
- (hyphen) operator, 32
' (single quote) operator, 31
, (comma) operator, 33
/ (forward slash) operator, 32
: (colon) operator
  navigating worksheets, 34
  for ranges, 33
+ (plus sign) operator, 32
= (equal sign) operator, 31, 35
! (exclamation point) operator, 34
(pound sign), 302
% (percent) operator, 32
% Difference From analysis, 416
% of Column Total percentage calculation, 419
% of Grand Total percentage calculation, 419
% of Parent Column Total percentage calculation, 419
% of Parent Row Total percentage calculation, 419
% of Parent Total percentage calculation, 419
% Of percentage calculation, 419
% of Row Total percentage calculation, 419
& (ampersand) operator, 33
* (asterisk) operator, 32, 313–314, 613–614, 617
? (question mark) wildcard, 313–314, 617
@ (at sign) operator, 33, 607
[ ] (square brackets) operator, 35
~ (tilde) wildcard, 617
< (less than) operator, 32, 268, 427
> (greater than) operator
  COUNTIF function, 158
  SUMIF function, 268

Numbers
24-hour time, 287

A
Above Average rule, conditional formatting, 325, 639
ABS function, 256
absolute references
  absolute addressing, 147–148
  applying, 40–41
  recording macros with, 686–689
absolute value, 256
accelerated depreciation schedule, 231–233
accessibility, enhancing, 68–69
Accessibility Assistant
  defined, 14
  launching, 68
Accessibility Checker, 14, 53
Accounting format, Format Cells dialog box, 56
Activate command, Manage Relationships dialog box, 505
Activate dialog box, 13
active windows, 124
ActiveX controls, 696
Add Scenario dialog box, 353
addition calculations
  dates and times, 46–47
  overview, 39
  PEMDAS sequence, 35, 150, 193
address
  cell, 137–138
  ranges, 139
AGGREGATE function, 92–94
  Array form, 94
  LARGE operation, 92
  MEDIAN operation, 92
  MODE.SNGL operation, 92
  PERCENTILE.EXC operation, 93
  PERCENTILE.INC operation, 93
  QUARTILE.EXC operation, 93

AGGREGATE function *(continued)*
  QUARTILE.INC operation, 93
  Reference form, 93
  SMALL operation, 93
AI (artificial intelligence), 380
All Charts tab, Insert Chart dialog box, 382
alt text, 68–69
ampersand (&) operator, 33
Analyze tab, PivotTable, 397
  adding subtotals, 426
  editing custom calculations, 433–434
  filtering data, 410
  grouping data, 405–406
  overview, 11
  refreshing data, 401–402
  summary calculations, 415, 417, 420–424
analyzing data
  conditional formatting
    based on formulas, 331–332
    cell values, 326–329
    color scales, 327–328
    creating custom rules, 329–330
    data bars, 326–327
    editing rules, 332–334
    finding duplicate values, 323–324
    icon sets, 328–329
    removing rules, 334–335
    setting criteria, 322–323
    top/bottom rules, 325–326
  consolidating data from multiple worksheets
    by category, 340–341
    by position, 339–340
  data models, 321
  data tables
    one-input, 344–346
    recalculating workbooks and, 349
    two-input, 346–348
  future value calculation, 349–351
  Goal Seek tool, 349–351
  grouping related data, 337–338
  overview, 320–321
  raw data, 320

scenarios
  applying, 354
  creating, 352–354
  deleting, 354–355
  editing, 354–355
Solver
  adding constraints, 361–363
  advantages, 356
  finding optimal result, 359–361
  loading add-in, 358–359
  saving solution as scenario, 364
  when to use, 356–358
  workings, 356
summarizing data with subtotals, 335–336
what-if analysis, 321
Answer report, Solver Results dialog box, 361
Aptos Narrow font, 69
arguments, function
  AGGREGATE function, 93–94
  `array` argument, 51, 94
  `Array` argument, 608–610
  AVERAGE function, 48
  AVERAGEIF function, 50
  AVERAGEIFS function, 50
  CHOOSE function, 597
  DB function, 235
  DDB function, 233
  defined, 18–19, 161
  DROP function, 184
  EXPAND function, 183
  Function Arguments dialog box, 155–156, 165–167, 172
  FV function, 226–227
  HLOOKUP function, 592
  IPMT function, 217
  IRR function, 237
  LARGE function, 51
  NPER function, 220
  overview, 153–154, 166
  PPMT function, 219
  PV function, 226
  RANDBETWEEN function, 260

RATE function, 224
ROUND function, 246
SEQUENCE function, 261
SLN function, 230
SMALL function, 51
SUBSTITUTE function, 306
SUBTOTAL function, 90, 264-265
SUM function, 19, 44
SYD function, 232
TAKE function, 185
TEXTJOIN function, 298
TRUNC function, 254
using RefEdit to enter, 156
arithmetic operators, 32, 46
Arrange All dialog box, 21
array argument
  Array form, 51
  SMALL or LARGE functions, 94
Array argument
  FILTER function, 611
  SORT function, 608
  SORTBY function, 609
  UNIQUE function, 610
arrays
  changing shape of, 183-186
  defined, 177
  dynamic arrays
    FILTER function, 611-614
    functions, 607-617
    overview, 602-604
    referencing spill ranges, 606-607
    software compatibility, 604
    SORT function, 608
    SORTBY function, 608-610
    spill ranges, 604-605
    UNIQUE function, 610-611
    XLOOKUP function, 614-617
  in formulas, 179-183
  functions returning, 186-190
  overview, 178-179
artificial intelligence (AI), 380
ascending sorts, 80

asterisk (*) operator, 32, 313-314, 613-614, 617
at sign (@) operator, 33, 607
auditing formulas, 107, 136, 200-202
Auto Data Tips option, VBE Editor tab, 711
Auto Indent option, VBE Editor tab, 711
Auto List Members option, VBE Editor tab, 711
Auto Quick Info option, VBE Editor tab, 711
Auto Syntax Check option, VBE Editor tab, 710
AutoCalculate Functions option, Status Bar, 14
Auto-Detect command, Manage Relationships dialog box, 505
Autofill
  date series, 43
  formulas, 42-43
  number series, 43
  text patterns, 43
AutoFilter setting, 12, 14
AutoFilter Status option, 13
AutoSum feature, 19, 44, 163, 245-246
AVERAGE calculation, SUBTOTAL function, 90
Average calculation, Value Field Settings dialog box, 414
AVERAGE function
  arguments, 48
  MAX function and, 159
  using in formulas, 152-153
  using with arrays, 183
average_range argument, AVERAGEIF function, 50
averages
  conditional, 49-50
  weighted, 48-49
Azure databases, 551

B

backups, workbook, 750-751
Banded Columns option, Table Design tab, 102
base field, 421
Below Average rule, conditional formatting, 325, 639
Between rule, conditional formatting, 322, 637
Blanks option, Go To Special dialog box, 119

Index   755

Bold command, Home tab, 54
Boolean variables, 719
borders
  active cells, 137
  de-emphasizing, 570, 621–623
  removing from picture, 658
  text boxes, 66
Borders command, Home tab, 54
Bottom 10 Items rule, conditional formatting, 325, 639
Bottom 10% rule, conditional formatting, 325, 639
Break All option, Workbook Links pane, 196
Break Links option, Workbook Links pane, 197
break-even analysis, 357, 361
Breaks command, Page Layout tab, 75
broken links, 196–197
bullet graphs
  adding data to, 671–672
  creating, 668–671
  formatting
    horizontal bullet graphs, 674–675
    qualitative bands, 673
By Changing Variable Cells box, Solver Parameters dialog box, 359–360
By_Array argument, SORTBY function, 609–610
By_col argument
  SORT function, 608
  UNIQUE function, 610–611

C

caches, Power Query, 553–554
CALCULATE function, 527
Calculate Status option, Status Bar, 13–14
calculated columns
  adding to table, 105–106
  creating, 514–515
  formatting, 516
  hiding, 517–518
  referencing in other calculations, 516–517
  unhiding, 518
Calculated Field feature, 430–431
Calculated Item feature, 431–433

calculated measures
  creating, 526–529
  defined, 514
  editing and deleting, 529
Calculation group, Formulas tab, 136
Camera tool
  enhancing dashboard with, 658–659
  finding, 656
  using, 656–658
capital assets, 228
Caps Lock indicator, Status Bar, 15
Cascade view, 21
CASE function, 309–310
cash flows, 210
category axis, PivotCharts, 437
category items, PivotCharts, 437
CEILING function, 248–251
Cell Mode indicator, Status Bar, 13
cells
  active, 137
  active cells, 137
  analyzing cell values
    with color scales, 327–328
    with data bars, 326–327
    with icon sets, 328–329
  changing cells
    applying scenarios, 354
    creating scenarios, 352–353
    defined, 352
    editing scenarios, 354–355
    objective cell formula, 357
    saving Solver solution as scenario, 364
  conditional highlighting, 322–323
  constraint cells, 357
  entering formulas and functions in, 174–175
  Format Cells dialog box
    accessing, 142–143
    currency, 299
    custom number formats, 57–59
    numbers, 55–57
  Highlight Cells Rules, 636–638
  highlighting based on formulas, 331–332

highlighting top or bottom values in range, 325–326
marquee, 147
merging and centering
  centering across selection, 64
  merging across columns, 63
objective cells, 356, 733–734
overview, 137–138
references
  absolute, 40–41
  mixed, 40
  relative, 40
styles
  applying and identifying, 61
  creating custom styles, 60–61
  modifying predefined styles, 60
  transferring between workbooks, 61–62
target cells, 733–734
Center Across Selection feature, 64
Change Chart Type dialog box, 669–670, 676–677
Change Constraint dialog box, 364
Change Source option, Workbook Links pane, 197
changing cells
  applying scenarios, 354
  creating scenarios, 352–353
  defined, 352
  editing scenarios, 354–355
  objective cell formula, 357
  saving Solver solution as scenario, 364
chart categories, PivotCharts, 436
chart data series, PivotCharts, 436
Chart Design tab
  Chart Elements menu, 384
  Chart Filters option, 385
  Chart Styles option, 385
chart sheets, 387
chart values, PivotCharts, 436
charts
  area charts, 382
  axes, 384
  axis titles, 384
  bar charts, 382
  bubble charts, 383
  chart title, 384
  Clustered Columns chart, 384
  column charts, 382
  combo charts, 383
  customizing, 384–385
  data labels, 385
  data tables, 385
  deconstructing, 383–384
  doughnut charts, 382
  error bars, 385
  gridlines, 385
  hierarchy charts, 382
  inserting, 382–383
  legends, 385
  line charts, 382
  maintaining data, 385–386
  moving and resizing, 387–388
  overview, 379–380
  pie charts, 382
  PivotCharts
    adding data labels to, 447–448
    adding titles to, 449–451
    building from Excel range or table, 441–443
    category axis, 437
    category items, 437
    changing type of, 446–447
    chart data series, 436
    creating from PivotTable, 439–440
    data series axis, 437
    data series items, 437
    displaying data table with, 452–453
    dynamic, 436
    filtering, 436, 444–446
    limitations of, 438–439
    moving legend in, 451–452
    moving to another sheet, 443–444
    overview, 435–436
    pros and cons, 436–437
    report filter, 437–438
    sorting, 448–449

Index 757

charts *(continued)*
  value area, 437
  x-axis, 436
  y-axis, 436
Recommended Charts, 380–382
scatter charts, 383
statistic charts, 383
templates
  creating and applying, 389–390
  managing, 390
thermometer-style, 666–667
transferring formatting and elements, 388–389
trendlines, 385
up/down bars, 385
waterfall charts, 383
Cheat Sheet for book, 3
CHOOSE function
  applying formulas in data models, 597–598
  `Index_num` argument, 597
  overview, 595–596
  `Value` argument, 597
circular references, 194–195
circumference, calculating, 257
Clustered Columns chart, 384
coauthoring workbooks, 28–29
Code Colors option, VBE Editor Format tab, 712
Code pane, Visual Basic Editor
  defined, 703
  getting VBA code into module, 707–709
  resizing windows, 706–707
collaboration
  adding comments, 29–30
  coauthoring simultaneously, 28–29
  sharing static copies of workbooks, 27
collections, Worksheets, 717
colon (:) operator
  for navigating worksheets, 34
  for ranges, 33
colors
  analyzing cell values with color scales, 327–328
  Color Scales, 641
  in data table design, 620–621
  numbers, 632
Column area, PivotTables, 394
Column Differences option, Go To Special dialog box, 119
Column field header, PivotTables, 394
column-level actions, Power Query, 542–543
columns
  adjusting widths, 69–70
  calculated columns
    adding to table, 105–106
    creating, 514–515
    formatting, 516
    hiding, 517–518
    referencing in other calculations, 516–517
    unhiding, 518
  grouping, 72–73
  headers, 137
  hiding, 71
  unhiding, 71–72
comma (,) operator, 33
comments
  adding to workbooks, 29–30
  Notes vs., 30
common-separated values (CSV) files
  importing into Power Query, 546–548
  number formats, 56
comparison operators, 32, 268
component questions, 565
CONCATENATE function, 296–297
conditional averages, 49–50
Conditional Formats option, Go To Special dialog box, 120
conditional formatting
  Above Average rule, 325, 639
  adding custom formatting rules manually, 642–646
  analyzing cell values
    with color scales, 327–328
    with data bars, 326–327
    with icon sets, 328–329
  based on formulas, 331–332

758 Microsoft 365 Excel All-in-One For Dummies

Below Average rule, 325, 639
Bottom 10 Items rule, 325, 639
Bottom 10% rule, 325, 639
Color Scales, 641
custom rules
  creating, 329–332
  editing, 332–334
  removing, 334–335
data bars, 640–641
A Date Occurring rule, 322, 637
Duplicate Values rule, 322–324, 637
Equal To rule, 322, 637
finding duplicate values, 323–324
Greater Than rule, 322–323, 637
Highlight Cells Rules, 636–638
icon sets, 642, 650–652
Less Than rule, 322, 637
removing rules, 334–335
Between rule, 322, 637
setting criteria, 322–323
showing data bars and icons outside cells, 648–650
showing only one icon, 646–648
Text That Contains rule, 322, 637
Top 10 Items rule, 325, 639
Top 10% rule, 325, 639
top/bottom rules, 325–326, 638–640
Conditional Formatting Rules Manager dialog box, 333–334, 646–647
consolidating data
  by category, 340–341
  by position, 339–340
Constants option, Go To Special dialog box, 119
constraint cells, 357
containers, 659–660
Copy link option, Workbook Links pane, 197
COUNT calculation, SUBTOTAL function, 90
Count calculation, Value Field Settings dialog box, 414
Count Numbers calculation, Value Field Settings dialog box, 414
COUNTA calculation, SUBTOTAL function, 90
COUNTA function, 606

COUNTIF function, 20, 158
  DAY function and, 277
  HOUR function and, 288
Create Links to Source Data check box, Consolidate dialog box, 340
Create Relationship dialog box, 503
Create Rule by Hand tab, workbooks, 643–644
`criteria` argument
  AVERAGEIF function, 50
  database functions, 366
CSV (common-separated values) files
  importing into Power Query, 546–548
  number formats, 56
currency
  format, 38
  formatting, 210–212
  separators, 212–213
Currency format, Format Cells dialog box, 56
Current Array option, Go To Special dialog box, 119
Current Date command, Header & Footer tab, 77
Current Region option, Go To Special dialog box, 119
Current Time command, Header & Footer tab, 77
custom calculations, PivotTables
  calculated field, 427
  deleting, 434
  editing, 433–434
  field references, 429
  formulas for, 427
  limitations, 428–429
  operands, 427
  operators, 427
  types, 428
Custom Lists dialog box, 84–85
Custom Views feature
  applying, 123–124
  creating custom views, 125–126
  defined, 12
  freezing, 111
  Quick Access Toolbar shortcut, 126–127
Customize Regional Options dialog box, 272–273

customizing
  charts, 384–385
  page layout, 124
  PivotTable reports
    applying numeric formats to data fields, 479
    changing PivotTable layout, 476–477
    changing summary calculations, 479–481
    customizing field names, 478–479
    hiding or showing items without data, 485–486
    showing and hiding data items, 483–485
    sorting PivotTables, 486–488
    suppressing subtotals, 481–483
  Quick Access Toolbar, 12
  Ribbon, 11
  Status Bar, 15
  Visual Basic Editor
    Docking tab, 714
    Editor Format tab, 712–713
    Editor tab, 710–712
    General tab, 713–714

D

dashboards. *See also* data modeling
  defined, 562–563
  design principles
    layout and placement, 571–572
    number formats, 572
    simplicity, 569–571
    titles and labels, 572–573
  enhancing with Camera tool, 658–659
  formatting, 570, 572
  reports defined, 562
  user requirements
    data sources, 566–567
    dimensions and filters, 567
    drill-down features, 568
    establishing audience and purpose, 564–565
    key performance indicators, 565–566
    refresh schedule, 568
data, defined, 320

data analysis
  conditional formatting
    based on formulas, 331–332
    cell values, 326–329
    color scales, 327–328
    creating custom rules, 329–330
    data bars, 326–327
    editing rules, 332–334
    finding duplicate values, 323–324
    icon sets, 328–329
    removing rules, 334–335
    setting criteria, 322–323
    top/bottom rules, 325–326
  consolidating data from multiple worksheets, 338–341
    by category, 340–341
    by position, 339–340
  data models, 321
  data tables
    one-input, 344–346
    recalculating workbooks and, 349
    two-input, 346–348
  future value calculation, 349–351
  Goal Seek tool, 349–351
  grouping related data, 337–338
  overview, 320–321
  raw data, 320
  scenarios
    applying, 354
    creating, 352–354
    deleting, 354–355
    editing, 354–355
  Solver
    adding constraints, 361–363
    advantages, 356
    finding optimal result, 359–361
    loading add-in, 358–359
    saving solution as scenario, 364
    when to use, 356–358
    workings, 356
  summarizing data with subtotals, 335–336
  what-if analysis, 321

data delivery formulas
  CHOOSE function
    applying in data models, 597–598
    overview, 595–597
  HLOOKUP function
    applying in data models, 592
    overview, 591–592
  SUMPRODUCT function
    applying in data models, 595
    filtering values, 594–595
    overview, 592–594
  VLOOKUP function
    applying in data models, 588–589
    data validation drop-down lists, 589–591
    overview, 587
data entry
  functions and, 18–20
  overview, 15–17
data labels
  charts
    adding to PivotCharts, 447–448
    defined, 386
  in dashboards, 572–573
  in data table design, 625–626
data modeling
  best practices
    limiting data amount, 582–584
    separating data, analysis, and presentation, 576–579
    structuring data, 579–582
    testing before building reporting components, 585–586
    using tabs, 584–585
  data delivery formulas
    CHOOSE function, 595–598
    data validation drop-down lists, 589–591
    HLOOKUP function, 591–592
    SUMPRODUCT function, 592–595
    VLOOKUP function, 586–589
  dynamic arrays
    FILTER function, 611–614
    functions, 607–617

    overview, 602–604
    referencing spill ranges, 606–607
    SORT function, 608
    SORTBY function, 608–610
    spill ranges, 604–605
    UNIQUE function, 610–611
    XLOOKUP function, 614–617
  Excel tables
    converting back to range, 601–602
    converting range to, 599–601
data models, 321
Data Preview Group, Power Query Editor, 556
data profiling
  options, 556–557
  overview, 555–556
  quick actions, 557–558
data ranges
  address, 139
  comparing to tables, 98
  converting Excel tables to, 601–602
  converting table to, 112
  converting to Excel tables, 599–601
  creating PivotCharts from, 441–443
  defined, 138
  determining workdays in range of dates, 283
  grouping related data, 337–338
  reference operators, 33–34
  removing conditional formatting from, 334
  SUM function and, 243–244
data series axis, PivotCharts, 437
data series items, PivotCharts, 437
Data Source Settings dialog box, 554
Data tab
  automatic subtotals, 335–336
  clearing filters, 89
  consolidating data, 340–341
  Filter feature, 88
  grouping related data, 337
  grouping rows and columns, 72–73
  importing data, 545–551
  managing queries and connections, 364, 506, 532, 537, 540–541

Data tab (continued)
  overview, 10
  reapplying filters, 90
  removing duplicates, 86–87
  scenarios and, 352–355
  Solver, 358–359, 362, 364
  sorting mixed data, 80–84
  Subtotal feature, 94–95, 111
  summarizing data with subtotals, 335
data tables. *See also* tables
  design principles
    borders, 621–623
    colors, 620–621
    labels and headers, 625–626
    number formatting, 624–625
  number formatting
    applying custom colors, 632
    basics, 627–629
    dates and times, 633–634
    in thousands and millions, 629–631
    zeroes, 631–632
  one-input, 344–346
  overview, 343–344, 619
  recalculating workbooks and, 349
  two-input, 346–348
data validation
  drop-down lists, 589–591
  Go To Special dialog box, 120
database functions
  calculating column's variance, 375–376
  column's values
    averaging, 371–372
    counting, 369–370
    determining maximum and minimum values, 372–373
    multiplying, 373–374
    summing, 368–369
  database argument, 366
  DAVERAGE function, 371
  DCOUNT function, 369–370
  DCOUNTA function, 369–370
  deriving column's standard deviation, 374–375
  DGET function, 367–368
  DMAX function, 372–373
  DMIN function, 372–373
  DPRODUCT function, 373–374
  DSTDEV function, 374–375
  DSTDEVP function, 374–375
  DSUM function, 368–369
  DVAR function, 376
  DVARP function, 376
  outliers, 372
  overview, 365–367
  retrieving single value from table, 367–368
database systems, importing into Power Query
  Azure databases, 551
  connection process walk-through, 552–553
  ODBC connections, 551
  OLAP database, 550
  other data systems, 551
  relational database, 550
datasets
  filtered, 91
  tabular, 581–582
DATE function, 274–275, 281
A Date Occurring rule, conditional formatting, 322, 637
Date section, Format Cells dialog box, 56
date series, 43
dates
  adding and subtracting, 46–47
  converting from text, 278–280
  DATE function, 274–275, 281
  formatting, 273–274, 633–634
  overview, 272–273
  splitting
    DAY function, 276–277
    MONTH function, 278
    YEAR function, 278
  TODAY function
    counting days from specific date, 281
    counting days to specific date, 280–281

WEEKDAY function, 281–282
workdays
  NETWORKDAYS function, 283–284
  WORKDAY function, 284–285
years, 272–273
DAVERAGE function, 371
DAX functions
  CALCULATE function, 527
  for calculated columns, 518–520
  enhancing calculated columns, 520–521
  nesting, 525–526
  referencing fields from other tables, 523–525
  RELATED function, 524–525
DAY function, 276–277
DB function, 235–236
DCOUNT function, 369–370
DCOUNTA function, 369–370
DDB function, 233
Deactivate command, Manage Relationships dialog box, 505
decimals
  INT function and, 253
  TRUNC function and, 254
Default to Full Module View option, VBE Editor tab, 712
Defined Names group, Formulas tab, 136
deleting
  calculated measures, 354–355
  custom calculations, 434
  scenarios, 354–355
  worksheets, 26
dependents, formula, 200–201
Dependents option, Go To Special dialog box, 119
depreciation
  accelerated schedule, 231–233
  depreciable cost, 229
  Double Declining Balance method, 233–234
  midyear schedule, 235–236
  returned value, 232
  straight-line, 230–231
descending sorts, 80
design principles

dashboards
  layout and placement, 571–572
  number formats, 572
  simplicity, 569–571
  titles and labels, 572–573
data tables
  borders, 621–623
  colors, 620–621
  labels and headers, 625–626
  number formatting, 624–625
Design tab
  managing existing relationships, 466
  overview, 11
  Table Design tab, 99–102, 105, 112, 461–462
DGET function, 367–368
diameter, calculating, 257
Difference From analysis, 416
difference summary calculations, 416–418
Dim statement, 710
dimensions, dashboard, 567
directional icon sets, 329
#DIV/0! error, 151
division calculations
  overview, 38–39
  PEMDAS sequence, 35, 150, 193
DMAX function, 372–373
DMIN function, 372–373
Docking tab, Visual Basic Editor, 714
DOLLAR function
  formatting currency, 299–300
  rounding feature, 300–301
Double Declining Balance depreciation method, 229, 233–234
double variables, 719
DPRODUCT function, 373–374
Drag-and-Drop Text Editing option, VBE Editor tab, 711
drill-down features, dashboard, 568
DROP function, 184
DSTDEV function, 374–375
DSTDEVP function, 374–375
DSUM function, 368–369

Index   **763**

duplicates
  Duplicate Values rule, 322–324, 637
  finding duplicate values, 323–324
  removing
    across multiple columns, 87
    from single column, 86–87
DVAR function, 376
DVARP function, 376
dynamic arrays
  basics, 602–604
  compatibility and, 604
  functions
    FILTER, 611–614
    SORT, 608
    SORTBY, 608–610
    UNIQUE, 610–611
    XLOOKUP, 614–617
  software compatibility, 604
  spilling and spill range
    defined, 603
    overview, 604–605
    referencing, 606–607
dynamic PivotCharts, 436

E

Edit command, Manage Relationships dialog box, 505
Edit in Formula Bar option, Error Checking dialog box, 205
Edit Points feature, 662
editing
  applying basic formatting, 17–18
  credentials for data source, 555
  custom rules, 332–334
  with functions, 18–20
  macros, 685–686
  PivotTables, 433–434, 529
  scenarios, 354–355
Editor Format tab, Visual Basic Editor, 712–713
  Code Colors option, 712
  Font option, 713
  Margin Indicator Bar option, 713
  Size option, 713
Editor tab, Visual Basic Editor
  Auto Data Tips option, 711
  Auto Indent option, 711
  Auto List Members option, 711
  Auto Quick Info option, 711
  Auto Syntax Check option, 710
  Default to Full Module View option, 712
  Procedure Separator option, 712
  Require Variable Declaration option, 710–711
effective interest rate, 222
empty strings, 308
Enable Iterative Calculation check box, Excel Options dialog box, 194–195
entering data
  functions and, 18–20
  overview, 15–17
equal sign (=) operator, 31, 35
Equal To rule, conditional formatting, 322, 637
ErrExit label, 725
Error Checking dialog box, 204–205
Error Checking feature, formulas, 198–200
error handlers
  On Error GoTo 0, 726–727
  On Error GoTo SomeLabel, 725–726
  On Error Resume Next, 726
Error statements, 725
Error Trapping setting, Options dialog box, 714
errors
  #SPILL! error, 605
  in formulas
    broken links, 196–197
    circular references, 194–195
    evaluating and checking in formulas, 204–205
    IFERROR function, 205–206
    ISERROR function, 205–206
    mismatched parentheses, 192–194
    overview, 149–151
  #VALUE! error, 313
ETL (Extract, Transform, and Load)
  defined, 531
  Power Query

    column-level actions, 542–543
    data profiling, 555–558
    data source settings, 553–555
    importing data from database systems, 550–553
    importing data from files, 545–550
    managing existing queries, 540–541
    overview, 531–532
    query steps, 538–539
    refreshing data, 539–540
    starting query, 532–537
    table actions, 544–545
  Power Query Editor
    adding file attributes, 550
    Close & Load command, 536
    Close & Load To command, 536
    column-level actions, 542–543
    Data Preview Group, 556
    Query Settings pane, 538
    table-level actions, 545
Evaluate Formula dialog box, 204
EVEN function, 248, 251–252
event macros, 730
event procedures
  workbooks
    overview, 723–724
    `Worksheet_BeforeClose` event, 724
    `Worksheet_BeforeSave` event, 724
    `Worksheet_Open` event, 724
    `Worksheet_SheetChange` event, 724
  worksheets
    overview, 721–722
    `Selection Change` event, 722
    `Worksheet_Activate` event, 723
    `Worksheet_BeforeDoubleClick` event, 723
    `Worksheet_BeforeRightClick` event, 723
    `Worksheet_Calculate` event, 723
    `Worksheet_Change` event, 722
    `Worksheet_Deactivate` event, 723
    `Worksheet_SelectionChange` event, 722
EXACT function, 310–312
`Exactly_once` argument, UNIQUE function, 611

Excel object model
  collections, 717
  methods, 718
  objects, 716
  overview, 715–716
  properties, 717–718
Excel Options dialog box
  Enable Iterative Calculation check box, 194–195
  Formula AutoComplete, 175
  installing bundled add-ins, 358–359
  Quick Access Toolbar tab, 12, 126, 136
exclamation point (!) operator, 34
Existing Connections dialog box, 507
Expand Formula Bar button, 8–9
EXPAND function, 183–184
exponents
  overview, 37–38
  PEMDAS sequence, 35, 150, 193
External Data Source dialog box, 506–507
Extract, Transform, and Load (ETL)
  defined, 531
  Power Query
    column-level actions, 542–543
    data profiling, 555–558
    data source settings, 553–555
    importing data from database systems, 550–553
    importing data from files, 545–550
    managing existing queries, 540–541
    overview, 531–532
    query steps, 538–539
    refreshing data, 539–540
    starting query, 532–537
    table actions, 544–545
  Power Query Editor
    adding file attributes, 550
    Close & Load command, 536
    Close & Load To command, 536
    column-level actions, 542–543
    Data Preview Group, 556
    Query Settings pane, 538
    table-level actions, 545

F

Few, Stephen, 569, 667
field argument, database functions, 366
file extensions
  charts, 389
  macro-enabled, 691
  types of, 132
File Name command, Header & Footer tab, 78
File Path command, Header & Footer tab, 77
File tab
  creating workbooks, 21
  opening workbooks, 21
  overview, 9
  saving workbooks, 20
Fill Color command, Home tab, 54
fill handle
  AutoFill and, 42–43
  copying formulas with, 148–149
  data analysis and, 47
filtering data
  AutoFilter setting, 12, 14
  AutoFilter Status option, 13
  Filter area, PivotTables, 394
  Filter Buttons option, Table Design tab, 102
  Filter feature, 88–90
  Filter fields, 488–490
  FILTER function, 611–614
  filtered datasets, 91
  filters
    applying, 124
    clearing, 89
    dashboard, 567
    reapplying, 90
  nonfiltered data, 92
  PivotCharts
    overview, 444–446
    report filter, 437–438
  PivotTables
    adding report filters, 474
    with report filter field, 407–408
    row or column items, 408–409
    with slicers, 410–411
    values, 409–410
  SUMPRODUCT function, 594–595
Find All option, Find and Replace dialog box, 115
FIND function, 312–313
Find Next option, Find and Replace dialog box, 115
Find What field, Find tab, 114
finding and replacing data within cells, 114–116
First Column option, Table Design tab, 102
flat files in data models, 581
FLOOR function, 248–251
folders, importing data from, 549–550
Font Color command, Home tab, 54
Font option, VBE Editor Format tab, 713
Font section, Home tab, 54
Font Size drop-down list, Home tab, 54
fonts
  readability of data, 69, 626
  setting default font style, 69–70
Footer command, Header & Footer tab, 77
footers, adding, 77–78
form controls, 694–696
Format All Cells Based on Their Values rule, 644
Format Cells dialog box
  curreny, 299
  formatting borders, 622–623
  formatting dates, 273
  formatting numbers, 627–629, 633
  formatting time, 286–287
  Number tab, 301
Format Only Cells That Contain rule, 644
Format Only Top or Bottom Ranked Values rule, 644
Format Only Values That Are Above or Below Average rule, 644
Format option, Find tab, 114–115
Format Slicer pane, 492–493
Format tab
  charts, 384, 451
  defined, 11
  Shape Format tab, 66, 388
  VBE Editor Format tab

Code Colors option, 712
Font option, 713
Margin Indicator Bar option, 713
Size option, 713
formatting
  adjusting row heights and column widths, 69–70
  borders, 622–623
  bullet graphs
    horizontal bullet graphs, 674–675
    qualitative bands, 673
  calculated columns, 516
  cells
    applying and identifying styles, 61
    centering, 64
    creating custom styles, 60–61
    merging across columns, 63
    modifying predefined styles, 60
    transferring between workbooks, 61–62
  commands, 54
  conditional formatting
    Above Average rule, 325, 639
    adding custom formatting rules manually, 642–646
    analyzing cell values, 326–329
    based on formulas, 331–332
    Below Average rule, 325, 639
    Bottom 10 Items rule, 325, 639
    Bottom 10% rule, 325, 639
    Color Scales, 327–328, 641
    creating custom rules, 329–332
    custom rules, 329–335
    data bars, 326–327, 640–641
    A Date Occurring rule, 322, 637
    Duplicate Values rule, 322–324, 637
    editing rules, 332–334
    Equal To rule, 322, 637
    finding duplicate values, 323–324
    Greater Than rule, 322–323, 637
    Highlight Cells Rules, 636–638
    highlighting cells that meet some criteria, 322–323
    highlighting top or bottom values in range, 325–326
    icon sets, 328–329, 642, 650–652
    Less Than rule, 322, 637
    removing rules, 334–335
    Between rule, 322, 637
    setting criteria, 322–323
    showing data bars and icons outside cells, 648–650
    showing only one icon, 646–648
    Text That Contains rule, 322, 637
    Top 10 Items rule, 325, 639
    Top 10% rule, 325, 639
    top/bottom rules, 325–326, 638–640
  currency, 210–212
  in dashboards, 570, 572
  date and time, 273–274, 633–634
  enhancing accessibility, 68–69
  Format Cells dialog box
    accessing, 142–143
    currency, 299
    custom number formats, 57–59
    numbers, 55–57
  grouping rows and columns, 72–73
  hiding and unhiding workbooks, 74
  hiding rows and columns, 71
  inserting images, 67–68
  numbers, 624
    applying custom colors to, 632
    basics, 627–629
    custom number formats, 57–59
    in dashboards, 572
    with Format Cells dialog box, 55–57
    in thousands and millions, 629–631
    zeroes, 631–632
  page setup
    adding headers, footers, and print titles, 77–78
    setting print ranges and page breaks, 76
  subtotals, 95–96
  tables
    establishing custom styles, 103–104
    manually, 102
    setting default styles, 104

Index   767

formatting *(continued)*
  text boxes, 65–67
  time, 286–287, 633–634
  unhiding rows and columns, 71–72
  wrapping text, 64–65
Formula Auditing, 107, 136, 200–202
Formula AutoComplete, 108, 175
Formula Bar
  entering formulas and functions in, 173–174
  Name Box, 138
  overview, 8
Formula Box, 138
formulas
  applying conditional formatting based on results of, 331–332
  arrays in, 179–183
  auditing, 107, 136, 200–202
  automatic subtotals, 335–336
  automating with Autofill, 42–43
  basic, 144
  constructing, 149–151
  copying with fill handle, 148–149
  copying with keyboard shortcuts, 41–42
  entering, 144–146
  in entering in cells, 174–175
  entering in Formula Bar, 173–174
  entering ranges into, 244
  Error Checking feature, 198–200
  errors
    broken links, 196–197
    circular references, 194–195
    evaluating and checking, 204–205
    IFERROR function, 205–206
    ISERROR function, 205–206
    mismatched parentheses, 192–194
    overview, 149–151
  errors while entering, 191–200
  functions in
    Function Arguments dialog box, 155–157
    inputs, 153–154
    Insert Function dialog box, 154–155
    nested functions, 158–160

highlighting cells based on, 331–332
implicit intersection, 607
overview, 143–144
PEMDAS sequence, 150
references, 146–148
self-expanding in tables, 109–110
at sign (@), 607
Watch Window, 203–204
Formulas option, Go To Special dialog box, 119
Formulas tab, 10, 135–136
forward slash (/) operator, 32
Fraction format, Format Cells dialog box, 56
Full Screen command, Quick Access toolbar, 12
Function Arguments dialog box
  editing functions, 172
  entering arguments, 155–156
  selecting function that takes no argument, 165–167
Function Library group, Formulas tab, 136
`function_num` argument
  Array form, 94
  Reference form, 93
`function_num` code, 90
functional math
  ABS function, 256
  PI function, 257
  POWER function, 261–263
  PRODUCT function, 263–264
  raising number to a power, 261–263
  random numbers
    RAND function, 258–260
    RANDBETWEEN function, 260–261
  rounding numbers
    CEILING function, 249–251
    EVEN function, 251–252
    FLOOR function, 249–251
    INT function, 253–254
    negative numbers, 250, 253–254
    ODD function, 251–252
    in one direction, 248–252
    ROUND function, 246–247
    ROUNDDOWN function, 249

ROUNDUP function, 248
TRUNC function, 254–255
SEQUENCE function, 261
SIGN function, 255
SUM function, 242–246
summing numbers
SUBTOTAL function, 264–266
SUMIF and SUMIFS functions, 268–270
SUMPRODUCT function, 266–267
functions
for data delivery
CHOOSE, 592–598
HLOOKUP, 591–592
SUMPRODUCT, 592–595
VLOOKUP, 586–591
database functions
calculating column's variance, 375–376
column's values, 368–374
database argument, 366
DAVERAGE function, 371
DCOUNT function, 369–370
DCOUNTA function, 369–370
deriving column's standard deviation, 374–375
DGET function, 367–368
DMAX function, 372–373
DMIN function, 372–373
DPRODUCT function, 373–374
DSTDEV function, 374–375
DSTDEVP function, 374–375
DSUM function, 368–369
DVAR function, 376
DVARP function, 376
outliers, 372
overview, 365–367
retrieving single value from table, 367–368
dates
DATE, 274–275
DATEVALUE, 278–280
DAY, 276–277
MONTH, 278
NETWORKDAYS, 283–284
TODAY, 280–281

WEEKDAY, 281–282
WORKDAY, 284–285
YEAR, 278
DAX functions
for calculated columns, 518–520
enhancing calculated columns, 520–521
nesting, 525–526
readability of data, 529
referencing fields from other tables, 523–525
in dynamic arrays
FILTER, 611–614
SORT, 608
SORTBY, 608–610
UNIQUE, 610–611
XLOOKUP, 614–617
editing with Function Arguments dialog box, 172
entering in cells, 174–175
entering in Formula Bar, 173–174
finding, 163–164
in formulas
entering arguments, 154–157
inputs, 153–154
nesting, 158–160
Insert Function dialog box
entering cells, ranges, named areas, and tables as function arguments, 168–171
entering functions, 164–172
finding correct function, 163–164
getting help in, 171–172
overview, 162–163
overview, 18–20
passive, 310–315
returning arrays, 186–190
statistical functions
AVERAGE, 48
conditional averages, 49–50
finding smallest and largest values, 51
weighted averages, 48–49
text
CONCATENATE, 296–297
DOLLAR, 299–301
EXACT, 310–312

Index   769

functions *(continued)*
    FIND, 312–313
    LEFT, 292–293
    LEN, 295–296
    MIDDLE, 293–295
    REPLACE, 304–306
    REPT, 303–304
    RIGHT, 293
    SEARCH, 313–315
    SUBSTITUTE, 307–308
    TEXT, 301–303
    TEXTJOIN, 298
    TEXTSPLIT, 295
    TRIM, 308–309
    time
        HOUR, 288–289
        MINUTE, 289
        NOW, 290
        SECOND, 290
future value calculation, 349–350
future value (Fv) argument
    IPMT function, 217
    Nper function, 220
    PMT function, 215
    PPMT function, 219
    PV function, 226
    RATE function, 224
FV function, 226–228

G

General format, Format Cells dialog box, 55
General tab, Visual Basic Editor, 713–714
Go To command, 101, 118
Go To dialog box, 71–72
Go To Special command, 118–120
Goal Seek tool, 349–351
gradient-fill data bars, 327
greater than (>) operator
    COUNTIF function, 158
    SUMIF function, 268
Greater Than rule, conditional formatting, 322–323, 637

GRG Nonlinear method, Solver, 360
grouping data
    grouping related data, 337–338
    rows and columns, 72–73
    worksheets, 27
guess argument, RATE function, 224

H

Header & Footer tab
    Current Date command, 77
    Current Time command, 77
    File Name command, 78
    File Path command, 77
    Footer command, 77
    Header command, 77
    overview, 11
    Page Number command, 77
    Picture command, 78
    Sheet Name command, 78
Header command, Header & Footer tab, 77
Header Row option, Table Design tab, 102
headers
    adding, 77–78
    column
        adding, 17
        labeling, 68
    in data table design, 625–626
Height command, Page Layout tab, 75
Help on This Error option, Error Checking dialog box, 205
Help system, 142–143
Help tab, 10
Hide/Show option, Navigation task pane, 117
hiding/unhiding
    rows and columns, 71, 124
    workbooks, 74
    worksheets, 26, 123–124
HLOOKUP function
    applying formulas in data models, 592
    basics, 591–592
Home tab

AutoSum feature, 163
  Font section, 54
  overview, 9
horizontal bullet graphs, 674–675
Horizontal view, 21
HOUR function, 288–289
HSTACK function, 186
hyperlink feature, workbooks, 698
hyphen (–) operator, 32

I

If_empty argument, FILTER function, 611–612
Ignore Error option, Error Checking dialog box, 205
images, inserting, 67–68
Immediate window, Visual Basic Editor, 703
implicit intersection, formulas, 607
Import Data dialog box, 510, 537
importing data
  from database systems
    Azure databases, 551
    connection process walk-through, 552–553
    ODBC connections, 551
    OLAP database, 550
    other data systems, 551
    relational database, 550
  from files
    CSV and text files, 546–548
    Excel workbooks, 545–546
    folders, 549–550
    PDF files, 548–549
Include argument, FILTER function, 611
Index summary calculation, 422–424
Index_num argument, CHOOSE function, 597
indicators icon sets, 329
indirect circular references, 194
Info tab, 132–133
infographic widgets, 661–662
initial investment argument, FV function, 226
inner fields, 416
inputs for functions, 153–154
Insert Chart dialog box, 381–382, 440
Insert dialog box
  choosing template via, 22–23
  keyboard shortcut to open, 110
Insert Function button, Ribbon, 8
Insert Function dialog box
  DAX functions, 519
  entering cells, ranges, named areas, and tables as function arguments, 168–171
  entering functions, 164
  finding correct function, 163–164
  function categories, 164
  functions with arguments, 166–168
  functions with no arguments, 165–166
  help feature, 171–172
  overview, 162–163
  using to multiply numbers, 154–155
Insert Slicers dialog box, 490–492
Insert tab
  adding headers and footers, 77
  inserting charts, 382–383
  inserting images, 67
  overview, 9
  Recommended PivotTables command, 395
  Tables group, 141
Insert Timelines dialog box, 495–496
INT function, 253–254, 259–260
interest rates
  calculating, 222–224
  effective interest rate, 222
  interest payments, 216–217
  internal rate of return, 237–239
  loans, 213
internal data model
  adding Excel tables to, 462–464
  creating new PivotTables, 506–508
  directly feeding data to, 499–504
  filling with multiple external data tables, 508–511
  limitations of, 459
  managing queries and connections, 506
  managing relationships in, 505
  overview, 458–459
  using in reporting, 467–468
  working directly with, 499–511

Index 771

internal rate of return (IRR), 237–239
Intersect method, 733–734
investment returns, 226–228
IPMT function, 154, 216–218
IRR function, 209, 237–239
irrational number, 257
Italics command, Home tab, 54
iterations, Goal Seek, 350–351

K

k argument
  Array form, 94
  SMALL or LARGE functions, 51
Keep Solver Solution option, 359
key performance indicators (KPIs), 565
Key Performance Indicators (Parmenter), 565
keyboard shortcuts
  activating worksheets, 121
  adding worksheets, 25
  applying absolute references, 40–41
  applying basic formatting, 17–18
  AutoSum, 44
  bold font, 54
  centering text, 64
  clearing filters, 89
  copying and pasting, 41–42
  Create Table dialog box, 99
  creating column charts, 382
  creating PivotChart from PivotTable, 439
  creating resizable range, 45
  creating workbooks, 21
  cutting and pasting, 444
  deleting worksheets, 26
  to edit cell contents, 8
  ending function, 189
  executing code, 709
  expanding Formula bar, 9
  Filter feature, 88
  find and replace, 114
  Format Cells dialog box, 55, 66, 622
  formatting subtotals, 96
  Go To command, 101, 118

  grouping worksheets, 27
  Help system, 143
  hiding/unhiding
    rows and columns, 71–72
    worksheets, 26
  Immediate window, 703
  Insert dialog box, 110
  inserting caret, 263
  italics, 54
  Multi-Select, 411
  opening workbooks, 21
  Project Explorer, 703
  Properties window, 706
  Quick Analysis feature, 97
  recalculating formulas, 13–14
  refreshing PivotTables, 401
  reordering worksheets, 121
  saving workbooks, 21
  Scroll Lock, 15
  searching menus, 10
  selecting
    cells, 17
    current region, 119
    multiple values, 491
    rows, 45
  sharing workbooks, 28
  starting new charts, 390
  switching between Code panes, 707
  tables, 110
  testing macros, 686
  turning array into formula, 181
  turning formula into array formula, 181
  underlining, 54, 622
  Undo command, 81, 87, 112, 116, 389, 708
  Visual Basic Editor, 684, 701, 708, 723, 730–731
KPIs (key performance indicators), 565

L

labels
  charts
    adding to PivotCharts, 447–448
    defined, 386

in dashboards, 572–573
in data table design, 625–626
LARGE operation, AGGREGATE function, 92
largest value, finding, 51
Last Cell option, Go To Special dialog box, 119
Last Column option, Table Design tab, 102
layout and placement of dashboards, 571–572
leading zeros, 57
LEFT function, 292–293, 305
LEN function, 295–296, 606
less than (<) operator, 32, 268, 427
Less Than rule, conditional formatting, 322, 637
level bars, 337–338
level numbers, 337–338
Limits report, Solver Results dialog box, 361
links, workbook, 34–35, 196–197
loans
  interest rate, 222–224
  payments
    calculating amount, 214–216
    calculating number of, 219–222
    calculating principal, 224–226
    interest payments, 216–217
    toward principal, 217–219
  PDURATION function, 221–222
  principal
    calculating, 224–226
    defined, 213
long variables, 719
Look In option
  Find tab, 115
  Replace tab, 116
Lookup_array argument, XLOOKUP function, 614–615
Lookup_value argument, HLOOKUP function, 592

M

macOS
  Quick Access Toolbar, 12
  serial numbering system, 272
Macro Recording option, Status Bar, 15

macros
  absolute references, 686–689
  assigning to form controls, 694–696
  building navigation buttons, 697–698
  defined, 681
  editing, 685–686
  error handlers
    On Error GoTo 0, 726–727
    On Error GoTo SomeLabel, 725–726
    On Error Resume Next, 726
  event procedures
    workbooks, 723–724
    worksheets, 721–723
  Excel object model
    collections, 717
    methods, 718
    objects, 715–718
    properties, 717–718
  installing in workbooks
    event macros, 730
    nonevent macros, 730
    Personal Macro Workbook, 730–731
    standard macros, 731
  one-touch reporting options, 699–700
  placing on Quick Access Toolbar, 696–697
  rearranging PivotTable data, 698–699
  recording, 682–691
  relative references, 689–691
  security
    macro-enabled file extensions, 691
    trusted documents, 692
    trusted locations, 692–693
  storing in Personal Macro Workbook, 694
  testing, 686
  variables
    assigning values to, 719
    declaring, 719
    defined, 718
    reasons to use, 720
  viewing, 684–685
  Visual Basic Editor
    activating, 684–685

Index   773

macros *(continued)*
   built-in module for worksheet, 721
   Code pane, 706–709
   customizing, 709–714
   Debug toolbar, 703
   defined, 701
   Edit toolbar, 703
   Immediate window, 703
   keyboard shortcuts, 708
   menu bar, 702
   overview, 701–702
   Project Explorer, 703–706
   Standard toolbar, 703
   UserForm toolbar, 703
   Visual Basic for Applications
      defined, 715
      On Error GoTo 0 error handler, 726–727
      Excel object model, 715–718
      variables, 720
      VBA module, 704–709
   when to use, 682
Manage Relationships dialog box, 505, 511
Margin Indicator Bar option, VBE Editor Format tab, 713
Margins command, Page Layout tab, 75
marquee, 147
Match Case option, Find tab, 115
Match Entire Cell Contents option, Find tab, 115
`Match_mode` argument, XLOOKUP function, 616
math, functional
   ABS function, 256
   PI function, 257
   POWER function, 261–263
   PRODUCT function, 263–264
   raising number to a power, 261–263
   random numbers
      RAND function, 258–260
      RANDBETWEEN function, 260–261
   rounding numbers
      CEILING function, 249–251
      EVEN function, 251–252
      FLOOR function, 249–251
      INT function, 253–254
      negative numbers, 250, 253–254
      ODD function, 251–252
      in one direction, 248–252
      ROUND function, 246–247
      ROUNDDOWN function, 249
      ROUNDUP function, 248
      TRUNC function, 254–255
   SEQUENCE function, 261
   SIGN function, 255
   SUM function, 242–246
   summing numbers
      SUBTOTAL function, 264–266
      SUMIF and SUMIFS functions, 268–270
      SUMPRODUCT function, 266–267
MAX calculation, SUBTOTAL function, 90
Max calculation, Value Field Settings dialog box, 414
MAX function, 159
Measure dialog box, 526–527
MEDIAN operation, AGGREGATE function, 92
menu bar, Visual Basic Editor, 702
merging across columns, 63
methods
   Double Declining Balance depreciation method, 229, 233–234
   Excel object model, 718
   `Intersect` method, 733–734
   Solver GRG Nonlinear method, 360
   straight-line depreciation method, 229
   sum of years' digits depreciation method, 229
Microsoft Access database, 508–509
Microsoft Query, 398–399
MIDDLE function, 293–295
midyear depreciation schedule, 235–236
military time, 287
MIN calculation, SUBTOTAL function, 90
Min calculation, Value Field Settings dialog box, 414
MINUTE function, 289
mixed references, 40, 148
MODE.SNGL operation, AGGREGATE function, 92

Modify Table Style dialog box, 103–104
monetary values
  cash flow, 210
  currency format, 299
  currency formats, 210–212
  separator symbols, 212–213
MONTH function, 278
Move Chart dialog box, 387
multiplication calculations
  overview, 38–39
  PEMDAS sequence, 35, 150, 193
My Table Has Headers check box, Create Table dialog box, 99

N

#N/A! error, 151
Name Box, 141. *See also* Formula Bar
  navigating with, 101, 120
  overview, 8
#NAME? error, 151
named areas, 178
naming
  tables, 100–101
  worksheets, 23–24, 133–134
navigating
  Custom Views feature, 123–127
    creating custom views, 125–126
    Quick Access Toolbar shortcut, 126–127
  finding and replacing data within cells, 114
  Go To command, 118
  Go To Special command, 118–120
  Name Box, 120
  Navigation task pane, 116–117
  replacing text within worksheet cells, 116
  searching within worksheet cells, 114–115
  to and from tables, 101–102
  worksheets
    activating, 120–121
    reordering, 121–122
    splitting windows, 122–123
    viewing two or more at once, 123
    zooming in and out, 127–128
navigation buttons, macros, 697–698
Navigation task pane, 116–117
negative numbers
  cash flows out, 210
  currency formatting and, 211
  formatting, 55–56
  as function arguments in TAKE function, 185
  FV function and, 227
  rounding, 250, 253–254
nesting functions, 158–160
NETWORKDAYS function, 283
New command, Manage Relationships dialog box, 505
New Formatting Rule dialog box, 330, 644
New Name dialog box, 178
New Sheet button, 132
New Window command, 123
Next option, Error Checking dialog box, 205
No Duplicate Values Found prompt, 86
nonfiltered data, 92
normal ranges, cells, 98
Not_found argument, XLOOKUP function, 615
Notes
  comments vs., 30
  searching, 115
Notes option, Go To Special dialog box, 119
NOW function, 290
NPER function, 215, 219–220
#NULL! error, 151
#NUM! error, 151
Num Lock indicator, 15
Number format option, Format Cells dialog box, 55
number series, 43
Number tab, Format Cells dialog box, 55, 301
number1 argument
  AVERAGE function, 48
  SUM function, 19, 44
number2...255 argument
  AVERAGE function, 48
  SUM function, 19, 44

numbers
  custom formats for, 57–59
  in data table design, 624–625
  formatting
    applying custom colors, 632
    basics, 627–629
    in dashboards, 572
    in thousands and millions, 629–631
    zeroes, 631–632
  random
    RAND function, 258–260
    RANDBETWEEN function, 260–261
  rounding
    CEILING function, 249–251
    EVEN function, 251–252
    FLOOR function, 249–251
    INT function, 253–254
    negative numbers, 250, 253–254
    ODD function, 251–252
    in one direction, 248–252
    ROUND function, 246–247
    ROUNDDOWN function, 249
    ROUNDUP function, 248
    TRUNC function, 254–255
  summing
    SUBTOTAL function, 264–266
    SUMIF and SUMIFS functions, 268–270
    SUMPRODUCT function, 266–267
  turning into text, 301–303

O

object variables, 719
objective cells, 356, 733–734
object-oriented programming, 715. *See also* Visual Basic for Applications
objects
  Camera tool and, 659
  defined, 380
  Excel object model
    collections, 717
    methods, 718
    overview, 715–716
    properties, 717–718
Objects option, Go To Special dialog box, 119
ODBC connections to nonstandard databases in Power Query, 551
ODD function, 248, 251–252
OLAP databases, 550
On Error GoTo 0 error handler, 726–727
On Error GoTo SomeLabel error handler, 725–726
On Error Resume Next error handler, 726
one-input data tables, 344–346
one-touch reporting options, macros, 699–700
online pictures, inserting into worksheet, 67
online resources
  Cheat Sheet, 3
  count functions, 370
  creating custom formatting rules, 643
  custom number formats, 302
  dashboard design, 569
  internal data model, 499
  linking tables to Power Pivot, 460
  macros
    basic, 681
    closing all workbooks at once, 747
    creating workbook backup, 751
    creating workbooks from scratch, 731
    determining if workbook exists, 745
    opening workbooks, 739, 741
    preventing workbook from closing, 749
    printing multiple workbooks, 747
    protecting worksheets, 737
    recording, 686
    saving workbooks, 733, 735
    unprotecting worksheets, 738
  organizing data, 79
  PivotTables, 469
  Power Pivot formulas, 513
  templates, 22
  VLOOKUP formulas, 588
Open Workbook option, Workbook Links pane, 197
operators

ampersand operator, 33
arithmetic, 32, 46
asterisk operator, 32, 313–314, 613–614, 617
colon operator
  for navigating worksheets, 34
  for ranges, 33
combining text, 33
comma operator, 33
comparison, 32, 268
equal sign operator, 31, 35
exclamation point operator, 34
forward slash operator, 32
greater than operator
  COUNTIF function, 158
  SUMIF function, 268
hyphen operator, 32
less than operator, 32, 268, 427
percent operator, 32
plus sign operator, 32
references
  ranges, 33–34
  sheets, 34
  workbooks, 34–35
at sign operator, 33, 607
single quote operator, 31
space operator, 33
square brackets operator, 35
options argument
  Array form, 94
  Reference form, 93
Options dialog box, 713–714
Options option, Error Checking dialog box, 205
order of operations
  addition, 39
  division, 38–39
  exponents, 37–38
  multiplication, 38–39
  parentheses, 36–37
  PEMDAS sequence, 35, 150, 193
  subtraction, 39
organizational trends, 665–666
organizing data

AGGREGATE function, 92–94
Filter feature
  clearing filters, 89
  reapplying filters, 90
Quick Analysis feature, 96–97
removing duplicates
  across multiple columns, 87
  from single column, 86–87
Sort feature
  applying sort options, 85–86
  basic sorting, 80–81
  creating custom sorts, 81–84
  custom lists, 84–85
  resolving mishaps, 81
Subtotal feature
  formatting subtotals, 95–96
  removing subtotals, 95–96
SUBTOTAL function
  differentiating, 91–92
  pairing with filters, 91
Orientation command, Page Layout tab, 75
outer fields, 416
outliers, 328, 372

P

page breaks, setting, 76
page layout and setup
  adding headers, footers, and print titles, 77–78
  customizing, 124
  managing, 75
  overview, 9
  setting print area, 76
  setting print ranges and page breaks, 76
Page Number command, Header & Footer tab, 77
parameters. *See also* arguments, function
  CHOOSE function, 597
  HLOOKUP function, 592
parentheses
  mismatched, 192–194
  overview, 36–37
  PEMDAS sequence, 35, 150, 193

Index 777

Parmenter, David, 565
passive functions
   EXACT function, 310–312
   FIND function, 312–313
   SEARCH function, 313–314
Paste Special dialog box
   abbreviated version of, 389
   transposing data, 189–190
payments, loan
   calculating amount, 214–216
   calculating interest, 216–217
   calculating number of, 219–222
   defined, 213
   payment periods, 213
   toward principal, 217–219
PDF files, 27, 548–549
PDURATION function, 221–222
PEMDAS sequence, 35, 150, 193
percent (%) operator, 32
percentage (%) Difference From analysis, 416
percentage calculations, 419
Percentage format, Format Cells dialog box, 56
percentage summary calculations, 418–420
PERCENTILE.EXC operation, AGGREGATE function, 93
PERCENTILE.INC operation, AGGREGATE function, 93
performance against target
   bullet graph
      adding data to, 671–672
      creating, 668–671
      formatting, 673–675
   organizational trends, 665–666
   range as target, 675–677
   showing with variances, 663–664
   thermometer-style chart, 666–667
Personal Macro Workbook
   installing macros in, 730–731
   storing macros in, 694
personalizing
   charts, 384–385
   page layout, 124

PivotTable reports
   applying numeric formats to data fields, 479
   changing PivotTable layout, 476–477
   changing summary calculations, 479–481
   customizing field names, 478–479
   hiding or showing items without data, 485–486
   showing and hiding data items, 483–485
   sorting PivotTables, 486–488
   suppressing subtotals, 481–483
Quick Access Toolbar, 12
Ribbon, 11
Status Bar, 15
Visual Basic Editor
   Docking tab, 714
   Editor Format tab, 712–713
   Editor tab, 710–712
   General tab, 713–714
PI function, 257
Picture command, Header & Footer tab, 78
PivotCharts
   adding data labels to, 447–448
   adding titles to, 449–451
   building from Excel range or table, 441–443
   category axis, 437
   category items, 437
   changing type of, 446–447
   chart data series, 436
   creating from PivotTable, 439–440
   data series axis, 437
   data series items, 437
   displaying data table with, 452–453
   dynamic, 436
   filtering, 436, 444–446
   limitations of, 438–439
   moving legend in, 451–452
   moving to another sheet, 443–444
   overview, 435–436
   pros and cons, 436–437
   report filter, 437–438
   sorting, 448–449
   value area, 437

x-axis, 436
y-axis, 436
PivotTable Fields dialog box, 507–508
PivotTable-driven data models, 581–582
PivotTables
  adding report filters, 474
  areas
    adding multiple fields to, 402–403
    pivoting field to different, 403–404
  building from new data connection, 399–400
  building from range or table, 395–397
  Calculated Field feature, 430–431
  Calculated Item feature, 431–433
  calculated measures
    creating, 526–529
    editing and deleting, 529
  changing and rearranging, 473–474
  creating
    from external data, 398–400
    overview, 470–473
    using internal data model, 506–508
  creating PivotCharts from, 439–440
  custom calculations
    deleting, 434
    editing, 433–434
    formulas for, 427
    limitations, 428–429
    types, 428
  customizing reports
    applying numeric formats to data fields, 479
    changing PivotTable layout, 476–477
    changing summary calculations, 479–481
    customizing field names, 478–479
    hiding or showing items without data, 485–486
    showing and hiding data items, 483–485
    sorting PivotTables, 486–488
    suppressing subtotals, 481–483
  embedding into worksheet, 439–440
  features, 394
  field subtotals
    displaying multiple, 425–426
    turning off, 425
  filtering data
    with report filter field, 407–408
    row or column items, 408–409
    with slicers, 410–411
    values, 409–410
  grouping data
    date and time values, 405–406
    numeric values, 404–405
    text values, 406–407
  macros and, 698–699
  Microsoft Query and, 398–399
  overview, 391–393
  refreshing data, 474–476
    automatically, 401–402
    manually, 401
  slicers
    controlling multiple PivotTables with one, 494–495
    creating standard type, 490–492
    creating Timeline type, 495–497
    customizations, 492–494
    data item columns, 493
    overview, 488–490
    settings, 493–494
    size and placement, 492–493
    sorting by month in Power Pivot–driven PivotTables, 522–523
  summary calculations
    changing default, 414–416
    difference, 416–418
    Index, 422–424
    percentage, 418–420
    Running Total In, 420–422
plus sign (+) operator, 32
PMT function, 214–215
pound sign (#), 302
POWER function, 261–263
Power Pivot
  calculated columns
    creating, 514–515
    formatting, 516
    hiding, 517–518

Power Pivot *(continued)*
    referencing in other calculations, 516–517
    unhiding, 518
  calculated measures
    creating, 526–529
    editing and deleting, 529
  DAX functions
    for calculated columns, 518–520
    enhancing calculated columns, 520–521
    nesting, 525–526
    referencing fields from other tables, 523–525
  internal data model, 458–460
  linking Excel tables to
    adding to data model, 462–464
    creating relationships between tables, 464–466
    managing existing relationships, 466–467
    overview, 461–462
    using data model in reporting, 467–468
  overview, 457–458
  Power Pivot–driven PivotTables, 522–523
Power Query
  column-level actions, 542–543
  data profiling, 555–558
    options, 556–557
    quick actions, 557–558
  data source settings, 553–555
  importing data from database systems
    Azure databases, 551
    connection process walk-through, 552–553
    ODBC connections, 551
    OLAP database, 550
    other data systems, 551
    relational database, 550
  importing data from files
    CSV and text files, 546–548
    Excel workbooks, 545–546
    folders, 549–550
    PDF files, 548–549
  M language, 538
  managing existing queries, 540–541
  overview, 531–532
  Power Query Editor
    adding file attributes, 550
    Close & Load command, 536
    Close & Load To command, 536
    column-level actions, 542–543
    Data Preview Group, 556
    Queries & Connections task pane and, 537
    Query Settings pane, 538
    table-level actions, 545
    query steps, 538–539
    refreshing data, 539–540
    starting query, 532–537
    table actions, 544–545
PPMT function, 217–219
precedents, formula, 200–201
Precedents options, Go To Special dialog box, 119
present value (Pv) argument
  FV function, 226
  PMT function, 215
Previous option, Error Checking dialog box, 205
primary key fields, 504
principal, loan
  calculating, 224–226
  defined, 213
Print Area command, Page Layout tab, 75
Print Gridlines command, Page Layout tab, 75
Print Headings command, Page Layout tab, 75
Print Titles command, Page Layout tab, 75
printing
  adding print tiles, 77–78
  from multiple workbooks in directory, 747–749
  setting print ranges, 76
priority zones, dashboards, 571
Procedure Separator option, VBE Editor tab, 712
PRODUCT calculation, SUBTOTAL function, 90
Product calculation, Value Field Settings dialog box, 414
PRODUCT function, 157, 263–264
profiling, data
  options, 556–557
  overview, 555–556
  quick actions, 557–558
Project Explorer, Visual Basic Editor

adding VBA module, 704–706
Code modules, 705
overview, 703
removing VBA module, 706
properties, Excel object model, 717–718
Pv (present value) argument
FV function, 226
PMT function, 215
PV function, 224–226

Q

QUARTILE.EXC operation, AGGREGATE function, 93
QUARTILE.INC operation, AGGREGATE function, 93
Queries & Connections task pane, 506, 540–541
Query Editor window, 534
Query tab, 11
question mark (?) wildcard, 313–314, 617
Quick Access Toolbar
adding Camera tool to, 656
Custom Views shortcut, 126–127
customizing, 12
placing macros on, 696–697
positioning, 136
saving workbooks, 21
quick actions, data profiling, 557–558
Quick Analysis feature, 96–97

R

R1C1 reference format style, 40
RAND function, 258–260
RANDBETWEEN function, 47, 260–261
random numbers
RAND function, 258–260
RANDBETWEEN function, 260–261
range argument, AVERAGEIF function, 50
Range_lookup argument, HLOOKUP function, 592
ranges, data
address, 139
comparing to tables, 98
converting Excel tables to, 601–602

converting table to, 112
converting to Excel tables, 599–601
creating PivotCharts from, 441–443
defined, 138
determining workdays in range of dates, 283
grouping related data, 337–338
reference operators, 33–34
removing conditional formatting from, 334
SUM function and, 243–244
RATE function, 222–224
ratings icon sets, 329
raw data, 320
readability of data
color and, 69
DAX functions, 529
fonts, 69, 626
formatting and, 142
sorting, 626
structured references and, 106
wrapping text, 65
Recommended Charts, 380–382
recording macros
with absolute references, 686–689
editing macros, 685–686
overview, 682–684
with relative references, 689–691
testing macros, 686
#REF! error, 151
RefEdit controls, 156, 169–170
references
circular, 194–195
in formulas, 146–148
operators, 33–35
ranges, 33–34
sheets, 34
workbooks, 34–35
relative, 40, 147–148, 689–691
structured
disabling, 108–109
dynamic range adjustments, 106
enhanced readability, 106
in tables, 106–108

Index 781

Refresh All option, Workbook Links pane, 196
refresh schedule, dashboard, 568
RELATED function, 524–525
relational databases, 550
relative references, 40, 147–148, 689–691
Remove Duplicates dialog box, 86–87
Rename option, Navigation task pane, 117
Replace Format button, Replace tab, 116
REPLACE function, 304–306
Replace With option, Replace tab, 116
Report Connections dialog box, 494
reports
  conditional formatting
    adding custom formatting rules manually, 642–646
    Color Scales, 641
    data bars, 640–641
    Highlight Cells Rules, 636–638
    icon sets, 642, 650–652
    showing data bars and icons outside cells, 648–650
    showing only one icon, 646–648
    top/bottom rules, 638–640
  defined, 562
  shapes in
    constructing custom infographic widgets with, 661–662
    creating containers with, 659–660
    layering to save space, 660–661
  symbols in, 652–655
Reports list, Solver Results dialog box, 361
REPT function, 303–304
Require Variable Declaration option, VBE Editor tab, 710–711
resources, online
  Cheat Sheet, 3
  count functions, 370
  creating custom formatting rules, 643
  custom number formats, 302
  dashboard design, 569
  internal data model, 499
  linking tables to Power Pivot, 460
  macros

    basic, 681
    closing all workbooks at once, 747
    creating workbook backup, 751
    creating workbooks from scratch, 731
    determining if workbook exists, 745
    opening workbooks, 739, 741
    preventing workbook from closing, 749
    printing multiple workbooks, 747
    protecting worksheets, 737
    recording, 686
    saving workbooks, 733, 735
    unprotecting worksheets, 738
  organizing data, 79
  PivotTables, 469
  Power Pivot formulas, 513
  templates, 22
  VLOOKUP formulas, 588
Restore Original Values option, Solver, 359
Return_array argument, XLOOKUP function, 614–615
returned value, depreciation, 232
returns on investment, 226–228
Review tab
  managing notes and comments, 30
  overview, 10
Ribbon
  customizing, 11
  disable commands, 111
  Expand Formula Bar button, 8–9
  Formula Bar, 8
  Insert Function button, 8
  Name Box, 8
  overview, 9–12
RIGHT function, 293
ROUND function, 246–247, 259–260
ROUNDDOWN function, 248–249
rounding numbers
  INT function, 253–254
  negative numbers, 250, 253–254
  in one direction
    CEILING function, 249–251
    EVEN function, 251–252

FLOOR function, 249–251
ODD function, 251–252
ROUNDDOWN function, 249
ROUNDUP function, 248
ROUND function, 246–247
TRUNC function, 254–255
ROUNDUP function, 248–249
Row area, PivotTables, 394
Row Differences option, Go To Special dialog box, 119
Row field header, PivotTables, 394
ROW function, 106
`Row_index_num` argument, HLOOKUP function, 592
rows
  adjusting heights, 69–70
  grouping, 72–73
  hiding/unhiding, 71–72, 124
  overview, 137–138
  tables, 141
  total rows in tables, 105
rules, conditional formatting
  Above Average rule, 325, 639
  Below Average rule, 325, 639
  Bottom 10 Items rule, 325, 639
  Bottom 10% rule, 325, 639
  A Date Occurring rule, 322, 637
  Duplicate Values rule, 322–324, 637
  Equal To rule, 322, 637
  Greater Than rule, 322–323, 637
  Less Than rule, 322, 637
  Between rule, 322, 637
  Text That Contains rule, 322, 637
  Top 10 Items rule, 325, 639
  Top 10% rule, 325, 639
Running Total In calculations, 420–422

S

salvage value, 229–230, 232, 234
saving
  Solver solution as scenario, 364
  workbooks

    before closing, 735–737
    `Intersect` method, 733–734
    overview, 20–21
Scale command, Page Layout tab, 75
Scenario Manager dialog box, 353–355
scenarios
  Above Average scenario, 639
  applying, 354
  Below Average scenario, 639
  Bottom 10 Items scenario, 639
  Bottom 10% scenario, 639
  changing cells, 352
  creating, 352–354
  A Date Occurring scenario, 637
  deleting, 354–355
  Duplicate Values scenario, 637
  editing, 354–355
  Equal To scenario, 637
  Greater Than scenario, 637
  Less Than scenario, 637
  overview, 351–352
  saving Solver solution as, 364
  Between scenario, 637
  Text That Contains scenario, 637
  Top 10 Items scenario, 639
  Top 10% scenario, 639
scientific notation, 38
Scientific notation, Format Cells dialog box, 56
Scroll Lock indicator, 15
search feature, Insert Function dialog box, 162–163
SEARCH function, 313–315
Search option, Find tab, 115
`Search_mode` argument, XLOOKUP function, 616
SECOND function, 290
security, macros
  macro-enabled file extensions, 691
  trusted documents, 692
  trusted locations, 692–693
Select All Sheets command, page setup, 74
Select Source Data dialog box, 386
self-expanding formulas, 109–110

Send Link dialog box, 28
Sensitivity report, Solver Results dialog box, 361
sentence case, 310
separators, currency, 212–213
SEQUENCE function, 261
serial numbering system
   dates, 272, 280
   time, 285
Set Objective field, Solver Parameters dialog
   box, 359
Shape Format tab, 66, 388
shapes
   constructing custom infographic widgets with, 661–662
   creating containers with, 659–660
   layering to save space, 660–661
shapes icon sets, 329
sharing
   coauthoring simultaneously, 28–29
   comments, 29–30
   static copies of workbooks, 27
Sheet Name command, Header & Footer tab, 78
Sheet Number option, Status Bar, 15
Sheet View, 125
Show Calculation Steps option, Error Checking dialog box, 205
SIGN function, 255
single accounting underlines, 622–623
single quote (') operator, 31
Size command, Page Layout tab, 75
Size option, VBE Editor Format tab, 713
slicers
   controlling multiple PivotTables with single, 494–495
   creating
      standard type, 490–492
      Timeline type, 495–497
   customizing, 492–494
   data item columns, 493
   overview, 488–490
   PivotTables, 410–411
   settings, 493–494
   size and placement, 492–493

SLN function, 230–231
SMALL operation, AGGREGATE function, 93
smallest value, finding, 51
smart tags, 197
solid-fill data bars, 327
Solver
   adding constraints, 361–363
   advantages, 356
   finding optimal result, 359–361
   loading add-in, 358–359
   overview, 355–356
   saving solution as scenario, 364
   usages, 356–358
   workings, 356
Solver Parameters dialog box, 359–360, 362–364
Solver Results dialog box, 361–363
Sort by Column dialog box, 522
Sort dialog box, 82–83, 86
Sort feature
   applying sort options, 85–86
   basic sorting, 80–81
   creating custom sorts, 81–84
   custom lists, 84–85
   resolving mishaps, 81
SORT function, 608
Sort Options dialog box, 85
Sort_index argument, SORT function, 608
Sort_order argument
   SORT function, 608
   SORTBY function, 609
SORTBY function, 608–610
space operator, 33
spaces
   readability and, 529
   removing from text, 308–309
   Sort feature and, 80
   in worksheet name, 34
Special number format, Format Cells dialog box, 56
spilling and spill ranges, dynamic arrays
   overview, 604–605
   referencing, 606–607

spreadsheets
  workbooks
    adding comments, 29-30
    automatically opening, 742-745
    backups, 750-751
    closing, 746-747
    coauthoring simultaneously, 28-29
    creating from scratch, 731-733
    creating new, 22
    data source, 546
    defined, 13
    event procedures, 723-724
    hiding and unhiding, 74
    hyperlink feature, 698
    importing into Power Query, 545-546
    installing macros, 730-731
    opening, 21
    opening to specific tab, 739-740
    overview, 132-135
    populating cells before closing, 749-750
    printing from multiple workbooks in directory, 747-749
    protecting worksheets, 737-738
    recalculating and data tables, 349
    reference operators, 34-35
    saving, 20-21, 733-737
    searching directory for, 745-746
    selecting workbook to open, 741-742
    sharing static copies of, 27
    templates for, 22-23
    unprotecting worksheets, 738-739
  worksheets
    activating, 13, 120-121
    active, 133
    adding, 25-26
    cells, 137-138
    changing tab color, 134
    collapsing sections of data, 337-338
    columns, 137
    consolidating data from, 338-341
    defined, 13
    deleting, 26
    event procedures, 721-723
    expanding sections of data, 337-338
    grouping, 27
    hiding/unhiding, 26
    inserting, 134
    moving or copying, 24-25
    named areas, 140-141
    overview, 132-135
    protecting, 737-738
    ranges, 138-139
    renaming, 23-24, 133-134
    reordering, 121-122
    rows, 137-138, 141
    splitting windows, 122-123
    tables, 141
    unprotecting, 738-739
    viewing two or more at once, 123
    zooming in and out, 127-128
square brackets ([ ]) operator, 35
standard deviation, 374-375
standard macros, 731
standard underlining, 622
statements, VBA module, 707-708
statistical functions
  AVERAGE function, 48
  conditional averages, 49-50
  finding smallest and largest values, 51
  overview, 47
  weighted averages, 48-49
Status Bar
  AutoCalculate Functions option, 14
  Calculate Status option, 13-14
  Caps Lock indicator, 15
  Cell Mode indicator, 13
  customizing, 15
  View Modes option, 14
  Workbook Statistics option, 15
  Zoom Slider option, 14
StdDev calculation, Value Field Settings dialog box, 414
StdDevp calculation, Value Field Settings dialog box, 414

Index   785

STDEV.P calculation, SUBTOTAL function, 90
STDEV.S calculation, SUBTOTAL function, 90
stock images, inserting into worksheet, 67
straight-line depreciation, 229–231
string variables, 719
strings, text
  breaking apart text, 291–296
  defined, 291
  empty string, 308
  putting text together, 296–298
structured references
  disabling, 108–109
  dynamic range adjustments, 106
  enhanced readability, 106
  in tables, 106–108
SUBSTITUTE function, 307–308
Subtotal feature
  formatting subtotals, 95–96
  overview, 94–95
  removing subtotals, 95–96
SUBTOTAL function
  argument values for, 265
  arguments, 90–91
  differentiating, 91–92
  pairing with filters, 91
  SUM function vs., 92
  syntax of, 264
subtotals
  formatting, 95–96
  PivotTable
    displaying multiple subtotals for field, 425–426
    turning off for field, 425
  removing, 95–96, 481–483
    all at once, 482
    grand totals, 483
    for only one field, 482–483
  summarizing data with, 335–336
subtraction calculations
  dates and times, 46–47
  overview, 39
  PEMDAS sequence, 35, 150, 193
SUM calculation, SUBTOTAL function, 91

Sum calculation, Value Field Settings dialog box, 414
SUM function
  adding numbers stored as text, 46
  arguments, 44
  AutoSum feature, 19, 245–246
  manual formula, 19
  number1 argument, 19
  number2...255 argument, 19
  overview, 242–245
  SUBTOTAL function vs., 92
  using in formulas, 152
  using ranges, 45–46
  using with arrays, 179–182
sum of years' digits depreciation method, 229
SUMIF function, 268–270, 277
SUMIFS function, 268–270
summary calculations, PivotTable
  changing, 479–481
  difference, 416–418
  Index summary calculation, 422–424
  percentage, 418–420
  Running Total In, 420–422
Summary of Action prompt, 86–87
summing numbers
  SUBTOTAL function, 264–266
  SUMIF and SUMIFS functions, 268–270
  SUMPRODUCT function, 266–267
SUMPRODUCT function
  applying formulas in data models, 595
  filtering values, 594–595
  overview, 266–267, 592–594
  using with arrays, 180
sums
  adding or subtracting dates and times, 46–47
  AutoSum, 44
  SUM function
    adding numbers stored as text, 46
    using ranges, 45–46
SYD function, 231–232
Symbol dialog box, 653
symbols, report, 652–655

T

Table feature
  Sheet View, 125
  Total Row option, 19
TABLE function, 348
Table_array argument, HLOOKUP function, 592
tables
  automating formulas and features, 104–110
    calculated columns, 105–106
    crafting self-expanding formulas, 109–110
    disabling structured references, 108–109
    structured references, 106–108
    total rows, 105
  calculating column's variance, 375–376
  column's values
    averaging, 371–372
    counting, 369–370
    determining maximum and minimum values, 372–373
    multiplying, 373–374
    summing, 368–369
  comparing data ranges to, 98
  converting back to range, 601–602
  converting range to, 599–601
  converting to data ranges, 112
  creating, 97–99
  creating PivotCharts from, 441–443
  data tables
    number formatting, 629–631
    one-input, 344–346
    overview, 343–344, 619
    recalculating workbooks and, 349
    two-input, 346–348
  Excel commands that work differently in, 110–111
  formatting
    adjusting manually, 102
    establishing custom styles, 103–104
    setting default styles, 104
  linking to Power Pivot, 460–468
    adding to data model, 462–464
    creating relationships between tables, 464–466
    managing existing relationships, 466–467
    overview, 461–462
    using data model in reporting, 467–468
  naming, 100–101
  navigating to and from, 101–102
  overview, 141, 598–599
  PivotTables
    adding report filters, 474
    building from new data connection, 399–400
    building from range or table, 395–397
    Calculated Field feature, 430–431
    Calculated Item feature, 431–433
    calculated measures, 526–529
    changing and rearranging, 473–474
    features, 394
    field subtotals, 425–426
    filtering data, 407–411
    macros and, 698–699
    Microsoft Query and, 398–399
    overview, 391–393
    refreshing data, 401–402, 474–476
    slicers, 488–497
    sorting by month in Power Pivot-driven PivotTables, 522–523
    summary calculations, 414–424
  resizing, 100
  retrieving single value from, 367–368
  standard deviation, 374–375
  Table feature, 599
tabs and data models, 584–585
tabular datasets, 581–582
TAKE function, 184–185
target cells, 356, 733–734
templates
  charts
    creating and applying, 389–390
    managing, 390
  overview, 22–23
testing
  data models, 585–586
  macros, 686

Index   **787**

text
  boxes, 65–67
  breaking apart
    LEFT function, 292–293
    LEN function, 295–296
    MIDDLE function, 293–295
    RIGHT function, 293
    TEXTSPLIT function, 295
  changing
    DOLLAR function, 299–301
    removing spaces, 308–309
    repeating text, 303–304
    REPLACE function, 304–306
    setting case, 309–310
    SUBSTITUTE function, 307–308
    swapping text, 304–308
    turning numbers into text, 301–303
  combining, 33
  comparing, 310–312
  converting dates from, 278–280
  FIND function, 312–313
  finding and replacing, 114–116
  importing text files into Power Query, 546–548
  putting together
    CONCATENATE function, 296–297
    TEXTJOIN function, 298
  SEARCH function, 313–315
  strings, 291
  text patterns, 43
  wrapping, 64–65
TEXT function, 301–303
Text number format, Format Cells dialog box, 56
Text That Contains rule, conditional formatting, 322, 637
TEXTJOIN function, 298
TEXTSPLIT function, 295
thermometer-style chart, 666–667
three-color scale, 328
tilde (~) wildcard, 617
Tiled view, 21
time
  adding and subtracting, 46–47

  formatting, 286–287, 633–634
  NOW function, 290
  overview, 285–286
  splitting into increments
    HOUR function, 288–289
    MINUTE function, 289
    SECOND function, 290
Time format, Format Cells dialog box, 56
Timeline slicers, 495–497
titles, dashboards, 572–573
To group, Solver Parameters dialog box, 359
TODAY function
  counting days from specific date, 281
  counting days to specific date, 280–281
tool tabs, Ribbon, 11
Top 10 Filter, 409
Top 10 Items rule, conditional formatting, 325, 639
Top 10% rule, conditional formatting, 325, 639
Total Row option, Table Design tab, 102
Total Row option, Table feature, 19
Trace Error command, 205
TRANSPOSE function, 187–189
TRIM function, 308–309
TRUNC function, 254–255
trusted documents, 692
trusted locations, 692–693
24-hour time (military time), 287
two-color scale, 328
two-input data tables, 346–348
type argument
  IPMT function, 217
  NPER function, 220
  PPMT function, 219
  PV function, 226
  RATE function, 224

U

Underline command, Home tab, 54
Undo command
  Group and Auto Outline commands and, 73
  sorting errors, 81

unhiding/hiding
  rows and columns, 71, 124
  workbooks, 74
  worksheets, 26, 123–124
Unicode characters, 652
UNIQUE function, 610–611
unknowns cells
  applying scenarios, 354
  creating scenarios, 352–353
  defined, 352
  editing scenarios, 354–355
  objective cell formula, 357
  saving Solver solution as scenario, 364
Use a Formula to Determine Which Cells to Format rule, 644–645
user interface
  activating worksheets, 13
  overview, 7–9
  Quick Access Toolbar, 12
  Status Bar, 13–15
  tabs, 9–11
user requirements, dashboard
  data sources, 566–567
  dimensions and filters, 567
  drill-down features, 568
  establishing audience and purpose, 564–565
  key performance indicators, 565–566
  refresh schedule, 568

V

Value area, PivotCharts, 437
Value area, PivotTables, 394
Value argument, CHOOSE function, 597
#VALUE! error, 313
#VALUE! error, 151
Value field header, PivotTables, 394
Value Field Settings dialog box, 414–415, 418
VALUE function, 303
Var calculation, Value Field Settings dialog box, 415
variable cells
  applying scenarios, 354
  creating scenarios, 352–353
  defined, 352
  editing scenarios, 354–355
  objective cell formula, 357
  saving Solver solution as scenario, 364
variables
  macros
    assigning values to, 719
    Boolean variables, 719
    declaring, 719
    defined, 718
    double variables, 719
    long variables, 719
    object variables, 719
    reasons to use, 720
    string variables, 719
    variant variables, 719
  variant variables, 719
variances
  calculating variance of column, 375–376
  showing performance against target with, 663–664
VAR.P calculation, SUBTOTAL function, 91
Varp calculation, Value Field Settings dialog box, 415
VAR.S calculation, SUBTOTAL function, 91
VBA (Visual Basic for Applications)
  defined, 715
  On Error GoTo 0 error handler, 726–727
  Excel object model
    collections, 717
    methods, 718
    objects, 716
    overview, 715–716
    properties, 717–718
  variables, 720
  VBA module
    adding to project, 704–706
    declarations, 704–705
    function procedures, 705
    getting VBA code into, 707–709
    removing from project, 706
    sub procedures, 705

Index **789**

VBE (Visual Basic Editor). *See also* macros
  activating, 684–685
  built-in module for worksheet, 721
  Code pane
    getting VBA code into module, 707–709
    overview, 703
    resizing windows, 706–707
  customizing
    Docking tab, 714
    Editor Format tab, 712–713
    Editor tab, 710–712
    General tab, 713–714
  Debug toolbar, 703
  defined, 701
  Edit toolbar, 703
  Immediate window, 703
  keyboard shortcuts, 708
  menu bar, 702
  overview, 701–702
  Project Explorer
    adding VBA module, 704–706
    overview, 703
    removing VBA module, 706
  Standard toolbar, 703
  UserForm toolbar, 703
Vertical view, 21
View Modes option, Status Bar, 14
View tab
  overview, 10
  Zoom section, 125
views, workbook, 21
Visible Cells Only option, Go To Special dialog box, 120
Visual Basic Editor (VBE). *See also* macros
  activating, 684–685
  built-in module for worksheet, 721
  Code pane
    getting VBA code into module, 707–709
    overview, 703
    resizing windows, 706–707
  customizing
    Docking tab, 714
    Editor Format tab, 712–713
    Editor tab, 710–712
    General tab, 713–714
  defined, 701
  Immediate window, 703
  keyboard shortcuts, 708
  menu bar, 702
  overview, 701–702
  Project Explorer
    adding VBA module, 704–706
    overview, 703
    removing VBA module, 706
  Standard toolbar, 703
  toolbars, 703
Visual Basic for Applications (VBA)
  defined, 715
  On Error GoTo 0 error handler, 726–727
  Excel object model
    collections, 717
    methods, 718
    objects, 716
    overview, 715–716
    properties, 717–718
  variables, 720
visualizations
  Camera tool
    enhancing dashboard with, 658–659
    finding, 656
    using, 656–658
  conditional formatting
    adding custom formatting rules manually, 642–646
    Color Scales, 641
    data bars, 640–641
    Highlight Cells Rules, 636–638
    icon sets, 642, 650–652
    showing data bars and icons outside cells, 648–650
    showing only one icon, 646–648
    top/bottom rules, 638–640
  shapes

constructing custom infographic widgets with, 661–662
creating containers with, 659–660
layering to save space, 660–661
symbols in, 652–655
VLOOKUP function
applying formulas in data models, 588–589
overview, 587
using data validation drop-down lists, 589–591
VSTACK function, 186

W

Watch Window, 136, 203–204
WEEKDAY function, 281–282
weighted averages, 48–49, 423
what-if analysis, 321, 343–349
Width command, Page Layout tab, 75
wildcards, 313–314, 616–617
Windows. *See also* keyboard shortcuts
coauthoring simultaneously, 28
creating new workbooks, 22
Customize Regional Options dialog box, 272–273
customizing Quick Access Toolbar, 12
customizing Ribbon, 11
dependency tree, 14
formatting date, 751
opening existing workbooks, 21
Scroll Lock, 15
Within option, Find tab, 115
workbook links, 34–35
Workbook Links pane, 196–197
Workbook Statistics option, Status Bar, 15
workbooks
adding comments, 29–30
automatically opening, 742–745
backups, 750–751
closing, 746–747
coauthoring simultaneously, 28–29
creating from scratch, 731–733
creating new, 22
data source, 546

defined, 13
event procedures, 723–724
hyperlink feature, 698
importing into Power Query, 545–546
installing macros
event macros, 730
Personal Macro Workbook, 730–731
standard macros, 731
opening, 21
opening to specific tab, 739–740
overview, 132–135
populating cells before closing, 749–750
printing from multiple workbooks in directory, 747–749
protecting worksheets, 737–738
recalculating and data tables, 349
reference operators, 34–35
saving
before closing, 735–737
`Intersect` method, 733–734
overview, 20–21
searching directory for, 745–746
selecting workbook to open, 741–742
sharing static copies of, 27
templates for, 22–23
unprotecting worksheets, 738–739
workdays
NETWORKDAYS function, 283–284
WORKDAY function, 284–285
worksheets
activating, 13
active, 133
adding, 25–26
cells, 137–138
changing tab color, 134
collapsing sections of data, 337–338
columns, 137
consolidating data from multiple
by category, 340–341
by position, 339–340
defined, 13
deleting, 26

Index   791

worksheets *(continued)*
  event procedures, 721–723
  expanding sections of data, 337–338
  grouping, 27
  hiding/unhiding, 26
  inserting, 134
  moving or copying, 24–25
  named areas, 140–141
  navigating
    activating, 120–121
    reordering, 121–122
    splitting windows, 122–123
    viewing two or more at once, 123
  overview, 132–135
  protecting, 737–738
  ranges, 138–139
  renaming, 23–24, 133–134
  rows, 137–138, 141
  tables, 141
  unprotecting, 738–739
  zooming in and out, 127–128
Worksheets collection, 717
wrapping text, 64–65

X

x-axis, PivotCharts, 436
XLOOKUP function, 614–617

Y

y-axis, PivotCharts, 436
YEAR function, 278
years, formatting, 272–273

Z

zeroes, hiding, 631–632
zooming, 14, 124–125, 127–128

About the Authors

Michael Alexander: Michael is senior consultant at Slalom Consulting with more than 15 years' experience in data management and reporting. He is the author of more than a dozen books on business analysis and has been named Microsoft Excel MVP for his contributions to the Excel community.

Ken Bluttman: Ken is a veteran software and web developer specializing in Excel/VBA and database-centric web applications. He has written numerous articles and books on a variety of technical topics. His latest projects include large-scale cloud-based applications and data analysis using Python and R. Ken and his wife live in North Carolina.

Dick Kusleika: Dick has been working with Microsoft Office for more than 20 years. He was named a Microsoft MVP for 12 consecutive years. Dick has written several books about Excel and Access.

Paul McFedries: Paul has been a technical writer for 30 years and has been messing around with spreadsheet software since installing Lotus 1-2-3 on an IBM PC clone in 1986. He has written more than 100 books that have sold more than four million copies worldwide. Paul's books include *Excel Data Analysis For Dummies*, *Teach Yourself VISUALLY Excel 365*, and *Teach Yourself VISUALLY Windows 11* (all published by Wiley).

David Ringstrom, CPA: David is the president of Accounting Advisors, Inc., an Atlanta-based consulting and training firm he founded in 1991. He specializes in helping clients streamline repetitive business processes and has delivered more than 2,500 live webinars on Excel and related topics. He also owns Students Excel, an online platform designed to help accounting professors teach Excel more effectively. Throughout his career, David has authored hundreds of articles on spreadsheets and accounting software, with some published internationally. He has served as the technical editor for more than three dozen books, including *QuickBooks Desktop For Dummies*, *Quicken For Dummies*, and *Peachtree For Dummies* (all published by Wiley) and is the author or coauthor of eight books, including *QuickBooks Online For Dummies* (published by Wiley). David lives in Atlanta, Georgia, with his children, Rachel and Lucas.

Publisher's Acknowledgments

Managing Editor: Sofia Malik
Executive Editor: Steven Hayes
Editor: Elizabeth Kuball

Production Editor: Magesh Elangovan
Cover Image: © South_agency/Getty Images
Special Help: Carmen Krikorian, Kristie Pyles